Women, Law, and Social Control

SECOND EDITION

Alida V. Merlo

Indiana University of Pennsylvania

Joycelyn M. Pollock

Texas State University at San Marcos

Boston   New York   San Francisco
Mexico City   Montreal   Toronto   London   Madrid   Munich   Paris
Hong Kong   Singapore   Tokyo   Cape Town   Sydney

To Kevin and Alexandra
A. V. M.

To Eric and Gregory
J. M. P.

Series Editor: *Jennifer Jacobson*
Series Editorial Assistant: *Emma Christensen*
Senior Marketing Manager: *Kelly May*
Production Editor: *Won McIntosh*
Editorial Production Service: *Walsh & Associates, Inc.*
Photo Researcher: *Image Quest*

Composition Buyer: *Linda Cox*
Manufacturing Buyer: *Megan Cochran*
Artist: *Asterisk, Inc.*
Electronic Composition: *Peggy Cabot*
Cover Administrator: *Kristina Mose-Libon*

For related titles and support materials, visit our online catalog at www.ablongman.com.

Between the time website information is gathered and then published, it is not unusual for some sites to have closed. Also, the transcription of URLs can result in typographical errors. The publisher would appreciate notification where these occur so that they may be corrected in subsequent editions.

Library of Congress Cataloging-in-Publication Data

Merlo, Alida V.
    Women, law, and social control / Alida V. Merlo, Joycelyn M. Pollock.—2nd ed.
        p.   cm.
    Includes bibliographical references and index.
    ISBN 0-205-44207-2
    1. Sex discrimination in criminal justice administration—United States.   2. Women criminal justice personnel—United States.   3. Women—Crimes against—United States.   4. Women prisoners—United States.   I. Pollock, Joycelyn M., 1956–   II. Title.
    HV9950.M47 2006
    364'.082'0973—dc22

                                                                                      2005047603

Printed in the United States of America

10 9 8 7 6 5 4 3 2 1   09 08 07 06 05

Photo Credits: p. 3, Bettmann/CORBIS; p. 32, © Getty Images/Hulton Archive; p. 47, AP/Wide World Photos; p. 64, AP/Wide World Photos, © John Pryke/Reuters/Landov; p. 91, © David M. Grossman/The Image Works; p. 111, © Jack Kurtz/The Image Works; p. 133, AP/ Wide World Photos; p. 149, © Rhoda Sidney/The Image Works; p. 170, © Jeff Greenberg/The Image Works; p. 191, © Bill Aron/PhotoEdit; p. 211, © Richard Hutchings/Photo Researchers, Inc.; p. 227, AP/ Wide World Photos; p. 251, © Robin Nelson/ PhotoEdit; p. 271, © Bob Daemmrich/PhotoEdit; p. 292, © CORBIS Saba; p. 315, AP/ Wide World Photos.

Contents

6   *Women Working in Prisons and Jail Settings:*
Progress and Prospects   **111**

by Mary Anne Farkas

Perspectives on Work Behavior   **112**

History of Women in Corrections   **113**

> Legal Challenges to Women Working in All-Male Institutions   115

Women Working as Correctional Officers   **116**

> Reasons for Women's Entry into Corrections   116 / Supervision Styles of Women
> Correctional Officers   117 / Perceptions of Supervisory Styles   120 / Views of
> Male Coworkers   120 / Attitudes of Male Inmates   121 / Attitudes of
> Correctional Administrators   121

Women in Management Positions   **122**

> Perspectives on Management Styles   122 / Management Styles of Female
> Wardens and Superintendents   123

Major Obstacles for Women   **124**

> Increased Occupational Stress   125 / Gender and Sexual Harassment   125

Conclusion   **127**

7   *The Practice of Law in the Twenty-First Century*   **133**

by Frances Bernat

History of Women in the Legal Profession   **134**

Stereotypes That Hurt Women Lawyers   **135**

Gender Bias Is Widespread and Persistent   **137**

> Salary Inequities Remain   138 / Female Lawyers of Color   139 / Women in the
> Judiciary   139 / Women in Law School   140

Balanced Lives   **141**

> Female Lawyers in the Criminal Justice System   142 / Redefining the Legal
> Profession   143

Conclusion   **144**

PART THREE • *Women as Victims*   147

8   *Rape Survivors: The Law and The Reality*   **149**

by Mittie D. Southerland and Rachel M. Southerland

Types and Definitions of Rape   **150**

> Types of Rape   150 / Perceptual Definitions of Rape   151 / Personal Definitions
> of Rape   152 / Legal Definitions of Rape   152

Preface

It has been about ten years since the first edition of this book was written. In that decade we have seen monumental changes in this country. The tragic loss of life on September 11, 2001, has forever changed our criminal justice system and the parameters of individual liberty and governmental power. Female police officers and female soldiers are commonplace today, and their deaths in the line of duty do not make headlines any more. Despite these changes, however, some things are remarkably the same. Girls are still socialized to value their bodies more than their minds, and in many areas of criminal justice there are still small percentages of women.

The last ten years has been a time of declining crime and increased imprisonment. The "drug war" has been called a "war on women" because the draconian sentencing of the federal sentencing guidelines in many states has impacted women severely.

In this new edition, we have asked many of the authors to update their chapters. However, we also have new chapters. Chapters 2 and 3 are new and discuss important concepts related to the historical treatment of women by formal and informal agencies of social control. Chapter 15 is also a new chapter and discusses the importance of race as a separate variable that affects women's lives. Chapter 12 focuses on women drug offenders because of their increased numbers and contribution to the imprisonment rates in the last decade. We have also added a chapter on female juvenile offenders.

We hope this new edition is met with approval by those who have used this text over the years.

Acknowledgments

There are a number of people who helped to make this second edition possible. First, we thank our editor at Allyn and Bacon, Jennifer Jacobson. She assisted us throughout the preparation of the manuscript and enthusiastically supported us. The editorial assistant, Emma Christensen, demonstrated her ability and her interest from the beginning. Both Jennifer and Emma were integral to this project, and we appreciate all that they did. We owe a debt of gratitude to our contributors who generously shared their knowledge. It was a pleasure and an honor to work with them on this second edition. Without them, this book would not have been possible. Our librarian, James Hooks, and the library staff, particularly William Daugherty, at Indiana University of Pennsylvania, provided invaluable reference assistance. I also thank my mother, Clara Merlo, for her love and support. Four special people have encouraged and assisted us in this endeavor—my husband, Kevin Ashley, whose love, generosity, wisdom, and humor make all things possible. Our daughter, Alexandra, makes every day memorable with her kindness and love. Joy thanks her husband, Eric Lund, and her son, Gregory Byrne, for their support and love. We feel very fortunate to have such wonderful families.

About the Contributors

Kate Bagley is Professor of Sociology and Chair of the Department of Sociology and Social Work at Westfield State College where she previously served as Coordinator of the Women's Studies Program. She received her Ph.D. in Sociology of Education from the University of California at Berkeley, and a J.D. from the University of Connecticut. Professor Bagley's scholarly and research interests are in the sociology of gender, women and religion, and discrimination law. She has coauthored articles and chapters on women and the criminal justice system and on juvenile justice and is the coeditor of *Women's Studies in Religion: A Multicultural Reader*, forthcoming from Prentice Hall.

Frankie Y. Bailey is Associate Professor in the School of Criminal Justice, State University of New York at Albany (SUNY), where she received her Ph.D. in Criminal Justice. Her area of research is crime and culture, focusing on two areas—crime history and crime and mass media/popular culture. She is the author of *Out of the Woodpile: Black Characters in Crime and Detective Fiction* (1991). She is the coeditor (with Donna C. Hale) of *Popular Culture, Crime, and Justice* (1998). She is the coauthor (with Alice P. Green) of *A Law Never Here: A Social History of African American Responses to Issues of Crime and Justice* (1999). She is the coeditor with Steven Chermak and Michelle Brown of *Media Representations of September 11* (2003). She is the coauthor (with Donna C. Hale) of *Blood on Her Hands: The Social Construction of Women, Sexuality, and Murder* (2004). She and Steven Chermak are the series editors for a five-volume set, *Famous American Crimes and Trials* (2004). As a mystery writer, Professor Bailey is the author of *Death's Favorite Child* (2000), *A Dead Man's Honor* (2001), and *Old Murders* (2003). Her most recent publication is a short story in the mystery anthology, *Shades of Black* (2004) (edited by Eleanor Taylor Bland). She is currently working on *Writing Justice: The Worldviews of African American Mystery Writers* (2005).

Peter J. Benekos is Professor of Criminal Justice and Sociology at Mercyhurst College and was a visiting professor with the School of Justice Studies at Roger Williams University (2003–2004). He received his Ph.D. in Sociology/Criminology from the University of Akron. Research interests include juvenile justice, corrections, and public policy. He is coeditor (with Alida V. Merlo) of *Controversies in Juvenile Justice and Delinquency* (2004) and coauthor (with Alida V. Merlo) of *What's Wrong with the Criminal Justice System? Ideology, Politics, and the Media* (2000). Professor Benekos is past president of the Northeastern Association of Criminal Justice Sciences and recipient of the Association's Fellows and Founders Awards.

Frances Bernat is Associate Professor in the Criminal Justice and Criminology Department at Arizona State University's West campus. She received a J.D. from the State University of New York at Buffalo and a Ph.D. in Political Science from Washington State University. Professor Bernat's research focuses on the criminal law and its policy and application in regard to disadvantaged populations. She is currently analyzing the degree to which present trends in criminological theory explain juvenile behavior. Over the past six years, her work has focused on school education and diversion programs aimed at keeping youth in the schools away from deviant behavior and lifestyles. She has published articles that focus on issues of gender, race and ethnicity, and affirmative action. In 1998, Professor Bernat received the following awards: the Governor's Spirit of Excellence Award from the State of Arizona; the Innovations in American Government Semi-Finalist Award from the Ford Foundation and the John F. Kennedy School of Government at Harvard University in partnership with the Council of Excellence in Government; and the Arizona State University's President's Medal for Team Excellence.

Lisa Growette Bostaph is Assistant Professor in the Department of Criminal Justice Administration at Boise State University. She received her Ph.D. in Criminal Justice from the University of Cincinnati with an emphasis in policing and criminal justice systems. Prior to earning her Ph.D., Professor Bostaph founded Project P.E.A.C.E., a domestic violence organization that works with three police departments in the Greater Minneapolis–St. Paul area and ran the Victim Assistance Program for the Chisago County Attorney's Office. Currently, her research interests include racial disparity and policing and the criminal justice system's response to the victimization of women.

Meda Chesney-Lind is Professor of Women's Studies at the University of Hawaii at Manoa. She received her Ph.D. in Sociology from the University of Hawaii at Manoa. She has served as Vice President of the American Society of Criminology and President of the Western Society of Criminology. Nationally recognized for her work on women and crime, her books include *Girls, Delinquency and Juvenile Justice,* which was awarded the American Society of Criminology's Michael J. Hindelang Award for the "outstanding contribution to criminology (1992)" *The Female Offender: Girls, Women and Crime* (1997), *Female Gangs in America* (1999), *Invisible Punishment* (2002), and *Girls, Women and Crime* (2004).

Sareta M. Davis received her Bachelor of Arts Degree in Psychology from the University of Texas at Austin in 1998. She worked as a parole officer for the state of Texas supervising sex offenders for six years. She completed a Master of Science Degree in Criminal Justice at Texas State University in San Marcos, Texas, while serving as a research assistant in the Criminal Justice Department. Davis was Outstanding Graduate Student of the year for the College of Applied Arts at Texas State University in 2004. Ms. Davis has published with Joycelyn M. Pollock, with whom she presented a related paper at the Academy of Criminal Justice Sciences Annual Meeting in 2004. Ms. Davis plans to continue her education in a joint Ph.D./J.D. program.

Mary Ann Farkas is Associate Professor of Criminology and Law Studies and director of the graduate program in the Administration of Justice at Marquette University. She received an interdisciplinary Ph.D. in criminal justice, sociology, and labor and industrial relations from Michigan State University. Professor Farkas is coauthor of *Correctional Leadership: A Cultural Perspective* and *The Dilemma of the Sexual Offender.* She has authored numerous chapters and articles on women working in corrections, correctional policy, and sex offender laws and policy. She serves on the editorial boards of the *International Journal of Offender Therapy and Comparative Criminology* and the *Journal of Criminal Justice Education.*

Carole Garrison is Professor and Chairperson of the Department of Criminal Justice and Police Studies at Eastern Kentucky University. In 1979 she received a Ph.D. in Public Administration at Ohio State University. She is currently working with the Kentucky Police Corps conducting a curriculum assessment of their academy and with the Madison County, Kentucky, School Board to enhance character development. Professor Garrison was formerly a police officer in Atlanta and was professor of criminal justice at the University of Akron from 1981 to 1999. In the mid-1990s she served as the Executive Director of the CCC, a coordination network of all humanitarian and developmental non-government organizations in Cambodia. She spent one year (1992–1993) as a District Electoral Supervisor in Cambodia serving with the United Nations' Volunteers as part of the UN peacekeeping mission.

Denise Kindschi Gosselin is Professional Educator in the Criminal Justice and Sociology Department at Western New England College. She has taught Domestic Violence at the Massachusetts State Police Academy, held a seminar on Cognitive Interviewing for the Justice System Training and Research Institute at Roger Williams University, and lectured at numerous state and community colleges. Her publications include *Heavy Hands: An Introduction to the Crimes of Family Violence* (3rd ed., forthcoming). She has authored chapters and encyclopedia entries on victim interviewing and child victimization. She is President of the Northeastern Association of Criminal Justice Sciences and has served on various committees for the Academy of Criminal Justice Sciences. She is a retired trooper from the Massachusetts State Police.

Katherine Irwin is Assistant Professor of Sociology at the University of Hawaii at Manoa. She received her Ph.D. in Sociology from the University of Colorado at Boulder. Her research interests include deviance, juvenile delinquency, youth violence, research methods, women and crime, drug use, ecology and crime, and youth culture. In addition, she has written about pregnancy and drug use, violence prevention programs, tattooing and social change, neighborhood contexts and youth violence, and research methods. She is currently conducting a study examining the social construction of at-risk youth.

Janice Joseph is Professor of Criminal Justice at Richard Stockton College of New Jersey. She received her Ph.D. in Sociology from York University in Toronto, Canada. She is the editor for the *Journal of Ethnicity in Criminal Justice.* Her broad research interests include violence against women, women and criminal justice, youth violence, juvenile delinquency, gangs, minorities, and criminal justice. She has published several articles, chapters, and books on delinquency, gangs, domestic violence, stalking, sexual harassment, and minorities in crime.

Marilyn D. McShane is Professor of Criminal Justice at the University of Houston-Downtown and Director of the Community Justice Institute. She received her Ph.D. in Criminal Justice from Sam Houston State University. Professor McShane has taught in doctoral, masters, and undergraduate programs since 1985. She has also been a department chair and director of both centers and institutes, has served and is serving on a number of national criminal justice professional organization boards, and serves as a reviewer of research proposals for the National Institute for Justice. Professor McShane has a substantial number of publications and research and training grants and has been involved in editorial work for book series and journals over the past twenty years. Her publications include two encyclopedias, more than a dozen books, and numerous journal articles.

Alida V. Merlo is Professor of Criminology at Indiana University of Pennsylvania. She received her Ph.D. in Sociology from Fordham University. Previously, she was a faculty member in the Criminal Justice Department at Westfield State College. She is Past-President of the Academy of Criminal Justice Sciences, and a corecipient (with Peter J. Benekos, William J. Cook, and Kate Bagley) of the Academy of Criminal Justice Sciences Donal MacNamara Outstanding Publication Award for 2002. She was also the recipient of the Academy of Criminal Justice Sciences Fellow Award in 2004 and the Founder's Award in 1997. Professor Merlo is coeditor (with Peter J. Benekos) of *Controversies in Juvenile Justice and Delinquency* (2004) and coauthor (with Peter J. Benekos) of *What's Wrong with the Criminal Justice System: Ideology, Politics, and the Media* (2000). She is coeditor (with Peter J. Benekos) of *Dilemmas and Directions in Corrections* (1992).

Barbara Owen is Professor of Criminology at California State University, Fresno. She received her Ph.D. from the University of California, Berkeley, in Sociology. She is a nationally known expert in the areas of women and girls, crime and prisons, substance abuse, and prison culture. Professor Owen was previously a senior researcher with the Federal Bureau of Prisons. Over the past twelve years, Professor Owen has concentrated her work in the areas of women, prisons, and crime, gender-specific programming, drug treatment systems, program evaluation, and applied research methods. She is the author or coauthor of over twenty articles, numerous technical reports, and two books, including *In the Mix: Struggle and Survival in a Women's Prison* (1998).

Joycelyn M. Pollock is Professor of Criminal Justice at Texas State University at San Marcos (formerly Southwest Texas State University). She received her Ph.D. in Criminal Justice at the State University of New York at Albany, and she received a J.D. from the University of Houston. Her books include *Morality Stories* (2004), coauthored with Michael Braswell and Scott Braswell; *Ethics in Crime and Justice: Dilemmas and Decisions* (2003); *Prisons and Prison Life* (2003); *Women, Prison, and Crime* (2002, 2nd ed.); *Sex and Supervision: Guarding Male and Female Inmates* (1986); *Counseling Women Prisoners* (1999); *Criminal Women* (1999); and *Prison: An American Institution* (editor) (1997). Professor Pollock has delivered training to police officers, probation officers, parole officers, constables, and other groups in the areas of sexual harassment, ethics, criminology, and other subjects. In 1998, she was awarded a Fulbright Teaching Fellowship at Turku

School of Law in Turku, Finland. She has served as President of the Southwest Association of Criminal Justice and Trustee-at-Large for the Academy of Criminal Justice Sciences.

Kathryn E. Scarborough is Professor of Criminal Justice and Police Studies at Eastern Kentucky University and earned her Ph.D. in Criminal Justice from Sam Houston State University. Prior to teaching at Eastern Kentucky University, she was a police officer in Portsmouth, Virginia, a United States Navy Hospital Corpsman, and a chemical dependency technician. Professor Scarborough is deputy director for research and evaluation for the Justice and Safety Center at Eastern Kentucky University. Her current teaching and research interests include women and policing, criminal investigation, law enforcement technology, cyber crime, and police administration. Professor Scarborough has contributed to journals such as *Police Quarterly,* the *Thomas Jefferson Law Review,* the *American Journal of Criminal Justice,* and *Crime Prevention and Community Safety: An International Journal.* She has also coauthored textbooks on women in law enforcement, workplace violence, and police administration.

Mittie D. Southerland is Professor Emeritus of Criminal Justice at Murray State University and Executive Director of the Academy of Criminal Justice Sciences. She received her Ph.D. in Social and Philosophical Studies in Higher Education at the University of Kentucky. Professor Southerland served for two years as public safety director and has been a criminal justice planner and juvenile counselor. She has published on administration and management, criminal justice education, rape, and workplace violence. She is a past president of the Academy of Criminal Justice Sciences and the Southern Criminal Justice Association and served two terms as Trustee for the Academy of Criminal Justice Sciences. Professor Southerland chaired the ACJS Committee on Minimum Standards for Criminal Justice Education and later the ACJS Academic Review Committee. She received the Southern Criminal Justice Association's Educator of the Year Award in 1997 and the ACJS Founder's Award in 2004.

Rachel M. Southerland is a premed student at Murray State University, majoring in Liberal Arts with concentrations in Chemistry and Multicultural, Class, and Gender Studies and a minor in Spanish. Her research interests include rape, domestic violence, and health issues of women and minorities. During the 2003–2004 academic year, she was a student in the Women's Studies Department of the University of New Mexico. After graduation she plans to pursue M.D. and M.P.H. degrees. Ms. Southerland works at the Women's Center on Murray State University's campus and belongs to the Pre-Health Professions Club, ROTARACT, and Students for Social Justice. She also volunteers at Angel's Community Clinic, a free medical clinic.

Mary K. Stohr is Professor of Criminal Justice at Boise State University. She received her Ph.D. in Political Science from Washington State University with emphasis areas in Criminal Justice and Public Administration. She has over sixty publications, and they tend to center on gender, management, and/or correctional topics, although she has also published in the areas of victimization and drug treatment evaluation research. She is currently the Treasurer for the Academy of Criminal Justice Sciences.

Frank P. Williams, III, is Professor of Criminal Justice at the University of Houston-Downtown and Director of the graduate Security Management Program. Professor Williams is Professor Emeritus at the California State University, San Bernardino. He received his Ph.D. in Criminology from Florida State University and has been in the criminal justice academic field since 1976. He has taught at doctoral, masters, and undergraduate levels and held positions as department chair, research director, and program coordinator. His academic credentials include a substantial publication record and numerous research projects. Professor Williams has held office and served on boards of several scholarly organizations. He has been an editor or deputy/associate editor for several journals and publishers' book and monograph series.

Part I

The Law and Social Control

In this first section, we present a series of chapters that identify several types of social control that affect what choices women make in their personal and professional lives. Chapter 1 presents a historical overview of the entire text, showing how the law and informal means of social control have constrained and restricted women's choices in the past. A common categorization of women's studies in criminal justice is to discuss women as practitioners, victims, and offenders. One of the themes of this text is that some women *cross over* from one category to another. The first chapter introduces this concept, and we encourage readers to keep this idea in mind as they read the other chapters.

Chapter 2 continues with the idea that images of women have been powerful means of social control, historically and even today. From the early Greeks, women have been portrayed as different from men and, usually, as inferior. Stories and songs of the past are similar in effect, if not in form, to the movies and digital images of today. Women are still sexualized, and they are still stereotyped.

Chapter 3 discusses how the law has been the most powerful formal social control of women. Women have had fewer rights and less protection from the law historically, and even today, while rights are supposedly equal, women find that their experiences in the legal system are not the same as men's. Even female attorneys are sometimes not treated as equals by legal colleagues. This male-centeredness of the legal system still has subtle effects in how the law interprets and judges the behaviors and experiences of women.

In Chapter 4, one particular element of the law's treatment of women is emphasized— the legal controls placed on women's bodies. While a common stereotype of women is that they are pawns of their biology, it is true that pregnancy and childbirth do set women apart from men. There is no parallel for men to the experience of having a law control such fundamentally private decisions as to whether to give birth or whether to undergo medical procedures related to prenatal care or childbirth. In these areas in which the law seeks to control women's decisions over their own bodies, we find that we have not come very far at all from the famous "mother of the species" argument, first voiced in the 1800s.

1

Gender, Justice, and Social Control

A Historical Perspective

Joycelyn M. Pollock

This chapter outlines women's experiences with formal agencies of social control. It examines women as offenders, victims, and practitioners. Rather than showing a linear progression of increasing rights and better treatment, history reveals that the progress of women has been more like a meandering river. At times, progress has been straightforward, but there have also been detours and even times when the gains of women have been reversed.

One can see patterns in the way that the images and stereotypes of women influence how they are viewed and their experiences with agencies of social control. For instance, women were hired by police agencies in the nineteenth century because of a belief that they could best handle female prostitutes and children. Beliefs about women's "special qualities" reemerged in the 1960s and 1970s when policewomen were assigned to sexual assault and domestic violence units. The efforts to control women's reproductive functions, leading to the incarceration of women for promiscuity and the criminalization of birth control in the late nineteenth century and early twentieth century, were precursors to the more current efforts to police reproduction found in fetal abuse statutes and in the criminalization of maternal drug use. The female victims of poverty, economic exploitation, and sexual segregation in women's work of the nineteenth century are hard to distinguish from the poor women today who struggle, as their foremothers did, to survive in a system where women's work is devalued. State childcare continues to be nonexistent, leaving women today with the same problem they have always had—the reality of economic responsibility versus the "myth" that women can and should limit themselves to the domestic sphere.

Images of Women and Social Control

Women's experiences with the agencies of social control can be understood only within the context of cultural definitions of femininity. These images of women shape beliefs about what women need and deserve and how they should be treated. Deviance is defined as different from normal, and normal is defined by stereotypes. Thus, if a normal woman is virtuous, passive, and maternal, then a woman who is not all of these things is, by definition, deviant, whether she is a prostitute (not virtuous), a professional (not maternal), or a victim of battering who fights back (not passive). Lest anyone think that these definitions of women are relegated to historical texts, one only has to compare the cult of true womanhood of the nineteenth century to the emphasis on family values today.

Faludi (1991) makes a good case that for every step forward for woman toward equal treatment in social and private spheres, there is a backlash that trumpets the "natural" differences between the sexes. This was true when the first edition of this book was published in the mid-1990s, and it continues to be true today. For instance, even though women are found in all professions, in Congress, and on the Supreme Court, there are still discussions in religious conferences of women's "natural place" as submissive to her husband. It is argued, for instance, that one of the reasons why Hillary Clinton aroused such negative passions was that she was an example of an intelligent, successful, professional woman who was clearly as strong, if not stronger, than her partner. President Clinton's spinmasters obviously didn't think the public was ready for such a woman, because they attempted to re-create her into a "softer" version, complete with cookie recipes that she shared with the nation. Whether or not women should hold political office while they have young children can still create a vigorous debate in a political race, but no one questions a man's decision to run for office when he is the father of young children.

One of the most obvious images of women's place in society was the signing of the Partial-birth Abortion bill enacted on November 5, 2003. The picture of this bill signing showed President Bush, surrounded by middle-aged white men.[1] The image was discomforting in that it ironically represented the reality that policymaking is still largely a male enterprise even when it profoundly affects women. Of course, there were many women who supported the bill as well, but the sponsors and voters of the bill were almost all men—a fact painfully obvious in the President's remarks and the photograph of him signing the bill. Historically, women's voices have been silent, and even today, women do not influence public policy in equal numbers to men.

Images of women are notoriously inconsistent. The *madonna-whore* duality points to the dichotomous portrait of women in popular literature and culture: a woman is either a mother/wife/virtuous paragon or an evil/Eve/seductress (Burford & Shulman, 1992; Feinman, 1992a). Typifications abound, from the Bible (Mary v. Eve) to movies (wife v. Alex in *Fatal Attraction*). Stereotypes in which women are forced into one slot or the other make it more difficult to understand reality. For instance, if a "good" woman is raped, then the rapist is viewed as worse than a murderer because he has violated her purity, which is seemingly more important than her life. By contrast, a "bad" woman cannot be raped according to this duality, and a bad woman is any woman who does not conform to the stereotype of femininity. Thus, acquaintance rape is an issue that the criminal justice system has difficulty resolving because the crime does not fit with the "good woman–stranger rapist" stereotype.

The general belief is that the woman who accuses an acquaintance of rape either caused or contributed to her own victimization. In the infamous 1992 Tailhook incident, U.S. Navy officers assaulted women and the Navy's response was originally "boys will be boys" until the public outcry led to a more serious investigation. Recently, a series of reports has shown that the military continues to be an unsafe place for women, with substantiated claims of sexual assault occurring in military academies, basic training, and even in combat units in Iraq. The *Washington Post* obtained data through the Freedom of Information Act that document that women stationed in Iraq, Afghanistan, and Kuwait have reported more than 100 cases of sexual assault or misconduct by male officers, and overall, the number of reported cases of sexual assault by army personnel have increased by 19 percent from 1999 to 2002 (from 658 reported cases to 783 reported cases). Even the army has acknowledged that these figures do not provide an accurate picture of the incidence of abuse and that these offenses are regularly underreported (Laurier, 2004, p. 1). The military's response to allegations of sexual misconduct by military personnel seems to be influenced by how public the charges are rather than how serious they are. Thus, things haven't changed all that much from over a decade ago.

The 1991 William Kennedy Smith and Michael Tyson rape trials bore witness to the vitality of the traditional image that good women do not go out alone, drink with a man, or spend time alone with men, and those who do deserve to be assaulted (*The Economist,* 1991; Jefferson, 1997; McDonald, 1991). Over a decade later, the Kobe Bryant case is yet the latest example of the trial strategy of painting the woman who alleges sexual assault as promiscuous, thereby negating her claims (see, for instance, Young, 2004). Defense attorneys use

---

[1]See http://www/whitehouse.gov/news/releases.2003/11/print/20031105-1.html

the power of image—a sexually active woman cannot also be seen as a sexual assault victim—and argue that they are using such information simply to challenge the credibility of the complainant.

Another stereotype claims that women are ruled by their biology. Menstruation, lactation, childbirth, and menopause are all elements that contribute to the view that women are more closely tied to their bodily functions than are men. Men, by contrast, are associated with rationality and spirituality (Burford & Shulman, 1992; Noddings, 1989; Rafter & Stanko, 1982). Again, religion and literature abound with examples of this association. Women are seen as nonrational and emotional, ruled by biological function, and thus incapable of spirituality (justifying their exclusion from religion) or rational management (justifying their exclusion from government, commerce, and public enterprise). Psychological theories (both old and more recent) promote this view with theories about lactational insanity and premenstrual syndrome. Current cultural trends remind women of their biology, warning that "biological clocks" are ticking and that women *naturally* will mourn motherhood if they miss out on the chance to bear children. Current images of women's biological nature continue to revolve around pregnancy. The woman who chooses to remain childless is suspect, whether she is a politician or a movie star. When successful women do become pregnant, inevitably the imagery presented by the media is that regardless of what successes they have had prior to childbirth, they are only now "fulfilled" and childbirth and motherhood are their "greatest accomplishments." Note that these beliefs are no doubt real to the women who express them, but that they may very well be culturally inspired.

Young women today are just as sexualized as they have ever been, and sexual harassment continues unabated in our junior high and high schools. The message clearly received is that a woman's worth is based on her attractiveness and sexual allure rather than on her personal or intellectual qualities. This message is as current in the new millennium as it has ever been. We still have beauty pageants in which women are judged on their physicality with only a token nod to her other qualities. One of the most successful television series of the decade (*Sex and the City*), involved four successful career women, but the writers showed us their professions only a tiny fraction of time, and instead portrayed the female characters as obsessing over, involved in, or getting over sexual relationships. Nothing, evidently, was as important as their sexuality, except perhaps a high-priced pair of shoes. Cultural beliefs are notoriously hard to change and the reality is that women have entered the workforce in greater numbers than ever before in history, but they are still, by and large, also responsible for the home, and still, by and large, evaluated on their sexuality.

The most dominant theme in our culture is that women are *different from men,* and men are defined as the norm. The influence of this idea cannot be underestimated. Women are the "other" sex. In textbooks, women—not men—have special chapters allocated to them. It is women who are excluded from medical studies so as not to skew the sample results. In law, the "reasonable man" standard is clearly still a man. Men and male traits are utilized as the comparative norm in science, culture, and popular opinion; women are measured by their differences from these norms (Eisenstein, 1988).

Social Control

Social control refers to the limits and restriction on behavior and values experienced by each member of society. To some extent, we are all controlled by our socialization to think and behave in certain ways. Social control manifests itself in trivial ways (it influences how one behaves in an elevator or what clothes one chooses to wear) and in major ways (it influences one's choices regarding career, marriage, and lifestyle).

Social control is exerted in society by those institutions that influence and restrict behavioral choices. Informal forms of social control include the church and family. These forms of social control are called *informal* because the shaping occurs through a socialization process that is largely interrelational and conducted within the normal process of developing into a mature adult. One learns right from wrong and other values and appropriate goals through relationships with others, primarily from one's parents. Formal social control is more direct and is exerted through institutions such as schools, the military, and the criminal justice system. In these institutions, incorrect forms of behavior are sanctioned more formally by utilizing the coercive control of the state.

Both informal and formal institutions have always controlled women in a different way from men. As Howe (1990, p. 50) states, "Social control—like criminality—is profoundly gendered." Informal social control restricts a woman's choice of activities throughout her life, determining which toys are appropriate for her, which family chores she should perform, when she may go out and for how long, which occupations are appropriate for her, when she should be married and have children, and how she should look and dress. Of course, boys and men are also controlled by these same social forces. Formal social control exerts its power as well. In the past, women have been restricted not just socially but also *legally* from certain occupations. They have not had the rights to contract, own property, keep their own name upon marriage, or even retain the legal right to their children if divorced from their husbands. In almost all areas of life, men and women have been treated differently by legislation. Discrepancies existed in the income tax code, social security, divorce and child custody decisions, health benefits, military conscription, housing policies, and educational opportunities (Kirp, Yudof, & Strong Franks, 1986). In the remainder of this chapter we will discuss examples of informal and formal social control of women throughout the history of this country. We will also pay particular attention to the experiences of women as victims, offenders, and professionals in criminal justice, both historically and currently. The issues that we introduce in this beginning chapter will be reexamined and explored more fully in the chapters that follow.

Women's Role in Colonial America

In Colonial America, women were usually treated as appendages of men. Under the legal concept of "coverture," they had no legal identity of their own if they were married, being first under their father's control and then under the control of husbands. Blackstone, the famous legal jurist, wrote:

> By marriage, the husband and wife are one person in law, that is, the very being or legal existence of the woman is suspended during marriage, or at least is incorporated and consolidated into that of the husband; under whose wing, protection, and cover, she performs everything. (Blackstone, cited in Eisenstein, 1988, p. 58)

Those who did not enter into marriage were often relegated to family homes as spinster aunts or were dependent on the largesse of brothers-in-law or other relatives.

The "protection and cover" of marriage was often a brutal prison since the husband had, by law, the right to discipline his wife just as he had the right to discipline his children. Only minor restrictions existed, in the form of some laws that warned him against disturbing the peace or inflicting permanent injury. The law often treated the same act differently based on the gender of the offender. For example, the murder of a spouse was considered to be a much more serious offense when committed by a woman. In England during this time, women who murdered their spouses were burned at the stake, while men guilty of the same crime faced hanging. The punishment was more severe for women because it was considered treason, or a crime against the king, to murder one of his valued subjects. By contrast, men who killed their wives were viewed as committing a crime similar to the killing of a servant or animal (Burford & Shulman, 1992).

In England and in the colonies, married women could not sign contracts, own property, or retain title to the wages they earned. They had no legal claim to their children (Kirp, Yudof, & Strong Franks, 1986). It was true that equity courts were utilized in England, and in this country, to protect the property of some wealthy daughters upon marriage through the use of marriage contracts and equitable trusts. These legal maneuvers, however, were not relevant for the vast majority of women who did not have fortunes to protect and who depended on their husbands for economic survival (Hymowitz & Weissman, 1978).

On the other hand, there were very few women in the new colonies, and each person's contributions were vitally important. Accordingly, women were treated in society, if not by law, almost as equal partners in the settlement of the new land. Historians point to such women as Margaret Brent, who litigated over 100 cases as a lawyer in Maryland, and to scores of women who served during the Revolutionary War as farmers, business operators, nurses, spies, and even soldiers. Single women could and did own businesses, and there are ample accounts of women who stepped out of traditional female roles to be traders, tavern owners, silversmiths, newspaper publishers, morticians, and pioneers (Hymowitz & Weissman, 1978).

Some women came to the New World as indentured servants. These individuals traveled from England and Europe to seek economic and religious freedoms. Landowners paid for their passage in return for seven years of labor. Some men and women became indentured servants as an alternative to criminal punishment. Prostitutes and common criminals in England agreed to indenturement for seven to fourteen years as an alternative to hanging. During their indenturement, their master owed them housing and food; in turn, they owed him labor—sometimes backbreaking labor from dawn until dusk. A woman was not allowed to marry, and if she became pregnant, it would add a year onto her indenturement, even if the father was sometimes the landowner himself and the pregnancy occurred because of sexual assault. Because women were so much in demand as workers and as wives for landowners, there is some evidence that the courts of England could not provide enough of them and that shipowners kidnapped young women off the streets of London to sell into marriage or indenturement (Burford & Shulman, 1992; Hymowitz & Weissman, 1978).

While not much is known about criminal offenses in early Colonial America, it is clear that adultery was one of the worst crimes a woman could commit because of the importance of inheritance rules. Women who ran away from marriages were treated as criminals. A husband who had a runaway wife could advertise for her return and could inform the community that she had stolen his belongings, including the clothes on her back. There were certainly some women who escaped a brutal marriage by killing their husband, and these women were dealt with severely (Jones, 1980).

Some early Puritan communities also punished women for crimes that only applied to women, such as being a "common scold," a label given to a woman who berated her husband or was too vocal in public settings. The ducking stool (or cucking stool) and branks were two punishments that the settlers brought from England. The ducking stool's origins were Celtic. Originally a punishment for religious infractions, the purpose was to drown the victim. Eventually it was adapted to serve as a punishment for female scolds and other minor criminals, both male and female. The branks was a type of metal headgear fastened over the head of an offender (usually a woman accused of being a scold). The tongue piece on the device was adorned with sharp spikes designed to inflict injury if the individual tried to move her tongue while wearing it (Burford & Shulman, 1992).

The witch hunts that took place in the late seventeenth century in Salem, Massachusetts, and other communities are interpreted today as sanctions against women who threatened the male power establishment. There seems to be evidence that at least part of the impetus for labeling and prosecuting some women had to do with their outspokenness and informal power as healers or community leaders (Hymowitz & Weissman, 1978).

Women who were found guilty of crimes were treated harshly. Housed with men in common jails, they often were forced to prostitute themselves just to stay alive. The common conception was that a criminal woman was beyond redemption and pity. As the eighteenth century and the Revolutionary War drew to a close, there might have been cause to assume that the protections and freedoms envisaged by the founding fathers would extend to women as well. Abigail Adams's plea to her husband to "remember the ladies" in the writing of the Constitution illustrated this hope, but when the framers wrote it was self-evident that "all men were endowed by the creator with certain inalienable rights," they really did mean men, not women.

The Nineteenth Century: "Separate Spheres"

While women in the seventeenth and eighteenth centuries were treated as valuable partners in the settlement of a new country, the nineteenth century was a time when women were increasingly relegated to their "separate sphere." As men abandoned the farm for factories and a labor economy grew, women, at least middle-class women, became seen as dependents, and more like children than partners. The image of women also changed to one of a delicate flower and guardian of the hearth, home, and society's morals. Of course, this only applied to middle- and upper-class women; poor women continued to work hard to survive as domestics or seamstresses or entered one of the few other lines of work open to women—prostitution.

In the Northeast, starting around the 1820s, young, unmarried women began to work in the textile factories. They were paid one-third to one-half the amount of money that men earned. Twelve- or thirteen-hour days were common. The young women, who came from farms or domestic servitude, lived in factory-owned boarding houses, and their few free hours were strictly controlled. This arrangement was viewed as an inducement to convince farmers to allow their daughters to go alone to the city for work. "Good" girls could hope to marry and thereby escape the grinding poverty of factory work, but girls who became pregnant or acquired a reputation as sexually active were tainted and had little hope of ever entering the realm of domestic dependence (Hymowitz & Weissman, 1978).

These factory women organized and spoke out against their working conditions even before unions controlled by men found their voice; yet when the labor unions grew stronger during and after the Civil War, male members excluded female workers because they believed that women brought male wages down. Also, when large numbers of immigrants began arriving after the 1840s, factory owners replaced native-born female workers who complained with desperately poor Irish women (Hymowitz & Weissman, 1978).

Before emancipation, female slaves were expected to do the same work in the field as male slaves but also to cook and clean for their own families. They were also supposed to give birth to many children. Female slaves were doubly victimized: Not only were they brutalized as people, but they were also exploited sexually as women. They might have been coerced to have sex with masters and then forced to watch the children born from these unions sold to other slave owners. Historians believe that one of the effects of this cruel sexual bondage was the glorification of the Southern white woman as the epitome of delicate frailty. This image of white women was perhaps created to assuage male conscience, since the victimization of African American women was easier to rationalize if they were depicted as completely unlike white women in strength, sensibilities, and emotions (Hymowitz & Weissman, 1978).

Domestic violence was considered an unseemly topic of discussion for middle and upper classes, although it surely existed in these classes then, as it does today. Family violence was more apparent in the culture of the lower classes, with whom it was associated. In the 1860s, some reformers were able to get courts to abandon chastisement rules that provided legal legitimacy for a man's right to punish his children and wife (Tong, 1984). Even in 1864, however, states such as North Carolina had certain rules mandating intervention only if permanent injury occurred (Belknap, 1992). Thus, women had few recourses to domestic violence. Divorce was possible, but many women chose to endure domestic violence rather than the stigma of divorce.

The first formal removal of spousal assault from the criminal justice system into the realm of social work occurred with the creation of family courts in the first part of the twentieth century in some northeastern cities. These courts defined battering as a *problem* rather than a *crime*. The family courts were similar to juvenile courts in that both types utilized psychological and social investigation and remedies other than punishment. Battering was the most common complaint brought to family courts (Dobash & Dobash, 1992).

Women who experienced rape also received little protection from the law. Rape victims were tested under the "utmost resistance standard"; this basically meant that a woman who did not fight to death had not been raped but had rather tacitly consented to her assaulter. A woman who was victimized by rape became a social pariah—regardless of her innocence, loss of virtue was a stigma. Women were supposed to be the guardians of morals and virtue in society. Since men were seen as subject to their baser instincts, a rape victim was blamed for failing to control the man's sex drive. So-called "Lord Hale" instructions, named after a British judge who first used them, warned the jury that a rape charge was easy to make and hard to defend against. Juries at the time were comprised only of men (Dobash & Dobash, 1992). It is no doubt the case that most rape victims never reported the crime, preferring to suffer in silence rather than face the consequences of public humiliation.

Feminism in the Nineteenth Century

Many women who were active in the abolitionist movement were also avid supporters of women's rights. At the Seneca Falls Women's Rights Convention in 1848, women demanded suffrage and liberties in education, jobs, marital and property rights, birth control, health, and dress reform (Faludi, 1991). As would be repeated in subsequent historical cycles, this incipient women's movement was met with a counterreaction that warned that education would make women barren, independent women would be the cause of moral decay, and women ought to be careful because there was a shortage of men and they would die alone (Faludi, 1991).

One avenue an educated woman could take during the mid- to late nineteenth century was social service. Occupations in this area did not conflict with the nurturing maternal role thought to be a woman's biological destiny. The rise of the social work movement owed its existence, at least partly, to the numbers of intelligent, educated women who had no other means of fulfilling their ambitions (Ginzberg, 1990).

Women who organized and ran moral reform groups did so with the zeal of religious reformation but also with the skill of corporate executives. Ironically, they ran corporations before they had legal rights to contract. According to Ginzberg (1990), corporate charters took care to ensure that the husbands of married female officers would be accountable, since the women themselves could not contract or be sued.

The notion of women as the bedrock of social stability and morality runs through all historical analysis of the period (see, for instance, Brenzel, 1983). Women entered public life through petition gathering, creating and administering benevolent societies, and lobbying legislatures. As long as women's activity concerned women, children, or the poverty-stricken, it was acceptable to society. Thus, men and women were depicted as existing in "separate spheres" of influence. Men had control over the public world of politics, law, and commerce, and women lived in the private world of home, family, and child rearing. Activity in abolitionist groups was less acceptable, but because the groups themselves were fairly unconventional, women were grudgingly accepted. Some women, however, did not accept the "separate spheres" designation.

There were two distinct lines of feminist thought. One group who advocated equal rights believed that men and women were substantially similar. A second group celebrated women as the superior sex and sought more freedoms only in those areas that substantiated their view of women as morally and spiritually superior to men. Thus, women who sought entry into corrections and social work did so because of a shared belief that they had something special to contribute. Ginzberg (1990) notes that the characteristics of women's involvement in benevolent, abolitionist, and moral reform work changed between the 1830s and 1850s. In earlier decades, the participation of women was prevalent, vocal, and stemmed from the idea of special spheres—that is, women had some special and unique mandate to promote moral good. In the 1850s, however, their presence was much more limited, especially in abolitionist groups.

Yet Ginzberg (1990) suggests that far from being inactive, women's groups were engaged in a fundamental shift to a narrow definition of political action that emphasized electoral activity instead of more informal lobbying. As abolitionists became more respectable, interest narrowed to those who held votes, and women who had worked side by side with male abolitionists were asked to step aside to make room for male voters. This rejection caused women to confront the inevitable power issues and made them realize how important suffrage was.

A few women sought entry into traditionally male bastions. Arabella Babb Mansfield was admitted to the Iowa bar in 1869, the same year that Washington University Law School in St. Louis became the first law program to admit women. However, most professional women confined themselves to areas such as teaching, social work, and volunteer moral reform work. It was one woman's attempt to practice law, in fact, which prompted the Supreme Court to give judicial approval to separate spheres philosophy at the time (*Bradwell v. State,* 83 U.S. 16b Wall 130, 131 [1873]). The Court reasoned that because God designed the sexes to occupy separate spheres of action—the man commerce and business, the woman hearth and home—only men were to make, apply, and execute laws. Women could not practice law because they could not enter contracts, serve on juries, or meet clients in hotels and restaurants. Their delicate sensibilities would be injured by the rough and tumble world of the court, and they might even be exposed to obscenities.

In the latter half of the nineteenth century, some feminists focused on reforming prostitutes. The number of prostitutes had risen as a result of the Civil War, and this was seen as a sign of growing moral decay. Women's groups were successful in arguing that only women could provide the role models needed to reform errant women. Houses of Refuge and, later, reformatories for women were established. They presented uniquely feminine alternatives to more traditional jails or prisons. For instance, the Female Moral Reform Society was concerned with homeless and destitute women and was instrumental in the decisions of police departments to hire the first matrons to guard female prisoners. In the second half of the nineteenth century, more police departments hired women, but their role was strictly limited to dealing with female offenders and children (Heidensohn, 1992).

Women's groups were also instrumental in getting states and communities to separate female offenders from male offenders in prisons and to hire women to guard them. Elizabeth Fry first proposed separate institutions in 1813, and slowly women were removed to separate wings or rooms in penal institutions. However, it was not until 1840 that Elizabeth Farnham finally became the first woman to head an all-female wing of Sing Sing. The Women's Prison Association was founded in 1845, and its members established halfway houses for women. Later still, a separate reformatory for women was opened in 1873 in Indiana, followed by one in Framingham, Massachusetts (1877), and another in Bedford Hills, New York (1901) (Freedman, 1981; Heidensohn, 1992; Rafter, 1985).

Reformatories and other institutions for reform were not reserved for adult women. Young girls were believed to be even more amenable to change. In fact, Brenzel (1983) contends that the administrators of the Lancaster Reform School wanted girls to enter when they were 7 years old and stay until they were 16 or 18. Evidence of wantonness was enough to disqualify a girl from such schools. If she were already proven to be promiscuous, she would likely find herself in a more restricted and less benevolent placement. After the Civil War, however, there was a shift in function and ideology. The school became more custodial and took in "hardened" girls.

Ironically, the female professionals and reformers who championed separate institutions participated enthusiastically in a system that strongly discriminated against poor and immigrant women. Women and young girls were brought into the system of social control almost solely to control their sexual behavior. From the very beginning of the juvenile court system, more girls were detained for status offenses than boys (Chesney-Lind, 1981; Feinman, 1992a). The juvenile court was more interested in moral reform than in criminality. The result was that young women were often incarcerated for behavior that was considered normal and natural for males.

Ginzberg (1990) postulates that the moral reform movement became "masculinized" during the Civil War. The earlier emphasis on women's moral superiority and the unique value of femininity was replaced by an emphasis on professionalism. Women's groups gradually focused more on suffrage than on moral reform, leaving the institutions to female administrators who had more of a professional orientation than one infused with moral fervor.

In the mid-nineteenth century, Married Women's Property Acts were passed, repealing many of the earlier laws that had vested title in all real and personal property in the husband. Legal historians speculate that this probably had more to do with attempts by males to protect their property by hiding it under their wives' or daughters' names, but regardless of the motives, women at least had now gained some economic rights. However, the law was still largely an oppressive force for women. The use of contraception, abortion, and adultery were all punished under the law. While the law was used to control women, it did not necessarily protect them.

The Twentieth Century

Another surge of feminism occurred in the early twentieth century. The International Ladies' Garment Workers Union was founded in 1900; Margaret Sanger was a vocal advocate of birth control; and the National Women's Party was created in 1916 to fight for an equal rights amendment. In 1910, Alice Stebbins Wells was hired by the Los Angeles Police Department, and in 1915, the International Association of Policewomen was formed. By that time, there were some women in law enforcement agencies, even though they were placed in women's bureaus. These women's divisions did preventative work with children and women (Hale & Bennett, 1995).

By the time the vote came in 1920 (also the year that all states admitted women to practice law), the backlash had begun. By 1930, there were fewer female doctors than in 1910, and the Depression forced tens of thousands of women out of work (Faludi, 1991). The International Association of Policewomen was disbanded in the 1930s due to lack of members (Hale & Bennett, 1995).

A large part of the feminist agenda in the early twentieth century was equality in the workplace. While some feminists advocated fighting for workplace improvements for both men and women through union activity, others championed protectionist legislation based on women's different needs (with the belief that this protectionist legislation could be used as a stepping stone to improved working conditions for everyone) (Brophy & Smart, 1985, p. 5; Heidensohn, 1992). Ultimately, protectionist legislation was passed, but women learned that the protections were illusory. While legislation restricted the type of work women could perform and mandated hours and work conditions, there was no protection over wages. Thus, "women's work" became the lowest paid employment. At its peak in the 1930s, protectionist legislation only applied to about one-third of women workers, since the majority worked in unregulated industries (Kirp, Yudof, & Strong Franks, 1986, p. 37). Court cases that dealt with such legislation illustrated the intent, illusory or not, to protect women because of their more important role as "mother of the species." That is, government needed to make sure that any other work they did could not interfere with their ability to reproduce:

> The two sexes differ in structure of body, in the functions to be performed by each, in the amount of physical strength, in the capacity for long-continued labor particularly when done standing, the influence of vigorous health upon the future well-being of the race, the self reliance which enables one to assert full rights, and in the capacity to maintain the struggle for subsistence. This difference justifies a difference in legislation and upholds that which is designed to compensate for some of the burdens which rest upon her (*Muller v. Oregon*, 208 U.S. 412, 422-23 [1908]).

Interestingly, a more recent case also depended on the same argument. When Johnson Controls sought to restrict women from high-paying positions because of fears of "fetal endangerment," the Supreme Court was not persuaded that a woman's special role as "mother of the species" should restrict their work choice (*U.A.W. v. Johnson Controls, Inc.*, 111 S. Ct. 1196 [1991]).

In general, women in the early twentieth century were perceived as normal only if they acted in conformance to the ideals of separate spheres. Thus, women who sought professional careers, or women who were criminal, were considered not only deviant in a sociological sense, but in more profound ways. In the early twentieth century, biological determinism was still popular as a theory to explain criminality, especially female criminality. Lombroso (1895), writing in the late 1800s and early 1900s, explained that criminal women were atavistic throwbacks and that masculine traits in criminal women overpowered the normal feminine traits of passivity and maternalism as well as piety, conservatism, and conformity. He also wrote that it was not unusual that so many criminal women were prostitutes because criminals were primitives, and all primitive women were prostitutes. When a woman became criminal she was a "thousand times worse than a man" because she had no moral sentiments and no sympathy for her victims. This is the madonna-whore duality in scientific guise (for discussion, see Pollock, 1999).

In the first part of the twentieth century, Freud and other early psychologists gave scientific credence to the view that women had weaker mental constitutions, were inherently masochistic, were deficient in moral and emotional development, and suffered from a number of maladies unique to their sex. These traits described normal women. Freud believed that all women desired to be men, but normal women sublimated that desire by having children. Deviant women, however, either criminals or professional women, tried to become men by engaging in male activities.

Freud also helped to deny the realities of female victimization:

> Female victims were thought to be irrational and prone to illusions, fabrications and exaggeration. Freud's conception of incest as an expression of unconscious female desire is probably the best known example of the transformation of female experiences into fantasies. Female victims of crime such as sexual assault, rape, and violence in the home, who had in the past been characterized as prone to exaggeration, were now "confirmed" in these perceptions. . . . By the 1930s psychoanalysis had enshrined the myth of masochism into its conceptions of normal female psychology (Dobash & Dobash, 1992, p. 158).

In the 1940s World War II spurred the creation of a new image of women that supplanted the tender flower of earlier decades. "Rosie the Riveter" was strong, athletic, and capable of holding heavy industry jobs. Women did not merely help out at home in the war years; they also comprised 57 percent of all workers at war's end. Their contribution to the war effort was not overlooked. In the 1940s, Congress passed thirty-three bills serving to advance women's rights. Yet when the war was over and men needed their jobs back, a concentrated effort to chase women home began. Two million women were fired from heavy industry; companies revived prohibitions against hiring married women, with some jobs placing ceilings on women's salaries; and the government discontinued state-supported daycare (Faludi, 1991).

In criminal justice, the same exodus was seen. During the war years, women gained back the number of jobs lost during the 1930s in police work; however, after the war they were once again displaced. By this time, too, reformatories for women, which had been developed with the philosophy that they should be run by women, were almost all headed by male administrators because of a perception that women could not handle the responsibilities of administration. Though women could and did work in such institutions as matrons (many women who served in the war came back to matron jobs), they rarely were given managerial positions (see Pollock, 2003; Rafter, 1985).

Women did not completely abandon work for home in the 1950s, the time period often viewed as the good old days when women stayed at home. Actually, more women were employed in the 1950s than at the height of the war, but women traded highly paid industrial jobs for service positions. In effect, "Rosie the Riveter" became a secretary (Faludi, 1991). Even though women were an important component of this nation's labor force, work was seen as temporary until marriage or motherhood, and women's employment was seen as supplemental to the wage earning of the husband. This perception, however, was never true for minority women, poor women, or even middle-class women, whose earnings were always necessary for the family's survival.

The Second Wave of Feminism

The first wave of feminism is described as occurring in the mid- to late-1800s with the work of Susan B. Anthony and Elizabeth Cady Stanton, ultimately resulting in the 19th Amendment in 1920 (Burford & Shulman, 1992). The second wave of feminism occurred in the late 1960s and early 1970s. Interestingly, while the first wave of feminism might be described as arising from the abolitionist movement and some women's anger that the freedoms and rights fought for did not extend to them, the second wave of feminism might be described as arising from the civil rights movement and the anger of women who were told that they had no place in that movement other than "on their backs." Women's efforts resulted this time in getting Congress to pass the Equal Rights Amendment in 1971; however, since thirty-eight states did not ratify the amendment, it died and has not been resurrected.

As was true in the nineteenth century and early twentieth century, feminism is not monolithic. While some advocate complete equality in the law and other spheres, others view this stance as misguided and advocate recognition of the special qualities and needs of women. Discussion on this subject bears striking similarities to discussions that took place over 100 years ago. Whether the issue concerns female criminals, victims, or professionals, the "equality versus special needs" argument emerges. For instance, while some argue that female criminals deserve equal treatment by police and equal sentencing and punishment options from the courts, others maintain that women are different and therefore should be treated differently. The argument over women as *victims* follows a similar pattern: Some hold that women should receive the same treatment from the system; others argue that female victims need special attention, that is, special laws such as the Violence Against Women Act. In law, commerce, law enforcement, and corrections, contributions of female professionals are described as equal to men's or, alternatively, that they bring special qualities to the job. In the sections that follow, we will examine societal changes that affected women in the last half of the twentieth century, paying special attention to the experiences of these three categories of women.

Women as Criminals

Criminologists largely ignored women's criminality until the 1970s. Traditional theories either completely ignored women or were stretched and manipulated to attempt to explain female criminality. Pollak (1950) was about the only researcher interested in female criminals, and he held the view that women were just as criminal as men, but their crimes were hidden and/or not prosecuted. The main reason that women were so ignored by the field was that their numbers were too few to be of concern, especially in serious and/or violent crime areas. In the 1970s female criminals were the subject of more interest. The women's liberation movement was identified as the impetus for a "new breed" of female criminal who was more violent (Adler, 1975), or, at least, engaged in more nontraditional forms of property crime (Simon, 1975).

The idea that women have become more violent is a perennially favorite topic for academics and journalists alike. Those who attempt to prove such a phenomena use percentage increases to show that women's percentage increases are higher than men's. However, the reason they are so high is because percentage increases are highly influenced by small base numbers. Because so few women commit violent crime, it is easy to achieve large percentage increases (Pollock & Davis, 2004). It is clear, however, that women's percentage of total arrests for all areas of property crime has increased in the last several decades (Steffensmeier & Streifel, 1992; Pollock, 1999). However, once again, the numbers must be used with caution because they come from official definitions. It may be the case that women are more likely to commit criminal acts today, and/or it may be that women are more likely to be arrested and formally charged today.

The so-called "chivalry factor" explanation of women's small numbers explained that women were less likely to be arrested, charged, convicted, or sentenced to prison than men. After an examination of all the sentencing studies, one may conclude that women, or at least some women, did receive somewhat more favorable treatment in the courts (Erez, 1992). The studies, however, are contradictory, and there is evidence that women may receive harsher sentences for some crimes, or that some women (those who do not fit female stereotypes) receive more punitive sentences than men (Chesney-Lind, 1981; Erez, 1992; Nagel & Hagan, 1983; Pollock, 1999). Social control theory, as described by some researchers, explains that women who are under informal social control (i.e., marriage) may be less likely to receive formal social control (i.e., prison sentences). This relationship applies only to women, not to men. Other studies find that having dependents (being a mother) seems to be more important than being dependent (as a wife), and that this feature applies to men as well as women (Eaton, 1986; Erez, 1992; Koons-Witt, 2002).

While there has been a definite increase in the number of women arrested, there was an even greater increase in the number of female offenders sentenced to prison. In the last half of the century, the number of women in prison went from several thousand to over 100,000 (from about 4 percent of the total prisoner population to closer to 10 percent). States that did not have separate facilities for women had all built one by the end of the 1970s; however, by the end of the century they found that they needed to build additional facilities to house the increasing numbers of women being sentenced (see Pollock, 2003, for discussion).

Also, in eerie reflections of past eras, crimes unique to women were defined and prosecuted in the 1980s and 1990s. For instance, pregnant drug addicts were arrested in some states for child abuse or neglect (Feinman, 1992b; Pollock-Byrne & Merlo, 1991). When judges would not accept prosecutors' attempts to manipulate current laws to punish women, states responded by passing fetal endangerment statutes that redefined the fetus as a legal entity with rights equal to that of the pregnant woman. In these laws, pregnancy is not considered a health concern of the woman, but rather a state interest that is legislated and controlled by state actors. Supporters of abortion rights are rightfully concerned that these laws are only the latest in the many attempts to challenge *Roe v. Wade,* 410 U.S. 113 (1972). This issue is explored more fully in Chapter 4.

Thus, women are no longer overlooked or forgotten in corrections or criminology. Some would say that is not necessarily a good thing. Equality seems to mean that women are increasingly being sent to prison. Women do commit more crime today than ever before, at least from what we can tell from official statistics. However, their crimes are not usually violent. Women's criminality will be addressed more fully in Chapter 10.

Women as Victims

The women's movement of the 1970s dramatically changed public perceptions toward rape victims and battered women and also law enforcement's treatment of these victims. Law enforcement and the courts had to be cajoled, prodded, and threatened before they began to change their traditional attitudes of neglect. Grassroots feminist organizations created and operated rape crisis centers and battered women's shelters in the 1970s. Women's Advocates in Minnesota and Transition House in Boston in 1973 and 1974 were the first battered women's shelters to open in this country. These American shelters were preceded by the women's shelter in Chiswick, England, which had opened after the need for such a place had been expressed in women's consciousness-raising groups (Dobash & Dobash, 1992, p. 26). Once public attention was focused on this area, the criminal justice system responded, and the movement grew to encompass a broader perspective under the victims' rights movement.

Domestic Violence.   Once shelters were created, legislators had to be pressured into providing governmental funds. Shelter fundraisers still confront the belief that it is antifamily to provide a place for battered women to find assistance. Dobash and Dobash (1992) noted that while the movement to provide services for battered women started out as a grassroots effort, professionals became interested in the problem when money became available. Similarly, the movement to provide rape crisis hotlines and other services started at the grassroots level and then was coopted by professionals. The influx of professional helpers has created a split in focus among women's groups today. Some believe that battering and rape are fundamentally social and political issues that need to be addressed by social action, while other groups approach battering as an individual problem and focus on counseling and assistance for the individual woman (Dobash & Dobash, 1992).

In the 1970s and early 1980s, social and economic reasons were given to explain a woman's plight in battering relationships. Professional therapists identified the battering experience as a syndrome. The learned helplessness theory was borrowed from other social-psychological literature. This syndrome, and the elements of the learned helplessness theory, became a defense for women who killed their attackers (Walker, 1984). Actually, accounts of many battered women showed that they tried to leave many times and returned only because their husbands threatened them or family members; and that they had sought help from every imaginable agency to no avail. Often the killing took place either after a dare from the husband, as in "Here's the gun—shoot me before I kill you," or because women believed that their death was imminent.

Women who killed spouses who had routinely and systematically beaten them over a number of years have been punished with convictions and prison sentences, even if the attack came during or immediately after an attack by the husband. Case files do not always show that women kill abusers while they are asleep or defenseless. Very often, the abuser is actively terrorizing her at the time, yet prosecutors still reject self-defense claims (Browne, 1987). Ironically, one prosecution stratagem in trial has been to challenge the woman's belief that she was in imminent danger of losing her life (an element of self-defense) because, after all, she had been beaten many times in the past and the attacker had never killed her.

The learned helplessness argument has been somewhat successful as a defense strategy in helping women with acquittals or mitigation of charges. It is interesting to speculate as to why self-defense claims are rejected unless they are presented under the theory of the battered woman syndrome. This theory presumes that the woman perceives herself as completely *helpless* in a cycle of violence that she is unable to break. Then she erupts in a temporary moment of fatal violence. Note what defense attorneys must prove in order for this to happen. The woman must have been victimized over a period of time by physical and emotional violence, she must give the appearance of passivity in the face of such violence (otherwise, she and her attacker are mutual combatants), and she must exhibit signs of poor self-image and weak ego. If she is sufficiently pathetic, the justice system may let her defend herself, provided she seek long-term counseling to help her discover why she is so masochistic as to attract brutal men.

It would seem to make more sense for the courts to recognize the differences between men and women when applying traditional self-defense arguments rather than to create a whole new defense. After all, mere differences in physical size would indicate that women may have to resort to weapons sooner than men and may be forced to use lethal violence. By contrast, men responding to similar threats may be able to utilize less than lethal violence to achieve the same purpose. Also, the social and environmental reality of women in these situations must be recognized. The creation of an entirely different defense for women may have more to do with stereotypes and myths of women as passive, or as emotionally unstable, than it does with the reality of battering.

The learned helplessness theory was never accepted by all courts, and recently has been less visible in the popular news and in jurisprudence. Ironically, the rise of battered women's shelters has seemed to result in a decrease in the number of husbands killed by wives, even though there has not been much of an effect on the number of wives killed by abusive husbands (Pollock, 1999, p. 31).

One of the results of the victim's rights movement has been to effectively change law enforcement's handling of domestic violence. Until recently, the response of police to such calls has been neglect and scorn. Those officers who wanted to do something to prevent the abuse were largely hamstrung by rules that required the woman to file a complaint unless the officer actually saw the assault. Women who feared further violence or who only wanted the violence to stop often refused to file, leading to the widespread belief among officers that women did not want to help themselves out of a violent relationship.

In the 1960s, there was a trend to adapt crisis intervention techniques in handling domestic assaults. The Law Enforcement Assistance Administration (LEAA) funded several model projects to train and employ civilian social workers and police officers that would act alone or in teams to respond to such calls. Despite popular opinion, these programs showed little or no success in reducing violence. In New York, violence calls rose threefold, and there were more domestic homicides in the study area than in the control area (Dobash & Dobash, 1992, p. 160).

In a few court cases, police departments have been held liable for not providing protection to women. These cases have been extremely important in changing departmental policies. *Thurman v. City of Torrington,* 595 F. Supp. 1521 (D. Conn. 1984), involved a woman who was beaten, stomped, and stabbed in front of her child, on a front sidewalk. Incredibly, this act took place while a police officer sat in his car on the street. The case led to a landmark ruling that held that police have a duty to protect women from violence from their husbands; failure to do so has been identified as sex discrimination and may result in large settlements against the department and city. The fact that such a case needed to be litigated at all in 1984 is the most troubling aspect of the holding.

The pressure for law enforcement to react to domestic violence with formal arrest led to mandatory arrest policies wherein officers were trained to arrest if they believed that violence had occurred or would continue. Research indicated that all officers did not always enforce the policy. In one study, only one-third of police indicated a pro-arrest philosophy (Dobash & Dobash, 1992, p. 208). There is emerging evidence, however, that mandatory arrest policies have not been the panacea for female victims that supporters envisioned.

There is some evidence that officers who are trained and must abide by mandatory arrest policies are more likely to arrest either both parties or the woman—even if she was the complainant (Chesney-Lind, 2002; Ferraro, 1998). This may, in fact, account for women's increased number of arrests in assault and aggravated assault categories (for a discussion, see Pollock & Davis, 2004). Why would the female victims of domestic violence be arrested? It has never been true that most women who are beaten by partners are helpless victims who do not fight back. Many women defend themselves when they are assaulted. When police arrive on the scene, they may see evidence that the abuser has been hit or scratched. Further, the woman may be more emotional than the male assailant. Faced with a "he said/she said" situation, the officer may choose to arrest both parties.

In the 1970s, many states enacted laws allowing no-fault divorces, which helped women escape from abusive relationships but also put more responsibility on the women themselves to do something about their victimization. While the legal right to leave an abusive mate, even without having to prove the abuse in court, exists today, it has done nothing to change the structural restraints that keep women in such marriages. Studies have shown that women's living standard goes down 30 percent after a divorce, while men's goes up 10 to 15 percent (Singleton, 1990, p. 41). More recent studies also indicate that after divorce, 43 percent of custodial mothers were living below the poverty line while only 10 percent of noncustodial fathers lived below the poverty line (Bartfeld, 2000). Economic reasons for remaining in an abusive marriage are real and will continue as long as women earn less than men and as long as child care remains expensive and unattainable for many.

Survivors of Rape.   As previously mentioned, early grassroots and feminist groups began organizing rape crisis hotlines and services for rape victims in the 1970s. Myths of rape, such as "it is impossible to rape a resistant woman," and "only young, attractive women are raped," were identified and repudiated (Goodstein & Lutze, 1992). Large numbers of female rape victims (some figures put the number at half or even nine out of ten) never reported their rape to criminal justice agencies because of the poor treatment they would receive. This was one impetus for hiring female police officers, who were perceived to be better at interviewing rape victims (Goodstein & Lutze, 1992).

Official agencies and professionals have supplanted the earlier grassroots organizations that were created to help rape victims. This has been a crucial development in gaining acceptance by law enforcement agencies. Police and prosecutors' offices often did not trust and were not cooperative with groups perceived to be feminist. The antagonistic relationship that often existed between such groups and formal justice agencies was eased if and when the feminist groups became more mainstream and when formal agencies employed professionals with a service agenda (as opposed to a political agenda) to address the needs of rape survivors.

Legal changes were fought for and won in the 1960s and 1970s. Among the features that were abandoned were marital exemption rules that defined rape as possible only outside of marriage; the requirement that resistance had to be physical or result in injury; corroboration requirements for each element of the offense; and the use of cautionary instructions to the jury. Most importantly, rape shield laws were enacted that prevented the defense from attacking a woman's credibility through evidence of her sexual history (Tong, 1984). Even today, however, prosecutors' offices may drop cases that do not fit the innocent victim–stranger attacker mode.

Feminists' recognition of female crime victims led a move to change the language applied to women who have been raped. The term *rape survivors* replaced *rape victims* in the popular lexicon of service providers. This change may have been simply semantic, but it did shed light on the crucial fact that women who had been battered and raped felt, above all, that they were without power during the crime and even after the justice system took over. Intervention agents were taught that women needed to have choices, including the choice to prosecute or not, and the choice to seek treatment or not.

The focus on female crime victims has spilled over into a more general victims' rights movement. Today there are victim–witness programs in many prosecutors' offices or police departments, as well as victims' rights legislation and victim compensation programs. Dobash and Dobash (1992) suggest that LEAA-inspired victim–witness programs might be seen as Trojan horses because they have allowed ideas and programs started by feminists to enter the criminal justice machinery (p. 205). Indeed, these programs often have disproportional numbers of women employed, and their orientation toward counseling and assistance as opposed to punishment and enforcement seems to be a particularly feminine addition to the criminal justice system.

Violence toward Women.   While the myths about rape and battering victims have slowly been brought out and exposed in the public arena, there is a disturbing persistence of violence directed against women, especially the gratuitous violence that is seen on television and movie screens in the "slasher" movies, and even in fashion advertisements. Pornography has proved to be a contentious issue for feminists since some find themselves aligned with conservatives and conservative right organizations in their wish to punish and censor pornography producers. Other feminist groups fear that censorship is too high a price to pay for the sexist degradation of pornography and its images of women as sexual slaves (Eisenstein, 1988). Part of the problem is that definitions of pornography are muddled. To the conservative right, pornography is sexual explicitness; to feminists, it is the portrayal of women as objects to be used and injured by males (Tong, 1984; Smart, 1989). These definitions still leave plenty of room for confusion and argument.

In 1994, Congress enacted the Violence Against Women Act, sponsored by Senator Joseph Biden. This measure allowed women to bring civil cases for attacks committed against them because of their gender and mandated educational programs against domestic violence and stiffer laws against spouse abuse. The Supreme Court overturned the provision of the Act that allowed for federal civil remedies for gender-based crimes, arguing that it exceeded the authority of Congress to legislate and punish private behavior (*United States v. Morrison,* 529 U.S. 598, 2000). The legislation was amended in 2000 with changes that adhered to the Supreme Court ruling. The Violence Against Women Office of the Department of Justice acts as a clearinghouse of information and annually funds programs designed to reduce domestic violence and other violence against women (Paulson, 2000). The Act expires at the end of every five years and must be passed again by Congress in 2005. The issues of women as victims of domestic violence and sexual assault will be covered in Chapters 8 and 9.

Women as Professionals

One of the most dramatic changes in the last forty years has been the entry of women into the workplace. In 1950, women comprised about 29 percent of the workforce, but in 1980 women made up 50 percent of the workforce. One out of seven women is the sole wage earner for her family. The most dramatic changes have taken place in the working habits of women who have small children. In 1940, fewer than 10 percent of mothers with children under 6 worked. In 1992, more than 65 percent of them did (Kirp, Yudof, & Strong Franks, 1986, p. 141; U.S. Bureau of the Census, 1993, p. 400). Since the first edition of this book, the increase has slowed but continued. In 2002, 75 percent of mothers with children under 18 were in the workforce, and 61 percent of women with children under 3 were in the workforce (U.S. Bureau of Labor Statistics, 2002).

Despite increases in numbers, however, women are still largely relegated to "women's" positions in teaching, clerical work, food service, nursing, or domestic service. In 1993, three-fourths of all working women were found in these occupations. For this reason—as well as due to wage discrimination, lack of seniority, sex-segregated assignments within an occupation, and career gaps—women still earned only 75 cents to every dollar men earned (U.S. Bureau of the Census, 1993, p. 426). In 2002, things had not changed all that much. While 98 percent of preschool and kindergarten teachers were women, only 19 percent of dentists and 10 percent of engineers were women. Women's earnings rose slightly to 78 percent of men's by 2002 (U.S. Bureau of Labor Statistics, 2002).

Federal laws (Title VII of the 1964 and 1972 Civil Rights Acts) and court decisions have prohibited hiring and promotional decisions based on sex. Even pregnancy is not to be used as a reason for firing or denying promotion or for forcing a maternity leave (Pregnancy Discrimination Act of 1978). While increasing numbers of women are working, these women report that the workplace is not an especially friendly environment. Women in traditionally male occupations (i.e., law enforcement, law, and engineering) faced issues of tokenism, sexual harassment, and role conflicts in the 1970s and 1980s. Today they face "mommy track" pressures and the difficulties of balancing work and family responsibilities.

Entry into criminal justice agencies has been especially problematic for women because of the "macho" nature of these professions and the strong subculture that emphasizes characteristics such as toughness, strength, bravery, risk, and danger. There is no doubt that men felt threatened by a loss of status when women entered these occupations, and their insecurity has been supported by referring to the women's *special* skills in interviewing female victims, calming explosive inmates, being especially powerful and sympathetic litigators for child abuse and rape cases, and being perfect undercover agents in narcotics and prostitution investigations.

While their numbers have increased, women still comprise only a fraction in any subsystem of criminal justice. When the 1995 edition of this book was published, we wrote that approximately 10 percent of sworn police officers, 18 percent of lawyers and judges, and 11 percent of federal correctional officers were women (Bernat, 1992, p. 302; Erez & Tontodonato, 1992, pp. 228–241; and Maguire, Pastore, & Flanagan, 1993). Ten years later those numbers have not increased much in law enforcement, and women appear to have made their greatest strides in the field of law and corrections. For example, 24 percent of attorneys are women. In the judiciary, women make up about 19 percent of federal judges and 20 percent of state judges. In correctional institutions on the federal level, women comprise 25.4 percent of the correctional officers. Women are still only about 11 percent of sworn female police officers out of the 440,920 full-time sworn personnel in local police departments as of June 2001 (Hickman & Reaves, 2003, p. 4; Maguire & Pastore, 2002). In other areas, women's gains have been similarly modest.

Women in the Law.   Women have entered the legal profession in increasingly large numbers only in the last decade or so. Bernat (1992, p. 307) noted that between 1970 and 1986, the number of female attorneys increased from 4 percent to 17 percent, but the real growth occurred only over the last decade. Corporate, tax, and litigation firms are still largely male bastions. In more recent years, women comprise close to half of all entering law school classes, and about 24.6 percent of all lawyers, but do not seem to be making great strides in achieving partnership or other measures of success (U.S. Department of Labor, 1995). For instance, Werner (2004) writes that only about 12 percent of partners in law firms are women.

The reason for this is only partially explained by the fact that women tend to continue to favor public agencies and small firms. More importantly, they earn significantly less than their male colleagues. There are 215,000 female attorneys and judges who earned an average of $1206 weekly compared to 420,000 male attorneys and judges who earned an average of $1615 weekly in 2002 (U.S. Dept. of Labor, 2003, p. 12).

A decade ago, gender discrimination studies found that female attorneys were subjected to demeaning treatment by judges and harassment and sexist remarks from colleagues (Schafran, 1990, p. 32). Unfortunately, more recent studies report that such behavior continues, albeit less often (Hemmens, Strom, & Schlegal, 1998).

While some judges have gained notoriety by refusing to address a female attorney by her maiden name or refusing to allow female attorneys to wear pants in their courtrooms, male lawyers are cited as the worst offenders. They are described as refusing to take direction from female court employees, treating them as personal secretaries, and intentionally using profane or sexist strategies to make female opponents uncomfortable. While some describe such practices as mere trial tactics, others point out that to utter a racist remark to a black opponent would never be allowed, regardless of its effectiveness (Schafran, 1990, p. 32). Chapter 7 covers the issues surrounding women in legal professions in more detail.

Women in Law Enforcement.   While female lawyers may encounter sexual slurs, female police officers have often been faced with more life-threatening discrimination. This was especially true for the first female officers who were integrated into the patrol ranks. Some reported that male partners refused to back them up on calls or, alternatively, forced them to stay in the car in a misguided effort at protection. In the late 1960s, female police officers first started to sue for equal employment opportunities. Up until this time, most large police departments had small numbers of policewomen who were given special titles, assignments, and less pay than male patrol officers. Women sued for equal pay and the right to take the exam for sergeant. They challenged the validity of height and weight requirements and demanded the right to be treated equally in promotional tests (Hale & Bennett, 1995).

Various factors influenced change. The Crime Control Act of 1973 made it illegal to discriminate against women in any agency or organization that received Law Enforcement Assistance Administration funds. Departments began to demilitarize their agencies, and training expanded to utilize more interpersonal strategies. Heterogeneity was viewed as a positive change in hiring practices. These factors, as well as the court actions of individual women, led to the sexual integration of patrol. Indianapolis was the first city to bring women into patrol work in 1969, followed by Washington, D.C., in 1969 (Greene, 2003; Heidensohn, 1992; Martin, 1992).

Female police officers were refused their own uniforms, had to use public restrooms because there were no locker facilities, and were faced with sexual harassment daily. This harassment took the form of rumors about their sexual habits, propositions, crude jokes, and other means used to make it clear that women were out of place in the masculine world of policing. As one female officer noted: "You're a butch-queer or you're laying everybody in sight" (cited in Heidensohn, 1992, p. 140).

In a survey of seventy female officers in five large urban areas in the early 1990s, two-thirds reported that they had experienced sexual discrimination, and three-fourths reported that they had experienced sexual harassment (Martin, 1992, p. 290). Female officers today still experience some degree of harassment, especially in academies, but nothing like that experienced by the first female officers. Yet the number of women in policing has not appreciably increased. About 10 percent of sworn employees in municipal departments are women, as are about 12 percent of sworn employees in county departments (Maquire & Pastore, 2002, p. 44, 45). The number of female chiefs or sheriffs also has continued to be remarkably small and shows no signs of any substantial increase.

In order to understand why women have not entered law enforcement in greater numbers, it is helpful to know that the entry of women in policing corresponded to the emergence of crisis teams, victim assistance, community outreach, outreach programs for juveniles (i.e., D.A.R.E.), and community policing. While these programs have never been given much status by the informal police subculture, and those who worked in these divisions are considered "soft cops" or not really doing police work, the positions were desirable to and considered appropriate for women (Miller, 1999).

Whether women have feminized police work or whether police organizations moved in that direction and only then were receptive to the entry of females is debatable. In any event, it seems that with the demise of federal funds for community policing and with the concerns over homeland security that have arisen since 9/11, policing has increasingly shed its "soft cop" image and the trend is now toward "traditional policing." One might speculate that this has discouraged women from entering academies; however, it could also be that there are only a certain number of women who are interested in law enforcement as a profession and that their numbers will never exceed what they are today.

Criminal justice programs have seen an increase in the number of female undergraduates so that today female criminal justice or criminology majors either equal or outnumber male students; however, evidently not very many of these women enter law enforcement. Informal interest surveys indicate that female criminal justice majors are interested in federal law enforcement or police-related occupations (such as forensic psychologists or crime analysts). They are not, however, much interested in patrol work. Reasons for their lack of enthusiasm include the danger of the position, as well as shift work, and the difficulties of accommodating family schedules to the demands of an academy.

Thus, women in a police uniform do not engender the same degree of curiosity or derision that they did thirty years ago. Images of female officers in television and movies have become increasingly common. Yet there are still elements of a sex-infused titillation factor that Hollywood cannot seem to resist when portraying women in law enforcement. Female officers' dress and make-up especially strain credibility; however, some television and movies have provided realistic portrayals of women's experiences. The issues of women in law enforcement will be explored in Chapter 5.

Women in Corrections.   While women have been employed in corrections since the late nineteenth century, it was only in the 1970s that they were able to work in institutions for men. This change was important because, first, there are many more prisons for men than there are for women; consequently, more jobs exist with access to those institutions. Second, women found that promotional opportunities were stunted because of their inability to have a range of experience in the correctional system. Third, in some states at least, the pay scales between those who worked in prisons for women and those who worked in prisons for men were different. Again, the impetus for integrating women into male correctional ranks came largely because of lawsuits, even though the only case that reached the Supreme Court supported keeping women out of male prisons (*Dothard v. Rawlinson,* 433 U.S. 321, 97 S.Ct. 2720, 53 L.Ed.2d 786 [1977]). In a later case, which did not reach the Supreme Court, it was held that women's right to equal employment overrode even the inmates' right to privacy (*Gunther v. Iowa,* 462 F.Supp. 952 [1979]). By the 1980s, all but four states employed women in prisons for men, and women comprised 6 percent of the correctional officer staff in those prisons. Seventeen percent of all correctional officers in 1993 were women (Maguire, Pastore, & Flanagan, 1993, p. 98; Zupan, 1992, p. 326;), by 1995 the percentage was 29 percent, and by 2000 the percentage was 33 percent (Maguire & Pastore, 2002, Table 1100).

As with female police officers, the first women to be employed in men's prisons in the 1970s encountered a great deal of sexual harassment and discrimination. Today the resistance is not as extreme, but it has not entirely disappeared either (Erez & Tontodonato, 1992). Resentment is fostered by a perception that women get the best assignments and are exempted from distasteful duties such as strip searches. As is true with the resistance toward women in law enforcement, there is an abiding belief that women cannot perform adequately in physical encounters. Chapter 6 covers the issues surrounding female correctional officers.

Sexual Discrimination and Harassment.   One would think that sexual discrimination would not exist in this new millennium. Even if social and cultural beliefs about women are resistant to change, at least one could assume that discrimination in hiring and promotion have ceased to exist. Sadly, this does not seem to be the case. In July 2004, Morgan Stanley agreed to pay $54 million to settle a lawsuit brought by dozens of women employees who contended that the firm had refused them promotions and pay increases. Allison Schieffelin, a Morgan saleswoman of securities, who had filed with the EEOC in the late 1990s, led the women. Included in the settlement was a $12 million payment to Ms. Schieffelin. In reaching the settlement, Morgan Stanley promised to take additional steps to preclude such practices from occurring again. Morgan Stanley will hire an outside monitor to review its antidiscrimination practices and to resolve complaints as well as improve its antidiscrimination training; and the monitor will file the reports with Morgan Stanley and the EEOC at least once each year (Kelly & DeBaise, 2004, pp. A1–A2). A similar sex discrimination suit was brought in the late 1990s against Merrill Lynch and Smith Barney, and both firms settled before trial. To date, they have each paid out more than $100 million to address the claims (McGeehan, 2004, p. C7).

One issue that is shared by women in all three subsystems of criminal justice is sexual harassment. Women experience more harassment in male-dominated professions, and almost all criminal justice occupations are male dominated. Tong contends that "economic power is to sexual harassment as physical force is to rape" (1984, p. 87). The term *sexual harassment* was coined in 1977 at a conference at Cornell University. It is used to designate those personal interchanges where the sexual role is acted upon over the role of worker (Erez & Tontodonato, 1992, p. 229). Sexual harassment is sexual discrimination because sex becomes the basis of employment either as quid pro quo ("submit or lose your job" or "you get this promotion only if you cooperate") or because hostile working conditions force an individual to quit. In effect, a worker is fired due to sex because the abusive conditions make continued employment impossible, as in *Meritor Savings Bank v. Vinson,* 106 S.Ct. 2399, 2406 (1986). Just as in rape and battering cases, there are widespread myths about sexual harassment, such as the following (Erez & Tontodonato, 1992, p. 234):

> Women should expect it if they want to be part of the workplace.
> Women who are virtuous never get harassed.
> Harassment is really a trivial matter.
> Women secretly enjoy it.
> If women would just ignore it, it would go away.
> Women make it up vindictively when a love affair goes sour.

These myths act in the same way as the myths about rape and battering. They trivialize or deny the existence of injury to women, or they place the blame for the injury on the women themselves.

The EEOC is the federal enforcer and litigator unless they choose not to be. If the commission refuses a case, the individual complainant has a right to retain a private attorney and continue the lawsuit. In recent years, many governmental agencies and private employers have instituted sexual harassment training and grievance policies that are designed to protect the agency or company against liability. Despite these efforts some observers and researchers note that the level of harassment has not appreciably changed (Grossman, 2002).

Crossovers

One of the themes of the first edition of this book and one that we continue with this edition is the idea of *crossovers*—women who are both victims and criminals, or professionals and victims. Battered women who kill their attackers have been recognized more as victims than offenders. Another type of crossover is the woman who left home because of abuse and entered into the world of prostitution and drug use and thereby becomes a criminal. Statistics show that a majority of prostitutes (65 percent) were raped as children (Tong, 1984). Many studies of female offenders in prison show over a third have been victims of childhood sexual abuse (for a review see Pollock, 2002). Some write that inherent in our society are economic inequalities between men and women that make selling sex an economically attractive proposition for women over other occupations and that economic inequality is itself a form of victimization (Heidensohn, 1986). Even if her choice is free, the life of a prostitute is a precarious one. She enjoys even less legal protection from rape and abuse than other women and may suffer from disproportional prosecution compared to her male clients.

Female professionals in criminal justice may experience harassment similar to the harassment experienced by female offenders—perhaps even by the same harassers whether they are patrol, jail, or prison officers. All women experience similar issues with childcare responsibilities. All women experience similar issues with societal definitions of how they should behave. In short, there are shared experiences in the lives of all women—whether they are criminals, victims, or professionals.

We should also note, however, that other factors may affect how women experience social control, and, especially, the criminal justice system. We note that race, especially, is a very powerful factor and that minority women experience social control differently, whether they be criminals, victims, or professionals in the criminal justice system. Chapter 15 begins to explore the very important issue of race and how it combines with gender to influence women's lives.

Conclusion

From *Reed v. Reed*, 402 U.S. 71 (1971), which eliminated the male preference in assigning executors, to *Mississippi University for Women v. Hogan*, 458 U.S. 718 (1982), wherein the court lambasted state decisions based on "stereotyped, anachronistic notions about women's role," women have increasingly been seen as deserving equal treatment in legislation. This, in turn, has affected the lives of many women, whether they are criminals, victims, or professionals.

Case law developed along the following lines. Different treatment was defined as "suspicious" and was defended by pointing to "important" governmental objectives, with the treatment substantially related to the achievement of such objectives (*Craig v. Boren*, 429 U.S. 190 [1976]). The only differences allowed to remain are those that are based on "essential differences" between the sexes; for example, in *Rostker, Dir. of Selective Services v. Goldberg*, 453 U.S. 74 (1981), the Supreme Court let stand a sex difference in draft registration and left to a later date to decide the legality of the underlying sex difference standards for military conscription. In *U.A.W. v. Johnson Controls, Inc.*, 111 S.Ct. 1196 (1991), the Supreme Court rejected the essential difference of fertility as a reason for restricting women's employment opportunities by a company's fetal protection policies. However, what are considered to be essential differences may be no more than the current myths and stereotypes believed by the court to be natural. The winds of change are fickle, and what are considered to be essential differences today may be different in future court decisions.

Some feminists argue that reliance on the law to protect women's rights would be a mistake, since the legal system is still largely paternalistic and utilizes male definitions, priorities, norms, and perceptions of reality (Daly, 1989; Eisenstein, 1988; Smart, 1989). Legal equality may be irrelevant if social institutions are unchanged, and legal equality almost always means being treated equally to men. The question is: Why do the standards of justice utilize male norms and definitions?

Regardless of formal legal equality, women are still years away from achieving economic equality. Males' and females' relative median incomes are still not equal. While about 27 percent of female-headed households live below the poverty line, only 12 percent of male-headed households (with no woman present) live below the poverty line (U.S. Bureau of Census, 2003). As mentioned before, women tend to be employed in those occupations with lower pay, and even when they are in high-income occupations, they tend to specialize in certain areas that are characterized by less income. Further, women seem to reach a "glass ceiling" in many professions and seldom rise to the level of partner, CEO, or chief. Government aid, never very generous for women with small children, has been cut back. The Personal Responsibility and Work Opportunity Reconciliation Act of 1996 replaced Aid to Families with Dependent Children (AFDC) with TANF (Temporary Assistance to Needy Families). This Act transferred the responsibility for providing financial support to the poverty stricken to states and limited the benefits to a maximum of five years.

While the number of women in Congress has risen, it is still not very impressive. In 2003, there were fourteen women in the Senate and sixty women in the House of Representatives. The strength of conservative groups and their emphasis on family values and pro-life are thinly disguised attacks on the feminist agenda. The recent passage of the Unborn Victims of Violence Act that criminalizes injury to a fetus in any federal crime has been described as the latest step in the dismantling of abortion rights for women.

The true test of equality, however, is to be found not in the courtrooms and legislative halls, but rather in the offices and homes, the boardrooms and the bedrooms of this nation. If legal equality is to be a reality, then social equality must exist. Women must have real choices when it comes to employment and procreation. These opportunities must exist for women of all races and economic classes, and not just for middle-class white women. Finally, we must move away from the idea that *equal* means being equal to men and that *equal rights* necessarily means rights equal to the rights of men.

Review Questions

1. Discuss some images of women and how they affect women as offenders, victims, and practitioners.

2. In what way does informal social control affect women? What about formal social control?

3. What was the legal status of women in colonial America?

4. Discuss the woman's role in the 1800s. What was the "separate spheres" idea?

5. How did the largely female moral reform groups affect corrections for women?

6. What were the Married Women's Property Acts?

7. What was the difference between those who advocated protectionist legislation and those who advocated unionism?

8. Discuss the "mother of species" argument and how it hindered women workers.

9. Explain the different approaches of feminist grassroots efforts versus those of professional counselors to such issues as battering and rape.

10. What is law enforcement's general response to battering today?

11. Describe the change that has taken place in the American workforce in the last fifty years.

12. Compare the entries of women into law enforcement and corrections.

13. What are "crossovers?"

Key Terms

Social control: informal versus formal
"Separate sphere"
Pregnancy Discrimination Act of 1978
Alice Stebbins Wells
Equal Rights Amendment

Women in corrections
Sexual harassment
Learned helplessness
Rosie the Riveter
Title VII of the 1964 and 1972 Civil Rights Act

References

Adler, F. (1975). *Sisters in crime: The rise of the new female criminal.* New York: McGraw-Hill.

Bartfeld, J. (2000). Child support and post-divorce economic well-being of mothers, fathers, and children. *Demography 37*(2), 203–313.

Belknap, J. (1992). The perceptions of woman battering. In I. Moyer (Ed.), *The changing roles of women in the criminal justice system* (2nd ed.; pp. 181–203). Prospect Heights, IL: Waveland Press.

Bernat, F. (1992). Women in the legal profession. In I. Moyer (Ed.), *The changing roles of women in the criminal justice system* (2nd ed.; pp. 307–321). Prospect Heights, IL: Waveland Press.

Brenzel, B. (1983). *Daughters of the state.* Cambridge: MIT Press.

Brophy, J., & Smart, C. (1985). *Women-in-law.* London: Routledge and Kegan Paul.

Browne, A. (1987). *When battered women kill.* New York: Free Press.

Burford, E. J., & Shulman, S. (1992). *Of bridles and burnings: The punishment of women.* New York: St. Martin's Press.

Chesney-Lind, M. (1981). Judicial paternalism and female status offenders: Training women to know their place. In L. H. Bowker (Ed.), *Women and crime in America* (pp. 354–366). New York: Macmillan.

Chesney-Lind, M. (2002). Criminalizing victimization: The unintended consequences of pro-arrest policies for girls and women. *Criminology and Public Policy 2* (1), 81–90.

Daly, K. (1989). Criminal justice ideologies and practices in different voices: Some feminist questions about justice. *International Journal of the Sociology of Law 17* (1), 18–26.

Daly, K., & Maher, L. (1998). *Criminology at the crossroads: Feminist readings in criminal justice.* New York: Oxford Press.

Dobash, R. E., & Dobash, R. (1992). *Women, violence, and social change.* London: Routledge.

Eaton, M. (1986). *Justice for women? Family, court and social control.* Philadelphia: Open University Press.

Economist (The). (1991). Voyeurs all: The Kennedy-Smith rape trial. 321 (7726), A26–28.

Eisenstein, Z. (1988). *The female body and the law.* Berkeley: University of California Press.

Erez, E. (1992). Dangerous men, evil women: Gender and parole decision making. *Justice Quarterly 9* (1), 105–127.

Erez, E., & Tontodonato, P. (1992). Sexual harassment in the criminal justice system. In I. Moyer (Ed.), *The changing roles of women in the criminal justice system*

(2nd ed.; pp. 227–252). Prospect Heights, IL: Waveland Press.

Faludi, S. (1991). *Backlash: The undeclared war on American women.* New York: Crown Publishers.

Ferraro, K. (1998). Policing woman battering. In K. Daly & L. Maher (Eds.), *Criminology at the crossroads* (pp. 209–325). New York: Oxford University Press.

Feinman, C. (1992a). Criminal codes, criminal justice, and female offenders. In I. Moyer (Ed.), *The changing roles of women in the criminal justice system* (2nd ed.; pp. 57–68). Prospect Heights, IL: Waveland Press.

Feinman, C. (1992b). *The criminalization of a woman's body.* New York: Haworth.

Freedman, E. (1981). *Their sisters' keepers: Prison reform in America, 1830–1930.* Ann Arbor: University of Michigan Press.

Ginzberg, L. (1990). *Women and work of benevolence: Morality, politics and class in the nineteenth-century United States.* New Haven: Yale University Press.

Goodstein, L., & Lutze, F. (1992). Rape and criminal justice system responses. In I. Moyer (Ed.), *The changing roles of women in the criminal justice system* (2nd ed.; pp. 153–179). Prospect Heights, IL: Waveland Press.

Greene, H. (2003). Women in policing. In J. Joseph & D.Taylor, *With justice for all: Minorities and women in criminal justice* (pp. 79–88). Upper Saddle River, NJ: Prentice-Hall.

Grossman, J. (2002). *Sexual harassment in the workplace.* Findlaw (May). Retrieved July 1, 2004 from http://www.writ.news.findlaw.com/grossman/20020507.html.

Hale, D., & Bennett, C. L. (1995). Realities of women in policing: An organizational cultural perspective. In A. Merlo and J. Pollock (Eds.), *Women, law, and social control* (pp. 41–54). Boston: Allyn and Bacon.

Heidensohn, F. (1986). Models of justice: Portia or Persephone? Some thoughts on equality, fairness, and gender in the field of criminal justice. *International Journal of the Sociology of Law 14*, 287–298.

Heidensohn, F. (1992). *Women in control? The role of women in law enforcement.* New York: Clarendon, Oxford University Press.

Hemmens, C., Strom, K., & Schlegal, E. (1998). Gender bias in the courts: A review of the literature. *Sociological Imagination 35*, 22–42.

Hickman, M. J., & Reaves, B. A. (2003). *Local police departments 2000.* U.S. Department of Justice: Washington, DC: U.S. Government Printing Office.

Howe, A. (1990). Sweet dreams: Deinstitutionalizing young women. In R. Graycar (Ed.), *Dissenting opinions: Feminist explorations in law and society.* Sydney, Australia: Allen and Unwin.

Hymowitz, C., & Weissman, M. (1978). *A history of women in America.* New York: Bantam Books.

Jefferson, T. (1997). The Tyson rape trial: The law, feminism and emotional "truth." *Social and Legal Studies* 6 (2), 211–301.

Jones, A. (1980). *Women who kill.* New York: Holt, Rinehart and Winston.

Kelly, K., & DeBaise, C. (2004). Morgan Stanley settles bias suit for $54 million. *The Wall Street Journal,* 13 July, A1, A2.

Kirp, D., Yudof, M., & Strong Franks, M. (1986). *Gender justice.* Chicago: University of Chicago Press.

Koons-Witt, B. (2002). The effect of gender on the decision to incarcerate before and after the introduction of sentencing guidelines. *Criminology* 40 (2), 297–327.

Laurier, J. (2004). Reports find pervasive and increasing sexual abuse in the U.S. military. Retrieved July 15, 2004 from http://www.wsws.org/articles/2004/jun2004/mili-j10.shtml.

Lombroso, C. (1895). *The female offender.* London: Fisher Unwin.

Maguire, K., Pastore, A. L., & Flanagan, T. J. (Eds.). (1993). *Sourcebook of criminal justice statistics—1992.* Washington, DC: U.S. Department of Justice, Bureau of Justice Statistics.

Maguire, K., & Pastore, A. L. (Eds.). (2002). *Sourcebook of criminal justice statistics—2002.* Washington, DC: U.S. Department of Justice: Bureau of Justice Statistics. Retrieved on June 28, 2004 from http://www.albany.edu/sourcebook/1995/pdf/t162pdf.

Martin, S. (1992). The changing status of women officers. In I. Moyer (Ed.), *The changing roles of women in the criminal justice system* (2nd ed.; pp. 281–305). Prospect Heights, IL: Waveland Press.

McDonald, M. (1991). Beyond the trial. *Maclean's* (Dec 23), 1104(51), 16–20.

McGeehan, P. (2004). Discrimination on Wall Street? Run the numbers and weep. *New York Times,* 14 July, C1–C7.

Miller, S. (1999). *Gender and community policing.* Boston: Northeastern Press.

Moyer, I. (Ed.). (1992). *The changing roles of women in the criminal justice system* (2nd ed.). Prospect Heights, IL: Waveland Press.

Nagel, I., & Hagan, J. (1983). Gender and crime: Offense patterns and criminal court sanctions. In M. Tonry & N. Morris (Eds.), *Crime and justice: An annual review of research* (pp. 91–144). Chicago: University of Chicago Press.

Noddings, N. (1989). *Women and evil.* Berkeley: University of California Press.

Paulson, C. (2000). First lady urges Congress to take up violence against women act. *CNN.com.* Retrieved July 15, 2004 from http://www.cnn.com/2000/ALLPOLITICS/stories/06/12/hre/violence.

Pollak, O. (1950). *The criminality of women.* New York: A.S. Barnes & Co.

Pollock, J. (1999). *Criminal women.* Cincinnati, OH: Anderson.

Pollock, J. (2002). *Women, prison and crime.* Pacific Grove, CA: Brooks/Cole.

Pollock, J., & Davis, S. (2004). *The myth of the violent female criminal.* Paper presented at the Academy of Criminal Justice Sciences Annual Meeting, Las Vegas, Nevada, March, 2004.

Pollock-Byrne, J., & Merlo, A. V. (1991). Against compulsory treatment: No "quick fix" for pregnant substance abusers. *Criminal Justice Policy Review* 5 (2), 79–99.

Rafter, N. (1985). *Partial justice: State prisons and their inmates, 1800–1935.* Boston: Northeastern University Press.

Rafter N., & Stanko, E. (1982). *Judge, lawyer, victim, thief: Women, gender roles and criminal justice.* Boston: Northeastern University Press.

Schafran, L. (1990). Overwhelming evidence: Reports on gender bias in the courts. *Trial* 26, 28–35.

Simon, R. (1975). *Women and crime.* Lexington, MA: Lexington Books.

Singleton, S. (1990). Gender bias skews justice for women. *Trial* 26 (2), 39–41.

Smart, C. (1989). *Feminism and the power of the law.* London: Routledge, Kegan Paul.

Steffensmeier, D., & Streifel, C. (1992). Time-series analysis of the female percentage of arrests for property crimes, 1960–1985: A test of alternative explanations. *Justice Quarterly* 9 (1), 77–105.

Tong, R. (1984). *Women, sex, and the law.* Totowa, NJ: Rowman and Littlefield.

U.S. Bureau of Census. (1993). *Statistical abstract of the United States: 1993* (113th ed.). Washington, DC: U.S. Government Printing Office.

U.S. Bureau of Census. (2003). *People and families in poverty by selected characteristics.* Retrieved June 30, 2004 from http://www.gov/prod/2003pubs/p60-222.

U.S. Bureau of Labor Statistics. (2002). *Women in the labor force: A databook.* Retrieved June 27, 2004 from http://www.stats.bls.gov/cps/wlf-intro.pdf.

U.S. Department of Labor. (1995). *Employment and earnings.* Washington DC: U.S. Government Printing Office, pp. 175–180.

U.S. Department of Labor. (2003, September). *Highlights of women's earnings in 2002.* Bureau of Labor Statistics. Report 972. Washington, DC: U.S. Government Printing Office.

Werner, W. (2004). Where have the women attorneys gone? *Law Practice Today.* Retrieved on June 28, 2004 from http://www.abanet.org/lpm/lpt/articles/mgt05041.html

Young, C. (2004). Kobe's rights: Rape, justice, and double standards. *Reason* 35 (January), 22–24.

Zupan, L. (1992). The progress of women correctional officers in all male prisons. In I. Moyer (Ed.), *The chang-ing roles of women in the criminal justice system* (2nd ed.; pp. 323–333). Prospect Heights, IL: Waveland Press.

Cases Cited

Ada v. Guam Society of Obstetricians and Gynecologists, 121 L.Ed.2d 564 (1992)

Bradwell v. State, 83 U.S. 130 (1873)

California Fed. Savings and Loan Association et al. v. Mark Guerra et al., 758 F.2d 390 (9th Cir. 1985), aff'd 479 U.S. 272 (1987)

Craig v. Boren, 429 U.S. 190 (1976)

Dothard v. Rawlinson, 433 U.S. 321, 97 S.Ct. 2720, 53 L.Ed. 2d 786 (1977)

Gunther v. Iowa, 462 F.Supp. 952 (1979)

Harris v. Forklift Systems, Inc., 114 S.Ct. 367 (1993)

Meritor Savings Bank v. Vinson, 106 S.Ct. 2399 (1986)

Mississippi University for Women v. Hogan, 458 U.S. 718 (1982)

Muller v. Oregon, 208 U.S. 412 (1908)

Reed v. Reed, 402 U.S. 71 (1971)

Roe v. Wade, 410 U.S. 113 (1972)

Rostker, Dir. Of Selective Services v. Goldberg, 453 U.S. 74 (1981)

Thurman v. City of Torrington, 595 F. Supp. 1521 (D. Conn. 1984)

U.A.W. v. Johnson Controls, 111 S.Ct. 1196 (1991)

United States v. Morrison, 529 U.S. 598 (2000)

2

Images of Women

Frankie Y. Bailey[*]

*With thanks to Dr. Donna C. Hale, Shippensburg University, who read a draft of this chapter and made comments and suggestions.

Distorted images of women based on sex roles and sexuality affect all women who partici-pate in the criminal justice system, whether as victims, offenders, or practitioners. In the nine-teenth century, Cesare Lombroso, the "father of positivist criminology," began his theorizing about criminal behavior by focusing on male criminals. When he later turned his attention to women, they were described in contrast to males, as the antithesis of everything masculine. To the extent that a woman was "manly" in features or behavior, she was abnormal. Yet, at the same time, Lombroso's description of the "normal" female left much to be desired. In fact, unflattering images of women can be traced back to the ancient Greeks and can still be found today (Bailey & Hale, 2004). Women in the criminal justice system bear the burden of these images that were created by males and have been sustained, perpetuated, and elaborated on over the centuries. In this chapter, the author examines these images and considers policy implications and the future directions scholars might take in response to this stereotyping.

Historical Images of Women

As noted above, stereotypes of women show remarkable historical continuity. Certain images persevere even in the midst of revolutionary social changes in the status of women in West-ern society. For example, in the world of sports, women have made significant strides in the last decade. During this period, the number of women participating in sports in high school and college has risen from 1.99 million to 2.64 million. At the same time, women have been spending about $21 billion dollars a year to purchase athletic apparel and sports equipment for themselves and their families (Wearden & Creedon, 2003, p. 189). This is remarkable given the long tradition in the United States and elsewhere of portraying sports as a pursuit for boys and men. However, a gender hierarchy continues to exist which "holds that female athletes are both 'other than' and 'less than' their male counterparts" (Wearden & Creedon, 2003, p. 189). At the same time, advertisers—who arguably in the past have been instrumen-tal in perpetuating stereotypes of women as physically inactive, noncompetitive, and house-bound—have offered some new, nonsexist images in response to the rise of female athletes such as the members of the Women's National Basketball Association (WNBA). These new images of women as active, competitive, and fit were presented by advertisers during the broadcast of WNBA games on television, but so were more traditional images (Wearden & Creedon, 2003).

Women have made inroads in both physically demanding professional sports and in other male-dominated occupations such as business and criminal justice. Yet ancient beliefs about the inferiority of "woman" as a creature whose destiny is determined by her anatomy (specifically her menstrual cycle and childbearing) and by her sexuality (i.e., passivity or sex-ual voraciousness) have not been completely eradicated. The stereotypes that are still a part of contemporary discourse about gender can be traced to the early creation myths of gods and goddesses. Some feminist scholars argue for a prepatriarchal universe in which The Goddess (the Earth Mother) was the source of life and death, birth and destruction. These scholars argue that this female Supreme Being became splintered into her various facets, dichotomized into "good" and "evil," when men seized control and created a patriarchal pan-theon in which a male god dominated (e.g., Getty, 1990). As such, one of the legacies of ancient Greek civilization is the mythology that shaped the religious rituals of the Greeks. In these myths, the roles played by the goddesses paralleled those played by their mortal coun-terparts—wives, mothers, sisters, and daughters. The existence of "warrior goddesses" was counterbalanced by the fact that they were virgins and/or androgynous and that they tended to intervene in human affairs on behalf of various males. For example, the goddess Athena provides Perseus with a shield of polished bronze that he uses as a mirror to avoid looking upon the face of the Gorgon, Medusa (whose gaze could turn men to stone). With this aid from Athena, Perseus is able to slay Medusa (for discussion of the roles of the goddesses in Greek mythology see Hamilton, 1942 [1999]).

Mortal women fared poorly in both the codes of law and the medical literature of ancient Greece. Women moved from the homes of their fathers to those of their husbands, controlled always by males. Women were described in medical works by Hippocratic physi-cians as inferior to males, being softer, warmer, moister, more porous, quicker to age, and subject to such malfunctions as the "wandering womb." According to ancient Greek physi-cians, a woman who was not sexually active and/or who had not produced children was prone to this affliction, in which the womb, deprived of moisture, detached itself from its custom-ary resting place and moved about the body causing a variety of unpleasant symptoms that varied according to where it moved (Demand, 1994, p. 55).

Concerns about lack of chastity on the part of virgins or adultery on the part of married women resulted in restrictions on the freedom of movement of women. The matter of the family bloodline, and thus citizenship, was a crucial concern for male citizens, and if this meant that women were restricted from active participation in public life (with the exception of religious rituals), then that was a sacrifice men were willing to make. Women, whose voices are not heard in the ancient records, apparently had little say in the matter.

What we do know is that in the myths, and later in the comedies and dramas created by Greek and Roman playwrights, the stories of certain women entered the Western conscious-ness. Such women included Medea, the daughter of a king, who fled with Jason and is reputed to have taken revenge when he deserted her for a princess. Medea murdered her two sons by Jason. She is the "murdering mother," whose legend echoes in descriptions of female offenders such as Susan Smith and Andrea Yates. At the same time, Medea and Circe, her aunt, are linked to the early images of female witchcraft. Circe is the beautiful temptress who turns the crew of Odysseus's ship into swine to ensure that he will tarry with her on her island. Odysseus's faithful wife, Penelope, offers contrast to the witch Circe. It is in her role as a loyal spouse, who holds off her suitors for two decades until her husband returns from his adventures, that Penelope lays claim to recognition as a "good woman."

The mythology of the ancient world also included the Amazons, the wild, warrior women who mate with men only to obtain female children. The respect of the Greeks for these women as warriors is reflected in the tales about their encounters with male heroes. However, this respect is tempered by the fact that triumph for the male hero is to tame (domesticate in marriage) or to slay the Amazon warrior (Lefkowitz, 1986, pp. 19–20).

Other women come down to us in legend—including Medusa of the snake locks who can turn men to stone with a glance from her fiery eyes, and Pandora, the curious mortal who opens a box and releases trouble into the world. Among the goddesses themselves, even Hera, the powerful sister-wife of Zeus, emerges in the myths as the often cheated-upon spouse who responds with fury to her husband's adultery—frequently directing her rage toward the other woman. Even the goddesses who are benefactors and protectors of mortals are not above responding like female humans to the injustices done them by their male counterparts (Hamilton, 1942 [1999]).

Equally influential in creating lasting images of women, the Bible served to perpetuate the inferior status of women that began with the Greeks and Romans. With the ancient holy fathers, the dichotomy of women as "virgins" or "whores" became firmly established. Mary, the Madonna, the Virgin Mary, who had given birth to the savior of mankind, was the feminine ideal. In contrast, Adam's two wives, the immortal Lilith who had deserted him, and Eve, who had been instrumental in their expulsion from the Garden of Eden, symbolized the danger inherent in the female being. The same was true of other "wicked women" of the Bible such as Jezebel, Salome, and Delilah, who used their sexual wiles to win favor, seduce, and/or betray (see e.g., Milne, 2002).

Although feminists since the nineteenth century have attempted to counteract these biblical images, they remain a potent source of depictions of women. This is also true of the fairy tales that emerged as literature with Perrault in the eighteenth century and later Hans Christian Andersen and the Brothers Grimm in the nineteenth century. These fairy tales grew out of folklore and featured women who were wicked stepmothers and/or evil witches. These women did their best to destroy the innocent young children and the lovely young women who stood in the way of their greed or lust for adoration. Unfortunately, these fairytale images would later be immortalized by the Disney films of the twentieth century. However, in an odd twist on this stereotyping, Claire Etaugh finds that in American children's books published between 1970 and 1999, it is only those women who are cast as wicked stepmothers or witches who demonstrate strength. Although girls are now portrayed as more adventurous than in the past, upon reaching adulthood, female characters in modern children's books tend to assume traditional women's roles (cited in Martin, 2001).

One aspect of folklore that was crucial to the images of women was that having to do with witchcraft. By the Middle Ages and into the Renaissance, the belief that witches existed and that they could wreck havoc among their neighbors had gained credence. The witch-hunters' guide, *Malleus Maleficarum* (1486), written by two Dominican monks, Heinrich Kramer and James Sprenger, emphasized the role of women in this deviance. Women were said to be particularly susceptible to temptation and therefore more prone to seduction by the devil. In their roles as caregivers, particularly as midwives and as nursemaids, female healers employed their knowledge of herbal medicine to ease their patients' suffering. In the case of childbirth, this defied the biblical decree that the daughters of Eve—all women—should bring forth their infants in pain and suffering. Related to this was a superstitious concern that a midwife/witch might harm the newborn infant because she sought not only its soul but also the umbilical cord and body fat that were reputedly used in demonic rituals (Forbes, 1966).

Images of Women as Criminals

If by the nineteenth century the belief in witches had disappeared from Western consciousness, the belief in the witchlike behavior of women had not. Here again wives, daughters, and caregivers—those who might engage in "malice domestic" were especially subject to suspicion. As Robb (1997) relates, in England, a moral panic developed around the female poisoner. This public fear of the woman who used her intimate contact with her victim to slowly poison him (or her) to death was at the heart of several high-profile cases involving upper-class women accused of murder. In the United States, this concern about the female poisoner appears in numerous trial narratives, including that of Lizzie Borden, the alleged (but legally acquitted) hatchet murderer. Borden was alleged to have attempted to purchase poison prior to the murders of her father and stepmother.

This concern about women as poisoners had appeared even earlier in tales of upper-class women in ancient Rome. It appeared again in the mid-twentieth century, in the work of Otto Pollak, who described poison as the favorite weapon of women. In *The Criminality of Women* (1950), Pollak argued that women engaged in much more criminality than was suspected or detected. He asserted that women were able to do this because women were socialized (by the need to conceal their menstrual cycle) to be devious and deceptive. Women, he claimed, preyed upon the people who trusted them and the people who were in their care. Women hid behind men, engaging in secret criminality and getting away with it.

In fact, Cesare Lombroso, the nineteenth-century "father of positivist criminology," began this social science tradition of presenting women in a negative light with the 1893 publication of his book *The Female Offender (La donna delinquent)*. According to Lombroso and the other Italian positivists, women were inherently inferior to men in both body and mind. Because of their natural tendency toward colorless passivity, few women engaged in violent crime. Instead, criminality for women was equivalent to prostitution. However, when a woman did engage in a crime such as murder, she was inherently worse than a man. Because she had engaged in a crime that was so at odds with the nature of woman, the female murderer was said to be "manlike." She could be expected to exhibit physical characteristics that were more masculine than feminine. She could also be expected to act with a cold-blooded lethalness (see Gibson, 2002).

Women fared little better in the early twentieth century with Sigmund Freud. Freud described the neuroses of his female patients. He attributed to females in general "penis envy," felt first by the young girl at her discovery that she lacked the symbol of masculinity that her brother and other males could claim. If males experienced an "Oedipal complex," then women had an equivalent "Electra complex" (named for the Greek maiden who avenges her father's murder by her mother). This Freudian description of female neuroses would figure in the high-profile trial of Ruth Snyder and her lover Judd Gray for the murder of her husband. This 1927 case inspired books and films about the femme fatale wife and her lover who conspire to remove an unwanted husband (e.g., *Double Indemnity* [1944] and *The Postman Always Rings Twice* [1946]).

In the 1920s, the Hollywood film assumed its place as popular entertainment for a cross section of the American public and meant that the images of women that had existed for thousands of years would now be captured on celluloid. The ancient narratives of women and crime, of women as offenders, would now receive modern treatment. Hollywood films were only one aspect of the mass media that emerged between the mid-nineteenth century and the early twentieth. With newspapers, popular fiction, photography, and radio, the movies were important purveyors of images of crime, victims, and offenders. Later in the twentieth century, television and the Internet would be added to this list.

The Emergence of Mass Media

The arrival of the "penny press" in the 1840s was a significant moment in the evolution from religious to secular crime coverage in the United States. Crime narratives that had begun with the gallows sermons of Puritan ministers such as Cotton Mather now took the form of legal narratives presented by lawyers in the courtroom and reports by journalists that appeared in urban newspapers. The editors of the pennies and their reporters moved center-stage as interpreters of crime in the cities. The circulation of these newspapers that sought readers among the working class was aided by two high-profile New York City cases involving female victims. The first involved Mary Rogers, the "beautiful cigar girl," the daughter of a boarding-house owner, who was found floating in the Hudson River. The newspapers used her swollen, blackened body as the object upon which to write their narratives of crime in the city, speculating in this unsolved case about how Rogers had come to her death, whether from gang rape or as the result of a botched abortion. There was no doubt how Helen Jewett, the second high-profile victim, had died. She had been murdered and then set on fire in her room in the brothel where she was employed. In the trial that followed, the accused was a young clerk, who, like Jewett, was a migrant to the city. His acquittal came in the midst of debate about the dangers of the city, not only for women but also for impressionable young men. Even as Rogers and Jewett were profiled in the press as victims, they were also presented as, to lesser or greater extent, complicit in their own demises (see Cohen, 1999; Halttunen, 1998).

In this respect the penny press presented narratives about female victims that resembled the "murdered girl" ballads of the nineteenth century that told tales of young women who had been seduced and then murdered by their lovers when they became pregnant or demanded marriage. The figure of the female victim of seduction, rape, and/or murder might begin as an innocent, but in the popular lore and the emerging mass media of the nineteenth century, she could still be held to some extent accountable for her victimization. In these narratives, women were weak and prone to male seduction. A woman who was naïve or reckless or foolish enough to lose her chastity might expect to come to a bad end.

Thus reformers worried about the temptations that young women encountered as workers in the industries that were springing up in mill towns and in cities. They worried about the leisure-time recreations that brought young men and women together in places such as the theaters and the new amusement parks and, by the late nineteenth century, the movie theaters. The reformers worried about abortion and "white slavery." The media of the day reflected these images and these concerns about women as victims. But, once fallen, the female victim of male seduction would then become the temptation that might lure an upstanding young man away from the straight and narrow.

Evolving Images of Women in the Mass Media

Images of women in the mass media reflect changes that occur in society. For example, in the commercial advertising of the late nineteenth century to the mid-twentieth century, the images of women reflected the changes that were occurring in society at that time. The mid-nineteenth century image of the middle-class matron who was the heart and soul of her home, and the embodiment of virtue and true womanhood, was superseded by the younger, more free-spirited "new woman" of the late nineteenth century. This new woman rode bikes, strolled out with young beaus, and attended college. She was younger and more independent than the matron, not yet a wife and mother. She was wholesome, fresh, and athletic. In contrast, the "vamp" (who had her origins in Theda Bara's 1915 film portrayal of "The Vampire" in *A Fool There Was*) was seductive, calculating, and, in her most threatening persona, foreign-born. However, by the 1920s, the image of the flat-chested, short-skirted, smoking, drinking flapper, the product of Prohibition and post-war ennui, had taken center stage. By this era, Hollywood movie stars were also important female images, from the ever-childlike Mary Pickford to the voluptuous and naughty Mae West (who was a focal point of the call for movie censorship leading to the creation of the Motion Picture Production Code). The bad girls of 1920s and 1930s movies included the gangsters' molls, the girlfriends of characters played by male actors such as Humphrey Bogart and James Cagney. These women were presented as hard-bitten, tough-talking "dames."

Examining popular culture images of prostitutes in American fiction and films, 1900–1930, Fishbein (1989, p. 409) finds evidence of some change over time:

> The earliest fiction and film shared the assumption of the cult of true womanhood, namely that the true woman embodied the virtues of purity, piety, submissiveness, and domesticity and that any fall, especially that occasioned by a sexual lapse, was an irrevocable one. Ironically, these works coincided with the appearance of the "new woman."

As Fishbein notes, the appearance of the new woman reflected the movement of significant numbers of women into the workplace and increasing freedom in manners and morals for women (1989, p. 409). In fiction, the prostitute (harlot) was often portrayed as "a victim of man's lust, ignorance, and greed." However, the degree of sympathy with which the fallen woman was portrayed evolved over time, reflecting social changes. One significant change from the earliest period to the 1930s was the question of whether a fallen woman could ever be redeemed sufficiently to become a wife and mother. By the 1930s, the harlots were often spunky social critics and sometimes did marry. However, this change in depiction came in the aftermath of a moral panic about prostitution in the early teens that had affected the film interest. During this earlier era, the film industry had responded to several urban vice commission reports by producing a "spate of white slavery films" about innocent young women who were coerced into prostitution (Fishbein, 1989, p. 413).

The 1940s produced "Rosie the Riveter," the nickname given to the female war-industry worker, embodied in the poster image that was used in the campaign aimed at bringing women into the workforce. The war years provided opportunities for some women, such as women of color and working-class women, to move into better-paying jobs. Other women, who had never worked outside their homes, gained a new sense of their own competence. The experiences of such women on the home front were captured in popular films such as *Since You Went Away* (1944).

At the same time, the 1940s also produced images of lethal women in *film noir*—the claustrophobic black-and-white films in which the story was often about a seductive woman and a willing male involved in an adulterous triangle or criminal scheme that spiraled downward to a climax that left one or both dead. In retrospect, some scholars have argued that these female characters of *film noir* represented a high point of women's images in the cinema. Compared to the female characters in post–World War II films, the women in *film noir* were able to hold their own with men. In the post–World War II films, women existed in a male-dominated world. "Sex kittens" and "teen queens" replaced *femme fatales*. The *femmes* would not rise again and become a mainstay of films until the 1980s.

Images of Criminal Women and Criminal Justice Practitioners

As for images of criminal women, Morey (1995, p. 1) examines four important "women's prison films" from 1950–1962, and finds:

> . . . prison is presented as an agent to return women to domesticity. In these films, however, the agent typically fails at its task because it brutalizes and masculinizes both female inmates and female staff members. While domesticity is valorized as an appropriate aim . . . prison is the site of contradictions.

These contradictions occur because in the gender ideology of the 1950s, women are assumed to be "innately homemakers and civilizers and should not require correctional institutions to educate them to do their jobs" (Morey, 1995, p. 1). Ironically, in these films, the women who enter prison as wives and mothers fare worse. Yet, men who "drive women to prison in the first place" are also presented as the means by which the female inmate will achieve successful reintegration into society. In these prison films, the women corrupt each other or become unhinged in their state of isolation from men (p. 5).

It is worth noting that in the 1970s and into the 1990s, another series of women in prison films focused even more intensely (no longer constrained by the Motion Picture Production Code) on the female inmate behind bars. Known in the video store jargon as "girls in prison" or "women behind bars," these movies focus on the plight of the new inmate, often wrongly imprisoned, who finds herself in a female jungle, peopled by brutal and corrupt staff, aggressive and violent lesbian inmates, and other women who are doing whatever they must to survive. While the prison films of the 1950s and 1960s dealt in stereotypes of domesticity and women who had gone astray, these latter films offered fantasies about sex and violence behind bars.

On the flip side, there are the images of women who participate in the criminal justice system as practitioners—police officers, lawyers, corrections officers. These women, too, have faced stereotypes based on their sex. In mass media and popular culture, even as their struggles to assimilate were chronicled, stereotypes about female criminal justice practitioners were perpetuated and exaggerated.

Examining the portrayal of female police officers in popular films, 1972–1996, Hale (1998, p. 175) finds that "although Title VII extended the legal standings for women to enter police work as sworn officers, the [films] produced during the past 25 years still show policewomen in the stereotypical roles ascribed to women." Bailey et al. (1998) find less blatant emphasis on the sexuality and physical appearance of female attorneys than Hale notes of police officers (who are often seen undercover as prostitutes). However, in many of the films that Bailey et al. (1998) analyzed, the female attorneys—although competent—were routinely presented as "women in jeopardy." These celluloid attorneys often found themselves in danger because of a problematic relationship, professional and/or romantic, with a man.

The film images of female corrections staff have been discussed earlier in this chapter. As noted, these cinematic images, from the earliest prison films to the more recent "women behind bars" movies, have tended to offer stereotypes of female officers and wardens. Even in serious films that attempt to explore prison life, the images of women who work in prison as tough and aggressive (i.e., masculine) or as too soft for the demands of the job, are the most prevalent images.

In Search of Positive Images for Women

The question of what is a positive image for women on the screen has been and is still debated. In the modern era, in films ranging from *Aliens* to *Kill Bill 2*, women have been increasingly violent. They kick, punch, blow up, and otherwise demolish their opponents. The debate among critics and scholars is whether the use of violence by women should be taken as a symbol of increasing equality with men in the world of films. Scholars have long argued that a "male gaze" predominates in Hollywood films. Historically, women have been "sexualized" (defined in terms of their sexuality) in films. Thus, scholars generally agree that the use of violence by female heroes and villains must be examined with this historical use and abuse of female sexuality in mind (on the male gaze, see Kaplan, 1983; Macdonald, 1995).

Given this history of women in film, the viewer might well ponder whether it is a step back or a step forward when Halle Berry and Sharon Stone engage in a "cat fight" in *Cat Woman* (2004), an echo of earlier female "cat fights" such as that between Alexis and Krystle on the television prime-time soap opera *Dynasty.* Or are images of women better served by those such as the female police chief in *Fargo* (1996) or the female psychiatrist and female police detective who team together to catch a serial killer in *Copycat* (1995)?

Although portrayals of violent women in hip-hop gangster films have often been dismissed as exploitive, Smith-Shomade (2003, p. 29) called for a more nuanced reading of these films. She writes:

> Most "boyz-n-the-hood" movies situate black women as bitches and "hoes" while foregrounding the inhumanity of blacks and crime. Very few of these films distinguish organized crime from poverty-induced greed. In those films that do examine structured crime, however, progressive roles for and images of African American women emerge. *New Jack City, Sugar Hill,* and *Set It Off* offer multiple examples of black women's work and roles.

However, these films are limited in number, and as Smith-Shamade notes, they occur within a subgenre in which the emphasis is on violent action in a context that invites racial stereotyping.

Images of Women in Music and Comics

The images that emerge in films over a hundred-year period have parallels to images in other mediums. In music, the "murdered girl" ballad was mentioned above. Recall such popular favorites as "Tom Dooley." Bluegrass and country music also offer images of women as victims of male violence. Male singers such as Kenny Rogers and Garth Brooks have recorded songs in which violence toward women is contemplated or realized by jealous men. Currently experiencing a renewal of his popularity, pop music icon Tom Jones has made "Delilah" one of his standards. This song—to which audiences sing along— is about a man who kills his unfaithful lover after seeing her with another man.

Reflecting what could well be interpreted as a double standard in the music industry, the response to female artists who record songs about women who engage in violent self-defense or seek vengeance when abused has often been negative. A recent example is the controversy surrounding the Dixie Chicks's award-winning album, featuring the single "Goodbye Earl." In this dark comedy song, an abused wife poisons her husband and with the help of her friend disposes of his body. Although showing little concern about songs by males about abusing and killing women, a number of country radio stations refused to play "Goodbye Earl," arguing that it might incite women to violence (Williamson, 2000).

In the music that comes out of the African American experience, blues, and rap, images of male violence toward female victims are also present. In this regard, it should be noted that heavy metal and rock music also present images that have been described as misogynistic. With regard to rap, in May 2004, a group of students at Spelman, the renowned black women's college, protested and succeeded in canceling a scheduled visit by rap superstar Nelly. The rapper was coming to the campus to appear at a charity event intended to encourage students to sign up for a bone marrow registry. Although the women acknowledged that this was a worthy cause, they felt compelled to protest Nelly's visit because of his music, particularly a recently released video in which he swiped a credit card through a woman's backside (Conwell, 2004).

Of course, Nelly is not the only male performer who has been accused of presenting misogynistic images of women in music videos. In *Dreamworlds II* (1995), a documentary that evolved from the materials that he developed for one of his courses, Sut Jhally examines the portrayal of women in MTV music videos. Juxtaposing scenes from over 165 music videos with the gang rape scene from *The Accused* (1988), Jhally (1995) makes a persuasive argument that in these videos, women are presented as interchangeable, as highly sexualized body parts. They are there for the males to gaze at, to use, and occasionally to abuse. These videos are aimed at an audience composed predominantly of young males.

The appeal to young men also seems to drive the visual images of female superheroes and villains in comic books. In an examination of the images of women in comic books over the past four decades, Lavin (1998) finds that even though comic books are read and collected by adults of both sexes, and even though women work as comic book artists, the images of comic book women have become increasing sexualized over the decades. If Wonder Woman's costume was modest when she appeared in 1942, the female superheroes and villains in modern comic books often have bodies that are impossibly voluptuous and costumes that are incredibly skimpy. Along with these visual images, Lavin points to an inherent tension in the portrayals. Even as the female superheroes are presented as powerful and strong, they are also objects of desire, with alluring costumes (Lavin, 1998). As Lavin notes, the trend toward superheroines as sex objects is evidenced by the swimsuit issues, which debuted in the early 1990s from both Marvel and Image. As for the comic book villains, Lavin identifies a class of female supervillains who are female martial arts assassins or vigilantes. Reflecting the artwork, these villains are known by comic book fans as "nimbos (ninja bimbos)."

The appeal to an audience by combining elements of sex with violence is not the domain of any one medium. Returning to popular films, among the offering are "rape-revenge" films in which a female protagonist (or group of females) avenge rape by seeking out the male offender(s). These movies present women who are, or who become, aggressive enough to seek out and often kill their offenders. Admittedly, the rapes are generally presented as brutal, violent acts that do physical and psychological harm to the victims. However, the victims then respond by becoming vigilantes. Classic early examples of this subgenre include *Lipstick* (1976), *I Spit on Your Grave* (1977), *Sudden Impact* (1983), and *The Ladies Club* (1986).

Another subgenre that combines R-rated sex and violence are "slasher" films, horror films in which violence by the unstoppable killer often follows sex scenes between the next victims. Although both men and women are the victims in such films, it is the sexual behavior of the women that is the focus. In *Scream,* a tongue-in-cheek film, one of the characters explained that a rule for survival in a slasher film is not to have sex. This is particularly important for the "last girl" protagonist, the virgin, who must slay (at least temporarily) the killer. Research suggests that the combination of sex and violence in R-rated movies may be more harmful with respect to desensitizing males to violence against women than X-rated pornographic films (Demare et al., 1993; Donnerstein & Linz, 1986). However, some feminists have argued for censorship of pornography (as opposed to erotica) because it objectifies women, shows unequal relationships, and perpetuates "rape myths" in some adult films (see e.g., Dworkin, 1981; MacKinnon, 1984).

News Coverage of Victims and Offenders

Examining how the press covers sex crimes, Benedict (1992) focuses on four high-profile cases that occurred between 1978 and 1990. She concludes that the press has tended to portray victims as "virgin" or "vamp." By the 1990s, rather than depicting rape as a "societal problem," the press was "reverting to its pre-1970s focus on sex crimes as individual, bizarre, or sensational case histories" (p. 251). Looking at the social construction of rape as a sexual problem in Canada, through sexual assault legislation in 1983, Los and Chamard (1997) suggest that such recognition may have mixed results with regard to media coverage of sex crimes. Responding to the feminist criticism of the attention given to stranger rape, the media moved away from coverage of this "ideal type" of sexual assault. However, the subsequent coverage of acquaintance rape cases by the press tended to present the complainant as the sexual partner of the accused rather than as a victim.

In the United States, the recent coverage of the Kobe Bryant case—as in the past with other celebrity acquaintance rape cases—has led to renewed debate about media coverage. The privacy rights of the alleged victim, rape shield laws, and the presence of the media in the courtroom were all issues in the Bryant case. These are not new issues, but the celebrity defendant brings into focus the social construction of rape in the media and the continuing existence of rape myths, as well as the continuing debate about the rights of male defendants in the face of accusations of sexual offending.

The ability of a woman to claim the status of victim may rise or fall on the perception of that woman or a group of women as "good" or "bad." Chesney-Lind (1997) raises this issue with regard to women who are sexually abused in prisons. Their stigmatization as bad women, as women who are immoral, makes it more difficult for such inmates to successfully pursue justice or even relief from continuing abuse.

In the midst of attempts to create new policies to deal with crimes that have become the focus of public concern, women may be neglected because of the focus on males. Danner and

Carmody (2001) argue that this was the case when the media, researchers, and policy makers responded to the school shootings of the late 1990s. Because the shooters were male and because they shot both males and females, commentators failed to consider gender as it applied to the female victims. They failed to account for the fact that 59 percent of the victims were females, and, in at least one case, the violence seemed to be related to the male shooter's rejection by a female. The explanation of this male violence left women and girls out of the research and out of the recommendations.

On the other hand, female offenders are sometimes the focus of too much attention. Aside from the media commentary on what homemaking guru/businesswoman Martha Stewart wore to court (although admittedly such commentary also occurs with male celebrity offenders), the tone of coverage of Stewart (convicted for lying to the government) provoked heated debate about whether it reflected media bias against Stewart. This came in tandem with assertions from some quarters that Stewart had become a scapegoat for prosecution of white-collar offenders because she was a woman with an image as hard-driving and aggressive. In this respect, recall hotel owner Leona Hemsley, known in the media as "the queen of mean" during her trial for tax evasion. As with celebrity males, celebrity female defendants often engage in attempts at impression management. In one recent example, film star Winona Ryder, accused of shoplifting from a Beverly Hills store, made a positive impression on the media as she arrived each day for court. Her attire during the trial received high marks from the press for both style and appropriateness.

With lower-class women who find themselves in the criminal justice system, there is little hope of controlling their images. They often experience group stigmatization as "bad women" or "bad mothers." In the media, poverty and criminality are presented as closely linked. Thus, in the "war against drugs" fought in the inner cities of the United States, poor women of color became the focus of media coverage. The war on drugs became a war that included not only drug dealers, but also "crack moms," who gave birth to addicted babies, and "crack hoes" who traded their bodies for drugs. Images of such women became commonplace on the news and in films and on television crime shows. A moral panic developed around these women and the children they were producing, as it had earlier around women who abused alcohol and gave birth to babies suffering from fetal alcohol syndrome (for discussion see Golden, 1999; Humphries, 1999; also see Chapters 4 and 11 in this text).

Clearly, the images of women in the criminal justice system are distorted. This distortion is only one aspect of the general distortion of crime and justice that occurs in the mass media and in popular culture. The final section considers the implications of this for future research and education.

Conclusion

In the discourse about women, crime, and justice, various sources offer sometimes complementary, sometimes competing, images. For example, Aileen Wuornos, the female serial killer, received little positive coverage from the news media. The portrait of Wuornos that emerged from the coverage was that of a "lesbian man-hater" who roamed the highways seeking men to rob and murder (e.g., Hart, 1994). However, the image of Wuornos that emerged from the feature film *Monster* (2003) offered more room for consideration of how Wuornos came to commit the homicides that led her to death row and finally to her execution.

Although feminist scholars have given some attention to depictions of women as victims, offenders, and practitioners in the news media and in popular culture, more analysis remains to be done. This social construction of images of women occurs in a complex environment of media conglomerates, politics (gender, race, and class), and societal change. Myriad factors affect what and who is portrayed and how. The neglect of coverage of crimes against women of color is one example of the impact of these factors on media coverage.

It is important that researchers deconstruct these images and engage in discourse about the role of these images in shaping perceptions and responses to women in the criminal justice system. As Young and Maguire (2003) discuss in their article titled "Talking about Sexual Violence," the language used to describe an event and the images that language conjures up can be crucial to how the event is perceived by those involved (including the victim herself). How victims see themselves, and how victims are perceived by others, is affected by images in news and entertainment media, by words and the pictures. One only need think of Glenn Close as the woman scorned in *Fatal Attraction,* with her increasingly wild (Medusa) blonde curls and maniacal obsession with revenge. Or think of Myra Hindley, the partner of Ian Brady in England's "moors murders." On the occasion of Hindley's death in prison, journalists described her as an icon of evil who lured children to their deaths.

Images—whether print, visual, or auditory—have meaning and have resonance. It is important that we examine those images closely and challenge stereotypes of women that may affect their treatment in the criminal justice system. Commenting on images of women in the United States and Afghanistan, Franks (2003, pp. 150–151) asserts:

> In any given major U.S. city, one will confront hundreds of images of women in a day—but none of these will be images that seek to highlight the problems of violence and sexual exploitation that women so often face. . . . In both Afghanistan and in the United States the fantasy of women reigns supreme; a constructed and artificial femininity is everywhere on display while the facts of violence and exploitation remain hidden.

It is important to look deeply at these images and strip away the fantasy.

Review Questions

1. Discuss the images of women that emerge from ancient Greece. What distinctions were made between men and women?

2. Discuss the theories of Lombroso, Freud, and Pollak and the images these social scientists offered of women criminals.

3. Discuss the impact of the Mary Rogers and the Helen Jewett cases in the context of images of women in the city and in the emerging press.

4. Discuss the film images of women as victims, offenders, and practitioners.

5. Do you agree or disagree with the argument that the use of violence by women is a sign of empowerment?

6. Discuss Franks's assertion about the images of women in the United States and in Afghanistan. Do you agree or disagree with her statement that a "fantasy" of women reigns supreme?

Key Terms

Gender hierarchy
Amazons
Malleus Maleficarum
Electra complex

Vamp
Film noir
Acquaintance rape
"Crack moms"

References

Armstrong, E. G. (2002). Devil music and gangsta rap: A comparison of sexual violence in blues and rap lyrics. *Arkansas Review: A Journal of Delta Studies* 33 (3), 182–194.

Bailey, F. Y., & Hale, D. C. (2004). Blood on her hands: *The social construction of women, sexuality, and murder.* Belmont, CA: Wadsworth/Thomson Learning.

Bailey, F. Y., Pollock, J. M., & Schroeder, S. (1998). The best defense: Images of female attorneys in popular films. In F. Y. Bailey & D. C. Hale (Eds.), *Popular culture, crime, and justice* (pp. 180–195). Belmont, CA: West/Wadsworth Publishing.

Barrett, D. (2004). Star Trek icon condemns Hollywood's "violence against women." *The Press Association Limited,* Home News, March 5. Retrieved on June 4, 2004.

Benedict, H. (1992). *Virgin or vamp: How the press covers sex crimes.* New York: Oxford University Press.

Block, P. (2000). Sexuality, fertility, and danger: Twentieth-century images of women with cognitive disabilities. *Sexuality and Disability* 18 (4), 239–254.

Campbell, B. (2004). Focus: One of these women is an evil murderer. *Independent on Sunday* (London), May 16, Features, 18. Retrieved June 4, 2004.

Chesney-Lind, M. (1997) *The female offender: Girls, women, and crime.* Thousand Oaks, CA: Sage Publications.

Cohen, P.C. (1999). *The murder of Helen Jewett.* New York: Vintage.

Conwell, V. (2004). Spelman rap protest derails charity event. *The Atlanta Journal-Constitution,* April 1, Features, 2F. Retrieved May 11, 2004.

Cooper, B. L. (1999). From Lady Day to Lady Di: Images of women in contemporary recordings, 1938–1998. *International Journal of Instructional Media* 26 (3), 353–358.

Danner, M. J. E., & Carmody, D. C. (2001). Missing gender in cases of infamous school violence: Investigating research and media explanations. *Justice Quarterly* 18 (1), 87–114.

Demand, N. (1994). *Birth, death, and motherhood in classical Greece.* Baltimore and London: John Hopkins University Press.

Demare, D, Briere, J., & Lips, H. (1993). Sexually violent pornography, anti-women attitudes, and sexual aggression: A structural equation model. *Journal of Research in Personality* 27, 285–300.

Donnerstein, E., & Linz, D. (1986). Mass media sexual violence and male viewers. *American Behavioral Scientist* 29, 601–618.

Dworkin, A. (1981). *Pornography: Men possessing women.* New York: G. P. Putnam's Sons.

Fishbein, L. (1989). The harlot's progress in American fiction and film, 1900–1930. *Women's Studies* 16, 409–427.

Forbes, T. R. (1966). *The midwife and the witch.* New Haven: Yale University Press.

Franks, M. A. (2003). Obscene undersides: Women and evil between Taliban and the United States. *Hypatia* 18 (1), 135–156.

Getty, A. (1990). *Goddess: Mother of living nature.* London: Thames and Hudson.

Gibson, M. (2002). *Born to crime: Cesare Lombroso and the origins of biological criminology.* Westport, CT: Praeger.

Golden, J. (1999). "An argument that goes back to the womb": The demedicalization of fetal alcohol syndrome. *Journal of Social History* 33 (2), 269–298.

Gruner, E. (1993). Merging fear and fantasy: Images of women at West Point. *ATQ* 7 (3).

Gussow, A. (2002). *Seems like murder here: Southern violence and the blues tradition.* Chicago and London: University of Chicago Press.

Hale, D. C. (1998). Keeping women in their place: An analysis of policewomen in videos, 1972–1996. In F. Y. Bailey & D. C. Hale (Eds.), *Popular culture, crime, and justice* (pp. 159–179). Belmont, CA: West/Wadsworth Publishing.

Hajewski, D. (2003). Forum focuses on effect of ads on images of women. *Milwaukee Journal Sentinel,* October 20, Business, 01D. Retrieved May 5, 2004.

Halttunen, K. (1998). *Murder most foul: The killer and the American gothic imagination.* Cambridge, MA: Harvard University Press.

Hamilton, E. (1942 [1999]). *Mythology: Timeless tales of gods and heroes.* New York: Warner Books.

Hart, L. (1994). *Fatal women: Lesbian sexuality and the mark of aggression*. Princeton, NJ: Princeton University Press.

Humphries, D. (1999). *Crack mothers: Pregnancy, drugs, and the media*. Columbus: Ohio State University Press.

Jhally, S. (1995). *Dreamworlds II* [Videorecording]: Desire/sex/power in music video. Northampton, MA: Media Education Foundation.

Johnson, B. D. (1994). Femme fatale revisited. *Maclean's* 107 (10), March 7, 58–59.

Kaplan, E. A. (1983). *Women and film: Both sides of the camera*. New York: Methuen.

Kurtz, J. (1997). Dream girls: Women in advertising. *USA Today Magazine* 125 (2620), 70.

Lavin, M. R. (1998). Women in comic books. *Serials Review* 24 (2), 1–8.

Lefkowitz, M. R. (1986). *Women in Greek myth*. Baltimore: Johns Hopkin University Press.

Lombroso, C., & Ferrero, G. (1893, pub. in English, 1895 [1980]). *The female offender*. Littleton, CO: Fred B. Rothman.

Los, M., & Chamard, S. E. (1997). Selling newspapers or educating the public? Sexual violence in the media. *Canadian Journal of Criminology*, 293–328.

Macdonald, M. (1995). *Representing women: Myths of femininity in the popular media*. London: Edward Arnold.

Mackinnon, C. (1984) Not a moral issue. *Yale Law Policy Review* 2, 321–345.

Martin, N. (2001). Why Harry Potter is under the spell of sex stereotypes. *The Daily Telegraph (London),* July 5, 11. Retrieved May 11, 2004.

Milne, P. J. (2002). Voicing embodied evil: Gynophobic images of women in post-biblical and intertestamental text. *Feminist Theology* 30, 61–69.

Morey, A. (1995). "The judge called me an accessory": Women's prison films, 1950–1962. *Journal of Popular Film & Television* 23 (2), 80–87.

Naylor, B. (2001). Reporting violence in the British print media: Gendered stories. *The Howard Journal* 40 (2), 180–194.

Pollak, O. (1950, reprint 1978). *The criminality of women*. Westport, CT: Greenwood Press.

Pollock, J. M. (1994). *Images of violence against women*. Paper presented at the Academy of Criminal Justice Sciences Meeting, Chicago.

Pollock, J. M. (1995). Gender, justice, and social control: A historical perspective. In A. Merlo & J. Pollock (Eds.), *Women, law, and social control* (pp. 3–36). Boston: Allyn and Bacon.

Quinn, R. G. (2004). Mothers, molls, and misogynists: Resisting Italian American womanhood in *The Sopranos. The Journal of American Culture* 27 (2), 166–174.

Robb, G. (1997). Circe in crinoline: Domestic poisoning in Victorian England. *Journal of Family History* 22 (2), 176–190.

Smith-Shomade, B. E. (2003). "Rock-a-bye, baby!": Black women disrupting gangs and constructing hip-hop gangsta films. *Cinema Journal* 42 (2), 25–40.

Wearden, S. T., & Creedon, P. J. (2003). "We got next": Images of women in television commercials during the inaugural WNBA season. *Sports, Media, Culture,* 189–210.

Williamson, L. (2000). Song boycott a cryin' shame. *Toronto Sun,* April 9.

Young, S. L., & Maguire, K. C. (2003). Talking about sexual violence. *Women and Language* 26 (2), 40–52.

3

Current Issues in the Law and Women

What Would a Reasonable Woman Do?

Mary K. Stohr and Lisa Growette Bostaph

The law is a peculiar weapon in that it has been employed for both good and evil purposes across the course of human history. In the case of women, for much of that time, it has been used as a method of social control to keep women separate, unequal, and ultimately oppressed. For female victims, offenders, and professionals in the criminal justice system, this has meant that they are valued and believed less (in the case of victims), blamed more (in the case of offenders), and excluded from valued work (in the case of professionals).

For the last 200 years, and primarily in Western cultures, a mammoth effort was launched by women and men of goodwill to marshal the force of law behind the idea that women are entitled to as many liberties and legal protections as men. Because, and only because, of these efforts, women and girls now have the law more often than not on their side. However, this does not mean that gender discrimination has ended in all spheres of human existence, including the criminal justice system. Nor does it mean that implementation of the law is handled in a gender-neutral way by criminal justice actors. In fact, informally and in the public and private spheres of criminal justice organizations, religious institutions, and families, it is still not true that women are accorded the same rights and liberties as men.

Clearly, much has been accomplished, but much more needs to be done. In this chapter we will chronicle some of the historical issues that shaped current practice of the law. For instance, we will explore the *reasonable man* standard in the law and the separate spheres that men and women occupy. In this chapter, we will explore how a "reasonable woman standard" might better befit the circumstances involving some crimes that are faced by female victims, offenders, and professionals. In such cases we will ask: What Would a Reasonable Woman Do? We will also note how women's experiences in the legal process are shaped by the informally held attitudes of courtroom actors. We will also examine how the sword of law formally can mandate great good in one action but informally can be wielded for its opposite purpose.

Law as a Gendered Entity

In most societies, laws are formally sanctioned social control mechanisms. They tend to represent the interests of those groups who have money and power. In our culture, and in practically every other known human society, this bias toward money and/or power has meant that the male gender's interests are those most recognized and protected by the law (Gowing, 1994). But those prosecuting the law have been faced with a conundrum: How should these interests of the males be balanced when they compete with other males or females? The *reasonable man* standard in the law was developed as a way to leaven the capriciousness that sometimes creeps into judicial decision making. It gave judges a means of measuring whether a particular behavior was acceptable by asking the question: What Would a Reasonable Man Do? In essence, this question forces the decision maker to consider whether what this defendant/victim or professional did fits within the boundaries of reasonable behavior—for a man, that is. Note that this standard was not initially intended to cover women, as women historically were considered to be inherently unreasonable. So rather than the popularly used, and abused, acronym WWJD (What Would Jesus Do), in the law the standard for judging behavior is WWARMD (What Would A Reasonable Man Do).

This standard was set at the very birth of our nation by the documents that established and maintained the republic that were written by men, for men. In both the Declaration of Independence and the U.S. Constitution there is no mention made of women. Instead, their authors used only male pronouns. Similarly, in the Federalist Papers (numbers 10 and 51), which were anonymous newspaper editorials used by male founders to argue points regarding the Constitution and its Amendments, only men are referred to as citizens with legal status. Moreover, in the Constitution only a "he" could serve in Congress or as President.

But these facts are not that surprising given that the male founders of this country were shaped by their culture and its social norms. Their political acts were influenced by male philosophers, such as Thomas Hobbes, John Locke, and Jean-Jacques Rousseau, who, writing in the sixteenth and seventeenth centuries, had little regard for the rights of women. Hobbes and Locke allowed that women deserved some rights, though limited, vis à vis their relationships with men (Coole, 1993). Since they were naturally inferior to men, they were to have only the right to exist and to keep possessions not acquired in marriage, otherwise they were to be subordinate to men (Hobbes, 1978 [1651, 16th printing]).

In fact, when reading Hobbes, Locke, and Rousseau, it becomes clear that women and girls were invisible to these authors. For Hobbes and Rousseau, all children worth educating are male, all persons capable of reason are male, all founders of civilization, makers of contracts with the sovereign, and all thoughtful persons are male (Durant & Durant, 1967; Hobbes, 1978). Rousseau, though a champion of rights in his writing for all men (he meant only white men), believed that women simply could not be citizens as they did not possess the ability to reason fully (Coole, 1993). If you were a woman, by Rousseau's definition, you were unreasonable.

Also under common law, which formed the basis for the U.S. system of jurisprudence, adult women were not accorded the rights and liberties of men. Blackstone (1765–1769) in his four volumes *Commentaries on the Laws of England,* which served as the intellectual rampart for interpreting common law, thought that women were essentially *chattel* or property. Moreover, once married, the man and woman became one and that one, for legal purposes, was the man. "Known as *coverture,* this doctrine would later be compared to slavery, in that it effectively stripped married women of any legal rights except the right to be prosecuted for heinous crimes . . . in general married women could not own land, retain their own wages, enter into contracts, or sue anybody" (Dusky, 1996, pp. 252–253; Naffine, 1990).

Mary Wollstonecraft, an early English feminist writing in *A Vindication of the Rights of Woman* (1792), argued in direct contradiction to Rousseau, that women's ability to reason cannot be compared to men's unless and until they are given the same educational opportunities as men. A girl's education, if she got one at all, was usually short and geared toward her likely servant or domestic role in the future; she wasn't given the requisite knowledge to prepare her for citizenship. Instead superficial matters, such as her looks, were too often focused upon and her mind was neglected. A social commentator today might see a similar focus in our present culture, though certainly not to the extent that it was true in the 1700s when Wollstonecraft wrote. Wollstonecraft (1967/1792, pp. 49–50) argued that law and social practice culturally limit the true ability of women to reason.

We know now that Wollstonecraft and others like her argued in vain. The male founders of this country meant "men" when they wrote "men" in our constitution (Dusky, 1996). They never intended that women should have full citizenship rights. Even John Adams when asked in a letter by his wife, Abigail, in 1776 to "remember the ladies" when liberties and rights are accorded, replied, "Depend on it, we know better than to repeal our masculine systems" (Dusky, 1996, p. 253). Abigail Adams had been asking that abused women have some recourse to escape tyrannical husbands, something that common law did not allow.

Thomas Jefferson, the author of the *Declaration of Independence*, concurred with John Adams, writing that "Even were our state a true democracy there would still be excluded from our deliberations women, who, to prevent deprivations of morals and ambiguity of issues, should not mix promiscuously in gatherings of men" (Dusky, 1996, p. 254). Therefore, Jefferson meant only men, and only white men who owned property, when he wrote in the *Declaration,* "We hold these Truths to be self-evident, that all Men are created equal. . . ."

Some have claimed retroactively that the *reasonable man* standard was intended to apply to women. It wasn't. Some claim that it encompasses women. It doesn't. According to the founders of this country, women could not be encompassed under the *reasonable man* standard for judging conduct, simply because they were never considered to be capable of reason. Yet in law, this standard has been applied as if we all were men negotiating our way in the world.

Of course female scholars of justice have commented on the invisibility of women and girls in the scholarship and law affecting the criminal justice system (e.g., see Belknap, 1996; Chesney-Lind & Sheldon, 1998; Joseph & Taylor, 2003; see also chapters in Datesman & Scarpitti, 1980; Merlo & Pollock, 1995; Muraskin, 2003; Price & Sokoloff, 1995). We know from them that this lack of recognition in the law by political philosophers, who subsequently influenced the founders of this country and its legal system, still profoundly affects the criminal justice system and women's treatment by it today.

What Would a Reasonable Woman Do?

In practice, the *reasonable man* standard has been particularly unfair when it is applied to crimes or civil offenses in which women are the primary victims (e.g., domestic violence, sexual assault, and sexual harassment). The application of the *reasonable man* standard in these cases is unfair for two reasons: (1) Most men and boys are not the usual victims of these crimes and therefore what they might consider a "reasonable" response might not be "reasonable" from a female victim's viewpoint, and (2) women and girls are typically physically smaller than men and boys, and their response to such crimes is tempered and shaped by that fact.

As most males do not usually face these types of crimes as victims they may have a hard time understanding the victim's perspective. They might not interpret the repeated unwanted telephoning of a victim or repeatedly showing up at her workplace as a threat, the way women do. They might see jokes that degrade women and unwanted touching in the workplace or at school as benign rather than as a threat. When faced with a physical conflict, they may choose to behave differently than a woman, who is physically smaller or weaker than her assailant, would. Notably, in combination, a history of abuse, or exposure to it through friends and family, coupled with less physical capabilities, give the *reasonable woman* facing domestic violence, sexual assault, or sexual harassment situations, a wholly different perspective than that of a *reasonable man.*

Yet, the law has been slow to recognize these realities (Feder, 1999; Lentz, 1999; Schlanger, 2002; Spencer, 1987). Rather, the standard has been the reasonable man. As Schlanger (2002) notes, the legal casebooks of old rarely addressed whether a person was old or young, male or female, but not so the cases and commentary by judges. In an 1856 definition of negligence in the case *Blyth v. Birmingham* the judge stated that it was the "[o]mission to do something which a reasonable man, guided upon those considerations which ordinarily regulate the conduct of human affairs, would do, or doing something which a prudent and reasonable man would not do" (Schlanger, 2002, p. 769). In a 1933 oft-quoted case regarding this standard, a reasonable man was allegedly defined by the judge as "the man who takes the magazines at home and in the evening pushes the lawn mower in his shirt sleeves" (Schlanger, 2002, p. 770 quoting from *Hall v. Brooklands* [1933]).

Rarely has the law considered the *reasonable woman* standard (or WWARWD) as the appropriate basis for judging behavior (Schlanger, 2002). What would a reasonable woman do when faced with battering, sexual assault, or harassment? Given the likelihood that she, or girls or women close to her, have been victims of this abuse before and given the fact that she is likely physically smaller and/or less strong than her abuser, would she not, if she is rational, act differently than a reasonable man? Would not we, as reasonable people, expect her to?

Case Law and the Reasonable Woman Standard

Most courts now use the "reasonable person" standard to correct for the male bias inherent in the "reasonable man" standard (Ranney, 2004) and/or because this term has been used throughout our history to refer to both men and women (Schlanger, 2002). But some feminists believe that this standard fails to take into account the female gender perspective in crimes such as battering and sexual and gender harassment (MacKinnon, 1987; Schlanger, 2002). It is argued that the traditions and conventions of our culture assign reasonableness to men, therefore a standard that does not explicitly recognize women is not gender neutral. Simply put, a "person" acting reasonably is assumed to be a man. Instead, the proper standard for such crimes, where the typical victim is female, should be the "reasonable woman standard." Or, to put it in the vernacular of the current cultural discourse: WWARWD?

The first case to establish the "reasonable woman" standard in sexual harassment cases was the Ninth Circuit's *Ellison v. Brady* case in 1991. In that case, Kerry Ellison, who was a revenue agent for the Internal Revenue Service in San Francisco, was repeatedly harassed by a coworker, Gray, who constantly watched her, wrote her notes, repeatedly asked her out, and sent her letters. He continued this behavior even after she asked him to stop. After she complained to her supervisor, the harasser was moved to another office but was moved back after six months. She then asked for a transfer herself and filed a complaint with the IRS, who concluded that she was not harassed. She then complained to the Equal Employment Opportunity Commission (EEOC), who found she was harassed but determined that the IRS had taken care of it. She then filed suit at the district court level, lost, and appealed to the Ninth Circuit, where she won.

The court held that Ellison, despite being frightened and upset by the harasser's actions, had acted as a "reasonable woman" would. She had refused advances, did not engage in questionable behavior that might have signaled to the harasser that his behavior was "welcome," and she complained. Unfortunately, this standard has not caught on in case law, even as it relates to sexual harassment.

Nor has a related defense to battering, "the battered woman syndrome," been that successful in court. According to this syndrome, the battered woman employs violent behavior to defend herself and/or her children from continued abuse. Instead, the courts have tended to use the "reasonable person" perspective to be "gender neutral" in their determinations of reasonableness (Schlanger, 2002).

Civil Protection Orders That Encompass the Reasonable Women Standard

Civil protection order laws in some states, ones used primarily in domestic violence cases, do seem to represent the interests of a reasonable woman and victims in such instances. In the 1990s, several states (e.g., New Jersey, New Mexico, and New York) passed laws that made it easier to obtain a civil protection order based on "threatening and controlling behaviors" associated with domestic violence, sexual assault, and harassment (Fernandez, Iwamoto, & Muscat, 1997; Finn, 1991; Klein & Orloff, 1999, p. 32). According to Klein and Orloff (1999, p. 32), "Among the states that include harassment as grounds for protection, the definitions vary, but may include following the victim, threatening the victim, driving around the victim's home, moving near the victim's home and calling the victim repeatedly at work." Most states have made stalking a crime, and protection orders can be used in a few states (e.g., New Mexico, New Jersey, Oklahoma, Rhode Island) to restrict contact between victims and stalkers. Emotional abuse of the victim or preventing her from exercising her liberty (e.g., to leave the home or to call the police) are behaviors that are allowed to serve as the basis for protection orders in some states, but far from all (Klein & Orloff, 1999).

The remedies afforded in such instances can vary from preventing behavior by the defendant to requiring it (Klein & Orloff, 1999). For instance, protection orders can prevent contact between the parties but require that compensatory and punitive damages be paid. They can also transfer real estate and order child support.

These orders become problematic, however, in those states that allow mutual protection orders without considering the separate circumstances that exist between a victim and offender in a domestic violence case. In fact, the Violence Against Women Act discourages judges from issuing mutual protection orders when there is no evidence that both parties were the victims of abuse. Klein and Orloff (1999) also argue that mediation in civil protection order matters is not helpful to female victims who often have less bargaining power in a situation in which all parties are supposed to be equal.

Civil protection orders are also problematic if they are not enforced (Finn, 1991). This means that the victim must report and the police and courts must respond. In most states, violation of a civil protection order is a crime, but it also can lead to a civil contempt hearing, which has been the more traditional route for enforcement.

Fernandez and her colleagues (1997) found that restraining orders work best when the victim is not dependent on the abuser and when the abuse is not severe. Because of their dependence on and fear of the abusers, victims are less likely to pursue a restraining order under these circumstances. This, of course, is ironic, as these are precisely the victims who most need official, and other, assistance. Both the "reasonable woman" standard and civil protection orders are two relatively current issues in the law. They have provided women with a means to address inequalities and misperceptions in law and practice. But for women to harness the full force of the law to their advantage, they needed to cross the bridge from their "outsider" position to that of an insider.

Separate Spheres

Because of this presumption in law, culture, and custom that women and men differed profoundly in their abilities to reason and act logically, they have historically occupied "separate spheres." Middle- to upper-class women, especially, have been homebound for much of the last two centuries in this country. However, poor white women and/or minority women were always expected to work outside of the home, though usually in traditional female jobs and for less pay than men. It has only been since the women's movement of the 1970s and the slow implementation of its precepts in our culture that men and women have been allowed more freedom in choosing who stays at home with the kids, if anyone, and who is the "breadwinner," if not both parents.

When much of America was mostly agrarian, the roles and spheres of influence for men and women intersected and overlapped more. Women were allowed to occupy more of a partnership role in the operation of the family farm. However, after industrialization, the world of work moved largely outside the home and became the province of men. It was not a coincidence that the first states to afford women suffrage were those "frontier" states (e.g., Wyoming 1869, Utah 1870, Colorado 1893, and Idaho 1896) where women were needed as equal helpmates on farms and ranches. In other words, because women in these Western states were not confined to their "sphere" of influence, the home and family exclusively, their abilities to reason and negotiate, and thus act responsibly as citizens, were demonstrated and somewhat accepted by men. In this sense, Mary Wollstonecraft's point made at the founding of our country was finally validated in the late 1800s in some states. But it was not until 1920, with the ratification of the Nineteenth Amendment, that women across the country were given what should have been theirs from the beginning, the right to vote.

The Legal Bridge into the Male Sphere

After more than a century and a half of trying, the first wave of feminists (1776 to 1920), achieved the right to vote for women. The second wave, beginning in the 1970s, focused on rights that more fully define women, and all others, as citizens. These rights encompass the right to own and transfer property and educational and employment opportunities (Brenner, 1996). The second wave has also focused on "outing" male violence against women and children (e.g., domestic violence, sexual assault, and sexual harassment). This second wave of the feminist movement followed on the heels of the successful civil rights movement of the 1960s. As any student of these movements and their predecessors know, it is rare that complete or sometimes even real reform occurred immediately as a result of these movements. Rather the implementation of change has been a long-term process with many steps forward, and a few steps back.

Supreme Court decisions helped in establishing women's rights in law. In 1973 (*Reed v. Reed*, 404 U.S. 71, *Frontiero v. Richardson*, 411 U.S. 677) and in 1975 (*Duran v. Missouri*, 439 U.S. 357), Supreme Court cases established that women could administer estates, were entitled to equal benefits from the government, and were granted their right to serve on juries. But perhaps the most important laws to establish women's ability to cross into the traditionally male sphere are the laws associated with civil rights, particularly as these are associated with equal employment opportunity. Civil rights legislation first appeared in 1866 and 1871 and was concerned with employment discrimination that might be faced by ex-slaves. Beginning with Franklin Roosevelt in 1941, several presidents have issued executive orders barring employment discrimination in federal employment and those organizations having federal contracts. Criminal justice agencies were not affected, for the most part, by this legislation or the executive orders.

In 1961 President Kennedy's executive order imposed the first requirement for affirmative action. Affirmative action (AA) simply means that an organization takes positive steps to ensure that its hiring practices are fair and that they do not disparately impact a targeted underrepresented group. President Kennedy required that federal agencies and those with federal contracts institute a "plan" and implement a program to ensure that the methods used for employment practices were nondiscriminatory. Affirmative action plans were also to address the methods used to compensate for past discriminatory practices in employment. In other words, affirmative action plans were premised on fair employment in the present and provided a remedy for past employment discrimination. Both Presidents Johnson and Nixon reaffirmed the importance of affirmative action with their own executive orders.

In 1964, however, the Civil Rights Act (CRA) was passed and included several titles. This act made it illegal to discriminate in voter registration requirements, public accommodation and facilities, and employment. The Act also created the EEOC to review complaints, although the EEOC's ability to enforce change was weak. The most important Title of the CRA of 1964, for our purposes, was Title VII, which became enforceable with an amendment to the Act in 1972 (the Equal Employment Opportunity Act). Title VII essentially made it unlawful to discriminate in the hiring, maintaining, or discharging of people because of their race, color, religion, sex, or national origin.

The Civil Rights Act of 1964 originally only covered employers of more than twenty-five persons but was eventually extended to cover both private and public employment agencies, including those on the state and local level that employed fifteen or more people. With the passage of this Act and its amendment in 1972, criminal justice agencies of any size were required to reform their hiring practices and to institute affirmative action plans. Also in 1972, Title IX of the Higher Education Act was passed constraining the ability of law schools (and other schools) to discriminate based on gender. Those that did faced the threat of the loss of federal assistance (Martin & Jurik, 1996). All of a sudden, the last vestiges of the formal legal barriers precluding admission to professional schools and jobs were eliminated. But actual compliance with these laws came only gradually and incrementally and took several years and countless lawsuits.

Women in Criminal Justice Agencies

Beginning in the early 1970s, and continuing through the 1980s and 1990s, the number of women employed has steadily increased in policing, corrections, and courts (Maguire & Pastore, 2004). According to data reported in the *Sourcebook of Criminal Justice Statistics,* the percentage of women employed as full-time sworn police officers in local police and sheriff's departments in 2000 (the latest date for which we have figures) ranges, on average, from 11 to almost 17 percent (Maguire & Pastore, 2004). Large departments in cities of 250,000 or more employ the most women and have seen the greatest increases in the percentage of women employed from 1990 to 2000 (about 5 percent). Some such cities (e.g., Philadelphia, Detroit, Washington, DC, and Pittsburgh) report that over 24 percent of their sworn officers are women. In contrast, the percentage of women employed as sworn officers in other small and large cities (e.g., Corpus Christi, El Paso, San Jose, and San Antonio) is in the single digits. Similarly, the number of women employed as full-time federal officers varies widely from agency to agency. For instance, 28 percent of Internal Revenue Service officers with arrest and firearms authority are women, but only about 9 percent of such officers for the Veterans Health Administration and Drug Enforcement Administration are women.

The percentage of correctional officers in jails who are women averaged 28 percent in 1999 (the latest date for which we have figures) (Maguire & Pastore, 2004). In federal, state, and private correctional facilities, the percentage of women employed, though not necessarily as correctional officers, was about 33 percent in 2000. This represents a 4 percent increase in women employed from 1995 to 2000 (from 29 to 33 percent).

Unfortunately, the *Sourcebook* does not include information on the number of women employed in traditionally male positions in the courtroom (judges, defense and prosecution attorneys, bailiffs, court reporters, and others) (Maguire & Pastore, 2004). The *Sourcebook* does, however, contain information on the number of women nominated for U.S. Court of Appeals judgeships from 1963 and the Johnson administration through 2002 and the George W. Bush administration. The general trend has been that more women are nominated recently, but with some decided differences from president to president. Only 2.5 percent of President Johnson's appointees were women, but none of Presidents Nixon's or Ford's appointees, who followed Johnson, were women. President Carter's appointees were almost 20 percent women, and both of the Bush presidents appointed about 19 percent women. But President Clinton appointed the most women as judges to the federal appellate courts—about 33 percent of his appointees were women.

Collectively, we gather from these data the sense that the employment picture for women has improved since the 1960s and 1970s when almost no women were employed in criminal justice agencies. It is not a coincidence that the increase in the number of women hired happened after the second wave of the feminist movement, after the 1972 amendment to the CRA of 1964, and after affirmative action plans were established and women sued to gain equal employment opportunity. History tells us that none of these changes would have happened without these efforts and initiatives (Martin, 1992; Martin & Jurik, 1996; Pollitz Worden, 1997; Zupan, 1992).

Employment Discrimination Continues

Furthermore, despite the clear evidence that women have made great strides in gaining equal employment in traditionally male spheres, we should be mindful that discrimination still exists in both the private and public sectors. Blumrosen and Blumrosen (2002), in a recent analysis of employment data provided to the EEOC by those who employed over fifty people in 1999, supported by the Ford Foundation, found that there is a continuing pattern of wide-spread intentional discrimination in employment that impacts both minority group men and women (African Americans, Hispanics, Asian/Pacific Islanders, Native Americans) and white women. The researchers found that this pattern of discrimination occurs across virtually all of the states. Though they did not have data for criminal justice organizations, what they found illustrates that discrimination in employment did not end with the institution of affirmative action plans.

For their study, Blumrosen and Blumrosen (2002) defined the existence of intentional discrimination when the employment of minorities and women fell two standard deviations below what the average employment was for those groups in that industry, job category, and metropolitan area. Their state by state study indicates that while agencies and corporations have come a long way in implementing equal employment in this country, there is still much room for improvement.

Reverse Discrimination

Unfortunately, reverse discrimination, or the discrimination against a majority group or its member who may be equally or more qualified in some ways than a minority group or its member, is always a possibility when affirmative action plans are implemented. Clearly, such discrimination does exist, but majority groups may overestimate its amount. Research by Camp, Steiger, Wright, Saylor, and Gilman (1997) on four years of promotions in the Federal Bureau of Prisons found that the majority group (in this case white men) often overestimated the advantage that the minority group (minority group men and women and white women) gain from affirmative action. What they found instead was that sometimes affirmative action advantaged the minority group in promotion and sometimes it did not. They conclude that rather than advantaging one group over another, affirmative action had the effect of "leveling the playing field" in personnel actions.

The Supreme Court in the *University of California Regents v. Bakke* (438 U.S. 265 [1978]) and *Grutter v. Bollinger et al.* (288 F. 3d, affirmed, U.S. 02-241 [2003]) dealt directly with reverse discrimination. Both cases are concerned with admissions to professional schools at prestigious universities. In the *Bakke* case, a white male claimed that he was the victim of reverse discrimination because applicants with lower academic qualifications were admitted to the University of California's Medical School while he was denied admission. He alleged that this occurred because he was white and the lesser-qualified applicants were minority group members, some of whom were admitted to the school under a special admissions program that, in practice, only was used to admit minority group members. Justice Powell, writing for the majority, agreed in part with this assessment, and the Supreme Court ordered Bakke's admission to the Davis Medical School and invalidated the special admissions program. But the majority did not say that race as a consideration in admissions was illegal. Justice Stevens, writing in support of this contention, noted that more than academic credentials might be considered when developing criteria for admissions. In other words, the court conceded that *reverse discrimination* had occurred in *Bakke,* but it also did not condemn the use of affirmative action in some cases.

In the more recent *Grutter* case (2003), Grutter, a white female applicant to the University of Michigan's Law School, maintained that she was denied admission because of her race (she is white), again while applicants with lesser academic credentials were admitted.

Women, particularly white women, now make up about 50 percent of law school entrants, and they are rarely accorded protected status requiring affirmative action for such institutions any more. Justice O'Connor, writing for the majority, argued that the consideration of race as one factor in admissions policies was lawful. She noted that the law school's admission policy that places a value on diversity does not define that term only in relation to racial and ethnic origin. She argued that the majority opinion in this case was in keeping with the *Bakke* decision, which allowed some consideration of race and ethnicity in admissions policies.

How the *Grutter* case impacts employment in criminal justice is not yet completely clear. It may mean that cases where the plaintiff alleges reverse discrimination will continue to be given "strict scrutiny" by the courts, but that race, ethnicity, and gender of applicants can be considered when making employment decisions. It also may mean, however, that once groups that formerly were in the minority are now proportionally represented in the workplace—as with white women in many law schools—they are no longer able to use affirmative action to gain admittance. In fact, another minority group can use affirmative action against them.

Women's Experiences in the Law

As with policing and corrections, it was not until the 1970s that women were admitted to law schools and to the practice of law in any large number (Martin & Jurik, 1996; Pollitz Worden, 1997; Zupan, 1992). As mentioned previously, often such victories only came, despite the laws, after equal opportunity was litigated in the courts. As indicated by the *Grutter* case, women, but particularly white women, have successfully integrated law schools around this country. According to the Princeton Review's *The Best Law Schools, 1998 Edition,* 44 percent of students entering law schools in the mid-1990s were women (Harrington, 1994; Hollander & Tallia, 1997). By 2002, the American Bar Association (ABA) and Law School Admissions Council (LSAC) publication on law schools indicated that 49 percent of attendees were women, and 48 percent of law school graduates were women (ABA-LSAC, 2004).

Krakauer and Chen (2003) note in their article on gender barriers in the legal profession that, although the entry of women into the legal profession has increased dramatically in the United States and Canada since the 1980s, their exit from the profession exceeds that of men. "However, despite their advances in gaining admittance to law school, women continue to face gender-based barriers once they enter the profession, and partly as a result, they are leaving the profession at significantly higher rates than their male peers are leaving it" (p. 66).

In the Princeton publication, Hollander and Tallia (1997) reported that 28 percent of faculty and administrators of law schools, 16 percent of tenured law professors, 8 percent of the deans, and 12.9 percent of the partners in law firms were women. They noted that, overall, women comprised 24 percent of those working in the legal profession. By 2002, the ABA and the LSAC found that the number of female professors in law schools was 29 percent of the total, though this figure, unlike Princeton's, included both full- and part-time professors.

The Gender Bias Studies

This discussion of who is trained in legal work, and who does the training, is relevant because it sometimes determines whether the practices and procedures in courts are fair. As the number of women increase in these law school and professional positions, it is likely that bias against them in the courtroom will decrease. In a review of thirty state gender bias studies done over a fifteen-year period, ending in 1997, Hemmens, Strom, and Schlegel (2004) found that men and women are not treated the same in the courts and that most often this means that women are the victims of gender bias that disadvantages them *vis à vis* men. The definition of gender bias that was used for these studies was "[a]ctions or attitudes that negatively impact an individual or group primarily because of gender" (Washington, 1989, as cited in Hemmens, Strom, & Schlegel, 2004, p. 261).

Hemmens et al. (2004) found bias noted in these state studies in the areas of domestic violence, sexual assault, divorce, and in the behavior of courtroom actors. Domestic violence cases presented a particular set of circumstances whereby victims, who were primarily women (e.g., in Nebraska 98 percent of the victims were women), were not believed, their cases were not prosecuted, they encountered obstructions, and they were even discouraged from securing a protection order from courtroom actors. Even once the orders were secured, there was no guarantee that they would be enforced.

The authors believed that many of these problems stem from the belief that domestic violence is a private family affair and has no place in the courtroom (as was found in the Washington 1989 study). Or it may be that domestic violence is not taken as seriously as violence between strangers (as was found in the Utah 1990 study). Moreover, in some states (e.g., Massachusetts), the study authors found that juries expect more physical injuries for domestic violence than they do for other types of crime. A state trial judge in Utah (1990) was quoted as saying, "I have difficulty finding where this defendant's [the husband] done anything wrong, other than slapping her [his wife]. Maybe that was justified" (Hemmens et al., 2004, p. 260).

In some states, there were court personnel who thought that the abuse was exaggerated or that such crimes should not be brought to court. "The California (1996) task force found that 53 percent of the male court personnel surveyed 'agreed' or 'strongly agreed' that declarations of abuse are often exaggerated. Only 26 percent of the female court personnel surveyed felt this was the case" (Hemmens et al., 2004, p. 260). Also in California, 40 percent of the male and 20 percent of the female personnel felt such cases should be diverted to counseling and should not be prosecuted. Among victims there was also doubt that the police and prosecutors would handle the cases seriously.

As previously mentioned, protection orders do represent a possible remedy for women and men interested in preventing their abuser or stalker from pursuing them. Unfortunately, Hemmens et al. (2004) found that here, too, the state gender bias studies uncovered problems. In four states, the courtroom actors who were surveyed had little confidence in the court personnel to provide assistance in securing a protection order, though they noted that many women did not know how to go about getting one. They also indicated that there were long delays in obtaining the order, and that petitioners were rarely represented by counsel. In some states they also found that the orders were not enforced and that there was inherent bias against women in the awarding of mutual protection orders.

In seven of the state studies the authors found that most women do not report sexual assault for easily understandable reasons: the police will not believe or will blame the victim, and judges and juries will not believe the victim. For instance, as Hemmens et al. reported in the Minnesota study (Hemmens et al., 2004, p. 894), one judge remarked, "Rape is simply a case of poor salesmanship."

Half of the female attorney respondents in the Texas study (1994) thought that the police either do not believe or blame the victim for the sexual assault. Forty percent thought that judges and prosecutors believed the victims were less credible. Sixty-four percent of the prosecutors and public defenders responding to the Massachusetts study (1989) believed that juries were more skeptical regarding rape charges and victims than other types of crimes. The same court practitioners thought that if no injuries were present, then juries were even less likely to convict offenders. Perhaps this bias exists because gender stereotypes prevail in courtrooms, as 75 percent of attorneys and 63 percent of judges in the Vermont study (1991) claimed. In the Connecticut study (1991), the authors found such stereotypes when the dress and past behavior of the victim were regarded as relevant by some courtroom actors. About a quarter of the responding judges in the Connecticut (1991) and Washington (1989) studies thought that the dress and past sexual behavior of the victim either invited the offense or should factor into a determination of how serious the offense was. Such beliefs are unsettling because they reflect a belief that women are still property under the law and once "damaged" by sexual activity, were "worth" much less.

The gender bias studies that relate to divorce indicate that alimony, division of marital property, child support awards, and their enforcement can all lead to discrimination against women, but also, against men. Six of the studies indicate that women suffer the most financially following a divorce. Women were accorded less property and child support, and men were much less likely to be awarded child custody. Several of the state studies indicated that some bias exists against men in the area of child custody. In eight state studies, a majority of respondents, usually more male attorneys than female, thought that judges had a bias toward the mother over the father in awarding custody of the children.

Another major area of gender bias that is covered by Hemmens et al. (2004) is the bigoted behavior that is directed at female attorneys. In fourteen of these studies the female attorney respondents indicated that they experienced biased behavior by either other attorneys or judges. Such behavior took the form of demeaning remarks about women, being treated differently, according less credibility to their statements (by judges), comments on their personal appearance, sexist remarks or jokes, or being repeatedly questioned about whether they are, in fact, attorneys.

This bias against female attorneys does not just exist in the courtroom. Many of the female respondents to these bias studies also believed that their chances of being hired, paid, and promoted in the legal profession were much less they were for men (e.g., Kansas 1992, New Mexico 1990, California 1996, Ninth Circuit 1993, Michigan 1989, and New Mexico 1990).

Hemmens et al. (2004) noted that several of the state studies indicate that judges rarely intervene when gender bias comes to their attention. Yet the authors speculate that this failure to intervene by judges inevitably negatively affects case outcomes. They concluded by noting that gender bias is pervasive across the states, and that it exists "[i]n all aspects of the court system, and in virtually all courts" (Hemmens et al., 2004, p. 275). They note that female respondents to these studies perceive more bias than males, but that "[t]he evidence suggests it is the males who misperceive the situation" (Hemmens et al., 2004, p. 275).

Policy Implications

The information presented in this chapter indicates that women and girls, even in a Western culture such as our own, still must struggle to ensure that they are accorded equal rights and protections under the law. We metaphorically stand at the point on a mountain where we can see below us all the pettiness and prejudice that kept women "in their place," but as we turn our eyes skyward it is clear there are other like ridges to scale in the future. The struggles of the past have led to the recognition that we are not all reasonable men—about 50 percent of us are women. This recognition has shaped the law as it applies to civil protection orders, it has helped bridge the "separate spheres" as applied to employment and property rights for women, and it has spurred research on the treatment of female lawyers, defendants, and victims/plaintiffs in the courts.

Specifically, the research on the "reasonable woman/person/man" standard and how it applies to cases in which women experience a disparate impact as victims (e.g., domestic violence, stalking, sexual harassment) has yet to be definitively determined. At this point in time, the courts appear to be settling into an acceptance of a "reasonable person" standard in determining the appropriateness of actions and reactions by all and the application of law.

Clearly, the employment opportunities for women have exploded since the implementation of the Civil Rights Act of 1964 and affirmative action plans. The employment history of criminal justice agencies and law school admissions make it quite clear that without affirmative action, none of this progress was likely to have been made. The courts have tempered and narrowed the use of affirmative action plans in professional schools, recognizing that any one group does not forever retain the benefit of underrepresented status, when they are no longer underrepresented (i.e., white women in the *Grutter v. Bollinger et al.* [2003] case). Therefore, it appears that affirmative action as a legal remedy for past and present discrimination will continue but will evolve to reflect the changing employment practices and makeup of agencies and admission practices in professional schools.

Finally, the Gender Bias Studies indicate that courtroom actors believe that discrimination against women (and in child custody cases, men) is still pervasive in the courts across this country. Collectively, these studies effectively rebut those claims that gender discrimination no longer exists. If the executive is the head, and the legislative branch the heart, then the courts are the very bowels of this democracy, where justice gets processed. If the guts, or the courts, are twisted by prejudice, then the attainment of justice for women, and men, is attenuated. Training judges, as the tertiary leaders in the courtroom, on the necessity of treating women and girls appropriately (and men in custody cases) is crucial to ensuring that the courtroom processing is fair and just.

Conclusion

What is a reasonable woman (or man) to do when faced with the realities of the world? It is true that we live in a time when women in Western countries are enjoying the penultimate prize for all the efforts made on their behalf by feminists: the protection and support of their liberties and rights under the law. The outlook is not nearly so optimistic for women living in the Middle East and parts of Asia where laws, religion, and customs severely restrict the ability of women and girls to learn and live as full human beings.

But there is much that needs to be done in the West, too. As discussed in this chapter, the law fails to recognize the value of a "reasonable woman" standard for crimes and situations that specifically affect women. Women have made great inroads in employment in criminal justice agencies, thanks to affirmative action plans. But those plans are under attack and need defending—not just for women, but for minority men. Finally, the gender bias studies indicate that women, and sometimes men, still experience bias in the courtroom.

How one perceives the realities of bias in courtrooms and our world at large has always depended to some degree on one's gender. The benefits that will accrue for the human race, once the full potential of women and girls is realized and protected in law and the courts, is inestimable. One means of achieving these benefits is to ensure that gender does not matter before the law, or after it.

Review Questions

1. Did the founders of this country intend that women and girls be considered full citizens under the law? Why or why not?

2. What did John Adams say in response to his wife's request that he "remember the ladies" when constructing the Constitution?

3. What did Mary Wollstonecraft claim was the problem with women and girls' abilities to reason?

4. Why is it not "reasonable" to apply the "reasonable man standard" to crimes where women are the primary victims? What standard would work best in such instances and why?

5. What standard is applied in the *Ellison v. Brady* case and why?

6. What are the benefits and drawbacks of civil protection orders? How do they encompass the concept of the reasonable woman perspective?

7. How did the Civil Rights Act of 1964 become a means for changing the employment status for women.

8. What are the benefits and drawbacks of affirmative action in criminal justice employment?

9. What did the Supreme Court decide in the *Bakke* and the *Grutter* cases regarding reverse discrimination?

10. How many women, on average, are employed in police, sheriff, jail, and corrections departments? How and why has their employment changed in the last ten to twenty years?

11. What did the gender bias studies find regarding the treatment of men and women in the courts?

Key Terms

WWARWD
Reasonable man
Reasonable person
Reasonable woman
Chattel
Coverture

Affirmative action
Intentional discrimination
Reverse discrimination
Gender bias
Civil Rights Act of 1964
EEOC

References

ABA-LSAC (2004). *Official guide to ABA-approved law schools.* Newtown, PA: Law School Admissions Council.

Belknap, J. (1996). *The invisible woman: Gender, crime and justice.* Belmont, CA: Wadsworth Publishing Company.

Blackstone, W. (1769). *Commentaries on the laws of England* (4 volumes). Chicago: University of Chicago Press.

Blumrosen, A., & Blumrosen, R. (2002). *The reality of intentional job discrimination in metropolitan America—1999.* Available at www.EEO1.com.

Brenner, J. (1996). The best of times, the worst of times: Feminism in the United States. In M. Threlfall (Ed.), *Mapping the women's movement* (pp. 17–72). London: Verso.

Camp, S. D., Steiger, T. L., Wright, K. N., Saylor, W. G., & Gilman, E. (1997). Affirmative action and the "level playing field": Comparing perceptions of own and minority job advancement opportunities. *The Prison Journal* 77, 313–334.

Chesney-Lind, M., & Sheldon, R. G. (1998). *Girls, delinquency, and juvenile justice* (2nd ed.). Belmont, CA: West/Wadsworth.

The Constitution of the United States. (1988, first published in 1787). In S. Welch, J. Gruhl, M. Steinman, & J. Comer (Eds.), *American government* (2nd ed.; pp. A3–A15). St. Paul, MN: West Publishing Company.

Coole, D. (1993). *Women in political theory: from ancient misogyny to contemporary feminism* (2nd ed.). Boulder, CO: Lynne Rienner Publishers.

Datesman, S. K., & Scarpitti, F. R. (Eds.) (1980). *Women, crime, and justice.* New York: Oxford University Press.

The Declaration of Independence. (1988, first published in 1776). In S. Welch, J. Gruhl, M. Steinman, and J. Comer (Eds.), *American government* (2nd ed.; pp. A1–A2). St. Paul, MN: West Publishing Company.

Dusky, L. (1996). *Still unequal: The shameful truth about women and justice in America.* New York: Crown Publishers.

Durant, W., & Durant, A. (1967). *The story of civilization: Part X, Rousseau and revolution: A history of civilization in France, England and Germany from 1756, and the remainder of Europe from 1715 to 1789.* New York: Simon and Schuster.

Feder, L. (1999). Domestic violence: An interdisciplinary approach. *Women & Criminal Justice* 10, 1–8.

Fernandez, M., Iwamoto, W., & Muscat, B. (1997). Dependency and severity of abuse: Impact on women's persistence in utilizing the court system as protection against domestic violence. *Women & Criminal Justice* 9, 39–64.

Finn, P. (1991). Civil protection orders: a flawed opportunity for intervention. In M. Steinman (Ed.), *Woman battering: Policy responses* (pp. 155–190). Cincinnati, OH: Anderson Publishing Company.

Gowing, L. (1994). Language, power, and the law: women's slander litigation in early modern London. In J. Kermode & G. Walker (Eds.), *Women, crime, and the courts in early modern England.* London: University of College London Press.

Harrington, M. (1994). *Women lawyers: Rewriting the rules.* New York: Alfred A. Knopf.

Hollander, D. A., & Tallia, R. (1997). *The Princeton review: The best law schools, 1998 edition.* New York: Random House.

Hemmens, C., Strom, K., & Schlegel, E. (2004). Gender bias in the courts: A review of the literature. In G. L. Mays, & P. R. Gregware (Eds.), *Courts and justice: A reader* (3rd ed.; pp. 258–280). Long Grove, IL: Waveland Press.

Hobbes, T. (1978). *Leviathan: parts one and two.* Indianapolis, IN: Bobbs-Merrill Company.

Joseph, J., & Taylor, D. (2003). Domestic violence and Asian Americans. In J. Joseph & D. Taylor (Eds.), *With justice for all: Minorities and women in criminal justice* (pp. 3–18). Upper Saddle River, NJ: Prentice Hall.

Klein, C. F., & Orloff, L. E. (1999). Protecting battered women: Latest trends in civil legal relief. *Women & Criminal Justice* 10, 29–47.

Krakauer, L., & Chen, C. P. (2003). Gender barriers in the legal profession implications for career development of female law students. *Journal of Employment Counseling* 40, 65–79.

Lentz, S. A. (1999). Revisiting the rule of thumb: An overview of the history of wife abuse. *Women & Criminal Justice* 10, 9–27.

MacKinnon, C. (1987). *Feminism unmodified: Discourses on life and law.* Cambridge, MA: Harvard University Press.

Maguire, K., & Pastore, A. L. (Eds.). (2004). *Sourcebook of criminal justice statistics [Online].* Available at www.albany.edu/sourcebook/.

Martin, S. E. (1992). The changing status of women officers: Gender and power in police work. In I. L. Moyer (Ed.), *The changing roles of women in the criminal justice system* (2nd ed.; pp. 281–306). Prospect Heights, IL: Waveland Press.

Martin, S. E., & Jurik, N. C. (1996). *Doing justice, doing gender.* Thousand Oaks, CA: Sage Publications.

Merlo, A. V., & Pollock, J. M. (1995). *Women, law, and social control.* Boston: Allyn and Bacon.

Muraskin, R. (2003). *It's a crime: Women and justice* (3rd ed.). Upper Saddle River, NJ: Prentice Hall.

Naffine, N. (1990). *Law and the sexes: Explorations in feminist jurisprudence.* North Sydney, Australia: Allen and Unwin.

Pollitz Worden, A. (1997). Gender and professional values in the criminal bar. *Women & Criminal Justice 83,* 1–28.

Price, B. R., & Sokoloff, N. J. (1995). T*he criminal justice system and women: Offenders, victims and workers* (2nd ed.). New York: McGraw-Hill.

Ranney, F. J. (2004). What's a reasonable woman to do? The judicial rhetoric of sexual harassment. *NWSA Journal* 9, 1–27. Available at iupjournals.org/nwsa.

Schlanger, M. (2002). Gender matters: Teaching a reasonable woman standard in personal injury law. *Saint Louis University Law Journal* 45, 769–778.

Spencer, C. C. (1987). Sexual assault: the second victimization. In L. L. Crites & W. L. Hepperle (Eds.), *Women,* the courts, and equality (pp. 54–73). Newbury Park, CA: Sage.

Stohr, M. K. (2000). Women and the law. In T. Walsh & C. Hemmens (Eds.), *From law to order: The theory and practice of law and justice* (pp. 269–298). Lanham, MD: American Correctional Association.

Walsh, T., & Hemmens, C. (2000). *From law to order: The theory and practice of law and justice.* Lanham, MD: American Correctional Association.

Wollstonecraft, M. (1967, first published in 1792). *A vindication of the rights of woman.* New York: W.W. Norton and Company.

Zupan, L. L. (1992). The progress of women correctional officers in all-male prisons. In I. Moyer (Ed.), *The changing roles of women in the criminal justice system* (pp. 323–344). Prospect Heights, IL: Waveland Press.

Cases Cited

Blyth v. Birmingham Water Works, 156 Eng. Rep. 1047, 1049 (Ex. 1856)

Duran v. Missouri (439 U.S. 357[1975])

Ellison v. Brady (924 Fed. Rep. 2d ser. 872 [9th Cir. {1991}])

Frontiero v. Richardson, 411 U.S. 677[1973]

Grutter v. Bollinger et al. (288 F. 3d, affirmed, U.S. 02-241 [2003])

Hall v. Brooklands Auto Racing Club 1 K.B. 205, 224 (1933)

Reed v. Reed (404 U.S. 71 [1973])

University of California Regents v. Bakke (438 U.S. 265 [1978])

4

Regulating and Controlling Women's Bodies

Kate Bagley and Alida V. Merlo

This chapter deals with the control of women's bodies in the areas of prenatal child abuse and the acquired immunodeficiency syndrome (AIDS). Charges of prenatal child abuse levied against pregnant women who use drugs have increased since the first edition of this book was published. Drugs are also implicated in the growing number of women who suffer from AIDS. Women who engage in unprotected heterosexual activities and/or who are intravenous (IV) drug users run an increased risk of contracting the human immunodeficiency virus (HIV) that causes AIDS. It is in these areas, treated separately and together, that we see clearly how "law, science, and the state" collude "in regulating and controlling women's lives" (Maher, 1992, p. 159).

As we noted in the first edition, heightened controls have not translated into adequate programs or services for women, especially for poor women of color, and this continues to be true as we move into the twenty-first century. Instead, the attention these women receive focuses on how their conduct negatively affects others' lives. Women's own health needs and their economic and social circumstances are frequently ignored or trivialized, and the women themselves are stigmatized and blamed for conditions that originate in structural inequalities and consequently require institutional remedies.

Pregnant Women and Drugs

Pregnant women are much less likely to use illicit drugs, alcohol, or tobacco than are women who are not pregnant, according to the 2002 National Survey on Drug Use and Health (Department of Health and Human Services, 2002; hereafter DHHS, 2002). When pregnant women do use these substances, alcohol and tobacco are the drugs of choice rather than illicit substances, the survey found.

Only 3.3 percent of pregnant women aged 15 to 44 reported using illicit drugs in the month prior to the survey. The rate of alcohol use among this group was higher: 9.1 percent reported using alcohol in the past month and 3.1 percent reported binge drinking (defined as having five or more drinks on the same occasion). Tobacco use was even higher: Slightly more than 17 percent of these women reported smoking cigarettes in the month prior to the survey (DHHS, 2002).

The survey found that rates of alcohol, tobacco, and illicit drug use vary with ethnicity/race. Pregnant African American women were more apt to report the use of illicit drugs in the month prior to the survey than were white, non-Hispanic women (6.2 percent and 3.6 percent, respectively). However, a higher proportion of pregnant white, non-Hispanic women reported using cigarettes (24.1 percent) than did African American women (7.3 percent) or Hispanic women (6.0 percent). Alcohol use was also higher among pregnant white women (11.5 percent) than among African American women (4.9 percent) or Hispanic women (6.3 percent) (DHHS, 2002).

Overall, these data show that many more pregnancies are exposed to alcohol and tobacco than to illicit drugs (see also National Abandoned Infants Assistance [hereafter NAIA] Resource Center, 2004). Even though statistics demonstrate that very few women abuse illicit drugs during their pregnancies, many states and localities have moved to require the testing of pregnant women for these substances. Most of these jurisdictions also compel health care providers to report women who have tested positive for illicit substances to local child welfare or criminal justice agencies, prompting charges of child abuse and/or civil commitment to an inpatient treatment program (Alan Guttmacher Institute, 2004). Even in jurisdictions where testing is discretionary, there is evidence that most of the testing occurs in public hospitals that serve low-income communities. Typically, it is poor minority women who are subjected to these tests and their consequences (Logan 1999).

Prosecution of Pregnant Women for Substance Abuse

To date, only South Carolina specifically criminalizes a pregnant woman's use of illicit drugs, but other states' interpretation of existing laws on child abuse and neglect or the delivery of drugs to a minor have been used to force women into treatment and to remove their children from their custody (NAIA Resource Center, 2004). The women who are targeted in these cases are overwhelmingly poor and members of racial and ethnic minorities.

At least thirty-five states have arrested and prosecuted women for substance abuse while they were pregnant (Jos, Perlmutter, & Marshall, 2003). Cooper (2003) reports that more than 200 pregnant women have been arrested since 1985 on charges related to the use of illicit drugs while pregnant; Talvi (2003) puts the number at over 275. In addition to criminal prosecution, states may seek a court order involuntarily committing a woman to a treatment center or other setting in order to "protect" her fetus (Jos et al., 2003). In some cases, the "other setting" is a jail cell. Mothers may not always be sent to jail; the state may remove their newborn babies from their custody or order mothers into a treatment program, which may mean that they effectively lose custody of their children.

The Ferguson Case.   Perhaps the most notorious case involving substance abuse during pregnancy is that of Crystal Ferguson. In 1989, the medical center of the Medical University of South Carolina (MUSC), in collaboration with local police and prosecutors, initiated a policy to test all pregnant women for cocaine. The tests were conducted without the women's consent, and positive results were reported to the local police. More than forty African American women and one white woman were arrested. The white woman had a "black boyfriend," which some commentators believe is the reason for her arrest given that this irrelevant information was included in her medical chart (Gagan, 2000; Jos et al., 2003).

The MUSC testing and reporting policy was clearly aimed at poor women of color. No other hospital in the state implemented a similar policy; the hospital in which the policy was carried out served primarily poor patients, and women who tested positive for cocaine were referred to the criminal justice system while women who used other substances such as methamphetamine and heroin were referred to social services (Gostin, 2001). Cocaine was the only drug for which women were tested ("Drug Testing of Pregnant Women," 2000). Implementation of the policy was aggressive.

> In some cases a team of police tracked down expectant mothers in the city's poorest neighborhoods. In others, police invaded the maternity ward to haul away patients in handcuffs and leg irons, hours after giving birth. One woman spent the final weeks of pregnancy detained in a dingy cell in the Charleston County Jail. When she went into labor she was transported in chains to the hospital and remained shackled to the bed during the entire delivery. (Roberts, 1997, p. 3)

Crystal Ferguson was one of the women arrested under this policy. After testing positive for cocaine, Ferguson was arrested when she did not comply with an order to enter a residential treatment program, even though her failure to comply was due to her inability to find child care for her other two children. Eventually, Ferguson became the named plaintiff in a class action lawsuit that ultimately found its way to the United States Supreme Court (*Ferguson et al. v. City of Charleston et al.,* 532 U.S. 67 [2001]).

At the Supreme Court, the only issue that remained to be decided was whether the state had violated the plaintiffs' Fourth Amendment protection against unreasonable search and seizure (the plaintiffs had prevailed on other constitutional issues in the lower courts). The city of Charleston argued that testing for drugs without the women's consent was permissible under the "special needs" exception to the Fourth Amendment, the "special need" here being the city's interest in protecting the fetus from harm (Gagan, 2000). The Supreme Court, in a six to three decision, rejected that argument, pointing out that the "immediate objective of the searches was to generate evidence for law enforcement purposes" rather than to protect the fetus (*Ferguson,* 532 U.S. at 82-83).

One commentator has described the Ferguson decision as a "landmark" case that rests on the principle that the "government of this country should not be permitted to police its pregnant citizens through their umbilical cord" (Weyrauch, 2002, p. 90). Such an optimistic reading of the case may be premature, however. The case was narrowly focused on the issue of a nonconsensual search; the larger question of the state's right to arrest and prosecute women for behavior during their pregnancy (in this case, the use of cocaine) was not addressed. And, the three staunch conservatives on the court, Justices Scalia, Rehnquist, and Thomas, dissented. A change in the makeup of the court could alter the court's response to cases like this one. In the meantime, women have continued to be prosecuted for using illegal drugs while pregnant, as the following case illustrates.

The McKnight Case. In 2001, after deliberating for less than fifteen minutes, a South Carolina jury found Regina McKnight guilty of the murder of her stillborn baby (*State v. McKnight,* No. 2000-GS-26-0432 [Ct. Gen. Sess. S. C. May 14, 2001]). McKnight had used cocaine during her pregnancy. Under South Carolina law, a pregnant woman who engages in behavior that may harm her fetus can be criminally charged under the state child abuse laws when the use, and resulting harm, occur at the stage of fetal viability (*Whitner v. South Carolina,* 1997, ruling that a viable fetus is a "person" for purposes of the South Carolina Children's Code). McKnight became the first person convicted of murder under this interpretation of the law, although there was no good evidence that her use of cocaine had contributed to the death of her baby (Jos et al., 2003; Talvi, 2003).

Organizations such as the American Public Health Association, the American Nurses Association, and the American Society of Addictive Medicine joined in filing an amicus brief on McKnight's behalf. The brief stated that "[t]he prosecution, conviction, and sentencing of Ms. McKnight for her stillbirth not only distorts the law, but contradicts the clear weight of available medical evidence, violates fundamental notions of public health, and undermines the physician-patient relationship . . ." (Talvi, 2003). On appeal, the South Carolina State Supreme Court upheld Ms. McKnight's conviction (*State v. McKnight,* 352 S.C. 635; 576 S.E.2d 168 [2003]).

Ironically, as Paltrow (2004) points out, if McKnight had had a third trimester illegal abortion, the longest sentence she could have received would have been two years; she is presently serving a twelve-year sentence for causing the baby's stillbirth. The two State Supreme Court judges who dissented from the majority opinion noted this disparate outcome. They contended that the legislature did not intend the homicide-by-child-abuse statute under which Ms. McKnight had been convicted to be applicable to fetuses.

The McKnight case is instructive for several reasons. First, the state's argument rested on a distortion of research data on the effects of cocaine on a fetus. Second, it reflects the selective prosecution of women who use cocaine, rather than other illegal drugs, during their pregnancy, women who are likely to be poor and members of ethnic and racial minorities. And third, it signals the growth of a movement to define a fetus as a legal "person" with rights independent of the mother.

The Effects of Crack Cocaine on Fetuses

Gómez (1997) discusses the hysteria generated in the 1980s and 1990s by the so-called epidemic of "crack babies." In her study of California's response to this "epidemic," Gómez (1997, p. 13) points to the hypocrisy that surrounded this issue:

> [W]hile heroin is widely recognized to be a more dangerous drug than cocaine, its use and abuse does [*sic*] not generate the same elite or popular concern. With respect to prenatal exposure, concern over cocaine use eclipses that for heroin, despite the medical consensus that the latter causes more severe withdrawal effects in more infants. . . . Over two decades (1970 to 1990), only 21 articles on prenatal heroin exposure appeared in American or international medical journals, compared to 80 on cocaine exposure that appeared in the same journals in a recent five-year period (1985–1990).

Gómez (1997, p. 15) also notes the contrast in the media's portrayal of powder cocaine versus crack cocaine users. The former were often glamorized while the latter were described as "'addicts' bereft of redeeming human qualities." This should not be surprising since the latter are more likely to be poor people of color.

In February 2004, in an effort to elevate the level of discourse, thirty medical doctors, scientists, and psychologists wrote an open letter to the media protesting the use of terms such as "crack baby" and "crack-addicted baby," noting that these terms "lack scientific validity and should not be used" (Open Letter to the Media, 2004). The letter went on to say that, after nearly twenty years of research, science had found no evidence for the existence of a "crack baby" syndrome or condition. The writers also noted that research findings have been mixed on whether prenatal exposure to cocaine causes any developmental delays, with some research finding "subtle effects" and other research finding no effect. Signatories to the letter included professors of pediatrics at Harvard Medical School, the director of neonatology at Boston University School of Medicine, and the director of the Infant Development Center at Brown University Medical School.

A Slippery Slope?

The Whitner, Ferguson, and McKnight cases represent only the proverbial "tip of the iceberg." As Barbara Risman, cochair of the Council for Contemporary Families in Raleigh,

North Carolina, has said, "across the country [there] is a movement toward a state apparatus that can control women's lives when they are pregnant" (quoted in Jonnson, 2001, p. 1). Many states are following South Carolina's lead.

As we have seen, the focus of government authorities has been on pregnant women who use illegal drugs, notably cocaine, but a number of observers have pointed to the "slippery slope" that these policies create. Pregnant women who engage in a variety of activities, not all of them illegal, may risk losing custody of their children or face criminal prosecution. And pregnant women who refuse to follow medical advice, even when that advice is of questionable value, may find themselves referred to law enforcement or child welfare agencies. For example, Paltrow (n.d.) discusses cases from Pennsylvania and Georgia in which doctors asked the courts to order two women to undergo caesareans. In both cases, the women fled and delivered healthy babies vaginally. More recently, in Utah, Melissa Rowland was arrested for allegedly refusing a cesarean section. After one of the twins she was carrying was stillborn, law enforcement authorities ordered her arrested and attributed the baby's death to Rowland's refusal to follow medical advice (Paltrow, n.d.). Because Rowland decided not to have a cesarean section (which the doctor advised her to do to save the babies' lives) immediately, the prosecutor originally charged her with homicide, but later withdrew the charges. Rowland subsequently entered a guilty plea to child endangerment (Johnson, 2004, p. A23). While Rowland had a troubled history, the cases Paltrow describes involved women who had no record of similar problems—they simply disagreed with their doctors' advice. Critics have frequently pointed to the widespread overreliance on cesarean births in the United States (Pollitt, 2004). Involving the courts in these decisions erodes women's autonomy and intrudes into the doctor–patient relationship. In addition, there is no guarantee that forcing a woman to have a cesarean section will save a child's life (Johnson, 2004, p. A23).

The unintended consequences that may result from starting down this slippery slope were pointed out in an amicus brief submitted by medical and public health organizations to the South Carolina Supreme Court in 2001 in the case of *State v. Peppers* (346 S. C. 502, 552 S.E.2d (2001) (a case in which a mother was arrested for child abuse after tests showed cocaine in her stillborn baby's body).

> [T]he extension of child abuse statutes to include maternal conduct that may endanger a fetus leads to absurd, unintended, and dangerous results. Health and social services professionals, among others, must guess whether, for example, a pregnant woman's failure to obtain prenatal care, to quit smoking or drinking, to stop taking over-the-counter medicine, or to refrain from playing rigorous sports constitutes unlawful behavior (American Public Health Association et al., 2001, p. 8).

The issue is, simply, to what standard of care should pregnant women be held? Should pregnant women stop drinking coffee, stop riding motorcycles, play doubles rather than singles tennis, and avoid eating too many sweets? While these questions may seem silly, what about a woman who stays in a violent relationship during her pregnancy? As Paltrow notes, "The pregnant woman who 'allows' herself to be battered, and the woman who misses prenatal care appointments are both now vulnerable to prosecution for murder should something go wrong in the pregnancy" (Paltrow, 2004, p. 2).

While slightly more than 3 percent of pregnant women have reported using drugs during their pregnancies, nearly three times as many reported drinking alcohol, and more than five times as many reported the use of tobacco (DHHS, 2002). The effects of alcohol on fetal development are well-known; research shows that it is much more dangerous to the fetus, especially when women drink to excess (five or more drinks a day), than any other substance the woman may ingest (Carroll, 2003). Tobacco use and exposure to second-hand smoke are associated with low birth weight and sudden infant death syndrome (SIDS) (DiFranza et al., 2004). There is also some research that suggests that smoking cigarettes during pregnancy is "a prenatal risk factor for offspring's criminal behavior across race and cultures" (Piquero, Gibson, Tibbetts, Turner, & Katz, 2002, p. 232).

We are not advocating the arrest and prosecution of women who use alcohol or tobacco during their pregnancies. Our point is that there are many risk factors associated with pregnancies. Singling out poor pregnant women who use cocaine and other illegal drugs for arrest and prosecution appears to be prompted by interests other than a concern with the well-being of the unborn child. Our skepticism is supported by data that show that health care for infants and children is not a priority for the actors involved in these efforts. South Carolina, the state that has most aggressively pursued this course of action, ranks forty-seventh among states in low birth weight babies, forty-fifth in infant mortality, and forty-third in the percent of babies born to mothers who received early prenatal care (Children's Defense Fund, 2003).

Defining the Fetus as a Person

Samuel Casey, executive director of the Christian Legal Society and anti-abortion activist, has said, "In as many areas as we can we want to put on the books that the embryo is a person. . . . That sets the stage for a jurist to acknowledge that human beings at any stage of development deserve protection—even protection that would trump a woman's interest in terminating a pregnancy" (Michelman, 2004). This statement reflects what Zitner (2003) has called "a loose and evolving legal effort to try to elevate the legal status of the embryo in a variety of arenas" with the goal of overturning *Roe v. Wade* 410 U.S. 113 (1973).

In what plainly seems to be efforts to limit a woman's right to an abortion, courts and legislatures have moved recently to define a fetus or embryo as a legal person with rights independent of, and, perhaps, superseding, those of its mother. Although state laws have long allowed criminal prosecution and negligence actions for the death of, or serious injury, to a woman's viable fetus (with an exception for legal abortions) (Fenwick, 1998), over sixty fetal homicide bills were proposed in state legislatures during 2003 (Center for Reproductive Rights, n.d.). Some of these bills defined the fetus as a separate person.

A number of recent cases reflect these changes in the law. In 2003 in Pennsylvania, Corinne Wilcott was convicted of third-degree murder after she kicked the abdomen of a rival who had become pregnant by Ms. Wilcott's husband and killed the fetus she was carrying (Pennsylvania: Guilty of Fetal Homicide 2003, p. A12). In 2002, a Michigan woman, Jaclyn Kurr, quarreled with her boyfriend, who had impregnated her. After he punched her in the stomach, she testified that she stabbed him and killed him. She was 16 to 17 weeks pregnant at the time of the crime. Although she argued self-defense, the jury convicted her. The Michigan Court of Appeals reversed her conviction and ordered a new trial. The judges ruled that a woman who is pregnant can "use deadly force to protect her fetus even when she does not fear for her own life" (Liptak, 2002, p. A16). In fact, the judges argued that the trial judge erred by not letting her argue that "she was defending not only herself, but also 'her unborn children.'" Ms. Kurr was pregnant with quadruplets at the time of the murder (Liptak, 2002, p. A16). This decision suggests that in Michigan a pregnant woman whose fetus cannot survive outside the womb has both the right to an abortion and a legal defense for the use of deadly force to protect her fetus (Liptak, 2002, p. A16).

Most recently, in March 2004, the U.S. Congress passed, and President Bush signed, the Unborn Victims of Violence Act (UVVA). The UVVA criminalizes assaults that cause harm to "a child in utero," recognizing "everything from a zygote to a fetus as an independent 'victim,' with legal rights distinct from the woman who has been attacked" (Paltrow, 2004, p. 1). Note that the UVVA extends the reach of criminal prosecution beyond the stage of fetal viability. Representative Jerrold Nadler from New York noted the implications of this legislation prior to its passage; "It [UVVA] is another battle in the war of symbols in the abortion debate, in which opponents of a woman's right to choose attempt to portray fetuses, from the earliest moments of development, as children" (Liptak, 2002, p. A16).

The UVVA is not the first time the federal government has defined a fetus as a person with rights recognized by law. In 2002, the Bush administration issued new regulations under the State Children's Health Insurance Program (SCHIP). SCHIP was originally designed to provide states with federal funding that could be used to offer health insurance to children who would not otherwise be eligible for Medicaid. The new regulations changed the definition of "child" to include unborn children. Thus, a mother who would not herself be eligible for Medicaid could receive prenatal care for her fetus under the SCHIP program (Catholic Charities USA, n.d.; Pear, 2001). Ironically, while the fetus would be covered for its health care needs, the woman within whose womb the fetus resided would not receive any health care benefits under this program other than those included in her prenatal care.

How these developments will play out is difficult to forecast. Obviously, there are challenges ahead. For example, pregnant women and their health care providers may well be faced with the dilemma of choosing whether to treat the woman and risk harming the fetus or to treat the fetus while causing risk to the woman:

> As technology has allowed doctors greater access to the fetus, they have learned how to treat certain defects before the baby is born. Increasingly, therefore, treatments may be beneficial to the fetus which are harmful, or at least risky, to the mother. As the technology expands in this area, mothers may be asked more often to jeopardize their own well-being to allow access to the fetus. (Fenwick, 1998, p. 59)

Coercive Contraception

Efforts to force poor women and those who use illegal drugs to use long-term contraception or to undergo sterilization have been reported for decades. In the infamous case of *Buck v. Bell* (274 U.S. 200 [1927]), the United States Supreme Court upheld a Virginia law permitting the involuntary sterilization of "imbeciles." Between 1924 and 1972, over 7,500 involuntary sterilizations were performed in Virginia (Tribe, 1988, p. 1339). As Paltrow (1999, p. 1054) notes, *Buck v. Bell* has never been overturned by the Supreme Court. Not until 1978 did the federal government issue regulations prohibiting the use of federal funds for involuntary sterilizations (Chavkin, Draut, Romero, & Wise, 2000; Silver, 2004).

Unfortunately, the attitudes and beliefs that legitimated these inhumane acts continue. In December 1990, the *Philadelphia Inquirer* published an editorial advocating the use of Norplant to reduce the numbers of the underclass (Kimelman, 1990). Following the publication of the editorial, every state and the District of Columbia began covering Norplant under Medicaid, the medical insurance for poor people. When Norplant's serious side effects could no longer be ignored, attention turned to other forms of long-term contraception such as Depo-Provera, even though it, too, may produce dangerous side effects (Roberts, 1997).

While Norplant is implanted under the skin, Depo-Provera is injected approximately every three months. Depo-Provera is marketed by Pharmacia-Upjohn, whose Web site describes it in glowing terms: "Birth control doesn't get much better than this. Convenient, reliable protection you don't have to think about every day" (Depo-Provera, n.d.). When Depo-Provera is used as directed, it is more than 99 percent effective in preventing conception.

The effectiveness of Depo-Provera and other long-term forms of contraception, and the fact that these methods could ensure contraception without "thinking about them" led to the creation of CRACK ("Children Requiring a Caring Kommunity"). Barbara Harris, whose four adopted children were born to a mother addicted to drugs, created the organization in 1998 (Trapnell, 2000). CRACK guaranteed payment of $200 to women (and men), addicted to drugs or alcohol (and, typically, poor), who agreed to undergo sterilization (tubal ligation or vasectomy) or to use some form of long-term contraception such as Depo-Provera. In response, the American Public Health Association (APHA) issued a policy statement in 2001 opposing coercive family planning and the CRACK program in particular. The APHA warned that programs such as this "violate principles of human rights, civil rights, and reproductive freedoms" in a number of ways. It noted that CRACK did not address the issues of racism, sexism, poverty, and violence that led to the use of illegal drugs, nor did it encourage people to seek drug treatment, and it did not offer contraceptive options that would protect against HIV/AIDS or other sexually transmitted diseases (American Public Health Association, 2001).

Controlling Women with AIDS

In 2003, almost half of all the adults worldwide who were infected with HIV were women (Ogden, Ogden, Mthembu, & Williamson, 2004). The estimated number of AIDS cases that have been diagnosed through 2002 totaled 886,575. Of that number, 159,271 were women. In the United States, women comprised 20 percent of the individuals living with AIDS in 1999. By contrast in 1992, women comprised 14 percent of all infected adults (Centers for Disease Control, [CDC], 2004b, para. 1). One of every four new AIDS cases is a woman, and each year there are approximately 40,000 new cases of HIV infections in the United States (Tasker, 2004, para. 1; UNAIDS, 2004, UNAIDS, Key Facts section, para. 5).

HIV/AIDS disproportionately affects minority women who suffer more adverse consequences from the disease than white women. The Centers for Disease Control and Prevention (CDC) has been following the progress of the AIDS epidemic since the first cases were reported in the United States in 1981. The CDC reports that black women, who represent approximately 12 percent of the female population of the United States, comprise approximately 64 percent of new female HIV infections (CDC, cited by Tasker, 2004, para. 8). Not only are black women more likely to be infected with the HIV/AIDS virus, but they are also more likely to die from it (Villarosa, 2004, p. A11). For black women between the ages of 25 and 34, AIDS is the leading cause of death (UNAIDS, 2004, Key facts, para. 5). Black women in the 25 to 44 age category have a death rate that is more than thirteen times greater than that of white patients (Villarosa, 2004, p. A11).

One of the difficulties that black women face regarding treatment for HIV is the cost associated with the treatment. Black women are more likely to be uninsured or underinsured when compared to white women who have the virus. At a minimum, the antiviral drugs cost $12,000 per year for each patient. The President announced in June of 2004 that he was adding $20 million to the AIDS Drug Assistance Program—a program that assists those who are infected and unable to pay for their medications to get the requisite treatment. Despite that increased funding, many experts believe that ten times that amount is needed to make it possible for HIV/AIDS-infected individuals to receive treatment (Villarosa, 2004, p. A11).

Another difficulty is the quality of care that black women infected with HIV/AIDS receive. In 2002, the Institute of Medicine found that blacks ". . . were less likely to be given the most sophisticated treatments for H.I.V. than whites, even when money was not a factor" (Villarosa, 2004, p. A11). Finally, black women are more likely to have a host of other medical conditions that complicate their treatment.

Black women are also at increased risk of infection because of the high rate of incarceration of black men. Black men make up almost 40 percent of the approximately 2.1 million inmates in the United States. This puts black men at higher risk of HIV infection because of the elevated rate of HIV/AIDS in prisoners. In states like North Carolina, blacks comprise more than 70 percent of all current HIV/AIDS cases and approximately 60 percent of the state's prison population. These factors put black men's female sexual partners at higher risk of HIV infection (Clemetson, 2004, p. A16).

The relationship between sexually transmitted diseases (STDs) and AIDS has also heightened concern and awareness. The presence of a STD in either the person infected with the HIV virus or their sexual partner increases the likelihood of transmission. Additionally, women are more vulnerable than men to HIV infection. Male-to-female transmission during sexual contact is about twice as likely as female-to-male infection (UNAIDS, 2004, para. 1). Historically, heterosexual contact has been the leading avenue of transmission of HIV/AIDS to women. The second leading cause of the disease in women has been intravenous (IV) drug use when needles are shared with other users (CDC, 2004b, para. 4). And, when women have sex with an IV drug user, they are also at increased risk of contracting the virus.

Attention also has begun to focus on adolescent and young women who are infected with AIDS. In 2002, young girls and women between the ages of 15 and 24 represented 35,460 AIDS cases (CDC, 2004a, Cumulative Cases by Age Section, para. 1). Beginning in 2000, girls and young women comprised almost half (47 percent) of the HIV cases in this age group. As the age of initial sexual intercourse and other sexual contact declines, girls and young women are at increased risk of acquiring HIV/AIDS, and this age group is perceived as vulnerable to infection because more girls and young women have begun to engage in high-risk behaviors (CDC, 2004b, para. 5).

Women who are HIV positive and women with AIDS have been largely ignored until very recently, except in the sense that they have been regarded as threats to "innocent" third parties such as male sex partners and fetuses. Activists on behalf of HIV-positive women have brought pressure on the CDC and other branches of government as well as on the medical community to focus more attention on the health needs of women and to expand the AIDS definition to recognize the ways AIDS is manifested in women.

In February 2004, Dr. Julie Gerberding of the Centers for Disease Control and Prevention focused on the critical problems regarding women and newborns. Dr. Gerberding noted that "Women disproportionately suffer the burden of poverty, are the victims of widespread and persistent discrimination in all areas of life and put their lives at risk every time they become pregnant" (Gerberding, quoted in Altman, 2004, p. A13). Specifically, she emphasized the importance of providing new diagnostic tests and more effective information programs to improve the control of infectious diseases, including HIV/AIDS, that infect women and their infants (Altman, 2004, p. A13).

Controlling Pregnant Women with AIDS

In the first edition of this book, we noted that most of the attention paid to women with AIDS focused on their role as child bearers (Zarembka & Franke, 1990, p. 524). This emphasis has continued, and it has resulted in some positive as well as negative outcomes for mothers and their babies. Although the situation has improved in the last ten years, there is some evidence that women who are HIV-positive continue to face hurdles when trying to obtain abortions. Women are not always provided with voluntary HIV counseling and testing when they decide to terminate their pregnancy, and they may not have the same opportunities for care after the abortion has been performed (deBruyn, 2003). Unfortunately, very little is known about abortion among HIV-infected women because little research has been conducted. There are some reports of health care providers encouraging HIV-infected pregnant women to terminate the pregnancy and to undergo sterilization (deBruyn, 2003). The introduction of antiretroviral drug regimens has resulted in fewer women who are HIV-positive opting for abortions in the United States than in the past, but the newer treatments do not appear to have affected the sterilization rates (deBruyn, 2003).

Access to abortion for poor women is particularly problematic. According to deBruyn, in 2002, abortion was not covered by Medicaid for HIV-positive women in 28 states except when the pregnancy resulted from rape or incest or when the woman's life was in danger (deBruyn, 2003). Even when abortion is covered by a woman's medical insurance, women who are HIV-positive might not be aware of the procedures for obtaining a safe and legal abortion in their communities. Or, they may have financial concerns that preclude them from visiting a private provider. They may also be deterred by the anticipated or actual negative reaction that they receive when they seek such care from providers. In addition, they may be uninformed about postabortion counseling and treatment. All of these barriers preclude poor pregnant women who are HIV-positive from making informed choices and having equal access to prenatal care including abortion (deBruyn, 2003).

For those women who decide to continue their pregnancy, the health risks are serious. Women who are HIV-positive face more critical complications than do other women when they undergo obstetrical and gynecological procedures. This is particularly problematic for women who have a cesarean section. In a study of 235 surgical procedures performed on

HIV-infected and non-HIV women, the researchers found that women who were HIV-positive had more complications after the procedures. The use of antiretroviral drugs and routine antibiotics did not reduce the complications (Grubert, Reindell, Kästner, Belohradsky, Gürtler, Stauber, & Dathe, 2002).

Another difficulty in treating women who are HIV-positive is identification. Determining who is at risk, notifying the authorities of the findings, and maintaining the confidentiality of the findings are recurring issues. Questions about where and to whom the test results will be disseminated may be especially worrisome for the person who is infected. From a purely medical research position, testing everyone in the United States in order to determine who is HIV-positive would be ideal. However, the possibility of placement on a state register of HIV-positive residents may discourage individuals from seeking diagnostic tests. Individuals who are considering testing may be concerned that a positive test and placement on a state register could affect their employment, health insurance, and housing. In addition, they may fear violence from their partners and spouses (Kaeser, 1998).

In order to promote healthy babies and successful pregnancies, the Institute of Medicine (IOM) in 1998 called for universal HIV testing with patient notification, but without counseling prior to administration of the test, as a part of routine prenatal care. This recommendation is troubling for several reasons. First, AIDS advocates contend that without comprehensive individualized counseling prior to the test, women might not comprehend the implications of being tested for HIV or what being HIV-positive means. Second, women do not have equal access to treatment, and some women lack adequate treatment. Given the fact that there is tremendous variation in health care among the states and that appropriate resources are lacking for treating pregnant women who are HIV-positive, testing all pregnant women when it is not completely voluntary seems particularly untenable and possibly unethical (Kaeser, 1998).

On the other hand, testing can be beneficial. The Centers for Disease Control and Prevention (CDC) report that not all prenatal care providers offer HIV testing to their patients. The CDC conducted a survey of pregnant women and found that when testing was offered, some women indicated that they chose not to undergo the tests because they (the women) perceived that their health care providers did not consider it important. A second problem that affects testing is the setting in which the prenatal care occurs. Women who receive care from a private provider are less likely to be offered HIV testing. By contrast, women who seek medical care through providers in public settings are more likely to be offered the diagnostic test (CDC, 2004c).

The fact that women who are seeking prenatal care in public facilities are more likely to be tested for HIV/AIDS illustrates one of the ongoing debates about testing pregnant women. If women who seek care in public facilities are predominantly lower class, poor, and minority women, perhaps they are also more likely to be singled out for special treatment and to be labeled. Most troublesome is the fact that women who are using drugs are often the least likely to seek prenatal care during their pregnancy (CDC, 2004c, para. 6). Their reluctance has been partly attributed to the policies discussed earlier in this chapter. If identified as drug users, the women could lose custody of their newborns and be prosecuted.

For the women who do seek prenatal care and are tested and diagnosed with the HIV virus, the prospects for treatment are excellent. According to the CDC, the actual number of perinatally acquired AIDS cases declined 75 percent from 1992 to 1998 in the United States.

A larger percentage of women volunteered to be tested for HIV in 1995 compared to 1993, and once diagnosed, they began a treatment regimen that included AZT (CDC, 2004c, para. 3). An antiretroviral drug, AZT (zidovudine) is administered to pregnant women to decrease their likelihood of transmitting the virus to their newborn babies (CDC, 2004d, para. 1).

One study demonstrated that, in 1996 as compared to 1993, more women in four states, Michigan, New Jersey, Louisiana, and South Carolina, accepted treatment for their infection after diagnosis, but 15 percent of HIV-infected women in those states did not seek prenatal care. As a result, they were excluded from this intervention (CDC, 2004c, para. 3). We do not know why these women did not seek prenatal care. Without the testing and treatment interventions, it is estimated that approximately 25 percent of HIV-positive pregnant women in the United States will transmit the virus to their newborns each year, resulting in over 1,700 HIV-infected infants. The lifetime cost of medical care for those undiagnosed and untreated infants is estimated at $282 million (CDC, 2004c, para. 4).

Another controversy concerns mandated testing of newborns for the HIV-virus. Thus far, New York and Connecticut mandate the testing of newborns when there is no information about whether the mother is HIV-positive when the baby is born (CDC, 2003b). Opponents of testing newborns contend that these policies are simply a "backdoor approach to testing the woman *without her consent*—opening the door for her potential prosecution in states that criminalize transmission" (Kaeser, 1998, Newborn Testing Section, para. 2). Proponents argue that these tests provide the opportunity to treat the newborn and to offer the mother treatment (Kaeser, 1998). Unfortunately, it would seem that it is the poor and minority women who would be most adversely affected by state infant testing policies. They may also be the ones that would be least likely to know how to secure and manage treatment in the community prior to giving birth.

HIV/AIDS in Prison

One need look no farther than prisons to see the impact of the AIDS crisis in America. Every year since 1991, state and federal prisons confirm that their inmates have a higher rate of documented AIDS cases (more than three times higher) than are found in the general U.S. population (Maruschak, 2004, p. 5). By the end of 2001, 3.2 percent (approximately 2,300) of the female state prison inmates were diagnosed as HIV-positive, compared to 2 percent (approximately 21,000) male inmates in state prisons (Maruschak 2004, p. 1). Although these state prison data reflect a slight decrease from the previous year, the increase in the federal prison system for 2001 was the highest since data collection began in 1991 (Maruschak, 2004, pp. 2–3). Once again, New York leads the country with the highest number of female inmates infected with HIV, with Florida and Texas in second and third place. In New York, Rhode Island, and Nevada, more than 10 percent of all the female state prison inmate population were diagnosed as HIV-positive. In no state were 10 percent of the male prison population HIV-positive. In fact, New York was the only state where HIV-positive male inmates comprised more than 5 percent of the total inmate population (Maruschak, 2004, p. 3).

Women in prison have frequently been involved in high-risk behaviors that are related to HIV infection. With the inmates' persmission, Cotton-Oldenburg, Martin, Jordan, Sadowski, and Kupper (1997) examined medical and self-report interview data on 700 female inmates in the North Carolina Correctional Institution for Women. Their findings indicate that women who exchanged sex for money or drugs had the greatest likelihood of being HIV-positive; over 75 percent of the participants had not used condoms regularly during vaginal intercourse (Cotton-Oldenburg et al., 1997, p. 284).

In a survey of eighty Texas inmates who had been diagnosed with mental illness, Brewer, Marquart, Mullings, and Crouch (1998, p. 110) found that over 65 percent of the women inmates indicated that they had injected drugs, over 45 percent indicated that they had engaged in oral sex, and over one-third of the women indicated that they had been involved in prostitution. These findings suggest that the study participants had participated in at least one HIV/AIDS-related risk behavior, and more than half of the respondents had participated in two or more activities that are considered to be HIV/AIDS-related risks (1998, p. 113).

Peugh and Belenko (1999, p. 25) interviewed over 13,000 women in prison in 1991. They found that the combination of drug use and risky or criminal sexual activity places these women at risk of contracting STDs and HIV as well as increasing their chances of being sexually abused, arrested, and incarcerated. However, their findings also indicate that women in prison who engaged in substance abuse have a much higher rate of sexual abuse than male inmates. In fact, the women in their study were seven times more likely to have been abused sexually than the men who used substances (1999, p. 31). Sadly, one-third of the women involved in substance abuse experienced sexual abuse before their eighteenth birthday (1999, p. 32).

In another study of a sample of 445 newly incarcerated women in two Texas prison facilities in 1998, Mullings, Marquart, and Hartley (2003) found that women inmates who were sexually abused as children were more likely than female inmates who had not been abused to have participated in prostitution, to have had unprotected sex with multiple partners six months prior to incarceration, and to have had unprotected sex with a crack cocaine user within thirty days prior to incarceration (2003, p. 450). In this sample, childhood sexual abuse was a significant predictor of sexual activities that was associated with a higher risk of HIV infection (Mullings et al. 2003, p. 454).

Because of their histories of abuse and involvement in behaviors that place them at risk of infection, we might expect that correctional administrators in state prisons and local facilities would place a high priority on testing and treatment of HIV/AIDS. In their study of a mega jail (more than 1,000 male inmates on a daily basis), Vaughn and Smith (1999) interviewed the court monitor, relevant jail and court personnel, medical staff, and analyzed inmate letters about health care. Their findings indicate that inmates who were HIV-positive were discriminated against in the jail setting. Although medical staff made certain promises to the inmates about care, they did not always follow through with obtaining the requisite medications in a timely manner. Inmate letters and interviews confirmed that HIV/AIDS infected inmates were taunted, humiliated, teased, and threatened in the jail setting studied (Vaughn & Smith 1999, pp. 194–195). There is no reason to believe that female HIV/AIDS infected inmates would be subjected to different treatment if they were studied.

Female inmates' perceptions about the likelihood of contracting the HIV virus are another area of concern. In research by Brewer et al. (1998) and Collica (2002), the inmates appeared to have an unrealistic perception of their chance of contracting HIV/AIDS. These findings suggest that prison might be an opportune time to educate women about the risks of HIV/AIDS. Similarly, Comfort, Grinstead, Faigeles, and Zack (2000, p. 70) found that women who are visiting men in prison were willing to participate in an AIDS awareness and educational program in California. The authors created a program using peers to educate the women about the risks of HIV while they were waiting for visitation.

Despite the fact that a higher percentage of women than men who are incarcerated have the HIV/AIDS virus, de Ravello (1999, p. 1) notes that "with the exception of the Federal prison system, there is no authoritative body which guarantees a standard level of health care for female or male inmates across all correctional facilities" (1999, p. 1). Caruso (2000) contends that only seven prisons in 1999 had mandatory HIV testing. Even the staff who treat inmates who are HIV-positive or who have AIDS experience adverse consequences. Prevention specialists working in the prison system report that they are often humiliated and subject to negative stereotyping by the correctional officers (Reuters Health, 2003). There is also variation in the delivery of services to HIV-infected inmates depending upon the resources available in the community where the prison is located or on whether the health services are contracted to an outside provider. In short, both men and women who are incarcerated are subject to sporadic and sometimes uneven health care services including diagnosis and testing, treatment, and follow-up care.

State-by-state variations in diagnosis and treatment lead to a number of adverse consequences for inmates, both female and male. They may not receive the medications that they need in a timely manner, and/or they may be uninformed about the consequences of their infections if left untreated. In addition, prison inmates are not eligible for Medicaid. Between their actual release from prison and the time that they are found to be eligible to receive Medicaid, some women may run out of their medication. There is research that indicates that correctional systems in some states provide inmates who have been released with only five days of medication (Reuters Health, 2003). Unfortunately, in some communities there is insufficient follow-up with these women to make sure that they have enough medication to last until their eligibility is established. Or, when there are programs that will provide the medication on a short-term basis, some women do not know about these services (Caruso, 2000).

Historically, women have not received good health care in prisons. Ross and Lawrence (1998) contend that the lack of health care afforded women in prisons and jails is a result of ". . . insidious attitudes, behaviors and beliefs which influence government policy" (Ross & Lawrence 1998, Future Directions sec., para. 1). Limited access to health care is a serious problem for women offenders (Acoca, 1998). There is a recent trend among the states to charge women inmates for their health care. Although the cost for such services is nominal, most women offenders do not have the income to pay for these services (Pollock, 2002, p. 78).

Another problem associated with prisons and HIV-positive women concerns the institution's decision to segregate women who are diagnosed as HIV/AIDS positive. There are advocates and opponents of this approach. Proponents contend that segregation reduces the spread of HIV/AIDS in the population through unprotected sex and intravenous drug use. Opponents note the difficulties associated with the accuracy of the test results and in determining when the testing would be administered. There are also the additional costs associated with the duplication of treatment services that would have to be offered to a segregated population (see Robinette & Long, 1999). Currently, only Alabama provides segregated housing and programs to inmates who are HIV-positive (Wagster, 2001). However, it was not until

2001, after a battle that lasted ten years, that Mississippi decided to open educational, vocational, and drug-treatment programs to HIV/AIDS inmates. The new Commissioner of Corrections for that state, Robert Johnson, established a fifteen-member HIV/AIDS task force in November 2000. That group's recommendation prompted the new Commissioner to make these programs available (Wagster, 2001). And, in June of 2004, a federal magistrate, Judge Jerry Davis, ordered the Mississippi Department of Corrections to allow inmates who are HIV-positive to participate in Community Work Centers. Previously, they had been excluded (Gates, 2004).

The Criminal Justice System's Response to Women Infected with HIV/AIDS

In search of the "quick fix" to deal with HIV/AIDS epidemic, legislators have enacted state statutes criminalizing the transmission of HIV/AIDS to another person. Some of these laws have specifically mentioned prostitutes who either solicit, agree to commit prostitution, or engage in sexual relations when they know that they are HIV-infected. In 2000, six states, Florida, Kentucky, Oklahoma, Pennsylvania, South Carolina, and Utah, made these acts a felony (American Civil Liberties Union, 2004). Twenty-nine states permit any HIV/AIDS-infected person who transmits the virus via sexual contact, needle sharing, blood, or bodily fluids to be charged with a felony or misdemeanor and have his or her sentence enhanced due to the act of transmission (Lamda Legal, 2004).

According to the HIV Criminal Law and Policy Project, between 1986 and 2001 there were over 300 individuals (male and female) prosecuted for either exposing someone to or transmitting HIV. The most common method by which people were exposed was through sexual activity, including prostitution, solicitation of prostitutes, consensual sex, or sex where consent was unclear (HIV Criminal Law and Policy Project, 2004).

These statutes are troubling for a number of reasons. First, as previously stated, treatment is not always equally available. Second, there is no guarantee that incarcerating these offenders will reduce the spread of HIV/AIDS. Third, there is no evidence that these kinds of laws act as a deterrent. Fourth, while incarcerated, there is no evidence that criminal penalties reform the person. Fifth, the women selected for prosecution are typically poor and uneducated, and frequently they have been sexually and physically abused as children. Finally, there is concern that these kinds of laws may be applied to those individuals who are socially as well as economically marginalized (see Elliott, 2002, p. 7).

Policy Implications and Future Goals

Great strides have been made during the last ten years in efforts to prevent Fetal Alcohol Syndrome (FAS) and Fetal Alcohol Effects (FAE). Two states, Minnesota and Washington, have been leaders in the provision of prevention, education, treatment, and advocacy services for women and their infants. Their state legislatures have funded programs designed to work with women who are at risk including women who may be abusing alcohol and drugs during their pregnancy. From intervention and advocacy for women who are drug- or alcohol-dependent to family support networks, these states have created greater awareness of FAS/FAE and provided significant support for these families (Streissguth, 1998, pp. 19–20). Other states ought to emulate these kinds of programs to ensure that all children will have an opportunity for a healthy start.

Providing services to ensure healthy babies and healthy parents is a laudable goal. Accessible and affordable health care is essential if women and their children are to receive good prenatal care, treatment for STDs, testing and treatment for HIV/AIDS, and help with alcohol and drug problems. Unfortunately, the lack of health insurance is an ongoing and serious problem in the United States. Recent research by the Centers for Disease Control National Center for Health Statistics indicates that the percent of children with health insurance has continued to decline since 1997. In 2003, 10 percent of children were without health insurance. In the same year, the percent of citizens between the ages of 18 to 64 who did not have health insurance rose to 20 percent (over 46 million Americans), an increase from previous years. Hispanics were the least likely to have health insurance. Approximately 33 percent, one in 33, were without health insurance compared to 17 percent of blacks and 11 percent of whites (CDC, National Center for Health Statistics, 2004; Dooren, 2004, p. D4). Rather than focus on women with drug problems or HIV in a reactive manner, legislators and policy makers should make the provision of health care for all citizens a top priority.

In addition to health care for all women and children, states could offer adequate benefits to meet the nutritional needs of women and children; provide alcohol and drug counseling and treatment to all who need these services; and protect women from abusive relationships, especially during their pregnancies. Support services that include housing, child care, parenting classes, and educational and vocational programs would be more beneficial than testing pregnant women for drugs and taking custody of their newborns.

With respect to pregnant women, HIV testing has not yet become a regular part of prenatal care. Providers have to be educated as to its importance, and they have to adopt testing as routine practice (CDC, 2004c). Prenatal HIV testing offers the best likelihood for preventing perinatal HIV transmission (CDC 2002b, Editorial note section, para. 1). For those women not tested during their routine prenatal care visits, there is some preliminary research to suggest that women can also be tested when they are admitted to hospitals for labor and delivery. In 2002, in four Chicago hospitals, over 200 women who were evaluated and determined to be eligible for rapid HIV testing consented to participate. Using point-of-care testing, those women who tested positive for HIV and their newborn infants received antiretroviral therapy during the labor and delivery process. Not one of these infants was infected with HIV (CDC, 2003a). These point-of-care tests and treatment are essential.

Recently, the Department of Health and Human Services announced that it was funding the Catholic Charities Diocese of Fort Worth to assist pregnant women with HIV/AIDS to deliver babies that are healthy (Mitchell, 2004). This kind of initiative is important and needs to be expanded to other states where women who have AIDS or are HIV-positive have historically not been given special attention and services.

Women face more serious risks than men related to HIV/AIDS infection, and they are more vulnerable to contracting the virus in sexual relationships. Fortunately, there are a number of strategies to prevent them from becoming infected and spreading the disease. However, successful programs must be not only gender specific but also relevant to the ethnic and racial populations they serve.

In particular, women have to be aware of the importance of reducing risky sexual behaviors such as exchanging sex for drugs or money. In addition, community services that are specifically targeted for women have to be increased. From parenting classes to health care and employment services in the community, a special effort has to be made to make certain that women are receiving support (Cotten-Oldenburg et al., 1997, p. 284; Peugh & Belenko, 1999, p. 33).

Clearly, policymakers have to focus on the incidence of child sexual abuse. The ramifications of child sexual abuse are devastating. According to Greenberg et al. (1999, p. 155), "women sexually abused in childhood, even when compared to other high-risk women, may lack the psychological resources necessary to assert themselves with sex partners." Programs designed to assist these victims must include some kind of sexual "reeducation" that utilizes techniques for sexual negotiation, definitions of responsibilities and rights, and partner selection skills (Greenberg et al., 1999, p. 155).

There is also the need to make certain that programs are appropriate for those racial/ethnic groups that are particularly vulnerable. DiClemente, cited by Tasker (2004), studied African American girls, aged 14 to 18, who had some sexual experience. The girls were divided into two groups: one group received information on nutrition and exercise; the other group was presented with information about gender pride, HIV knowledge, healthy relationship skills, and how and when to use a condom. In two follow-ups, six and twelve months later, the group that had received the HIV information was 50 percent more likely to indicate that they were using condoms, had fewer new sexual partners, and were less likely to be pregnant (Tasker, 2004).

Similarly, Marcus and Bibace (1993) interviewed 113 female inmates in the Texas prison system in an effort to assess their understanding of AIDS compared to male inmates (p. 242). Although they found that the female inmates and the male inmates as a whole appeared to have identical levels of understanding, female Hispanic inmates did not score as high as the white participants. The researchers contended that educational programs had not been as effective with Hispanic inmates, and they advocated educational programs designed to provide information to Hispanics in a realistic and relevant manner (Marcus & Bibace, 1993, p. 251).

In a qualitative study of female inmates in Northeastern State Prison, West (2001) used focus groups to gather information. Her findings indicate that the heterogeneous racial/ethnic composition of prison populations have been largely ignored when programs on AIDS education have been implemented. West recommends peer educators who are Hispanic, with an emphasis on increasing the participants' perceived level of self-control through empowerment strategies and preventive measures. In addition, community support services are essential for Hispanic women when they are released from prison (West, 2001, p. 38).

Whenever possible, peers should conduct HIV/AIDS awareness programs. Research suggests that the more effective programs for education and prevention are those in which the participants are peers of the instructors (Collica, 2002; Comfort et al., 2000, p. 70). Programs also should reflect the research that suggests that women need not only to be aware of the disease but also to learn how to successfully negotiate with their sexual partners regarding condoms (Cotton-Oldenburg et al., 1997, p. 284). The programs must be offered on an ongoing basis during an adolescent's or adult's lifetime and during incarceration. For example, participating in an HIV/AIDS program at the beginning of incarceration might not be useful for a woman serving a 23-to-life sentence. Requiring such programs at the beginning and at the end of a woman's prison experience is more appropriate (Collica, 2002, p. 121).

Louisiana has implemented a new program funded by the federal and state governments to increase inmates' knowledge about the disease and to coordinate services for them in the community when they are released. In addition to using inmates as peer counselors at intake and using support groups and books to educate the inmate population and to encourage testing and treatment, there is now better coordination between the community and the prison for the aftercare phase of treatment. Prior to leaving the prison, inmates are introduced to caseworkers in the community who will be working with them. Appointments for treatment with community health specialists are also arranged. Although the results of this project will not be known for a few years, it illustrates the importance of collaboration between prison and community in HIV/AIDS treatment and prevention (*Sunday Advocate,* 2003).

Some promising strategies for pregnant women offenders have been established in local institutions. In Santa Rita County, California, a $174 million facility and a $21 million service contract accommodate the gynecological and obstetrical needs of female inmates. In addition to providing pregnancy testing and testing for sexually transmitted diseases, these women are offered treatment for substance abuse and HIV infection. The institution provides an exercise program, social services, and good quality medical care (Ross & Lawrence, 1998).

Viable programs must be offered in the community for adolescents and adults who are not in school. Whether at runaway shelters, detention centers, teen centers, or through churches, greater emphasis has to be placed on communicating information about HIV/AIDS to young women and their parents. Better diagnosis, treatment, and prevention of STDs are also important to reduce the risk of HIV/AIDS infection (CDC, 2004b).

Conclusion

We have documented the increasing controls over women's bodies that have occurred in the last ten years. Women and girls, many of whom have been the victims of crime, may be labeled as criminals for behaviors ranging from refusing a cesarean section, using drugs during pregnancy, to transmitting HIV. In addition, the fetus has been afforded new rights and protections that may override those of the mother. We do not know how these developments will change in the next few years. One thing that appears fairly certain is that women, particularly poor and minority women, will continue to be prosecuted and convicted for behaviors that they may be ill-equipped to address.

Research indicates that when a young child is the victim of sexual abuse, the consequences are often long term and traumatic. Rather than promoting more policies that would seek to prevent child abuse, the system is focused on punishing offenders. Greater attention must be paid to the prevention of child abuse, whether sexual, physical, or emotional. Numerous strategies can be implemented, from parenting classes to community support networks. However, none of these is likely to succeed if citizens, experts, and elected officials do not prioritize these strategies.

To achieve the goals of a healthy pregnancy and a positive birth outcome, policies will have to be established that deal with the needs of women and their families who are involved in substance abuse. Clearly, these interventions are more economically and emotionally sound and socially desirable than the costs of neonatal intensive care units or the separation of mother and child at birth (Farr, 1995, p. 242). In addition, greater emphasis must be placed on the effects of licit as well as illicit drugs on pregnant women. Stress and poor nutrition and diet as well as environmental contaminants can harm both mother and fetus; these factors must also be addressed (Lyons & Rittner, 1998, p. 319).

Some research suggests that women who use drugs during their pregnancy and seek treatment are more aware of the deleterious effects of drugs than are women who do not seek treatment. Perry, Jones, Tuten, and Svikis (2003) found that the lack of awareness of non-treatment-seeking drug users demonstrates the need for more community-based education and prevention programs about the negative effects drugs can have on fetal development. These programs should be available in areas where drug use is widespread (Perry et al., 2003, p. 7).

If there is true concern for the welfare of drug-affected newborns, programs should be developed that empower addicts who are pregnant to be good mothers (Logan 1999, p. 137). Rather than zeroing in on the fetus exclusively, greater attention ought to be paid to the woman. Efforts to provide education, prevention awareness, good-quality prenatal care, and decent living conditions to promote the healthy development of the fetus can be enhanced. Women who are HIV-positive should not have to fear being arrested and prosecuted when they seek counseling or treatment (UNAIDS, 2004). There must be a concerted effort to revise or rescind these kinds of laws. In particular, researchers have to work with policymakers to ascertain that the information that is presented to the public is accurate and balanced.

Finally, greater attention has to be focused on the spread of HIV/AIDS among black and Hispanic women and adolescent girls of all ethnic backgrounds. Efforts must be made to ensure that they are aware of the risks, and that they are prepared to confront situations in which they may be engaging in risky behaviors. At the very least, they have to have access to health care, family planning, education, vocational training, and support systems that will help them navigate their way through the dangerous waters that surround many of them.

Review Questions

1. Why is the prosecution of pregnant women who use illegal drugs described as a slippery slope?

2. What behaviors engaged in by pregnant women do you think should result in criminal prosecution or referral to child welfare agencies? Should the response of the government be different if a woman does not know she is pregnant when she engages in these behaviors? Explain your reasoning.

3. What steps should be taken by the government, other than the arrest and prosecution of individual women, to deal with the problems discussed in this chapter?

4. What legal rights, if any, should a fetus have? At what point should a fetus's rights "trump" the legal rights of its mother?

5. Research shows that exposure to secondhand smoke can harm fetuses. Should the partner of a pregnant woman be charged with child abuse for smoking in that woman's presence? Should a pregnant woman be charged if she works in or frequents an establishment that permits smoking?

6. What do we know about the incidence of HIV/AIDS in the general population and among adolescent girls and young women? What are some strategies that can be undertaken in prisons

to deal with HIV/AIDS prevention and awareness?

7. Should HIV/AIDS inmates be segregated from the general population in prison? Why? What specific steps should be taken to deal with HIV/AIDS infected inmates?

8. Should HIV/AIDS infected women be subjected to coerced abortions and sterilization? When, if ever, is it appropriate to pay someone to use contraception or to be sterilized? Explain your reasoning.

Key Terms

Binge drinking
Peer counseling
Fetal viability
Norplant
HIV/AIDS Testing of Pregnant Women
Roe v. Wade

Prenatal care
Coercive contraception
Slippery slope
Standard of care
Perinatal HIV transmission
Heterosexual spread of HIV/AIDS

References

Acoca, L. (1998). Defusing the time bomb: understanding and meeting the growing health care needs of incarcerated women in America. *Crime and Delinquency* 9, 49–69.

Alan Guttmacher Institute. (2004, May 1). *State policies in brief: Substance abuse during pregnancy.* Retrieved May 3, 2004, from http://www.agi-usa.org/pubs/spib_SADP.pdf.

Altman, L. K. (2004). Action urged on diseases with dangers for women. *New York Times,* February 28, A13.

American Civil Liberties Union. (2004). State criminal statutes on HIV transmission (June, 2000). Retrieved from http://archive.aclu.org/issues/aids/HIV_criminalization.html.

American Public Health Association (2001). Opposition to coercion in family planning decision making. Retrieved May 3, 2004 from http://www.apha.org/legislative/policy/policysearch/index.cfm?fuseaction=view&id=261.

American Public Health Association, South Carolina Medical Association, American Nurses Association, South Carolina Nurses Association, American Academy on Physician and Patient, American Academy of Addiction Psychiatry, Association of Maternal and Child Health Programs, Institute for Health and Recovery, Ira J. Chasnoff, M.D. (n.d.). *Brief as amici curiae in support of appellant, Brenda Peppers.* Retrieved April 24 from http://dpf.org/docUploads/peppers.pdf.

Brewer, V., Marquart, J., Mullings, J., and Crouch, B. (1998). AIDS-related risk behavior among female prisoners with histories of mental impairment. *The Prison Journal* 78, 110–118.

Carroll, L. (2003). Alcohol's toll on fetuses: Even worse than thought. *New York Times* (November 4), F, p. 1.

Caruso, K. (2000). *Correctional facilities.* Retrieved on November 10, 2004 from www.corrections.com/ncchc.

Catholic Charities USA (n.d.). *New regulations allow unborn children to be covered under SCHIP.* Retrieved May 5, 2004 from http://www.catholiccharities.org.

Centers for Disease Control, National Center for Health Statistics. (2004). *More children than ever had health insurance in 2003, but coverage for working-age adults declined.* Retrieved August 13, 2004 from http://www.cdc.gov/nchs/pressroom/04news/insur2003.htm.

Centers for Disease Control. (2004a). *Basic statistics.* Retrieved on May 28, 2004 from http://www.cdc.gov/hiv/stats/htm.

Centers for Disease Control. (2004b). *HIV/AIDS among US women: Minority and young women at continuing risk.* Retrieved May 28, 2004 from http://www.cdc.gov/hiv/pubs/facts/women.htm.

Centers for Disease Control. (2004c). *Perinatal HIV prevention programs: Background.* Retrieved on July 14, 2004 from http://www.cdc.gov/hiv/projects/perinatal/background.htm.

Centers for Disease Control. (2004d). *Section 7: AZT counseling for HIV-seropositive women and new mothers.* Retrieved on November 9, 2004 from http://www.cdc.gov/hiv/pubs/HAC-PCG/section7.htm.

Centers for Disease Control. (2004e). *STD general information/fact sheet.* Retrieved on August 5, 2004 from http://www.cdc.gov/std/STDFact-STD&HIV.htm.

Centers for Disease Control and Prevention. (2003a). *Rapid point-of-care testing for HIV-1 during labor and delivery—Chicago, Illinois, 2002.* Retrieved on August 5, 2002 from http://www/cdc.gov/mmwr/preview/mmwrhtml/mm5236a4.htm.

Centers for Disease Control and Prevention. (2003b). *Department of Health and Human Services.* Retrieved on August 17, 2004 from http://www.cdc.gov/hiv/rapid_testing/materials/LDRT_appendices.pdf.

Centers for Disease Control and Prevention. (2002a) *HIV/AIDS surveillance report 2002.* Atlanta, GA: Centers for Disease Control and Prevention.

Centers for Disease Control and Prevention. (2002b). *HIV testing among pregnant women—United States and Canada, 1998–2001.* Retrieved on August 5, 2004 from http://www.cdc.gov/mmwr/preview/mmwrhtml/mm5245a1.htm.

Center for Reproductive Rights (n.d.). *2003 year-end report.* Retrieved April 22, 2004 from http://www.reproductiverights.org.

Chavkin, W., Draut, T. A., Romero, D., & Wise, P. H. (2000). Sex, reproduction, and welfare reform. *Georgetown Journal on Poverty Law & Policy* 7, 379–393.

Children's Defense Fund (2003, January). *Children in South Carolina.* Retrieved May 10, 2004 from http://www.childrensdefense.org/familyincome/childreninthestates2003/sc.pdf#xml=http://childrensdefense.org.master.com/texis/master/search/mysite.txt?q=child+poverty+in+South+Carolina&order=r&id=4810500b60b1203e&cmd=xml.

Clemetson, L. (2004). Links between prison and AIDS affecting blacks inside and out. *New York Times,* August 6, A1, A16.

Collica, K. (2002). Levels of knowledge and risk perceptions about HIV/AIDs among female inmates in New York State: Can prison-based programs set the stage for behavior change? *The Prison Journal* 82, 110–124.

Comfort, M., Grinstead, O. A., Faigeles, B., & Zack, B. (2000). Reducing HIV risk among women visiting their incarcerated male partners. *Criminal Justice and Behavior* 27, 57–71.

Cooper, C. L. (2003). *Pregnant and punished.* Retrieved May 3, 2004 from http://www.fordfound.org/publications/ff_report/view_ff_report_detail.cfm?report_index=382.

Cotton-Oldenburg, N. U., Martin, S. L, Jordan, B. K., Sadowski, L., & Kupper, L. (1997). Preincarceration risky behaviors among women inmates: Opportunities for prevention. *The Prison Journal* 77, 281–288.

deBruyn, M. (2003). Safe abortion for HIV-positive women with unwanted pregnancy: A reproductive right. *Reproductive Health Matters* (11), 152–162. Re-trieved August 27, 2004 from http://imail.iup.edu/Session/513264-7NikWlrTFQdx0pHVsXa1-kmbczau/Message.wssp?Mailbox=INBO.

Department of Health and Human Services, Substance Abuse and Mental Health Services Administration, Office of Applied Studies. (2002). *National survey on drug use and health: National findings.* Retrieved May 5, 2004 from http://www.oas.samhsa.gov/nhsda/2k2nsduh/Results/2k2Results.htm#chap2.

Depo-Provera. (n.d.). Retrieved June 14, 2004 from http://www.depo-provera.com/.

de Ravello, L. (1999). *Current reproductive health and HIV prevention issues for incarcerated women.* Centers for Disease Control and Prevention. Retrieved on August 27, 2004 from www.aegis.com/aidsline/2000/may/A0051499.html.

DiFranza, J. R., Aligne, C. A., & Weitzman, M. (2004). Prenatal and postnatal environmental tobacco smoke exposure and children's health. *Pediatrics* 113, 1007–1015.

Dooren, J. C. (2004). Health coverage in U.S. rises for children, but slips in total. *Wall Street Journal,* July 1, 2004, D4.

Drug testing of pregnant women: The Fourth Amendment and America's war against narcotics (November 2000). *Supreme Court Debates* 3, 225.

Elliot, R. (2002). *Criminal law, public health, and HIV transmission: a policy options paper.* Geneva, Switzerland: UNAIDS.

Farr, K. A. (1995). Fetal abuse and the criminalization of behavior during pregnancy. *Crime & Delinquency* 41, 235–245.

Fenwick, L. B. (1998). *Private choices, public consequences: Reproductive technology and the new ethics of conception, pregnancy, and family.* New York: Dutton.

Gagan, Bryony J. (2000). *Ferguson v. City of Charleston, South Carolina:* "Fetal" abuse, drug testing, and the Fourth Amendment. *Stanford Law Review* 53, 491–518. Retrieved April 14, 2004 from the Lexis-Nexis database.

Gates, J. (2004). Rights group: Consent decree for HIV inmates still needed. *Clarion-Ledger.* Retrieved on August 27, 2004 from CDC National Prevention Network, http://ww.cdcnpi.org/scripts/utilities/DocView.asp?K2DocKey=http%3A%2F%2Fwww%2Ecdcnpin%.

Gómez, L. E. (1997). *Misconceiving mothers: Legislators, prosecutors, and the politics of prenatal drug exposure.* Philadelphia: Temple University Press.

Gostin, L. O. (2001). The rights of pregnant women: The Supreme Court and drug testing. *Hastings Center Report* 31, 8–9. Retrieved April 20, 2004 from Academic Search Elite database.

Greenberg, J., Hennessy, M., Lifshay, J., Kahn-Krieger, S., Bartelli, D., Downer, A., & Bliss, M. (1999). Childhood sexual abuse and its relationship to high-risk behavior in women volunteering for an HIV and STD prevention intervention. *AIDS and Behavior* 3, 140–156.

Grubert, T. A., Reindell, D., Kästner, R., Belohradsky, B. H., Gürtler, L., Stauber, M., & Dathe, O. (2002). Rates of postoperative complications among human immunodeficiency virus-infected women who have undergone obstetric and gynecologic surgical procedures. *Clinical Infectious Diseases* (34), 822–830.

Highleyman, L. (2004). State review calls for HIV names reporting. *Bay Area Reporter,* August 19. Retrieved August 28, 2004 from http://www.lcdcnpin.org/scripts/News/Newslist.asp.

HIV Criminal Law and Policy Project. (2004). *Prosecutions.* Retrieved August 9, 2004 from www.hivcriminallaw.org/prosecutions/index.cfm.

Johnson, R. (2004). C-sections and the real crime. *New York Times,* Op-Ed, April 12, A23.

Jonsson, P. (June 28, 2001). South Carolina tests the bounds of a fetus's rights. *Christian Science Monitor,* p. 1. Retrieved May 5, 2004 from Lexis-Nexis database.

Jos, P. H., Perlmutter, M., & Marshall, M. F. (2003). Substance abuse during pregnancy: Clinical and public health approaches. *Journal of Law, Medicine, and Ethics* 31, 340–347. Retrieved March 23, 2004 from the Lexis-Nexis database.

Kaeser, L. (1998). Confidentiality, consent remain central as policymakers, activists address changing face of HIV/AIDS. *The Guttmacher Report on Public Policy* (1), December. Retrieved on August 18, 2004 from http://www.guttmacher.org/pubs/journals/gr010603.html.

Kimelman, D. (1990). Poverty and Norplant: Can contraception reduce the under-class? *Philadelphia Inquirer,* December 12, A-18.

Lamda Legal. (2004). *State criminal statutes on HIV transmission 2002.* Retrieved August 5, 2004 from www.thebody.com/lamda/crimina_law.html.

Liptak, A. (2002). Ruling opens new arena in the debate on abortion. *New York Times,* October 16, A16.

Logan, E. (1999). The wrong race, committing crime, doing drugs, and maladjusted for motherhood: The nation's fury over "crack babies." *Social Justice* (26), 115–138.

Lyons, P., & Rittner, B. (1998). The construction of the crack babies phenomenon as a social problem. *American Journal of Orthopsychiatry* 68, 313–320.

Maher, L. (1992). Punishment and welfare: Crack cocaine and the regulation of mothering. In C. Feinman (Ed.), *The criminalization of a woman's body* (pp. 157–192). New York: Harrington Park Press.

Marcus, D. K., & Bibace, R. (1993). A developmental analysis of female prisoners' conception of AIDS. *Criminal Justice and Behavior* 20, 240–253.

Maruschak, L. (2004). *HIV in prisons, 2001.* Washington, DC: U.S. Department of Justice, 1–8.

Michelman, K. (2004). *Prenatal politics.* Retrieved April 12, 2004 from http://tompaine.com/feature2.cfm/ID/10153.

Mitchell, M. (2004). $1.9 million will help area HIV/AIDS patients. *Fort Worth Star-Telegram,* August 26. Retrieved from http://www.cdcnpin.org/scripts/News/NewsListasp on August 27, 2004.

Mullings, J., Marquart, J., & Hartley, D. (2003). Exploring the effects of childhood sexual abuse and its impact on HIV/AIDS risk-taking behavior among women prisoners. *The Prison Journal* (83), 442–463.

National Abandoned Infants Assistance Resource Center (2004). *Perinatal substance exposure.* Retrieved May 3, 2004 from http://aia.berkeley.edu/publications/fact_sheets/perinatal_substance.html.

Ogden, L., Ogden, J., Mthembu, P., & Williamson, N. (2004). Impact of HIV on women internationally (conference summary). *Emerging Infectious Diseases.* Retrieved on November 9, 2004 from http://www.cdc.gov/ncidod/EID/vol10no11/04-06234_01.htm.

Open letter to the media from thirty medical doctors, scientists, and psychologists. (2004, February 25). - Retrieved April 24, 2004 from http://www.advocatesforpregnantwomen.org/articles/crackbabyltr.htm.

Paltrow, L. (1999). Pregnant drug users, fetal persons, and the threat to *Roe v. Wade. Albany Law Review* 62, 999–1055. Retrieved June 16, 2004 from Lexis-Nexis database.

Paltrow, L. M. (2004). *The pregnancy police.* Retrieved April 12, 2004 from http://www.alternet.org/print.html?StoryID=18321.

Paltrow, L. M. (n.d.). Coercive medicine. Retrieved March 23, 2004 from www.tompaine.com/feature2.cfm/ID/10103.

Pear, R. (2001, July 6). Bush plan allows states to give "unborn child" medical coverage. *New York Times,* A, p. 1. Retrieved May 5, 2004 from Lexis-Nexis database.

Pennsylvania:Guilty of fetal homicide. (2003). *New York Times,* March 28, A12.

Perry, B., Jones, H., Tuten, M., & Svikis, D. (2003). Assessing maternal perceptions of harmful effects of drug use during pregnancy. *Journal of Addictive Diseases* (22), 1–18.

Peugh, J., & Belenko, S. (1999). Substance-involved women inmates: Challenges to providing effective treatment. *The Prison Journal* 79, March, 23–44.

Piquero, A. R., Gibson, C. L., Tibbetts, S. G., Turner, M. G., & Katz, S. H. (2002). Maternal cigarette smoking during pregnancy and life-course-persistent offending. *International Journal of Offender Therapy and Comparative Criminology* 49, 231–247.

Pollitt, K. (2004). Pregnant and dangerous. *Nation* 278, 9. Retrieved June 3, 2004 from Academic Search Premiere database.

Pollock, J. (2002). *Women, prison, and crime* (2nd ed.). Belmont, CA:Wadsworth Thomson Learning.

Reuters Health (2003). *HIV prevention, treatment needs in prisons: report.* http://www.cdcnpin.org/scripts/utilities/DocView.asp?K2DocKey=http%3A%2F%2Fwww%2Ecdcnpin%. Retrieved August 27, 2004 from CDC National Prevention Information Network.

Roberts, D. (1997). *Killing the Black body: Reproduction and the meaning of liberty.* New York: Pantheon Books.

Robinette, P. A., & Long, B. (1999). Is the segregation of HIV-positive inmates ethical? *The Prison Journal* 79, 101–119.

Ross, P. H., & Lawrence, J. E. (1998). Health care for women offenders. *Corrections Today* 60 (122). Retrieved on August 27, 2004 from http://imail.iup.edu/Session/513264-7NikWlrTFQdx0pHVsXa1-kmbczau/Message.wssp?mailbox=INBO.

Silver, M. G. (2004). Eugenics and compulsory sterilization laws: Providing redress for the victims of a shameful era in United States history. *George Washington Law Review* 72, 862–891. Retrieved June 16, 2004 from Lexis-Nexis database.

Steissguth, A. (1998). Attaining human rights, civil rights, and criminal justice for people with fetal alcohol syndrome. *TASH Newsletter*, September, 18–20.

Sunday Advocate (Baton Rouge, LA). (2003). HIV/AIDS after prison. http://www.cdcnpin.org/scripts/utilities/DocView.asp?K2DocKey=http%3A%2F%2Fwww%2Ecdcnpin%. Retrieved August 27, 2004 from CDC National Prevention Information Network.

Talvi, S. J.A. (2003, December 11). Criminalizing motherhood. *Nation.* Retrieved April 20, 2004 from http://advocatesforpregnantwomen.org/.

Tasker, F. (2004). Women catching up with HIV rate in men. *Miami Herald.* Retrieved July 20, 2004 from http://www.aegis.org/news/mh/2004/MH040714.html.

Trapnell, S. (2000, August 14). Group pays addicts cash for birth control. *Lancaster New Era,* p. B-1. Retrieved June 14, 2004 from Lexis-Nexis database.

Tribe, L. H. (1988). *American constitutional law.* Mineola, NY: Foundation Press.

UNAIDS. (2004). *Women and AIDS—A growing challenge.* Fact sheet. Retrieved on August 4, 2004 from http://www.unaids.org/html/put/publications/factsheet04FS_ Women_ en_pdf/FS_Women . . .

Vaughn, M. S., & Smith, L. G. (1999). Practicing penal harm medicine in the United States: Prisoners' voices from jail. *Justice Quarterly* (16), 175–231.

Villarosa, L. (2004). Patients with HIV seen as separated by a racial divide. *New York Times,* August 7, p. 1, A11.

Wagster, E. (2001). *Mississippi opens education, drug-treatment programs to HIV-positive inmates.* Associated Press, May 1, 2001. http://www.cdcnpin.org/scripts/utilities/DocView.asp?K2DocKey=http%3A%2F%2Fwww%2Ecdcnpin%. Retrieved August 27, 2004.

West, A. D. (2001). HIV/AIDS education for Latina inmates: The delimiting impact of culture on prevention efforts. *The Prison Journal* 81, 20–41.

Weyrauch, S. (2002). Inside the womb: Interpreting the Ferguson case. *Duke University Journal of Gender Law and Policy* 9, 81–90. Retrieved May 5, 2004 from Lexis-Nexis database.

Zarembka, A., & Franke, K. M. (1990). Women in the AIDS epidemic: A portrait of unmet needs. *Saint Louis University Public Law Review* 9, 519–541.

Zitner, A. (2003, January 20). As *Roe v. Wade* anniversary nears, challenges mount. *Salt Lake Tribune.* Retrieved May 19, 2004 from http://www.sltrib.com/2003/Jan/01202003/nation_w/21911.asp.

Cases Cited

Buck v. Bell, 274 U.S. 200 (1927)

Ferguson et al. v. City of Charleston et al., 532 U.S. 67 (2001)

Roe v. Wade, 410 U.S. 113 (1973)

State v. McKnight, No. 2000-GS-26-0432 (Ct. Gen. Sess. S.C. May 14, 2001)

State v. McKnight, 352 S.C. 635; 576 S.E.2d 168 (2003)

State v. Peppers, 346 S.C. 502; 552 S.E.2d 288 (2001)

Whitner v. South Carolina, 328 S.C. 1, 492 S.E.2d 777 (1997)

Part II

Women Practitioners in the Criminal Justice System

In this section, the chapters concentrate on women in each of the subsystems of criminal justice. We find that the images and stereotypes of women that were discussed in the last section have hindered women's full participation in these areas of employment. Historically, women were considered too frail, passive, emotional, and weak to engage in criminal justice professions, including law, corrections, and law enforcement. Each of the professions are characterized by traits that have been inconsistent with women's nature—or, at least, the stereotypes of women that have been so powerful in the past.

The historical legacy of exclusion has been mediated quite dramatically, especially in law school admissions, where women appear to have reached parity with male applicants. However, the small numbers of women who reach partner status or gain a judicial position bears witness to the fact that law, like corrections and law enforcement, is still a nontraditional occupation for women. They comprise fairly small percentages in all areas, except corrections for women and juveniles.

Each of the authors in this section echoes the themes that have been previously introduced. Women are controlled by images and stereotypes in that people expect them to behave in certain ways. There is a continuing controversy as to whether women do, in fact, perform their roles differently from men. While some researchers indicate that women are different (the gender model), other research indicates that they perform similarly to men (the job model).

What seems to be less controversial is that women have different familial obligations that impact their job stress. While much has changed in society regarding women's employment, less has changed regarding their responsibilities at home. This means that women cannot, and perhaps do not want to, prioritize work responsibilities over family responsibilities. This has some effects, however. For example, women may be less interested in law enforcement because of the shift work. Female attorneys are "mommy tracked" to areas of the firm where they are not expected to put in the long hours necessary for litigation. These patterns have effects in salary inequities and job satisfaction.

The chapters are remarkably similar in discussing the history, current status, and continuing obstacles facing women in criminal justice occupations. Some of these same themes will be addressed again in later sections of this text.

5

Police Women in the Twentieth-First Century

Kathryn E. Scarborough and Carole Garrison

Police are the primary agents of social control in the United States. Ironically, female police officers experience a great number of social controls. Historically, women in policing were relegated to positions that were considered more "appropriate," based on gender expectations. This means that women began working with children and other women as police matrons because that was consistent with their designated role. Their professional opportunities and their possibilities for advancement were limited.

It has been almost a decade since the first edition of this book, but an important question for women and policing still remains. What are the realities that affect their everyday lives? The women themselves can help us answer this question. Media, academic research, and existing policies and procedure can also shed light on women who face challenges in a dynamic, male-dominated profession that reinforces stereotypical gender roles and the informal and formal social control of women in the United States today.

It has been over twenty years since Penny Harrington became the first female chief in a large metropolitan organization. Beverly Harvard followed as the first black female chief in a large urban organization more than a decade later. More recently, within a six-month period, four women have been selected to lead the police in major cities: Boston, San Francisco, Milwaukee, and Detroit (Associated Press, 2004). However, the representation of women in police organizations is still limited, especially when compared to women's representation in the total work force, which is more than 50 percent.

Nontraditional occupations, like policing, are defined as those that employ less than 25 percent of the gender that is considered not necessarily "appropriate" for the occupation. Therefore, policing is considered a nontraditional occupation for women. According to U.S. Bureau of Labor Statistics (BLS) comparison data (1983–2002) for women's employment in nontraditional occupations, the only occupation that has shown an increase for women in the last twenty years is Protective Services, which also had an increase in male representation. The increases for both men and women represent about three-tenths of 1 percent over this time period (see Table 5.1).

The representation of women is difficult to determine because there is no single source that provides these figures. Representation varies by size of organization based on population served and type of organization (local, state, or federal). Some interesting themes can be identified when comparing differences in representation based on type of organization.

The average number of women in all local organizations is 10.6 percent. Table 5.2 provides the most recent numbers of full-time sworn female officers in local organizations, with a breakdown by race. As is the case in county organizations, white women outnumber women of color at the rate of 2 to 1 in most instances. There is a range of representation of women in police organizations, from only 3.2 percent of the total in the smallest organizations to 8.8 percent of the total in organizations serving 250,000 to 499,000 people. It is not surprising that the larger an organization is, the more women are employed. Typically, medium and large agencies have specialized units, which are often roads for advancement after serving in uniformed patrol. However, women are less likely than men to be promoted into these units and have less opportunity to attend special training that supports the units (U.S. Department of Justice, 2003c).

Only about 12.5 percent of sworn officers in sheriff's organizations are women. Table 5.3 provides the most recent numbers of full-time, sworn female officers in sheriff's (county) organizations, with a breakdown by race. The range of percentage of women in sheriff's

TABLE 5.1 *Percentage of Women in Nontraditional Protective Occupations*

	Total Employees (in thousands)	Percent of Women
Supervisors/managers of police and detectives	2,727	20.7
Firefighters	258	3.6
Bailiffs, correctional officers, and jailers	371	26.2
Detectives and criminal investigators	112	23.6
Police and sheriff's patrol officers	612	12.4
Private detectives and investigators	64	34.5
Security guards and surveillance officers	781	21.1

Source: U.S. Department of Labor. (2002). *Nontraditional Occupations for Women in 2002.* Washington, DC: Bureau of Labor Statistics. Retrieved on July 1, 2004 from http://www.dol.gov/wb/stats/main.htm.

organizations is 7.1 percent in organizations serving populations of less than 10,000, to 13.8 percent in organizations serving populations from 500,000 to 999,000. Again, white women are represented in organizations at a ratio of almost 2 to 1 when compared to women of color (U.S. Department of Justice, 2003d).

Table 5.4 identifies the numbers of full-time sworn women in state police organizations. Women comprise only about 1 percent of the South Dakota Highway Patrol, and 14 percent (the highest percentage of any state) of the Wisconsin Highway Patrol. No breakdown by race and ethnicity was available.

TABLE 5.2 *Percent of Women in Local Law Enforcement*

Population	White	Black	Hispanic	Other
Total Number of Women	6.5%	2.7%	1.1%	0.3%
1,000,000 or More	7.8%	5.1%	3.1%	0.4%
500,000 to 999,000	7.7%	6.5%	0.8%	0.5%
250,000 to 499,000	8.8%	4.0%	1.1%	0.3%
100,000 to 249,999	7.5%	2.1%	0.7%	0.4%
50,000 to 99,999	6.4%	1.1%	0.5%	0.1%
25,000 to 49,999	5.7%	0.8%	0.4%	0.1%
10,000 to 24,999	4.8%	0.5%	0.2%	0.2%
2,500 to 9,000	4.6%	0.4%	0.4%	0.1%
Less than 2,500	3.2%	0.3%	0.1%	0.3%

Source: U.S. Department of Justice, Bureau of Justice Statistics. (2003). *Local Police Departments, 2000.* Bulletin, p. 4. Washington, DC: U.S. Government Printing Office.

TABLE 5.3 *Women in County Law Enforcement (Sheriff's Organizations)*

Population	White	Black	Hispanic	Other
Total Number of Women	9.1%	2.3%	0.8%	1.4%
1,000,000 or More	8.3%	2.9%	2.2%	0.4%
500,000 to 999,000	9.6%	2.9%	1.1%	0.3%
250,000 to 499,000	9.7%	2.7%	0.8%	0.2%
100,000 to 249,999	10.2%	2.9%	0.4%	0.1%
50,000 to 99,999	10.2%	1.3%	0.1%	0.1%
25,000 to 49,999	8.3%	1.7%	0.5%	0.1%
10,000 to 24,999	6.6%	1.4%	0.3%	0.1%
Less than 2,500	6.9%	0.0%	0.0%	0.2%

Source: U.S. Dept. of Justice, Bureau of Justice Statistics. (2003). *Sheriff's Offices: 2000.* Bulletin, p. 4. Washington, DC: U.S. Government Printing Office.

TABLE 5.4 *Percent of Women in State Police Organizations*

Organization	% of Women	Organization	% of Women
Alaska Dept. of Public Safety	3	Nebraska State Patrol	3
Alaska State Troopers	8	Nevada Highway Patrol	6
Arizona Dept. of Public Safety	6	New Hampshire State Police	9
Arkansas State Police	6	New Jersey State Police	3
California Highway Patrol	5	New Mexico State Police	3
Colorado State Patrol	5	New York State Police	8
Connecticut State Police	7	North Carolina State Highway Patrol	2
Delaware State Police	10	North Dakota Highway Patrol	6
Florida Highway Patrol	10	Ohio State Patrol	9
Georgia State Patrol	3	Oklahoma Highway Patrol	4
Idaho State Police	5	Oregon State Police	9
Illinois State Police	9	Pennsylvania State Police	4
Indiana State Patrol	5	Rhode Island State Police	8
Iowa State Patrol	3	South Carolina Highway Patrol	3
Kansas Highway Patrol	3	South Dakota Highway Patrol	1
Kentucky State Police	3	Tennessee Department of Safety	5
Louisiana State Police	3	Texas Department of Public Safety	5
Maine State Police	5	Utah Highway Patrol	4
Maryland State Police	10	Vermont State Police	7
Massachusetts State Police	9	Virginia State Police	4
Michigan State Police	12	Washington State Patrol	7
Minnesota State Police	8	West Virginia State Patrol	3
Mississippi Highway Safety Patrol	2	Wisconsin State Patrol	14
Missouri State Highway Patrol	4	Wyoming Highway Patrol	2
Montana Highway Patrol	7		

Source: U.S. Dept. of Justice, Bureau of Justice Statistics. (2003). *Law Enforcement Management and Administrative Statistics, 2000.* Data for Individual State and Local Agencies with 100 or More Officers, Bulletin, p. 243. Washington, DC: U.S. Government Printing Office.

Table 5.5 shows the representation of women in federal law enforcement, including total personnel numbers by organization. A breakdown by race was not available. Women in federal law enforcement organizations represent from 8.6 percent in the Drug Enforcement Administration to 28 percent in the Internal Revenue Service. No breakdown by race was available for women in federal law enforcement.

There is a greater representation of women in federal law enforcement than in local organizations, with state police having the least women. This is not surprising since state police organizations tend to be the most militaristic of all categories of law enforcement organizations, meaning that social control mechanisms are more likely to be stronger and more prevalent.

It is true that women have made important strides, but it is also arguable whether a 6 percent increase in women's representation in law enforcement over the course of thirty-five years is truly significant. In 1988, the U.S. 7th Circuit Court of Appeals decided *Equal Employment Commission v. Sears, Roebuck & Company* 839 F.2d 302 (1988), agreeing with Sears that women being underrepresented in higher-paying commission sales jobs was the result of women's preference to stay in the less competitive hourly jobs and not because of discriminatory practices by Sears. Since then, we have often heard that low numbers of women in policing are the result of choice. While we do not assume that all women who are eligible would want a career in law enforcement, we can confidently say that the current status of women in law enforcement warrants further examination. There is certainly information that suggests that good recruiting and retention practices can dramatically help change these preferences and increase the numbers of women in departments who are using these strategies.

Hale and Bennett (1995) examined the realities of women in policing from an organizational perspective in the first edition of *Women, Law, and Social Control*. The current chap-

TABLE 5.5   *Women in Federal Law Enforcement*

Agency	Total Number of Personnel	Percent of Women
Immigration and Naturalization Services	19,407	12.1
U. S. Customs	11,977	18.6
Federal Bureau of Investigation	11,398	18.0
U.S. Secret Service	4,266	9.7
Drug Enforcement Administration	4,111	8.6
U.S. Postal Inspection Service	3,175	17.7
Internal Revenue Service	2,868	28.0
U.S. Marshal's Service	2,692	11.6
Bureau of Alcohol, Tobacco, & Firearms	2,362	12.9
National Park Service	2,148	15.2
U.S. Capitol Police	1,225	18.8
U.S. Fish and Wildlife Service	728	11.1
G.S.A., Federal Protective Services	709	9.3
U.S. D.A. Forest Service	611	21.9
Bureau of Diplomatic Security	592	9.6

Source: U.S. Dept. of Justice, Bureau of Justice Statistics. (2003). *Federal Law Enforcement Officers, 2002*, p. 7. Washington, DC: U.S. Government Printing Office.

ter builds on their work by examining these realities from an organizational perspective through a descriptive policy analysis, which is informed by a "view from the street," that is, hearing from the women themselves, through a focused discussion group and survey research. Included is an updated presentation of women police in the media, grounded in a review of current research on women in policing.

Media Images of Policewomen

In the last ten years, television images of female crime fighters have become more complex and more sophisticated, with strong female characters appearing in popular weekly dramas including *Law and Order, NYPD Blue, CSI, Law and Order: SVU, Cold Case, Without a Trace,* and *Third Watch.* For over a decade, Lt. Anita Van Buren has had a key role in solving crimes in *Law and Order.* Van Buren is a middle-aged, black woman who supervises two male detectives, one black and one white. Van Buren not only brings wisdom and restraint, but she also directs the male detectives in very fundamental aspects of criminal investigation, sharing her experience and knowledge with them. She is a clear example of television's move to more realistic portrayals of female crime fighters (Reep, 2004).

Along with *Law and Order, NYPD Blue* (NBC) has had a significant impact on the portrayal of female police during the past ten years. The female detectives in this series are generally mature and portrayed as people dealing with realistic personal problems. Detectives Diane Russell and Jill Kirkendall handle gritty crimes and face serious personal problems. Russell, a recovering alcoholic, struggles with grief after her husband, another detective, died from an infection after being attacked. Kirkendall, Russell's partner, has dealt with an abusive ex-husband. Nevertheless, the women are thoroughly professional in their work, and yet show the emotional trauma and uncertainties caused by complicated life situations that women often face.

CSI (CBS), another top-rated program, features Catherine Willows, a blood spatter specialist, and a woman with a past that has included an ex-husband and a former career as an exotic dancer. *Law and Order: Special Victims Unit* (NBC) has Detective Olivia Benson, a mature and capable investigator. Benson empathizes with the victims and frequently works through her own troubled past.

Although most characters are still white, *Without a Trace* (CBS) includes black investigator Vivian Johnson, who is tough and sensitive to families suffering loss. *Third Watch* (NBC) includes Sergeant Maritza Cruz as the leader of an anticrime unit, who consistently struggles with her role as a leader who rose out of a troubled past full of personal betrayal and drug use. In all of these portrayals, the female crime fighters are part of the team (Reep, 2004). While there are now stronger female characters in television's popular crime dramas, it is of note that there tends to be a greater emphasis on the personal lives of these women and their emotional struggles when compared to the strong male characters that have so long been a part of the world of crime drama. Whether this is good, in that the women are portrayed as sensitive and empathetic, or these portrayals have the potential to render the female role as incapable because they cannot separate their personal lives from their work lives, is debatable.

Lemberg (2004) suggests that the reason some women have been appointed to chief positions is because of "corruption and allegations of police brutality, stale public safety initiatives and a recent spike in the number of violent crimes" (p. 1). He quotes Margaret Moore, current director of the National Center for Women and Policing, "Things need to be constantly changing to stay relevant . . . and women bring a different style. The infusion of different points of view is essential. I'm not saying women are the answer to every police department's problems, but they have to be given a chance" (Moore cited in Lemberg, 2004, p. 1). Heather Fong, recently appointed police chief of San Francisco, is quoted as pointing out: "There's a militaristic culture in most law enforcement agencies—power, image, use of force. It's a very authoritarian attitude. But good policing isn't in the shoulders; it's in the head" (Fong, cited in Lemberg, 2004, p. 2).

Popular culture depictions of women in policing may have both positive and negative effects. While attention is brought to the fact there are more women in policing, much is left to the interpretation of the general public and their assessment of how "real" these portrayals are. Additionally, the lack of media coverage on the status of women could possibly negate or distort any positive effects popular culture may have.

Research on Policewomen

Assessing the realities of women in policing has been done through a variety of research techniques, including but not limited to survey research, observation, and interviewing. The research has been presented from several different academic perspectives, such as criminal justice, sociology, and public administration. Points of focus have included competency, attitudes toward and of women in policing, stress, legal issues, or simply works attempting to describe the current status of women in policing, with regard to types and numbers of women. Morash and Greene (1986) assessed the validity of numerous previous works and found gender bias in several works.

Early research on women in policing increased significantly following the gender integration of patrol officers in the early 1970s. Much of this increase was not necessarily due to an interest in how or to what extent women were being used, but rather the research was being done to evaluate women's competency in this male-dominated role in the police organization. Prior to this time period, women were primarily relegated to stereotypical positions, such as police matrons or support positions.

The initial competency research examining policewomen found women to be as capable as their male counterparts, with only a few exceptions. Unfortunately, these findings did not result in a significant increase in either the number of women in policing or related research activities. As a matter of fact, the results may have been a disincentive to hire more women because women were then seen as competitive threats, which had not previously been the case.

With the exception of Martin's seminal work and follow-up works (1980, 1990), Schulz's historical work (1995), Heidensohn and Brown's comparative studies (2000), and Miller's work on gender and community policing (1999), only sporadic efforts examining the current status of women and policing have been published.

Research in the last ten years includes Haar's (1997) use of qualitative methods to examine attitudes toward women in policing, specifically focusing on the effects of gender and race on patterns of interpersonal interaction. Wertsch (1998), following Ott (1989) and Kanter (1977), used interviews to examine tokenism as a barrier to advancement for women in policing. Scarborough and Hemmens (1998) looked at gender differences in Section 1983 claims against law enforcement in the U.S. Circuit Court of Appeals. Lersch (1998) also examined gender differences in complaints against police using content analysis. Leger (1997), using telephone survey research, assessed citizens' perceptions of women in policing. Zhao, Thurman, and He (1999) and Dantzker and Kubin (1998) examined job gender differences and job satisfaction using survey research. Gossett and Williams (1998) explored female officers' perception of discrimination in the police organization using interviews. Morash and Haar (1995) used participant observation and interviews to describe womens' experiences at work, and their conceptualization of problems and stresses. They continued their work, further evaluating stress and coping, through an examination of gender and race (Morash & Haar, 1999). Finally, for the last three years, the National Center for Women and Policing (NCWP) and Eastern Kentucky University (EKU) have surveyed a limited number of organizations to describe the current status of women in policing (NCWP, 2002), but these works only give a very limited piece of the big picture.

Applied Research

Besides the research previously cited, much of the field looks to professional organizations such as the Police Foundation, International Association of Chiefs of Police (IACP), and the Police Executive Research Forum (PERF), for news, policy, and analyses of law enforcement activities. Professional organizations tend to be very practical, using applied research, as compared to more theoretically based academic work typically emanating from universities. However, a look at the following prominent organizational Web sites illustrates that there is *even less* work that has been done or is currently in progress that focuses on women in policing, as compared to the academic research reported above.

The Police Foundation.   According to their literature, the Police Foundation is "[a]n independent and unique resource for policing [and it] acts as a catalyst for change and an advocate for new ideas" (Police Foundation Home Page, 2004). The Police Foundation also promotes "a way of thinking about law enforcement and a set of skills honed over thirty years of real-world experience in how to convert that thinking into practical programs that can be objectively evaluated and applied to improve the quality of public safety" (Police Foundation, 2004). While "Women and Policing" was listed topically in their index of available publications, there was no research listed on their Web site that has been done on women in policing in the past fourteen years, and there were only five publications listed. The most recent were Martin's book (1990) and a summary report (1989). Other available publications included a status report done in 1981 by Sulton and Townsey, a multivolume seminal study by Bloch and Anderson (1974), and a manual published in 1974 (Milton et al., 1974). It is important to note that the Police Foundation funded all of these publications. In the same section listing available publications, there were various reports that were listed as available, but which were funded by other means and published by other presses. The focus of some of these publications includes ethics, police administration, and intelligence gathering. No other works about women and policing were listed as available by the Police Foundation.

International Association of Chiefs of Police.   The home page of the International Association of Chiefs of Police (IACP) describes the organization as "the world's oldest and largest nonprofit membership organization of police executives, with over 19,000 members in over 89 different countries." The IACP's leadership consists of the operating chief executives of international, federal, state, and local agencies of all sizes. According to the vision statement in their Strategic Plan, the IACP "works to promote and support diversity, equality, tolerance, professionalism and sustained high standards throughout the professional police service (IACP, 2004, p. 4). In support of this vision, the IACP indicates that it engages in projects that "serve to examine barriers to the recruitment of minorities for police work and the development of strategies to increase their representation" (IACP, 2004, p. 14). Women are not mentioned in the IACP Strategic Plan.

A significant component of the IACP is the National Law Enforcement Policy Center, which was developed in 1987 through a cooperative agreement with the U.S. Justice Department's Bureau of Justice Assistance. The primary objective of the center is to assist law enforcement agencies developing and refining law enforcement policy. Model policies available through the center are developed because "they represent some of the most difficult issues facing law enforcement administrators" and those issues that are also described as high "priority areas" (IACP, 2004). Interestingly, of the ninety-two different available policies only one was related to women in policing—Harassment and Discrimination-Workplace.

Of the twenty reports available on their Web site, only one focused on women in policing, *Future of Women in Policing: Mandates for Action*. The survey was undertaken by the IACP following an ad hoc committee's recommendation to examine the role of women in policing and potential issues of concern. Findings from the survey indicate that the IACP members believe that "it is essential to strengthen the position of women in policing—their number, their professional development, their progress to positions of leadership, and their contribution to the public service and safety" (IACP, 2004). Additionally, the "IACP intends to act, in collaboration with a variety of other agencies, on the recommendations as immediately as is practicable" (IACP, 2004). Interestingly, the report was published in 1998, with no subsequent policy development or research on women and policing since then.

Police Executive Research Forum.   The Police Executive Research Forum (PERF) is "dedicated to improving policing and advancing professionalism through research, public policy debate, provision of management services and executive development training, and publishing" (PERF, 2004). PERF has publicly available completed research reports as well as status reports on active research projects and other types of publications available through the organization, but not necessarily funded by PERF. The public document area includes twenty broad categories, none of which are women, but include topics such as terrorism, budgeting, and information technology. There are sixty-one additional publications available, also none including women.

In the active research projects that are funded directly by PERF, only one out of thirty-six deals with women, "Cop Crunch: Identifying Strategies for Dealing with the Hiring

Crisis." This project includes a national survey designed to "identify department-level policies and practices that facilitate the recruiting and hiring of quality personnel, with a particular focus on successful strategies to recruit women and minorities" (PERF, 2004). None of
the eleven completed research projects deal with women.

The current work relies on going directly to the women in the field and asking them to
describe their reality, state their priorities, and voice their concerns, using a broad-based
roundtable and survey research. The following section highlights some of what has been
learned from these new efforts.

Voices from Women in the Field

Where should police departments focus their attention in order to attract and retain women in
the twenty-first century? What policy areas should be addressed so that women are utilized
to their full potential? A research roundtable was held at the 2003 conference of the NCWP,
which brought together academic researchers with women from law enforcement agencies of
varying type, size, rank, and geographical regions. Approximately forty women participated
in this roundtable, in which academic researchers presented women professionals with existing research on women in policing.

After this presentation, the professionals identified additional needs that were not currently met with existing research and prioritized all areas that were identified for future
research. Through a process of discussion and voting, participants generated a list of topics
that represent the range of existing needs and priorities. Twenty-three topics were identified
through this method. Students interested in doing research on women and policing should
consider investigating one or more of these topics. These issues represent an action agenda
promulgated by the women in the field and are of great importance to them, their careers, and
most importantly, their ability to perform their jobs. The topics also complement previous
research done on women in policing. Since women represent less than 20 percent of sworn
officers and less than 3 percent of upper management, their concerns, insights, and suggestions more often than not go unnoticed, resulting in no response. Research goals were also
identified with the topics. A detailed description of the topics can be found in Appendix A.

The twenty-three topics were then presented to another group of women professionals
in summer 2003 at an International Association of Women Police (IAWP) conference. The
women were asked to complete a survey at the conference, either by choosing a paper survey
or using an available laptop computer. Additionally, the survey was available online following the conference through the IAWP Web site. The goal was to present the topics to a much
wider and more representative sample of police women for additional clarification and prioritization. That process resulted in a similar set of five areas of concern, which are presented
as follows:

1. **Recruitment and retention** (#1 on the NCWP list). This includes policies dealing with
   prehiring screening, physical fitness tests, education, age, and height and weight requirements. This also includes policies and/or practices affecting recruitment
   approaches and target locations for recruitment.
2. **Women in upper level positions** (#3 on the NCWP list). Promotion to higher supervisory and administrative ranks. This includes promotion policies and/or practices.

3. Sexual hostility/harassment in the work place (#5 on the NCWP list). This includes any policies or practices establishing reporting and grievance procedures, definitions of harassment, or informal practices for handling such situations.
4. Effectiveness of interagency collaboration (#16 on the NCWP list). This includes policies and/or practices for establishing task forces and for assigning personnel.
5. Impact of child abuse on victims (#17 on the NCWP list). This includes concern on the part of the participants as to how child abuse affects the victims in the long run.

Following the identification and prioritization of the topics by the two groups of women, an assessment of police department policy on four of the top five topics was done. Recruitment, promotions, sexual harassment, and interagency collaboration policies were examined. While a pertinent and timely issue, the impact of child abuse on victims was not examined in this assessment. A limited, random, geographically diverse sample of fifty police organizations nationwide was selected for this descriptive policy evaluation. The departments were contacted to request their participation in this study, and only ten departments agreed to participate (Orchard Park, NJ; Joplin, MO; Bayonne, NJ; Edison, NJ; Fort Wayne, IN; Tallahasee, FL; Indianapolis, IN; Austin, TX; Virginia Beach, VA; and Birmingham, AL). The initial random selection was more geographically representative; however, the final sample did not include any organizations from the western United States. The ability to generalize this work is limited; however, the descriptive information provides useful guidance for further research related to women's concerns and existing policy. Table 5.6 identifies the existing policies in the departments studied.

Recruitment and Retention

Three responding agencies had a recruitment and retention policy in place to recruit women to their agency. These agencies at least mentioned women in their policy. Of the three agen-

TABLE 5.6 *Police Department Policies*

	Recruitment and Retention	Promotions	Sexual Harassment	Interagency Collaboration
Orchard Park, NY			X	
Joplin, MO			X	
Bayonne, NJ			X	
Edison, NJ	X		X	
Fort Wayne, IN	X		X	
Tallahassee, FL			X	
Indianapolis, IN			X	
Austin, TX			X	
Virginia Beach, VA	X		X	
Birmingham, AL			X	

X = POLICY DIRECTLY RELATING TO WOMEN

Source: Data gathered as part of the authors' research described in the chapter.

cies, the Fort Wayne Police Department (FWPD) had the most comprehensive policy in place. Part of their policy reads, "Women and minorities are aggressively invited to be members of the Fort Wayne Police Department" (Fort Wayne Police Department, 2001, p. 2). Further, "Fort Wayne Police Department will work to ensure that women and other minority members are sought out as potential recruit applicants. . ." (Fort Wayne Police Department, 2001, p. 3). Women are also used to represent the department at Career Day functions at various colleges and universities within a 150-mile radius of the city. The FWPD has also implemented an Equal Employment Opportunity Plan relating to recruitment of women that contains these four goals:

1. Ensure the availability of job posting information to white and black females through the Fort Wayne Women's Bureau and similar organizations within a 600-mile radius of the city.
2. Place advertisements in periodicals that are targeted toward the recruitment of women and attend Job Fairs and Career Days locally that may focus on the recruitment of minorities.
3. Target females during college recruitment activities and job fairs.
4. Encourage more female officers to take promotion tests for sergeant and lieutenant (Fort Wayne Police Department, 2001, pp. 3–4).

The Edison, New Jersey, Police Department and Virginia Beach, Virginia, Police Department also focus on recruiting women. The Edison Police Department (EPD) has a recruitment program in place specifically for women. It establishes and utilizes women's organizations as employment recruiters. The EPD is also the only department with a separate physical agility scale for women.

The Virginia Beach Police Department (VBPD) conducted a comparison of current workforce demographics against the community labor statistics that indicated the department underutilizes women in several areas. They continue to strive toward a department that closely matches the demographics of the community. They continue to research and evaluate new methods for recruiting and hiring qualified applicants and are currently utilizing the study "Mobilizing the Community for Minority Recruitment and Selection" published by the IACP in December 2003. The VBPD also asks female officers for new recruiting ideas or suggestions. One recruitment strategy is, "one-on-one recruitment activity in a variety of venues, such as presentations at the Naval Base for transitioning military personnel, participation in community events and college job fairs, website recruiting, etc." (Jacocks, 2002, p. 3). With the increased attention toward women, the VBPD has seen an increase in female police recruits, with women in the VBPD now constituting approximately 12.7 percent of personnel; 17 percent of their current recruits are women (Jacocks, 2002).

Promotion Findings

None of the responding police departments had policies relating to women and promotions. All of the participating departments have some type of promotion selection system and/or procedure in place. These systems/procedures usually consist of a variety of stages including tests, review boards, and a number of other things. Experience, education, and training are also taken into consideration. However, as mentioned previously in the recruitment and retention section, the FWPD encourages female officers to take promotion tests.

Sexual Harassment Findings

As expected, all of the selected agencies have some type of sexual harassment policies. Departments must comply with Title VII of the Civil Rights Act of 1964 for dealing with sexual harassment. Departments also often refer to the Equal Employment Opportunity Commission Guidelines. More recently, U.S. Supreme Court decisions required departments to review their policies (Graham, 1998). Departments can be held liable for sexual and gender harassment, even if an employer is unaware of the harassment (NCWP, n.d.). All departments can defend harassment charges by demonstrating they have a policy, have communicated the policy, trained supervisors, and followed the policy.

The sexual harassment policies reviewed in this study included a number of components such as: definitions of sexual and gender harassment with general and specific examples, reporting procedures, investigation procedures, and supervisor responsibilities. Some departments also designate an officer/s to focus on sexual harassment (Bayonne Police Department, 1998; Indianapolis Police Department, 1995).

Interagency Collaboration Findings

While it is not clear whether the concern of policewomen about interagency collaboration was due to organizational issues or gender issues, there are no specific written policies that address either issue. Most agencies indicate they cooperate and maintain open communication with other agencies in their surrounding areas. Women were not the focus of this collaboration, however.

Summary of Findings

Recruitment and retention is the number one concern of women in law enforcement today, according to those who participated in the NCWP summit and completed the IAWP survey. Respondents believe more attention must be focused on these areas and current research supports this concern. A number of agencies, Tucson, AZ (29 percent women); Miami Beach, FL (28 percent women); Madison, WI (26 percent women); Pittsburgh, PA (22 percent women); and Birmingham, AL (19 percent women) changed their recruitment strategies and have seen positive results. Although the numbers of women in these departments are still nowhere equal to men, there was a substantial increase in the number of women being recruited into these agencies.

Almost all police agencies have sexual harassment policies in place. However, according to the concern raised by the IAWP, the NCWP, and previous research, these policies are still not effective in eradicating the problem in the workplace. Policies must be routinely reviewed and updated and support current law. Given the evident level of concern, sexual harassment is still a serious problem and may have a negative impact on both recruitment and retention.

There is no evidence to suggest that there are any policies—and certainly no women-focused policies—on either promotion or interagency collaboration. If women are to be promoted proportionately to their numbers or in numbers sufficient to influence law enforcement policy or police culture, then they must be assigned to positions that lead to promotion and advancement.

The literature review identified a limited number of model policies developed by national agencies or associations. Policies that do exist were developed in the early 1990s by departments and may be outdated. With the absence of policies at the agency level and absence of model policies at the national level, it is doubtful that the concerns identified by women in the field can or will be systematically addressed.

The NCWP assessment guide, *Recruiting and Retaining Women,* stresses that family-friendly policies recognizing women's roles as wife and mother, as well as realistic and more liberal work expectations for pregnant women, would go a long way in recruiting and retaining women in policing. Some specific suggestions are that these family-related policies be fair, flexible, and safe. Supporting this policy focus is the IACP's survey examining the future of women in policing, which listed the top reasons for women's resignations in order of importance: family, children, birth, better career opportunity, better pay, career change, and better advancement opportunities.

Conclusion

The dynamic, multifaceted nature of policing, along with the complex organizational structures and strong subculture, make the occupation difficult to study. Painting an accurate picture of the occupation is challenging, and focusing on women increases the challenge enormously. Women are "outsiders" in a traditionally male-dominated profession, fraught with stereotypical perceptions of "appropriate" behavior both for women generally, and for women in a nontraditional occupation specifically. Our perceptions of women in law enforcement are often shaped more by media portrayals, which are attempting to be more realistic, than by systematic study or research.

As the authors can attest, having been officers in the 1970s and 1980s, anyone who was an officer in the early days of TV media portrayals of policewomen will tell you that the media has "come a long way baby!" Just as policewomen in the 1970s often had to wear short skirts and blue panty hose as their uniforms, early TV police shows sexualized women and portrayed them as needing a male rescuer. Television policewomen today display their acumen across police tasks and even star as rather aggressive and competent heroines and yet manage to remain feminine.

In academia, research on women tends to be valued less than traditional "mainstream" research. Similarly, women in policing have not been able to make inroads into policy agendas except through legal actions. Most policies have been a response to class action lawsuits resulting in consent decrees or by media pressure by women's groups. Also, the influence of professional organizations, or lack thereof, may be significant, considering the paucity of information about women.

In the current research, when women were asked to identify those issues most salient to them, there was surprising agreement on the important issues: recruitment and retention, promotion to policy making positions, sexual harassment in the workplace, and cooperative interagency activities. While there have been some successes in recruitment and retention, the number of women in upper-level positions remain small. After decades of policies on sexual harassment, women are still struggling to get updated, effective policies either developed or implemented. We could find nothing that directly speaks to interagency cooperation and the role of women, but it is not surprising that women would find a cooperative activity important and thus of interest. Also, depending upon the type of interagency project, participation in these activities can often lead to promotion and financial award. Women who do not get these assignments are not only kept out of the activity itself, but also prevented from reaping potential rewards.

Policies should facilitate better opportunities for advancement by assigning women to those areas of policing that traditionally lead to advancement. For women to be more successful in twenty-first century policing, these pertinent timely issues must be adequately addressed.

Review Questions

1. How does research contribute to the picture of women in policing?

2. What is the importance of having women promoted into upper-level positions in law enforcement? What are some strategies to get women into these positions?

3. In 2003–2004, policewomen identified four topics they thought were of the most immediate concern to women in law enforcement: recruitment and retention, women in upper-level positions, sexual harassment in the work place, and effectiveness of interagency cooperation. Take one issue and discuss its possible importance to women's careers and to the overall effectiveness of policing.

4. Do you think the media portrayal as discussed in this chapter is a realistic depiction? Is it a positive view of women in law enforcement or does it have a negative connotation?

5. Do you think we have reached a plateau in the number of women in law enforcement? Why or why not?

6. If police departments want to focus on recruitment and retention of women and minorities, what would you recommend that they do? Have you ever talked with a police recruiter at a career fair at your college or university? Why?

7. What should future research on women in policing focus on?

Key Terms

Stereotypical
Gender bias
Bureau of Labor Statistics
Nontraditional occupation
Mentoring

Policy
International Association of Chiefs of Police
Police Executive Research Forum
National Center for Women and Policing
International Association of Women Police

Appendix A: 2003 NCWP Roundtable Topics

1. Recruitment and Retention

Goal: Evaluate the effectiveness of various innovative practices for successfully recruiting top quality applicants and retaining valued employees—especially women and minorities.

2. Advantages of Women vs. Men in Law Enforcement

Goals: Expand the existing research on the advantages that women bring to law enforcement, and compare with the advantages that men bring to the field. Using quantitative and/or qualitative methods, explore the comparative strengths of female versus male personnel within law enforcement agencies. Explore the effect that women in law enforcement have on their community, especially with respect to community organizations.

3. Women in Upper-Level Positions

Goals: Identify women in upper-level positions within law enforcement and analyze the variables that explain their presence and/or their absence within an agency. Determine the point at which a "critical mass" of women is achieved within the upper ranks of law enforcement agencies, and explore the ways in which their presence has an effect on the culture, policy and practice of those agencies. Examine potential differences in the leadership style of men versus women in law enforcement.

4. Perceptions of Women in Law Enforcement

Goals: Measure perceptions of women in law enforcement—among practitioners, political elites, and within the community. Determine whether these perceptions differ from those of men within law enforcement, and explore potential similarities and differences with traditional gender stereotypes.

5. Sexual Hostility/Harassment in the Workplace

Goals: Expand existing research on sexual harassment in the law enforcement workplace by documenting how often it occurs, what it looks like, what kind of effect it has on women, and the potential costs for law enforcement agencies. Explore potential avenues for addressing this problem and analyze the links with women's "sexual status" (e.g., married, single, divorced, dating, heterosexual, lesbian).

6. Physical Agility Testing/Training

Goals: Measure the impact of physical agility testing and/or training requirements on the recruitment, performance, and retention of female law enforcement officers. Analyze the existing standards for physical agility testing/training within law enforcement agencies, and the recommendations and/or requirements of state regulatory agencies (i.e., Peace Officer Standards and Training). Examine the validity of physical agility tests by researching the potential link between test standards and various criteria for successful job performance.

7. Women's Networks and Competition

Goals: Explore the question of formal and informal networks available to women within law enforcement agencies—and between agencies. Document any consequences for the relationships among women. Examine the competition between women in law enforcement agencies, and determine whether there is any link with the existing formal and/or informal networks. Evaluate whether there are consequences of women's networks and/or competition for the workplace environment, level of performance, opportunities for promotion, and retention.

8. Gender and Excessive Force

Goals: Document any link between gender and the likelihood of using excessive force. Explore possible gender differences in the type of excessive force used by law enforcement personnel and the consequences for law enforcement agencies and community relations.

9. Effect of Consent Decrees on Increasing the Number of Women

Goals: Expand existing research on the effects of consent decrees on increasing the number of women within law enforcement throughout the rank structure. Explore potential links between consent decrees mandating the hiring and/or promotion of women and/or minorities. Analyze the factors that make a consent decree more or less likely to have a positive effect on women's representation, and document what happens when the consent decree expires.

10. New Information on Police Officer Domestic Violence

Goals: Expand the existing research on domestic violence perpetrated by law enforcement officers to better understand how often it happens, what it looks like, what the consequences are for victims, and the response of law enforcement agencies. Explore the unique dynamics of domestic violence that are perpetrated by a police officer against a partner who is also a police officer, possibly even within the same agency.

11. Extent and Impact of Sexual Assault on Women in Law Enforcement

Sexual assault always has a wide range of serious negative effects on victims, but research has not focused on the unique dynamics that are experienced by victims who are police officers—especially if the perpetrator is also a police officer. The goal is to explore this topic by examining how often this happens, whether it is linked with sexual harassment within the workplace, and what the consequences are for the physical, psychological, and professional well-being of victims.

12. Gender and Nontraditional Occupations

Goal: Expand the existing research on women in nontraditional occupations and explore potential links with the experiences of women within law enforcement specifically.

13. Critical Mass of Women in Law Enforcement

Goals: Document the effects of increasing the number of women recruited and retained within a law enforcement agency. Identify the variables that explain their increasing numbers, and determine the point at which a "critical mass" of women is achieved within a law enforcement agency. Explore the effect of this "critical mass" on the culture, policy, and practice of law enforcement agencies.

14. Effectiveness of Restraining Orders

Goals: Evaluate the effectiveness of restraining orders in preventing domestic violence and homicide. Analyze the factors that influence a victim's likelihood of obtaining a restraining order and the effectiveness of that order in deterring future violence.

15. Enhanced Communication for Domestic Violence Victims

Goals: Evaluate the effectiveness of providing cell phones and other communication devices to victims of domestic violence to increase their access to law enforcement and other services. Analyze the factors that influence a victim's likelihood of obtaining and using such enhanced communication, and document any potential effect on preventing future violence.

16. Effectiveness of Interagency Collaboration

Goals: Evaluate the effectiveness of partnerships between law enforcement and victim services in areas such as domestic violence, sexual assault, and child abuse.

17. Impact of Child Abuse on Victims

Goals: Expand the existing research on the many negative effects of child abuse on victims, both in childhood and into adulthood. Measure negative effects on the physical and psychological well-being of victims and explore the positive effects of intervention.

18. Conflict Resolution within Law Enforcement Agencies

Goals: Explore the process for internal conflict resolution within law enforcement agencies. Examine the types of conflicts that men and women experience within law enforcement organizations, how they resolve these conflicts with coworkers, whether and how they utilize the resources within the law enforcement agency, and whether there are differences by gender.

19. Access to Information Within and Between Law Enforcement Agencies

Although a great deal of information within law enforcement agencies is supposed to be accessible—to those within the organization, in other law enforcement agencies, or in the community—this access is inconsistently achieved. The goal is to explore how men and women within law enforcement agencies access the information they need to perform their jobs successfully and to determine whether there any implications of gender for providing and/or obtaining information.

20. Lack of Women in Special Operations and Intelligence

Goals: Measure the representation of women in specialized positions such as intelligence and operations (e.g., SWAT). Determine whether men and women in these positions perform their duties differently and what the consequences are for the quality of law enforcement services and community relations.

21. Use and Impact of Technology

Technology in the field of law enforcement is changing at an incredible pace, yet research has not explored any potential effect of gender on its use and impact. The goal is to explore whether men and women in law enforcement utilize technology differently, to determine whether there are any consequences for women's performance and promotion, and to document any effects on the quality of law enforcement services and community relations.

22. Women in Small/Rural Agencies

Most research on women in law enforcement has been conducted in large, urban police agencies. The goal is to explore the experiences of women within small/rural law enforcement organizations and to document similarities and differences with their female counterparts in larger urban agencies.

23. Women in State and Federal Agencies

Goal: Explore the experiences of women within state and federal law enforcement organizations, and document similarities and differences with their female counterparts in municipal police agencies.

References

Associated Press. (2004). *Women top police ranks in several cities.* Retrieved June 18, 2004 from http://www.etopics.com/index.asp?layout=print&doc_id=NEh0527068.4ap&usderid=2003.

Bayonne Police Department. (1998). *Sexual harassment.* Bayonne, NJ: Author.

Bloch, P., & Anderson, D. (1974). *Police women on patrol: Final report.* Washington, DC: Urban Institute.

Dantzker, M. L., & Kubin, B. (1998). Job satisfaction: The gender perspective among police officers. *American Journal of Criminal Justice* 23, 1, 20–31.

Fort Wayne Police Department. (2001). *Recruitment.* Fort Wayne, Indiana.

Gossett, J. L., & Williams, J. E. (1998). Perceived discrimination among women in law enforcement. *Women and Criminal Justice* 10 (1), 53–73.

Graham, G. Inter-Office Communication, Office of Personnel. City of Birmingham, Alabama.

Haar, R.N. (1997). Patterns of interaction in a police patrol bureau: Race and gender barriers to integration. *Justice Quarterly* 14 (1), 53–85.

Haar, R. N., & Morash, M. (1999). Gender, race, and strategies of coping with occupational stress in policing. *Justice Quarterly* 16 (2), 303–336.

Hale, D. C., & Bennett, C. L. (1995). Realities of women in policing. In A. V. Merlo & J. Pollock (Eds.), *Women, law and social control* (pp. 41–54). Boston: Allyn and Bacon.

Heidensohn, F., & Brown, J. (2000). *Gender and policing: Comparative perspectives.* London, England: Palgrave Macmillan.

Indianapolis Police Department. (1995). *Sexual harassment, No. 7.02.* Indianapolis, IN: Author.

International Association of Chiefs of Police. (1998). *The future of women in policing: Mandates for action.* Alexandria, VA: IACP. Retrieved on November 9, 2004 from http://www.theiacp.org/documents/index.cfm?fuseaction=document&document_type_id=1.

Jacocks, A. M. (2002). *EEOP short form introductory information.* Virginia Beach, VA: Virginia Beach Police Department.

Kanter, R. M. (1977). *Men and women of the corporation.* New York: Basic Books.

Leger, K. (1997). Public perceptions of female police officers on patrol. *American Journal of Criminal Justice* 21 (2), 231–249.

Lemberg, J. (2004). Women reach top of police ranks, growth still slow. *Women's E News.* Retrieved July 1, 2004 from http://www.womeensenews.org/article.cfm/dyn/aid/1759/context/archive.

Lersch, K. M. (1998). Exploring gender differences in citizen allegations of misconduct: An analysis of a municipal police department. *Women and Criminal Justice* 9 (4), 69–79.

Manning, J. (2004). From matron to major. *Kentucky Law Enforcement News* 3 (1), 50–54.

Martin, S. E . (1980). *Breaking and entering: Policewomen on patrol.* Berkeley, CA: University of California Press.

Martin, S. E. (1990). *On the move: the status of women in policing.* Washington, DC: Police Foundation.

Miller, S. L. (1999). *Gender and community policing: Walking the talk.* Boston: Northeastern University Press.

Milton, C., Abramowitz, A., Crites, L, Gates, M., Mintz, E., & Sandler, G. (1974). *Women in policing: A manual.* Washington, DC: Police Foundation.

Morash, M., & Greene, J. (1986). Evaluating women on patrol: A critique of contemporary wisdom. *Evaluation Review* 10, 230–255.

Morash, M., & Haar, R. N. (1995). Gender, workplace problems, and stress in policing. *Justice Quarterly* 12 (1), 113–136.

National Center for Women and Policing. (2002). *Equality denied: The status of women in policing 2001.* Los Angeles: National Center for Women and Policing.

National Center for Women and Policing. (n.d.). *Recruiting and retaining women: A self assessment guide for law enforcement.* Los Angeles: NCWP.

Ott, M. E. (1989). Effects of the male-female ratio at work: Policewomen and male nurses. *Psychology of Women Quarterly* 13, 41–57.

Police Executive Research Forum. (2004). *Police executive research forum home page.* Retrieved July 1, 2004 from http://policeforum.

Police Foundation. (2004). *Police Foundation home page.* Retrieved on July 1, 2004 from http://www.policefoundation.

Reep, D. (2004). *Television cops.* Unpublished essay.

Scarborough, K. E., & Collins, P. A. (2002). *Women in public and private law enforcement.* Woburn, MA: Butterworth-Heinemann.

Scarborough, K. E., & Hemmens, C. (1999). Section 1983 suits against law enforcement in the circuit courts of appeals. *Thomas Jefferson Law Review* 21 (1), 1–21.

Schulz, D. M. (1995). *From social worker to crime fighter: Women in United States municipal policing.* London, England: Praeger.

Stuart, H. (2004). *Model policy request.* Personal e-mail.

Sulton, C. G., & Townsey, R. D. (1981). *Women in policing: A progress report.* Washington, DC: Police Foundation.

U.S. Department of Defense. (2001). *Active duty military personnel by rank/grade.* Washington, DC: U.S. Government Printing Office.

U.S. Department of Justice, Bureau of Justice Statistics. (2003a). *Federal law enforcement officers, 2002,* Bulletin 199995. Washington, DC: U.S. Government Printing Office.

U.S. Department of Justice, Bureau of Justice Statistics. (2003b). *Law enforcement management and adminis-* *trative statistics, 2000: Data for individual state and local agencies with 100 or more officers.* Bulletin 203350, p. 243. Washington, DC: U.S. Government Printing Office.

U.S. Department of Justice, Bureau of Justice Statistics. (2003c). *Local police departments, 2000.* Bulletin 196002, p. 4. Washington, DC: U.S. Government Printing Office.

U.S. Department of Justice, Bureau of Justice Statistics. (2003d). *Sheriff's offices: 2000.* Bulletin 196534, p. 4. Washington, DC: U.S. Government Printing Office.

U.S. Department of Labor. (2002). *Nontraditional occupations for women in 2002.* Washington, DC: Bureau of Labor Statistics. Retrieved from July, 1. 2004 from http://www.dol.gov/wb/stats/main.htm.

Wertsch, T. L. (1998). Walking the thin blue line: Policewomen and tokenism today. *Women and Criminal Justice* 9, 3, 23–61.

Zhao, J. Q., Thurman, Q., & He, N. (1999). Sources of job satisfaction among police officers: A test of demographic and work environment models. *Justice Quarterly* 16 (1), 153–173.

6

Women Working in Prisons and Jail Settings

Progress and Prospects

Mary Ann Farkas

Women working as correctional officers and managers in prisons and jails face unique challenges and obstacles to their full integration and utilization. In correctional work, "the removal of legal and formal barriers to employment has been only the first step. The larger task of removing the less tangible human barriers of the workplace remains" (Etheridge, Hale, & Hambrick, 1991, p. 66). Women may have been granted the legal right to work in all areas of corrections but that does not guarantee acceptance by male colleagues (Zimmer, 1986). Women entering traditionally and predominantly male occupations confront negative stereotyping and adverse expectations about their ability to do the job (Pollock, 1995). The tradition of a male occupation creates a work culture that is an extension of male culture, and the numerical dominance of men heightens the visibility and hostility toward women invading their domain (Gruber, 1998).

Corrections work has been described as a "highly sex-typed male job requiring qualities of dominance, authoritativeness, and aggressiveness" (Pogrebin & Poole, 1997, p. 42) and an allegiance to male norms of behavior. Gendered organizational logic in corrections is predicated on the underlying assumption that workers are men, the requisite or valued job skills are distinct to men, and divisions along lines of gender are constructed formally and informally (Britton, 1997, p. 797). Ways to perform the work and standards used to judge performance are also based on masculine norms and values (Crouch, 1985).

Perspectives on Work Behavior

The suitability and capability of women to work in all positions in prisons for men has been the subject of considerable discussion. A related issue is whether women and men bring different qualities and attitudes to the job of correctional officer or administrator, and thus, whether women perform the job differently or as effectively as men. Four principal perspectives, the "gender model," the "job model," the "integrated model," and the "interactionist perspective," have been used in the sociological and organizational literature to analyze the work behavior of women. The gender model posits that women's special qualities, traits, values, sex role socialization, prior experiences, and preferred modes of interaction shape their orientation, approach to the job, and their work experience (Feldberg & Glenn, 1979; Statham, 1987). In other words, "women's relationship to their work (their occupational choices, attitudes toward the job, occupational behavior, commitment, and the like) are [*sic*] determined by factors directly related to their female status" (Zimmer, 1986, p. 193).

The job model asserts that work-related variables, including organizational structure, occupational socialization, task complexity, and work conditions, influence the female worker's orientation, behavior, approach to the job, and interactions with others (Feldberg & Glenn, 1979), as well as her intellectual and psychological functioning (Miller, Schooler, Kohn, & Miller, 1979). In effect, these aspects of the job will supercede gender-related factors. Moreover, the job model also suggests that gender differences in work behavior lessen over time and become "homogenized" by exposure to similar work experiences and conditions, and a distinct set of occupational values (Britton, 1997; Crouch, 1985; Van Voorhis, Cullen, Link, & Wolfe, 1991).

Feldberg and Glenn (1979) proposed an integration of the two models as a more comprehensive way to view the occupational behavior and experience of men and women. The "integrated model" theorizes that both job and gender-related factors are critical to an understanding of women's work experience and approach to the job.

> Women's occupational behavior differs from men's not only because of differences in their organizational positions, the effects of tokenism, or the sexist attitudes of others in the organization, but also because in contemporary American society, female workers often enter employment settings with skills, attitudes, beliefs, and prior experiences that are different from their male coworkers. (Zimmer, 1986, p. 205)

Zimmer (1986, pp. 208–209) supports the integrated model, but also contends that it is not enough to simply include both organizational and gender variables in an explanation of work behavior. She proposes a fourth model, the "interactionist perspective," as a means of understanding women's occupational experience. This perspective focuses on the process of how job and gender-related factors combine and *interact* to produce particular outcomes. In other words, women may have a unique philosophy, orientation, or skill, but features of the job, such as the hierarchical structure of authority or occupational socialization, inhibit or alter their work behavior.

Throughout this chapter, the ongoing debate over these perspectives will become evident as we examine the supervisory and management styles and the work experiences of women employed as correctional officers and wardens and superintendents. We will explore the available evidence and their implications for workers and managers in corrections. First, however, we will explore the history of women in corrections as the starting point for our discussion.

History of Women in Corrections

In the 1800s, female inmates were housed in the same prisons as men; however, they were gradually separated in wings, rooms, and attics (Feinman, 1986). The institutions were administered and staffed by men and as a result, female inmates had no female supervision to provide protection from sexual or other abuse (Morton, 1992). Women imprisoned in these facilities were neglected, sexually exploited, and kept in overcrowded, unsanitary conditions (Feinman, 1986; Rafter, 1990). Prison reform groups in the United States were mobilized by the horrid conditions for women inmates and the influential work of an English Quaker named Elizabeth Fry. Fry stressed the importance of a personal approach and continuous, useful labor for incarcerated women. She proposed banning all males from the daily supervision of female inmates (Dobash, Dobash, & Gutteridge, 1986). Inspired by Fry, the Womens' Christian Temperance Union, the Moral Reform Society, and the Womens' Prison Association lobbied for separate reformatories for women, run by women.

In 1822 the first female matron was hired in Maryland. In 1830, separate buildings were designated for women prisoners in several states. The first correctional facility for women opened in 1873 in Indiana, staffed largely by women (Zupan, 1992). This facility was separate from men's institutions in administration and location, although its architecture and operation still resembled the male custodial prison (Hawkes, 1991). Superintendent Sarah Smith and her matron staff created a homelike atmosphere and reinforced women's traditional roles through the teaching of domestic skills. The matrons were hired on the basis of their good reputations and their maternal abilities.

According to Parisi (1984), the term "matron" connotes a distinct role and philosophy. The matron role served as an example of a virtuous, dutiful woman and provided mothering and nurturing to female prisoners to teach the skills of domesticity to them. The matron philosophy incorporated many of Elizabeth Fry's correctional theories (Freedman, 1974). Women in prison would be rehabilitated and redirected toward the path of true womanhood through faithful domestic service and sexual chastity until marriage (Harris, 1998, p. 78). The women were taught orderly habits and household skills, including cooking, sewing, washing and ironing, and gardening in preparation for employment and a life of domesticity.

Rehabilitating and reforming female prisoners was the domain of matrons who alone possessed the unique abilities to accomplish these tasks. This reliance on domestic routines and training as a form of rehabilitation never entirely disappeared from correctional facilities for women (Freedman, 1974). In the 1940s, the title of matron was gradually changed to "cottage officer/supervisor" (for those women in charge of cottages), and eventually to "correctional officer" in the 1970s (Hawkes, 1991).

From the 1930s to the 1970s, women worked in corrections in a variety of capacities: administrators, officers, and counselors; however, their employment was circumscribed to female and juvenile facilities (Martin & Jurik, 1996). Women were permitted to enter the correctional system as long as they directed their efforts toward female prisoners and did not encroach on guard work in male prisons. This sex-segregated prison system limited women's employment opportunities in three ways: only a small number of female officers could work in the system at any time; promotions to supervisory and administrative positions were very limited and seldom available; and women were restricted to one prison in a single geographic area with no opportunity to transfer to institutions in other areas of the state (Feinman, 1986, p. 143).

Because of the greater numbers of institutions for men, the greater opportunity for promotion, and the higher pay, women had a large stake in obtaining employment in these facilities. "Recognition of the limited opportunities and salary inequities for women in the corrections field are documented in the newsletter of the Women's Correctional Association during the 1960s" (Hawkes, 1991, p. 105).

A major impetus for women's entry into prisons for men was the passage of an amendment to Title VII of the 1964 Civil Rights Act. The original act prohibited employment discrimination on the basis of sex, but this proscription applied only to private sector employment. In 1972, Congress passed an amendment that extended the prohibition to public employers. Armed with Title VII, women were then able to bring suits against officials who refused to hire them as correctional officers in all-male prisons (Farkas & Rand, 1997).

Prison administrators were opposed to employing women in facilities for men based on security and order concerns. They felt women were in danger of assault by inmates and would disrupt institutional order. Nonetheless, administrators almost immediately began to hire women as guards in institutions for men. The first step toward officer integration took place when New York voluntarily admitted female officers in facilities for men (Zimmer, 1986). In 1973, California merged the job titles of men and women and placed female officers in facilities for men. Zimmer (1986) suggests that their motivation may have been to circumvent the seniority system that allowed experienced, skilled guards to bid for low-contact posts in towers and control rooms. Hiring women to fill these posts would then free these male guards for reassignment to high-risk, inmate contact positions.

Legal Challenges to Women Working in All-Male Institutions

In 1977, a critical ruling by the U.S. Supreme Court threatened to thwart the equal employments prospects for women (Farkas & Rand, 1997). *Dothard v. Rawlinson,* 433 U.S. 321, became the first and only case of unlawful sex discrimination in the hiring of female correctional officers to reach the nation's highest court. Diane Rawlinson used Title VII to challenge the validity of an Alabama statute specifying the minimum height and weight requirements of 5'2" and 120 pounds for employment as a prison guard, as well as a prison regulation prohibiting the hiring of women as prison guards in contact positions that required continual close proximity to inmates. Rawlinson was rejected as a prison guard after failing to meet the minimum height requirement. The Supreme Court overturned the use of height and weight restrictions unless the state could demonstrate that they were related to the job. However, the Court ruled that the Alabama regulation barring the hiring of women guards in contact positions at all male prisons fell within the ambit of section 703 (e) of Title VII, which permits sex-based discrimination where sex is a *bona fide* occupational qualification (BFOQ).

The Court reasoned that the use of women as guards in contact positions in the particular conditions of the Alabama prison system would pose a substantial security problem directly related to the sex of the prison guard. Nevertheless, *Dothard* was a narrow ruling applying only to the Alabama prisons. Conditions in the prisons had been characterized by "rampant violence" with no attempt to classify or segregate inmates in the male dormitory style prisons according to offenses or dangerousness. The *Dothard* ruling had very little impact on women's employment simply because no court has ever found the prison conditions in other states to match the "jungle-like," unconstitutional conditions that served as the basis for women's exclusion in Alabama (Zimmer, 1989).

The other legal challenge to female officers in prisons for men has been in the area of inmates' right to privacy. In *Gunther v. Iowa State Men's Reformatory,* 462 F. Supp. 952 (1979), the court held that privacy shall not take precedence over female correctional officers' right to promotion, but that it may not be necessary to open every post to women. The court opined that adjustments could be made without jeopardizing the privacy rights of prisoners or disrupting the efficient management or core goals of the prison. In *Grummet v. Rushen,* 779 F.2d. 491 (1985), the court agreed that inmates have a privacy interest in not being viewed naked by members of the opposite sex, but declared that the infrequency of viewing nude male inmates by female guards precluded relief.

Concern with inmate privacy may be heightened, however, when male correctional officers work in prisons for women. "Some courts have recognized that women are socialized to have greater privacy needs than men in our society, and there are more potential dangers (sexual exploitation or assault) in having men observe women in their living units and patting down inmates than are raised by female officers supervising men" (Pollock, 2002, p. 165). In *Jordan v. Gardner,* 986 F. 2d. 1521 (9th Cir. 1993) (*en banc*), the court considered whether a prison policy allowing the cross-gender clothed body search of female inmates by male guards violated the Eighth Amendment (Farkas & Rand, 1999).

The *Jordan* court was convinced that because of their histories of victimization, female inmates were more likely to be psychologically harmed by cross-gender searches, and thus such a policy was cruel and unusual in violation of the Eighth Amendment (Pollock, 2002, p. 167). Whether *Jordan v. Gardner* will set a precedent for deciding future cases involving cross-gender searches of female inmates remains unclear. A recent case, *Carl v. Angelone* (883 F. Supp. 1433 [1995]), raised questions regarding its precedential power.

Thus, the standards governing cross-gender searches are quite complicated, involving a balancing of institutional security, equal employment rights, and inmate rights to privacy. Bennett (1995), Farkas and Rand (1999), and Pollock (2002) analyzed numerous inmate privacy cases brought by male and female inmates and reached the following conclusions. First, in cases involving observation of nude inmates by opposite-sex officers, courts generally have not found constitutional violations, upholding instead equal employment opportunities for officers. The frequency of the observations by opposite-sex officers is considered in court rulings. Cross-gender routine strip searches and body cavity searches are viewed as much more objectionable, although they may be justified in emergency situations. Finally, pat searches and clothed body searches of male inmates by female officers are acceptable, but searches of female inmates by male officers may constitute cruel and unusual punishment. Thus "the courts have narrowed the scope of prisoner privacy to the point where only a few posts and a few activities clearly fit within the BFOQ exemption" (Zimmer, 1989, p. 69).

Women Working as Correctional Officers

Overall women comprise 28 percent of officers working in jails, 24 percent of those working in state facilities, and 14 percent of women employed as officers in the federal system (American Correction Association, henceforth ACA, 2003). Approximately 45 percent of female correctional officers are women of color. Since the passage of the 1972 amendment to Title VII, women have progressed slowly in their employment as officers in prisons for men. Women accounted for only 6.6 percent of correctional officers employed in facilities for males in 1978 and 12.9 percent of officers in prisons for men in 1988 (Morton, 1991a). In 2003, 18 percent of officers in state prisons for men were women, and women constituted only 8 percent of those working in federal institutions for men. However, most of the female correctional officers employed in corrections are working in prisons for men.

Reasons for Women's Entry into Corrections

Women entered correctional work for a variety of reasons. As aforementioned, women fought to work in male institutions because of the greater availability of jobs and the higher pay scales. A study by Jurik and Halemba (1984) cited intrinsic factors, such as the nature of the work and inmate rehabilitation, as the primary reasons for women's entry. Many female officers entered corrections because of the encouragement and support of male relatives already employed in the field (Jurik, 1985a). Zimmer (1986) found the major incentive to become a prison guard was financial. A majority of the women in her study had worked at various lower-paying jobs before seeking prison employment. Likewise, Maghan and McLeish-Blackwell (1991) reported salary as the most important factor in the decision of African

American women to become correctional officers. This finding was attributed to the historically high percentage of African American families headed by women.

> The Black woman, as head of her family, will direct her energies to those areas where there is a solid equal employment ground, good benefits, and the opportunity to earn a pay comparable to that of her male counterparts. (Maghan & McLeish-Blackwell, 1991, p. 89)

Belknap's (1991) research found that female jail officers chose the job for the salary, benefits, and the work experience, with many women hoping to obtain a job in law enforcement.

Supervision Styles of Women Correctional Officers

Despite the unpredictability and danger of the job, correctional work is "essentially custodial and bureaucratic, managing the movement of inmates from place to place and dealing with innumerable forms and regulations" (Britton, 1997, p. 803). Officers are required to see that inmates "do things," obey rules, and arrive and leave food, recreation, or work areas on time (Lombardo, 1989). Correctional work is also largely "people work" requiring a general understanding of human behavior (Farkas & Manning, 1997). Despite the emphasis on self-defense and custodial techniques in training, communicating and interacting with inmates consume a large portion of the day for officers in contact positions. A female officer working in a prison for men explains:

> They don't prepare you [in training], they try to prepare you for the physical part. But that's not what gets to you, it's the mental part. Playing games with the inmates, they're constantly trying to figure out a way to get over you. (Britton, 1997, p. 804)

An officer's choice of style affects his or her ability to accomplish these tasks and obtain inmate compliance. It is also important to recognize that the supervisory style of women may vary by age, seniority level, marital status, and race/ethnicity (Belknap, 1991; Martin & Jurik, 1996; Zimmer, 1986).

Female correctional officers have been described as using a unique style or philosophy, a "softer" approach to the job (Pollock, 1986; Wright & Saylor, 1991; Zupan, 1986). A human service or rehabilitative approach to working with inmates was also characteristic of women officers (Jurik & Halemba, 1984; Jurik, 1985b; Walters, 1992). Female staff were more likely to use a nonphysical means to gain inmate compliance (Kissel & Katsampes, 1980), whereas males were more likely to use threats, intimidation, and physical coercion (Belknap, 1991; Pogrebin & Poole, 1997, 1998). They were also more likely to communicate with inmates and observe their behavior to understand the nature of the problem. Communication and crisis management were used by women officers to prevent an escalation to a physical confrontation (Jurik, 1985a).

Other research has concluded that any differences in orientation, supervision styles, or job performance of women and men is a function of work-related variables. Jurik and Halemba (1984) stated that the attitudes of working women were a function of their position in the organizational structure and immediate working conditions. Belknap (1991) acknowledged that even though the gender and job models both explained the gender differences in jail supervisory style, job-related aspects were the more salient variables.

Several research studies have used hypothetical situations to explore the supervisory style of correctional officers. Farkas (1999) incorporated hypotheticals in her study of officer/inmate interactions. She found that male and female officers performed the job similarly in confrontational situations in which they could apply strategies learned during training. However, women tended to be stricter, adhered more closely to rules, and asserted their authority more often in situations that called for more discretionary decision making. Conversely, male officers were more likely to talk things out with inmates. This stricter, more authoritative approach by female officers was attributed to ongoing problems with acceptance by male coworkers and the pressure many women felt to prove themselves. The job model appeared to be a stronger explanation for gender differences with resistance by male staff as a strong organizational influence on women's supervisory style.

Jenne and Kersting (1996) also used hypotheticals to examine gender differences in the use of aggression by correctional officers. Their findings indicated that male and female officers responded similarly to most inmate incidents and did not generally resort to physical force. Nevertheless, when force was called for, women were as aggressive as their male counterparts in most situations. Where differences existed, female correctional officers tended to be more aggressive than their male peers. The authors suggested that direct challenges to authority may evoke a sense of vulnerability on the part of female officers and the need to take charge by a show of aggression. The findings lend support for the job model in that occupational socialization and the demands of the job accounted for similarities in handling inmates between genders. Moreover, distinctions in job performance resulted from gender-specific barriers confronting women correctional officers.

Gender and reciprocity (the tendency to overlook minor rule violations) were the focus of another study by Jenne and Kersting (1998). The authors measured aggressiveness in inmate encounters through the use of a series of hypothetical prison confrontational situations. Results indicated no differences between women and men working in prisons for men. Female correctional officers did not overlook minor rule violations more frequently than male officers; and similar to their male coworkers, women followed up on their actions with written reports. The type of facility appeared to be a more salient factor than gender. In other words, women and men working in prisons for men faced many of the same exigencies and consequently performed the job in similar ways. The authors added that questions remain concerning whether women were learning to act more like men who have essentially defined the correctional officer role or whether occupational socialization and the demands of the job counter any potential gender differences.

Freeman (2003) also explored gender differences in rule enforcement. In his survey of correctional officers, he found that both male and female officers used similar criteria in determining what behavior constitutes a rule violation. He suggested that occupational socialization and job demands account for similarities in rule enforcement and that differences in rule violation reporting were not a function of gender-specific interpretation.

Although Zimmer (1986) relied primarily on unstructured interviews with female officers, her study was also among a handful of studies that utilized behavior observation. She was able to conduct observations of male and female officers in lunch rooms, locker rooms, and administrative offices. She concluded that female officers must adopt a style that addresses problems basic to the job, but also problems specific to women, including discrimination, harassment, and tokenism. She identified three general patterns of adaptation among female subjects working in prisons for men. The "institutional role" was a style characterized by inflexibility about rule violations and adherence to the established system of rewards and punishments for inmates. This role was used as self-protection from any criticism from male staff. A professional distance was also maintained in relations with inmates and coworkers as a strategy to minimize harassment.

Women in the "modified role" believed that women are inherently unable to perform the job on an equal basis with men. Acknowledging their limitations, these women generally worked safe, noncontact posts and relied on male officers for help with duties and protection from inmates. They tolerated jokes, teasing, and gender-related remarks by the men in exchange for protection and better work relations. Finally, the "inventive role" allowed female officers to adopt a more flexible approach to rules and regulations and to overlook minor violations. Women in this role preferred to work with inmates and developed personalized relations with many of them in order to obtain compliance.

Zimmer's (1986) findings offer support for her interactionist model of women's occupational behavior. Gender-related variables interact with organizational-level factors to produce gender differences in inmate supervisory style. Women often failed to receive adequate socialization during their on-the-job training and were denied access to important information about formal and informal techniques for handling inmates while on the job (Zimmer, 1986, pp. 422–423). This resistance and "freezing out" by male coworkers resulted in women developing a variety of supervisory styles that allowed them to utilize their unique abilities, attitudes, and life experience, yet protected them from scrutiny and harassment.

Thus, the available research is inconclusive in determining whether women employ a unique inmate supervisory style based on their distinctive qualities, attitudes, socialization, and life experience or whether aspects of correctional work influence their approach to the job, or whether both gender-related variables and aspects of the job combine and interact to shape their style. Some scholars attribute the inconsistencies of these research findings to the type of methodology employed. For example, Pollock (2002, p. 197) asserts that the use of hypotheticals may place officers in unrealistic situations in which there is no background or buildup to the incident. "Hypotheticals cannot capture the day-to-day interactions between officers and inmates that builds a relationship and influences how each treats the other." Similarly, surveys and interviews may also be unable to capture the realities and situational exigencies of interactions with inmates.

Actual observation of correctional officers and inmates in the prison environment may be the most suitable method of study. Yet many researchers have been forced to compromise due to the constraints of correctional research. These limitations, such as denial of access and mobility and time constraints, have been identified in a number of studies (Farkas, 1992; Taylor & Tewksbury, 1995; Unnithan, 1986).

Although Zimmer (1986) was able to observe inmate/officer interactions, her observations were circumscribed to certain areas of the prison because of safety and security concerns. This does not mean that researchers should stop trying to access correctional work settings to conduct observations. With increased numbers of women entering correctional work and assuming management positions, more research will be needed to examine how supervisory styles are affected in a changing workplace. As the next few sections demonstrate, even though there is a lack of consensus among researchers, most female and male officers, inmates, and supervisors believe that women do have a different style.

Perceptions of Supervisory Styles

Women overwhelmingly believe that they perform the job as effectively as men or better (Belknap, 1991; Kissel & Katsampes, 1980). Moreover, surveys of female officers also identified a different supervisory style than men. In Belknap's study (1991), 91 percent of female officers asserted that women bring different abilities, skills, and life experiences to the job. The women claimed that female officers are less likely to use force and more likely to talk things out with inmates. In the Kissel and Katsampes (1980) study, female officers described how inmates were better able to relate to women and admitted certain inclinations and feelings to them.

Female jail officers reported that they possessed more effective communication skills, were more efficient at handling inmates, and that inmates responded better to their softer approach (Pogrebin & Poole, 1998). The women equated effective inmate management techniques as analogous to good parenting skills. Farkas (1999) found that female correctional officers viewed themselves as using a more personalized, service-oriented approach to inmates.

Views of Male Coworkers

The attitudes of male officers are generally based on stereotypical assumptions that correctional work is a man's job and that physical strength, aggressiveness, and dominance are the skills/qualities necessary to work effectively in a prison. In a study by Farkas (1999), male correctional officers complained that women were not assertive and authoritative in handling inmates and became too friendly with inmates. As one correctional officer stated:

> Women do not assert themselves with inmates. They lack self-confidence, mainly. I always advise females to forget their manners and trying to be nice. They need to talk louder and act more aggressive. If they act timid, they won't get any respect from inmates. (Farkas, 1999, p. 35)

A major concern was the supposed "lack of toughness, both physically and psychologically, to handle the dangers of prison work" (Walters, 1993, p. 49). Male officers claimed that their personal security and the security of the prison was compromised by the hiring of women (Horne, 1985). A study by Lawrence and Mahan (1998) found that 61 percent of male officers in their sample believed that their female coworkers were in more danger in prison. Many male correctional officers expressed a concern that women did not have the physical strength to deal with a situation that calls for force (Jurik, 1985a; Lawrence & Mahan, 1998; Szockyj, 1989).

Many male officers also acknowledged an instinctive, protective attitude toward female coworkers (Bowersox, 1981; Kissel & Katsampes, 1980; Szockyj, 1989; Zimmer, 1986). Some officers feared that male inmates would assault female officers (Parisi, 1984). This perception was perhaps bolstered in some institutions by the informal division of job assignments into "safe" and "unsafe" with unsafe positions considered inappropriate for women by both male and female officers, as well as supervisors (Britton, 1997). Male staff also voiced a concern about whether women would be able to render assistance to another officer in trouble (Jurik, 1985a; Parisi, 1984; Peterson, 1982) and accordingly expressed a preference for male backup in a volatile situation (Szockyj, 1989).

Although male officers, and even some female staff, believe that women are more vulnerable to physical assault; there is no empirical evidence to support this. Female officers are not assaulted or injured more often than their male colleagues (Lawrence & Mahan, 1998; Rowan, 1996; Wright & Saylor, 1991). Rowan (1996) reported that male officers were assaulted 3.6 times more often than their female counterparts.

Some research has indicated that as female officers increase in numbers and demonstrate their ability to do the job, men will become more accepting of them. Lawrence and Mahan (1998) found that regardless of the reservations of some male officers concerning their physical abilities, most agreed that women can effectively supervise, write reports, maintain personal control under stress, and control verbal confrontations with inmates. Walters (1992, 1993) reported that male officers claimed good working relationships and a higher level of acceptance of women as coworkers.

Moreover, recent findings indicate that resistance to women as coworkers and lack of confidence in their abilities stemmed more from older, more experienced officers (Lawrence & Mahan, 1998), while less experienced, newer staff held the highest opinions of the abilities of female staff (Hemmens, Stohr, Schoeler, & Miller, 2002). This may be attributed to some staff experiencing cynicism in midcareer, which manifests itself in negative attitudes toward groups unlike themselves or in perceived competition (Hemmens et al., 2002, p. 483). Younger, newer officers have also been working in integrated work environments from their date of hire and thus may be more open and accepting of women as coworkers.

Attitudes of Male Inmates

Inmates relayed mixed feelings about women working in prison. They had three basic attitudes: neutral, strongly favored, or adamantly opposed (Zimmer, 1986). To some inmates, the sex of the guard made no difference. Other inmates felt that female officers humanized the prison, were less abusive, and were more willing to talk (Horne, 1985). They also thought female officers were more helpful, understanding, and compassionate (Zimmer, 1986). Petersen (1982) claimed that inmates liked female officers because they fulfilled a role as a sex object.

The inmates who were opposed to women voiced several concerns. They were worried that women would not be able to protect them and some feared for the women's safety (Kissel & Katsampes, 1980). Inmates also resented taking orders and being guarded by a woman; they found it demeaning and a denigration of their masculinity (Horne, 1985; Zimmer, 1986). Inmates also complained that their privacy was violated by the presence of female officers when the women walked by as they were taking showers, dressing, or using the toilet. Finally, some inmates felt the employment of women made the lack of sex more frustrating (Kissel & Katsampes, 1980; Petersen, 1982).

Attitudes of Correctional Administrators

Initially, male prison administrators held a negative attitude toward women working in prisons for men, largely due to safety and security concerns. Moreover, the legal mandate to hire women presented a host of legal problems. Horne (1985) discussed the problems in implementing Title VII's requirements and the burden of lawsuits filed by male and female guards and male inmates. In more recent years, male administrators have developed a more favorable attitude toward the entry of women in prisons for men. In a recent nationwide survey, male administrators reported that "female officers listen better, seldom act 'macho,' have a calming effect, are less confrontational, and often control without using force," (Rowan, 1996, p. 188).

Women in Management Positions

Since the late 1800s, women have held supervisory positions in corrections but only in prisons for women. The Civil Rights legislation of the 1970s was integral to providing women employment in prisons for men and paving the way toward advancement opportunities, for one important reason: "Agencies frequently required staff to have experience in medium or maximum security facilities as a prerequisite for promotion to supervisory or management positions" (Morton, 1991a, p. 37). Given that prisons for women did not have medium and maximum-security levels, the women were not eligible for promotional opportunities. Women slowly rose in the ranks once they were allowed to work in male facilities. In 1979, Margaret Hambrick became the first female warden of a federal, all-male, correctional institution (Altendorf, 2003). The numbers of women working in management positions has increased steadily, especially in male facilities. "In 1991, women accounted for less than 10 percent of management staff in adult correctional institutions, including women's prisons" (Martin & Jurik, 1996, p. 164). Approximately ten years later, women accounted for 25 percent of state wardens and superintendents and 17 percent of federal correctional administrators (ACA, 2003). African American women comprised 5 percent of state managers and 6 percent of managers in the federal system. Of note is that over half (56 percent) of the 525 female state wardens and superintendents administered prisons for men. In 2003, there were only eight women working at the executive level in the state corrections system, as commissioner, director, or secretary of corrections. In the federal system, Kathleen Hawke has held the highest administrative position since 1992 (Kim, Devalve, DeValve, & Johnson, 2003).

Despite these gains, women still face many challenges as wardens, superintendents, and as directors/commissioners in a field and a workplace defined by masculine values and sex-based stereotypes. As the proportion of women in correctional management continues to increase, it will be interesting to discover if their style of management is different and how their numbers and style impact the organization.

Perspectives on Management Styles

Gender differences in management styles, attitudes, or values have also been a subject of debate. Eagly and Johnson (1990, p. 236) suggest that "ingrained sex differences in traits and behaviors, a 'spillover' of gender roles onto organizational roles, and subtle differences in the structural positions of men and women could cause behavior to be somewhat sex differentiated." There is evidence that men and women have distinctive approaches to management based on gender-based qualities or attributes. In Statham's study (1987), female managers were characterized as "person-invested" and "task-engrossed." The women focused on accomplishing the task, and they used their people orientation to motivate, support, organize, and make the most effective use of staff. They tended to be hands-on managers, becoming involved in all tasks. Male managers, on the other hand, were seen as "image-engrossed" and "autonomy-invested." Men in management were focused on the importance of their job to the organization and emphasized the need for autonomy for themselves and their subordinates. Good management meant delegating responsibility and letting employees be responsible for their actions.

Female managers tended to adopt a more democratic or participative style, whereas men used a more autocratic or directive style, according to a study by Eagly and Johnson (1990). Women used a collaborative, participative style to win acceptance from others, to gain self-confidence, and to become more effective.

Styles of management have been referred to as "feminine" and "masculine" depending on the stereotypic sex-based qualities or values expressed. Loden (1985) discussed a masculine mode of management characterized by the qualities of competitiveness, hierarchical authority, high control for the leader, and unemotional and analytic problem solving. The feminine management style, preferred by women, was characterized by cooperativeness, collaboration with subordinates, lower control for the leader, and problem solving based on intuition and empathy, as well as rationality. Sloan and Krone (2000) contend that the feminine style of management operates from more traditional feminine values that invite participation, new ideas, and the sharing of organizational information.

Although the feminine style has been more closely associated with female managers, it can also be employed by men. On the other hand, women may adopt a masculine management style even though it is more common among male managers (Sloan & Krone, 2000; Statham, 1987). Eagly and Johnson (1990) found that when there were few women in leadership roles, they tended to abandon a stereotypically feminine style of management to establish authority.

Workers perceive men and women managers in different ways and have different expectations of them. Statham (1987) indicated that, in general, female employees preferred the feminine style of management and men preferred the masculine style of management. Female staff appreciated the support and the time and energy invested in their development by women managers. Male workers seemed to enjoy the autonomy provided by male managers.

For women entering male-dominated and traditionally male work domains, such as corrections, the temptation may be to assume a more masculine style of management. Women working as wardens and superintendents of male institutions confront the challenge of an occupation defined historically, and at present, by masculine values. It is an occupation shaped by a long line of male leadership holding these values and perceptions of their work.

Management Styles of Female Wardens and Superintendents

Research on the management styles of women employed as wardens and superintendents is very sparse. Only a handful of studies have investigated the orientation, management styles, and work experience of women correctional administrators. Kim et al. (2003) examined whether there were gender differences in managerial philosophy, job satisfaction, and attitudes of wardens toward inmate programs, prison goals, and factors influencing prison operations. They surveyed 641 wardens of state adult correctional facilities. Approximately 85.9 percent of the sample were male and 14.1 percent were female. The majority of female wardens were Caucasian and slightly younger than their male peers with a mean age of 45. They were also more highly educated than the men with 61 percent having completed post-baccalaureate educational coursework.

Results revealed that female wardens (89.9 percent) were slightly more likely than their male peers (83.3 percent) to emphasize the importance of rehabilitation. They were also less inclined than their male counterparts to make prison conditions more harsh for the sake of deterrence. The women were more likely to reduce amenities that could potentially promote violence in prison and to be more concerned about health conditions of inmates. They were also more receptive to suggestions from line staff for policy recommendations. In addition, female wardens were also less likely to seek support from colleagues to address stresses of the job, while their male counterparts pointed to more staff with whom they could talk about the job. This finding was attributed to a lack of comfort felt by the women in discussing their decisions for fear of appearing weak or incompetent in the minds of their colleagues.

Altendorf (2003) conducted in-depth interviews with twenty-nine female wardens from twenty-one states. Most of the women were Caucasian with the exception of one African American woman. The wardens worked primarily in institutions for men. The women believed that they brought distinctive skills to their position, including the ability to communicate well, to create a supportive environment, to work with staff, and to organize and multitask. They overwhelmingly agreed that they had to work much harder that their male peers to prove themselves. They also felt under greater scrutiny and held to higher standards of professionalism. The female wardens tried to create professional relations with coworkers and inmates. They accomplished this by being careful not to discuss personal issues and maintaining a distance. Socializing with colleagues was also avoided.

Dealing with the stereotypes of women working in traditionally male fields was a major complaint of the women. These stereotypes included the notion that they worked in a "masculine occupation" because they either hate men or were looking for a husband, or that they became a warden by sleeping their way to the position or having political connections. Female wardens in the study felt resentment from both female and male coworkers, which they ascribed to a dislike of having a female supervisor on the part of some employees. Most women indicated that they were not interested in being "one of the boys," and that they have tried to maintain their "femininity." The following quote is illustrative:

> Yes, I have maintained my femininity because I like who I am. I can still mix with the boys; but I have no desire to spit tobacco, scratch, lower my face, or curse. By the same token, I do not appear to be a withering flower who needs a man to protect her while walking the inmate yard. (Altendorf, 2003, p. 16)

Female wardens reported trying to find a management style that works for them. They were working hard to incorporate their own values and beliefs about how coworkers and inmates should be managed. However, they were not immune from the problems of gender-based expectations, stereotypes, and harassment in the workplace. In fact, their visibility at the top resulted in greater scrutiny and evaluation of their behavior and decision making.

Major Obstacles for Women

Masculine-defined work environments may be more hostile and intimidating to women because women are perceived as challenging deeply held beliefs about male superiority for that type of work (Swerdlow, 1989). Women's greater visibility in this type of work environment draws attention and underscores gender-based status differences (Gruber, 1998). Women face major obstacles, including a heightened level of job stress and gender and sexual harassment, in the correctional workplace.

Increased Occupational Stress

A higher level of stress has been identified in several studies on women working in corrections (Cheek & Miller, 1983; Savicki, Cooley, & Gjesvold, 2003; Cullen, Link, Wolf, & Frank, 1985; Lovrich & Stohr, 1993; Pogrebin & Poole, 1998; Wright & Saylor, 1991). Cullen et al. (1985) reported that female officers experienced an increased level of job stress, particularly if employed at male institutions. They questioned whether the women's stress was "caused by the inherent nature of the job, and constraints by fellow male officers, and sustained by the administration's organizational policies" (Cullen et al., 1985, p. 524).

Women also reported greater work-related stress than men in a study by Wright and Saylor (1991). The authors concluded that the higher stress level was related to the vulnerability to physical assault identified by female prison staff. Moreover, the sexist environment of prison work, resistance by male coworkers, sexual harassment by inmates and fellow staff, and conflicting occupational and gender-role demands were also suggested as contributing factors (p. 522).

Lovrich and Stohr (1993) found that female officers reported greater psychosomatic stress, including obsessive compulsiveness, interpersonal anxiety, and anxiety than their male counterparts. Another study by Triplett, Mullings, and Scarborough (1999) identified a greater level of work–home conflict among female officers leading to a greater level of work-related stress. The findings suggested that "women are still dealing with the conflict engendered by a culture that holds one set of role expectations for women at home and another set for them at work" (Triplett et al., 1999, p. 384).

Harassment, especially gender-based harassment, was also a significant and unique source of stress for women officers (Pogrebin & Poole, 1997, 1998; Savicki et al., 2003). Derogatory remarks by male coworkers and the denigration of women's job performance contributed to their level of stress. Moreover, the job stress was exacerbated by their lack of informal types of occupational support, such as the peer groups used by their male coworkers (Pogrebin & Poole, 1997, 1998). Women, in effect, were denied a means of validating the stressfulness of their job; as well as an important way to mitigate stress.

Race was also an important variable related to stress in a handful of studies. Van Voorhis et al. (1991) found that African American women were more likely to perceive their work as dangerous, stressful, or dissatisfying. This finding was somewhat mitigated by organizational support. Although Britton (1997) discovered that African American female officers felt less stress, the women also reported that their jobs were less satisfying, regardless of the institutional context in which they worked. This decreased job satisfaction was attributed to interactions with coworkers. Caucasian women reported higher levels of job satisfaction and pointed to supervision as the most important aspect. Britton suggested that Caucasian women may compare themselves with minority women in assessing their own levels of satisfaction and feel relatively less deprived.

Differences in coping mechanisms have also been identified between female and male officers. Hurst and Hurst (1997) found that although there were no differences in how men and women were affected by stress; they did process stress differently. Women sought social and emotional support to deal with stress; whereas males used "planful problem solving" (deliberate analysis of a solution). "Female officers were more likely to seek tangible and informational support to cope with the event, while male officers were slightly more likely to look for an analytical solution first" (Hurst & Hurst, 1997, p. 133). The findings indicated that correctional officers followed traditional sex roles in coping with occupational stress.

Gender and Sexual Harassment

Gender harassment refers to nonsexual negative comments about a woman's ability to perform the job, while sexual harassment refers to offensive sexual comments or behaviors (Belknap, 1991). Occupations that are traditionally and predominantly male have an increased risk of both types of harassment (Belknap, 1991; Gruber, 1998; LaFontaine & Tredeau, 1986; Savicki et al., 2003; Stohr, Mays, Beck, & Kelley, 1998). The resistance of male coworkers to women working in correctional facilities has been documented in numerous studies (Fry & Glaser, 1987; Jurik, 1985b; Jurik & Halemba, 1984; Peterson, 1982; Zimmer, 1986). Although male staff members were largely opposed, these attitudes varied depending on a number of factors. As one experienced correctional administrator observed:

> The level of opposition by male staff to the integration of women varied dramatically among institutions. This was apparently due to differences in organizational culture, such as officer cliques or tradition. In some cases, individual women were accepted while the concept of women working in the prisons was rejected. Strong personalities were a major factor, with some individuals affecting, either positively or negatively, whole institutions or shifts within the facility. (Johnson, 1991, p. 11)

Gender harassment is the most common type experienced by women working in prisons for men. This harassment includes gender-based insults, condescending and demeaning behavior toward women, and paternalistic treatment. Female officers complained of male coworkers making overt statements of opposition to their presence, spreading rumors about them, reporting them to supervisors, and undermining their chances of receiving favorable performance appraisals (Johnson, 1991, p. 94). Belknap (1991) found an overwhelmingly majority (70 percent) of female officers in her sample believed that women as a group tended to be "put-down" and demeaned by male officers. In a study by Savicki et al. (2003, p. 617) gender was four times as likely to be identified as a primary source of harassment. Gender harassment was not only a significant contributor to stress for female officers but also played a role in reducing organizational commitment and in increasing intentions to leave.

Sexual harassment includes sexual propositions, sexual innuendos, jokes, pranks, and unwanted touching. Males maintain their occupational and situational dominance by sexualizing the work environment through such actions (Martin & Jurik, 1996; Pogrebin & Poole, 1997). Swerdlow (1989) asserts that the sexualization and objectification of female coworkers are really modes of accommodation used by men to minimize the threat produced by the entry of women. According to sex role spillover theory (Gutek & Morasch, 1982), sexual harassment occurs because traditional gender-based roles "spill over" into the workplace. This spillover is more likely to occur when men have the numerical advantage. Male-skewed work groups set the stage for the playing out of traditional sex roles (Goldberg, 2001). Not surprisingly, male workers employed in male-dominated jobs are less inclined to define their behavior as sexual harassment than men employed in gender-integrated jobs (Konrad & Gutek, 1986).

"In criminal justice workplaces, males tend to have more achieved, ascribed (by virtue of their gender), and situational power than women. Men are more likely to be supervisors, to be paid more, and to be privy to more information (achieved power)" (Stohr et al., 1998, p. 139). Several studies have indicated that female correctional officers experience more sexual harassment on the job than their male counterparts (Belknap, 1991; Petersen, 1982; Pogrebin & Poole, 1998; Savicki et al., 2003). Altendorf (2003) also found that female wardens experienced discrimination and sexual harassment in the workplace. The women spoke of rumors concerning their sexuality and "sleeping their way to the top."

One study by Petersen (1982, p. 453) described the sexual rumor mill working informally in prisons for men. Sexual interactions and liasions were alleged between certain female officers and male staff or inmates. Very few of these rumors were investigated or substantiated and so the women were forever labeled and under suspicion. These allegations of sexual misconduct serve the purpose of superimposing sexual identities on the women officers and reinforcing traditional dominant and subordinate roles for the sexes. Relating to women who are defined in sexual terms is less ambiguous and less intimidating for male staff (Swerdlow, 1989).

Interestingly, many female correctional officers and managers who experienced harassment did not pursue formal channels but rather tried to handle the matter on a personal level (Altendorf, 2003; Belknap, 1991). Caucasian women officers are more likely than African American women to report sexual harassment (Martin & Jurik, 1996). Part of the reason may be that gender and racial discrimination becomes blurred for African American women since they experience both types of behavior (Maghan & McLeish-Blackwell, 1991). The women may also feel that their claims will be taken less seriously than those of their Caucasian counterparts and that their "outsider status" will be furthered reinforced (Martin & Jurik, 1996).

In a study of sexual harassment and women jail officers, Stohr et al. (1998) noted that few victims of sexual harassment used the complaints process. Victims were reluctant to report the harassment for a number of reasons: a belief that it will do no good, a preference to resolve the matter informally, uncertainty about whether the behavior was actually prohibited by law, or fear of further harassment or retaliation (Stohr et al., 1998; Zimmer, 1986, 1989). Altendorf (2003) found that most female wardens handled discrimination or harassment by accepting it as part of the job, ignoring it, or confronting it on a personal level. The women stated that they would have filed a grievance or a lawsuit if they were working at a lower level in the organization. They felt that formally addressing harassment would bring negative attention to their position and have a negative effect on their career prospects.

As women achieve more situational and achieved power in the workplace, the hope is that harassment will be reduced. Stohr et al. (1998) reported a low level of harassment in jails where women were in a majority and occupied some of the midlevel management positions. However, recent findings from the interviews with women wardens occupying the highest position in their prisons indicates that harassment still is a problem that warrants attention and ongoing preventive and corrective efforts.

Conclusion

This chapter has examined the occupational experience of women working as correctional officers in prisons and jails. We explored gender differences in the orientation and supervisory or management styles of the women. Although support was shown for the gender model, this model alone does not provide an adequate explanation for differences in the work behavior of women in corrections. The job model asserts that gender differences may be superceded by aspects of the job and even homogenized over time and with exposure to occupational socialization and a strong male culture. The correctional workplace with its hierarchical structure, paramilitary organization, and masculine norms and values, most certainly has a significant influence on women's occupational behavior. The question remains whether "homogenizing" the supervisory style of women to a "male model" of supervision is the most appropriate or effective strategy for integrating women into corrections or even for managing inmates.

The importance of the interactionist perspective was also demonstrated in explaining the dynamics that occur in the correctional institution. As previously mentioned, the interactionist model posits that women's occupational behavior is the sum of the interaction of their unique characteristics, including attributes, orientation, and life experience (the gender model), and the characteristics and conditions of the work place (the job model). Utilizing a male model of inmate supervisory style may simply increase the job stress for women as they attempt to reproduce this style and submerge their orientation and unique style. The hostility and harassment toward women may also increase as male officers evaluate women's job performance according to this standard. The study by Eagly, Makhijani, and Klonsky (1992) showed that when women occupying male-dominated roles adopted a stereotypically masculine style, employees evaluated them more negatively. Women adopting this style received negative reactions, resistance, and a lack of acceptance by coworkers.

The reality is that there will be different styles of inmate supervision based on individuals, male or female (Pollock, 1995, p. 114). Male officers should be flexible in their approach, utilizing "feminine-defined" skills of communication and responsiveness, and alternatively, women should be flexible in employing a "masculine" style, becoming assertive or authoritative as the situation warrants. Neither gender should feel pressure to adopt a style that does not fit with their orientation or values. Each individual officer and manager needs to find an approach that works, yet still be willing to find out what style is most effective in specific situations. One female correctional administrator summed it up:

> [Managers] need to recognize that all employees bring different gifts and talents to the workplace. Both genders know that protecting society is important, but methods to achieve this goal may differ since we all have unique gifts to contribute. Managers need to embrace inclusiveness. They cannot afford to exclude creative, talented individuals who try new approaches. (Libolt, 1991, p. 138)

Harassment and resistance to women working in prisons for men were also discussed in this chapter. Despite the increasing numbers of women entering corrections as officers and managers, recent evidence shows that this continues to be a significant problem for women. Gender and sexual harassment continue to impede the full integration and utilization of women in corrections. The consequence of this harassment is that women approach the job in a defensive manner trying to protect themselves from the scrutiny and abuse of their male colleagues. They become hesitant to use their own style of supervision for fear of criticism.

Additional consequences of harassment are increased work stress and problems with the retention of female officers. Harassment plays a large role in increasing intentions to leave the job for women in corrections (Savicki et al., 2003). This has huge implications for correctional administrators if labor force projections hold true. The construction of new prisons and the expansion of existing facilities will create an estimated 25,300 openings for correctional officers to be filled each year for the next ten years (Kieckbush, 2001). With women comprising approximately half of our labor pool, their recruitment and later retention will become priorities for correctional managers (Stojkovic & Farkas, 2003).

In a study by Gruber and Smith (1995), women responded more assertively to unwanted sexual attention when policies, a complaint procedure, and a training program were in place. They were more likely to file a complaint or tell someone in a position of authority. However, it is not enough to simply establish policies and procedures; employees must perceive organizational intolerance to harassment and visible and credible methods of addressing the problem (Gruber, 1998). Women officers need to know that their complaints will be taken seriously and acted upon. Male officers need to know that hostile, harassing, and discriminatory behavior will not be tolerated and that there will be consequences. For the correctional workplace to change, correctional administrators need to become change agents.

Women who hold management positions in corrections have additional responsibilities in addressing harassment and discrimination. As managers, they must take a proactive, visible stance to change workplace norms that encourage or tolerate sexist or racist behavior and lead by example. As victims of gender and sexual harassment and discrimination, they must not try to handle it informally, but pursue formal channels. A change in attitude, behavior, and work culture must start at the top level, and women administrators are assuming positions to institute that change.

Review Questions

1. Discuss the four explanatory models or perspectives of women's occupational behavior.

2. What were the goals of separate prisons for women? Describe the role of the matron. Why did women want to work in prisons for men?

3. What were the two legal arguments utilized to prevent women from working in prisons for men?

4. Describe the characteristics of a sex-typed male occupation or masculine occupation.

5. Describe the attitudes of male coworkers, inmates, and supervisors to women working as correctional officers in prisons for men.

6. What are the research findings regarding gender differences in the supervisory styles of men and women correctional officers?

7. Discuss how stereotypes and gender-based expectations affect the job performance of women correctional officers.

8. Identify some of the obstacles facing women working as correctional officers.

9. What are the research findings regarding gender differences in the management styles of men and women?

10. Discuss how stereotypes and gender-based expectations affect the job performance of women wardens and superintendents.

11. Identify some of the obstacles facing women working as wardens and superintendents.

12. Define and give examples of gender harassment and sexual harassment.

13. Discuss how the full integration and utilization of women as correctional officers in male institutions can be accomplished.

Key Terms

Sex-typed male occupation
Gendered organizational logic
Gender model
Job model
Integrated model
Interactionist perspective
Bona fide occupational qualification (BFOQ)
Sex-role spillover theory

Institutional role
Modified role
Inventive role
Feminine management style
Masculine management style
Gender harassment
Sexual harassment

References

Altendorf, K. (2003). *Success strategies of female prison wardens: Managing gender identity in a nontraditional occupation.* Unpublished doctoral dissertation. Oklahoma State University, Stillwater.

American Correctional Association. (2003). *Directory of adult and juvenile correctional departments, agencies, and probation and parole authorities.* Lanham, MD: American Correctional Association.

Belknap, J. (1991). Women in conflict: An analysis of women correctional officers. *Women and Criminal Justice* 2 (2), 89–115.

Bennett, K. (1995). Constitutional issues in cross-gender searches and visual observation of nude inmates by opposite-sex officers: A battle between and within the sexes. *The Prison Journal* 75 (1), 90–112.

Bowersox, M. S. (1981). Women in corrections. Competence, competition and the social responsibility norm. *Criminal Justice and Behavior* 8 (4), 491–499.

Britton, D. (1997). Perceptions of the work environment among correctional officers: Do race and sex matter? *Criminology* 35 (1), 85–105.

Cheek, F. E., & Miller, M. (1983). The experience of stress for correction officers: A double-bind theory of correctional stress. *Journal of Criminal Justice* 11, 105–120.

Crouch, B. (1985). Pandora's box: Women guards in mens' prisons. *Journal of Criminal Justice* 13, 535–548.

Cullen, F. T., Link, B. G., Wolfe, N. T., & Frank, J. (1985). The social dimensions of correctional officer stress. *Justice Quarterly* 2, 505–533.

Dobash, R. P., Dobash, R. E., & Gutteridge, S. (1986). *The imprisonment of women.* New York: Basil Blackwell.

Eagly, A. H., & JohnsonB. T. (1990). Gender and leadership style: A meta-analysis. *Psychological Bulletin* 108 (2), 233–256.

Eagly, A. H., Makhijani, M. G., & Klonsky, B. G. (1992). Gender and the evaluation of leaders: A meta-analysis. *Psychological Bulletin* 111 (1), 3–22.

Etheridge, R., Hale, C., & Hambrick, M. (1991). Coping strategies for women in all-male correctional facilities.

In J. Morton (Ed.), *Change, challenge, and choices: Women's role in modern corrections* (pp. 59–81). Laurel, MD: American Correctional Association.

Farkas, M. A. (1992). The impact of the correctional field setting on the research experience: A research chronicle. *Journal of Crime and Justice* 15 (2), 177–184.

Farkas, M. A., & Rand. K. (1997). Female correctional officers and prisoner privacy. *Marquette Law Review* 80 (4), 995–1030.

Farkas, M. A., & Rand, K. (1999). Sex matters: A gender-specific standard for cross-gender searches of inmates. *Women and Criminal Justice* 10 (3), 31-55.

Farkas, M. A., & Manning, P. K. (1997). The occupational culture of corrections and police officers. *Journal of Crime and Justice* 20 (2), 51–68.

Farkas, M. A. (1999). Inmate supervisory style: Does gender make a difference? *Women and Criminal Justice* 10 (4), 25–45.

Feinman, C. (1986). *Women in the criminal justice system* (2nd ed.). New York: Praeger.

Feldberg, R. L., & Glenn, E. N. (1979). Male and female: Job vs. gender models in the sociology of work. *Sociology of Work* 26 (2), 524–537.

Freedman, E. B. (1974). Their sisters' keepers. An historical perspective in female correctional institutions in the United States: 1870–1900. *Feminist Studies* 2 (1), 77–95.

Freeman, R. (2003). Social distance and discretionary law enforcement in a womens' prison. *The Prison Journal* 83 (2), 191–205.

Fry, L. J., & Glaser, D. (1987). Gender differences in work adjustment of prison employees. *Journal of Offender Counseling Services and Rehabilitation* 12 (1), 39–52.

Goldberg, C. B. (2001). The impact of the proportion of women in one's workgroup, profession, and friendship circle on males' and females' response to sexual harassment. *Sex Roles* 4 (5/6), 359–374.

Gruber, J. E., & Smith, M. (1995). Womens' response to sexual harassment. A multivariate analysis. *Basic and Applied Social Psychology* 17, 543–562.

Gruber, J. E. (1998). The impact of male work environments and organizational policies on women's experiences of sexual harassment. *Gender and Society* 12 (3), 301–320.

Gutek, B. A., & Morasch, B. (1982). Sex ratios, sex role spillover and sexual harassment of women at work. *Journal of Social Issues* 38, 55–74.

Harris, M. K. (1998). Women's imprisonment in the United States. *Corrections Today* 60, 74–80.

Hawkes, M. G. (1991). Women's changing roles in corrections. In J. Morton (Ed.), *Change, challenge, and choices: Women's role in modern corrections* (pp. 100–110). Laurel, MD: American Correctional Association.

Hemmens, C., Stohr, M. K., Schoeler, M., & Miller, B. (2002). One step up, two steps back. The progression of perceptions of women's work in prisons and jails. *Journal of Criminal Justice* 30, 473–489.

Horne, P. (1985). Female correction officers. *Federal Probation* 49, 46–54.

Hurst, T. E., & Hurst, M. M. (1997). Gender differences in mediation of severe occupational stress among correctional officers. *American Journal of Criminal Justice* 22 (1), 121–137.

Jenne, D. L., & Kersting, R. C. (1996). Aggression and women correctional officers in male prisons. *The Prison Journal* 76 (4), 442–460.

Jenne, D. L., & Kersting, R. C. (1998). Gender, power, and reciprocity in the correctional setting. *The Prison Journal* 78 (2), 166–185.

Johnson, P. (1991). Why employ women? In J. Morton (Ed.), *Change, challenge, and choices: Women's role in modern corrections* (pp. 6–12). Laurel, MD: American Correctional Association.

Jurik, N. C., & Halemba, G. J. (1984). Gender, working conditions, and the job satisfaction of women in a nontraditional occupation: Female correctional officers in men's prisons. *The Sociological Quarterly* 25 (4), 551–566.

Jurik, N. C. (1985a). An officer and a lady: Organizational barriers to women working as correctional officers in mens' prisons. *Social Problems* 32 (4), 375–388.

Jurik, N. C. (1985b). Striking a balance: Female correctional officers, gender role stereotypes, and male prisons. *Sociological Inquiry* 58 (3), 291–305.

Kieckbush, R. G. (2001). The looming correctional work force shortage: A problem of supply and demand. *Corrections Compendium* 26 (4), 1–3, 24–25.

Kim, A., Devalve, M., DeValve, E. Q., & Johnson, W. W. (2003). Female wardens: Results from a national survey of state correctional executives. *The Prison Journal* 83 (4), 406–425.

Kissel, P. J., & Katsampes, P. L. (1980). The impact of women corrections officers on the functioning of institutions housing male inmates. *Journal of Offender Counseling, Services, and Rehabilitation* 4 (3), 213–231.

Konrad, A. M., & Gutek, B. A.(1986). Impact of experiences toward sexual harassment. *Administrative Science Quarterly* 31, 422–438.

Lafontaine, E., & Tredeau, L. (1986). The frequency, sources, and correlations of sexual harassment. *Administrative Science Quarterly* 31, 422–438.

Lawrence, R., & Mahan, S. (1998). Women corrections officers in men's prisons: A acceptance and perceived job performance. *Women and Criminal Justice* 9 (3), 63–86.

Libolt, A. (1991). Bridging the gender gap. *Corrections Today* 53 (7), 136–138.

Loden, R. (1985). *Feminine leadership or how to succeed in business without being one of the boys.* New York: Times Books.

Lombardo, L. X. (1989). *Guards imprisoned. Correctional officers at work* (2nd ed.). Cincinnati: Anderson Publishing Company.

Lovrich, N., & Stohr, M. (1993). Gendered jail work. Correctional policy implications of perceptual diversity in the workplace. *Policy Studies Review* 12, 66–85.

Maghan, J., & McLeish-Blackwell, L. (1991). Black women in correctional employment. In J. Morton (Ed)., *Change, challenge, and choices: Women's role in modern corrections* (pp. 82–99). Laurel, MD: American Correctional Association.

Martin, S., & Jurik, N. (1996). *Doing justice, doing gender.* Thousand Oaks, CA: Sage.

Merlo, A. V., & Pollock, J. M. (Eds.). (1995). *Women, law and social control.* Boston: Allyn and Bacon.

Miller, J., Schooler, C., Kohn, M. L., & Miller, K. A. (1979). Women and work: The psychological effects of occupational conditions. *American Journal of Sociology* 85, 66–94.

Morton, J. (1991a). Women correctional officers: A ten-year update. In J. Morton (Ed.), *Change, challenge, and choices: Women's role in modern corrections* (pp. 19–39). Laurel, MD: American Correctional Association.

Morton, J. (1991b). What does the future hold? In J. Morton (Ed.), *Change, challenge, and choices: Women's role in modern corrections* (pp. 111–114). Laurel, MD: American Correctional Association.

Morton, J. (1992). Women in corrections. Looking back on 200 years of valuable contributions. *Corrections Today* 18, 76–87.

Parisi, N. (1984). The female correctional officer: Her progress and prospects for equality. *The Prison Journal* 64, 92–109.

Peterson, C. (1982). Doing time with the boys: An analysis of women correctional officers in all-male facilities. In

B. P. Raffel & N. J. Sokoloff (Eds.), *The criminal justice system and women. Women offenders, victims, and workers* (pp. 437–460). New York: Clark Boardman.

Pogrebin, M., & Poole, E. (1997). The sexualized work environment: a look at women jail officers. *The Prison Journal* 77 (1), 41–57.

Pogrebin, M., & Poole, E. (1998). Women deputies in jail work. *Journal of Contemporary Criminal Justice* 14 (2), 117–134.

Pollock, J. M. (1986). *Sex and supervision: Guarding male and female inmates.* New York: Greenwood Press.

Pollock, J. M. (1995). Women in corrections: Custody and the "caring ethic." In A. V. Merlo & J. M. Pollock (Eds.), *Women, law, and social control* (pp. 97–116). Boston: Allyn and Bacon.

Pollock, J. M. (2002). *Women, prison, and crime.* Belmont, CA: Wadsworth Thomson Learning.

Rafter, N. H. (1990). *Partial justice: Women, prison, and social control.* New Brunswick, NJ: Transaction Books.

Rowan, J. L. (1996). Who is safer in male maximum security prisons? *Corrections Today* 58 (2), 186–189.

Savicki, V., Cooley, E., & Gjesvold, J. (2003). Harassment as a predictor of job burnout in correctional officers. *Criminal Justice and Behavior* 30 (5), 602–619.

Sloan, D. K., & Krone, K. J. (2000). Women managers and gendered values. *Women's Studies in Communication* 23 (1), 111–130.

Statham, A. (1987). The gender model revisited: Differences in the management styles of men and women. *Sex Roles* 16 (7/8), 409–429.

Stohr, M. K., Mays, G. L., Beck, A. C., & Kelley, T. (1998). Sexual harassment in women's jails. *Journal of Contemporary Criminal Justice* 14 (2), 135–155.

Stojkovic, S., & Farkas, M. A. (2003). *Correctional leadership. A cultural perspective.* Belmont, CA: Thomson/Wadsworth Learning.

Swerdlow, M. (1989). Men's accommodation to women entering a nontraditional occupation. A case of rapid transit operatives. *Gender and Society* 3 (3), 373–387.

Szockyj, E. (1989). Working in a man's world: Women correctional officers in an institution for men. *Canadian Journal of Criminology* 31 (3), 319–328.

Taylor, J. M., & Tewksbury, R. (1995). From the inside out and the outside in: Team research in the correctional setting. *Journal of Contemporary Criminal Justice* 11 (2), 119–134.

Triplett, R., Mullings, J. L., & Scarborough, K. E. (1999). Examining the effect of work-home conflict on work-related stress among correctional officers. *Journal of Criminal Justice* 27 (4), 371–385.

Unnithan, P. (1986). Research in a correctional setting: Constraints and biases. *Journal of Criminal Justice* 14, 401–412.

Van Voorhis, P., Cullen, F. T., Link, B.G., & Wolfe, N. T. (1991). The impact of race and gender on correctional officers' orientation to the integrated environment. *Journal of Research in Crime and Delinquency* 28 (4), 472–500.

Walters, S. (1992). Attitudinal and demographic differences between male and female correctional officers. *Journal of Offender Rehabilitation* 18, 173–189.

Walters, S. (1993). Changing the guard: Male correctional officers' attitudes toward women as co-workers. *Journal of Offender Rehabilitation* 20 (1/2), 47–60.

Wright, K., & Saylor, W. G. (1991). Male and female employees' perceptions of prison work: Is there a difference? *Justice Quarterly* 8, 505–524.

Zimmer, L. (1986). *Women guarding men.* Chicago: University of Chicago Press.

Zimmer, L. (1989). Solving women's employment problems in corrections: Shifting the burden to administrators. *Women and Criminal Justice* 1, 55–79.

Zupan, L. (1986). Gender-related differences in correctional officers' perceptions and Attitudes. *Journal of Criminal Justice* 14 (4), 349–361.

Zupan, L. (1992). The progress of women correctional officers in all-male prisons. In I. Moyer (Ed.), *The changing roles of women in the criminal justice system* (2nd ed.; pp. 323–343). Prospect Heights, IL: Waveland Press.

Cases Cited

Carl v. Angalone 8883 F. Supp. 1433 (1995)

Dothard v. Rawlinson 433 U.S. 321 (1977)

Gunther v, Iowa State Men's Reformatory 462 F. Supp. 952 (1979)

Grummet v. Rushen 779 F.2d. 491 (1985)

Jordan v. Gardner 986 F.2d. 1521 (9th Cir. 1993) *(en banc)*

7

The Practice of Law in the Twenty-First Century*

Frances Bernat

*An earlier version of this paper was presented at the *Academy of Criminal Justice Sciences* annual meeting. Las Vegas, NV, March 9–13, 2004.

The number of women practicing law and attending law schools has been continually increasing since the 1970s (Kim, 2001). In the early 1970s, very few women were admitted to law schools and the percentage of women practicing law was small. By the end of the 1970s, due in large part to affirmative action laws and litigation, women accounted for about one-third of those students admitted into law schools. Presently, approximately one-half of any given law school class is comprised of women. The percentage of women practicing law has been slowly but steadily increasing since the 1970s. According to the American Bar Association's Commission on Women in the Profession (American Bar Association, hereafter ABA, 1995a), in 1960 and in 1971, only 3 percent of the 286,000 and 355,000 practicing attorneys, respectively, were women. Women accounted for 8 percent of the 542,205 lawyers in 1980 and 13 percent of the 655,191 lawyers in 1985.

By the early 1990s, women comprised 20 percent of the 805,872 lawyers. In recent years, the profession has exceeded one million members, with women accounting for 27 percent of all lawyers in 2000, and 29 percent of all lawyers in 2003 (ABA, 1995b; ABA, 2003). Women account for only about 6 percent of law school tenured faculty but hold a majority of the part-time and clinical practice positions (ABA, 2003; Wald, 1989; White, 1999). In 2002, law school faculties reported that 33 percent of their faculty were women, with 52 percent of female law faculty holding the rank of assistant professors and only 21 percent employed full time (ABA, Commission on Women in the Profession, 2003).

Despite the increased numbers, female attorneys still voice strong concerns about employment opportunity, equality, acceptance of their work, and the contributions they make to their firms. The ABA Commission on Women in the Profession held hearings throughout 2003 in order to determine the status of women in the legal profession with a focus on equality for female lawyers (Tebo, 2003). Many female attorneys still report experiencing a "glass ceiling" that prevents them from advancing in their careers. In 2000, women accounted for 16 percent of law partners and 14 percent of those serving as general counsel in Fortune 500 companies (Catalyst, 2001). When evaluating which lawyers to promote and which lawyers are most valuable to the firm, law firms appear to ignore particular contributions made by female associates. Gendered evaluation practices maintain a prevailing belief that women will leave their work for their family or that women are less committed to their jobs than men.

History of Women in the Legal Profession

In the first half of the twentieth century, the legal profession excluded women. The almost total exclusion of women was based on social, cultural views of women (Bernat, 1992; Pollock & Ramierez, 1995). In one of the earliest cases to articulate the reasons why courts are no places for ladies, the U.S. Supreme Court in *Bradwell v. Illinois* (83 U.S. 130 [1873]) held that women did not have a fundamental privilege to participate in every profession. The court's majority focused on a strict interpretation of the Fourteenth Amendment's privileges and immunities clause. Justice Bradley's concurring opinion highlights the moral attitude underlying the decision:

> Man is, or should be, women's protector and defender. The natural and proper timidity and
> delicacy which belongs to the female sex evidently unfits it for many of the occupations of

civil life. The constitution of the family organization, which is founded in the divine ordinance, as well as in the nature of things, indicates the domestic sphere as that which properly belongs to the domain and functions of womanhood. (Cited in Wortman, 1985, p. 257)

Courts routinely denied women's access to the practice of law by reasoning that women's nature would be harmed by work outside the home or by work that required mental tenacity. Courts argued that women were too emotional and sentimental and as such were unfit for legal practice.

Slowly, standards for entrance into the profession began to change. States and law schools, particularly in the West, began to remove gender language that would bar women from admission. The most common way for women to gain entrance during this time was by attending law school. Women had a difficult time finding a practicing lawyer who would provide them with a clerkship, the prevailing method of legal entry in the nineteenth century. As law school education gained preference during the first part of the twentieth century as the primary requirement qualifying a person to take bar examinations necessary for admission into the profession, women began to enroll in progressive schools that were increasingly willing to educate them. However, school charters in the provincial Eastern states specifically excluded women as students. Entrance in the older and more prestigious institutions required removal of the gendered language before women could be eligible for admission. Harvard Law School's charter, for example, was one of the last to be changed and that school admitted twelve female students in 1950. Not surprisingly, women did not account for a large percentage of lawyers during this time. In 1910, 558 women accounted for only 1.1 percent of the profession. In 1920, the year that women achieved suffrage, only 1.4 percent (1,738) of lawyers were women. Between 1950 and 1970, women accounted for about 4 percent of the profession (Bernat, 1992).

Stereotypes That Hurt Female Lawyers

Stereotypes of female attorneys are beginning to change; however, negative assumptions about women's capabilities persist. In general, people believe that women lawyers are less competent than men (Hasuike, 1996). According to studies on the legal profession, male lawyers tend to think that because there are more women in the legal profession today women have equal opportunities to excel as lawyers. Female attorneys, however, indicate that gender bias continues and that despite some gains, many obstacles remain.

The more common myths about female lawyers are that they are too emotional, not tough enough to handle the stress of the job, not aggressive enough to handle a case, too aggressive at the office, and not committed to their employers because of family or personal matters and demands (ABA, 1997). Female lawyers, for example, may be viewed more negatively in a courtroom if they engage in overt displays of hostility (e.g., use sarcasm) or if they are not as courteous as their male counterparts (Hasuike, 1996). The consequence of stereotypical assumptions about women is that female attorneys may use less effective courtroom techniques and are held to a higher performance standard than their male peers. In short, female lawyers are evaluated more harshly and must work harder to obtain credibility. According to one woman law associate in a large firm (ABA, 1997, p. 15):

There are really two tracks in a law firm. One track is related to performance, and the other is political. The political track is very gender sensitive because there are no checks and balances, and language and unconscious assumptions are allowed to play a major role. You can make the grade on the performance track, but still not make it to partner because of the political track.

Problematically, the myths about women's competence and commitment to their jobs may become a double-edged sword. On the one hand, if a male supervising attorney believes that a woman is less competent and not as committed to her job as a male lawyer, the supervisor will not mentor the woman or assign her more lucrative assignments and cases (Foster, 1995; Rhodes, 1996/1997). Female attorneys therefore remain outside the circle of employment opportunities that may provide them with the informal and formal supports necessary for success and acceptance (Wald, 1989).

Female attorneys are also believed to place more importance on their family than their jobs (Rhodes, 1996/1997). A common stereotype that hurts female lawyers is that their family responsibilities *should* take precedence over their careers and that women *should* be homemakers (Bisom-Rapp, 1996; Foster, 1995). While many female attorneys with children are more likely to be responsible for child rearing than their husbands or partners, such responsibilities are in addition to and *not* a replacement for their job duties. Women take their legal careers seriously and are willing to find a balance between their home life and work responsibilities.

Initially, women who entered the legal profession delayed starting families in order to devote time to their careers, but presently women are having families as the opportunities present themselves. As with other professions and occupations, family responsibilities tend to fall more heavily on women. Accordingly, workplaces may find that the initial costs associated with flex-time and family leave result in the greater productivity, morale, and retention of women (Rhodes, 1996/1997). Women with families want meaningful lives, lives that include family time. However, this value is at odds with a male view that work commitments take precedence over all else, including family (Ballard, 1998).

Two prevailing and opposite views on the changing view of women's competence are reflected by the following perspectives expressed by the ABA and Janet Rhodes. One view is that as more women slowly advance into leadership roles and contribute to a diversified field that responds to the myriad of needs of a firm's clientele, the negative views on women's professionalism and legal competence will change (ABA, 1995a). The ABA reports that blatant gender bias and discrimination is waning as more women proceed into positions throughout the various employment options that exist (ABA, 1995b). Rhodes (1996/1997) states, however, that gender disparity will not dissipate by "time alone." Rhodes (1996/1997, p. 587) indicates, for example, that:

Among law firm partners, only about half of female attorneys but three quarters of male attorneys have equity status. Although some 40 percent of in-house corporate lawyers are women, only 17 percent of surveyed companies have female attorneys heading their legal divisions.

In order to offset the view that women are not committed to their careers and should receive lower evaluations, senior legal partners and management divisions must be committed to using gender-neutral evaluation systems. If one considers employment discrimination suits filed by women who were not promoted to partner, then it is evident that simply having written promotional and job performance criteria does not alleviate gender bias. Systemic masculine definitions of the practice of law solidify glass ceilings and walls as divergent styles expressed by women may be viewed as less effective or less intellectually astute (Bisom-Rapp, 1996). Personal characteristics of women seem to account for the difficulty women lawyers face in achieving the highest levels in their field (Radford, 1989–1990). Women's job performances must be assessed in regard to the full range of characteristics and contributions that they make in the legal field (ABA, 1997) if female lawyers are to benefit in terms of power, economics, and status in their employment settings.

Gender Bias Is Widespread and Persistent

In order to ascertain the particular problems women face in the practice of law, the ABA and some states have commissioned task forces to determine the nature and extent of gender bias in the bar. Task forces on gender bias and discrimination in the legal profession have been constituted in more than forty states and several federal circuits (North Dakota Law Review, 1996). Initially, gender bias considerations were the provinces of state courts, but in 1990, federal courts began to take action. The various studies and task forces have asked difficult questions about the status of women in the legal profession (Epstein, Sauté, Oglensky, & Gever, 1995; Foster, 1995; Resnik, 1996).

Research on elite or top law firms have found that despite some initial progress in hiring women in a variety of practice areas, the progress is eroding and glass ceilings endure (Epstein et al., 1995; Foster, 1995). The top New York law firms, for example, are losing their best female attorneys because glass ceilings limit their advancement opportunities (Foster, 1995). Hiring women has not, in and of itself, resolved gender inequity (Association of the Bar of the City of New York, 1996). One-third of students who graduated from law school in 1980 were women, but by 1991, an ABA study indicated that only 18 percent had become partners in their firms (Foster, 1995).

In 1990, the ABA's Commission on Women in the Profession found that gender bias and discrimination are endemic throughout the profession (Slotkin, 1996). Each task force found that gender bias is pervasive against women lawyers, litigants, and court employees. For example, in North Dakota, most attorneys agree that subtle forms of gender bias exist against women but that such bias is less than in years past (North Dakota Law Review, 1996). Although few judges and male attorneys reported that they witnessed verbal sexual harassment, 39 percent of female lawyers stated that women lawyers experience verbal sexual harassment.

In this same study, female attorneys also noted that they were more likely to be called by their first names or terms of endearment in the courtroom setting than their male peers. Such terms demean or undermine the integrity of women before the court, juries, and others. Many female lawyers preferred judges to intervene when inappropriate and insensitive gendered verbal comments are made; although male lawyers thought that judges might intervene in such situations, many favored judicial inaction over action (North Dakota Law Review,

1996). The Commission in North Dakota recommended that overt forms of gender bias be dealt with and that the legal profession needed to improve its programs on how to identify and respond to gender bias within the courts.

Similarly in New York state, a committee asked to review the status of women in the judiciary found that gender bias existed and had negative impacts on both the women and the profession. The committee expanded the scope of its work as it also worked with local communities to identify problems, acted as a resource for information on how the system can be reformed, and worked to lay a foundation for a court system free of gender bias and insensitivity (New York Judicial Committee, 1992). In some states these reports have been used to change existing policies and practices that disadvantage women. In New York, for example, sexual harassment policies were developed, and canons of ethics were revised as a result of a task force report (Resnik, 1996).

Task forces and studies on gender in the legal profession generally find that as a consequence of bias, women experience inequity, embarrassment, emotional stress, professional inequity and deprivation, and economic disadvantage. Partnerships are overwhelmingly given to male attorneys. Successful women appear to adopt male normative employment traits and behaviors (aggressive, competitive, and with a single focus on one's job). They "assimilate" to, rather than alter, the legal workplace to accommodate female traits and needs (cooperation and a focus on multiple concerns and their family). Women are more dissatisfied with their jobs than their male peers and are leaving firms to work in small private firms or as in-house counsel (Foster, 1995).

Salary Inequities Remain

Gender bias in the practice of law is prevalent despite ABA admonitions that standards of equity apply in the legal profession to the same degree that lawyers seek to impose employment equality in other businesses. When thirty-seven female attorneys were asked what their firms valued most, all women indicated that clients and money were the most important values expressed by their employers (Ballard, 1998). When women hit a glass ceiling in a firm or are devalued in evaluations and not provided with choice client assignments, their wage-earning capacity concomitantly lags behind their male peers. In 1993, for example, female lawyers with one to three years experience earned $30,806 compared with $37,500 for male peers; women earned $49,191 compared with $57,511 for male peers with four to nine years experience; and they earned $68,466 compared with $90,574 for male peers with ten to twenty years experience. With more than twenty years experience, women's salaries were only slightly less than their male peers, $102,500 to $104,103 respectively (ABA, 1995a).

Some of the pay inequities discussed above have been attributed to differences in the profit sharing rules and gender-influenced job assignments (ABA, 1995b); women may not be given "choice" clients and assignments that might otherwise be rewarded when merit salary adjustments are made. However, when corporate lawyers are compared, female lawyers with similar job assignments to their male peers were paid less at all levels of the corporate legal departments (ABA, 1995b). According to Kornhauser and Revesz (1995, note 82), although stark gender differences in employment are waning, one study showed that male lawyers earned about 13 percent more than women even after controlling for demographic characteristics, family situation, work hours, and job setting. Salary inequity, according to the ABA (1995b, p. 51), "is too persistent to be an anomaly: it is a systemic problem."

Female Lawyers of Color

If women in the legal profession face endemic challenges to equity, women of color face additional challenges. Limited data exist on the status of women lawyers of color, but Rhodes (1996–1997) reports that these women account for less than 3 percent of lawyers and judges and that their retention rates in law firms are poor. Kornhauser and Revesz (1995) report that lawyers of color accounted for 1 percent of the profession in 1970, 5 percent in 1980, and 7 percent in 1990. More recent statistics indicate that in the sixteen states that reported data, 19 percent of lawyers are a racial or ethnic minority (ABA, 2003). In 2003, a survey on the presence of women and minority attorneys in the profession revealed that both male and female minority attorneys account for only 4 percent of partners in the nation's major law firms (NALP, 2004).

Minority female lawyers self-report that they are treated very badly and are "ghettoized" in the least prestigious areas of legal practice that are among the least compensated (ABA, 1994; Slotkin, 1996). According to an ABA report (1994) on recent law school graduates in 1993, larger percentages of women of color obtained employment in the government sector (20.8 percent) and at public interest law firms (6.3 percent) compared to white men (11.4 percent and 1.2 percent, respectively), minority males (19.2 percent and 4.0 percent, respectively), and white women (12.4 percent and 2.8 percent, respectively). In 1992, the majority of attorneys who became "partner" in California were white men, 25 percent were women, and 9 percent were minority (Pinder, 1993). Minority lawyers indicate that they had difficulty in finding employment when they graduated from law school. One lawyer, for example, stated:

> When I graduated from law school, there was no law firm that would even interview me. . . . In white society they were saying, "Women can't do it." In Black society, they were saying "Women do too much." (Pinder, 1993, p. 1065)

Once employed, female lawyers of color report frustration with a lack of respect in their employment environments from both their staff and peers. Problematically, many minority lawyers indicate that they are mistaken for their criminal clients, janitors, legal assistants, or clerks when they appear in court and are told they have to have thick skins if they want to be respected by their firms (Pinder, 1993). Minority female attorneys indicate they have to repeatedly prove their legal skills and are being held back in their careers despite their talent or efforts (ABA, 1995a; Pinder, 1993). Although the number of women from various ethnic and racial backgrounds has been increasing, these women continue to feel invisible and disadvantaged within the profession (ABA, 1994). According to Pinder (1993), although most law firms have not tried to diversify, race and gender discrimination is not an insurmountable obstacle *if* employment discrimination is viewed as unquestionably wrong.

Women in the Judiciary

Many of the women who become members of the appellate courts pioneered in the practice of law when many firms refused to hire them and viewed them as liabilities. Women were slowly appointed to state judicial positions in the late nineteenth and early twentieth centuries. In 1928, the first woman was appointed to the federal bench, a customs court (Barteau, 1997;

Cedarbaum, 1993). Three barriers existed for women to become judges: they needed to be politically powerful, have a legal education, and be experienced attorneys (Barteau, 1997).

Although two women presently serve as justices on the U.S. Supreme Court, the number of women serving on federal and state appellate courts is still low. It was not until 1980 that every state had at least one female judge serving at some judicial level (Barteau, 1997). In 2004, women comprised approximately 20 percent of all the federal judiciary (Gender gap in government, 2004). When compared to 1995, when 12 percent of judges on the federal bench were female (2 Supreme Court Justices, 32 Court of Appeals judges, 109 District Court judges, and three Court of Claims judges), women have made significant progress in being appointed to the federal bench (ABA, 1995b). In 1991, women accounted for only 9 percent of state judges. In New York State, female judges seem to be concentrated in lower courts (e.g., in the New York City family, criminal, and civil courts) rather than appellate or county courts (New York Judicial Committee, 1992).

At both the state and federal levels, female lawyers are overrepresented among support personnel for the courts (administrators, law clerks, court aides) compared to their representation on the bench. In 1991, for example, female lawyers accounted for 39 percent of state court support personnel and 32 percent of federal court support personnel but only 9 percent and 7 percent, respectively, of the judgeships (ABA, 1995b). In 2002, two of the nine justices serving on the U.S. Supreme Court were women, and women comprised 16 percent of U.S. Circuit Court and 15 percent of U.S. District Court judgeships (ABA Commission on Women in the Profession, 2003). Twenty-eight percent of state supreme court justices are women (ABA Commission on Women in the Profession, 2003).

Women in Law School

In the early 1970s, women made up a very tiny portion of all law students. Presently, female law students account for almost half of all law school enrollments (ABA Commission on Women in the Profession, 2003; Foster, 1995). Minority law students are underrepresented given their percentage in the population. According to Kornhauser and Revesz (1995), 7 percent of the law students were black, 5 percent were Latino, 5 percent were Asian American, and less than 1 percent were Native American in 1993. Thus, in 1993, minority law students accounted for 18 percent of all students, but they accounted for about 26 percent of the United States population. Most men and women indicate satisfaction with their law schools, but a significant percentage of minority female law students (31 percent) indicate that they are dissatisfied or very dissatisfied compared to white females (18 percent) and males (12 percent) with their experiences (Krauskopf, 1994).

Among the reasons that women go to law school and want to become lawyers are to achieve economic independence, to make a difference in the lives of others, and to pursue legal practice because it seems interesting (Ballard, 1998). Nonetheless, female law students continue to express concerns about sexual harassment by professors and "overt animosity" from male law students (ABA, 1995a, p. 6; Neumann, 2000). According to the American Bar Association (ABA, 1995a), although sexual harassment of female students seems to be declining, female students continue to indicate that they have experienced overt hostility that is similar to that experienced by women prior to the 1980s. Minority law students face the negative assumption that they were accepted primarily on the basis of affirmative action policies and that they had lower qualifications than other students (Haddon, 1997). Women of color believe that they have to work harder to prove themselves than their law school peers (Ebben & Gaier, 1998). Diversifying law school classes requires law schools to develop and maintain hospitable environments.

Analysis of the economic inequities that create inequalities of opportunities for qualified students to gain entrance into law schools and the profession must be undertaken. Debt burdens are increasingly being cited as reasons why candidates choose particular law schools or enter into particular fields of legal practice (Haddon, 1997; Kornhauser & Revesz, 1995). Many students support their legal education through loans, as opposed to grants and scholarships. Kornhauser and Revesz (1995) estimate that more than one-third of law school graduates choose a job in the not-for-profit sector over a higher-paying job in for-profit elite and non-elite law firms if a loan forgiveness program is offered. Latino and black women attorneys indicate that an important factor in accepting employment in the not-for-profit legal sector is loan forgiveness programs. In general, women may enter law school and indicate that they will seek employment in the not-for-profit sector, and they are "channeled" toward the for-profit jobs while in law school (Kornhauser & Revesz, 1995).

Balanced Lives

The legal profession has maintained a masculine identity and culture despite increasing numbers of women who choose to practice law. In order to understand the dynamics that affect women in the legal profession it is important to understand the particular concerns that women experience, the ethical and pragmatic concerns that face women, and the employment disappointments that women continue to experience (Leiper, 2001). Women must try and adjust to a male-defined and dominated profession or leave. Many women earn less than their male peers and will leave large firms where they know that will stay at the rank of associate and not be promoted to partner. About one-third of legal aid and public defender lawyers are women, and many women become solo practitioners (ABA, 1995b). The work environment in law firms is aimed at childless lawyers (or lawyers whose partners can stay at home to care for their children) and advocates male argumentative work styles (Slotkin, 1996). Despite increased numbers of women, the legal profession employs women disproportionately in specific areas of law (Epstein et al., 1995; Foster, 1995; Gellis, 1991; Kim, 2001; Wald, 1989).

According to Kim (2001), female lawyers are more likely to work as in-house legal counsel or in the public sector than in large private law firms, and their upward mobility is somewhat limited. Women usually are not lead counsel in lucrative personal injury and contract dispute cases (*Judicature,* 1990). The question remains whether women are choosing these employment opportunities or they are tracked away from the more lucrative corporate positions (Foster, 1995).

The practice of law demands lawyers to work exceptionally long hours. One reason that lawyers work long hours is that firms are in competition with each other. Lawyers are people who have throughout their academic and professional lives competed with others to be the best, and such competition continues to be played out in the desire to work for firms to earn the most money (Foster, 1995; Schiltz, 1999). Job satisfaction and the ability to balance family and professional lives are the highest priorities among those lawyers working for the government or in legal services and lowest amongst lawyers working in private practice (Schiltz, 1999; Wald, 1989). Thus, it might not be too surprising that women who aim to balance their professional and personal lives work in the public sectors or small law firms.

In addition to long work hours, lawyers indicate that they are depressed, suffer from alcoholism, think about committing suicide, and are, not surprisingly, unhappy with their lives (Schiltz, 1999). Women also report substantially higher divorce rates and are significantly less likely to remarry than women in other professions like medicine and academia (Schiltz, 1999). Female lawyers experience role conflict and problems with balancing their career and personal lives (Leiper, 2001; Slotkin, 1996). Although Slotkin (1996) found that female lawyers are experiencing less role conflict than they did twenty years ago, women must still find ways to balance their responsibilities for work, home, and family. The level of stress and strain felt by female lawyers is higher than that felt by men but consistent with the types of difficulties that women express in other employment settings (Taber et al., 1988). It is time also that law firms find ways to enable women to balance each of these important responsibilities.

Female Lawyers in the Criminal Justice System

Public sector legal employment in the criminal justice system usually entails working as a prosecutor or a public defender. Every jurisdiction will have a prosecuting attorney office to handle criminal cases. In 2001, half of the nation's prosecuting attorney offices employed fewer than ten people, with 65 percent having at least one assistant attorney being employed full time (Bureau of Justice Statistics, 2004). Not all jurisdictions in the United States utilize a public defender system to provide legal representation to indigent defendants; rather, some states assign indigent defendants to members of the local bar or contract with private firms to handle indigent criminal defense work. In 1994, for example, the percent of defendants being represented only through a public defender program comprised 21 percent of state prosecutions. In the nation's largest counties, public defender programs are more commonplace and accounted for 68 percent of legal representation for felony defendants in 1996 (Bureau of Justice Statistics, 2000).

Women are attracted to prosecutor and public defender employment because it provides a stable work environment. Women believe they will encounter less gender bias in terms of salary compensation, work assignments, and the ability to balance a family life with their career since their employment evaluations will not depend on the amount of money that is brought into the firm (Bernat, 1992). Nevertheless, female prosecutors and defense counsel may have their trial work assessed on the basis on gender characteristics. For example, female criminal lawyers may be viewed as too kind or too harsh to witnesses, or too passive or too aggressive in litigating the case. Hahn and Clayton (1996) found in their study on the effect of attorney presentations and style on juror decisions that aggressive defense attorneys were more likely to win an acquittal for their clients than passive attorneys and that male aggressive attorneys were more successful than aggressive female attorneys. In the criminal trial arena, jurors expect a commanding style of speech. This expectation places female prosecutors and defense counsel in a double bind. If the women are too aggressive, they are viewed as cold and unfriendly; if they are too passive, they will not prevail in the litigation (Hahn & Clayton, 1996). According to Pollock and Ramirez (1995), female prosecutors may be more astute trial lawyers than male prosecutors because they listen to witnesses more carefully, spend more time preparing for trial, and may appear less aggressive to victims. Interestingly, Pollock and Ramirez (1995) report female prosecutors indicated that hiring committees worried if the women were not "aggressive enough" for the position. Thus, even in the criminal law sector of practice, gender assumptions about women's ability to handle cases persist; women are not given the same measure of credibility that men have when they enter the courtroom (Bogoch, 1999).

Redefining the Legal Profession

Women's experiences in the practice of law and in the judiciary indicate that full inclusion and employment equity have not been achieved. Most people, when asked to depict their image of a lawyer, will describe a male person in a suit carrying a briefcase. Women in the legal profession articulate any number of stories in which they are described as being a woman, as being a person of color, or as possessing an innate "female" trait, in addition to being a lawyer or judge. The legal profession may be one employment setting in which simply increasing the numbers of women will not change or redefine the parameters of the job (Bisom-Rapp, 1996). Power, success, and leadership are masculine traits that are deeply entrenched in the normative practice of law. If the male norm continues to define the legal profession, then it is not possible for women to achieve parity and overcome the subliminal double bind that will continue to devalue their work through sexual stereotyping. Women who exhibit male power strategies will be viewed as unlikable, but if they exhibit female power styles then they will be deemed "unreliable" (Radford, 1989–1990, p. 501).

The legal profession and legal education are based upon a model that one must "win" and that lawyers must beat their opposition in argument, in analytical thinking, and legal strategy. Sturm (1997) describes this presumed model of practice as a "gladiator model" of lawyering. The gladiator model persists despite the range of roles and the range of practice styles that women and minorities have brought to the legal profession in recent years. When the emphasis of legal success is defined by "winning and losing" or being the "top dog," women and minorities who may accentuate the emerging lawyering styles of cooperation, mediation, and diffusion of conflict may be viewed as unsuccessful. The legal profession must transition itself to accept multiple views of lawyer success. In this new forum, the professional legal role will openly acknowledge that lawyers can work together as problem solvers and are not merely adversaries winning a competition.

Cultural change of the profession is difficult to achieve but a worthwhile goal nonetheless. If the profession can modify the standards that depict legal success using only male norms, then emergent legal trends toward mediated dispute resolutions can be more fully accommodated. Such accommodation is necessary as the profession continues to diversify in terms of gender, race, ethnicity, and in terms of legal practice, legal roles, legal styles, and legal competence. Having multiple avenues and definitions of success in the practice of law will help ensure that women and minority attorneys are viewed as contributing to the development of law and legal professionalism and not viewed (or treated) as the proverbial "worker bee."

Law school education can assist in redefining the profession if law school curriculum is broadened from Socratic analysis alone to the link between scholarship and experience

(Sturm, 1997). It is important to understand that men and women may develop a variety of styles of legal practice and that the profession should transform itself so that it can recognize and reward alternative methods of practice (Cahn, 1992). Gender bias is difficult to eradicate because well-meaning individuals may believe that they are engaged in equitable practices but can be operating upon deeply ingrained social and cultural notions that systemically discriminate or perpetuate bias.

Conclusion

Women still express serious concern about employment equity and equality despite the larger numbers of female attorneys today. It is hoped that the discrimination that currently exists will not just diminish but end as more women advance up the ranks and become partners, as more women teach in law schools, as more women become judges, and as the profession itself redefines itself away from traditional male norms and expectations of success. Some women may wish to pull the ladder up behind them, others, due to their youth, may not fully appreciate the struggles that faced the women before them. To change the persistent tide of gender inequity female and male lawyers must help redefine the practice of law and look ahead to a day when legal practice is not just for men any more. Changing the characterization of the profession away from male norms and expectations is a difficult but necessary endeavor if the profession is to create new standards of evaluation, refine methods of rewards, and generate new avenues for women to work. Glass ceilings are not just a problem for women to solve and are not going to dissipate merely because more women are practicing law. Systemic barriers need to be identified and removed.

Review Questions

1. What are the principal myths that resulted in women's exclusion from legal practice?

2. What percentage of practicing lawyers are women? What types of law do they practice?

3. Describe the challenges faced by women lawyers of color.

4. Describe the formal and informal mechanisms by which gender bias continues to exist for women attorneys.

5. Describe how women lawyers attempt to achieve balanced lives.

6. What are the possible ways in which women can achieve parity with men in the practice of law and in the judiciary?

7. What can be done to encourage women to study law and to practice in law firms?

Key Terms

Bradwell v. Illinois
Law firm partner
Criminal law practice
Public sector law
Task forces on gender bias in the legal profession

Salary inequity
Appellate judge
Sexual harassment
Law school diversity
Gladiator model of lawyering

References

American Bar Association. (1994, August). *The burdens of both, the privileges of neither. A joint report from the American Bar Association Commission on Women in the Profession and the Commission on Opportunities for Minorities in the Profession.* Chicago, IL: American Bar Association.

American Bar Association. (1995a, December). *Unfinished business: Overcoming the Sisyphus factor. A report from the American Bar Association Commission on Women in the Profession.* Chicago, IL: American Bar Association.

American Bar Association. (1995b, December). *Women in the law: A look at the numbers. A report from the American Bar Association Commission on Women in the Profession.* Chicago, IL: American Bar Association.

American Bar Association. (1997). *Fair measure: Toward effective attorney evaluations. A report from the American Bar Association Commission on Women in the Profession.* Chicago, IL: American Bar Association.

American Bar Association. (2003). 2003 *National lawyer population survey.* Chicago, IL: ABA Market Research Department.

American Bar Association, Commission on Women in the Profession. (2003). *A current glance of women in the law.* Retrieved from http://www.abanet.org/women/glance2003.pdf.

Association of the Bar of the City of New York, Commission on Women in the Profession. (1996). Responses to glass ceilings and open doors: Women's advancement in the legal profession. *Fordham Law Review* 64, 561–564.

Ballard, N. H. (1998). *Equal engagement: Observations on career success and meanings in the lives of women lawyers.* Wellesley, MA: Wellesley College, Center for Research on Women.

Barteau, Honorable B. (1997). Thirty years of the journey of Indiana's women judges 1964–1994. *Indiana Law Review* 30, 43–202.

Bernat, F. P. (1992). Women in the legal profession. In I. L. Moyer (Ed.), *The changing roles of women in the criminal justice system: Offenders, victims and professionals* (2nd ed.; pp. 307–321). Prospect Heights, IL: Waveland Press.

Bisom-Rapp, S. (1996). Scripting reality in the legal workplace: Women lawyers, litigation prevention measures, and the limits of anti-discrimination law. *Columbia Journal of Gender and Law* 6, 323–385.

Bogoch, B. (1999). Courtroom discourse and the gendered construction of professional identity. *Law and Social Inquiry* 24, 329–375.

Bureau of Justice Statistics. (2000). *Defense counsel in criminal cases: Special report.* NCJ 179023, November 2000.

Bureau of Justice Statistics. (2004). *Prosecution statistics.* Retrieved from http://www.ojp.usdoj.gov/bjs/pros.htm.

Cahn, N. R. (1992). Styles of lawyering. *Hastings Law Journal* 43, 1039–1069.

Catalyst (2001). *Women in law: Making the Case.* Accessed on 8/31/2004. http://www.catalystwomen.org/press_room/factsheets/fact_sheet_women_in_law.htm.

Cedarbaum, M. G. (1993). Women on the federal bench. *Boston University Law Review* 73, 39–45.

Ebben, M., & Gaier, N. G. (1998). Telling stories, telling self: Using narrative to uncover Latinas' voices and agency in the legal profession. *Chicano-Latino Law Review* 19, 243–263.

Epstein, C. F., Sauté, R., Oglensky, B., & Gever, M. (1995). Glass ceilings and open doors: Women's advancement in the legal profession: A report to the Committee on Women in the Profession, The Association of the Bar of the City of New York. *Fordham Law Review* 64, 291–560.

Foster S. E. (1995). The glass ceiling in the legal profession: Why do law firms still have so few female partners? *UCLA Law Review* 42, 1631–1689.

Gellis, A. J. (1991). Great expectations: Women in the legal profession, a commentary on state studies. *Indiana Law Review* 66, 941–976.

Gender gap in government: The federal government. (2004). Retrieved on November 7, 2004 from gendergap.com/government.htm.

Haddon, P. A. (1997). Keynote address: Redefining our roles in the battle for inclusion of people of color in the legal profession. *New England Law Review* 31, 709–725.

Hahn, P. W., & Clayton, S. D. (1996). The effects of attorney presentation style, attorney gender, and juror gender on juror decisions. *Law and Human Behavior* 20, 533–554.

Hasuike, R. (1996). Credibility and gender in the courtroom: What jurors think. In J. M. Snyder & A. B. Greene (Eds.), *The woman advocate* (pp. 121–135). Chicago: Publications, Planning and Marketing, American Bar Association.

Judicature. (1990). Different voices, different choices? The impact of more women lawyers and judges on the justice system. *Judicature* 74, 138–146.

Kim, H. (2001). The changing patterns of career mobility in the legal profession: A log-linear analysis of Chicago lawyers (1975 and 1995). *Sociology of Crime, Law and Deviance* 3, 3–24.

Kornhauser, L. A., & Revesz, R. L. (1995). Legal education and entry into the legal profession: The role of race, gender, and educational debt. *New York University Law Review* 70, 829–964.

Krauskopf, J. M. (1994). Touching the elephant: Perceptions of gender issues in nine law schools. *Journal of Legal Education* 44, 311–340.

Leiper, J. M. (2001). Gendered views of time and time crunch stress: Women lawyers' responses to professional and personal demands. *Contemporary Perspectives on Family Research* 3, 251–280.

NALP. (2004). NALP Research—Women and attorneys of color. http://www.nalp.org/nalpresearch/mw_indx. htm.

Neumann, Jr., R. K. (2000). Women in legal education: What the statistics show. *Journal of Legal Education* 50, 313–357.

New York Judicial Committee. (1992). Five year report of the New York Judicial Committee on Women. *Fordham Urban Law Journal* 19, 313–390.

North Dakota Law Review. (1996). Supreme Court Commission on gender fairness in the courts. *North Dakota Law Review* 72, 1127–1146.

Pinder, W. W. (1993). When will Black women lawyers slay the two-headed dragon: Racism and gender bias? *Pepperdine Law Review* 20, 1053–1070.

Pollock, J. M., & Ramirez, B. (1995). Women in the legal profession. In A.V. Merlo & J. M. Pollock (Eds.), *Women, law and social control* (pp. 79–95). Boston: Allyn and Bacon.

Radford, M. F. (1989–1990). Sex stereotyping and the promotion of women to positions of power. *Hastings Law Journal* 41, 471–535.

Resnik, J. (1996). Gender in the courts: The task force reports. In J. M. Snyder & A. B. Greene (Eds.), *The woman advocate* (pp. 7–21). Chicago: Publications, Planning and Marketing, American Bar Association.

Rhodes, D. L. (1996–1997). Myths of mediocrity. *Fordham Law Review* 65, 585–594.

Schiltz, P. J. (1999). On being a happy, healthy, and ethical member of an unhappy, unhealthy, and unethical profession. *Vanderbilt Law Review* 52, 871–951.

Slotkin, J. H. (1996). You really have come a long way: An analysis and comparison of role conflict experienced by women attorneys today and by educated women twenty years ago. *Women's Rights Law Reporter* 18, 17–48.

Sturm, S. P. (1997). From gladiators to problem-solvers: Connecting conversations about women, the academy, and the legal profession. *Duke Journal of Gender Law and Policy* 4, 119–147.

Taber, J., Grant, M. T., Huser, M. T., Norman, R. B., Sutton, J. R., Wong, C. C., Parker, L. E., & Picard, C. (1988). Gender, legal education, and the legal profession: An empirical study of Stanford law students and graduates. *Stanford Law Review* 40, 1209–1297.

Tebo, M. G. (2003). Far to go: Hearings seek to pinpoint issues that resonate with female lawyers. *ABA Journal* 89, 73.

Wald, Judge P. M. (1989). Breaking the glass ceiling. *Human Rights* 16, 40–43, 54.

White, R. (1999). *Association of American Law Schools. 1998-1999 Statistical Report on Law School Faculty and Candidates for Law Faculty Positions.* www.aals. org/statistics/rpt9899w.html.

Wortman, M. S. (1985). *Women in American law: From colonial times to the New Deal,* vol. 1. New York: Holmes and Meier Publishing.

Cases Cited

Bradwell v. Illinois, 83 U.S. 130 (1873)

Part III

Women as Victims

In this section, our focus is on female victims. The criminal justice system has changed dramatically in its response to female victims of crime. The women's rights groups and advocates in the 1970s were successful in their attempts to get police departments and courts to provide equal protection for female victims. Legal reforms have included changes in the legal definitions of sexual assault and in the powers of police to arrest perpetrators of domestic violence. Law enforcement reforms have included training on sexual assault and domestic violence and mandatory arrest policies.

These crimes are no longer hidden. Further, services are available for victims in most towns and cities. However, there are some troubling signs that progress is not as rapid as we might think. In Chapter 8, the authors note that the Kobe Bryant case brings up all the issues of "prosecuting the victim" that have been around as long as there have been prosecutions for rape. They also note that the victimization rate is racially disproportional. Black and Hispanic women are much more likely to be sexually assaulted, and there are troubling signs that the system does not protect or defend them as vigorously as white women. In Chapter 9, the author points out that, although the frequency of intimate assault has declined, this is truer for men than for women. Interestingly, the numbers of male victims of intimate partner homicide have declined more rapidly than the numbers of female victims.

We recognize that the sections we have created in this volume are arbitrary. That is, it may not be that the women who suffer as victims are different from those we have previously discussed as professionals, or those who we will discuss in the next section as offenders. Women live their lives with greater fears than do men. This may be partially due to the fact that if they are victims, they are most likely to be victimized by those close to them.

8

Rape Survivors

The Law and the Reality

Mittie D. Southerland and Rachel M. Southerland

Historically, society has viewed sexual violence against women as the victim's problem. Rape was a dark secret not openly discussed. The woman was pathologized—something within her caused the incident, she was a victim of her own actions and choices. Since the early 1960s, significant attention has been devoted to redefining women's experiences of rape as assault of a sexual nature. In the late 1960s the women's movement gave public voice to this previously private problem; "sexual" assault received national attention. Laws were revised and established, and organizations were created with the purpose of protecting, researching, and counseling rape victims. The Law Enforcement Assistance Administration funded the first publicly funded rape crisis centers in 1972. The first completely revised sexual assault statute was adopted that year by the Michigan legislature (Marsh, Geist, & Caplan, 1982). The National Center for the Prevention and Control of Rape was established in 1975. Much later, the 1994 Violence Against Women Act called for the development of the National Violence Against Women Prevention Research Center. These efforts have drawn attention to the goals of preventing rape and assisting rape victims to survive.

This chapter presents the types and definitions of rape, legal reforms, data regarding rape victimization and reported rape, the effects of rape on victims, the characteristics and motivations of rapists, and policy implications. *Rape* is the term under which all forms of sexual assault are subsumed except when statistics specific to the victimization category "sexual assault" are examined. *Victim* or *survivor* refers specifically to women and girls throughout the chapter—male rape victims are excluded from consideration.

Types and Definitions of Rape

Defining rape is not as easy as it might seem. Reliance on a legal definition is one way to proceed, but law is vague and, at times, contradictory. In his study of forcible sex offenses, LaFree (1989) found that victims, police, and other legal agents are influenced by extralegal characteristics of the rape incident. Police officers view rape as a serious offense but in practice rarely encounter cases that fit their preconceived definitions. Rape cases involve both sex and force, call for legal agents to respond to events they do not actually observe, and rarely include eyewitnesses. Criminal justice professionals must frequently interpret and process cases based solely on the victim's and offender's testimony. Interpretation of law falls on professionals and jurors whose perceptions regarding rape have been shaped by the cultural messages they have accepted. LaFree (1989) hypothesizes that the more similar the characteristics of rape victims, offenders, and offenses to the typification of rape held by the various justice processing agents, the more likely a conviction of the accused.

Types of Rape

   1. **Hate Rape.** A new category of rape currently raised in feminist discussion attempts to redefine rape as a hate crime in some instances. Targeted rape, or hate rape exists when

a perpetrator chooses a victim solely based on her ethnicity—racism is the perpetrator's only motivation.

2. **Stranger Rape.** Stranger rape means the victim and assailant did not know each other before the rape. Of all violent crimes, this type of rape is the most feared but least perpetrated.

3. **Acquaintance Rape.** Acquaintance rape is a type of rape in which nonconsensual sex occurs between a victim and rapist who know each other. It is the most frequently perpetrated form of rape.

4. **Date Rape.** The most well-known type of acquaintance rape is date rape, which is nonconsensual sex between people who are on a date. In this form of rape, the victim willingly accompanies a man who then becomes violent toward her.

5. **Campus Rape.** A special form of date rape occurs as campus rape. In the typical rape on a college campus, a man assaults a woman he met at a party. These rapes often involve excessive use of alcohol by one or both of the persons involved.

6. **Gang Rape.** Gang rape involves a victim with two or more perpetrators. The victim and at least one of the perpetrators usually know each other. Occurring more frequently in college settings than in other types of communities, this type of rape is not as readily accepted in our society as other forms of rape.

7. **Stalker Rape.** Stalker rape occurs when the rapist knows the victim even if the victim does not know the rapist. The rapist, in this form of acquaintance rape, usually lives in the vicinity and has been watching or stalking the victim.

8. **Marital Rape.** Marital rape is nonconsensual intercourse between people who are married.

Perceptual Definitions of Rape

Bourque (1989), Gordon and Riger (1989), and Williams and Holmes (1981) analyze the way rape is defined in U.S. society. Perceptual definitions of rape range from the view that rape cannot occur to the view that any unwanted sexual advance—verbal or nonverbal—constitutes rape. The context (in a marriage, on a date, with a stranger) of such behaviors should be irrelevant but it shapes perceptual definitions (Bourque, 1989). This wide range of perceptions causes confusion for victims, criminal justice professionals, and jurors. Such confusion shapes the ways the victim responds to the rape event. It also shapes the way society responds to rape in terms of treatment of rape victims, the legal definitions of rape, policy making, and criminal justice system responses. Additionally, since rape victims often fail to perceive their experience as rape, the validity of rape victimization data is placed in question.

Stranger rape, the most common perceptual definition of rape, rarely occurs. The picture is a woman walking through an unlit area, a man jumps out from behind bushes or a doorway and rapes her. In contrast, acquaintance rape is a widespread problem but a hidden crime (Bechhofer & Parrot, 1991). It is hidden predominantly because victims of this form of rape fail to see themselves as legitimate crime victims (Estrich, 1987; Koss, 1985). Evidence of this is the fact that many women answer "yes" when asked if they have had unwanted sex with a man because he used physical force against them. At the same time these women adamantly respond "no" when asked if they have been raped (Allison & Wrightsman, 1993).

Personal Definitions of Rape

Gordon and Riger (1989) studied personal definitions of rape and reported that the perceptions of men and women regarding what constitutes rape are very similar to legal definitions. When physical force was included in the definition, 99 percent of both men and women defined unwanted intercourse as rape. Despite their consistency on the previous definitions of rape, 20 percent of both men and women were unwilling to define, as rape, unwanted sexual intercourse when on a date. Our society's accepted dating system "legitimizes the consensual 'purchase' of women as sexual objects and obliterates the crucial distinction between consent and nonconsent" (Gordon & Riger 1989, p. 60). Women who are victims of date rape may not recognize that the behavior by their date was rape (Warshaw, 1988), having been socialized concerning the exchange nature of dating with sex as payment.

Legal Definitions of Rape

Two legal categories of rape are defined: forcible and statutory. Statutory rape is sexual intercourse with a minor. Forcible rape refers to all other types of rape in which consensual sex could have been possible.

Although states have varying definitions of statutory and forcible rape, three elements have traditionally been crucial for successful prosecution of forcible rape cases. First, the rapist must be identified by the victim; second, force must be threatened or used; and third, the victim must be penetrated against her will. Victims often have difficulty presenting evidence to substantiate all three of these aspects, especially to prove that penetration was against their will. Rape has also been difficult to prove, because the victim is often the only witness and her veracity is frequently doubted, particularly when her history of sexual activity causes her respectability to be questioned.

How much resistance is sufficient to negate consent and thus show that the act was against the victim's will? The most stringent standards require "utmost resistance." That is, the victim must do everything possible, use every physical means within her power, to prevent the completion of the assault. All courts now use the "reasonableness standard" requiring sufficient resistance to make nonconsent reasonably manifest. In the changing legal context, courts generally have come to accept that a victim's submission due to reasonable fear does not constitute consent. Nevertheless, many rape victims who escaped physical harm, other than sexual penetration, as a result of the rape are made to feel by police, court personnel, and others who learn of the crime that they failed to use sufficient resistance.

For acquaintance rape, implied consent has been more problematic than for stranger rape because sexual encounters are a real possibility when people know each other. Bechhofer and Parrot (1991) report three situations in which the aggressor argues that he mistakenly assumed consent: if there have been one or more previous instances of sex between the parties; if the victim has had sex with numerous other individuals and has a "loose reputation"; and if the victim is drunk or asleep, in which case she is "fair game." In such circumstances, perpetrators falsely assume implicit consent on the basis of present or past behavior or no explicit refusal by the victim.

Legal Reforms

From 1962 to 1990, traditional rape laws were modified or repealed, and evidentiary reforms were enacted in all fifty states (Spohn & Horney, 1992). The Model Penal Code of the American Bar Association sought to eliminate the element "against her will" from the statutes in an attempt to reduce the degree of resistance required of the rape victim. Nevertheless, the woman remained obligated to offer more than "token initial resistance." The Model Code somewhat shifted the focus of attention to the perpetrator's conduct in its requirement that the assailant "compel" the victim to submit by use of force or by threatening the victim with imminent death or other serious bodily injury, threatening extreme pain, or threatening kidnapping (Spohn & Horney, 1992).

The Violence Against Women Acts of 1994, 1998, and 2000 attempt to provide protection of women through federal legal reform. Both the National Organization for Women Legal Defense Education Fund (2004) and the U.S. Department of Justice (2004b) delineate progress toward reform:

- Repeat offenders may be sentenced to twice the previously authorized time.
- Defendants must pay victims restitution, including attorneys' fees, lost income, transportation, childcare expenses, medical services, and civil protection order fees—regardless of the defendant's economic circumstances.
- Grants provide funding to train law enforcement officers, prosecutors, judges, and court personnel to more effectively handle, prosecute, and adjudicate violent crimes against women.
- Funds are provided for government entities to assume the full costs of forensic rape medical exams.
- Rape crisis centers or other nongovernmental organizations receive funding for rape education, prevention, and intervention.

These legal reforms are meant to provide victims with adequate support systems to facilitate recovery from their assault. The laws may be effective with regard to providing victims support but do little to deter rape.

Marital Exemption for Rape

Most states grappled with the conflict that nonconsensual intercourse should be rape regardless of marital status, but evidentiary problems make it extremely difficult for a married victim to meet the necessary burden of proof of nonconsent. Many states handled this conflict by determining that, legally, rape can occur within marriage only when the spouses are living apart at the time of the rape (Margolick, 1984). In 1993, the last state adopted a marital rape statute (Bergen, 1999). Marital rape was then a crime in all fifty states, although the statutes of thirty-three states provided husbands some exemption from rape prosecution. This conflict over marital rape demonstrated the tension in society between those who wanted all women to be protected from rape and those who were concerned about protecting husbands from frivolous charges.

Rape Shield Laws

Because of the legal requirement that victims prove nonconsent, evidence of the victim's sexual history typically has been admissible in the rape trial. The inference is that a history of intercourse, especially with multiple partners, establishes a propensity to consent. Most states in the 1970s adopted rape shield laws prohibiting the admission of evidence about a victim's previous sexual conduct, history, or reputation. Rape shield laws established that such information is irrelevant to the allegations and serves only to discredit the alleged victim, prejudicing the jury. Rape victimization is traumatic and reliving the experience on the witness stand is excruciating. According to Nnamdi (2004), placing rape victims on trial for their past sexual conduct is tantamount to telling them they cannot tell the difference between consensual sex and nonconsensual sex. Strong rape shield laws encourage victims to report their rape and pursue prosecution and trial. These laws apply primarily to criminal cases; few states extend them to civil cases (National Center for Victims of Crime, 2004a).

Four types of rape shield laws are delineated by Anderson (2002). First, legislative exception laws ban all admission of a victim's prior sexual history but provide an exception for the history between the defendant and alleged victim. Second, constitutional catchall laws are legislative exception laws but authorize judges to protect the defendant's and alleged victim's constitutional rights. Third, evidentiary purpose laws, the weakest laws, are found in two different forms: Either they establish that the victim's prior sexual history may be used to determine the victim's credibility but not consent or they establish that her sexual history is admissible to show the victim's propensity to consent, but not to determine her credibility. Fourth, judicial discretion laws allow judges to decide whether the prejudicial nature of the evidence outweighs the relevance. Under such laws, judges have the same discretionary position as before the enactment of the law—nothing changes.

Colorado's rape shield laws are examples of judicial discretion laws. In the 2004 rape case against Kobe Bryant, the defense team took advantage of the weak nature of Colorado's laws in their pretrial motions. They petitioned for evidentiary admission of the victim's sexual history (both with other partners and the defendant), her mental health, and her reluctance to discuss her sexual past. The pretrial motions and leaks to the press regarding the woman's name and personal information served to prejudice the jury pool against the alleged victim by tarnishing her character and credibility before the jury was chosen and before the case went to trial (Anderson, 2004).

Campus Reforms

The Campus Sexual Assault Victims' Bill of Rights amendment to the Student Right-to-Know and Campus Security Act of 1990 required colleges and universities to establish policies identifying behaviors that constitute acquaintance rape and to establish administrative processes for dealing with rape. Such policies must be disseminated to all students and explained in the campus's annual security report (Fisher, Cullen, & Turner, 2000). The intent of these reforms is to teach students to recognize rape and sexual assault and to prevent rape. Unfortunately, students rarely read such publications or student handbooks, thus the policies have little or no effect on victimization rates.

Hate Rape

Federal law allows prosecution of bias crimes committed on the basis of race, color, religion, or national origin. On June 15, 2004, the Senate approved the Local Law Enforcement Enhancement Act. The Act expands federal hate crime legislation, by adding new protected categories of gender, sexual orientation, and disability (Erickson & Shevin, 2004). This bill was not supported, but its passage would have allowed prosecutors to expand charges of rape to define the incident as a hate crime, if applicable.

Prevalence and Correlates

The Uniform Crime Reports (UCR) compiles data from police records sent to the Federal Bureau of Investigation. The UCR subsumes all attempted and completed carnal knowledge of a female that is forcible and against her will under the category forcible rape. Statutory rape and other sex offenses are excluded. According to the 2002 UCR (U. S. Department of Justice, 2003c), an estimated 95,136 forcible rapes were reported to law enforcement agencies—64.8 per 100,000 female inhabitants. This represented a 3.5 percent increase over 2001, but a 15.6 percent decrease since 1993. On average, one reported forcible rape occurred every six minutes. The highest percentage of forcible rapes was reported in the warmest months. The rate of rape per female inhabitant was highest in the Midwest. Surprisingly, Alaska has the highest rate of reported rape—an extreme outlier—and New York has one of the lowest rates. In fact, contrary to expectation, the Northeast had the lowest rate and was well below the national average in both rate of rape and overall crime index. A loose regional pattern exists; however, there are significant state-by-state differences within each region. The risk of rape was highest for women living in a city outside a Metropolitan Statistical Area and lowest in rural counties. Preliminary 2003 data released in May 2004 report the incidence of forcible rape down by nearly 2 percent from 2002 (U. S. Department of Justice, 2004a).

In contrast to the UCR, the National Crime Victimization Survey (NCVS) compiles data from responses to interviews of victims. The NCVS underwent an extensive redesign that was first used in 1992. NCVS interviewers began to ask questions specific to the category of sexual assault (Eigenberg, 1990) and cued interviewees regarding non-stereotypical crimes involving acquaintances. Kindermann, Lynch, and Cantor (1997) report that these new interviewing procedures produced a 157 percent increase in the rate of victimization for the crime of rape. They conclude that the redesign achieved its intended purpose to capture a larger portion of the unreported incidence of rape and sexual assault.

Though all rapes are assaults of a sexual nature, the redesigned NCVS uses the term *sexual assault* to refer to a specific form of assault that is separate from and less than rape. The 2002 NCVS Criminal Victimization Glossary (U.S. Department of Justice, 2003b) defines rape as forced penetration of the vagina, anus, or mouth by the offender or by a foreign object. Force includes both psychological coercion and physical force. Attempted rape is uncompleted penetration and also includes verbal threats of rape. Sexual assault is defined as any sexual victimization that does not meet the definition of either rape or attempted rape, including attacks or attempted attacks that may or may not involve force. Sexual assault includes behavior such as fondling or grabbing. A continuum of rape based on the NCVS definitions moves from rape (the most serious category) through attempted rape to sexual assault (the least serious category).

Trends and the 2002 Victimization Data

Data presented in Table 8.1, when calculated as a percent of all violent victimizations, show that rape/sexual assault decreased only 0.9 percent from 9.5 percent (in 1993) to 8.6 percent (in 2002) of the violent victimizations of women per 1,000 persons age 12 or older. Though rape/sexual assault remained relatively stable as a percent of all violent victimizations from 1993 to 2002, the incidence of rape was down by more than 50 percent. This change was consistent with the change in crimes of violence as a whole. The within-year differences of the three categories of rape, attempted rape, and sexual assault remained relatively constant with minor discrepancies from 1993 to 2002.

Rape continues to be the least frequently occurring violent crime. However, when specific types and degrees of violent crimes are examined (see Table 8.1), the incidence of rape/attempted rape in 2002 was higher than robbery with injury and virtually equal to aggravated assault with injury.

TABLE 8.1   *Selected Rates* of Female Criminal Victimization and Percent Change,** 1993–2002*

Type of crime	1993	1994	1995	1996	1997	1998	1999	2000	2001	2002	Percent change 1993–2002
Crimes of violence	42.3	42.5	36.5	34.6	33.0	30.4	28.8	23.2	23.0	20.8	–50.8
Completed violence	14.8	14.1	12.2	11.3	11.0	10.9	9.8	8.7	8.0	7.8	–47.3
Rape/sexual assault	4.0	3.7	2.8	2.3	2.5	2.7	3.0	2.1	1.9	1.8	–55.0
Rape/attempted rape	2.7	2.7	1.9	1.5	1.5	1.6	1.5	1.2	1.2	1.2	–55.6
Rape	1.4	1.5	1.2	0.7	0.9	0.9	1.1	0.8	0.7	0.7	–50.0
Attempted rape	1.3	1.3	0.7	0.8	0.7	0.7	0.4	0.5	0.5	0.5	–61.5
Sexual assault	1.4	1.0	0.8	0.8	0.9	1.1	1.5	0.9	0.7	0.6	–57.1
Completed/attempted robbery with injury	1.1	1.4	1.0	1.1	0.9	1.0	0.9	0.5	0.6	0.7	–36.4
Aggravated assault with injury	2.7	2.5	1.9	1.8	2.1	1.4	1.3	1.0	1.2	1.3	–51.9
Simple assault with minor injury	6.7	6.5	6.1	5.6	5.5	5.1	4.6	4.5	4.2	4.2	–37.3

*Victimization rates per 1,000 persons age 12 or older or per 1,000 households

**Calculated change from 1993 to 2002 does not account for any changes in the intervening years 1994–2001.

Data included in this table are from U.S. Department of Justice, Bureau of Justice Statistics (1996, 1997, 2000a, 2000b, 2000c, 2000d, 2001, 2002, 2003a, 2003b), *Criminal Victimization in the United States, Statistical Tables* for the years 1993–2002, adapted from Table 2: Number of victimizations and victimization rates for persons age 12 and over, by type of crime and sex of victims.

The Crime.   The NCVS data (U.S. Department of Justice, 2003b) show that rape and sexual assault most frequently occurred while involved in leisure activities away from home or in some activity at home other than sleeping. Just over half of all rape/sexual assaults occurred in a place where women typically feel secure: at or near their own home; at or near a friend's, relative's, or neighbor's home; or inside a school building/on school property. Rape and sexual assault are crimes of known places and crimes of the night. Seventy-five percent of all rapes and sexual assaults occur within five miles of home. Two-thirds of all incidents occur between 6 P.M. and 6 A.M.

Victims reported that no weapon was used in 85 percent of rape/sexual assault cases. Of all violent crimes, rape and sexual assault victims were the least likely to report the use of a weapon in the crime. The estimates of weapon use in rape cases are of questionable reliability since they are based on ten or fewer cases. These estimates show that weapons were more likely to be used by strangers. The weapon of choice for strangers was handguns while acquaintances used knives (U.S. Department of Justice, 2003b).

Victims used self-protective measures in over 80 percent of all rape/sexual assault victimizations—12 percent more often than for crimes of violence as a whole. Rape survivors were more likely to take self-protective measures when dealing with acquaintances. Females, whites, and individuals age 20 to 34 were most likely to use self-protective measures. Though data indicate that all victims age 65 and over took self-protective measures, this result is based on too few cases to be reliable. The most frequently used self-protective measures were resisting the offender, running away, or persuading the offender. In those situations in which self-protective measures were used, survivors believed that they helped the situation in just over half the cases and hurt the situation in about one-fourth of the cases. Survivors viewed the self-protective measures as helpful when they were able to escape, avoid injury, or scare the offender away. Victims believed measures taken by other individuals to assist them rarely hurt the situation and helped in just under half the cases. Rozee (2004) suggests that at the first sign of verbal or physical aggression potential victims should immediately use physical resistance to avoid rape and injury. Women who used such strategies were no more likely to suffer physical injury as a result of their actions.

The Victim.   Women were six times more likely than males to be victims of rape/sexual assault in 2002 (Rennison & Rand, 2003). According to the NCVS (U.S. Department of Justice, 2003b), the categories of women with the highest rate of rape/sexual assault were blacks, persons age 16 to 19, persons who had never married, and urban dwellers. Black women are more than twice as likely to be assaulted as whites or Hispanics. Urban areas have significantly higher victimization rates for all race/ethnicity groups. Those who have lived in their current residence for less than six months at the time of their interview for the NCVS were more than twice as likely to have been raped as those who have lived in their residence for longer than six months (U.S. Department of Justice, 2003b, Table 50).

Of the estimated 216,090 female rape/sexual assault victims in 2002, two-thirds were acquaintance rape victims (U.S. Department of Justice, 2003b). Hispanics were more likely than any other group to be assaulted by a stranger. Rapes reported in the 2002 victimization study were typically intraracial when there was a lone offender—the rape was most likely to be white-on-white or black-on-black.

The Offender.   The victimization data (U.S. Department of Justice, 2003b) report that lone assailants commit the vast majority of all rape victimizations. Seventy percent of the lone offenders were under the age of 30, over half were white, and virtually all were male. Some form of drug and alcohol usage by the offender was reported in almost half of all rape incidents.

Gang rape is relatively rare, accounting for 15 percent of all victimizations. Sixty-four percent of the gang rape cases were acquaintance rape with at least one of the offenders well known by the victim in one-fourth of these incidents. A male offender was involved in every reported gang rape, with over 85 percent of gang rapes committed by only male offenders. One-fifth of these incidents were committed by offenders of mixed race and over 40 percent by offenders of mixed age.

The Effect on the Victim.   Less than 15 percent of all rapes/sexual assaults resulted in loss of time from work by the survivor (U.S. Department of Justice, 2003b). Of those almost 40 percent were away from work for less than one day. Less than one-third of all rape/sexual assault survivors received medical care. Over half of those who did receive medical care went to an emergency room, a hospital, or a doctor's office or clinic. Assistance to survivors aids the healing process, but more than 80 percent of all survivors report receiving no assistance. When assistance was received, it was most likely to come from a government agency.

Reporting to Police.   Reporting to the police has long been a problem for rape and sexual assault victims. In 1993, approximately 30 percent of female rape victims indicated that they had reported their assault to the police. By 2002, over 55 percent reported the rape. Rape was more likely to be reported than sexual assault. Reporting increased dramatically for women who were victimized by strangers (U.S. Department of Justice, 2003b). The female reporting rate for rape in 2002 was higher than the overall rates for violent crime, attempted/threatened violence, assault, and simple assault, as well as the individual reporting rate for simple assault without injury (see Table 8.2). The rate for violent crime reporting to the police by women increased 9 percent from 1993 to 2002, while the reporting of rape/sexual assault increased by over 25 percent. Only "attempts to take property" showed more dramatic increases in violent crime reporting by women (see Table 8.2).

Campus Rape.   Campus rape statistics vary widely depending on the study used to analyze events. The NCVS statistics, averaging victimization rates from 1995 to 2000, reported 6.8 incidents of rape or sexual assault per 1,000 female students (U.S. Department of Justice, 2003d). The National College Women Sexual Victimization (NCWSV) study, of the 1996–1997 academic year, reported 27.7 victims of completed and attempted rape per 1,000 female students. Due to victims reporting multiple victimizations, the rate of incidents was higher: 35.3 per 1,000. These discrepancies between studies are most likely due to the wording of interview questions. In the NCWSV interviewers asked direct, descriptive questions of the victim and perpetrator's behavior, while the NCVS questions were not behaviorally spe-

TABLE 8.2   *NCVS Percent of Crime Reported to the Police by Females by Type of Crime, 1993 and 2002*

Type of Crime	1993	2002	Percent Change
Violent crime	43.9	53.0	+9.1
Completed violence	52.1	61.6	+9.5
Attempted/threatened violence	39.5	47.8	+8.3
Rape/sexual assault*	30.2	55.8	+25.6
Robbery	61.9	79.3	+17.4
Completed/property taken	69.7	79.4	+9.7
With injury	76.2	85.3	+9.1
Without injury	66.7	74.6	+7.9
Attempted to take property	46.1	78.7	+32.6
With injury	*55.7	**100.0	+44.3
Without injury	42.6	**70.6	+28.0
Assault	43.5	50.3	+6.8
Aggravated	58.3	62.8	+4.5
With injury	58.4	58.8	+0.4
Threatened with weapon	58.2	65.2	+7.0
Simple	38.8	47.3	+8.5
With minor injury	52.8	59.0	+6.2
Without injury	34.1	42.3	+8.2

*Includes verbal threats and threats of sexual assault.

**Estimate is based on about ten or fewer sample cases.

Data included in this table are from U.S. Department of Justice (1996 and 2003b), Table 93: Percent of Victimizations Reported to the Police, by Type of Crime, Victim–Offender Relationship, and Sex of Victims.

cific. Rather than asking "have you been raped," NCWSV used questions such as, "Since school began in fall 1996, has anyone made you have sexual intercourse by using force or threatening to harm you or someone close to you? Just so there is no mistake, by intercourse I mean putting a penis in your vagina" (Fisher et al., 2000, p. 6). With wording exceptions, the NCWSV study used the same methodology as the NCVS (Fisher et al., 2000).

Most college sexual victimizations occur in residences (apartments, homes, dorm rooms, or fraternities), at night, with men the victims know. NCWSV reported that approximately 90 percent of victims knew their attacker and less than 5 percent reported their attack to the police (Fisher et al., 2000). Lack of reporting of campus rape is partially due to victims not defining their experience as rape. Fisher et al. (2000) found in their study that half of the respondents who answered yes to the description of a completed rape replied "no" when asked if they had been raped. Other reasons the women gave for not reporting the sexual victimization included desire of secrecy from family members and friends, lack of proof of their victimization, doubt as to the seriousness of incident or the belief that others would doubt it, and fear of hostility from the criminal justice system.

Aftermath of Rape

Rape is a severe, traumatic, and often life-threatening event from which many victims never fully recover (Resick & Schnicke, 1993). With all forms of rape, attempted or completed, victims and those who know them experience fear and emotional trauma. Stranger rape causes victims and their loved ones to feel powerless to prevent such attacks because the event happens without warning and with no prior contact with the offender. Acquaintance rape is emotionally harrowing because it breaks an expectation of trust, leaving victims feeling no one can be trusted.

Rape Trauma Syndrome

Burgess and Holstrom (1974) conducted rape victimization research interviewing victims admitted to hospital emergency wards. They discovered rape trauma syndrome (RTS), which is an acute stress reaction resulting in a combination of emotional and physical reactions to rape. Victims of RTS go through three phases in their attempt to cope with the stress of rape (see Figure 8.1). One-fourth of the rape victims Burgess and Holstrom interviewed still did not feel that they had fully recovered four to six years after the rape. A primary post-rape focus of all the victims was on protecting themselves from future attacks.

Resick and Schnicke (1993) present RTS as another example of posttraumatic stress disorder. The National Center for Victims of Crime (2004b) does not discuss RTS, but rather rape-related posttraumatic stress disorder (RR-PTSD). The four major symptoms of RR-PTSD are re-experiencing the trauma, social withdrawal, avoidance behaviors and actions, and increased physiological arousal.

FIGURE 8.1   *Rape Trauma Syndrome*

Phase 1: *Immediate* *Reaction*	• 0–3 weeks after rape • Fear of death or physical harm • Feelings: fear, humiliation, embarrassment, anger, revenge, self-blame • Actions: crying, sobbing, smiling, restlessness, controlled calmness
Phase 2: *Recovery* *Phase*	• Phase may last months, years, or indefinitely—length varies based on victim's support structure, ego strength, and treatment received as victim • Increased fears and awareness of idiosyncratic factors associated with their rapes • Nightmares frequent • Actions: increased number of visits to family and friends, change of address and/or telephone number common
Phase 3: *Transition* *Phase*	• Begins several months after rape • Victims become survivors • Survivors more or less return to normal lives • Significant number of women never fully recover • Actions: focus on protection from future attacks

Information included in this table is from Burgess and Holstrom (1974).

Gordon and Riger (1989) found that whether victims blame themselves or not, their stories indicate the devastating realities of rape. There is no typical rape, no typical rape victim, and no typical rapist. Those who know a rape victim and have learned about the victim's experiences incorporate this knowledge with their own feelings; this knowledge becomes an important component of their own reaction to rape.

Postrape Adjustment

Victims respond to rape with two predominant styles: an expressed style in which the victim openly expresses her feelings, and a controlled style in which the feelings may be masked by calm. Reactivating symptoms of previous traumatic experiences such as physical illness, psychiatric problems, or social difficulties may also compound the rape victim's reaction. Responses to rape under such conditions can be negatively influenced by previous social and emotional difficulties (Koss & Harvey, 1987). The severity of a victim's reactions does not depend on severity of the assault. Instead the victim's social support system, ego strength, life stress, age, and life stage determine the severity of her response (McCahill, Meyer, & Fischman, 1979).

Winkel and Koppelaar (1991) found that the victim's self-presentation determines whether the victim will be secondarily victimized by those in the victim's environment. When victims' self-presentation after rape was emotional, they were seen as exhibiting caution in the rape incident and therefore were not assessed responsibility for the rape. However, a controlled style of self-presentation resulted in secondary victimization. An example of society's propensity for victim-blaming, these victims were perceived as less credible, less careful, and more responsible for the rape occurrence.

Child victims appear to experience the least short-term problems in reaction to rape, yet they face serious long-term consequences (Koss & Harvey, 1987). Children may accommodate and assume responsibility for the victimization or they may deny the reality of the rape if met with disbelief or rejection when reporting the rape incident. Adolescents are very reluctant to tell anyone about rape, to seek help, or to return after an initial counseling session. A newly emancipated young adult may experience conflict about separation and independence, fearing the rape will be used as evidence that she should not live alone and cannot take care of herself.

Women with children are concerned about their children's reaction. They are also concerned with finding caretakers during their absence that may result from undergoing therapeutic counseling or attending the offender's trial. Other women worry that they may become emotionally unable to care for their children as a result of their failure to cope with rape. Middle-aged women often get little support from spouses who discount the severity of the rape crisis. Elderly women often react with extreme and paralyzing fears (Koss & Harvey, 1987).

Successful therapy to transition rape victims to survivors helps the victims:

• To accept and integrate the rape as a reality that cannot be ignored or discarded.
• To experience the full range of emotions attached to the rape.
• To explore how their prior experiences and beliefs affected their reactions.
• To explore how their prior experiences and beliefs were affected by this traumatic incident. (Resick & Schnicke, 1993)

Motivation for Rape

Researchers offer several theories to explain rape, and these various theoretical propositions have been examined empirically and explicitly (Ageton, 1983; Baron & Straus, 1989; Dietz, 1978; LaFree, 1982; Williams & Holmes, 1981). However, the sociologists, criminologists, and feminist scholars who study this social problem do not agree on any single primary motivation for rape. Perhaps this is due to the two frameworks from which rape can be viewed: rape as multiple isolated incidents with each perpetrator having his own motivation, and rape as a socially instituted act of violence toward the female gender.

Before 1970, most research approached rape psychoanalytically. The sexual dysfunction of the rapist resulted from inappropriate child-rearing behaviors of mothers or the sexual inadequacies of wives. Later studies adopted the learned personality disorder perspective, in which researchers studied motivation, sexual and aggressive impulses, and descriptive features of the rape itself. Knight, Rosenberg, and Schneider (1985) identified three categories of rapists. One is aggressive during the offense either to enhance his sense of power or masculinity or to express feelings of mastery and conquest. Another commits rape out of anger toward women and seeks to hurt, humiliate, and degrade his victim. He becomes sexually aroused in response to violence and commits brutal, sometimes bizarre assaults. The final type has an extensive criminal history; sexual offenses are only one component of an impulsive, antisocial lifestyle.

Feminist Theories

For feminist researchers, rape is ultimately a result of gender role stereotyping (Bourque, 1989). They argue that society labels behavior as feminine or masculine based on early socialization. Gender role theory provides a source of hope for those interested in changing the roles that reinforce assaultive behaviors and their acceptance. What is learned can be unlearned; gender expectations can be changed.

Research consistently shows that rapists have conservative positions and behavior regarding sex, women, and sex roles. They are more likely than other men to have been sexually abused and their attitudes are more likely to support violence. Gordon and Riger (1989) report that over 70 to 80 percent of rapists have been sexually abused as children compared to 30 to 40 percent in the general prison population. Men who assault women are less likely to call the assault a rape and are more likely to view their behavior as within accepted sex roles.

Feminist theorists view rape as an extreme form of sexual exploitation violently keeping women in their place. From the feminist perspective, male dominance in the form of rape is merely aggressive behavior toward women—an inevitable part of maintaining their position of power within the culture. A lack of equal pay, access to resources, and status with males subordinate females. Additionally, males are socialized to be aggressive seducers and women to be passive prey and sex objects.

The most comprehensive and often cited research on imprisoned rapists is that of Groth (1979). Based on his research, rapists agree with the feminists' contention that rape is an act of power—these convicted rapists did not report passion or lust as a motivation for their rapes. They reported desire to exert control over or to possess the women, desire to lash out or attack the victim, or a combination of power and anger as motivation.

Men maintain positions of power by raping women and through women's fear of being raped. Women develop fear through exposure to friends' or acquaintances' rapes, their personal victimization experiences, and media portrayal of rape. Society's propensity to blame women for rape results in a higher use of precautionary behaviors, often restricting their movement within society (Rozee, 2004). Portrayals of men as essential guardians to protect females are ironic, because male acquaintances and dates commit most rapes. The most problematic aspect of male violence is that no matter what precautionary behaviors women use or how virtuous their character, violence still occurs (Pharr, 2001).

Individualistic Theories

Many individualistic theories explain rape as a result of men's biology. One theory says that rape occurs because men are overcome by a sexual urge and cannot control themselves. A second biological explanation is that men rape due to a need to reproduce. Another individualistic theory claims the perpetrator has a psychopathological condition, some mental or emotional illness, that makes him not "normal" (Janinski, 2001). Other theories place the blame on either prior sexual abuse of the perpetrator or on alcohol use by the rapist.

Limitations of Rape Motivation Theories

No individual theory is adequate for explaining the motivation of rape. Feminist theories do not explain the differences between males, because all males do not commit rape. Their theories assume that a social condition can predict an individual's thoughts or actions. Biological, psychopathological, sexual abuse, or alcohol-related explanations negate an individual's control over his actions. None of these singular explanations make sense to victims because victims rarely experience rape as a mere act of political dominance, power, or anger or resulting from the nature of the rapist. From the victim's point of view, rape is a complex phenomenon of sexual and physical violence. Several interlocking theories must be used to address motivation and to combat this social problem.

Policy Implications

Many policy and legal changes have focused on unveiling the "hidden" nature of rape. Baumer, Felson, and Messner (2003) found that by the early 1990s there was no longer a significant difference in reporting to police of incidents committed by strangers and acquaintances. While this finding is encouraging, the fact remains that many incidents are still not reported to anyone and many survivors still fail to recognize their experience as rape. Only when women believe that the stigma against rape reporting has vanished and that the criminal justice system acts without prejudice toward rape victims will rape be reported at rates equal to that of other violent crimes. Governments and communities must act to improve the societal and justice system responses to rape.

Preventing Acquaintance Rape

Society continues to ignore the acquaintance rape problem. Though acquaintance rape makes up approximately 70 percent of all rape incidents, the media and police place emphasis on stranger rape. The precautions typically recommended for preventing stranger rape (e.g., locking doors and windows, walking in groups, not letting strangers in) are not useful for acquaintance rape. Children and adult women are taught to be afraid of strangers who might attack them, but little or no attention is paid to the need to be alert to the behaviors of acquaintances.

The concrete danger signals of acquaintance rape fall in four areas: sexual entitlement, power and control, hostility and anger, and interpersonal violence (Rozee, Bateman, & Gilmore, 1991). Dangerously inappropriate behaviors are found in each category:

- *Sexual entitlement:* touching women without regard to their wishes, inappropriately sexualizing relationships that are not sexual, using conversation that is inappropriately intimate, telling sexual jokes at inappropriate times or places, and making inappropriate comments about women's bodies or sexuality
- *Power and control:* interrupting women, exhibiting inappropriate competitiveness, being a "bad loser," using intimidating body language, and game playing
- *Hostility and anger:* exhibiting a quick temper, blaming others when things go wrong, and transforming other emotions into anger
- *Interpersonal violence:* using threats when displaying anger, using violence in situations that do not clearly call for it, approving observed violence, and justifying violence

Several of these behaviors may overlap or interact. Education must be provided regarding these behavioral indicators to forewarn potential victims. Women must also be taught strategies that have been successful in stopping rape. Both acquaintance and stranger rape research has found that women who fight back when assaulted are less likely to be harmed (Bart & O'Brien, 1985; Ullman & Knight, 1992).

Law Enforcement Issues

Police should receive annual training regarding rape that includes awareness and prevention as well as investigative knowledge and skills. Lauritsen's and Schaum's (2004) findings lead to the recommendation that police executives develop methods for police to be the "guardians" in communities where most households are headed by single females. Landlords of apartment complexes and housing authorities should be cognizant of the need to place tenants specifically for guardianship to be available. Kraska and Kappeler (1999) explored instances of police sexual violence against women and found that some forms of sexual violence may be institutionally supported. Therefore, specific policies should be enacted to guard against improper use of authority by police or others placed in such "guardianship" roles.

Sexual assault nurse examiner programs that utilize specially trained nurses in the initial forensic medical exam should be available as described by Littel (2001). These programs enhance health care, reporting, and prosecution of rape cases (Crandall & Helitzer, 2003).

The predictors of rape victimization include prior rape (indicative of a failure in healing) and use of alcohol or other drugs. The justice system cannot be the only recourse—therapeutic intervention in the form of access to mental health care and substance abuse treatment are essential.

Urine and hair samples should be obtained from rape victims when there is any reason to believe that a date-rape drug may have been used. The findings of Negrusz (2001) indicate that special testing procedures can detect traces of the drugs in urine fourteen days after administration of a single dose of Rohypnol,® while traces remain in hair for at least one month.

Higher Education Issues

Institutions of higher education should provide a mechanism for rape victims to receive assistance, particularly in the evening and early morning hours when most campus rapes occur (Fisher et al., 2000). Karjane, Fisher, and Cullen (2002) reported that the contact person listed in the security brochures of almost half of the schools was not available 24 hours a day. This service must be provided 24 hours a day every day of the year.

Training on rape, its prevention, and appropriate response should be provided to the general student body, faculty, and staff on a continuing basis. Peer educators should be used in these training sessions. Karjane et al. (2002) report that only one-third of schools mandated training for faculty and staff, and 60 percent of schools provided no training to students on rape. When training was conducted for students, it was provided for student staff members in residence halls and student security officers.

Training should be provided for campus law enforcement/security officers and all people to whom formal complaints are likely to be made. Karjane et al. (2002) found that less than 40 percent of the schools required such training. Victim-related support services should be provided to special populations of students (e.g., those who are nonnative English speakers, who live off-campus, or are disabled). Karjane et al. (2002) found that such services are provided by only one-fourth of the schools.

Procedures for handling reported incidences of rape should be designed to facilitate and encourage reporting and to deal with the case expeditiously and fairly. Schools should provide for confidential and anonymous reporting and establish written protocols for law enforcement, medical, and victim assistance personnel to coordinate the campus and community crisis responses. Forensic medical evidence should be collected by sexual assault nurse examiners. Such procedures should assure that the survivor is not further victimized by any stage of the process and that survivors' needs are met.

NCVS Methodological Issues

The authors faced significant frustration by the fact that the estimates in many of the 2002 NCVS statistical tables with various demographic and descriptive breakdowns were based on cell frequencies with below ten sample cases. The validity of such data is suspect. Estimates based on less than ten sample cases first appeared in a major crime category in 1997. The NCVS should either over-sample every year or conduct larger samples every two years rather than average data over two years as done in recent research (Rennison & Rand, 2003).

The results of Fisher et al. (2000) suggest that the wording of NCVS questions regarding rape need reexamination. The extent of hidden rape remains significant due to lack of behaviorally specific questions. Full governmental commitment is needed to obtain valid data concerning rape victimization.

Conclusion

Rape produces fear in women, causes emotional and physical trauma, and restricts their social movements. Rape most often occurs within the victim's "comfort zone" and is perpetrated by an individual she trusts. Women and children must be taught to recognize dangerous relationships and to deal with them assertively. Education programs must teach successful resistance strategies.

Society must acknowledge that general attitudes toward women affect the treatment women receive at the hands of men they know. Our nation and its institutions must accept responsibility for changing the way rape victims are viewed and treated. Victim blaming must cease. No matter what clothing she wears, what her intoxication level, where she happened to be, how many times she has had sex and with how many partners, rape is never a woman's fault. In many ways, rape survivor advocates are still fighting the same battles of victim blaming and individuation of the problem of rape as they were before all the national attention and research began (Russo, 2001). Those interested in women's rights must stand vigilant, and work for and support research, education, and change throughout society.

Review Questions

1. Why might being labeled a victim be problematic for some women?

2. List all of the protective actions you take to personally avoid assault. Discuss your responses with someone of a different gender and compare your results. Are your responses different? Why or why not?

3. Can a prostitute be raped? Why or why not?

4. Compare and contrast perceptual and legal definitions of rape.

5. Briefly summarize the victimization data on rape. Who are the rapists? Their victims? Where do the rapes tend to occur? What other situational variables were reported? Why is the incidence of officially reported rape decreasing?

6. Summarize the theories and research on motivation.

7. What is the extent of acquaintance rape in American society? What can society do to prevent it?

8. What danger signals indicate the potential for assault from an acquaintance? What are some strategies you recommend or could implement to reduce the likelihood that you will be sexually assaulted by an acquaintance?

Key Terms

Rape victim
Rape survivor
Rape crisis center
Perceptual definition of rape

Personal definition of rape
Statutory rape
Forcible rape
Implied consent

Rape shield laws
Rape as a hidden crime
Stranger rape
Acquaintance rape
Date rape
Campus rape

Gang rape
Stalker rape
Marital rape
Hate rape
Rape trauma syndrome
Reasonableness standard

References

Ageton, S. S. (1983). *Sexual assaults among adolescents.* Lexington, MA: D.C. Heath and Company.

Allison, J. A., & Wrightsman, L. S. (1993). *Rape: The misunderstood crime.* Newbury Park, CA: Sage.

Anderson, M. (2004). Time to reform rape shield laws: Kobe Bryant case highlights holes in the armor. *Criminal Justice* 19 (2), 14–19.

Anderson, M. (2002). Chastity requirement to sexuality license: Sexual consent and a new rape shield law. *George Washington Law Review* 70 (1), 51–197.

Baron, L., & Straus, M. A. (1989). *Four theories of rape in American society: A state level analysis.* New Haven: Yale University Press.

Bart, P. B., & O'Brien, P. H. (1985). *Stopping rape: Successful survival strategies.* New York: Pergamon.

Baumer, E. P., Felson, R. B., & Messner, S. F. (2003). Changes in police notification for rape, 1973–2000. *Criminology* 41, 841–872.

Bechhofer, L., & Parrot, A. (1991). What is acquaintance rape? In A. Parrot & L. Bechhofer (Eds.), *Acquaintance rape: The hidden crime* (pp. 9–25). New York: Wiley and Sons.

Bergen, R. K. (1999). *Marital rape.* Retrieved October 2, 2004 from http://www.vaw.umn.edu/documents/vawnet/mrape/mrape.html.

Bourque, L. B. (1989). *Defining rape.* Durham, NC: Duke University.

Burgess, A. W. (Ed.). (1985). *Rape and sexual assault.* New York: Garland.

Burgess, A. W., & Holstrom, L. L. (1974). *Rape: Victims of crisis.* Bowie, MD: Brady.

Chrisler, J. C., Golden, C., & Rozee, P. D. (Eds.). (2004). *Lectures on the psychology of women.* New York: McGraw-Hill.

Crandall, C. S., & Helitzer, D. (2003). *Impact evaluation of a sexual assault nurse examiner (SANE) program.* (Final report, NCJ 203276, NIJ Grant # 1998-WT-VX-0027.) Retrieved July 12, 2004, from http://www.ncjrs.org/pdffiles1/nij/grants/203276.pdf.

Dietz, P. E. (1978). Social factors in rapist behavior. In R. T. Rada (Ed.), *Clinical aspects of the rapist* (pp. 59–115). New York: Grune and Stratton.

Eigenberg, H. (1990). The national crime survey and rape: The case of the missing question. *Justice Quarterly* 7, 655–671.

Erickson, J., & Shevin, C. (2004, June 18). *Senate approves federal hate crime legislation; fails to include all affected groups.* Retrieved July 17, 2004, from http://www.now.org/issues/violence.

Estrich, S. (1987). *Real rape: How the legal system victimizes women who say no.* Cambridge, MA: Harvard University Press.

Fisher, B., Cullen, F., & Turner, M. (2000). *The sexual victimization of college women.* (NCJ 182369. Bureau of Justice Statistics.) Washington DC: U.S. Department of Justice.

Gaines, L. K., & Cordner, G. W. (Eds.). (1999). *Policing perspectives: An anthology.* Los Angeles: Roxbury.

Gordon, M. T., & Riger, S. (1989). *The female fear.* New York: Free Press

Groth, N. A. (1979). *Men who rape: The psychology of the offender.* New York: Plenum.

Janinski, J. L. (2001). Theoretical explanations for violence against women. In C. M. Renzetti, J. L. Edleson, & R. K. Bergen (Eds.). *Sourcebook on violence against women* (pp. 5–18). London: Sage.

Karjane, J. K., Fisher, B. B., & Cullen, F. T. (2002). *Campus sexual assault: How American's institutions of higher education respond.* (Final report, NIJ Grant # 1999-WA-VX-0008.) Newton, MA: Education Development Center.

Kindermann, C., Lynch, J., & Cantor, D. (1997). *Effects of redesign on victimization estimates.* (NCJ 164381. Bureau of Justice Statistics, National Crime Victimization Survey.) Washington DC: U.S. Department of Justice.

Knight, R. A., Rosenberg, R., & Schneider, B. (1985). Classification of sexual offenders: Perspectives, methods and validation. In A. W. Burgess (Ed.), *Rape and sexual assault* (pp. 222–293). New York: Garland.

Koss, M., & Harvey, M. (1987). *The rape victim: Clinical and community approaches to treatment.* Lexington, MA: Greene.

Koss, M. P. (1985). The hidden rape victim: Personality, attitudinal, and situational characteristics. *Psychology of Women Quarterly* 9, 193–212.

Kraska, P. B., & Kappeler, V. E. (1999). Exploring police sexual violence against women. In L. K. Gaines & G. W. Cordner (Eds.), *Policing perspectives: An anthology* (pp. 324–341). Los Angeles: Roxbury.

LaFree, G. D. (1982). Male power and female victimization: Toward a theory of interracial rape. *American Journal of Sociology* 88, 311–328.

LaFree, G. D. (1989). *Rape and criminal justice: The social construction of sexual assault.* Belmont, CA: Wadsworth.

Lauritsen, J. L., & Schaum, R. J. (2004). The social ecology of violence against women. *Criminology* 42, 323–357.

Littel, K. (2001). *Sexual assault nurse examiner (SANE) programs: Improving the community response to sexual assault victims.* Washington, DC: U.S. Department of Justice.

Margolick, D. (1984). Top court in New York rules men can be charged with rape of wives. *New York Times,* December 1, 1.

Marsh, J. C., Geist, A., & Caplan, N. (1982). *Rape and the limits of law reform.* Boston: Auburn House.

McCahill, T. W., Meyer, L. C., & Fischman, A. M. (1979). *The aftermath of rape.* Lexington, MA: Heath.

National Center for Victims of Crime. (2004a). *FAQ: Rape shield laws.* Retrieved August 19, 2004, from http://www.ncvc.org/ncvc.

National Center for Victims of Crime. (2004b). *Rape-related posttraumatic stress disorder.* Retrieved August 19, 2004 from http://www.ncvc.org/ncvc.

National Organization for Women Legal Defense and Education Fund. (2004). *Violence against women act of 2000 as passed by Congress.* Retrieved August 23, 2004 from http://www.nowldef.org/html/issues/vio/vawapassed.shtml.

Negrusz, A. (2001). *Detection of "date-rape" drugs in hair and urine, final report.* (NCJ 201894.) Retrieved 07/12/2004 from http://www.ncjrs.org/pdffiles1/nij/grants/201894.pdf.

Nnamdi, K. (Moderator). (2004, March 10). *The Kojo Nnamdi Show.* National Public Radio: WAMU. Retrieved on August 27, 2004 from http://www.ncvc.org.

Parrot, A. (1991a). Institutional response: How can acquaintance rape be prevented? In A. Parrot & L. Bechhofer (Eds.), *Acquaintance rape: The hidden crime* (pp. 355–367). New York: Wiley and Sons.

Pharr, S. (2001). Homophobia as a weapon of sexism. In P. S. Rothenberg (Ed.), *Race, class, and gender in the United States: An integrated study* (5th ed.; pp. 143–152). New York: Worth.

Rada, R. T. (Ed.). (1978). *Clinical aspects of the rapist.* New York: Grune and Stratton.

Rennison, C. M., & Rand, M. R. (2003). *Criminal victimization, 2002.* (NCJ 199994. Bureau of Justice Statistics, National Crime Victimization Survey.) Washington DC: U.S. Department of Justice.

Renzetti, C. M., Edleson, J. L., & Bergen, R. K. (Eds.). (2001). *Sourcebook on violence against women.* London: Sage.

Resick, P. A., & Schnicke, M. K. (1993). *Cognitive processing therapy for rape victims: A treatment manual.* Newbury Park, CA: Sage.

Rothenberg, P. S. (Ed.). (2001). *Race, class, and gender in the United States: An integrated study* (5th ed.). New York: Worth.

Rozee, P. D. (2004). Women's fear of rape: Cause consequences, and coping. In J. C. Chrisler, C. Golden, & P. D. Rozee (Eds.), *Lectures on the psychology of women* (pp. 277–290). New York: McGraw-Hill.

Rozee, P. D., Bateman, P., & Gilmore, T. (1991). The personal perspective of acquaintance rape prevention: A three-tier approach. In A. Parrot & L. Bechhofer (Eds.), *Acquaintance rape: The hidden crime* (337–354). New York: Wiley and Sons.

Russo, A. (2001). *Taking back our lives: A call for action for the feminist movement.* New York: Routledge.

Spohn, C., & Horney, J. (1992). "The law's the law, but fair is fair": Rape shield laws and officials' assessment of sexual history evidence. *Criminology* 29, 137–161.

Ullman, S. E., & Knight, R. A. (1992). Fighting back: Women's resistance to rape. *Journal of Interpersonal Violence* 7, 31–43.

U.S. Department of Justice. (1996). *Criminal victimization in the United States, 1993 Statistical Tables.* (NCJ 151657.) Retrieved July 14, 2004 from http://www.ojp.usdoj.gov/bjs/pub/pdf/cvus93.pdf.

U.S. Department of Justice. (1997). *Criminal victimization in the United States, 1994 Statistical Tables.* (NCJ 162126.) Retrieved July 14, 2004 from http://www.ojp.usdoj.gov/bjs/pub/pdf/cvius94.pdf.

U.S. Department of Justice. (2000a). *Criminal victimization in the United States, 1995 Statistical Tables.* (NCJ 171129.) Retrieved July 14, 2004 from http://www.ojp.usdoj.gov/bjs/pub/pdf/cvus95.pdf.

U.S. Department of Justice. (2000b). *Criminal victimization in the United States, 1996 Statistical Tables.* (NCJ 174445.) Retrieved July 14, 2004 from http://www.ojp.usdoj.gov/bjs/pub/pdf/cvus96.pdf.

U.S. Department of Justice. (2000c). *Criminal victimization in the United States, 1997 Statistical Tables.* (NCJ 174446.) Retrieved July 14, 2004 from http://www.ojp.usdoj.gov/bjs/pub/pdf/cvus97.pdf.

U.S. Department of Justice. (2000d). *Criminal victimization in the United States, 1998 Statistical Tables.* (NCJ

181585.) Retrieved July 14, 2004 from http://www. ojp.usdoj.gov/bjs/pub/pdf/cvus98.pdf.

U.S. Department of Justice. (2001). *Criminal victimization in the United States, 1999 Statistical Tables.* (NCJ 184938.) Retrieved July 14, 2004 from http://www. ojp.usdoj.gov/bjs/pub/pdf/cvus99.pdf.

U.S. Department of Justice. (2002). *Criminal victimization in the United States, 2000 Statistical Tables.* (NCJ 188290.) Retrieved July 14, 2004 from http://www. ojp.usdoj.gov/bjs/pub/pdf/cvus00.pdf.

U.S. Department of Justice. (2003a). *Criminal victimization in the United States, 2001 Statistical Tables.* (NCJ 197064.) Retrieved July 14, 2004 from http://www. ojp.usdoj.gov/bjs/pub/pdf/cvus01.pdf.

U.S. Department of Justice. (2003b). *Criminal victimization in the United States, 2002 Statistical Tables.* (NCJ 200561.) Retrieved July 14, 2004 from http://www. ojp.usdoj.gov/bjs/pub/pdf/cvus02.pdf.

U.S. Department of Justice. (2003c). *Crime in the United States, 2002.* Retrieved August 5, 2004 from http:// www.fbi.gov/ucr/ucr/02cius.htm.

U.S. Department of Justice. (2003d). *Violent victimization of college students.* (NCJ 196143.)

U.S. Department of Justice. (2004a). *Preliminary annual uniform crime report, 2003.* Retrieved August 5, 2004 from http://www.fbi.gov/ucr/2003/03prelimucr.pdf.

U.S. Department of Justice. (2004b). *Violence against women act of 1994.* Retrieved August 23, 2004 from http://www.ojp.usdoj.gov/vawo/laws/vawa/vawa.htm.

Warshaw, R. (1988). *I never called it rape: The Ms. report on recognizing, fighting, and surviving date and acquaintance rape.* New York: Harper & Row.

Williams, J. E., & Holmes, K. A. (1981). *The second assault: Rape and public attitudes.* Westport, CT: Greenwood.

Winkel, F. W., & Koppelaar, L. (1991). Rape victim's style of self-presentation and secondary victimization by the environment: An experiment. *Journal of Interpersonal Violence* 6, 29–40.

9

Intimate Partner Violence Against and By Women

Denise Kindschi Gosselin

Violence against women is a practice with historical standing and global reach. It occurs within the boundaries of intimate and family relationships. Historically, it has been sanctioned through both law and societal bias. Revelations that intimate partner violence occurs against women began with the realization that violence against wives was considered a private matter.

Three dominant explanations for partner violence against women are the psychological perspective, the sociological perspective, and the legalistic model. From the psychological viewpoint, violence stems from social learning and modeling grounded in male and female marital role expectations. Patriarchy involves the idea of male superiority within the domestic sphere. The sociological approach attributes the problem to social stress factors that lead to the violence, such as poverty, unemployment, drinking, and isolation. The legalistic perspective views family violence as a personal choice. Control and punishment are central to choice theory. Arresting family lawbreakers is considered a form of punishment and a deterrent to future intimate partner violence.

The prominent explanations for lesbian intrafamily abuse rely on the feminist model of power and control. Seeing intimate partner violence in same-sex relationships as being similar to heterosexual abuses is helpful for understanding the problems involved, but it can narrow one's perspective and limit the range of service options. Current literature suggests that sexism, racism, homophobia, and heterosexism need to be incorporated into our understanding of intimate partner violence by and against lesbian women (McLaughlin & Rozee, 2001).

Historical Perspective

Patriarchy has been the dominant social arrangement since recorded history. The term comes from the Greek for patriarch, or *father as ruler.* Based on the assumption of male superiority, man was recognized as having power to rule his family. There is very little sociohistorical work that describes the condition of the family in ancient and medieval times; rare glimpses into legal sanctions for wife assault inform us about the expected code of behavior by husbands. Wives and children were considered property in ancient Greece; they were maintained and controlled at nearly every stage of their lives (Romano & White, 2002). The primary role of the woman was to bear children—preferably male—and to run the household. Under the civil Roman law, women, children, and slaves were property that could be bought or sold. Women had no legal status under the law, therefore they could not appear in court as a complainant. A transgression against a woman was considered an offense against the father if she was unmarried or an offense to the husband if she was married. These legal and social arrangements made by men were for the purpose of protecting the family and securing the safety of women (von Wormer & Bartollas, 2000).

As the Roman era declined, the Christian era embraced the subordination of wives by their husbands. Scriptures commanded women to be silent, obedient, and accepting of their husbands' authority. A passage from the New Testament, Ephesians 5:22–24, specifically states the role of a married woman according to the Church: "Wives submit yourselves unto your own husbands, as unto the Lord. For the husband is the head of the wife, even as Christ is head of the Church: and he is the saviour of the body. Therefore, as the church is subject unto Christ, so let the wives be to their own husbands in everything" (Holy Bible, 1968, p. 1045).

Patriarchy is not the only social arrangement between married people, but it has been the dominant one in Western civilizations. Under common law in England, women were no longer viewed as property, but the results were the same. The perspective was based on the belief that when two people are joined in marriage, they become one, socially and legally. The earliest case of intimate partner violence heard in the British court was in 1395. Margaret Neffield and witnesses testified that her husband attacked her with a dagger, causing several wounds and broken bones. The court was not satisfied that this constituted grounds for a judicial separation and ordered her to return to live with her husband (Lunn, 1991).

Attempts to protect women who were brutalized by husbands resulted in isolated legal attempts of protection. The "rule of thumb," which asserted that a husband had the right to beat his wife as long as the stick was no thicker than his thumb, is believed to have originated from an English case (Pagelow, 1984). Although the rule is thought harsh by most standards, it is believed to be a compassionate replacement for the law that allowed a husband to beat his wife with any reasonable instrument (Dutton, 1998).

Despite the English common law foundation for law in the colonies, there is no record of the rule of thumb being used in American courts (Pleck, 1989). The Puritans in colonial Massachusetts became the first in the world to prohibit intimate partner violence through legislation. From 1640 to 1680 the first reform against family violence resulted in laws against wife beating that provided penalties of fines, whipping, or both (Pleck, 2001). Since wife beating was considered a social problem that involved the community, enforcement included "holy watching" by neighbors.

The colonial American reform movement did not last long, and there is no indication of widespread acceptance. The legal perspective that condoned physical violence against women, as long as it was "reasonable," remained dominant. In *Commentaries on the Laws of England* (1765), William Blackstone explained the longstanding legal subjugation of women through the patriarchal order (cited in Ulrich, 1991, p. 7):

> By marriage, the husband and wife are one person in law; that is, the very being or legal existence of the women is suspended during the marriage, or at least is incorporated and consolidated into that of the husband; under whose wing, protection, and cover, she performs everything.

In the United States the status quo was illustrated in *Bradley v. State* (1824), a case where the court confirmed the right of a husband to inflict pain and physically "correct" his wife. The only question submitted to the court was whether a husband had the right to chastise his wife. A reform movement on behalf of battered women later occurred in the United States between 1874 and 1890 (Pleck, 2001). This period included one of the first policy responses to intrafamily violence, when family violence was "discovered" by social service agencies confronted with child welfare clients. The response to female victims was judgmental and prejudicial according to Gordon. There was a lack of effective legal remedies for the female victims (Gordon, 1988).

In 1887 Sigmund Freud of Austria published his seduction theory. It was one of the earliest research attempts to explain mental illness and symptoms of hysteria in women from the psychological perspective (Adams, 1992). The theory claimed that the majority of women suffering from these illnesses were experiencing the effects of being victimized from intrafamily rape and other sexual abuses. Faced with professional scorn, Freud recanted the theory in 1890 saying that the female clients fantasized the sexual abuse. Interest in the victimization of women was evidenced again in the 1940s when victim precipitation became the predominant approach to explaining intrafamily violence (Meadows, 1998).

The battered women's movement beginning in the early 1970s placed partner abuse within the context of economic and social subjugation. Battered women's shelters began to open in the United States in 1974; these gave safe refuge to women who had been abused. The criminalization of intimate partner violence emerged from this movement, along with other social service and policy responses (Fagan, 1996). Describing the situation within the framework of heterosexual relationships, early feminist activism labeled intimate violence as "wife-abuse." During the 1980s came the uncomfortable acknowledgment of partner abuse in lesbian relationships (Renzetti, 1992).

Intimate Partner Violence

Intimate partner violence is a phrase that refers to any act of violence that occurs within a legally or socially recognized domestic relationship. Frequently acknowledged categories include married and previously married persons; those that live together as husband and wife; persons that have a child in common; and partners of same-sex relationships. Some states expand on traditional meanings of domestic through the recognition of persons that live under the same roof, regardless of affiliation. Long-term dating relationships may also meet the definition. In some states with special legislation, victimization within a domestic relationship provides additional criminal and civil protections and increased sanctions. Most notable is the intimate partner violence restraining or protection order. This court order can be either a criminal or a civil protection order. The civil option may have specific provisions that carry the force of criminal sanctions when violated by the abuser.

Those victimized by identifiable family members are also afforded social protections through resources and services specific to meet the needs of intimate partner violence victims. Examples of the social systems response include crisis intervention, 24-hour hotlines, and temporary shelter.

Violence against women within recognized domestic relationships may also be termed *abuse*. This broad categorization describes an intentional pattern of emotional, physical, or psychological mistreatment. Multiple forms of violence exist within dysfunctional homes. Behaviors can include ongoing verbal, emotional, sexual, physical, psychological, and economic abuse. Examples of these tactics include hitting, kicking, and punching; preventing access to family finances; threatening to take custody of the children or threatening to take the children away; harming children as a punishment to one's partner; destroying property; harming pets; berating; threatening violence; restricting access to family and friends; accusations of infidelity; and forcing the partner to do sexual things she does not want to do or is uncomfortable with. The patterns of abuse that are recognizable in heterosexual abuse against women can be seen in violence among lesbian women. For this reason a definition that is inclusive of all female victims has been furthered by the National Coalition of Anti-Violence Programs (NCAVP, 2003, p. 10):

> Intimate partner violence is defined as a pattern of behaviors utilized by one partner (the abuser or batterer) to exert and maintain control over another person (the survivors or victim) where there exists an intimate, loving, and dependent relationship.

Since the term *domestic* refers to the relationship of the offender to the victim rather than a specific offense, any prohibited act may properly be considered as intimate partner violence. For example: An ex-husband who burns down the house of his estranged wife may be charged with the crime of arson; however, the victim is also entitled to intimate partner violence protections. For the determination of full social benefits and civil protections, the victim-to-perpetrator relationship must be clearly identified. At the same time, this status brings additional burdens to the victim who attempts to find redress through the criminal justice system.

Prevalence of Relationship Violence

The two largest survey attempts to measure violence against women are National Crime Victimization Survey and National Family Violence Survey. According to estimates from the National Crime Victimization Survey (NCVS), violent crimes committed by intimate partners against women have declined from 1.1 million in 1993 to 494,570 in 2002 (Catalano, 2004). This current report confirms earlier NCVS studies that intimate partner violence primarily involves female victims. Females included in the study are aged 12 and older. The definition of intimate violence includes the crimes of rape, sexual assault, robbery, aggravated assault, and simple assault. The NCVS reports that approximately 85 percent of intimate partner violence is perpetrated by men against women (Belknap, 2001). Since women are believed to be victimized more than once in a year, an earlier version of NCVS estimated that 5.3 million victimizations occur annually against women ages 18 and older in the United States (Rennison & Welchans, 2000). This violence results in approximately 2 million annual injuries, and more than 550,000 require medical attention (National Center for Injury Prevention and Control, 2003). Victimization rates for major crimes, including the offenses committed against women by an intimate, remained at the same levels in 2003 from 2002 (Catalano, 2004). These have been trending downwards since 1993 and appear to have stabilized, except for rape and sexual assault, which continued a small decline in 2003.

Contrary to these estimates, the National Family Violence Survey results suggest that women are more violent than men when it comes to family assaults. In minor violence (slap, spank, throw something, push, grab, or shove) the incident rates were found to be roughly equal for men and women. In severe violence (kick, bite, hit with a fist, hit or try to hit with something, beat up the other, threaten with a knife or gun, use a knife or gun) more men were victimized than women. Projecting the surveys onto the national population of married couples, the early survey results showed that 1.8 million women were victims of severe violence compared to 2 million male victims (Straus, Gelles, & Steinmetz, 1980). In 1993, Murray Straus reviewed more than thirty mostly American studies on married or college student dating couples. In each, the rate of women admitting the use of aggressive acts against their partner was roughly equal to the rate of men who reported using violent acts against women (Straus, 1993).

Understanding the prevalence of violence committed by intimates is not an easy task. An analysis by Schwartz (1987) based on a U.S. National Crime Survey confirmed that the seriousness of violent acts reported by partners was roughly equal for men (79.7 percent) and women (84.1 percent). Explaining that violence against women is different than female aggression against men, a significantly higher number of women in the study (981) received injuries than men (55). Even when both parties engage in acts of violence (83 percent of 199 couples), husbands were more likely to use severely violent tactics and are less likely to be injured (Schwartz, 1987).

The rates of victimization from the Family Violence Survey indicate a gender-symmetry, that women use violence against men as much as men use violence against men. It fails to tell us the context of the acts or show if many incidents took place in self-defense. In contrast, the NCVS clearly indicates that rates of intimate violence against women perpetrated by men are higher than rates of intimate violence perpetrated by women against men. NCVS results have been substantiated by studies when self-protection is included in the analysis (Bachman, 1998).

The Disabled Victim.   Women with developmental disabilities seem to have the highest rates of physical, sexual, and emotional violence by spouses, ex-spouses, boyfriends, and family members (Sigmon & Edmunds, 2002). Research confirms that women with disabilities are as likely to be victimized by all forms of intimate partner violence as the general population of women; some reports estimate that the victimization is as high as 85 percent of the population of women with disabilities (Fiduccia & Wolfe, 1999). Compared to women without disabilities, these victims frequently experience greater dependence on their abusers for personal care. Men perpetrate the vast majority of abuse toward women with disabilities. These women experience a high probability of victimization, repeat victimizations, and are subject to more severe abuse that occurs over longer periods of time, as compared to the general population of women (Milberger, LeRoy, Martin, & Israel, 2002).

Professional Women as Victims.   Professional women are not immune to victimization by a spouse or intimate. From a survey examining the prevalence of intimate partner violence among active-duty military women, results indicated that 22 percent of the women had been physically and/or sexually assaulted, and 36 percent indicated some type of abuse, including emotional abuse, from an intimate partner while serving in the military (Nicolaidis et al., 2003).

There are no recent studies on the extent to which police officers' families are at risk for intimate partner violence. Those studies conducted in the early 1990s may or may not be legitimate as the population can change dramatically with age and job attrition. There is no reason to suspect that police officers are *less* inclined to perpetrate family violence than the general population, however; old studies suggest that the opposite may be truer. What appears most significant is that when police officer abusers are suspected of committing violence against a family member, prosecution seldom is pursued or extremely light discipline results (National Center for Women and Policing, 2003). Victims of battering by an intimate who is also a police officer may fear calling the police due to the concern that the case will not be handled properly; a heightened apprehension results from the batterer's having access to a variety of weapons. This concern is given substance by a 1999 survey of the nation's 100 largest police departments that revealed only six cities acted against police officers through the Intimate Partner Violence Offender Gun Ban, and only eleven officers were affected (National Center for Women and Policing, 2003). Police officers have their records expunged or plead to a charge other than intimate partner violence in order to avoid losing their right to carry a weapon.

Minority Victims.   Contradictory information exists relative to the rate at which minority and underserved female populations experience partner violence. It is generally accepted that black women experience intrafamily violence at a higher rate than white women. Rennison and Welchans (2000), for instance, determined that black women had been victimized at a 35 percent higher rate than white women between the years of 1993 to 1998. Nearly one-third of African American women experience intimate partner violence in their lifetimes compared with one-fourth of white women, according to another source (Tjaden & Thoennes, 2000).

Women of color also appear to have the highest percentage of cases that are dropped prior to prosecution. A distrust of the criminal justice system, cultural differences, and beliefs that their experiences and needs differ in comparison to that of white women are among the reasons why this occurs (Vann, 2003). Accounting for socioeconomic factors, one recent study concluded the opposite, that the victim's race and rate of intimate partner violence are not significant (Rennison & Planty, 2003).

Lesbian Relationship Violence.   The battered woman's movement has been slow to recognize intimate partner violence perpetrated within female relationships, and few significant studies have documented its prevalence. From these rare and outdated studies come the suggestion that 50 percent of lesbian partnerships have experienced violence (NCAVP, 2003). A contrary finding is that women living with a female intimate partner experience less partner violence than heterosexual women (Tjaden & Thoennes, 2000). Reports compiled by the New York City Gay and Lesbian Anti-Violence Project estimate that partnership violence in the gay community occurs in 25 percent to 33 percent of relationships, which is consistent with the prevalence in heterosexual relationships (NCAVP, 2003). A few isolated studies are not sufficient to determine the extent of partner violence within this population. What is apparent is that there is a need to include lesbian families in future research on intimate partner violence.

The numbers of same-sex households have only recently been documented within the United States and are expected to reflect those that are openly lesbian. Approximately 300,000 same-sex female couples reported that status in the 2000 United States Census (Bradford, Barrett, & Honnold, 2002).

Crimes Against Women

Obedience and subservience to the husband was a religious duty as well as a legal obligation of wives in America since the seventeenth century (Ulrich, 1991). A wife could not own or acquire property, enter into a contract or write a will unless her husband was willing to sign a special contract prior to marriage. The wife was not permitted to sue in her own name; a wrong committed against her must be pursued by the husband. At the same time, the husband could be held legally responsible for the actions of his wife. For that reason the courts acknowledged his right to make moderate correction of his wife though physical punishment (*Bradley v. State,* 1824). Under this subservient social and legal status, it is no wonder that historically women did not appeal to the courts for protection from abuse by husbands. While the Massachusetts legislature had authorized divorce in 1838, gross negligence and extreme cruelty were not among the enumerated causes to obtain one (*Polly Pidge v. Palemon Pidge,* 1841). Crimes against a woman by her husband have historically been private matters in which the courts have hesitated to interfere.

In the last several decades, women victimized by intimates are at least more likely to be recognized and counted. The NCVS indicates that women separated from their husbands are victimized by an intimate at rates higher than married, divorced, widowed, or never married women (Rennison, 2001). Women are most vulnerable to intimate violent crime between the ages of 16 to 24 in all categories except for murder. Women aged 35 to 49 are the most vulnerable to intimate partner murder. It should also be noted that each year between 1993 and 1999 an average of 128,550 men were victimized by women. During the same period, 16,900 victimizations resulted from intimate violence against women by women.

Assault. An assault is considered a purposeful attempt or threat to inflict harm on another, together with the apparent ability to do so. An intentional display of force, such as a raised fist or gesture that would give the victim cause to fear or expect immediate bodily harm constitutes an assault. A simple assault might be charged if the person attempts to cause harm or knowingly causes bodily injury to another. Simple assault is the most common violent crime against an intimate partner in the United States. An estimated 421,550 simple assaults were committed against a female intimate partner in 2001 (Rennison, 2003).

An aggravated assault would be the purposeful attempt or actual causing of serious bodily injury to another. Aggravated assault of women by intimates occurs with less frequency. Approximately 81,140 aggravated assaults occurred against a woman by her intimate partner in 2001 (Rennison, 2003).

Rape. This crime against women was discussed in the last chapter. In this discussion, we will focus on sexual assault by intimate partners. The NCVS estimates that 41,740 females were raped or sexually assaulted by an intimate in 2001 (Rennison, 2003). There were less than ten rapes of males during the same period. During 2003, about seven in ten female rape and sexual assault victims stated the offender was an intimate, another relative, or a friend or an acquaintance (Catalano, 2004).

Until the late 1970s, a majority of states still had laws that said a husband was immune from prosecution and could not be charged with rape if he was legally married to the victim (Finkelhor & Yllo, 1985). The exclusionary language has since been removed; rape of a spouse is a crime in all fifty states and the District of Columbia (National Center for Victims of Crime, 2003). Marital rape accounts for about 25 percent of all rapes (Bergen, 1999). Still, trivializing the crime continues in less obvious ways. Some states mandate a shortened reporting period or provide a lesser punishment to the offender; others statutorily require the use of force versus the lack of consent (NCVC, 2003). It is estimated that more than three-fourths of rapes in which the perpetrator was a former husband or boyfriend are not reported to police (Rennison, 2002).

Stalking.   Once thought to be a crime committed only against celebrities and politicians, stalking became known as the crime of the 1990s. Stalking is not a new behavior. It has been prosecuted as harassment, annoyance, and under domestic violence laws. California passed the first antistalking law and coined the term in 1990; since then antistalking legislation has been passed in every state and in the District of Columbia. While each state law may differ slightly, many require a credible threat and describe prohibited behaviors. A credible threat requires the victim to reasonably fear for his or her safety, and the perpetrator must have intent and the ability to complete the threat.

In addition to the fear generated by stalking behaviors, it is estimated that stalkers are violent toward their victims between 25 and 35 percent of the time. Those most likely to be violent have had an intimate relationship with the victim (NIJ, 1998). The first national study to determine stalking prevalence was undertaken in the National Violence Against Women Survey (NVAW) in 1998 (Tjaden & Thoennes, 1998). Used in the survey was a general definition of stalking that is not specific to any particular state law:

> Course of conduct directed at a specific person that involves repeated visual or physical proximity; nonconsensual communication; verbal, written, or implied threats; or a combination thereof that would cause fear in a reasonable person (with "repeated" meaning on two or more occasions). (Tjaden & Thoennes, 1998, p. 16)

The NVAW survey found it was more prevalent than previously thought. Eight percent of women and 2 percent of men surveyed said they had been stalked at some time in their life. Estimating that approximately 1 million women and 371,000 men are stalked annually in the United States, the report concluded that stalking should be considered a serious criminal justice and public health concern. Almost one in three victims sought counseling as a result of the stalking, 18 percent sought help from friends or family members, and 17 percent obtained a gun (Tjaden & Thoennes, 1998).

Murder.   Statistics on murder in the United States have been collected from police reports for many years, but only recently has the relationship between the perpetrator and the victim been noted. The relationship between the victim and the perpetrator could not be determined for about one-third of murders (Catalano, 2004). Murder is the willful killing of a human being by another. When a husband murders his wife, it is referred to as *uxoricide. Femicide* is a word recently come in to use by scholars of domestic violence; it refers to the killing of a woman by her relative, friend, or lover (Radford & Russell, 1992).

According to Dawson and Langan, spousal homicides are committed by husbands in 51 percent of the cases; wives are the offenders who kill their husbands in 41 percent of these cases. The remaining intimate murders are committed by persons who are not in a marriage relationship with their victim (Dawson & Langan, 1994). The offenders are older than any other group of killers, an average of 39 years old, and they represent 6.5 percent of the total number of homicides in the United States. Recent trends indicate that the rate of intimate murders is declining. The number of spousal murders, the largest portion of intimate murder, is now half of what it was twenty years ago (Greenfield & Snell, 1999). This welcome decline in intimate homicide has been studied, and explanations are being offered to account for this downward trend. One explanation being offered is that people are not getting married as frequently. In one study, the decline in the number of people getting married was closely related to the decline in rates of spousal homicide (Rosenfeld, 1997).

A woman is nine times more likely to be killed by her spouse, an intimate acquaintance, or a family member than by a stranger according to the report *When Men Kill Women* (Brock, 2003). Over 60 percent of women murdered in 2001 were the wives, common-law wives, ex-wives, or girlfriends of the killer. The report further states that 327 women (nearly one woman a day) were shot and killed by either their husband or intimate acquaintance during the course of an argument (Brock, 2003).

Between 1976 and 2000, the proportion of all male murder victims killed by an intimate dropped 68 percent, while the number of women murdered by intimates fell only 22 percent (Rennison, 2003). Of all female murder victims, the proportion killed by an intimate was relatively stable until 1995, when the proportion began increasing (Catalano, 2004).

Brock (2003) reported that black women are at the greatest risk from intimate and acquaintance homicide. More than seven times as many black women as white women were murdered by men they knew (479 victims) than were killed by male strangers (67 victims) in single victim/single offender incidents in 2001. Of black victims who knew their offenders, 59 percent (281 out of 479) were wives, common-law wives, ex-wives, or girlfriends of the offenders.

Effects of Intimate Partner Violence

Violence against women results in physical injury, psychological trauma, and sometimes death. Victim reactions depend on the nature of the experience and the circumstances surrounding it, the characteristics of the victims themselves, and the degree of violence against them (Dutton, 1998). As a group, abused women experience more physical health problems and have a higher occurrence of depression, drug and alcohol abuse, and suicide attempts than women who are not abused (National Center for Injury Prevention and Control, 2003). Family violence has also been identified as a contributing factor for pregnancy and birth complications, sudden infant death syndrome, brain trauma, fractures, sexually transmitted diseases, HIV infection, depression, dissociation, psychosis, and other stress-related physical and mental disorders (Chalk & King, 1998). The most pervasive health concerns associated with violence against women include gastrointestinal disorders, chronic pain or fatigue, loss of appetite and eating disorders, and gynecologic and urologic disorders (Carlson, 2000).

The physical effects of domestic partner rape may include injuries to the vaginal and anal areas, lacerations, soreness, bruising, torn muscles, fatigue, and vomiting. Other physical symptoms may include broken bones, black eyes, bloody noses, and knife wounds that occur during the sexual violence. Approximately one-half of the survivors in a study on marital rape reported having been kicked or burned during sex (Bergen, 1999). Miscarriages, stillbirths, bladder infections, infertility, and the potential contraction of sexually transmitted diseases including HIV are specific gynecological consequences of marital rape. Survivors of rape often experience changes in their overall health. Sleep disorders such as insomnia or eating disorders often occur following rape or sexual assault. Some women experience nightmares and flashbacks. Others encounter body aches, headaches, and fatigue. Rape victims sometimes experience anxiety, depression, self-injury, and/or suicide attempts, as well as other emotional disorders. They sometimes try to cope with their feelings by indulging in alcohol or drugs.

Posttraumatic stress disorder (PTSD) is the diagnostic category most frequently used by psychotherapists to explain the psychological trauma associated with rape, battering, and sexual abuse. The Diagnostic and Statistical Manual of Mental Disorders defines posttraumatic stress disorder (PTSD) as a type of anxiety disorder caused by trauma and prolonged stress (American Psychiatric Association, 2000). Experienced as the result of traumatic events, PTSD varies with the severity of the stressor. Kilpatrick et al. found that 57.1 percent of rape victims developed PTSD after the incident (Kilpatrick et al., 1987).

Studies on victim reactions have raised the possibility that some battered women develop a unique relationship with their batterers known as the Stockholm syndrome. A bidirectional bonding between the captor and the hostage occurs between the abuser and battered women, prisoners of war, and people in hostage situations (Graham & Rawlings, 1998). The Stockholm syndrome is a survival strategy that develops as a victim perceives a threat to her survival along with the belief that the captor is willing to carry out that threat. Additional precursors include a victim perception that some small kindness from the captor occurred within the context of terror, isolation from perspectives other than those of the captor that narrows the victim's perception of the events, and the perception that the captive is unable to escape. There is no estimate on the numbers of battered women who suffer from this reaction to interpersonal violence.

Suman Kakar suggests that victims have both internal and external factors that explain why they tolerate violence (Kakar, 1998). The internal traits that victims possess may be natural or due to the experiences of the battering relationship. Examples are timidity and low self-esteem. Feelings of helplessness are acquired when the victims feel trapped and unable to escape. Through controlling tactics, the perpetrator "brainwashes" the victim, and a traumatic bonding occurs. Overly optimistic victims may feel that they love the offender and hope that they can change the abuser's behavior. External factors that influence the victim can be summed up through economic dependence on the perpetrator. Women often remain economically dependent on the man while they care for children in the home; they may delay their education and forgo employment outside the home. Social factors make up another external influencing factor. The lack of friends and supportive adults increase the sense of futility and the victim's feeling of isolation and despair.

"Why do women stay in violent relationships?" This question is often asked with a victim-blaming attitude. The fact is that women do leave their abusers. It simply is not up to us to determine when or if a woman should stay. In a recent study of married women who reported that an intimate had victimized them, 30 percent were separated and an additional 8 percent were divorced (Rennison, 2001). Female victims of abuse often hear that they must like or need such abuse, or they would leave. Others may be told that they are one of the many "women who love too much" or who have "low self-esteem." No one enjoys being beaten, no matter what his or her emotional state or self-image. A woman's reasons for staying are more complex than a statement about her strength of character. In many cases it is dangerous for a woman to leave her abuser. If the abuser has all of the economic and social status, leaving can cause additional problems for the woman. Leaving could mean living in fear and losing child custody, losing financial support, and experiencing harassment at work. Battered women experience shame, embarrassment, and isolation.

In addition to the physical and psychological problems, an increasing amount of literature suggests that violence against women is a contributing factor to homelessness. Domestic violence was cited as the primary reason for homelessness in 56 percent of the cities surveyed in 2000 (Lowe, 2000). According to another study, approximately half of all women and children experiencing homelessness are fleeing intimate partner violence (National Coalition for the Homeless, 1999). Citing the overwhelming economic effects of violence against a woman, the U.S. Department of Housing and Urban Development recently issued a policy suggestion that female domestic violence victims be given preference for low-income, affordable housing (HUD, 2003).

The effects of violence against women go beyond the victimized person. The impact to society at large comes in the high costs associated with intimate partner violence. In its recent report, the National Center for Injury Prevention and Control (2003) estimated that the costs of intimate partner rape, physical assault, and stalking exceed $5.8 billion each year, nearly $4.1 billion of which is for direct medical and mental health care services. The total costs include nearly $0.9 billion in lost productivity from paid work and household chores for victims of nonfatal violence and $0.9 billion in lifetime earnings lost by victims of intimate partner homicide. Additional costs of intimate partner violence include payments to victims of these crimes. Almost $1 million in compensation for medical expenses, mental health counseling, and economic support went to adult victims of intimate partner violence crimes in 2001 (Crime Victim Compensation Quarterly, 2003).

Responses to Intimate Partner Violence

The first response to women victimized by intimate partner violence came in the form of social action and direct practice activities. The shelter movement evolved into hotline and advocacy services and counseling programs for men that batter. Among the legalistic approaches that have emerged since the 1980s are the criminalization of domestic violence with mandated and preferred arrest policies, gun control, and protection orders.

Social Action Responses

In 1972, the first shelters for battered women opened in the United States in St. Paul, Minnesota, and in Pasadena, California. The use of battered women's shelters has grown to be among the most widely used source of intervention. At first, there were antagonistic relationships between the police and shelter services. Now institutionalized, shelters are widely supported. Approximately 2,000 intimate partner violence programs exist nationally, and at least 1,200 of these are in shelters (Carlson, 2000). Studies during the 1980s indicated that once a woman has received help and shelter support, she is less likely to return to her abuser (Dziegielewski, Resnick, & Krause 1996). Advocates claim that social service interventions have been successful in lowering the rate of domestic homicide. As services to female victims of intimate partner violence increased between 1976 to 1996, the rate of intimate partner homicide decreased (Duggan, Nagin, & Rosenfeld, 2003).

The social change mission of shelters challenged the inevitability of abuse in women's lives. The most immediate need of the battered woman is safety for herself and her children. The shelter or refuge home responds to that most basic need. Counseling and advocacy are also offered. Assisting the women in gathering information and applying for economic assistance or vocational training are ingredients for building self-esteem and self-reliance. Advocates familiar with the legal system facilitate a woman's efforts in obtaining restraining orders, contacting attorneys, and pressing charges.

Miscellaneous services to aid battered women include hotlines and legal advocacy. By establishing contact between the battered woman and a helping network, hotlines provide information and referrals for services that a woman might need to protect herself and her children from abuse. Information on alternative housing, financial help, legal aid, medical services, and vocational resources are among the issues that might be addressed. Hotlines are often the first attempt the woman makes at seeking help. Emergency hotlines are often operated by a shelter.

The first hotline for battered women started in St. Paul, Minnesota, in 1971. Since then national and local hotlines have been established to provide callers with crisis intervention, details on local resources, and information about intimate partner violence. Since its inception in 1996, the National Hotline has answered more than 1,014,209 phone calls from victims of intimate partner violence, family members, and friends from all over the world (National Domestic Hotline, 1999). This number reflects an 18 percent increase in calls from 2001 to 2002, averaging 15,000 phone calls daily.

Legalistic Responses

A lack of consensus on how police should respond to intimate partner violence in the civilian population is mirrored within the criminal justice community. The Minneapolis Domestic Violence Experiment in 1984 was the first to study the deterrent effects of arresting the family violence perpetrator (Liska & Messner, 1999). The study design called for officers in the Minneapolis Police Department to carry out one of three responses when they had probable cause to believe a misdemeanor assault had occurred between cohabitants or spouses: (1) arrest the suspect, (2) order one party out of the residence, or (3) advise the couple on how to solve their problems at the scene. The researchers reported that when the suspect was arrested, there were statistically significant reductions in reoffending in the official records of all the cases and in the cases with victim interviews. The preliminary report indicated that police *should* arrest abusers for crimes of intimate violence.

Within days of the initial report, the New York Police Department became the first to require police officers to arrest in family violence situations, citing the experiment as among the reasons for the new policy (Maxwell, Garner, & Fagan, 2003). Contributing to this policy change was the success of civil suits brought against police departments for the failure to provide equal protection to victims of intimate partner violence. A classic example is the successful 1982 suit brought by Tracy Thurman who was permanently disabled when Torrington, Connecticut, police failed to protect her against her estranged husband (*Thurman v. City of Torrington,* 1984).

Since 1984, all states, the District of Columbia, and the Commonwealth of Puerto Rico have each enacted some form of legislation specific to domestic violence. The first domestic abuse statutes applied only to adult married spouses of abusers and only to women as victims. Today's statutes have broadened the definitions and legislative protections; these definitions, provisions for protection, and enforcement vary widely from state to state. Mandatory arrest statutes require that police officers make a warrantless arrest of the abuser when called to the scene of a complaint of domestic violence and probable cause exists that the abuse occurred. A hybrid statute mandates an arrest in some circumstances and grants discretion to police officers under some other situations. Preferred arrest statutes suggest that an officer make an arrest whenever probable cause to do so exists but does not require that the officer make an arrest.

Proclaimed as one of the most significant advances to end intimate partner violence, the Intimate Partner Violence Offender Gun Ban was passed as part of the Omnibus Consolidated Appropriations Act of 1997. This makes it illegal for any person convicted of a misdemeanor or felony crime of intimate partner violence to ship, transport, possess, or receive firearms or ammunition. Hotly debated, opponents referred to the ban as excessive. Arguments focused on the failure of the ban to exclude police and military personnel from its provisions. It is now illegal for a person to possess a firearm while subject to a court order restraining such person from harassing, stalking, or threatening an intimate partner or the child of an intimate partner.

The most significant legislative change for protection against intrafamily violence is the civil protection order, sometimes called a restraining order, no-contact order, or temporary restraining order. Until recent times the use of protective orders has been restricted to protect crime victims and witnesses from harassment by defendants. Women who were unwilling to divorce at the same time as applying for protection were denied the legal process of the civil restraining order until the legal reforms of the 1970s (Fagan, 1996). These court orders are now available to adults in every state and in the District of Columbia (Hart, 1992).

Three components determine a civil order's scope of protection. The first component answers the question of who is eligible for this type of court order. Early statutes limited access to married persons and "family" or "household" members. Progressive jurisdictions extend protections beyond the traditional definition of family; these include unrelated household members and dating partners, for example. States differ substantially when answering the "Who is eligible?" question. The second component that civil protection orders have in common is that the order is addressed to a particular person. This is important since only the named individual can violate the court order, and only the court can dissolve the order. In other words, the named person ordered to "stay away," who then violates the order by going over to the house of the victim, cannot use the excuse that he was invited. He would be in violation of the order, regardless of any understanding or misunderstanding from the victim. In order to vacate the order the court must be asked by the person who petitioned for the protection.

The third common feature found in civil protection orders is that they specify the relief that is granted by the court. Forms of relief vary significantly between jurisdictions. Common are an order restraining the defendant from subjecting the victim to domestic violence; commanding the abuser to "stay away" from the victim; granting exclusive possession to the plaintiff of the residence or household regardless of ownership; specifying monetary relief;

and prohibiting the defendant from possessing firearms. Some courts also address custody and visitation issues in the civil protection order.

Interstate enforcement of protection orders was authorized by federal legislation through the Violence against Women Act (1994). This provision is referred to as having full faith and credit, which means that a person who receives an order of protection carries that protection with her to any other state where it must be enforced as if that place had issued the court order. Paving the way for the nationwide reciprocal enforcement of protection orders, the National Stalker and Intimate Partner Violence Reduction Act (1997) authorized civil restraining and abuse protection orders to be entered in all National Crime Information Center databases. Indications are that enforcement practices across the nation are inconsistent, however. Since the authorization in 1997 only nineteen states have begun to enter their data, less than 5 percent of the estimated 2 million eligible orders (OVC, 2002). A concerted effort to enter restraining orders into the database is needed for the effective nationwide enforcement of existing orders.

For women in lesbian relationships, protections afforded by a civil restraining order are difficult to obtain. Hawaii is the only state throughout the United States, Washington DC, and Puerto Rico whose statute specifically grants intimate partner violence protection orders to victims of same-sex abuse (NCAVP, 2002). In thirty-eight other jurisdictions, a victim should be able to obtain the protection when the statutes are construed liberally due to gender-neutral language. The legal language in seven states does not recognize same-sex couples; in Florida, for example, those who seek restraining orders may be required to acknowledge an illegal sexual relationship when petitioning for protection (NCAVP, 2002).

Conclusion

History indicates a long-standing subjugation of woman in relation to men. Social and legal impediments to equal protection have been challenged in the past, but no movement has been as successful as the present one. Feminist ideology has shaped the current response to intimate violence for the criminal justice response and social services approach. The movement has created interventions that have served millions of intimate partner violence victims since their inception. Crisis intervention shelters and hotline services continue to be in demand. Crimes against women are enforced, regardless of the relationship between the victim and the offender.

Future studies on prevalence rates need to be more inclusive of violence committed within same-sex relationships. In order to reduce confusion, the rates of violence, particularly for intimate homicide, need to be clearer where the relationship between the victim and the perpetrator is unknown. There is a lack of research concerning the effectiveness of any of these current interventions. For instance, while the Minneapolis study led to changes in arrest policies, replication studies that came afterward did not show a clear correlation between arrest and a reduction in violence (Dunford, Huizinga, & Elliot, 1990; Sherman, 1992). Thus we know that violence against women has declined, but we do not know why. It may be that the combination of social services and legal interventions has contributed to the overall declines, but we will have trouble determining future directions of preventing intimate partner violence. More research is needed to plan the course for the next part of the movement to protect women within their intimate partnerships.

Review Questions

1. Explain the three dominant theoretical approaches used to understand family violence.

2. Describe the historical social arrangement between men and women.

3. Define intimate partner violence; include examples of legally recognized domestic relationships.

4. Who is most affected by intimate partner violence?

5. Do women commit intimate partner violence?

6. What are the major categories of crimes committed by intimates?

7. Explain the effects of intimate partner violence on its victims.

8. What is the effect of intimate partner violence to society at large?

9. What are the primary responses that have developed to address intimate partner violence?

10. Describe the legislative responses towards violence against women.

Key Terms

Patriarchy

"Rule of thumb"

Seduction theory

Intimate partner violence

Battered women's movement

Uxoricide

Femicide

Stockholm Syndrome

Civil protection order

Minneapolis experiment

References

Adams, D. (1992). *Historical timeline of institutional responses to battered women.* Cambridge, MA: Emerge.

American Psychiatric Association. (2000). *The diagnostic and statistical manual of mental disorders* (4th ed.). Washington, DC: APA.

Bachman, R. (1998). *Incidence rates of violence against women: A comparison of the redesigned National Crime Victimization Survey and the 1985 National Family Violence Survey.* Retrieved September 22, 2004 from http://www.vaw.umn.edu/documents/vawnet/incidenc/incidenc.html.

Belknap, J. (2001). *The invisible woman: Gender, crime, and justice.* Belmont, CA: Wadsworth/Thompson Learning.

Bergen, R. K. (1999). *Marital rape.* Retrieved April, 2004 from http://www.vaw.umn.edu/library/dv/.

Black, H. C. (1990). *Black's law dictionary.* St. Paul, MN: West Publishing Co.

Bradford, J., Barrett, K., & Honnold, J. A. (2002). New York: The National Gay and Lesbian Task Force Policy Institute, the Survey and Evaluation Research Laboratory, and the Fenway Institute.

Brock, K. (2003). *When men murder women: An analysis of 2001 homicide data.* Washington, DC: Violence Policy Center.

Carlson, B. E. (2000). *Violence against women: Synthesis of research for service providers.* (Report No. NCJ 199578.) Washington, DC: U.S. Department of Justice.

Catalano, S. (2004). *Criminal victimization, 2003.* (Report No. NCJ 205455.) Washington, DC: Bureau of Justice Statistics.

Chalk, R., & King, P. A. (1998). *Violence in families: Assessing prevention and treatment programs.* Washington, DC: National Academy Press.

Crime Victim Compensation Quarterly. (2003). *Compensation at record heights!* Retrieved October 30, 2004 from www.ncvc.org/resources/statistics/costofcrime.

Dawson, J., & Langan, P. (1994). (Report No. NCJ 143498.) Washington, DC: U.S. Department of Justice.

Duggan, L., Nagin, D., & Rosenfeld, R. (2003). Do domestic violence services save lives? *National Institute of Justice Journal* (250), 2–29.

Dunford, F., Huizinga, D., & Elliot, D. (1990). The role of arrest in domestic assault: The Omaha experiment. *Criminology* 28 (2), 183–197.

Dutton, D. G. (1998). *The domestic assault of women: Psychological and criminal justice perspectives* (3rd ed.). Vancouver, BC: UBC Press.

Dziegielewski, S., Resnick, C., & Krause, N. B. (1996).

Shelter-based crisis intervention with battered women. In A. Roberts (Ed.), *Helping battered women: New perspectives and remedies* (pp. 159–171). New York: Oxford University Press.

Fagan, J. (1996). *The criminalization of domestic violence: Promises and limits.* Washington, DC: National Institute of Justice.

Fiduccia, B. W., & Wolfe, L. R. (1999). *Violence against disabled women.* Washington, DC: Center for Women Policy Studies.

Finkelhor, D., & Yllo, K. (1985). *License to rape: Sexual abuse of wives.* New York: Holt, Rinehart and Winston.

Gordon, L. (1988). *Heroes of their own lives: The politics and history of family violence.* New York: Penguin Books.

Graham, D., & Rawlings, E. (1998). Bonding with abusive dating partners: Dynamics of Stockholm syndrome. In B. Levy (Ed.), *Dating violence: Young women in danger* (2nd ed.; pp. 119–135). Seattle, WA: Seal Press.

Greenfield, L. A., & Snell, T. L. (1999). *Women offenders.* U.S. Department of Justice. Washington, DC: Bureau of Justice Statistics.

Hart, B. J. (1992). State codes on domestic violence: Analysis, commentary and recommendation. *Juvenile & Family Court Journal* 42 (4), 3–18.

Holy Bible. (1968). Nashville, TN: National Publishing Company.

HUD. (2003). *Public housing occupancy guidebook. Washington,* DC: U.S. Department of Housing and Urban Development.

Jerusalem Bible, The. (1996). New York: Doubleday.

Kakar, S. (1998). *Domestic abuse: Public police/criminal justice approaches towards child, spousal and elderly abuse.* San Francisco, CA: Austin and Winfield.

Kilpatrick, D. G., Saunders, B. E., Veronen, L. J., Best, C. L., & Von, J. M. (1987). Criminal victimization: Lifetime prevalence, reporting to police, and psychological impact. *Crime and Delinquency* 33, 479–489.

Liska, A., & Messner, S. F. (1999). *Perspectives on crime and deviance.* Upper Saddle River, NJ: Prentice Hall.

Lowe, E. T. (2000). *A status report on hunger and homelessness in America's cities, 2000: A 25-city survey.* Washington, DC: U.S. Conference of Mayors.

Lunn, T. (1991). Til death do us part. *Social Work Today* 29(8), 165–17.

Maxwell, C. D., Garner, J. H., & Fagan, J. A. (2003). The preventive effects of arrest on intimate partner violence: Research, policy, and theory. *Domestic Violence Report* 9 (1), 9–10.

McLaughlin, E. M., & Rozee, P. D. (2001). Knowledge about heterosexual versus lesbian battering among lesbians. In E. Kaschak (Ed.), *Intimate betrayal: Domestic violence in lesbian relationships* (pp. 39–58). New York: Haworth Press.

Meadows, R. J. (1998). *Understanding violence and victimization.* Upper Saddle River, NJ: Prentice Hall.

Milberger, S., LeRoy, B., Martin, A., & Israel, N. (2002). *A Michigan study on women with physical disabilities.* (Report No. NCJ 193769.) Washington, DC: U.S. Department of Justice.

National Center for Injury Prevention and Control. (2003). *Costs of intimate partner violence against women in the United States.* Atlanta, GA: Center for Disease Control and Prevention.

National Center for Women and Policing. (2003a). Police family violence fact sheet. Retrieved September 20, 2004 from www.womenandpolicing.org/violence FS.asp.

National Center for Victims of Crime. (2003b). Spousal rape laws: 20 years later. Retrieved September 20, 2004 from www.ncvc.org/policy/issues/spousal rape.

National Coalition for the Homeless. (1999). Domestic violence and homelessness. Retrieved August 2004 from http://www.nationalhomeless.org/domestic.html.

National Domestic Hotline. (1999). Hotline services. Retrieved August 2004 from www.ndvh.org/ndvh5.html.

NCAVP. (2002). *National report on lesbian, gay, bisexual, and transgender domestic violence in 2001.* New York: National Coalition of Anti-Violence Programs.

NCAVP. (2003). *National report on lesbian, gay, bisexual, and transgender domestic violence in 2002.* New York: National Coalition of Anti-Violence Programs.

Nicolaidis, C., Curry, M. A., Ulrich, Y., Sharps, P., Mcfarlane, J., Campbell, D., Gary, F., Laughon, K., Glass, N., & Campbell, J. (2003). Could we have known? A qualitative analysis of data from women who survived an attempted homicide by an intimate partner. *Journal of General Internal Medicine* 18 (10), 788–794.

NIJ. (1998). (Report No. NCJ 172204.) Washington, DC: U.S. Department of Justice.

OVC. (2002). *Enforcement of protection orders.* (Report No. NCJ 189190.) Washington, DC: U.S. Department of Justice.

Pagelow, M. D. (1984). *Family violence.* New York: Praeger.

Pleck, E. (1989). *Criminal approaches to family violence, 1640–1980. Family Violence* 11, 19–57.

Pleck, E. (2001). Domestic tyranny: The making of social policy against family violence from colonial times to the present. In C. Dalton, & E. Schneider (Eds.), *Battered women and the law* (pp. 10–17). New York: Foundation Press.

Radford, J., & Russell, D. E. H. (1992). *Femicide: The politics of woman killing.* New York: Twayne Publishers.

Rennison, C. (2003). Intimate partner violence, 1993–2001. (Report No. NCJ 197838). Washington, DC: U.S. Department of Justice.

Rennison, C. (2002). *Rape and sexual assault: Reporting to police and medical attention, 1992–2000.* (Report No. NCJ 194530.) Washington, DC: U.S. Department of Justice.

Rennison, C. (2001). (Report No. NCJ 187635.) Washington, DC: U.S. Department of Justice.

Rennison, C. M., & Welchans, S. (2000). *Intimate partner violence.* (Report No. NCJ 178247.) Washington, DC: U.S. Department of Justice.

Rennison, C., & Planty, M. (2003). Nonlethal intimate partner violence: Examining race, gender, and income. *Violence and Victims* 18 (4), 433–443.

Renzetti, C. (1992). *Violent betrayal: Partner abuse in lesbian relationships.* Newbury Park, CA: Sage.

Romano, I., & White, D. (2002). *Woman's life.* Retrieved October 29, 2003, from http://www.museum.upenn.edu/Greek_World/women.html.

Rosenfeld, R. (1997). (Report No. NCJ 166149.) Washington, DC: U.S. Department of Justice.

Schwartz, M. (1987). Gender and injury in spousal assault. *Sociological Focus* 20 (1), 61–75.

Sherman, L. (1992). *Policing domestic violence: Experiments and dilemmas.* New York: Free Press.

Sigmon, J., & Edmunds, J. (2002). Victimization of individuals with disabilities. *National Victim Assistance Academy: Foundations in victimology and victims' rights and services.* Washington, DC: Office for Victims of Crime.

Straus, M. (1993). Physical assaults by wives: A major social problem. In R. J. Gelles & D. L. Loseke (Eds.), *Current controversies on family violence* (pp. 67–87). Newbury Park, CA: Sage.

Straus, M. A., Gelles, R. J., & Steinmetz, S. K. (1980). *Behind closed doors: Violence in the American family.* Garden City, NY: Anchor Press/Doubleday.

Tjaden, P., & Thoennes, N. (2000). *Extent, nature, and consequences of intimate partner violence: Findings from the national violence against women survey.* (Report No. NCJ 181867.) Washington, DC: U.S. Department of Justice.

Tjaden, P., & Thoennes, N. (1998). *Prevalence, incidence, and consequences of violence against women: Findings from the national violence against women survey.* (Report No. NCJ 172837.) Washington, DC: National Institute of Justice.

Ulrich, L. T. (1991). *Good wives: Image and reality in the lives of women in northern New England 1650–1750.* New York: Vintage Books.

Vann, A. (2003). *Developing culturally-relevant responses to domestic abuse: Asha Family Services, Inc.* Harrisburg, PA: National Resource Center on Domestic Violence.

von Wormer, K. S., & Bartollas, C. (2000). *Women and the criminal justice system.* Boston: Allyn and Bacon.

Cases Cited

Bradley v. State, 1 Miss. 156, Supreme Court of Mississippi (1824)

Ligon v. Ford, 19 Va. 10; 1816 Va. LEXIS 2, Supreme Court of Virginia (1816)

Polly Pidge v. Palemon Pidge, 44 Mass. 257; 1841 Mass. LEXIS 122, Supreme Court of Massachusetts (1841)

Thurman v. City of Torrington, 595 F. Supp 1521 (1984)

Weiand v. State, 2 Fla. Coastal L.J. 125 (2000)

Part IV

Women Offenders

In this section, we examine women offenders and their treatment by the formal agents of social control. Although female criminality has generated a considerable amount of research and interest since the 1970s, it is only more recently that we have begun to explore the effects of factors like increased formal social control, economic marginalization, and drugs on women's involvement in crime. Some indications of women's inferior economic position in U.S. society can be found in the fact that women earn approximately $.75 for every dollar that men earn, the increasing number of children living in single-parent households headed by women, the alarming number of children who are living below the poverty line, and the differences in the median weekly incomes of men and women. Clearly, women have not attained economic equality in the labor market with men.

The number of arrests for drug possession and distribution, and the incidence of self-reported drug use by women in jails and prison just prior to and at the time of their offense, provide some insight into the pervasiveness of the drug problem and its effects on women. The government response to the problem persists; it depends on increased penalties for drug-related offenses and an insufficient number of treatment programs in the communities. In particular, there continues to be a small number of drug prevention and treatment options for women with children. The dramatic increase in female prison populations is largely due to the "war on drugs," which has adversely affected women. In short, arrest, prosecution, and incarceration rather than prevention and treatment have continued to be the dominant policies of the new millennium.

Typically, the female drug offender is not in the upper echelon of a major drug organization. She is usually poor, a minority, underemployed, and drug dependent. Treatment and prevention programs would be far more advantageous for women and their children than the deleterious consequences of violence and the reactive strategies that we currently authorize.

As illustrated in the chapters in this section, female offenders who use or sell drugs and who engage in violent acts are often the victims of violence. The pathways to violent offending often include long-term physical and sexual abuse. Women who kill may be killing their abuser. If we are really committed to reducing women's involvement in violent offending, we will need to institute policies and programs that prevent their victimization during childhood. In addition, we will have to provide meaningful employment options and equal remuneration for women who work.

10

Female Criminality

Ten Years Later

Sareta M. Davis, Alida V. Merlo, and Joycelyn M. Pollock

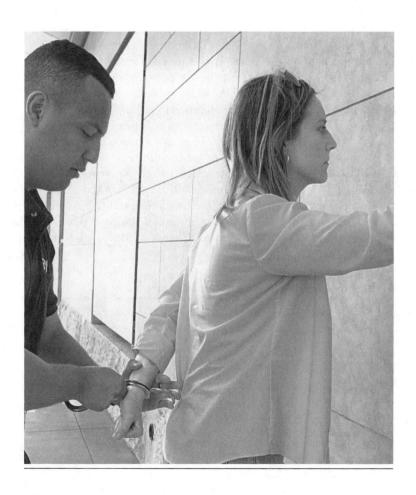

In the first edition of this book, Merlo (1995, p. 119) described the typical female offender as "not a corporate or computer criminal, a terrorist, a burglar, or a murderer." Rather, the typical female criminal was likely to engage in theft, fraud, drug offenses, forgery, embezzlement, and prostitution. Merlo (1995) pointed out that despite the reality of female offense patterns, the media and the public preferred to focus on the "glitzy exceptions," suggesting that women's involvement in crimes of violence (like serial murder) and property crimes (like industrial espionage) was increasing. Some explanations that have been offered, like the female emancipation hypothesis, have not been empirically substantiated. Others, like the feminist critical perspectives, are difficult to test empirically. However, an important dimension in understanding contemporary female criminality had emerged ten years ago: the female offender's use of drugs. It continues to merit close scrutiny as an important element in female criminality.

At first glance, the arrest data for men and women appear similar. In 1992, female offenders were most likely, in order of frequency, to be arrested for larceny-theft, driving under the influence, other assaults, drug abuse violations, and fraud. Men were most often arrested for driving under the influence, larceny-theft, drug abuse violations, other assaults, and drunkenness (U.S. Department of Justice, 1993, p. 226). In 2002, however, the order of frequency of arrests for the aforementioned crimes had changed. The new order of crime frequency for men and women is now slightly different, as Figure 10.1 indicates.

In 2002, the number of men and women arrested in the most frequent offense categories: larceny-theft, driving under the influence, and fraud decreased. However, arrests for drug abuse violations have increased substantially for both men and women (see Table 10.1). For men, arrests in this offense category increased from 769,800 to 903,656 arrests, and for women from 151,344 to 199,361 (U.S. Department of Justice, 1993, 2002).

Merlo (1995) noted that the number of arrests for men far exceeded the number of arrests for women in 1992, and official data indicate this continues to be the case in the new millennium. In 1992, men were responsible for 9,633,809 of the total 11,893,153 arrests in the United States (U.S. Department of Justice, 1993, p. 229). Although the total number of arrests in the United States has since decreased, men were still responsible for 7,478,623 of the total 9,807,735 arrests in 2002 (U.S. Department of Justice, 2002). For the four violent crimes—murder, rape, robbery, and aggravated assault—561,310 males and 79,940 females

FIGURE 10.1 *Rank Order of Crimes of Men and Women*

Men	Women
1. Drug Abuse Violations	1. Larceny-Theft
2. Larceny-Theft	2. Other Assaults
3. DWI	3. Drug Abuse Violations
4. Other Assaults	4. DWI
5. Fraud	5. Fraud

Source: U.S. Department of Justice (2002). *Uniform crime reports, 2002.* Washington, DC: U.S. Government Printing Office. Retrieved on July 7, 2004 from http://www.fbi.gov/ucr/cius_02/html/web/arrested/04-table42.html.

TABLE 10.1 *Female and Male Arrests in 1992 and 2002 by Most Frequent Offense Categories*

	Female		Male	
	1992	**2002**	**1992**	**2002**
Larceny-Theft	415,248	312,735	876,736	845,009
Driving Under the Influence	182,041	177,607	1,137,542	842,770
Other Assaults	156,584	**220,114**	755,933	701,562
Drug Abuse Violations	151,344	**199,361**	769,080	**903,656**
Fraud	145,948	105,191	200,366	127,896
Total	1,051,165	1,015,008	3,739,657	3,420,893

Source: U.S. Department of Justice. (1993, 2002). *Uniform Crime Reports, 1992, 2002.* Washington, DC: U.S. Government Printing Office. These data were taken from the table entitled "Total Arrests, Distribution by Sex, 1992," p. 234; and "Arrests, by Sex, 2002," Table 42 (http://www.fbi.gov/ucr/cius_02/html/web/arrested/04-table42.html).

were arrested in 1992; in 2002, the numbers of arrests for these crimes were 373,849 and 79,362, respectively (U.S. Department of Justice, 1993, pp. 229–231; U.S. Department of Justice, 2002).

For property crimes (larceny-theft, burglary, motor vehicle theft, and arson), 1,370,198 men and 467,076 women were arrested in 1992; in 2002, the arrest figures were 1,170,165 men and 359,591 women (see Table 10.2) (U.S. Department of Justice 1993, p. 234; U.S. Department of Justice, 2002, Table 42).

One of the most interesting observations one can make of this decade-long decline in crime for men and women is that in three crime categories, women have shown an increase. The number of arrests of women for "other assaults" has increased from 156,584 in 1992 to 220,114 in 2002, and the number of arrests of women for aggravated assault in 1992 was 64,539 and 68,532 in 2002. Finally, the number of women arrested for drug abuse violations in 1992 was 151,344 and 199,361 in 2002 (U.S. Department of Justice, 1993, pp. 229–231; U.S. Department of Justice, 2002).

This review of official arrests data proves that, as predicted by Merlo in 1995, women did not reach the levels of criminal behavior of men during the twentieth century as measured by arrests. However, any theory that seeks to explain women's criminal behavior must account for the increase in three crime categories: other assaults, aggravated assault, and drug abuse violations (see Tables 10.1 and 10.2).

Constructing a Theory of Female Criminality

Theories explaining female criminality must explain not only why women engage in less crime than men but also why their participation in some crime categories has increased in the last several decades. Early theories of female criminality focused on biological, physiological, and psychological explanations of crime (Pollock, 1999; Rasche, 1975). Before examining contemporary female criminality, it is important to summarize the theories that have been proposed to explain it.

TABLE 10.2   *Female and Male Arrests in 1992 and 2002 for Index Offenses by Crime Category*

Crime	Female		Male	
	1992	**2002**	**1992**	**2002**
Violent Crime				
Murder	1,899	1,092	17,592	9,015
Rape	420	278	32,965	19,884
Robbery	13,082	7,973	140,374	69,369
Agg. Assault	64,539	**68,532**	370,379	270,905
Total	79,940	77,875	561,310	369,173
Property Crime				
Larceny-theft	415,248	312,735	876,736	845,009
Burglary	33,129	27,330	326,570	178,806
MVT	18,516	17,724	152,753	89,463
Arson	2,183	1,802	14,139	10,031
Total	469,076	359,591	1,370,198	1,170,165

Source: U.S. Department of Justice. (1993, 2002). *Uniform Crime Reports, 1992, 2002.* Washington, DC: U.S. Government Printing Office. These data were taken from the table entitled "Total Arrests, Distribution by Sex, 1992," p. 234; and "Arrests, by Sex, 2002," Table 42 (http://www.fbi.gov/ucr/cius_02/html/web/arrested/04-table42.html).

In the past, theories designed to explain the criminality of men have been inappropriately and ineffectively used to attempt to explain the criminality of woman, or ignored women all together (this review relies largely on Pollock, 1999). The Classical Theory (Jeremy Bentham [1748–1832] and Cesare Beccaria [1738–1794]) assumed that all humans were rational beings, and as such, utilized free will to formulate "rational choices." However, women were not viewed as rational beings, and further, they were considered to be under the domain of their fathers or husbands, both morally and legally.

Positivist theorists, notably Cesare Lombroso (1835–1909), believed the key to criminality resided within the individual. Women commit less crime than men, according to Lombroso and other early positivists, because of essential, biological differences. Lombroso believed, for instance, that although women were less evolved intellectually and emotionally than men, they were held in check by elements of piety and passivity. Criminal women were more masculine than women and were even worse than criminal men because women, in general, were less evolved than men.

Other theories that have attempted to explain female criminality are psychological, social structure, or social process in nature. Psychological theories include psychodynamic, developmental, and learning theories. Psychodynamic theories are based on the assumption that normal development does not take place if one's parental ties are not properly established and/or a devastating childhood trauma occurs (Lykken, 1995, pp. 6–7). Individuals become criminals due to feelings of guilt and a need for punishment or due to a failure to develop adequate impulse control. The problem with applying psychodynamic theories to female criminals is that they are counterintuitive—they view male and female development and criminality as being different; however, they apply modified versions of theories designed to explain male criminality to females, without attempting to distinguish why men and women differ with regard to participation in crime.

Developmental theories revolve around the proposed developmental stages an individual goes through from birth to adulthood (Piaget, 1965). The inability of an individual to achieve or pass through all levels of development results in immaturity in all aspects of one's life, and this leads to criminal offending. The application of developmental theories to explain differences between the criminality of men and women holds promise, especially since some developmental schemes are able to identify differences between men and women that may affect criminal choices (Gilligan, 1982).

Learning theory posits that one is not necessarily "born" criminal, but becomes a criminal as a consequence of observing and emulating the behavior of those close to him or her, especially parents and close friends. The second component of "learning" in this sense includes reinforcement of the delinquent or criminal behavior via praise or some type of gain for the individual. Learning theory is helpful in providing explanations for two aspects of female criminality: why women in general are responsible for much less crime than men, especially violent crime, and why women, when criminal, typically engage in crimes involving financial fraud.

According to learning theory (Bandura, 1977), women are less likely to behave criminally because the socialization process for women in this country encourages them to be social, collective, conforming, and nonaggressive. Official data indicate women are more likely to engage in property crimes. Learning theory could explain this, because as a consequence of their socialization, women may be more likely to learn how to embezzle or steal via fraud, rather than by using violence or aggression to achieve financial gain. If learning theory can explain why women commit less crime, it might also explain why women are committing more crime in some crime categories. If the socialization of women changed, for instance, and the reward structure for criminal behavior changed, then we would expect to see differences in the pattern of criminal behavior.

Social structure theories seek to explain crime by describing and studying how some constructs of society cause those exposed to particular societal circumstances to become criminal. Social structure theories include cultural deviance theory and social strain theory. Cultural deviance theory (Shaw & McKay, 1969) proposed why those living in the so-called interstitial zones engaged in crime. The theory stated that those who resided in a subculture—a neighborhood or area rife with crime—were subject to receiving deviant morals transmitted via gang and group activities outside of the home. The problem with applying this theory to female criminals is that it specifically discusses male delinquents; no mention of women or girls was made. Men receiving deviant cultural cues from other men within their subculture were the focus of this theory, and the social relationships of women living in interstitial zones was not addressed.

Social strain theory (Merton, 1968) proposed the idea that everyone in our society is encouraged to obtain material items and wealth as a sign of "success," although everyone does not have access to the legitimate means to achieve these goals. Because the focus on gaining wealth and success is so strong in our society, those without access to the legitimate means (education, family wealth, community status, and good jobs) to obtain the goals of wealth and success will utilize other avenues, at times illegitimate or illegal, to reach those goals. The problem with applying this theory to criminal women is that it would predict that since women have historically had less wealth and power in our society than men, they should be committing more crime than men.

According to social strain theory, women should be committing more or as much crime as men, and they are not. One might argue that women aspire to different goals—not power and money, but, rather, marriage and strong relationship bonds. Thus, their crimes should relate to these goals. This idea, while having some potential, has not garnered strong empirical support.

Social process theories concentrate on how, or what, breaks the bonds between an individual and society, and how this leads to deviant or criminal behavior. Social process theories include differential association, control theory, and labeling theory. Differential association theory (Sutherland, 1937) goes one step further than subculture theories; it seeks to explain why one is susceptible to the influences that promote delinquent behavior within a subculture. This theory posits that although one may be submersed in a deviant subculture with criminal values and morals, the key to the individual actually adopting these criminal definitions as their own is reinforcement. Problematic in the application of this theory to female criminals is that women are not usually exposed to the same social bond building system as are men. In general, women receive socialization related to maintaining intimate ties, while men receive messages that support aggressive or risk-taking behavior that is often associated with deviant or criminal behavior.

Control theory (Hirschi, 1969) posits that one behaves in a criminal manner as a result of weak or nonexistent social bonds. Therefore, when one is poorly socialized, he or she will have no internal barriers to offending against society. Hirschi studied only young males in his development of control theory. Later studies have attempted to include women by exploring the increased social attachments of women relative to men (for a review, see Pollock, 1999). Control theory does seem to be consistent with the criminal patterns of men and women, since, it can be argued, women have closer "bonds" to others, at least during the young adult years, and in measurable ways.

Labeling theory (Lemert, 1951) proposes that individuals who are labeled as criminals by those in power or significant others in a society will then behave in a manner consistent with the label given. Those involved in the labeling facilitate this process by treating the labeled individual differently once the label has been affixed. Labeling theory might explain why women are less likely to commit criminal acts if we assume that they are less likely to be labeled. It might also explain why the number of arrests is increasing in some crime categories if we can assume that women are more likely to be labeled today. However, these assumptions have yet to be tested.

It was not until the 1970s that female criminality emerged as a separate and distinct academic research field (Rasche, 1975). The publication of Freda Adler's *Sisters in Crime* (1975) and Rita Simon's *Women and Crime* (1975) facilitated discussion and critiques of female involvement in criminal activities. Both Adler and Simon used women's liberation to predict that women would increase their involvement in crime. Adler (1975) suggested that liberation would finally free women; she argued that women have basically the same characteristics as men and, by nature, are no more law-abiding than men. Adler predicted that once women achieved equality, they would engage in the same kinds of crime and experience the same health problems as their male counterparts. As a consequence, Adler (1975) predicted that the numbers of women engaging in violent crime (murder, robbery, and assault) would also increase in conjunction with increased equality with men.

Simon (1975) hypothesized that liberation would result in greater opportunities for women in the marketplace and that there would be correspondingly greater opportunities for crime. Unlike Adler, Simon contended that the liberation movement would give women more opportunities for economic crime like forgery, fraud, and embezzlement but that their participation in murder and other violent crimes would decrease. Both theories proposed that social circumstances (i.e., limited opportunities and aspirations), not biological factors, prevented women from engaging in crime. Therefore, if the social circumstances were changed, women would be as prone to criminal activities as men.

Contrary to the expectations of both theories, female offenders were not influenced by the women's liberation movement, at least not measurably so; and women did not achieve economic equality with men (Daly & Chesney-Lind, 1988). Although women's arrest rates for property crimes have increased, these crimes have not been attributed to greater opportunities due to higher-level positions in employment as Simon predicted. The increased frequency of arrests of women for other assaults and aggravated assaults appears to lend credence to Adler's hypothesis; however, there are also other explanations that seem equally likely. These issues will be explored more fully later in the remainder of this chapter.

Recent Theories

Despite the fact that Adler's and Simon's theories have been refuted, both are credited with helping the field of female criminology to emerge as separate and distinct from male criminology. Adler and Simon have prompted critiques, discussions, further research, and a new body of literature. Some of the factors that explanations of female criminality need to take into account include women's socialization and their economic position relative to men, the inherent nature of a patriarchal society and how that affects criminal opportunities, the differences between African American and white female criminality, the differences in moral development between men and women, sex differences in childhood abuse and neglect, and increased formal social control, especially in domestic violence enforcement and how that affects women (Baskin & Sommers, 1993; Daly & Chesney-Lind, 1988; Datesman & Scarpitti, 1980; Feinman, 1986; Gilligan, 1982; Merlo, 1995; Pollock, 1999; Simpson, 1989; Smart, 1979; Spatz Widom, 1992; Steffensmeier, 1978).

Unfortunately, the interest in female criminality has not resulted in its inclusion in the literature on crime. Criminology texts barely mention its importance and influence. In an examination of criminology textbooks, Wright (1992) observed the extent of coverage of female criminology issues in criminology textbooks written from 1956 to 1965. He compared this time period with 1981 to 1990 (1992, p. 223). Although the number of pages devoted to women in crime increased from a mean of fourteen pages in 1956–1965 to 19.7 pages in 1981–1990, he notes that most of the coverage is devoted to discussions of rape; other topics are generally ignored (1992, p. 225).

In a recently released criminal justice textbook (Inciardi, 2004), the subject index contained no pages devoted to females or gender; and of 658 pages, only thirty-four specifically addressed issues related to women and crime. Further, none of the ten pages devoted specifically to theory mention feminist criminology. Although well-known criminologists have been actively involved in researching female offenders for over thirty years, they are still largely ignored in textbook treatments of criminology.

Since the liberation hypothesis has not been empirically supported (Daly & Chesney-Lind, 1988; Pollock, 1999; Steffensmeier & Cobb, 1981; Steffensmeier & Streifel, 1992), other theories have been used to explain increases in female criminality.

Steffensmeier and Streifel (1992) analyzed FBI female arrest data for property crimes for the twenty-six-year period from 1960 to 1985. They tested three hypotheses: increased formal social control, economic marginality, and female liberation. While they found no empirical support for the liberation or emancipation hypothesis, they did find strong support for the increased formal social control hypothesis and some support for the economic marginality hypothesis (Steffensmeier & Streifel, 1992, p. 92). These two theories are discussed in the next section.

Increased Formal Social Control.   Steffensmeier and Streifel (1992, p. 92) found that increased formal social control best explained the number of female arrests for property crime between 1960 and 1985. According to the theory of increased formal social control, the increase in female arrests during that time period was due, in part, to the more formal policing that led to more official documentation of female criminality. Improved social control resulted in increased police bureaucratization (including civilian personnel) and more specialized professionals, more sophisticated and computer-assisted recordkeeping services, formal and established procedures for handling deviant behavior, and more police officers (Feinman, 1986; Steffensmeier & Streifel, 1992). Social control proponents contend that the actual number of women involved in criminal activity may not be that different from previous years; they are just more likely to be apprehended and processed.

Similarly, in their research on police arrests between 1962 and 1980 in Lincoln, Nebraska, and Kansas City, Missouri, Ortega and Burnett (1987) found their results somewhat consistent with the position that it is not the incidence of female criminality that has increased but rather changes in the way the agents of social control conduct themselves. Research on female offenders in state courts by Greenfield and Snell (1999, pp. 5–6) indicates that 90 percent of the violent felony increase can be attributed to increases in the number of women convicted of aggravated assault; and they indicated this could be due to the increase in the number of domestic violence cases prosecuted (Greenfield & Snell 1999, p. 3).

According to the chivalry hypothesis, the arrest rates for women are generally lower than those of men because of "courtesy" or leniency afforded women by those in the criminal justice system because of their sex (Belknap, 2001; Pollock, 1999). If procedural changes like mandatory arrest and a greater likelihood of prosecution for certain crimes are considered, then this could explain the increase in the number of women arrested. For instance, police departments have adopted mandatory arrest policies for domestic violence. It may be that this policy change is responsible for at least some of the increase in arrests for assaults and aggravated assaults.

In arrests involving other assaults and/or aggravated assault, intimates are most likely to be women's victims. Greenfield and Snell (2000) report that two-thirds of the women arrested had a prior relationship with those they assaulted, and 40 percent of violent offenses committed by women occurred in close proximity to the victim's home or school (Greenfield & Snell, 2000, p. 43). Mandatory arrest policies in domestic violence cases have increased the likelihood of both men and women being arrested in these types of disputes (Chesney-

Lind, 2002; Humphries, 2002; Miller, 2001). In Canada, the arrest rates for women for domestic violence increased from 23 percent to over 58 percent after the implementation of mandatory arrest policies (Chesney-Lind, 2002, p. 83). These data suggest the importance of reviewing the arrest rates of women in the United States for assaults involving domestic violence. These policy initiatives could account for most of the increase in arrests of women for other assaults/aggravated assault.

Table 10.3 illustrates that although the crime rate for aggravated assault went down for women between 1992 and 2002, the numbers of arrests for this offense increased (see Table 10.2). This could be attributed to the fact that the population of women in the United States increased from 129,663,000 in 1992 to 146,610,000 in 2002. The number of arrests of women for aggravated assault was 64,539 in 1992, and 68,532 in 2002, a difference of only 3,993 arrests. It is possible that this increase was a combination of increased formal social control accompanied by the leveling effect of population growth (U.S. Department of Justice, 1992, 2003; World Bank, 2004).

Enhanced bureaucratization in police departments—with its attendant formalized policies and procedures, computerized recordkeeping, training, and the addition of more civilian employees—can be credited with improving the overall performance of police departments and in professionalizing police. Increased formal social controls have negatively affected women with regard to arrest rates, especially for assault. Women may not be committing any more assaults than they ever did; instead, the evolution of the definition of assault combined with changes in arrest policies can account for much of the rise in arrest rates.

TABLE 10.3 *Female and Male Crime Rates per 100,000 Population in 1992 and 2002 for Index Offenses by Crime Category*

Crime	Female		Male	
	1992	2002	1992	2002
Violent Crime				
Murder	1.46	.74	13.98	6.41
Rape	.32	.18	26.20	14.14
Robbery	10.08	5.43	111.57	49.33
Agg. Assault	49.77	46.74	294.39	192.65
Property Crime				
Larceny-theft	320.25	213.31	696.87	378.52
Burglary	25.55	18.64	259.57	127.15
MVT	14.28	12.08	121.41	63.62
Arson	1.68	1.22	11.23	7.13

Source: U.S. Department of Justice. (1993,2002). *Uniform Crime Reports, 1992, 2002.* Washington, DC: U.S. Government Printing Office. Data used to compute crime rates taken from table entitled "Total Arrests, Distribution by Sex, 1992," p. 234; and "Arrests, by Sex, 2002," Table 42 (http://www.fbi.gov/ucr/cius_02/html/web/arrested/04-table42.html).

Population data used to compute crime rates retrieved on August 2, 2004 from Worldbank, http://1180-devdata.worldbank.org.libproxy.txstate.edu/dataonline/.

Economic Marginalization.   The other major explanation for women's increased participation in property crime categories is economic marginalization. To assess economic marginality, Steffensmeier and Streifel (1992, p. 86) examined four variables: the percentage of single-parent households headed by women, the female unemployment rate relative to the male rate, the illegitimacy rate, and the divorce rate. Their study found that the economic marginalization thesis could account for some of the increase in officially recorded female criminality.

A number of other variables might provide a clearer picture of women's economic status and should be included in future research. Some of the specific factors that merit consideration and inclusion in documenting economic marginality and empirically testing its significance are the increases in the number of black single mothers, of women living in poverty, of children living with mothers who are living in poverty, and the differences in the level of college education between men and women. These variables illustrate women's economic position relative to men and suggest that their situation may actually be worsening.

The economic status of single and married women has not made the significant strides that were envisioned in the 1970s. More and more women have slipped into poverty. There were over 3.2 million women living below the poverty level in 1989 (U.S. Bureau of the Census, 1993, p. 385). Since the first edition of this book, the poverty level for women has not significantly improved. In 2000, 11.9 million women lived below the poverty level (U.S. Department of Health and Human Services, 2002). The problem was most pronounced for African American and Hispanic women, with 21.4 percent of African American women and 20.1 percent of Hispanic women living below the poverty level (U.S. Department of Health and Human Services, 2002).

As an indicator of economic marginality, recent census data indicate that more and more women are heads of single-parent households. In 1990, 65 percent of all births in the African American community were to unmarried women. In the white community, the figure was 20 percent (U.S. Bureau of Census, 1993, p. 78). Although single parenthood by mothers has increased for African Americans and whites, the phenomenon is far more prevalent among African Americans. In 1991, women headed 58 percent of all African American families with children, compared to only 19 percent of white families (Suro, 1992, p. A8). The reason for single parenthood given by female heads of families differed for African Americans and whites. Among white single mothers, the major reasons were divorce and separation, although the number of white mothers who had never married increased from less than 3 percent of one-parent families in 1970 to 19 percent in 1991. In 1992, 54 percent of single-parent African American families were headed by women who had never married (Suro, 1992, p. A8).

U.S. Census Bureau data indicate in 2002, that 33 percent of all births in the United States were to unmarried women (Downs, 2003, p. 5). In 2002, the number of out of wedlock births had increased to 25 percent for white women and remained at 65 percent for black women (Downs, 2003, p. 6). Thirty-six percent of births to Hispanic women were out of wedlock (Downs, 2003, p. 6). Though Downs (2003) reports that the majority of all births to teenagers continue to occur out of wedlock (89 percent), current data indicate that the rate of pregnancy and abortion for teenagers has declined in all states for all racial and ethnic groups (Editors of Health Day, 2004). Since 1990, rates of teen pregnancy have decreased by 28 percent, and from 1999 to 2000 they decreased another 2 percent. Black females experienced a 40 percent decrease in teen pregnancy since 1990 (Centers for Disease Control, 2003).

Since 1991, not much has changed for the economic position of single African American women and the households they must head. Although the reasons of divorce, separation, and never marrying are all legitimate to explain the disparity between single-parent households headed by African American women in comparison to those headed by white women, an issue that must also be addressed is the increasing number of African American men being incarcerated—and for longer periods of time—in the United States.

Single-parent families headed by women (both African American and white) are characterized by poverty, limited education, underemployment, and depression (Suro, 1992, p. A8). In 1993, 5.1 million 6-year-olds, or 22.4 percent of the total number of children aged 6, lived only with their mother. Of these, 3 million, or 57.5 percent of the total, lived below the poverty line (U.S. Bureau of the Census, 1993, p. 470). Although the size of these families is not provided, the poverty level for a four-person household in 1991 was $12,812.00 (U.S. Bureau of the Census, 1993, p. 474).

In 2000, the poverty level for a four-person household was $17,603. Over 11 million children age 18 and under were living below the poverty level, and 17 percent of children 6 years and younger were living in poverty (U.S. Bureau of the Census, 2000c). African American and Hispanic children comprised most of those children living in poverty, with 30 percent of African American children and 27 percent of Hispanic children living below the poverty level (U.S. Bureau of the Census, 2002). For the children living in poverty in 2000, 40 percent resided in a single-parent household headed by their mothers (U.S. Bureau of the Census, 2002). In 1999, 18.5 percent of households headed by women with no husband present had incomes of less than $10,000 per year (U.S. Bureau of the Census, 2000a). This constituted 2,307,019 of the households in the United States in 1999 (U.S. Bureau of the Census, 2000a, 2000b).

Census data suggest that the earnings of women who are employed do not equal those of their male counterparts. This factor contributes to their economic marginality (U.S. Bureau of the Census, 1993, p. 426). Median weekly earnings for men employed in 1992 were $505, and for women they were $381. In short, women earned approximately 75 cents on the dollar compared to men in 1992 (U.S. Bureau of the Census, 1993, p. 426). The largest percentage (44 percent) of women worked in the field identified as "Technical, Sales, and Administrative Support." Over 16 million women and 9.8 million men worked in positions so categorized. The median weekly salary for men in these positions was $519; for women it was $365 (U.S. Bureau of the Census, 1993, p. 426).

In this century, the average median income for men continues to be well above the average median income of women, and the disparate incomes of men and women in the United States continue to lend credence to the economic marginality thesis. For the third quarter of 2002, the median weekly earnings for women who worked full time were $528, compared to $676 for men (U.S. Department of Labor, 2002).

The educational attainment of women has continued to increase since 1992. In 1992, 24.3 percent of men and 18.6 percent of women aged 25 or older had four years of college or postbaccalaureate studies (U.S. Bureau of the Census, 1993, p. 153). In 2002, of the 84 percent of adults that completed high school or more, 25 percent of women and 29 percent of men have baccalaureate or postgraduate degrees (Spraggins, 2003, p. 3).

The economic position of women may help to account for their representation in official arrest data in the areas of larceny, theft, check and welfare fraud, and forgery of credit cards. Overall, the official arrest data depict that women, much more than men who violate the law, are minor property offenders (Steffensmeier & Streifel, 1992, p. 81). Greenfield and Snell (1999) reviewed defendants in state courts. They found that, in 1996, 41 percent of those convicted of embezzlement, forgery, and fraud were women (Greenfield & Snell, 1999, p. 8). Women comprised 23 percent of all felons convicted of property crimes in 1996 (Greenfield & Snell, 1999, p. 8). However, these numbers do not tell the whole story. They do not tell us, for instance, whether these property crimes were committed by women who were in positions of authority and involved large sums of money or whether they were by minimum wage earners whose crimes involved smaller losses than crimes committed by men.

The economic marginalization thesis is supported by Daly's (1989) study of 1,342 white-collar offenders who, between 1976 and 1978, were prosecuted and convicted in seven urban federal district courts for bank embezzlement, income tax fraud, postal fraud, false claims and statements, and bribery (1989, p. 770). In her sample, 14 percent of the embezzlers were women. At least half of the employed men in her sample were managerial or professional workers, but most of the employed women were clerical workers. Sixty-percent of the women in the sample worked as tellers and 90 percent worked in clerical positions. None attained any substantial financial gain from engaging in this type of criminal activity (1989, p. 773).

Daly (1989) predicted that if female arrests for fraud, embezzlement, and forgery increase, the increases will result from the following:

> (1) increasing numbers of women in highly monitored, money-changing types of clerical sales or service jobs and (2) increasing numbers of poor or unemployed women attempting to defraud state and federal governments or banks by securing loans, credit cards, or benefits to which they are not legally entitled. (p. 790)

Daly (1989) further noted that the women in the study cited their family financial needs as their primary motivation for engaging in criminal activity, lending some support to the economic marginalization hypothesis.

Holtfreter, Reisig, and Morash (2004) recently completed a study that appears to empirically support the economic marginalization hypothesis. They hypothesized that increased access of female offenders to "state capital," or government resources would decrease rates of recidivism (Holtfreter et al., 2004). A longitudinal study was completed using a sample of 134 females under community supervision who were convicted of felonies in an Oregon county and in Minneapolis and St. Paul, Minnesota (Holtfreter et al., 2004). Some of the probationers were serving deferred prison sentences in the community, and all were newly sentenced (Holtfreter et al., 2004). The women were asked to participate at their initial probation/parole interviews; those that chose to participate were interviewed immediately and again six months later (Holtfreter et al., 2004).

Holtfreter et al. (2004) found the factors of education/employment status and financial status to be highly correlated with poverty and recidivism. They also found that poor offenders (using the U.S. Bureau of the Census guidelines) in their sample who did not receive state capital were 3.3 times more likely to reoffend than poor offenders who received help (Holtfreter et al., 2004, p. 200). The critical aspect for those who did not recidivate appeared to be the availability of quick fix, or short-term but immediate, state benefits provided to the offenders (Holtfreter et al., 2004). Unfortunately, because of the short duration of the study, they could not apply the economic marginality thesis to long-term state capital benefits. However, the availability of short-term state capital did affect rates of recidivism, and this provides some support for the economic marginality hypothesis.

The economic marginalization and increased formal social control theories are useful for explaining some aspects of women's involvement in crime. However, drug use may be a significant factor as well. Criminologists have debated the relationship between drugs and crime for some time. Since the 1970s, criminologists have contended that poverty and drugs are major factors contributing to female criminality (Feinman, 1986). The increases in arrests for drug-related crimes, the increases in the prison and jail populations of women convicted for possession and distribution of drugs, and the increasing number of women under the influence of drugs at the time of their offenses suggest that drugs are, perhaps, one of the most important factors in female criminality today. We will highlight some points in this chapter, but leave the discussion of the female offender's drug use to be explored in greater detail in Chapter 11.

Drugs: Impact on Female Criminality

The number of arrests of women for drug abuse violations has increased from 151,344 in 1992 to 199,361 in 2002 (U.S. Department of Justice, 1993, 2002). Drug use and criminal activity are both directly and indirectly related.

In data collected by the U.S. Department of Justice in 1992, it was found that in those cities where arrestees were tested for drug use, higher percentages of women than men tested positive for drugs in 13 of 21 cities (Maguire, Pastore, & Flanagan, 1993, p. 459; National Institute of Justice, 1993).

The 2002 Arrestee Drug Abuse Monitoring Program (ADAM) study found that although women constituted only 20 percent of those arrested in 2000, 63 percent of the women arrested had used illegal drugs compared to 64 percent of arrested men (Taylor, Newton, & Brownstein [NIJ], 2003, p. 47, 53). In sites tested, the drugs most often used by women were, in order, cocaine, marijuana, opiates, and methamphetamine (Taylor, Newton, & Brownstein [NIJ], 2003, p. 47). Men tested positive for marijuana, cocaine, opiates, and methamphetamine, in this order (Taylor, Newton, & Brownstein [NIJ], 2003, p. 12).

In 1991, an equal percentage of female and male state prison inmates reported having ever used drugs in the category that includes heroin, methadone, cocaine, PCP, and LSD. A larger percentage of women, however, used them *daily* in the month before their current offense, being under the influence at the time of their offense (Maguire, Pastore, & Flanagan 1993, p. 627). A third of female inmates in Texas and California reported that they used cocaine enough in their lives to consider the use to be problematic, and one-third of these inmates reported that alcohol/heroin use had caused problems for them in their lives (Pollock, 1999). Although drug use in the United States has been steadily declining since the 1980s, there was a 13 percent increase in the number of female drug offenders incarcerated in state prisons between 1995 and 2001 (Dorsey, Zawitz, & Middleton [BJS], 2004).

In 1991, of the female state prison inmates that indicated the need for drugs was the motive for their crimes, 17 percent committed violent offenses and 43 percent committed property crimes (Snell, 1991). In a later study, Greenfield and Snell (1999) reported that one in three female inmates reported committing their offense as a means to finance their drug habits (Greenfield & Snell, 1999, p. 9).

Although it is commonly assumed that female addicts will most likely engage in prostitution to support their drug habits, their involvement in property crimes is more common. In their sample of 197 female crack users in Miami, Inciardi, Lockwood, and Pottieger (1993) found that in the women's last ninety days on the street, 76 percent engaged in drug business offenses, 77 percent committed minor property crimes, and 51 percent engaged in prostitution (1993, p. 120). Anglin and Hser's sample (1987) showed no evidence that female prostitutes relied primarily on prostitution to support drug habits. They found that the women in their sample supported their habits with a variety of crimes, in addition to property crimes, to raise money. Although theft is the crime of choice for female drug users, the researchers found that their respondents also engaged in drug dealing (1987, p. 393). However, women are not likely to be considered drug "king-pins."

In a study of 211 female crack cocaine users in Brooklyn, New York, between 1989 and 1992, Maher and Daly (1996) found that most women were not "in charge" of or instrumental in any drug market, and only one female manager was identified. Additionally, the nature of the business did not allow for sexual relationships to develop between these women and the men in charge, and sex in exchange for drugs was not the norm. Rather, women worked in the lowliest positions, and they were given more extensive duties temporarily only in situations in which men refused to work or the police were actively investigating a certain area (Maher & Daly, 1996). Maher and Daly (1996) did not find that women were able to capitalize on and flourish in the new illegitimate positions created when crack cocaine emerged onto the drug scene in the 1980s. The drug market is dominated by the philosophy that one must possess the traditionally masculine traits of strength and ruthlessness. Since women are perceived as not being able to live up to this image, they are, as often occurs in legitimate corporate business, not allowed to enter the "boys' club."

Female involvement in drug use and drug trafficking is an interesting topic for a number of reasons. In 1975, Adler proposed that with respect to the economic marginality thesis, drug use would provide low-income and depressed women an opportunity to escape poverty and experience some modicum of pleasure regardless of how brief the period. She also contended that women might engage in more violent crime in an attempt to protect their territory and economic opportunity in the drug market. However, Maher and Daly (1996) found no evidence to indicate women have "equal opportunity" in the drug market. Most engage in low levels of these markets simply as a means of making fast money to survive and support their habits (Maher & Daly, 1996).

The war on drugs in the United States has been referred to as "a war on women" because of the rapidly increasing number of women being arrested and incarcerated for drug crimes (Chesney-Lind, 1997, p. 147). African American women age 20 to 29 have been the most severely affected by incarceration for drug offenses (Belknap, 2003; Lyman & Potter, 2003). There has been a dramatic increase in the number of women incarcerated for drug offenses (Belknap, 2001; Lyman & Potter, 2003; Pollock, 2002).

Women are not the only ones victimized by the war on drugs and the concommitant mandatory sentencing guidelines that often impose unreasonably long sentences. The war on drugs has also increased the number of men, most notably African American men, incarcerated in state and federal prisons. This leaves women to bear the burden of being single heads of households and the sole caretakers for children. Women who are addicted to drugs are further burdened by the threat of loss of their children if certain officials are made aware of their addictions. This makes it difficult for the female addict to seek pre- or post-natal care or drug treatment, because of the potential to be charged with child abuse, neglect, and even murder (Bagley & Merlo, 1995; Lyman & Potter, 2003; see also Chapters 4 and 11).

Once convicted of a drug offense, many women are denied access to many state and federal welfare benefits, and their children ultimately suffer. Federal funding for college tuition is also denied these women once convicted of a drug offense, as well as eligibility for many jobs available for high school graduates. Inability to support oneself or one's children legally ultimately leads to more criminal behavior as a means of survival (for a review of these issues, see Pollock, 2002).

Conclusion

In order to enhance our understanding of female criminality, every effort must be made to propose theories that examine not only the economic marginalization and the increased formal social control of female offenders, but also their drug use. Although drug use in the United States has been declining since the first edition of this book, data indicate drug use/addiction continues to be a significant factor in female criminality. Women who use drugs regularly and who get involved in street crime (including drug sales) to support their drug habits have been the targets of the war on drugs. The fact that they account for such a large percentage of recent felony convictions in state and federal courts and prison populations illustrates the enormity of the problem and the criminal justice system's inability to address it. The current strategy is costly, punitive, and ineffective. It would be far more humane and beneficial to provide these women with drug treatment, vocational training, employment, and health care. This issue is covered in greater detail in Chapter 11.

If a significant part of the increase in the female arrest rate for drug abuse violations, other assaults, and aggravated assault can be explained through a combination of increased economic marginalization, social control, and drug use, there are a number of social interventions that could ameliorate women's involvement with drugs and their inferior economic position. First, the federal government has to take the initiative to establish broad-based alcohol and drug prevention programs. In order to enable these programs to reach all those who need them, immediate and long-term funding will be essential. A concerted emphasis on prevention will represent a significant policy shift. It requires more than a campaign asking children to "just say no." It will involve, in part, examining the media and advertising images that associate drugs like alcohol and tobacco with sexual attractiveness, beauty, and health. Part of the prevention efforts have to be aimed at debunking these myths and honestly dealing with the long-term consequences of alcohol, tobacco, and illicit drug use. Such a stance is far more proactive than the traditional drug enforcement reactive policy that characterized the government's approach in the 1980s and 1990s.

Second, society needs to make treatment programs a priority. Specifically, women have to have access to drug treatment programs on a residential and an out-patient basis. In order to facilitate availability, poor women, pregnant women, and women who have dependent children living with them have to be encouraged to participate in treatment. They need to know that they will not be excluded because of their lack of health insurance or because of their pregnancy or motherhood status. The federal and state governments will be required to commit the requisite funding to establish and maintain such programs and to ensure that lack of private health insurance will not result in poor women being excluded. As indicated by Holtfreter, Reisig, and Morash (2004), the availability of state capital in the form of welfare, treatment, and health care to female offenders is positively correlated with reduced rates of recidivism. Women in need of drug treatment must also not be made to fear legal repercussions if they seek treatment while pregnant. The threat of the permanent loss of children if labeled an addict must also be removed so that women can feel safe when requesting treatment.

Third, although the actual number of female addicts is smaller than the number of male addicts, the female addicts seem to have more difficult problems to address. For example, it is estimated that women make up approximately 20 percent of the heroin addict population; yet they are more likely to be unemployed, unmarried, to have minor children to care for, lower self-esteem, other health problems, and to be perceived as more deviant and less amenable to treatment than male addicts (Andersen, 1993, p. 192; Lyman & Potter, 2003, pp. 332–333; Pollock, 1999, pp. 95–96). Therefore, female drug addicts require specialized treatment programs designed to address their problems and to assist them in developing the coping skills necessary to combat their addiction. Such programs need to include parenting and social skills, communication skills, health, diet and nutrition, and emotional and psychological support services.

Fourth, there is evidence that women are more frequently the victims of child abuse and maltreatment than males (Pollock, 1999; Taeuber, 1991) and that a significant percentage of female substance users were sexually and physically abused as children (Corea, 1992; Downs, Miller, & Gondoli, 1987; for a review of this literature, see Pollock, 2002). A study of 1,575 cases followed from childhood through early adulthood by Spatz Widom (1992, p. 2) found that being abused or neglected as a child increased the likelihood of arrest for females by 77 percent when they were compared to nonabused women.

A 1997 survey of state prison inmates reported that 19 percent of those interviewed indicated they had been sexually abused prior to their instant offense (Dorsey, Zawitz, & Middleton, 2004). The survey also revealed a possible correlation between being abused and current drug use (Dorsey et al., 2004). Of the total inmates surveyed who reported being abused, 76 percent of men and 80 percent of women admitted using illegal drugs on a regular basis; 65 percent of women and 68 percent of men that reported no abuse admitted to drug use regularly (Dorsey et al., 2004). These findings demonstrate the importance of preventing child abuse and neglect and establishing programs to provide the victims with counseling and support services (see Pollock, 1998). The effects of abuse, both in the short term and the long term, illustrate the exigency of appropriating resources to address it. Through prevention and early intervention, the risk of drug abuse might be reduced.

Fifth, high levels of social disorganization, physical and social segregation, decaying buildings, high infant mortality rates, disease, truancy, and violence often characterize the neighborhoods where poor women and their families reside. It is not enough to attempt to deal with drug abuse without also attempting to ameliorate the conditions that are conducive to women's returning to drugs and crime. In short, treatment cannot be focused only on the addict and ignore the broader social environment. The broader social environment must also be addressed when considering the potential future women face once convicted of a drug offense. Changes must be made in the government and society to decriminalize the way in which female addicts are viewed and treated by health care professionals, because negative views of these offenders reduce the likelihood that they will seek and receive treatment (Lyman & Potter, 2003).

Sixth, women have to be empowered to realize that their self-worth is not determined solely by their sensuality and physical attractiveness. Every effort must be made to encourage female teenagers, including teenage unmarried mothers, to continue their education. In order to facilitate the completion of high school, school systems may have to provide some type of day care programs or home tutorial assistance for young mothers. Additionally, vocational training programs and an opportunity to attend college should be stressed and encouraged. The educational system has to take steps to retain all female students and to facilitate their career development. It is through education that the young mothers and their children and all students will have the opportunity for better jobs and a higher standard of living.

Current research and official data suggest that drug abuse violations and other assaults are the dominant offenses for which women will be arrested in greater numbers. The two theses presented to explain female criminality, increased social control and drug use, require further testing. Holtfreter, Reisig, and Morash (2004) have provided empirical support for the economic marginality thesis, at least where short-term but immediate state capital resource allocation to poor offenders is concerned. There is also some preliminary evidence that childhood abuse and neglect are significant in predicting female adult criminality. Recognizing the deleterious effects of poverty, drugs, and child abuse, and implementing effective strategies to combat these, will be neither quick nor easy to achieve. However, the prevention of crime and a reduction in human suffering are certainly laudable goals that are worthy of a significant societal investment.

Review Questions

1. Discuss three theories presented in this chapter and explain why each theory failed/succeeded in attempting to provide insight into why women commit crime.

2. Women are currently responsible for only about 20 percent of the crime committed in the United States. Why do you think it is still important to research their crime commission and motivation to participate in criminal activity?

3. For which crimes are women and men most likely to be arrested in the United States? Have these crimes changed since the first edition of this book?

4. Explain Adler's and Simon's hypotheses regarding female criminality. Have their hypotheses been supported by the data? Explain.

5. How do men's and women's economic situations support the economic marginalization theory?

6. Explain why increased formal social control may have facilitated the rise in arrests for offenses involving assault committed by women.

7. Discuss how drug convictions might prevent women from successfully engaging in future legal activities as a means of survival.

8. Discuss some strategies society can undertake to reduce female involvement in criminality.

Key Terms

Classical theory
Positivist (theorists)
Developmental theories
Learning theory
Social structure theories
Social process theories
Cultural deviance theory

Strain theory
Interstitial zones
Control theory
Labeling theory
Liberation (or emancipation) theory
Economic marginalization theory
Increased formal social control theory

References

Adler, F. (1975). *Sisters in crime.* New York: McGraw-Hill.

Andersen, M. L. (1993). *Thinking about women* (3rd ed.). New York: Macmillan.

Anglin, M. D., & Hser, Y. (1987). Addicted women and crime. *Criminology* 25, 359–397.

Bagley, K., & Merlo, A. V. (1995). Controlling women's bodies. In A. V. Merlo & J. M. Pollock (Eds.), *Women, law, and social control* (pp. 135–153). Boston: Allyn and Bacon.

Bandura, A. (1977). *Social learning theory.* Englewood Cliffs, NJ: Prentice-Hall.

Baskin, D. R., & I. Sommers (1993). Females' initiation into violent street crime. *Justice Quarterly* 10, 559–581.

Belknap, J. (2003). Responding to the needs of women prisoners. In S. F. Sharp (Ed.), *The incarcerated woman: Rehabilitative programming in women's prison* (pp. 93–106). Upper Saddle River, NJ: Prentice Hall.

Belknap, J. (2001). *The invisible woman: Gender, crime, and justice.* Belmont, CA: Wadsworth/Thompson Learning.

Centers for Disease Control. (2003). *Teen birth rate continues to decline; African-American teens show sharpest drop.* Retrieved on March 12, 2005 from http://www.cdc.gov/nchs/pressroom/03facts/teenbirth.htm.

Chesney-Lind, M. (2002). Criminalizing victimization: The unintended consequences of pro-arrest policies for girls and women (electronic version). *Criminology & Public Policy* 2 (1), 81–89.

Chesney-Lind, M. (1981). Judicial paternalism and female status offenders: Training women to know their place. In L. H. Bowker (Ed.), *Women and crime in America* (pp. 354–366). New York: Macmillan,

Chesney-Lind, M. (1997). *The female offender: girls, women, and crime.* Thousand Oaks, CA: Sage.

Corea, O. (1992). *The invisible epidemic.* New York: HarperCollins.

Daly, K. (1989). Gender and varieties of white-collar crime. *Criminology* 27 (4), 769–794.

Daly, K., & Chesney-Lind, M. (1988). Feminism and Criminology. *Justice Quarterly* 5, 497–538.

Datesman, S. K., & Scarpitti, F. (Eds.). (1980). *Women, crime, and justice.* New York: Oxford University Press.

DeParle, J. (1993, December 1). An underground railroad from projects to suburbs. *New York Times,* A1, A12.

Dorsey, T. L., Zawitz, M. W., & Middleton, P. (2004). *Drugs and crime facts* (electronic version). U.S. Department of Justice, Office of Justice Programs, Bureau of Justice Statistics. Washington, DC: U.S. Government Printing Office.

Downs, B. (2003). *Fertility of American women: June 2002.* Current Population Reports, P20-548. U.S. Census Bureau, Washington, DC.

Downs, W. R., Miller, B. A., & Gondoli, D. M. (1987). Childhood experiences of parental physical violence for alcoholic women as compared with a randomly selected household sample of women. *Violence and Victims* 2, 225–240.

Editors of Health Day. (2004, February 21). Teen pregnancy, abortion rates drop in U.S. *Austin American Statesman,* Health News Archives: Health Highlights. Retrieved on August 10, 2004 from http://www.statesman.com/health/content/shared-auto/healthnews/prss/517556.html.

Feinman, C. (1986). *Women in the criminal justice system* (2nd ed.). New York: Praeger.

Flanagan, T. J., & K. Maguire (Eds.). (1992). *Sourcebook of criminal justice statistics–1991.* U.S. Department of Justice, Bureau of Justice Statistics. Washington, DC: U.S. Government Printing Office.

Gilligan, C. (1982). *In a different voice: Psychological theory and women's development.* Cambridge, MA: Harvard University Press.

Greenfield, L. A., & Snell, T. L. (1999). *Women offenders.* U.S. Department of Justice, Bureau of Justice Statistics. Retrieved on March 1, 2004 from http://www.ojp.usdoj.gov/bjs/pub/pdf/wo.pdf.

Greenfield, L. A., & Snell, T. L. (2000). About female offenders. *Women Police* 34 (1), 43–44.

Hirschi, T. (1969). *Causes of delinquency.* Berkeley, CA: University of California Press.

Holtfreter, K., Reisig, M. D., & Morash, M. (2004). Poverty, state capital, and recidivism among women offenders. *Criminology and Public Policy* 3 (2), 185–208.

Humphries, D. (2002). No easy answers: Public policy, criminal justice, and domestic violence (electronic version). *Criminology & Public Policy* 2 (1), 91–94.

Inciardi, J. (2004). *Criminal Justice* (7th ed.). New York: McGraw-Hill.

Inciardi, J. A., Lockwood, D. & Pottieger, A. E.. (1993). *Women and crack-cocaine.* New York: Macmillan.

Klein, D. (1973). The etiology of female crime: A review of the literature. *Issues in Criminology* 8, 3–30.

Lemert, E. (1951). *Social pathology: A systematic approach to the theory of sociopathic behavior.* New York: McGraw-Hill.

Lykken, D. T. (1995). *The antisocial personalities.* Hillsdale, NJ: Lawrence Erlbaum.

Lyman, M. D., & Potter, G. W. (2003). *Drugs in society: Causes, concepts, and control* (4th ed.). Cincinnati, OH: Anderson.

Maguire, K., Pastore, A. L., & Flanagan, T. J. (Eds.). (1993). *Sourcebook of criminal justice statistics—1992.* U.S. Department of Justice, Bureau of Justice Statistics. Washington, DC: U.S. Government Printing Office.

Maher, L., & Daly, K. (1996). Women in street-level drug economy: Continuity or change? *Criminology* 34 (4), 465–491.

Merlo, A. V. (1995). Female criminality in the 1990s. In A. V. Merlo & J. M. Pollock (Eds.). *Women, law, and social control* (pp. 119–134). Boston: Allyn and Bacon.

Merton, R. K. (1968). *Social theory and social structure.* Glencoe, IL: 1968.

Miller, B. A., Downs, W. R., & Gondoli, D. M. (1989). Delinquency, childhood violence, and the development of alcoholism in women. *Crime & Delinquency* 35, 94–108.

Miller, S. L. (2001). The paradox of women arrested for domestic violence (electronic version). *Violence Against Women* 7 (12), 1339–1376.

National Institute of Justice. (1993). *Drug use forecasting: 1992 Annual Report.* Washington, DC: U.S. Department of Justice, Office of Justice Programs: 2–31.

National Institute of Justice. (2003). *2000 Arrestee drug abuse monitoring: Annual Report, Part I, Chapter I: Overall findings and ADAM redesign.* Washington, DC: U.S. Department of Justice, Office of Justice Programs. Retrieved on August 2, 2004 from http://www.ncjrs.org/txtfilesl/nij/193013.txt.

Ortega, S. T., & Burnett, C. (1987). Age variation in female crime: In search of the new female criminal. *Journal of Crime & Justice* 10, 133–169.

Piaget, J. (1965). *The moral judgment of the child.* New York: Free Press.

Pollock, J. M. (1998). *Counseling women in prison.* San Francisco: Sage.

Pollock, J. M. (1999). *Criminal women.* Cincinnati, OH: Anderson Publishing Company.

Pollock, J. (2002). *Women, prison and crime* (2nd ed.). Belmont, CA: Wadsworth/Thompson Learning.

Rasche, C. E. (1975). The female offender as an object of criminological research. In A. Brodsky (Ed.), *The female offender* (pp. 9–28). Beverly Hills: Sage.

Shaw, C. R., & McKay, H. D. (1969). *Juvenile delinquency and urban areas.* Chicago: University of Chicago Press.

Simon, R. J. (1975). *Women and crime.* Lexington, MA: D.C. Heath and Company.

Simpson, S. S. (1989). Feminist theory, crime, and justice. *Criminology* 27, 605–631.

Smart, C. (1979). The new female criminal: Reality or myth? *British Journal of Criminology* 19, 50–59.

Snell, T. L. (1991). *Women in prison.* Washington, DC: U.S. Department of Justice, Office of Justice Programs: Bureau of Justice Statistics Special Report.

Spatz Widom, C. (1992). *The cycle of violence.* National Institute of Justice, Research in Brief (October):1–6. Washington, DC: U.S. Government Printing Office.

Spraggins, R. E. (2003). *Women and men in the United States: March 2002.* Current Population Reports, P20-544. Washington, DC: U.S. Census Bureau.

Steffensmeier, D. (1978). Crime and the contemporary woman: An analysis of changing levels of female property crime, 1960–75. *Social Forces* 57 (2), 566–584.

Steffensmeier, D., Allan, E., & Streifel, C. (1989). Development and female crime: A cross-national test of alternative explanations. *Social Forces* 68 (1), 263–283.

Steffensmeier, D. J., & M. J. Cobb (1981). Sex differences in urban arrest patterns, 1973–1979. *Social Problems* 29, 37–50.

Steffensmeier, D., & Streifel, C. (1992). Time-series analysis of the female percentage of arrests for property crimes, 1960–1985: A test of alternative explanations. *Justice Quarterly* 9, 77–103.

Suro, R. (1992, May 26). Single mothers tell of varied reasons for their situation. *New York Times,* A1, A8.

Sutherland, E. (1937). *The professional thief.* Chicago: University of Chicago Press.

Taeuber, C. (Ed.). (1991). *Statistical handbook on women in America.* Phoenix: Oryx Press.

Taylor, B. G., Newton, P. J., & Brownstein, H. H. (2003). *2000 arrestee drug abuse monitoring: Annual report, part I, chapter V—drug use among adult female arrestees*. U.S. Department of Justice, National Institute of Justice. Retrieved on August 2, 2004 from http://www.ncjrs.org/txtfilesl/nij/193013.txt.

U.S. Bureau of the Census. (1993). *Statistical abstracts of the United States: 1993* (113th ed.). Washington, DC: U.S. Government Printing Office.

U.S. Bureau of the Census. (2000a). *Census 2000 summary: Income distribution in 1999 of households and families*. From Census Summary File 3 (SF3)—Sample Data, Quick Tables and Demographic Profiles. Retrieved on August 15, 2004 from http://www.factfinder.census.gov/home/safflmain.html?lang=en.

U.S. Bureau of the Census. (2000b). *Census 2000 summary: Occupation by sex, 2000*. From Census Summary File 4 (SF 4)—Sample Data, Quick Tables and Demographic Profiles. Retrieved on August 2, 2004 from http://factfinder.census.gov/home/safflmain. html?_lang=en.

U.S. Bureau of the Census. (2000c). *Poverty 2000*. Retrieved on August 15, 2004 from http://www.census.gov.hheglpoverty/threshld/thresh00.html.

U.S. Bureau of the Census. (2002). *America's children 2002*. Retrieved on August 15, 2004 from http://www.childstats.gov/ac2002/indicators.asp?IID=14.

U.S. Department of Health and Human Services. (2002). *Women's health USA 2002*. Rockville, MD: Health Resources and Services Administration, Maternal Child Health Bureau. Retrieved on August 1, 2004 from http://www.mchb.hrsa.gov/whusa02/Page_17.htm.

U.S. Department of Justice. (1993). *Uniform crime reports, 1992*. Washington, DC: U.S. Government Printing Office.

U.S. Department of Justice. (2002). *Uniform crime reports, 2002*. Washington, DC: U.S. Government Printing Office. Retrieved on July 7, 2004 from http://www.fbi.gov/ucr/cius_02/html/web/arrested/04-table42.html.

U.S. Department of Labor, Bureau of Labor Statistics. (2002). *Usual weekly earnings of wage and salary workers: Third quarter 2002*. Retrieved on August 20, 2004 from ftp://ftp.bls.gov/pub/news.release/History/wkyeng.10212002.news.

Williams, L. (1992, February 6). Girl's self-image is mother of the woman. *New York Times,* 1, 6.

Worldbank. Retrieved on August 2, 2004 from http://1180-devdata.worldbank.org.libproxy.txstate.edu/dataonline/.

Wright, R. A. (1992). From vamps and tramps to teases and flirts: Stereotypes of women in criminology textbooks, 1956 to 1965 and 1981 to 1990. *Journal of Criminal Justice Education* 3, 223–236.

11

Women Drug Offenders

Marilyn D. McShane and Frank P. Williams, III

A Brief History of Drugs

The history of drug use and abuse is essentially inseparable from the history of humans. There is evidence that humans have long used a number of psychoactive substances. Alcohol from fermented plants and berries was likely one of the first drugs to be abused. Marijuana was also an early drug used in China and India. There are references to opium in written script from Sumer around 5,000 BC and ephedrine in 3,000 BC China. Early Incas used coca for altitude sickness, and people of that area still do today. Caffeine, in the form of coffee, was a staple in Africa. In North America, indigenous peoples discovered and used tobacco, peyote, mescaline, and psilocybin. Thus, we can say that humans have a long history of drug use. Perhaps more importantly, the sum of research into neurobiology demonstrates that humans have natural receptors for most drugs—meaning that we either evolved using drugs, or the body naturally produces similar compounds, or both. As a result, drug use for religious, medical, and recreational reasons is an established part of human history.

Drugs have also been economically important for a long time. Trade among various peoples has frequently included drugs as desirable commodities. In the fifteenth through seventeenth centuries, the search for new drug commodities was one reason for exploration and colonization of the Americas. For example, Europeans took tobacco from America to Africa and returned with coffee. Drugs provided wealth to the colonizing country and businesses were based on the drug trade. The largest business organization of the time, Britain's East Indies Merchants Association, purveyed drugs from continent to continent and, ultimately, was the architect of two wars (the Chinese Opium Wars) by which England, France, and the United States forced opium onto the Chinese (Latimer & Goldberg, 1981).

In the United States, the Civil War represented a major turning point in drug use. Before that point, opium was available in common trade. A derivative of opium, morphine became available as an injectable form of painkiller. The medical usage of morphine created the nation's first major drug epidemic (as long as one ignores alcohol and tobacco use), and addiction was called the "soldier's disease." From there, morphine usage became widespread among the nation's households. Goode (1999) even states that the common addict of the period could be characterized as a middle-class white woman. However, studies of the problem and attempts at rehabilitation focused on prostitutes and showgirls who often frequented opium dens (Fagan, 1994). These were the women sent to prison as the nation confronted the vices of the early twentieth century in a broad-based strategy of eugenics, confinement, moral instruction, and training for employment.

As the search for interventions continued, cocaine was developed as one possible solution to morphine addiction and as a general therapeutic drug. Unfortunately, the addictive properties of cocaine were not realized, and the cure was no better than the original problem. Similarly, heroin developed as a cure for both morphine and cocaine addiction (Courtwright, 1982).

Patent medicines, sold both by traveling hucksters and retail stores, were widely available with contents containing opium, morphine, cocaine, heroin, alcohol, or some combination of these drugs. In some ways, these medicines were successful in alleviating symptoms of illness, but also could result in addiction (Ray & Ksir, 1999). By 1890 to 1915, society perceived a new drug problem, an alcohol epidemic, and crusades against alcohol ultimately led to Prohibition, which, as a consequence, resulted in the spread of marijuana.

In one sense, Prohibition provided an important model for subsequent solutions to drug abuse. First, there was the notion of prohibition, or the prevention of access to drugs. Second, the federal drug agency—later to become the DEA—was placed in the Prohibition Unit of the Treasury Department. The combination of a prohibition mentality and the *Webb v. U.S.* (1919) decision in which a physician's narcotic prescriptions were ruled illegal was interpreted by the drug agency as meaning that prescribing any drug to an addict was illegal (Ray & Ksir, 1999). Because the solution was a law enforcement one, the agency orientation has remained the same for the past eighty years.

As one may surmise from this brief history, drug use and abuse is not a new problem in the United States. Moreover, the 1970s and 1980s were not an especially different period, even though we obviously believed that when we declared a "war on drugs." Indeed, it appears that the late 1800s were far and away the dominant period of drug abuse in the nation.

Moreover, the nature of criminal drug use (and, therefore, drug offenders) seems to vary by the groups perceived at the time as the dominant users of a particular drug. Time and again, the enactment of criminal drug legislation has been associated with a perception that those drugs were used by individuals defined at the moment as an undesirable element of society (e.g., opium was perceived to be part of the Chinese problem; cocaine, an African American problem; and marijuana, a Hispanic problem). It appears that drug laws are created and used, in part, in an effort to resolve other social problems. From these historical lessons we glean the following generalities:

1. The use of psychoactive substances is normal to humans.
2. Substances defined as undesirable vary across time.
3. The definition of substances as undesirable is a product of a historical moment's economy and social perceptions.
4. The definition of drug offenders is partially governed by what drugs are being defined as illegal and who uses those drugs.
5. Illegal drugs and, therefore, drug offenders are a product of social definitions reflecting undesirability and social reactions to perceived immorality.

Women as Drug Offenders

What do these generalities have to do with female drug offenders? Because of the historically common use of drugs, there is no reason to believe that men and women used them in drastically different ways. Even so, it is also true that some drugs were imbued with religious restrictions or were only to be used by certain classes of people—and that frequently excluded females. On the whole, though, drug use and abuse are not tied to gender. Both men and women have similar biological mechanisms at work, although there is some evidence that neurochemical reactions may differ slightly for certain drugs. Thus, any gender differences in the history of drug use and abuse are primarily social and cultural. This point will be important in discussing female drug offenders.

Female drug offenders have been typically similar to men in the war on drugs. However, unique aspects of gender including prostitution, childbearing, and primary responsibility for child rearing have evolved to make the issues affecting these women socially, legally, and politically controversial. While some of the measures to combat drug use are new, many theorists argue that the forces at work in this scenario are simply traditional avenues of gender oppression (Boyd, 1999). Feminists have used the double victimization scenario to describe women as harmed both by drugs and a sexist and patriarchal system of justice.

While it is still unclear why some people are more likely to become drug dependent than others, we do know much about the reasons people give for using drugs and the effects that the various drugs have on the body over time. Researchers point out that women are more likely to abuse legal prescription drugs and illegal drugs and to be controlled by the men in their lives who may also be involved in the use and sale of drugs. These factors all contribute to a more complex view of female offending that must be understood within the context of a male-dominated society.

Criminal Involvement with Drugs

Today there are over one million women under the supervision of the criminal justice system in this country (Bloom, Johnson, & Belzer, 2003). More than 71 percent of all female arrests are for drug-related offenses or larceny/theft. For comparison, it should also be noted that the 95 percent increase in female drug arrests from 1985 to 1996 far exceeded the 55 percent increase in male drug arrests during the same period (FBI, 1998, p. 231). In addition, convictions of women for drug offenses increased by 40 percent. It is fair to say that women's increasing rates of arrest, conviction, and incarceration on drug-related charges have outpaced men's. Female arrestees also reported higher levels of usage than men for every measure of prior drug use in a government survey (Greenfield & Snell, 2000).

Lest one think that these arrests are primarily for serious drug crimes, about one-third of women's total drug-related arrests in 1996 were for simple possession. Moreover, women are not arrested as drug kingpins or major traffickers, the ostensible focus of the war on drugs. Instead, women are primarily arrested for drug use, drug possession, and minor selling of drugs. The research reveals that women are simply "holders," or in domestic relationships with dealers, that household responsibilities keep them from assuming more active roles in trafficking, and that female users often perform dealing activities only until more fixed measures of obtaining drugs for their habits can be obtained (Fagan, 1994).

If the corporate world allegedly has a glass ceiling for women executives, the drug world has an iron one: Women are simply not counted among major distributors and traffickers. Instead, women are often legally in the roles of constructive possessor, aiding and abetting, or co-conspiring, all which carry harsh penalties (Goldfarb, 2002). They are used by men for such purposes as carrying and distributing drugs, hiding the man's own stash, and maintaining the laundered gains of drug dealing (e.g., property purchased with drug proceeds and placed under the woman's name).

As a result of the higher rates of arrest, there are also unprecedented rates of incarceration and longer sentences for female drug offenders. Although women represent only about 7 percent of those incarcerated, the number of women in prison is now growing faster than the number of men. And, the profile of the adult female offender has also changed over the years. In 1975, women were primarily incarcerated for larceny, forgery, embezzlement, and prostitution. By 1995, the most common commitments were more likely to be related to drugs and larceny. Approximately 34 percent of female state prisoners and 72 percent of female federal prisoners are serving drug sentences (Greenfield & Snell, 2000). Jails also hold a disproportionate number of women for nonviolent drug and property crimes (Bloom, Johnson, & Belzer, 2003).

It should also be noted that drug use is commonly associated with women's criminal behavior in general. According to recent government Arrestee Drug Abuse Monitoring data (ADAM), 67 percent of women arrested test positive for drugs at the time of arrest, usually cocaine and marijuana (National Institute of Justice [NIJ], 2001). A 1999 report indicated that while only 25 percent of women prisoners reported being on drugs at the time of the offense for which they were currently serving a state sentence, almost 60 percent admitted to having used drugs in the month leading up to that criminal event (Greenfield & Snell, 2000). Also, one-quarter of the women on probation in this country admitted to using alcohol at the time of their offense (Greenfield, 1998).

The Impact of the War on Drugs

The war on drugs, originally intended as a strategy to break up large drug distribution and trafficking networks, is most likely the reason that the percentage of incarcerated women who were serving time for a drug offense rose dramatically, from 12 percent to 33 percent in the period from 1986 to 1991. By 1996, the number of women incarcerated for drug offenses in state prisons was tenfold that in 1986 (Amnesty International, 1999).

Many feminists have referred to the war on drugs as a war on women (Bloom, Chesney-Lind, & Owen, 1994). The concept of a war, particularly a gender-based conflict, was furthered by the mid-1980s emergence of a "crack epidemic" among the poor. Media reports projected the image of the "crack mother" into mainstream crime coverage and began a prosecution frenzy not only on drug charges but on a new range of crimes for exposing children, and even fetuses, to the effects of a woman's addiction (Humphries, 1999).

One of the government's major weapons in the war on drugs was the 1988 Anti-Drug Abuse Bill. This legislation allowed for increased sentences for drug-related offenses, allocated additional resources and equipment for law enforcement interdiction efforts, and created an asset forfeiture system much like that developed under the RICO (Racketeer-Influenced and Corrupt Organization) Statutes a few years earlier (Miller & Selva, 1994). Ironically, in both organized crime and large-scale drug operations, women played little or no significant leadership role nor did they profit in any real sense from their operations. Despite the consistency of the evidence on this matter, women—particularly poor minority women—still appear to suffer the same harsh consequences of the laws as the men in their lives.

Laws developed to reduce access to illicit substances have not only had disparate effects upon women but also unintended consequences for families. Probation and parole officers, social workers, and child protective service caseworkers are constantly challenged by the lack of gender-responsive strategies available to address parenting, job, and personal skills development, as well as addiction and mental health needs. To be effective, interventions must be coordinated with all relevant agencies including the courts, corrections, treatment providers, public health, housing, child welfare, and community outreach centers.

Drug Offending and Women's Lifestyles

Unfortunately, studies of female drug offenders, like those of female offenders in general, tend to focus almost exclusively on those incarcerated. This means that many functioning drug users, undetected by the system, are missing from the databases of what we know about female drug users. This creates a bias in our information and, consequently, in the policies and programs that are derived from analysis of the known offenders.

Even the data on incarcerated female offenders tend to be ignored by policy makers. Data on female prisoners indicate that about 70 percent of the women in jails, prisons, and on probation have minor children (Greenfield & Snell, 2000). There is also evidence these women have a higher incidence of being under the influence of drugs at the time of their offense then men. Thus, it is difficult to consider female drug offenders without including the way that social values, laws, and policies impact their children as well.

Sources of Interaction

As a consequence of contemporary social values and perhaps political pressures, judges and prosecutors are more likely to find alternatives to incarceration less appropriate for mothers who commit crimes while under the influence. Feminists have long argued that, as primary caregivers, women bring more attention to themselves in the legal system and subsequently suffer more serious condemnation than men who are fathers. Throughout the criminal justice process, drug offenses become intertwined with perceptions about the proper role of women, prostitution, lifestyle, conditions of the home, care of the children, and potential fetal health risks that appear not only to complicate but to enhance the punitive aspects of sentencing dispositions (Belknap, 2001; Boyd, 1999).

To be realistic, the issue of drug use/abuse cannot be viewed in isolation, as a simple behavior or lifestyle; instead, one must analyze the many social and economic problems in effect including marginalized employment, discrimination, single parenthood, poverty and lack of access to medical care, domestic violence, and historical sexual victimization. It often is difficult to establish any temporal sequence or establish any consistent cause and effect relationships between these factors. Instead, they function more as coexisting variables that may aggravate and enhance each other as children are drawn into the network. In addition, any of the issues outlined in Figure 11.1 that remain untreated could become more serious over time or more difficult to resolve as the number of children increases.

Drugs and Social Issues

For years female offenders have been processed through a male-dominated criminal justice system with little thought to their special needs or circumstances. Although women remain a small percentage of those involved in the courts, they represent much greater percentages of those seeking treatment in civil and publicly funded drug programs (Harwood, Fountain, & Livermore, 1998).

Virtually all drug court programs, supervised release agreements, and other diversion contracts require that offenders hold regular jobs. For women, particularly single parents, the ability to balance the scheduling demands of work and a family, transportation issues, and the

FIGURE 11.1   *Factors Involved in Female Drug Offender Lifestyle*

Women	Children
Marginalized employment	Poverty
History of sexual and physical abuse	Poor school attendance
Single parenthood	Teen pregnancy
Poverty	Sexual/physical abuse
Lack of access to medical care	Inadequate health care
Low education/skills	Gang activity
Drug and alcohol abuse	Criminal justice system involvement
Domestic violence	Drug and alcohol abuse
Criminal record	
Prostitution/HIV/AIDS/STDs	
Inadequate housing/safety issues	
Loss of custody/termination of parental rights	

often break-even nature of working and paying for adequate child care is a daunting task. Add to that the pressures of paying supervision fees and the court costs associated with their criminal convictions, and it often seems like a vicious and self-defeating cycle.

Research has consistently found that women are more likely than men to succeed in their first year of parole (McShane, Williams, & Dolny, 2002) and that, for women, substance abuse history is less of a risk factor for predicting failure (Bonta, Pang, & Wallace-Capretta, 1995). Women are also more likely to be revoked from parole and probation for technical reasons than for new offenses. The use of technical grounds often implies that parole officer discretion is operating and that personal interpretations of a client's behavior are being used in making the decision to seek revocation. Norland and Mann (1984) found that when men violated for technical reasons, those charges were likely to be absconding or failure to work. In the case of female clients revoked for technical reasons, the charges were more often "absconding" and "improper associates." The difficulty with revoking a parolee for having improper associates is that it is usually a moralistic judgment call. Interviews with officers led Norland and Mann to conclude that women consume more of the officers' time and seek more emotional support. It has been suggested that having a higher service need may actually predispose supervising officers against the female client.

As Holtfreter, Reisig, and Morash (2004) argue, poverty factors, specifically unemployment and financial problems, seem to place women in higher risk categories for recidivism when assessed with traditional instruments like the LSI-R. In fact, when they controlled for poverty status, risk instruments failed to predict recidivism among the female offenders studied in their analysis. The link between poverty and involvement in the criminal justice system has been a major theoretical issue for both conflict and feminist criminologists.

Feminists argue that the female drug offender is symptomatic of the "pink collar ghetto" status of women that lingers in society today. Unemployed and underemployed, low-paid, unskilled female employees suffer the hopelessness of dead-end work, and seek to escape the pressures of single parenting while trying to make ends meet by long hours and difficult negotiations of hours, transportation, and child care.

The hopelessness of this position creates a situation in which women, particularly poor, minority women, are more likely to be attracted to drug use and criminal activity. Data consistently show that women of color are more likely to be prosecuted and incarcerated, lose custody of their children, have their parental rights terminated, and to have their pregnancies monitored and regulated by health and law enforcement systems.

For female drug offenders, economic issues are common and profoundly related to their lifestyle choices—even the decision to sell drugs is frequently related to the need to bolster family income.

Drugs and Criminological Theories

There are a number of sociological and psychological approaches to studying the female drug offender particularly in reference to victimization and abuse. Arguably, this group of women would be at greater risk of violence both inside and outside of the home as they continually find themselves in high risk places, situations, and relationships. Criminological theories such as routine activities, lifestyle, rational choice, conflict, and feminist perspectives would all see different roots of the problem. They would also suggest varied methods of treatment in the areas of diagnosis, prioritization of therapeutic goals, family reconciliation plans, and style of intervention used.

Bednar (2003) comments on the difficulty in unraveling the relationship between domestic violence and substance abuse. Over 40 percent of the women in prison and almost 60 percent of those in state custody report having been physically or sexually abused some time in their life. Most of those who were assaulted report that it occurred prior to their eighteenth birthday (Greenfield & Snell, 2000). Both the violent and the substance abusing family seem to exhibit the intergenerational transmission of dysfunctions, frequent crises, low self-esteem, and the dynamics of blaming, forgetting, isolation, and loss of control. These similarities may facilitate some cases in treatment and cause dilemmas for others.

Some experts argue substance abuse therapies, like those designed to respond to domestic violence, should separate clients by gender as men and women may have different circumstances contributing to their dysfunctional lifestyles, and thus different law enforcement, sentencing, and treatment plans might be more appropriate (Bloom, 1999; Shearer, 2003). Conflict and feminist perspectives have claimed that the failure to adopt gender-specific strategies is part of the patriarchal social structure that pervades not only our responses to female drug use but our theoretical consideration of it as well (Goode, 1999).

Treatment Issues

Officials often use evaluative criteria in determining who should be directed to drug treatment, particularly when there are not enough treatment programs, beds, or funds available to serve all those in need. Motivation and the desire to be in treatment is one of those factors, and given the consequences of losing one's children and one's freedom, women are most often eager to be involved in rehabilitation programs. According to Harwood et al. (1998), treatment issues for women also include access to treatment, mental illness, and abuse experiences, family and social support, work and welfare, and criminal justice system involvement.

Access to Treatment

To develop truly effective programming for female drug offenders, the system would need to provide a full range of prevention, intervention, and treatment services. Ideally, the goal would be to address as many of the social and personal problems contributing to substance abuse as possible. However, what we find is that programs are more likely to address only the most critical health issues and to react in ways that do not promote the maintenance of the independent family unit.

Many of the more intensive drug treatment programs are residential, and it is a challenge to find any of these willing to accept children (Miller, 2002), which limits the options available to single parents. Other criticisms of drug treatment programs are that they are difficult to attend because of transportation problems, they are too short, and do not offer enough transition services to needed social resources such as housing, skills development, jobs, and assistance with child care. Many programs require health insurance to subsidize the costs of drug treatment, which some women may not be able to obtain, or obtain quickly enough to avoid discouragement. Spotty employment, poor recordkeeping, and frequent moves may make eligibility status hard to verify.

Drug courts, perhaps a viable option for female offenders, have been dominated by male offenders (Belenko, 2001) and have not been particularly successful (Hoffman, 2000; Nolan, 1998). Unfortunately, many women do not receive comprehensive drug treatment until they are incarcerated and, even at that time, there is competition for limited programming resources.

Treatment for AIDS

Research indicates that female drug users, particularly those who engage in prostitution for drugs, are more likely to contract HIV/AIDs then men who engage in similar high-risk behaviors (Freeman, Rodriguez, & French, 1994). Female inmates also have higher rates of HIV and AIDS then men with about 2.5 percent of female jail inmates and 3.5 percent of female prison inmates classified as HIV positive (Hammett, Harmon, & Maruschak, 1999). And, as Mahan (1996) explains, women entering prison have higher rates of HIV infections, which are exacerbated by the low level of medical services available in most institutions.

There are many possible strategies for reducing the spread of AIDS infections. According to officials, needle exchange programs could reduce one of the primary causes of AIDS, and the use of safe injection facilities would replace crack houses where violence, victimization, and the spread of disease have been prevalent. Health officials also call for the provision of male and female condoms, onsite counseling, and testing for HIV and hepatitis, the provision of alcohol and bleach, as well as screening for tuberculosis and other sexually transmitted diseases (U.S. Centers for Disease Control, 2001).

Mental Health, Abuse, and Family Support Issues

As with drug courts and battered women's shelters, most drug treatment facilities and outpatient programs do not accommodate the mentally ill. Given the complex abuse histories of many women, it is common to find severe personality disorders and dissociative illnesses whose treatment most professionals would argue takes precedence over drug treatment. In fact, drug use is often characterized as a symptom of these psychic disturbances and is often viewed as a coping mechanism; a strategy for dealing with pain and suffering that must be dealt with outside of normal drug treatment curricula.

Other drug treatment strategies may involve family therapy or periods during which the patient is guided in attempting to repair relationships damaged by drug use and criminal activity. Incarcerated women may have more difficulty in utilizing these techniques because of physical and resource limitations. With far fewer female prisons, there is a greater likelihood that children and other family members are too far away to visit or participate in treatment sessions. Foster and even custodial relatives may be unwilling to promote relationships between female prisoners and their children. Many children, particularly teenagers, are angry at their mothers for the pain and separation they are experiencing and cut off communications, which often causes the prisoner to lose hope and drop out of programming. With almost 200,000 children at risk themselves and trying to cope with a mother behind bars (Greenfield & Snell, 2000), advocates campaign for more comprehensive, family-based approaches to drug treatment.

Policy Responses and Implications

There are three areas of drug law that have potential impact on women in ways that are different from men. Although most law equally impacts men and women, such as mandatory minimums, mandatory treatment, and asset forfeiture, other areas, such as pregnancy and the termination of parental rights, are directed almost exclusively at women.

Laws and Pregnancy

According to Mahan (1996), laws regulating pregnant female drug users fall into three categories: those that address the use of narcotics itself (such as delivering a controlled substance to a minor), those that criminalize more general behaviors such as fetal endangerment and fetal abuse, and those that regulate the conduct of informants such as health care workers who come into contact with pregnant women who may be abusing drugs.

Drug war rhetoric exploited the concept of illicit drug use and fetal abuse. One highly sensational report claimed that pregnant crack–cocaine users were delivering over 100,000 extremely damaged "crack babies" a year. The first studies (Chasnoff, Hunt, & Kletter, 1986; Riley, Brodsky, & Porat, 1988) reporting on the negative effects of maternal use of crack failed to control for various other drugs, unhealthy behaviors, and socioeconomic factors. Subsequent medical studies have responded with reliable indications that pregnancy issues were misrepresented and exaggerated (Bauchner et al., 1988; Hurt et al., 1997; Zucherman & Frank, 1992). They also demonstrated that the negative effects were approximately the same as tobacco use during pregnancy (Jacobson, Jacobson, Sokol, Martier, Ager, & Sankaran, 1994; Zucherman, Frank, & Hingson, 1989). Research has indicated that with intensive prenatal care, even serious cocaine users have shown significant improvements in fetal health and development (Youchah & Freda, 1995). Regardless of the research, drug policymakers have continued the crack baby claims, and politicians have used the hysteria to support criminal laws specifically focusing on pregnant women with drugs found in their systems.

In *Ferguson v. City of Charleston* (2001), the U.S. Supreme Court struck down a local policy that allowed women receiving prenatal care to be surreptitiously screened for drugs and arrested if the tests were positive. The local hospital advertised the prenatal care program for those on welfare and then at the urging of the prosecutor's office, reported any evidence of drug use. The justices refused to find a "special needs" exception when the intent of the test appeared to be the furthering of prosecution. It was determined that such a search was unreasonable as the patient had not consented to that type of procedure. Further, it appears that the court endorsed the research that associated prosecution for substance abuse with avoidance of prenatal medical care and social services, resulting in potentially harmful behavior by pregnant women (Cole, 1990; Koren, Gladstone, Roberson, & Robieux, 1992; Polan, Dombrowski, Ager, & Sokol, 1993).

Recently, a New York judge ordered a couple, both drug addicted and living in the streets, to stop having children after the woman was forced to give up her fourth child. Although arguably both parents could be jailed if the woman, Stephanie, becomes pregnant in contempt of the court, it is the status of the woman as pregnant that is the basis for the punitive sanction (Dobbins, 2004). While many hailed the judge's ruling as significant in its attempt to ensure that children have caring parents and a home, others saw it as a direct infringement on human rights. Ironically, two weeks before the Family Court's ruling was handed down, it was already determined that Stephanie was pregnant again.

On the other hand, there is little political concern about an estimated 12,000 infants who are born each year with symptoms related to fetal alcohol syndrome (Kelly, 2003), which appear to pose more serious, long-term effects than cocaine exposure. It is important to note, however, that there is disagreement about what the term "fetal alcohol syndrome" specifically means. There is also disagreement about the degree of impairment that is directly attributed to alcohol use versus other behaviors associated with alcohol use such as poor diet, lack of prenatal monitoring, and poverty. Similarly, the effects of smoking tobacco during pregnancy do not create social concern, even though there is evidence of various types of harm to the fetus and even an increased risk of diabetes (Montgomery & Ekborn, 2002).

Asset Forfeiture and Zero Tolerance Policies

Originally designed as a way to undermine the advantages of wealthy drug lords, asset forfeiture laws have become what critics describe as an overused mechanism for harassing and intimidating the poor. Over the years, the courts' tolerance for liberal asset forfeiture policies has resulted in many law enforcement agencies becoming dependent on the supplemental resources confiscated funds allow them. According to Miller and Selva (1994), the result was that law enforcement agencies tended to engage more in asset hunting than in traditional strategies for reducing drug trafficking. In 1999, the total of U.S. Government civil asset forfeitures was $957 million (Gibson & Huriash, 2000).

When female drug offenders and women who live with men who are targeted for drug-related arrests are faced with asset forfeiture, they may lose not only their homes, but access to transportation, work, and a secure environment for their children. One of the unintended consequences of these harsh policies is the impact on nondrug offending family members, particularly children, who may even end up in foster care. For example, the California Safe Streets and Anti-Terrorism Act was initially written with strict measures to confiscate the property of suspected gang members. However, the likelihood of mothers and caretakers losing their homes and assets was brought to the attention of lawmakers, and the measure was not passed until the provisions were removed. Zero tolerance policies relating to drug use in public housing affect women in the same way and endanger the stability of living arrangements for family members.

Termination of Parental Rights

Family law has traditionally decided cases based on the principle of *parens patriae,* which asserts the state's ultimate right to exercise an urgent interest in the welfare of the child and to fulfill its duty to protect that child. Under this doctrine the court will determine the "best interests of the child," which more recently has been through the assistance of a guardian or advocate who would speak on the child's behalf. With the passing of the Uniform Marriage and Divorce Act, the relevant factors used in making custody decisions include specific health concerns and this is where the dangers of exposure to drugs and drug use are weighed (Chinnock, 2003).

Women under evaluation for possible termination of parental rights are often assessed in terms of "cumulative environmental risk" to their children. Thus, officials may weigh any number of home factors including the physical and mental health of the parents; amount of space and cleanliness of the living areas; ability to provide meals, adequate clothing, schooling, and health care; and the presence of physical and mental health risks, weapons, drug use, and potential sexual victimization.

The Adoption and Safe Families Act of 1997 (Public Law 105-89) limits the time between the placement of a child in foster care and the processing of the petition to terminate a parent's rights. Goldfarb (2002) argues that this will likely speed up the rate at which female drug offenders, particularly those who are incarcerated, will lose their children. Given the connection between physical and sexual abuse, subsequent mental problems, and substance abuse, there is a strong likelihood that a mother's drug conviction, paired with a history of previous abuse, will result in a termination of parental rights.

Besinger et al. (1999) examined the cases of over 600 children removed from their homes for maltreatment, and almost 80 percent of the caregivers in those cases were known to be substance abusers. Overall, though, it may be easier for officials to find neglect than actual maltreatment as a basis for terminating parental rights. Parents who are involved in a drug-centered lifestyle may neglect their children by leaving them unattended for hours at a time and leaving them without food. In other cases, exposure to the passive smoke of marijuana or other drugs such as cocaine, methamphetamine, or heroin may be considered abuse or maltreatment.

Media attention surrounding the presence of children in homes used as methamphetamine labs has led to changes in child protection policies and laws in many states. The highly toxic and potentially explosive chemicals used in the manufacturing process have caused a number of deaths and injuries, particularly in younger children. In California, Bureau of Narcotics Enforcement agents are required to contact social workers any time children are found at a meth lab. Authorities are encouraging child advocates to test clients for drugs and other health-related risks as well as for evidence of child endangerment (Weikel, 1996).

Mandatory Minimum Sentences and Harsher Drug Laws

Women have been impacted in direct and indirect ways by harsher sentences for drug offenses, which have taken place as part of the drug war policies. First, sentences for all types of drug-related crimes have increased. Smaller quantities of drugs have reached felony status, and subsequent offenses also yield longer prison terms. And, a wider net has been cast over persons further removed from the actual criminal event. Relationships and associations draw others into the web of prosecution. For example, under the Rockefeller Drug Laws in New York, a judge must impose fifteen years to life for anyone convicted of selling 2 ounces or possessing 4 ounces of cocaine or heroin. As the Families Against Mandatory Minimums organization explains, many others who are caught in a nonviolent, low-level, addiction-related criminal pattern are also required to serve lengthy prison terms and only the prosecutor, not the judge, is allowed to make placements in drug treatment alternatives.

Under the California Street Terrorism and Enforcement Act, mothers whose children have been involved as gang members engaged in drug sales, or who have unknowingly benefited from the profits of those drug sales, may be facing criminal charges. All of these recent criminal enhancements and punitive sentencing measures have had a disparate impact on people of color. African American women appear to have been incarcerated for drug offenses at a much higher rate than white women (Harrison & Beck, 2002) and appear more likely to have been reported to child welfare agencies for prenatal drug abuse, although reported use rates were similar (Common Sense for Drug Policy, 2004; Sandy, 2003).

Conclusion

Women drug offenders are disproportionately represented in the criminal justice system. At the same time, they are overwhelmingly on the lower end of the drug seriousness spectrum. In many cases, their offenses are the product of roles undertaken in a male-dominated culture—as holders and purveyors of male drug property and paraphernalia. They have also been criminalized because of association with male drug users and sellers (especially gang members) and because of pregnancy. Much of this has less to do with actual offenses than with society's fear of a questionable drug epidemic and an overreaction to and politicization of that fear.

The reality of our drug concern has been that those guilty of minor drug offenses, and we have seen that women are overrepresented in that group and have been given longer mandatory sentences normally reserved for serious and violent crimes. There appears to be much truth in the statement that the drug war is a war against women, primarily because it is women who have borne the brunt of harsh sentencing for minor drug offenses.

Politicians continue to focus on illegal drug use rather than the myriad social problems plaguing our communities. Although smoking causes more deaths than alcohol, AIDS, cocaine, heroin, homicide, suicide, auto, and fire accidents combined each year (National Institute on Drug Abuse, 2003), the pursuit of illegal drug offenders dominates our political and criminal justice system agenda. And despite the fact that alcohol is more likely to be related to serious birth defects than cocaine, laws continue to be devised that, purposefully or not, target poor, inner-city women.

Critics argue that the failures of the drug war should lead us to adopt more humanistic approaches, such as harm reduction efforts that involve treatment and education. From methadone to clean needles to prevention programs and a range of subsidized therapies, the suggestions contain the core elements of family based, multi-agency, long-term neighborhood-level interventions. The lack of gender-specific services remains a serious defect in the rehabilitation and treatment field. As women appear to have different antecedents to drug use, patterns of substance abuse, barriers to treatment, and relapse triggers (Bloom, Owen, & Covington, 2003), many have advocated for more appropriate intervention strategies for more effective outcomes.

As we found in the overview of the history of drugs, the realities of time and place and sociopolitical environment continue to define crime and who becomes a criminal. Women drug offenders present a good example of this thesis.

Review Questions

1. Describe the history of drug use in human societies. What are the five conclusions reached by the author regarding the history of drugs?

2. Describe the arrest and sentencing patterns of female drug users.

3. What are some unintended consequences of drug laws?

4. What are the factors involved in the interactions between lifestyle and drug use?

5. What are the differences between men and women on parole?

6. What are some treatment issues relevant to female drug offenders?

7. What are the different laws that are discussed as relevant to female drug offenders?

Key Terms

Chinese opium wars
"Kingpins"
Prohibition
"War on drugs"
A.D.A.M.
"Crack babies"

Pink collar ghetto
Fetal abuse
Asset forfeiture
Parens patriae
California Street Terrorism and Enforcement Act

References

Amnesty International. (1999). *Not part of my sentence: Violations of the human rights of women in custody.* Washington, DC: Amnesty International.

Bauchner, H., Sucherman, B., McClain, M., Frank, D., Fried, L. E., & Kayne, H. (1988). Risk of sudden infant death syndrome among infants with in utero exposure to cocaine. *Journal of Pediatrics* 113, 831–834.

Bednar, S. G. (2003). Substance abuse and women abuse: A

proposal for integrated treatment. *Federal Probation* 67 (1), 52–57.

Belenko, S. (2001). *Research on drug courts: A critical review, 2001 Update.* New York: National Center on Addiction and Substance Abuse, Columbia University.

Belknap, J. (2001). T*he invisible woman: Gender, crime and justice* (2nd ed.). Belmont, CA: Wadsworth.

Besinger, B. A., Garland, A. F., Litrownik, A. J., & Landsverk, J. A. (1999). Caregiver substance abuse among maltreated children placed in out-of-home care. *Child Welfare* 78, 221–239.

Bloom, B. (1999). Gender-responsive programming for women offenders: Guiding principles and practices. *Forum on Corrections* 11 (3), 22–27.

Bloom, B., Johnson, J., & Belzer, E. (2003, September/October). Effective management of female offenders. *American Jails* 29–33.

Bloom, B., Chesney-Lind, M., & Owen, B. (1994). *Women in prison: Hidden victims of the war on drugs.* San Francisco, CA: Center on Juvenile & Criminal Justice.

Bloom, B., Owen, B., & Covington, S. (2003). *Gender-responsive strategies: Research, practice and guiding principles for women offenders.* Washington, DC: National Institute of Corrections.

Bonta, J., Pang, B., & Wallace-Capretta, S. (1995). Predictors of recidivism among incarcerated female offenders. *The Prison Journal* 75, 277–294.

Boyd, S. (1999). *Mothers and illicit drugs: Transcending the myths.* Toronto, Ontario, Canada: University of Toronto Press.

Chasnoff, I. J., Hunt, C., & Kletter, R. (1986). Increased risk of SIDS and respiratory pattern abnormalities in cocaine-exposed infants. *Pediatric Research* 20, 425A.

Chinnock, W. F. (2003). No smoking around children: The family court's mandatory duty to restrain parents and other persons from smoking around children. *Arizona Law Review* 45, 801–821.

Cole, H. M. (1990). Legal interventions during pregnancy: Court-ordered medical treatment and legal penalties for potentially harmful behavior by pregnant women. *Journal of the American Medical Association* 264, 2663–2670.

Common Sense for Drug Policy. (2004). *Drug war facts: Impact of the drug war on families.* Retrieved June 5, 2004 from http://www.drugwarfacts.org.

Courtwright, D. T. (1982). *Dark paradise: Opiate addiction in America before 1940.* Cambridge, MA: Harvard University Press.

Dobbins, B. (2004, May 16). Judge tells couple to stop having children. *Houston Chronicle,* A, p. 8.

Fagan, J. (1994). Women and drugs revisited: Female participation in the cocaine economy. *Journal of Drug Issues* 24, 179–225.

Federal Bureau of Investigation. (1998). *1997 Uniform Crime Report.* Washington, DC: U.S. Department of Justice.

Freeman, R., Rodriguez, G., & French, J. (1994). A comparison of male and female intravenous drug users' risk behaviors for HIV infection. *American Journal of Drug and Alcohol Abuse* 20 (2), 129–157.

Gibson, W., & Huriash, L. (2000, April 11). Drug cops may be reined in: Congress is likely to make it harder for the government to take money, homes, cars and other items in drug cases. *Orlando Sentinel,* A, p.1.

Goldfarb, P. (2002). Counting the drug war's female casualties. *Journal of Gender, Race and Justice* 6, 277–296.

Goode, E. (1999). *Drugs in American society* (5th ed.). Boston: McGraw-Hill.

Greenfield, L. (1998). *Alcohol and crime: An analysis of the national data on the prevalence of alcohol involvement in crime.* Washington DC: U.S. Department of Justice, Bureau of Justice Statistics.

Greenfield, L., & Snell, T. (2000). *Women offenders.* Washington, DC: U.S. Department of Justice, Bureau of Justice Statistics.

Hamid, A. (1998). *Drugs in America: Sociology, economics, and politics.* Gaithersburg, MD: Aspen Publishers.

Hammett, T., Harmon, P., & Maruschak, L. (1999). *1996–1997 update: HIV/AIDS, STDs and TB in correctional facilities.* Washington, DC: National Institute of Justice.

Harrison, P., & Beck, A. (2003). *Prisoners in 2002.* Washington, DC: U.S. Department of Justice.

Harwood, H., Fountain, D., & Livermore, G. (1998). *The economic costs of alcohol and drug abuse in the United States, 1992.* GPO 017-024-01629-2. Washington, DC: National Institute of Drug Abuse.

Hoffman, M. B. (2000). The drug court scandal. *North Carolina Law Review* 78, 1533–1534.

Holtfreter, K., Reisig, M., & Morash, M. (2004). Poverty, state capital, and recidivism among women offenders. *Criminology & Public Policy* 3, 185–208.

Humphries, D. (1999). *Crack mothers: Pregnancy, drugs and the media.* Columbus, OH: Ohio State University Press.

Hurt, H., Malamud, E., Betancourt, L., Braitman, L. E., Brodsky, N. L., & Giannetta, J. (1997). Children with in utero cocaine exposure do not differ from control subjects on intelligence testing. *Archives of Pediatrics & Adolescent Medicine* 151, 1237–1241.

Inciardi, J. (2002). *The war on drugs III.* Boston: Allyn and Bacon.

Inciardi, J. A., Lockwood, D., & Pottieger, A. (1993). *Women and crack-cocaine.* New York: Macmillan.

Jacobson, J. L., Jacobson, S. W., Sokol, R. J. Martier, S. S., Ager, J. W., & Sankaran, S. (1994). Effects of alcohol use, smoking, and illicit drug use on fetal growth in black infants. *Journal of Pediatrics* 124, 757–764.

Kelly, S. J. (2003). Cumulative environmental risk in substance abusing women: Early intervention, parenting stress, child abuse potential and child development. *Child Abuse & Neglect* 27, 993–995.

Koren, G. Gladstone, D., Roberson, C., & Robieux, I. (1992). The perception of teratogenic risk of cocaine. *Teratology* 46, 567–571.

Latimer, D., & Goldberg, J. (1981). *Flowers in the blood: The story of opium.* New York: Franklin Watts.

Leslie, H. (2001). *Ferguson v. City of Charleston:* A limitation on the "special needs" doctrine. *Loyola Journal of Public Interest Law* 3, 93–104.

Mahan, S. (1996). *Crack cocaine, crime and women.* Thousand Oaks, CA: Sage.

Montgomery, S. M., & Ekborn, A. (2002). Smoking during pregnancy and diabetes mellitus in a British longitudinal birth cohort. *British Medical Journal* 324, 26–27.

McShane, M., Williams, F. P., III., & Dolny, H. M. (2002). Do standard risk prediction instruments apply to female parolees? *Women & Criminal Justice* 13, 163–182.

Miller, A. F. (2002). Substance abuse treatment for women with children. In H. T. Wilson (Ed.), *Annual editions: Drugs, society and behavior* (17th ed.; pp. 210–213). Guilford, CT: McGraw Hill/Dushkin.

Miller, J. M., & Selva, L. H. (1994). Drug enforcement's double-edged sword: An assessment of asset forfeiture programs. *Justice Quarterly* 11, 314–335.

National Institute on Drug Abuse. (2003). *Nicotine addition.* Research Report. Retrieved on March 11, 2005 from http://www.nida.nih.gov/PubCat/ Pubsindex. html.

National Institute of Justice (NIJ). (2001). *Annual report on drug abuse among adult and juvenile arrestees.* Washington, DC: U.S. Department of Justice.

Nolan, J. L. (1998). *The therapeutic state.* New York: New York University Press.

Norland, S., & Mann, P. J. (1984). Being troublesome: Women on probation. *Criminal Justice and Behavior* 11, 115–135.

Polan, M. L., Dombrowski, M. P., Ager, J. W., & Sokol, R. J. (1990). Punishing pregnant drug users: Enhancing the flight from care. *Drug and Alcohol Dependence* 31, 199–203.

Ray, O., & Ksir, C. (1999). *Drugs, society, and human behavior* (8th ed.). Boston: McGraw-Hill.

Riley, J. G., Brodsky, N. L., & Porat, R. (1988). Risk for SIDS in infants with in utero cocaine exposure: A prospective study. *Pediatric Research* 23, 454A.

Sandy, K. (2003). The discrimination inherent in America's Drug War: Hidden racisim revealed by examining the hysteria over crack. *Alabama Law Review* 54, 665–693.

Scahill, M. C. (2000). *Female delinquency cases, 1997.* OJJDP Fact Sheet. Washington, DC: U.S. Department of Justice.

Shearer, R. (2003). Identifying the special needs of female offenders. *Federal Probation* 67 (1), 46–51.

Snell, T. L. (1994). *Women in prison: Survey of State Prison Inmates, 1991.* Washington, DC: U.S. Department of Justice, Bureau of Justice Statistics.

Stevens, S. J., & Wexler, H. K. (1998). *Women and substance abuse: Gender transparency.* Binghamton, NY: Haworth Press.

U.S. Centers for Disease Control. (2001, May 18). Update: Syringe Exchange Programs—United States, 1998. *Morbidity and Mortality Weekly Report* 50, 385.

U.S. General Accounting Office. (1999, December). *Women in prison: Issues and challenges confronting U.S. correctional systems.* (GAO/GGD-00-22). Washington, DC: U.S. Government Accounting Office.

Weikel, D. (1996, April 7). Meth labs: How young lives are put in peril. *Los Angles Times,* A, pp. 1, 18–19.

Youchah, C., & Freda, M. C. (1995). Cocaine use during pregnancy and low birth weight: The impact of prenatal care and drug treatment. *Seminars in Perinatology* 19, 293–300.

Zucherman, B., Frank, D. A., & Hingson, R. (1989). Effects of maternal marijuana and cocaine use on fetal growth. *New England Journal of Medicine* 320, 762–768.

Zucherman, B., & Frank, D. (1992). "Crack Kids": Not broken. *Pediatrics* 89, 337–339.

Cases Cited

Ferguson v. City of Charleston, 121 S.Ct. 1281 (2001)

Webb v. U.S., 249 U.S. 96 (1919)

12

Women as Perpetrators of Murder

Peter J. Benekos

Since 1892, when Lizzie Borden (then age 32) was accused of the brutal murders of her father and stepmother (actually, the father had 11 blows and the mother had 19), the interest and fascination in women as killers has generated both scholarly research as well as popular fiction (e.g., Bailey & Hale, 2004; Cantwell, 1992; Ewing, 2000; Jones, 1980; Lamb, 2003; Mann, 1996; McConnel, 1995; Muraskin, 2000; Pollock, 1999; Weisheit & Mahan, 1988). While research and fiction have also focused on women as victims of violence, the image of a woman deliberately and repeatedly swinging an ax to kill her parents represents a social and cultural anomaly: Women are to be protected from victimization, not feared as the victimizers.

Even though Lizzie Borden was acquitted of the charges, the suspicion has persisted that she committed the bloody killings in order to gain access to her father's inheritance (Cantwell, 1992). What appalled the citizens of Fall River, Massachusetts, who held this suspicion was the manner (violent) and the motive (greed) of the murders: They were un-feminine.

The case of Karla Faye Tucker, who also used an ax to murder her victims, further illustrates how female killers can gain media attention and captivate public sentiment. In 1983, in Houston, Texas, Tucker and her boyfriend, Daniel Ryan Garrett, used a pick ax to hack Jerry Lynn Dean (her ex-lover) and Deborah Thornton (his companion) while they were sleeping (Tucker Dies by Lethal Injection, 1998). Tucker, age 23 at the time, was a drug user and prostitute who was convicted and sentenced to death. (Garrett was also sentenced to death but died in prison in 1994.)

During her fifteen years in prison, Tucker became a born-again Christian (who married her chaplain, Dana Brown) and gained support from several groups who believed she should not be executed. The governor at the time, George W. Bush, refused to grant a reprieve; the U.S. Supreme Court also denied her petition for a stay of execution. In 1998, at age 38, Tucker became the first woman executed in Texas since 1863, and the first woman in the United States since 1984 (Tucker Dies by Lethal Injection, 1998).

A more contemporary case of unfeminine and similarly violent behaviors is that of Aileen Wuornos. At age 34, with motives of revenge and money, she became a predatory serial killer of seven men (Shipley & Arrigo, 2004, p. 95). Her story of childhood victimization and abuse, promiscuity, prostitution, crime, and murders (that began in 1989 and lasted until her arrest in January 1991), were popularized in the movie *Monster.* Wuornos was convicted and executed on October 9, 2002, in Florida (Shipley & Arrigo, 2004, p. 153).

The Borden, Tucker, and Wuornos cases illustrate the importance of gender-specific expectations in understanding the study of "[W]omen and crime" generally and of women and violence specifically. As perceptions of women have changed, system responses and social controls have also changed: "Women offenders must now manage a new public fear of the 'violent female' despite strong evidence that it is social and justice system responses to women offenders that are changing and not the nature of women's behaviour itself" (John Howard Society, 2001, p. 14). In this context of system responses, Leonard (2001, p. 74) describes how the justice system that "often fails to respond to woman abuse seems, in many cases, to prosecute vigorously the battered woman who kills."

This chapter describes women's roles as perpetrators and victims of murder and presents data on the extent and nature of women and homicide. In examining the gender distribution of murder, the findings reported here will focus on spouse/intimate murder. Since women are at greater risk to be victims and perpetrators of homicide in the family/intimate relationship, the conceptualizations that are useful for explaining this form of family violence will be reviewed. While other acts of violence are briefly noted (i.e., infanticide, suicide), the discussion of women and murder includes a review of the "sexual symmetry" issue in spouse abuse and violence and a summary of some policy implications based on the research findings.

Images of Murder: Women as Offenders and Victims

Data for homicide studies are available from five major sources: (1) the *Uniform Crime Reports (UCR)*, (2) the National Center for Health Statistics (NCHS), (3) city studies, (4) prison studies, and (5) "anecdotal" studies (Wilbanks, 1982, p. 155). While each has strengths and weaknesses, the availability of the *UCR* data provides researchers with descriptive information on the nature of murder and nonnegligent manslaughter. In critiquing the *UCR*, Hagan (2003, p. 119) cautions that researchers need to "be aware of the limitations of these statistics." For example, it is important to recognize the distinction between the terms *murder* and *homicide*. "Murder is a criminal homicide that involves both intent and premeditation," whereas homicide refers to "the killing of one human being by another" (Wilbanks, 1982, p. 153). In his discussion of this definitional issue, Wilbanks notes that homicide is a more inclusive term and that decisions on how deaths are classified may affect research conclusions. (See Wilbanks, 1982, for further critique of the definitional issue.)

Notwithstanding this caveat, data from the U.S. Department of Justice *Uniform Crime Reports* presented in Tables 12.1 and 12.2 indicate rather consistent patterns regarding the involvement of women in murder. As a percentage of "perpetrators" of murder, as measured by arrests, women generally account for about one in ten arrests for murder and nonnegligent manslaughter (Table 12.1). The pattern has been consistent from 1985 to 2002, with a slight decrease in arrests evidenced between 1992 and 1995. In 1992, about 10 percent of the 18,164 offenders arrested for murder and nonnegligent manslaughter (1,744) were women; in 1995, women were also arrested for about 10 percent of the murders (1,587); and in 2002, about 11 percent of the 10,107 offenders (1,092) were women (U.S. Department of Justice, 1986–2003).

Women are twice as likely to be murder victims as they are to be murder offenders. In 1992, women represented 22 percent of the 22,512 victims of murder (4,930), but they made up only 10 percent of those arrested for this offense. In 2002, women represented 23 percent of the 14,054 victims (3,246) but only 11 percent of those arrested for murder. Again, the figures suggest a fairly constant pattern in female victimization for murder, especially since 1989 (U.S. Department of Justice, 1986–2003).

When arrest and victimization data are reported as rates based on the population of males and females, the gender disparity becomes more evident. For each of the eighteen years reported in Table 12.2, women represent about two arrests for murder and nonnegligent manslaughter per 100,000, and the rate began to decrease in 1995. Arrests of men, however, increased from 12.96 per 100,000 in 1985 to 18.91 per 100,000 in 1994, and then decreased to 8.95 per 100,000 in 2002 (U.S. Department of Justice, 1986–2003).

TABLE 12.1   *Percentages of Arrests for Murder and Nonnegligent Manslaughter by Sex, 1985–2002*

	Sex of Offenders		Total Arrests
	Male	Female	
2002	89.2	10.8	10,107
2001	87.5	12.5	9,426
2000	89.4	10.6	8,709
1999	88.6	11.4	9,727
1998	88.8	11.2	12,335
1997	89.7	10.3	12,764
1996	89.7	10.3	14,447
1995	90.5	9.5	16,701
1994	90.4	9.6	14,485
1993	90.6	9.4	20,285
1992	90.4	9.6	18,164
1991	89.7	10.3	18,654
1990	89.6	10.4	18,298
1989	88.2	11.8	17,044
1988	87.9	12.1	15,311
1987	87.6	12.4	15,064
1986	87.7	12.3	16,066
1985	87.6	12.4	15,777

Source: U.S. Department of Justice (1986–2003), *Uniform Crime Reports, 1985–2002.* Washington, DC: U.S. Government Printing Office. These data are taken from tables entitled "Total Arrests, Distribution by Sex."

These rates indicate a male/female arrest ratio of 7.4:1 in 1985, a rate ratio of 9.7:1 in 1992, and a rate ratio of 8.5:1 in 2002. In other words, in 2002 for every woman arrested for murder and nonnegligent manslaughter, nine men were arrested for the same offense. Another way of explaining this is that in 1992, one woman in every 53,191 was arrested for murder and nonnegligent manslaughter compared to one man in 5,507; in 2002, one woman of every 95,611 compared to one man of every 11,171 was arrested for murder and nonnegligent manslaughter.

In his analysis based on data from 1963 to 1979, Wilbanks (1982, p. 162) also found that rates of arrest per 100,000 for males exceeded the rates for female arrests. He reported a male/female rate ratio that increased from 4.8:1 in 1963 to 6.6:1 in 1979 (1982, p. 162). In 2002, the ratio had almost doubled from 1963 to 9:1 (see Table 12.2) (U.S. Department of Justice, 1986–2003).

The information in Table 12.2 indicates that women have lower murder rates than men (as measured by arrest) and that these rates have also remained fairly consistent over time. These data would appear not to support the argument made by some researchers that women have become more violent (Adler, 1975; Hamlett, 1998; Pearson, 1997; Saunders, 1986).

When victimization rates per 100,000 population are compared, the information indicates that women are less likely to be murdered than men. For example, in 1992, one woman in 19,305 was murdered compared to one man in 5,144. In 2002, this changed to one female

TABLE 12.2 *Arrest Rates for Murder and Nonnegligent Manslaughter, by Sex, 1985–2002 (Rates are per 100,000 population)*

| | Sex of Offenders | |
	Male	Female
2002	8.95	1.05
2001	8.72	1.20
2000	8.70	1.00
1999	10.30	1.26
1998	12.09	1.45
1997	12.83	1.40
1996	14.01	1.53
1995	15.80	1.57
1994	18.91	1.91
1993	17.63	1.74
1992	18.16	1.88
1991	18.08	1.97
1990	17.38	1.92
1989	16.27	2.08
1988	15.57	2.06
1987	14.84	2.01
1986	14.56	1.95
1985	13.96	1.89

Source: The rates of arrest are calculated using (a) the number of arrests reported in the *Uniform Crime Reports* (U.S. Department of Justice, 1986–2003) in tables entitled "Total Arrests, Distribution by Sex" 1985–2002, and (b) the population figures are derived from the notation on the populations as reported in the *Uniform Crime Reports* tables. Populations of males and females were determined with the method used by Wilbanks (1982, p.162). For 1985–1999, the population of males was estimated at 48.7 percent and the population of females at 51.3 percent of the total population reported in the *Uniform Crime Reports* tables; for 2000–2002, the population of males was estimated at 49.1 percent and the population of females at 50.9 percent. These percentages represent the gender distribution of the population from 1985 to 1999 as reported in the *Statistical Abstract of the United States,* Washington, DC: U.S. Department of Commerce and from 2000–2002 as reported by the U.S. Bureau of the Census, www.census.gov. While the rates are estimates, they do provide comparative information regarding the arrest trends.

in 32,160 compared to one male in 9,345. This represents a rate ratio of 3.8 male murder victims for each female murder victim in 1992, and a ratio of 3.4 male victims to female murder victims in 2002. However, when a woman is murdered, it is very likely that the perpetrator is a man and someone she knows (U.S. Department of Justice, 1986–2003).

Offender/Victim Relationship

When the relationships between offenders and victims in incidents of murder are examined, the data indicate that when women do kill, they are more likely to kill a man than another woman; that is, the murders are intersexual (Whitson & Moyer, 1992; Wilbanks, 1982; Wolfgang, 1958).

The incidence of female-to-female murder is very rare. From 1985 to 1992, women accounted for less than 18 percent of the total victims of female perpetrators (U.S. Department of Justice, 1986–2003). In 1993, female-to-female murder represented 2.5 percent of cases when offenders and victims were known. In 2002, this was essentially the same at 2.7 percent: 183 female-to-female murders out of 6,817 cases when the sex of the offender and victim was known (U.S. Department of Justice, 1994, 2003). Similar to Wilbanks's conclusion (1982, p. 167), these data indicate that when the offender is female, the victim is most often a male, and when the victim is female, the offender is most likely to be a man. In addition, when the victim is male, the offender is likely to be male. In the incidents of intersexual murders, men murder about two to three times as many women as women murder men (Table 12.3). That is, the ratio of male-to-female victims ranges from 1:1.9 in 1985 to 1:2.5 in 1992 to 1:3.4 in 2002.

In addition to revealing the intersexual nature of female murder, researchers have also found that female offenders and victims are usually intraracial (Mann, 1990; Simpson, 1990; Weisheit, 1984; Wilbanks, 1982) and intra-familial (Browne, 1987; Kuhl, 1985; Wilbanks, 1982; Wolfgang, 1958). When women do murder other women, one image supported by some data is the "scorned lover response," where rejected women kill the current wife or

TABLE 12.3   *Percentages of Murders Committed by Males and Females in Intersexual Relationships, 1985–2002*

	Offender/Victim		
	Male/Female	**Female/Male**	**Total Intersexual Murders**
2002	77.1	22.9	2,306
2001	77.7	22.3	2,300
2000	76.8	23.2	2,235
1999	77.0	23.0	2,156
1998	74.8	25.2	2,475
1997	73.9	26.1	2,464
1996	74.3	25.7	2,635
1995	74.8	25.2	3,113
1994	72.0	27.9	3,459
1993	73.4	26.6	3,769
1992	71.1	28.9	3,518
1991	69.8	30.2	3,448
1990	67.5	32.5	3,449
1989	66.9	33.1	3,544
1988	68.9	31.1	3,618
1987	67.8	32.2	3,666
1986	66.1	33.9	4,075
1985	65.9	34.1	3,817

Source: U.S. Department of Justice. (1986–2003). *Uniform Crime Reports, 1985–2002.* Washington, DC: U.S. Government Printing Office. Based on data taken from tables entitled "Victim/Offender Relationship by Race and Sex" 1985–2002. The figures in this table are calculated using the "known" relationships.

lover of an ex-partner (Deadly Triangles, 1992). Another variation of the scorned lover response is when a woman kills the man who is trying to terminate a relationship.

A larger body of research, however, supports the finding that many murders committed by women are "victim-precipitated" (Browne, 1987; Jones, 1980; Kuhl, 1985; Mann, 1988; Saunders & Browne, 2000; Stark, 1990; Totman, 1978; Walker, 1984; Wolfgang, 1958). For example, Jones (1980, p. 319) reports that 40 percent of the women who murder are acting in self-defense. The National Clearinghouse for the Defense of Battered Women reports that for women who kill, self-defense is the motive in 83 percent of murders (Battered Women Who Kill, 1995, para. 2). Stark (1990, p. 18) describes the nature of abusive domestic relationships and the psychology of entrapment that presents murder as a "safe alternative." This image or scenario is often reported in popular magazines. For example, in *McCall's,* the theme of self-defense was emphasized in an article about five women who killed their abusive husbands or boyfriends (D'Antonio, 1991). The question of "killer or victim?" (i.e., anger or self-defense) is salient when women kill their husbands.

In 2004, in Oakland County, Michigan, Nancy Seaman, a 52-year-old elementary schoolteacher, claimed she killed her husband after years of physical abuse (Brasier, 2004). During one of his attacks, she used an ax to kill him. What makes this case newsworthy is the brutality of her "defensive" action: Her husband had numerous slash wounds, a severed throat, smashed bones, and a crushed skull (Brasier, 2004). In addition to claiming self-defense during allegations of murder, incarcerated women seek clemency or reduced sentences for murders they allegedly committed in self-defense (Gross, 1992; Killing the Enemy, 1991).

Studies of domestic/familial murder suggest that the dynamics of spousal/intimate interactions are important in understanding these types of homicide. Before reviewing this topic and violence in the family in general, the following is a summary of the characteristics of women and murder. The data on murder and the research on women who are offenders and victims suggest the following:

1. Women are arrested for about one in ten murders.
2. About one in four murder victims is a woman.
3. When women commit murder, it is mostly intersexual, intraracial, and intrafamilial.
4. When women are in abusive relationships, the abuser/victim's death may be "victim-precipitated." Arguments and fights may be precipitating factors in which self-defense leads to murder.
5. When women are killed, it is most likely by a male.

Marital Violence

While murder may be the most severe and visible form of violence in the family, there is increasing recognition that family violence is a "pervasive social problem" (Bersani & Chen, 1988, p. 57; Buzawa & Buzawa, 2002; Ewing, 2000; Gelles, 1987; Gosselin, 2003; Hagan & Sussman, 1988; Hamlett, 1998; Ohlin & Tonry, 1989; Straus & Gelles, 1990). Because of the family's unique characteristics as a social group, family members are at risk for violence-prone interactions and unchecked escalation of violence (Gelles, 1987, p. 15). The fact that much of the murder by and of females occurs in the family or in intimate relationships (i.e., intrafamilial, intersexual) raises important questions about the dynamics of spouse/intimate interactions. In this context, the research on spousal battering offers some insights on the nature of these relationships.

Spouse Battering and Violence. The data on domestic violence indicate that women are often victims of abuse and battering by their spouses/significant others. As a result, when women kill, the act is often victim-precipitated and in self-defense (Harlow, 1991; Kuhl, 1985; McLeod, 1984; Mann, 1988; Shupe, Stacey, & Hazlewood, 1987). The idea of women as instigators and initiators of violence against men seems "so absurd" that this "subject of female violence has been almost ignored" (Shupe, Stacey, & Hazlewood, 1987, p. 45). Controversial findings reported by Straus and Gelles (1986, p. 470), however, purport that "women are about as violent within the family as men." Data from two surveys in 1975 and 1985 have been used to argue that women initiate violence about as often as men (Straus & Gelles, 1990, p. 61). Straus and Gelles (1990) suggest that "husband battering" is not as anomalous as previously believed; their reports, however, have prompted critiques of their sexual symmetry conclusions.

The question of sexual symmetry in marital violence has been carefully reviewed by Dobash, Dobash, Wilson, and Daly (1992) and Melton and Belknap (2003), who concluded that qualitative differences in motivations and intentions, as well as in the actions and consequences in incidents of spousal violence, do not support the symmetry conclusions. Citing injury data, repetitiveness and patterns of violence, actual cases, and definitional differences, Dobash et al. (1992, p. 74) conclude that women are not as violent as men and their research supports findings that wives are "much more likely than husbands to be victims."

Melton and Belknap (2003, p. 346) reported similar results. They found that "men are generally more seriously violent toward their intimate female partners than women are toward their intimate male partners." In their study of intimate partner violence (IPV), they observed that in police-reported abuse cases (i.e., official data), male defendants were more likely to shove or push, grab or drag, physically restrain, and strangle their female victims as compared to female defendants. They also found that men had a greater number of abuse acts and caused greater fear in their female victims.

In evaluating self-report survey methodology, Dobash et al. (1992) found problems with data that tended to obscure the distinctions in the severity of violence. For example, respondents were presented with a list of "acts," including a "slap" that could encompass "anything from a slap on the hand chastising a dinner companion for reaching for a bite of one's dessert to a tooth-loosening assault intended to punish, humiliate, and terrorize" (p. 79). These definitional concerns raise doubts about the findings and tend to discredit the symmetry thesis of marital violence. Dobash et al. (1992, p. 83) conclude that the symmetry claims are "unfounded" and fail to comport with existing data or theoretical conceptions of violence. In other words, the findings "fail to establish the intention (e.g., assault or self-defense), consequence (e.g., injury), or extent of violent acts" (Stark & Flitcraft, 1988, p. 297).

Additional research by Steinmetz (1980) and Steinmetz and Lucca (1988) also examined the conclusion that family violence between men and women is more prevalent and also more symmetrical. While these researchers describe spousal hitting and battering as normative family behavior, some salient differences are reported. According to Steinmetz and Lucca (1988, p. 241):

The intention of men and women to use physical violence in marital conflicts is equal . . . the major difference appears to be the males' ability to do more physical damage during non-homicidal marital physical fights.

In the absence of weapons, the differences in physical strength and in the ability to restrain the abuser explained the greater degree of harm to women. In other words, since women are generally less able to restrain violent males, they are battered more severely. When women assault their spouses, not only are the women usually not as strong, but also men are better able to restrain the female attacker, thus minimizing the physical damage (Steinmetz & Lucca, 1988). Hagan (1990, p. 249) concludes that while both spouses use violence, husbands employ the most dangerous and injurious forms of violence and are more frequently repeaters.

Data from the 1999 General Social Survey on Spousal Violence in Canada also demonstrate that women are more likely to experience more severe forms of abuse than men (Jiwani, 2000). For example, 10 percent of male victims of spousal violence reported being beaten compared to 25 percent of female victims; 4 percent of males were choked compared to 20 percent of females; and 7 percent were threatened with or had a gun or knife used against them compared to 12 percent of female victims (Jiwani, 2000, para. 7). Jiwani concludes that "the severity of woman [*sic*] abuse outweighs the kinds of violence experienced by male spouses." Data from the Canadian survey indicate that "women were 5 times more likely to require medical attention as a result of the violence" (Jiwani, 2000, para. 12).

While official data reveal that "men and women are equally likely to be both perpetrators and victims of IPV" (intimate partner violence), Melton and Belknap (2003, p. 339) found that "female defendants were significantly more likely than male defendants to be involved in 'cross-complaints' or 'dual-arrest' cases where both partners were arrested for IPV." In other words, in the question of symmetry versus asymmetry in spouse/intimate violence, official data that report increases in female arrests for domestic violence (i.e., assault) may in fact reflect a change in policy that now requires police to arrest women who use violence even in self-defense. Pollock and Davis (2004) also support this argument. They conclude that mandatory arrest policies have contributed to increases in women's arrests for assault. "Thus, what we see in official statistics is a system change, rather than a real change in violent crime by women" (Pollock & Davis, 2004, p. 33).

Fatal Violence.   When lethal as opposed to nonlethal outcomes of marital violence are examined, "the near equivalence of body counts" does suggest a more symmetrical distribution of violence (Dobash et al., 1992, p. 80). However, the data reported by Kratcoski (1988), Maxfield (1989), Mercy and Saltzman (1989), and Wilson and Daly (1992) indicate that husbands kill their wives more often than wives kill their husbands.

Based on spouse homicides between 1976 and 1985 (16,595), Mercy and Saltzman (1989, p. 595) found that "the risk of being killed by one's spouse was 1.3 times greater for wives than for husbands." Similarly, in Canada, "3.4 wives are murdered for every one husband killed" (Locke, cited in Jiwani, 2000, para. 2). Mercy and Saltzman (1989, p. 596) also found that spouses were "equally likely to have been killed by a firearm" (71 percent for female victims; 72 percent for male victims). When firearms were not used, cutting instruments were more likely used against husbands (25 percent against husbands; 12 percent against wives) while bludgeoning was more prevalent against wife victims (12 percent against wives versus 2 percent against husbands). They observed that "the presence of a firearm in the home may be a key contributor to the escalation of nonfatal spouse abuse to homicide." In addition, they found that 67 percent of the homicides were associated with arguments (Mercy & Saltzman, 1989, pp. 596–598).

While Mercy and Saltzman (1989, p. 597) concluded that husbands and wives are at "similar" risks of being physically abused by each other, as noted earlier, "violent behavior by wives directed at their husbands may reflect acts of self-defense or retribution." Citing the history of physical abuse against women, the researchers note that wives often kill their husbands in this context. Others also utilize a theme of self-defense (Breyer, 1992; Browne, 1987; DeKeseredy, 2000; Flowers, 1987; Jones, 1980; Kandel-Englander, 1992; Kuhl, 1985; Wilson & Daly, 1992) and support the conclusions presented by Dobash et al. (1992) that the motives and intentions of wives and husbands who murder their spouses are not symmetrical. Their characterization of spousal murder suggests male aggressiveness and female defensiveness (Dobash et al., 1992, p. 81):

> Men often kill wives after lengthy periods of prolonged physical violence accompanied by other forms of abuse and coercion; the roles in such cases are seldom if ever reversed. Men perpetrate familicidal massacres, killing spouse and children together; women do not. Men commonly hunt down and kill wives who have left them; women hardly ever behave similarly. Men kill wives as part of planned murder-suicides; analogous acts by women are almost unheard of. Men kill in response to revelations of wifely infidelity; women almost never respond similarly, though their mates are more often adulterous. The evidence is overwhelming that a large proportion of spouse-killings perpetrated by wives, but almost none of those perpetrated by husbands, are acts of self-defense.

In contrast to the national murder data presented by the U.S. Department of Justice in the *Uniform Crime Reports,* the studies cited above suggest that in a family or intimate context, there is another image of women and murder. That is, while females represent a fraction of both those who commit murder (11 percent of the total arrests in 2002), and who are murdered (23 percent of the murder victims in 2002), some data on spousal murder suggest a more proportionate distribution of murder and victimization. Based on 16,367 spousal homicides from 1976 to 1985, 57 percent of the victims were wives and 43 percent were husbands (Mercy & Saltzman 1989, p. 596). In other words, from 1976 to 1985, for every 100 men who killed their wives, about 77 women killed their husbands.

However, based on 56,047 intersexual murders (i.e., not limited to intimate relationships) reported from 1985 to 2002, 71 percent of the victims of murder were females and 29 percent were males. More specifically, the data in Table 12.4 indicate that in intimate relationships, women are more likely to be murdered than men. For example, in 2002, about 3 percent of male victims were killed by their wives or girlfriends as compared to 32 percent of female victims who were killed by their husbands or boyfriends. That is, for every 1 male killed by his significant other, 12 females are killed by their significant others. These data suggest that women are at greater risk to be murdered by their intimates than are men.

Generally, data from the last twenty years indicate that homicides as well as other victimizations of intimate partners have declined. The declines, however, have been more evident for men than for women (Fox & Zawitz, 1999). Based on their review of recent studies, Wells and DeLeon-Granados (2004, p. 231) conclude that "male intimate partner victimiza-

TABLE 12.4 *Offender/Victim Relationship: Percentages of Murders Committed by Significant Others, 1985–2002*

	Percentages of Female Victims Killed by Husbands/Boyfriends	Percentages of Male Victims Killed by Wives/Girlfriends
2002	32.1	2.7
2001	32.2	2.8
2000	33.0	3.2
1999	32.0	3.0
1998	32.0	4.0
1997	29.0	3.0
1996	30.0	3.0
1995	26.0	3.0
1994	28.0	3.0
1993	29.0	3.0
1992	29.0	4.0
1991	28.0	4.0
1990	30.0	4.0
1989	28.0	5.0
1988	31.0	5.0
1987	29.0	6.0
1986	30.0	6.0
1985	30.0	6.0

Source: U.S. Department of Justice. (1986–2003). *Uniform Crime Reports, 1985–2002.* Washington, DC: U.S. Government Printing Office. Based on data taken from tables entitled "Victim/Offender Relationship by Race and Sex" (Single Victim/Single Offender). The figures are calculated using data from "known" relationships.

tion has declined at greater rates than female victimization" and specifically in cases of spousal homicide, "victimization rates declined more rapidly for husbands than for wives." Dugan, Nagin, and Rosenfeld (1999, p. 187) conclude that increases in services for victims of domestic violence have resulted in "exposure reduction" to violence "that helps to account for the especially pronounced decline in the rate at which married women kill their husbands." They also cite changed patterns of marriage and divorce, and the improved economic status of women as "factors which reduce exposure to violent relationships" (1999, p. 187).

Infanticide

Another topic that generates attention is the murder of children. The American Anthropological Association (AAA) reports that "more than 200 women kill their children in the U.S. every year" (2002). Some studies indicate that mothers murder their children more often than fathers (Daly & Wilson, 1988; Gelles, 1987; Mann, 1993). In their study of homicides in Canada between 1974 and 1983, Daly and Wilson found that of 141 solved homicides of victims under the age of 1 year, the mother was the accused murderer in 62.4 percent of the cases (1988, p. 62). They also found that younger, unmarried women were more likely to be perpetrators. However, other data indicate that older children are "as likely to be murdered by their fathers as by their mothers" (Lithwick, 2002, para. 3). In the United States, from 1976 to 2000, 30 percent of children under the age of five years were murdered by their mothers; this figure is similar to the 31 percent who were killed by their fathers (Bureau of Justice Statistics, 2002, p. 2).

Although cases of infanticide are limited in number, studies suggest that the women's role as primary caretaker may explain the overrepresentation of women in child filicide (cases where the victim is killed by a parent). In his review of research on gender and abuse, Gelles (1987, p. 55) observed that "one explanation for this is that the child threatens or interferes with the mother's identity and esteem more than it does the father's. Suggesting that unwanted/unplanned babies are at higher risk for filicide, Daly and Wilson (1988, p. 64) report that while single women delivered only 12 percent of the babies (1977–1983), they "were responsible for just over half of the 64 maternal infanticides known to police." This conclusion is also indirectly supported by a report that neonatal homicides decreased after *Roe v. Wade* (Lester, 1992). Daly and Wilson (1988, p. 69) also discuss medical explanations including lactational psychosis and postpartum depression. When mothers kill older children, however, characteristics of depression and other mental health concerns are more likely (Daly & Wilson 1988, p. 79).

The issue of mental illness and mothers who kill their children was dramatically reported in the 2001 case of Andrea Yates, who drowned her five children in a bathtub. Yates maintained that she was possessed by Satan and also suffered from postpartum depression after the miscarriage of her sixth child (Yates Claimed She Killed Kids to Keep Them from Going to Hell, 2002). The prosecution did not challenge her claim that she had a mental disease; instead the prosecution argued that she knew her acts were wrong and that they were premeditated (Yates Found Guilty of Murdering Her Children, 2002). Yates was convicted of murder and sentenced to life in prison (she will be eligible for parole in 2041).

While maternal filicide by mentally ill mothers is relatively rare—about 100 mentally ill mothers kill their children a year (Husband Forgives Wife in Child Killings, 2004)—historically mothers have been more likely to be hospitalized than imprisoned. In one 1969 study, 68 percent of mothers convicted of filicide were hospitalized, and 27 percent were sentenced to prison (Lithwick, 2002, para. 2). In contrast, fathers who killed their children were hospitalized in 14 percent of the cases but "were sentenced to prison or executed 72 percent of the time" (Lithwick, 2002, para. 2).

While the impact of child abuse on filicide varies, Stark and Flitcraft (1988) report that women who are battered by spouses are more likely to abuse their children. Their findings indicate that child abuse is five times as common among battered than nonbattered women (1988, p. 304). In a study that examined "gender inequality" as a social characteristic of each state, Baron (1993, p. 216) concluded that gender inequality and the child homicide rate for children below 5 years of age are directly related. The states with higher cirrhosis death rates and disproportionate numbers of single female-headed families with children also were more likely to have higher rates of child homicide.

In her descriptive study of women arrested for homicide in six major cities, Mann (1993, p. 228) found that only a few women were arrested for filicide. In 1979 and 1983, ten and fifteen women respectively were arrested for murdering their children. Although Mann's sample was small, she found that the majority of women were unemployed and occupied low economic status, several had records as child abusers, most committed the offense alone, and most claimed innocence or that the death was an accident.

Suicide

A brief note regarding suicide is warranted since this form of female violence, like spousal homicide and child abuse/infanticide, also has been linked to battering and abuse (Rasche, 1993; Stark & Flitcraft, 1988). Stark and Flitcraft (1988, p. 304) report that compared to non-battered women, battered women are 4.8 times more at risk for attempted suicide. While research findings are inconsistent, data suggest that abuse and marital conflict are salient precipitants of suicide attempts. According to the National Center for Health Statistics (NCHS), in 2001, the suicide rate for women was 4.0 per 100,000 as compared to 18.2 per 100,000 for men (2002). This makes suicide the nineteenth leading cause of death for females (compared to eighth for males) (National Institute of Mental Health, 2003).

In addition, women who commit suicide may also kill their children. This is explained as a form of altruism in which the children are murdered for reasons such as concern about their welfare after the mothers are gone (Rasche, 1993, p. 83). This differs from familicide, which is much more characteristic of males who kill their spouses and children, and then themselves. Their motivation seems to be that if they cannot have the children, no one will. The case of the divorced father in Baton Rouge, Louisiana, who poisoned his five children illustrates this motivation: He reportedly told his ex-wife "that if he could not have the children, he would kill them and himself" (Father Poisoned His 5 Children, Police Say, 1993).

Based on these findings of gender and intersexual murder and infanticide, female violence is most characteristic of a "family" phenomenon. As a result, some theoretical models of family violence will be reviewed in an effort to explain spousal violence and female murder.

Theories of Family Violence

In his study of families who kill, Kratcoski (1988) presented four theories to explain intrafamilial violence. Three theories—stress theory, systems theory, and exchange/social control theory—will be considered here to examine spousal violence. Of these, stress theory, which focuses on the inability to deal with increasing levels of stress and the accumulation of pressures, is especially relevant in understanding why women murder their spouses or intimates. When traumas, abuses, and crises add to the levels of stress and pressure, the resulting frustration, fear, helplessness, and inability to cope can precipitate expressions of violent behavior. Kratcoski cites the case of "battered wives killing their husbands as the catharsis of years of suffering abuse" to illustrate this theory (1988, p. 49).

In this model, the frustration and feelings of helplessness that reflect the nature of an abusive relationship reach levels in which a triggering incident releases an accumulation of emotions that can overcome internal and social controls against the use of violent retaliation. With a sense of insecurity and loss of self-esteem, feelings of self-deprecation and dependency make it more difficult to tolerate the abusive relationship (Kuhl, 1985). While increased stress can be internalized (expressed in depression or suicide), it can also be turned outward as a hostile, aggressive defensive response to the sense of perceived hopelessness. In this frustration-anger-aggression response, the level of stress (accumulation of abuse) is so high that the "homicidal reaction" occurs (Kratcoski, 1988, p. 49).

This model, however, fails to account for the individualized experience of stress and the different psychological consequences of abuse. "Evidence on how abuse affects self-esteem is mixed" (Stark & Flitcraft, 1988, p. 306). For example, some women have different thresholds of pain and may endure a longer history of abuse; others can tolerate less and respond sooner. In either event, when the stress reaches a critical level, the outcome (i.e., fight or flight) may be determined by the alternatives perceived to be available to the stressed individual.

In addition to stress theory, the integration of systems and exchange/social control theories also help in explaining spousal murder. In systems theory, the family unit becomes the basis of the stresses and demands. When family patterns and interactions are mutually satisfactory to the members, the family system is in a state of "homeostasis." When disruptions precipitate dysfunctions of the system, "explosive emotional incidents that result in violence and death are possible results" (Kratcoski, 1988, p. 50). Due to interaction opportunities, emotional involvement, life transitions, and age and power differentials, the family is set apart from other social systems and is more vulnerable to violence. Disruptions brought on by any number of circumstances can upset patterned interactions and balances of power; these can lead to expressive violence. "Violence is viewed as a system product rather than the result of individual pathology" (Gelles, 1987, p. 42).

The exchange/social control theory emphasizes the rewards and costs inherent in family relationships and recognizes that when reciprocal agreements regarding conduct and conformity are violated, anger may trigger aggressive responses in order to punish the norm violator and control the threatening behavior. For example, a husband who believes his wife has humiliated him may use violence to both punish her and control her future conduct.

Together, these theories present a model in which violence is viewed as an acceptable "cost" for the "reward" of maintaining the status (i.e., control) of the family system. This may also help explain why males are more prone to violent exchanges. As the traditional "head of the household," husbands have had a social responsibility to maintain family control (Bersani & Chen, 1988). In this patriarchal perspective, when a family member deviates from expected behavior, violence is used as an instrument of control that historically "was allowed unless the level of violence was evidenced by observable injuries or complaints from other community members" (Kratcoski, 1988, p. 52). In other words, if the social costs of spousal violence committed by men are less than those for women who use violence, then more male violence would be predicted.

In addition to these theories—stress, systems, and exchange/social control—Gosselin (2003) suggests that "family systems theory" offers additional perspective on intimate violence. This model focuses on "inadequate interpersonal skills and a dysfunctional relationship" that contribute to assaults and violence between intimates (p. 134). The issue of power inequality is also a dimension that contributes to "anger and frustration," which often leads to violence (p. 134).

In explaining family violence perpetrated by females, these theories would suggest that significant disruptions in the family system and/or increased costs and reduced rewards have reached such levels of imbalance or intolerance that violent exchanges are warranted. For example, the increased severity and frequency of battering, the added element of abusing the children, or fear of death can negate the rewards of staying and justify the costs of using violence against the male abuser. These explanations of spousal violence provide a framework for understanding the elements of family interaction but suggest the need for a more integrated and dynamic conceptualization.

Integrated Model

Additional explanations of violence have relied on models that incorporate both social and cultural variables as well as the dynamics of interpersonal interaction. According to Collins and Flewelling (1991, p. 2), since interpersonal violence is a "process of social interaction between individuals, it is guided by conduct norms which are emergent from individuals' interpretations and assessments of the meaning of interactions." These researchers have developed a model that assumes that violent behavior is guided by rules of social interaction that have meaning to the participants.

The Collins-Flewelling model, presented in Figure 12.1, attempts to incorporate several important variables into a systematic explanation of violence. The contextual variable indicates the setting (private or public), physical location (bar, street), presence of observers, availability of weapons, mobility of actors, and the definition of the situation to the participants. The individuals' relationships to each other also guide the transaction. Age, gender, family role, friendships, and the nature of the relationships determine how violence will be perceived.

During a specific interaction, the topic and temperament can also affect the likelihood of violence. Some of these factors would include the history between the individuals and whether the interaction is a character contest to save face or a power contest to gain or maintain advantage in the relationship. An individual's emotional state is also viewed as a mediating factor that can determine the norms of the interaction. Angry arousal, for example, may escalate a minor insult into an expressive outburst of violence. Collins and Flewelling (1991, p. 8) note that emotional arousal "is probably a precondition for the use of violence in individuals who are not normally violent."

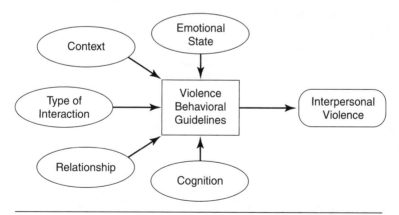

FIGURE 12.1 *Dynamics of Violence (Model to Explain Violent Acts)*

Source: J. Collins and R. Flewelling. (1991). *Interpersonal Violence as Normative Conduct.* Paper presented at the Annual Meeting of the American Society of Criminology, San Francisco, November.

Cognitive capacity refers to how information is perceived and processed during a transaction (Collins & Flewelling, 1991, p. 9). Cognitive impairments can be caused by psychiatric disorders, the influence of psychoactive substances, as well as emotional factors. If the cognitive process becomes irrational, decision making and consideration of risks and consequences of violence and retaliation may become distorted. For example, the presence of alcohol in cases of spouse abuse and spouse murder has been recognized (Mercy & Saltzman, 1989; Wilbanks, 1982; Wolfgang, 1958).

This integrative model can be useful for understanding the pattern of interpersonal violence between men and women. For example, in the context of a patriarchal social order in which male domination is prevalent and pro-violence norms are evident, stress on family systems or perceived threats to individual authority can precipitate interpersonal dynamics that escalate to instrumental or expressive use of violence. If alcohol, emotional distress, and a history of anger and abuse also coincide, it is not difficult to understand the prevalence of violence in the family.

Using Collins and Flewelling's model (Figure 12.1), we can predict that the incidents of intrafamilial murder (i.e., relationship) occur in the man's castle (i.e., context), during or after an argument (i.e., emotional state, type of interaction) in an expressive manner (i.e., cognitive impairment) in which the male initiates the violence (i.e., patriarchal society). This would also tend to support the observation made by Collins and Flewelling (1991, p. 7) that "violence is connected to issues of power and dominance in relationships." From a cultural perspective, Levy (1991) argues that men in American society learn to be sexist and violent toward women. To consider these motivations, we will devote the final section of this chapter to a discussion of the motives of violence between intimates.

Motives for Murder

In the context of intersexual violence between intimates, Rasche (1993) studied various motives for murder. Of fifty-four female offenders in her study, she found that 39 percent of these murdered for self-defense compared to only 4 percent of the 104 males. She also found that more than half of the males were motivated by possessiveness, compared to 24 percent of the females. Another motive for murder, arguments, characterized 24 percent of the female murders and 19 percent of the male murders. Rasche (p. 88) concluded that "females were at more risk from possessive and abusive mates, while males were at more risk from mates acting in their own defense or others responding to perceived dangers."

In discussing these findings, Rasche (1993, pp. 97–98) observed that motives having to do with "termination of a relationship" and "concern for the sanctity or security of the relationship" together explained "almost half of all homicides between intimates." This would support the systems/control model, in which disruptions or perceived disruptions in the relationship (which represents the system) and increased threats to individuals (i.e., the psychological and physical dimensions of the model) could justify the costs of using violence as a means to control the other intimate's behavior. The fact that 82 percent of the offenders who were motivated by "possessiveness" were male further suggests a patriarchal perspective in which control, authority, and gender inequality are important to the family system (Bersani & Chen, 1988, p. 73). That is, when this arrangement (superordinate–subordinate relationship) is threatened, males are more likely to resort to violence.

The themes of power, dominance, and control by males have also been used to explain violence in dating relationships (Gosselin, 2003; National Broadcasting Corporation, 1993). Possessiveness and jealousy as well as distorted conceptions of control and power can have lethal consequences (Lardner, 1993). As women try to leave or end abusive relationships, men exert more control. This pattern often results in the man killing his girlfriend or spouse then killing himself. This is consistent with the "backlash" hypothesis which posits that as women leave or attempt to leave abusive situations, male dominance and control are threatened thus provoking attempts to reassert control (Wells & DeLeon-Granados, 2004, p. 234).

In contrast to male possessiveness, women were the vast majority of murderers in the category of self-defense: 83 percent compared to 17 percent for males (Rasche, 1993, p. 88). This presents a different pattern of interpersonal dynamics for women who murder their intimates. The findings could suggest that high levels of stress, threats, or disruptions were operating in order for the women to have resorted to lethal violence against male intimates. In the language of exchange theory, the potential costs of violent retaliation by the male, arrest and imprisonment, and loss of status were apparently minimal in comparison to the threats and explosive, unpredictable, and unjustifiable attacks that the female victims endured (Gelles, 1987, p.17). As Silverman, Vega, and Danner (1993, p. 180) suggest, homicides committed by women are "more personalized events" and self-defense is a personal issue.

The self-defense motive appears to be gender-related. Rasche's data are consistent with a review presented by Silverman et al. (1993, p. 188) in which they report that "fights, arguments, and abusive situations were the predominant factors" when females committed homicide. While conclusions such as these tend to reduce the specific dimensions of homicide incidents to useful generalizations, they can also distort the various patterns of female homicide. As the Collins and Flewelling (1991) model suggests, the context and emotional state of interpersonal interactions influence and shape the outcomes of interpersonal violence.

In addition, as women seek to escape from abusive relationships by using available social services and community resources (i.e., exposure reduction), intimate male victimization (including homicide) can be expected to decline (Wells & DeLeon-Granados, 2004). As noted earlier, this trend has been demonstrated. Ironically, as women attempt to reduce their risk of victimization by leaving (risk reduction), they are at increased risk for violence (i.e., backlash). That is, male intimate victimization declines but female victimization declines less as a result of male efforts to exert control and dominance. This is a potential, unintended consequence of providing greater services and support for women seeking to leave abusive relationships (Wells & DeLeon-Granados, 2004, p. 234).

Conclusion

The data reviewed in this chapter indicate that the pattern of female murder has essentially remained consistent, and if any change is evident, it is toward a decline in homicides committed by women: Women perpetrate a small proportion of the murders. When they do murder, it is generally in a marital/intimate relationship in which the prevailing motivation is self-defense. Theoretical models suggest that the unique social organization of the family (as well as intimate partner relationships) makes it a "conflict-prone institution" (Gelles, 1987, p. 16) in which inequality, privacy, and sociocultural norms of violence increase the likelihood of violent interpersonal interactions and the risk of lethal consequences, especially for women.

The implications of these findings that women are at greater risk to be victims and perpetrators of murder in the family/intimate contexts are that both long-term social and cultural changes and short-term alternatives and support services are needed. Gelles (1987, p. 19) has observed that "no meaningful changes can occur" until cultural norms and the social organization of the family are changed. For Gelles (1987, pp. 18–19), this will require at least five steps: that the legitimacy and glorification of violence in society and the family are eliminated; that stressors on the family are reduced; that the sexist nature of society and the family are changed; that the cycles of violence that often begin in the family are broken; and that judicial policies and legal codes that view the family as a "sacred cow" are changed.

Similarly, Wells and DeLeon-Granados (2004, p. 235) identify four developments that can "reduce the exposure of men and women to abusive partners: social services that include community-based resources for victims of domestic violence, criminal justice response, the economic standing of women relative to men, and types of intimate relationships."

As some authors suggest, the availability of shelters and other supportive services may be providing some women avenues to escape self-defensive homicide as well as lethal victimization by their partners. As a result of public education and attention to domestic violence, several local and state programs offer services to victims and promote prevention through various community initiatives. Some of these initiatives have been successful in reducing intimate partner homicide. For example, in the early 1990s, the domestic abuse program in Quincy, Massachusetts, reported a reduction of domestic homicide to zero as a result of special prosecution teams and stringent enforcement (Witt, 1992).

Similarly, in an effort to reduce violence escalation, some police departments have specialized units to respond to domestic violence. The Domestic Abuse Response Team (DART) in Lakeland, Florida, is comprised of specially trained officers who handle domestic violence calls and also offer "guidance to other patrol officers" (www.lakelandgov. net/lpd/specialprogs/dart.htm). The Lakeland Police Department reports that (www. lakelandgov.net/lpd/specialprogs/dart.htm, para. 3):

> Since implementing the DART program in 1990, our domestic violence related homicides have dropped to below 10% per year. In 1999, there were no domestic violence related homicides in our city.

In North Carolina, under the direction of the Department of Corrections, a Domestic Abuse Officer Control Program provides offender assessment, treatment, and supervision. The goal is to reduce the "cycle of violence" by targeting at-risk offenders and coordinating efforts of police, service providers, victim advocates, and community corrections (www.doc. state.nc.us/dcc/programs/domestic%20abuse.htm). Also under the aegis of the Department of Corrections, in Vermont, a number of programs, including the Intensive Domestic Abuse Program (IDAP) and the Batterers Intervention Program (BIP), are offered throughout the state to victims and families of abuse and violence (www.doc.state.vt.us/domestic.htm). Notwithstanding the efforts of these programs, a 2003 National Institute of Justice report raises questions about the effectiveness of batterer intervention programs (BIP) (Jackson, Feder, Forde,

Davis, Maxwell, & Taylor, 2003). In their review of batterer programs in Brooklyn, New York, and Broward County, Florida, the authors found that programs had limited effectiveness in changing attitudes and behaviors of batterers (Jackson et al., 2003).

The information reviewed in this chapter suggests both a question for continuing research and a policy implication for reducing intimate homicides: What is the relationship between the availability of shelters and intimate homicide? That is, does an increase in the number of shelters reduce intimate homicide? As Dugan, Nagin, and Rosenfeld (1999) concluded in their study of intimate partner homicide, domestic violence services, along with other social changes, have contributed to declining homicides between intimate partners. And, as discussed by Silverman, Vega, and Danner (1993), if this is the case, then continuing to expand services for victims of abuse will provide alternatives to victimization and intimate partner homicide.

As society's tolerance for domestic violence has diminished, women have become more aware that economic support and legal services are available. Gosselin (2003, p. 107) concludes that recent accomplishments in responding to domestic violence, including "heightened public awareness," "enhanced intervention strategies," "protection and prevention efforts," and "batterers' programs," have helped reduce abuse and violence. If this observation is accurate, then women should be less likely to become victims of intimate murder or to resort to murder against their intimates. Trends in intersexual violence and murder support this observation. However, increased arrests of females for assault (i.e., cases of domestic violence) suggest that policy changes (i.e., mandatory arrest) have had unintended consequences for women and have contributed to images of women as perpetrators of violence. Nonetheless, programs such as those in Lakeland, Florida (DART), suggest that training police officers, coordinating services, and focusing on early intervention for domestic violence can reduce intimate partner violence and homicide.

Review Questions

1. What are some offender motives for intimate partner murder?

2. Discuss sexual symmetry in domestic violence.

3. Using three of the theories developed by Kratcoski, explain intrafamilial violence. How do you explain intimate partner violence?

4. What are the distinctions between the terms murder and homicide? What do the data show regarding the extent of women's involvement in murder?

5. Discuss the characteristics of women and murder. For example, who are their victims?

6. Explain the Collins-Flewelling integrated model of interpersonal violence. What is the contextual variable?

7. Explain the relationship between domestic violence and an increase in child abuse.

8. What resources in the community might assist in reducing female involvement in homicide? How do these services affect victims?

9. How can we reduce the incidence of homicide and assault in U.S. families?

10. Explain the effects of exposure reduction efforts on intimate partner victimization.

Key Terms

Backlash hypothesis
Conjugal violence
Child filicide
Exchange/social control theory
Familicide
Infanticide
Integrated model of interpersonal violence

Motives for murder
Risk reduction
Scorned lover response
Sexual symmetry
Stress theory
Systems theory
Victim precipitation

References

Adler, F. (1975). *Sisters in crime: The rise of the new female criminal.* New York: McGraw-Hill.

American Anthropological Association. (2002, March 25). *Why women kill their children.* Retrieved June 29, 2004 from www.aaanet.org/press/motherskillingchildren.htm.

Bailey, F. Y., & Hale, D. C. (2004). *Blood on her hands: The social construction of women, sexuality, and murder.* Belmont, CA: Wadsworth.

Baron, L. (1993). Gender inequality and child homicide: A state-level analysis. In A. V. Wilson (Ed.), *Homicide: The victim/offender connection* (pp. 207–225). Cincinnati: Anderson Publishing.

Battered women who kill. (1995). Retrieved June 11, 2004 from www.cybergrrl.com/views/dv/stat/statbwkill.html.

Belknap, J. (1996). *The invisible woman: Gender, crime and justice.* Belmont, CA: Wadsworth.

Bersani, C., & Chen, H. T. (1988). Sociological perspectives in family violence. In V. V. Hasselt, R. Morrison, A. Bellack, & M. Hersen (Eds.), *Handbook of family violence* (pp. 57–86). New York: Plenum Press.

Branan, K. (1991, October). Killer or victim? *Ladies Home Journal,* 128.

Brasier, L. L. (2004, July 26). Brutal slaying is full of questions: A wife's self-defense or rage? Jury must decide. *Detroit Free Press.* Retrieved August 5, 2004 from www.freep.com/news/locoak/over26_20040726.htm.

Breyer, H. (1992). The battered woman syndrome and the admissibility of expert testimony. *Criminal Law Bulletin* 28 (2), 99–115.

Browne, A. (1987). *When battered women kill.* New York: Macmillan/Free Press.

Bureau of Justice Statistics. (2002, November 21). *Homicide trends in the U.S.: Infanticide.* Retrieved June 30, 2004 from www.ojp.usdoj.gov/bjs/homicide/children.htm.

Buzawa, E. S., & Buzawa, C. G. (Eds.). (2002). *Domestic violence: The criminal justice response* (3rd ed.). Thousand Oaks, CA: Sage.

Cantwell, M. (1992, July 26). Lizzie Borden took an ax. *New York Times Magazine,* 18–21, 42, 44.

Collins, J., & Flewelling, R. (1991, November). *Interpersonal violence as normative conduct.* Paper presented at the Annual Meeting of the American Society of Criminology, San Francisco.

Daly, M., & Wilson, M. (1988). *Homicide.* New York: Aldine de Gruyter.

D'Antonio, M. (1991, October). Why she shot him. *McCall's,* 32.

Deadly triangles. (1992, June 8). *Time,* 1.

DeKeseredy, W. S. (2000). *Women, crime and the Canadian criminal justice system.* Cincinnati: Anderson Publishing.

Dobash, R., Dobash, R. E., Wilson, M., & Daly, M. (1992). The myth of sexual symmetry in marital violence. *Social Problems* 39 (1), 71–91.

Dugan, L., Nagin, D. S., & Rosenfeld, R. (1999). Explaining the decline in intimate partner homicide: The effects of changing domesticity, women's status, and domestic violence resources. *Homicide Studies* 3 (3), 187–214.

Ewing, C. P. (2000). *Fatal families: The dynamics of intrafamilial homicide.* Thousand Oaks, CA: Sage.

Father poisoned his 5 children, police say. (1993, January 5). *New York Times,* A7.

Flowers, R. B. (1987). *Women and criminality: The woman as victim, offender, and practitioner.* New York: Greenwood Press.

Fox, J. A., & Zawitz, M. W. (1999). *Homicide trends in the United States.* Washington, DC: U.S. Department of Justice.

Gelles, R. (Ed.). (1987). *Family violence.* Newbury Park, CA: Sage.

Gosselin, D. K. (2003). *Heavy hands: An introduction to the crimes of family violence* (2nd ed.). Upper Saddle River, NJ: Prentice-Hall.

Gross, J. (1992, September 15). Abused women who kill seek a way out of cells. *New York Times,* A1.

Hagan, F. (1990). *Introduction to criminology: Theories, methods, and criminal behavior* (2nd ed.). Chicago: Nelson-Hall.

Hagan, F. (2003). *Research methods in criminal justice and criminology* (6th ed.). Boston: Allyn and Bacon.

Hagan, F., & Sussman, M. (Eds.). (1988). *Deviance and the family.* New York: Haworth Press.

Hamlett, N. (1998). *Women who abuse in intimate relationships.* Minneapolis, MN: Dometic Abuse Project.

Harlow, C. W (1991). *Female victims of violent crime.* Washington, DC: U.S. Department of Justice, Bureau of Justice Statistics.

Husband forgives wife in child killings. (2004, June 20). *Erie Times-News,* 4A.

Jackson, S., Feder, L., Forde, D. R., Davis, R. C., Maxwell, C. D., & Taylor, B. G. (2003). *Batterer intervention programs: Where do we go from here?* Washington, DC: U.S. Department of Justice, National Institute of Justice.

Jiwani, Y. (2000, August). *The 1999 general social survey on spousal violence: An analysis.* Retrieved June 29, 2004 from www.harbour.sfu.ca/freda/reports/gss01.htm.

John Howard Society of Alberta. (2001) *Women and violence.* Retrieved July 29, 2004 from www.johnhoward.ab.ca/PUB/women.htm.

Jones, A. (1980). *Women who kill.* New York: Holt, Rinehart, Winston.

Kandel-Englander, E. (1992). On the incarceration of abused women who kill their batterers. *C J Update* 21, 1–2.

Killing the enemy. (1991, April 29). *National Review,* 13.

Kratcoski, P. (1988). Families who kill. In F. Hagan & M. Sussman (Eds.), *Deviance and the family* (pp. 47–48). New York: Haworth Press.

Kuhl, A. (1985). Battered women who murder: Victims or offenders? In I. Moyer (Ed.), *The changing roles of women in the criminal justice system* (2nd ed.; pp. 197–216). Prospect Heights, IL: Waveland Press.

Lamb, W. (2003). *Couldn't keep it to myself.* New York: ReganBooks/Harper Collins.

Lardner, G. (1993, January 4–10). How Kristen died. *The Washington Post National Weekly Edition,* 8–12.

Leonard, E. D. (2001). Convicted survivors: Comparing and describing California's battered women inmates. *The Prison Journal* 81 (1), 73–86.

Lester, D. (1992). *Roe v. Wade* was followed by a decrease in neonatal homicide. *The Journal of the American Medical Association* 207, June 10, 3027.

Levy, D. (1991, September 16). Why Johnny might grow up violent and sexist. *Time,* 16.

Lithwick, D. (2002, March 12). *When parents kill: Why fathers do it. Why mothers do it.* Retrieved June 29, 2004 from www.slate.msn.com/?id=2063086.

Mann, C. R. (1988). Getting even? Women who kill in domestic encounters. *Justice Quarterly* 5 (1), 33–51.

Mann, C. R. (1990). Black female homicide in the United States. *Journal of Interpersonal Violence* 5, 176–201.

Mann, C. R. (1993). Maternal filicide of preschoolers. In A. V. Wilson (Ed.), *Homicide: The victim/offender connection* (pp. 227–246). Cincinnati: Anderson Publishing.

Mann, C. R. (1996). *When women kill.* Albany: State University of New York Press.

Maxfield, M. (1989). Circumstances in supplementary homicide reports: Variety and validity. *Criminology* 27 (4), 671–695.

McConnel, P. (1995). *Sing soft, sing loud.* Flagstaff, AZ: Logoria.

McLeod, M. (1984). Women against men: An examination of domestic violence based on an analysis of official data and national victimization data. *Justice Quarterly* 2 (1), 171–193.

Melton, H. C., & Belknap, J. (2003). He hits, she hits: Assessing gender differences and similarities in officially reported intimate partner violence. *Criminal Justice and Behavior* 30 (3), 328–348.

Mercy, J., & Saltzman, L. (1989). Fatal violence among spouses in the United States, 1976–85. *American Journal of Public Health* 79 (5), 595–599.

Mills, T. (1984). Victimization and self-esteem: On equating husband abuse and wife abuse. *Victimology* 9 (2), 254–261.

Muraskin, R. (2000). *It's a crime: Women and justice* (2nd ed.). Upper Saddle River, NJ: Prentice-Hall.

National Broadcasting Corporation. (1993). *Dateline: Date violence.* Broadcast January 7.

National Center for Health Statistics. (2002). *Death rates for suicide, according to sex, race, Hispanic origin, and age: United States, selected years 1950–2001.* Retrieved June 29, 2004 from www.cdc.gov/nchs.

National Institute of Mental Health. (2003). *In harm's way: Suicide in America.* Retrieved June 28, 2004 from www.nimh.nih.gov/publicat/harmaway.cfm.

Ohlin, L., & Tonry, M. (Eds.). *Family violence.* Chicago: University of Chicago Press.

Pearson, P. (1997). *When she was bad: Violent women and the myth of innocence.* New York: Penguin Group.

Pollock, J. M. (1999). *Criminal women.* Cincinnati: Anderson Publishing.

Pollock, J. M., & Davis, S. (2004). *The continuing myth of the violent female offender.* Paper presented at the Annual Meeting of the Academy of Criminal Justice Sciences, Las Vegas (March).

Rasche, C. E. (1993). "Given" reasons for violence in intimate relationships. In A. V. Wilson (Ed.), *Homicide: The victim/offender connection* (pp. 75–100). Cincinnati: Anderson Publishing.

Saunders, D. G. (1986). When battered women use violence: Husband-abuse or self-defense? *Violence and Victims* 1, 47–60.

Saunders, D. G., & Browne, A. (2000). Intimate partner homicide. In R. T. Ammerman & M. Hersen (Eds.), *Case studies in family homicide* (pp. 415–449). New York: Plenum Press.

Shipley, S. L., & Arrigo, B. A. (2004). *The female homicide offender: Serial murder and the case of Aileen Wuornos.* Upper Saddle River, NJ: Pearson/Prentice Hall.

Shupe, A., Stacey, W., & Hazlewood, L. (1987). *Violent men, violent couples: The dynamics of domestic violence.* Lexington, MA: D. C. Heath.

Silverman, I., Vega, M., & Danner, T. (1993). Die female murderer. In A. V. Wilson (Ed.), *Homicide: The victim/offender connection* (pp. 175–190). Cincinnati: Anderson Publishing.

Simpson, S. (1990). Caste, class, and violent crime: Explaining differences in female offending. *Criminology* 29 (1), 115–137.

Stark, E. (1990). Rethinking homicide: Violence, race, and the politics of gender. *International Journal of Health Services* 20 (1), 3–22.

Stark, E., & Flitcraft, A. (1988). Violence among intimates: An epidemiological review. In V. V. Hasselt, R. Morrison, A. Bellack, & M. Hersen (Eds.), *Handbook of family violence* (pp. 293–317). New York: Plenum Press.

Steinmetz, S. (1980). Women and violence: Victims and perpetrators. *American Journal of Psychotherapy* 34, 334–350.

Steinmetz, S., & Lucca, J. (1988). Husband battering. In V. Van Hasselt, R. Morrison, A. Bellack, & M. Hersen (Eds.), *Handbook of family violence* (pp. 233–246). New York: Plenum Press.

Straus, M., & Gelles, R. (1986). Societal change and change in family violence from 1975 to 1985 as revealed by two national surveys. *Journal of Marriage and the Family* 48, August, 465–480.

Straus, M., & Gelles, R. (1990). *Physical violence in American families: Risk factors and adaptations to violence in 8,145 families.* New Brunswick, NJ: Transaction Publishers.

Totman, J. (1978). *The murderess: A psychological study of criminal homicide.* San Francisco: R and E Research Associates.

Tucker dies by lethal injection. (1998, February 3). CNN Interactive. Retrieved July 29, 2004 from www.cnn.com/US/9802/03/tucker.executed/index.html.

U.S. Department of Justice (1985–2002). *Uniform Crime Reports* (annual publications). Washington, DC: U.S. Government Printing Office.

Walker, L. (1984). *The battered woman syndrome.* New York: Springer Publishing.

Weisheit, R. (1984). Female homicide offenders: Trends over time in an institutional population. *Justice Quarterly* 1 (4), 471–489.

Weisheit, R., & Mahan, S. (1988). *Women, crime, and criminal justice.* Cincinnati, OH: Anderson Publishing.

Wells, W., & DeLeon-Granados, W. (2004). The intimate partner homicide decline: Disaggregated trends, theoretical explanations, and policy implications. *Criminal Justice Policy Review* 15 (2), 229–246.

Whitson, M., & Moyer, I. (1992). Patriarchy, power differentials and women offenders. In I. Moyer (Ed.), *The changing roles of women in the criminal justice system* (2nd ed.; pp. 31–56). Prospect Heights, IL: Waveland Press.

Wilbanks, W. (1982). Murdered women and women who murder: A critique of the literature. In N. H. Rafter & E. Stanko (Eds.), *Judge, lawyer, victim, thief: Women, gender roles, and criminal justice* (pp. 151–180). Boston: Northeastern University Press.

Wilson, M., & Daly, M. (1992). Who kills whom in spouse killings? On the exceptional sex ratio of spousal homicides in the United States. *Criminology* 30 (2), 189–215.

Witt, E. (1992). Quincy, Massachusetts: Batterers, beware. *Governing,* October, 41.

Wolfgang, M. (1958). *Patterns in criminal homicide.* Philadelphia: University of Pennsylvania Press.

www.doc.state.nc.us/dcc/programs/domestice%20abuse. htm. North Carolina Department of Correction, Division of Community Corrections, Domestic Abuse Offender Control Program. Retrieved August 5, 2004.

www.doc.state.vt.us/domestic.htm. Vermont Department of Corrections, Domestic Abuse Services. Retrieved August 5, 2004.

www.ilcadv.org. Illinois Coalition Against Domestic Violence. Retrieved August 6, 2004.

www.lakelandgov.net/lpd/specialprogs/dart.html. City of Lakeland, Domestic Abuse Response Team, D.A.R.T. Retrieved August 6, 2004.

www.mass.gov/gcdv/help.htm. Governor's Commission on Domestic Violence. Yates claimed she killed kids to keep them from going to hell. (2002, March 1). Retrieved June 30, 2004 from www.courttv.com/trials/yates/030102_pm.html.

Yates found guilty of murdering her children. (2002, March 13). Retrieved July 1, 2004 from www.cnn.com/2002/LAW/03/13/yates.trial/index.htm.

Part V

Girls and Women in the System

In this edition, we devote a separate section to the issues of girls and women who are detained in either juvenile or adult facilities, and we look at the intersection of race/ethnicity, class, and gender and how women of color are affected The treatment of girls and women has always been different from men's, but not necessarily better. These institutions have a historical legacy of paternal/maternal treatment derived from a belief that women and girls were less criminal, less violent, and more in need of treatment. Unfortunately, this belief, historically and today, does not translate into better treatment for women. In fact, one sees disturbing parallels to the treatment of girls and women today compared to their treatment in much earlier decades. We have a pattern of holding girls for lesser offenses, even though detention is often a place of victimization, not treatment. We do the same for women today with the increased rate of minor drug offenders being sentenced for long terms of imprisonment.

Women offenders have the same profile today as they did almost ten years ago when the first edition of this book was published. They are still overwhelmingly poor and disproportionately minority. They are likely to be mothers of young children and have a history of drug problems, unemployment, and dysfunctional family background. The only difference is that there are many more of them today. These chapter authors also demonstrate the significant effect that race or ethnicity and class have on the treatment of offenders, victims, and professionals in the system.

13

The Context of Women's Imprisonment

Barbara Owen

In the past decades, issues surrounding women in prison have become more visible. Partially due to the exponential increases in the female prison population and partly due to vigorous attention by feminist scholars, the knowledge about women in prison has also increased. This chapter reviews this knowledge in terms of the context of women's imprisonment across several dimensions: gender and social control, women's pathways to prison, the origin of women's prisons, the contemporary prison, issues affecting women in prison, and reentry. The chapter concludes with a discussion of gender and criminal justice policy.

As Belknap (2001) contends, women conventionally have been invisible in studies of the criminal justice system and in the literature of the prison. In making this argument, the critical gender differences related to imprisonment are described through prior research (see particularly Bloom, Owen, & Covington, 2003; Owen, 1999, 1998) and incorporate the findings of increasingly rich scholarship on gender differences in the broad area of criminology over the past few decades (Belknap, 2001; Chesney-Lind & Palmore, 2004; Pollock, 1999, 2002). Understanding the social and political context of female criminality and subsequent imprisonment shifts our attention to a feminine—as opposed to a masculine—perspective that enriches our understanding about women and prison.

Gender and Social Control

Women's prisons must also be understood in the context of gender and social control. Patriarchy is one key element of this relationship. Kurshan (1992, p. 330) argues that the imprisonment of women in the United States is tied directly to their status under patriarchy. Like other feminist scholars, she argues that the imprisonment of women "as well as all other aspects of our lives, takes place against a backdrop of patriarchal relationships." Kurshan (1992, p. 331) defines patriarchy as "the manifestation and institutionalization of male dominance over women and children in the family and the extension of male dominance over women in society in general." She continues in suggesting that "Women's 'crimes' have often had a sexual definition and have been rooted in the patriarchal double standard. Therefore the nature of women's imprisonment reflects the position of women in society."

The study of women in prison must be framed through the lens of patriarchy and its implications for the everyday lives of women. When women's imprisonment itself is examined separately, it may well be that the rising numbers of women in prison are a measure of the society's failure to care for the needs of women and children who live outside the middle-class protection afforded by patriarchy. The rising numbers of women in prison reflect the cost of allowing the systematic abuse of women and children, the problem of increased drug use, and a continuing spiral of marginalization from conventional institutions (Owen, 1998).

These same processes continue to control and constrain women's behavior during incarceration. For men, the concept of "dangerousness" represents the threat to social order through the potential harm men can do through physical violence or damage to property. For women, "dangerousness" has traditionally been seen as the threat of harm to conventional morality and the oppressive patriarchal order. In her review of gender and social control, Pollock (1995, p. 4) argues that women's experiences with prisons and other agencies of social control should be understood within the context of cultural definitions of femininity and their virtue. Women who do not conform to a "normal" standard based on virtue, passivity, and maternalism become, by definition, "deviant" and in need of social control.

Prisons and their punitive nature evolved to control the violent and destructive behavior associated with male criminality. As such, prisons have been used to respond to women's criminal behavior with little thought to the unintended consequences for women, their children, and the community. While there can be no dispute that the imprisonment of men is also damaging across these elements, the evidence is clear that gender mediates the overall effect of the prison on women. For the huge majority of imprisoned women, incarceration is a sanction disproportionate to the harm they cause to society through their lower-level property and drug offenses. Prisons for women have been modeled after those designed for their "louder and bigger brothers" (Griggs, 2004), and, in most cases, punish women incommensurate with the level of threat they present to society. As the numbers of women imprisoned in contemporary America increase, these issues require an investigation with a gendered lens.

The Gendered Context of the Imprisonment Binge

There is a clear gendered effect of the imprisonment binge (Bloom, Chesney-Lind, & Owen, 1994; Bush-Baskette, 1999; Mauer, Potler, & Wolf, 1999; Owen 1999; Women's Prison Association, 2004). The continued criminalization of drug use among women has fueled much of the rise in female prison populations in the past decades. Since 1980, the rate of increase in the female prison population has risen much faster than that of males. In absolute numbers, the number of women incarcerated in state and federal prisons has risen nearly eightfold, from 12,000 in 1980, to almost 98,000 mid-2003 (Harrison & Beck, 2003). While the total number of male prisoners between 1990 and 2000 grew 77 percent, the number of female prisoners increased 108 percent during the same period. The data on arrests demonstrate that the number of women under criminal justice supervision has risen disproportionately to arrest rates. In 2004, the Women's Prison Association (WPA) analyzed the trends in sentencing and arrests for women, using *Uniform Crime Reports* data. They show that arrest and subsequent imprisonment rates for every 1000 women have risen dramatically between 1986 and 2000. In 1986, one woman was admitted to prison for every 87 arrests. By 2000, the incarceration rate increased with one woman admitted to prison for every 31 arrests. Table 13.1 displays this trend.

Another way to look at this data is to compare the percentage change in arrests across these offense categories to the percentage change in prison admissions, as shown in Table 13.2. The reason for this population increase differs between women and men. Although Bureau of Justice Statistics data (Harrison & Beck, 2003) indicate that violent offenses are the major factor in the growth of the male prison population, this is not the case for women. For women, drug offenses represent the largest source of growth. Almost 50 percent of male prisoners are locked up for a crime of violence, with 18 percent doing time for property offenses, 19 percent for drug crimes, and 11 percent for public order offenses.

Women, in marked contrast, have a much more even distribution across the three major offenses categories: 32 percent of incarcerated females are serving time for a violent offense; 26 percent for property offenses; 30 percent for drug crimes, with the remaining 12 percent convicted of public order and other crimes (Harrison & Beck, 2003). The BJS data shows that

TABLE 13.1 *Rate of Women Imprisoned*

| Offense Category | Number Imprisoned for Every 1,000 Female Arrests | | |
	1986	2000	Percent Increase
Drugs	29	91	+214
Property	13	33	+154
Violent	26	31	+19
Public Order	2	7	+250

Source: Women's Prison Association (2004). Retrieved on September 4, 2004 from www.wpaonline.org.

female violent offenders are more likely to know their victims and less likely to cause serious physical harm to them (Greenfield & Snell, 1999). As Table 13.3 shows, the majority of offenses committed by women in prisons are nonviolent drug and property crimes.

Nationally, women make up about 7 percent of the U.S. prison population. For that small number of women, the pathways to prison are shaped by structural conditions and personal experiences related to gender as well as race and class. The majority of women who wind up in prison struggle in a world structured by poverty and experience racial and gender discrimination within a patriarchical society. Like incarcerated men, most women in prison are poor, with little stake in the work or school worlds.

However, several measures demonstrate that imprisoned women are more marginalized from conventional institutions than their male counterparts. They are less likely than male offenders to be employed at arrest or to be looking for work when unemployed, less likely to be married, and more likely to come from single-parent families. Women are also more likely to come from families where parents used drugs and alcohol (Belknap, 2001; Chesney-Lind & Palmore, 2004; Bloom, Owen, & Covington, 2003; Pollock, 2002).

These gendered offense patterns illustrate the differential impact of drug policy on women. Several sources show that this increase in prison population cannot be explained by increasing crime rates, as illustrated in Table 13.2. According to the Bureau of Justice Statistics (Greenfield & Snell, 1999), the crime rate for women has risen only about 32 percent in the last two decades, while the imprisonment rate has increased 159 percent. Steffensmeier

TABLE 13.2 *Percentage Change in Arrests & Prison Admissions 1986–2000*

Offense Category	Change in Arrests	Change in Prison Admissions	Increase after 1993
Drugs	+63%	+403%	20%
Property	–23%	+ 89%	20%
Violent	+75%	+110%	32%
Public Order	–18%	+235%	53%

Source: Women's Prison Association (2004). Retrieved on September 4, 2004 from www.wpaonline.org.

TABLE 13.3   *Offenses of Women in Prison 2001 Data*

Offense	Number	Percent
Violent	24,400	32
Property	20,000	26
Drug	23,200	30
Public Order	8,300	10
Other	400	2
Total	**76,200**	**100**

Source: Derived from Harrison & Beck (2003), p.10.

and Allan (1998, p. 11) confirm that an increase in crime and arrest rates cannot alone account for the explosion in the female prison population. The root of female crime, they argue, is found in the criminalization of drug use and "female inequality and economic vulnerability that shape most female offending patterns."

According to Bloom, Owen, and Covington (2003, p. 4), additional offense data indicate the following:

1. Women in prison are less likely than men to have long criminal histories. Approximately 51 percent of incarcerated women have one or no prior offenses. Among males, only 39 percent have one or no prior offenses.
2. The per capita rate of murder committed by women in 1998 was the lowest recorded since 1976; the rate of murder by women has been declining since 1980.
3. Three of four women offenders serving time for a violent offense committed simple assault.
4. An estimated 62 percent of women offenders serving time for a violent offense had a prior relationship with the victim as an intimate, relative, or acquaintance; of the 60,000 murders committed by women between 1976 and 1997, more than 60 percent were against an intimate or family member.

Pathways to Imprisonment: A Contextual Approach

A contextual approach examines the realities of women's lives as embedded in structural and institutional frames. On an institutional level, these frames include the pervasive effects of gender and such accompanying concepts as patriarchy, sexism, and discrimination on the lives of women. Investigations of the corresponding effects of family, school, and work on women are also critical to understanding their imprisonment (Owen, 1998). At the individual level, these influences play out in terms of behavior in conflict with the law. These behaviors are illuminated in the types of crimes women commit, the development of female criminal identities, the gendered harm of imprisonment, and their lives upon release. Gender shapes the context of women's imprisonment, subjecting them to punishment and social control differently than men, incommensurate to the level of harm caused by their criminal behavior.

Bloom, Owen, and Covington (2003) describe the ways in which women's imprisonment differs from that of men:

- Levels of violence and threats to community safety in their offense patterns.
- Responsibilities for children and other family members.
- Relationships with staff and other offenders.
- Vulnerability to staff misconduct and revictimization.
- Differences in programming and service needs while under supervision and in custody, especially in health and mental health, substance abuse, recovery from trauma, and economic/vocational skills.
- Differences in reentry and community integration.

The pathway perspective draws on multiple empirical methods and multidisciplinary conceptual frameworks in explaining female criminality (Belknap, 2001; Bloom, Owen, & Covington, 2003). This view suggests that criminality and experiences with the prison system have both structural and personal components. On a macro level, social control—both informal and formal—is delivered to women under different rationalizations and in different ways. On a micro level, the experience of imprisoned women prior to imprisonment, during incarceration and upon release, varies widely from that of men.

Class and race combine with gender to create what Bloom (1996) calls "triple jeopardy" for women enmeshed in the prison system. Combining macro- and micro-level analysis provides attention to personal experience within the context of material and social conditions. Another point of investigation includes the effects of criminal justice processing, such as labeling and gender discrimination within the system, and the ways in which girls and women react to this processing. A theory of "multiple marginalization" combines descriptions of personal experience and structural effects in explaining women's pathways to imprisonment (Owen, 1998).

Women and men embark on the path to criminality and subsequent incarceration in ways quite different from male offenders (Bloom, Owen, & Covington, 2003). This evidence centers on several gender-based interrelationships: violence and trauma, substance abuse, and economic marginalization.

Violence and Trauma

Girls and women are subjected to a greater degree of personal violence and consequent trauma than their male counterparts (Harlow, 1999). Although the level of personal violence in the lives of boys and young men has likely been underreported, women currently report violence many times the rate of males. These experiences with intimate violence create pathways to prison in two ways: First, trauma is typically untreated and is tied to initial entry into substance abuse—the primary reason for increasing female imprisonment. Second, repeated victimization in the lives of women can lead to defensive violence and other criminal behavior (Belknap, 2001; Bloom, Owen, & Covington, 2003; Browne, Miller, & Maguin, 1999; Owen, 1998; Pollock, 1998). Snell and Greenfield (1999) also find a correlation between victimization and future offenses. Women convicted of violent offenses were more likely to have had serious personal violence committed against them. Widom (2000, 1995) and Richie (1996) also found this connection.

Substance Abuse

For women, substance abuse and addiction are highly correlated with criminal behavior (Bloom, Owen, & Covington, 2003; Merlo, 1995; Pollock, 2002). The Center for Substance Abuse Treatment (CSAT, 1997) estimates that approximately 80 percent of women in state prisons have substance abuse problems (Center for Substance Abuse Treatment [CSAT], 1997). The Bureau of Justice Statistics (BJS) (Greenfield & Snell, 1999) has found that that about 50 percent of female offenders in state prisons had been using alcohol, drugs, or both at the time of their offense, with nearly one in three reporting that they committed their offenses in order to obtain money to support a drug habit. About half describe themselves as daily users. For many traumatized women, drug and alcohol use becomes a psychological survival strategy, further reducing their options and life chances.

Economic Marginalization

Like men, women in prison are among the poorest citizens in the United States. This reflects the fact that, in the general population, men continue to out-earn women across almost every occupational category. Among imprisoned populations, this gender gap in employment income is even wider: BJS (Greenfield & Snell, 1999) found that while about 60 percent of men reported working prior to their imprisonment, only 40 percent of the women were similarly employed. Of the women that worked, two-thirds reported that they had never made more than $6.50 an hour.

In a 1995 study of women in California prisons, Owen and Bloom (1995) found that 37 percent of the sample reported working at a legitimate job. Twenty-two percent had been on some kind of public support, 16 percent had made money from drug dealing, and 15 percent had been involved in prostitution, shoplifting, or other illegal activities. About half of the women in the representative sample had never worked, and more than half had been unemployed in the year before this prison term. One-third of the women indicated that their ongoing substance abuse problems had prohibited them from working; others said they made more money from illegal pursuits; and about 12 percent said child care and other responsibilities had kept them at home. Fewer than 10 percent said that their partners or families had provided them with support. These data show that women have been marginalized from the conventional world of work.

These pathways are also mediated by race and ethnicity. In addition to gender differences between male and female crime, women's arrest and incarceration rates vary by race and ethnicity. Minority women are disproportionately represented in the U.S. prison population, and the percentage of incarcerated African American women continues to grow. In 1991, this group made up about 40 percent of the female prison population; by 1995, this population had grown to 48 percent. The percentage of Hispanic and Latina women is also growing but at a somewhat slower rate. In 2002, the number of sentenced women per 100,000 residents varied significantly across race and ethnicity. For all women, 61 per 100,000 were sentenced prisoners: for white women, the proportion was 35 per 100,000; for black women, 191 per 100,000, and for Hispanic women, 80 per 100,000 residents (Harrison & Beck, 2003).

Origins of the Prison

In Western societies, the prison evolved as the primary mechanism for controlling threats to the social and economic order. While there is some overlap in the history of prisons for men and women, it is clear that the development of women's prisons were based on the need of men to control behavior that challenged the gender order rather than social or economic institutions.

Throughout history, the female criminal has been cast as "double-deviant"; first, because she violated the criminal or moral law and, second, perhaps more importantly, because she has violated the narrow strictures of the female role within society (see Belknap, 2001, and Pollock, 2002, for further discussion). In almost every Western society, women have been cast as second-class citizens, subservient to the will and wishes of men. Women who violated the law also violated their subservient position and were seen as morally suspect as well as criminal.

As a precursor to the contemporary prison, the workhouse, in its various forms, was used to confine a range of less serious offenders, including penniless women and prostitutes. Fathers or husbands who wanted to punish unruly, disobedient, or unchaste women could send them to bridewells, poorhouses, or nunneries.

In the American colonies, incarceration was relatively uncommon. Crimes committed by women were fewer and less serious than those committed by men, but punishments for women were tied to their status in society. Public humiliations, such as the ducking stool and the "Scarlet Letter," were delivered to women behaving outside the traditional gender role expectations or engaging in sexual practices that are tolerated for men.

America developed the penitentiary system in the 1830s. Women, however, were excluded from imprisonment in the emerging penitentiary with its promise of reformation because "the common conception was that a criminal woman was beyond redemption" (Pollock 2002, p. 9). By 1850, only about 4 percent of the U.S. prison population was women, but examples of the harm they experienced because they were women are found in the historical record (Freedman, 1981; Rafter, 1985). Johnson (1997, p. 32) writes that women and minorities were "barely considered human," and thus not fit candidates for the penitentiary's regime. The harsh treatment of women was justified by the argument that "women convicts were more depraved than men, since having been born pure, they had fallen further than their male counterparts in crime" (Freedman, 1981, p. 78).

In the New World, prisons for women were dirty, crowded, unsupervised, and without adequate material provisions (Pollock, 2002). Typically, women were held in local jails rather than a centralized prison. Women were often locked away in rooms above the guardhouse or mess hall. Left without consistent supervision, women were vulnerable to attacks by one another and had fewer opportunities to work and exercise. Male staff also sexually and physically abused women in these early prisons. Freedman (1981, p. 60) states that women were subjected to the "worst debasement at the hands of the prison officials and guards" and that sadistic beatings, rape, and illegitimate births combined to make the prison experience even more terrifying. Matrons were eventually hired to supervise women prisoners and protect them from the sexual advances of the male staff and prisoners. Pollock (2002) describes research that shows matrons were paid less than their male coworkers, and those working in institutions for white women were paid more than those employed in facilities housing African American women.

The Reformatory

By the mid-nineteenth century, prisons for women then diverged into two directions, custodial institutions and the reformatory (Rafter, 1985). The custodial model was the traditional prison, adopting the retributive purpose, high-security architecture, male-dominated authority and harsh discipline of the male prison (Rafter, 1985). While some women—typically young, white and often middle-class—were locked up in the new reformatory, the lower class and women of color remained confined to the male prison. In the 1870s, the reformatory movement led to the development of separate women's prisons. These unwalled reformatories were built on large parcels of land, usually in a rural area with small cottages representing the ideal of domesticity, replacing the cell block structure found in the male prisons built at that time. The reformatory was a new form of punishment designed specifically to house women in entirely separate institutions, with female matrons and programs planned to reform women by promoting appropriate gender roles. Training in cooking, sewing, laundry, and other domestic arts were designed to return the women prisoner to free society as either a well-trained wife or domestic servant.

Rafter (1985) offers evidence that minority women were more likely to be sent to the more brutal custodial prison, whereas white women, particularly young, white women who had committed minor offenses, were more likely to be seen as ideal candidates for redemption in the reformatory. Alderson Federal Prison in West Virginia and the California Institute for Women represent the reformatory model and were still in use at the end of the 1990s. After the 1930s, Rafter suggests that the custodial and reform institutions merged, combining elements of their two styles with differing results throughout the United States.

By the 1940s and 1950s, a new philosophy of punishment, based on a medical model of treatment, emerged in the United States. Called "correctional institutions," these prisons moved away from the harsh discipline and work orientation of the custodial prison and instead attempted to introduce treatment to a newly defined inmate—rather than convict—population (Johnson, 2002). "Correctional officers" replaced prison guards, and women as well as men were introduced to a treatment regime that attempted to diagnose, classify, and treat the inmate prior to release.

The Contemporary Prison

Beginning in the late 1970s, prison systems began to return to a custodial or "warehouse" model, with few prisons offering rehabilitative programs. This trend continues. By the 1980s, the number of women in prison began to increase exponentially, due primarily to enhanced and punitive sanctions against drug offenders. Some states began to build new prisons for women, with California and other states building large institutions, using designs based on male prisons.

While many of the reformatory prisons remain in use, the majority of modern prisons for women are now run as custodial, rather than rehabilitative, institutions. These "new generation" prisons typically have two types of housing: Special housing units intended to hold disciplinary problems, and the much larger general population units made up of either dormitory housing or separate rooms holding two to eight women for the vast majority of prisoners. Most states have a relatively small number of prisons for women and thus house female prisoners at one or two geographically isolated prisons. California, Texas, Illinois, Florida, and the Federal Bureau of Prisons are exceptions with multiple facilities.

In 2002, over one-third of all women prisoners were held in the three largest jurisdictions, Texas (13,051), the federal system (11,234), and California (10,050). At year end 2002, one in every 1,656 women and one in every 110 men were incarcerated in a state or federal prison (Harrison & Beck, 2003, p. 5).

Throughout the country, housed far from home, friends, and family, female prisoners are distant from services more available in urban communities. Some states with small female prison populations ship their female prisoners to other states for a price. Hawaii is the most extreme example with its policy of shipping women from its institutions to Oklahoma. In contrast, men typically are transferred to other state or federal custody for security reasons. While male prisoners are assigned to the more numerous facilities with a wider range of security levels, the majority of women in the United States are confined to prisons that encompass all classification and security levels in one facility. Today, the "tyranny of the numbers" of male prisoners disadvantages women in terms of policy, programs, and services within the contemporary prison (Owen, 2003).

Programming

For both women and men, the contemporary prison has introduced a range of programming theoretically designed to address the individual-level problems that bring both women and men into prison. While there is significant disagreement about the efficacy of these programs in all prisons, the problems in providing effective programs for women also have gendered elements. Prison systems in the United States have been sued by women prisoners and their legal advocates about the system's failure to provide equal programming in female institutions. Litigation since the 1980s has established that female prisoners have equal rights when it comes to programming, although many jurisdictions have been unable to provide comparable programming for both women and men (Raeder, 2003).

Glover v. Johnson (1979), one of the most famous cases, was adjudicated in Michigan, where women sued under the equal protection clause of the Fourteenth Amendment (Pollock, 2002). In this case, the comparison between the female and male programs showed a dramatic difference across several areas. Male prisoners had access to twenty-two vocational programs, where women had access to three. Jobs in the women's facilities were fewer in number, lower-paying, and sex-stereotyped. In the same job classification, women were paid less than their male counterparts. Men had access to college classes at the bachelor level; women had only high school courses. Prisons for men had fully equipped libraries while the institutions for women did not. Perhaps most unfair, women did not have any opportunity to earn earlier release through good time as did the men. The Court found in favor of the female prisoners and ordered the state to improve and increase their programming for women and instituted heavy fines for these discriminatory practices over the twenty-year monitoring period. Other state systems have also been found to provide diminished programming for women in terms of visits, work release, and recreational programs (Pollock, 2002).

Another gendered element in programming involves the provision of gender-responsive, or women-centered, services. The National Institute of Corrections (Bloom, Owen, & Covington, 2003) report builds on prior work by Bloom and Covington in identifying the ways in which programs and policies designed for male offenders are inappropriate and often damaging for female prisoners. One specific example lies in current research on in-prison drug programming for women. Although female offenders are very likely to have an extensive history of drug and alcohol use, a relatively small percentage of women receive any treatment within the justice system (Kassebaum, 1999). A large body of empirical research agrees that treatment within criminal justice systems is less intense, modeled after programs for men and thus does not meet the special needs of women (Kassebaum, 1999; Pollock, 1998). Prison drug treatment has been designed for men by men, with provision of services to females as an after-thought. Many prison drug programs often use curricula designed for men (with pictures of men and use of male pronouns), do not provide treatment staff with women-specific information, and continue to use confrontational approaches that do not work well with women (Owen, in progress).

Issues Affecting Women in Prison

The experience of imprisonment does considerable harm to female and male prisoners in obvious and subtle ways, both during incarceration and upon release. Some of this harm is directly related to the intended "pains" that are inherent in imprisonment. Much of the harm, however, stems from other features of imprisonment that do not overtly intend harm but have long-term consequences on their lives over time (Irwin & Owen, forthcoming). Women in prisons face specific pains and deprivations arising from their imprisonment. Pollock (1998, 2002) has described the range of pains and deprivations experienced by female prisoners and their consequences. She argues that stress shapes the daily life of female inmates and has three primary sources: arbitrary rule enforcement; assaults on self-respect that are endemic to prison life; and the loss of children. This section discusses issues that affect women during their incarceration.

Separation from Children.   Female prisoners react differently than men to the separation from children and significant others. Most research describes the importance of family, particularly children, in the lives of imprisoned women (Bloom, Owen, & Covington, 2003; Pollock, 2002). National surveys of women prisoners find that three-fourths were mothers, with two-thirds having children who were under the age of 18 (Greenfield & Snell, 1999). For mothers, separation from their children is the most painful aspect of incarceration. Bloom and Chesney-Lind (2000) state that distance between the prison and the children's homes, lack of transportation, and very limited economic resources compromise a female prisoner's ability to maintain these relationships.

Slightly over half of the women responding to Bloom and Steinhart's 1993 survey of imprisoned mothers reported never receiving visits from their children. Lord (1995, p. 266), a prison warden in New York, has stated that while men in prison "do their own time," women "remain interwoven in the lives of significant others, primarily their children and their own mothers. . . ." Connections to the free world can make it much harder to "do time," particularly for those with a long time to serve. A female prisoner points out:

> You cannot do your time in here and out on the streets at the same time. That makes you do hard time. You just have to block that out of your mind. You can't think about what is going on out there and try to do your five, ten (years) or whatever in here. You will just drive yourself crazy. ("Divine," quoted by Owen, 1998, p. 129)

Pregnant Women.   Acoca (1998) argues that pregnancy during incarceration must be understood as a high-risk situation, both medically and psychologically, for inmate mothers and their children. She notes that deficiencies in the correctional response to the needs of pregnant inmates include lack of prenatal and postnatal care, little education regarding childbirth and parenting, and inadequate preparation for separation from the infant after delivery.

Legal Services for Prisoners with Children (LSPC, 2004) has reviewed the treatment of pregnant women in prison. Their investigation in California has uncovered cases where obvious danger signs such as high blood pressure, no fetal heartbeat, and vaginal bleeding have been ignored. This has led directly to late-term miscarriages, premature deliveries, still births, and sick infants. One of the most troubling aspects of in-prison pregnancies involves shackling pregnant women. Shackling of all pregnant prisoners appears to be the policy in almost all state and federal prisons. This restraint policy has many negative effects on the delivery, including hemorrhage or decrease in fetal heart rate.

Mental Heath.   Mental health disorders appear to be more prevalent for female prisoners. While few studies accurately assess the prevalence and incidence of these conditions, estimates suggest that 25 percent to over 60 percent of the female prison population require mental health services (Acoca, 1998; Leonard, 2002; Singer et al., 1995). The violent and traumatic experiences of female prisoners contribute to increased levels of mental health disorders. Prison policies and everyday operational practices have also been shown to aggravate posttraumatic stress disorders in female prisoners (Bloom, Owen, & Covington, 2003). Heavy medication is often used to control the behavior of women rather than treating mental health problems with corresponding therapy (Leonard, 2002).

More so than males, female inmates are often dually diagnosed, experiencing both substance abuse and mental health problems. Singer et al. (1995) report that incarcerated women have had experience with both the criminal justice and mental health systems. Teplin, Abraham, and McClelland (1996) found that over 60 percent of female jail inmates had symptoms of drug abuse, over 30 percent had signs of alcohol dependence, and one-third had posttraumatic stress disorder. Women's prisons are ill-prepared to deal with these complex mental health needs.

Rule Enforcement.   Although prisons for men typically hold a much greater percentage of violent offenders and have a higher rate of in-prison violence, women tend to receive disciplinary infractions at a greater rate than men. In her comparative study of Texas prisons, McClellan (1994) found that women were cited more frequently and punished more severely than men. The infractions committed by the women in McClellan's Texas sample were overwhelmingly petty and, she suggests, were perhaps a result of a philosophy of rigid and formalistic rule compliance expected of the women but not of the men. The most common infractions among the women were "violation of a written or posted rule" and "refusing to obey an order." She also found that women were more strictly supervised than men and cited for behavior that would be overlooked in an institution for men. Pollock (2002) also suggests that reasons for this disparate practice can be found in staff expectations and differential responses to the behavior of women and men. The patriarchal patterns of social control that propel women into the prison may also be responsible for the differential rule enforcement patterns between male and female institutions.

Physical and Psychological Safety.   Compared to prisons for men, almost all women's prisons are physically safer. Physical violence between female prisoners is infrequent, with serious assaults involving weapons even less frequent. Verbal threats and loud arguments are more typical expressions of conflict. Physical fights do occur but typically occur in the context of a personal relationship or, less often, as a result of a drug deal or other material conflict. Organized conflicts related to gangs and ethnic strife are extremely rare (Owen, 1998). Women strike or scratch each other but usually do not inflict serious injury. Occasionally, women will resort to a "lock in a sock" as an improvised weapon. The extremely rare stabbing may occur with a pair of scissors or a tool in a spontaneous fight. Riots and other collective disturbances are also atypical.

Female prisoners, like women in the free community, are at a much greater risk of violence and sexual assault from males. Multiple reports of staff sexual misconduct have been released from Human Rights Watch Women's Rights Project (1996), Amnesty International (1999), and other women's rights advocates (Moss, 1999; Smith, 2001). For example, the Human Rights Watch investigators identified four specific issues: (1) the inability to escape one's abuser, (2) ineffectual or nonexistent investigative and grievance procedures, (3) lack of employee accountability (either criminally or administratively), and (4) little or no public concern. They bluntly state "Our findings indicate that being a woman in U.S. state prisons can be a terrifying experience" (Human Rights Watch Women's Rights Project, 1996, p. 1). As Bloom and Chesney-Lind (2000) note, the sexual victimization of female prisoners is difficult to uncover due to inadequate protection of women who file complaints and an occupational subculture that discourages complete investigation of these allegations. Additionally, they suggest, the public stereotype of women as "bad girls" compromises the legitimacy of their claims. While these issues affect most women while incarcerated, perhaps the greatest harm of imprisonment is its effect on their post-release life chances.

Reentry and the Gendered Problems of Parole

Both women and men face overwhelming odds in reintegrating into the free community. Bloom, Owen, and Covington (2003) argue that these challenges—complying with conditions of supervised release, achieving financial stability, accessing health care and housing, and attempting to reunite with their families—are complicated by gender. Reunification with children is one example of these gendered problems, as are their requirements for safe housing, economic support, medical services, and other needs including the ability to take care of their children.

The majority of incarcerated mothers expect to take responsibility for their children once they are released and rarely receive any financial or emotional support from the children's fathers. Families who have taken care of the children of imprisoned women often expect the paroled woman to take custody of her children immediately following release. For those without formal custody of their children, reunification with children is an important but often elusive goal of released mothers. If a child has been placed in foster care or state custody while the mother has been incarcerated, it is especially difficult for the released mother to demonstrate to state agencies that she is able to take care of and provide for her child adequately. Many states now require that a paroled offender (female or male) repay the state for any child-related welfare or foster care expenses incurred during incarceration (Bloom, Owen, & Covington, 2003).

The Experience of Parole for Women

Eaton (1993, p. 54) describes the disorganization of the self that occurs during the parole period. In her study of women in the United Kingdom, she states that imprisoned women return to society "disoriented and disempowered." Eaton continues by saying that the woman is expected to be effective in a world from which she has been estranged.

Two current studies examine the experience of parole for women. Brown (2003) investigates the role of motherhood in the parole process in her sensitive description of parole in Hawaii. O'Brien (2001) examines the transition from prison into the free world through case studies of eighteen women returning to the community. Housing is a central problem for both female and male offenders. O'Brien (2001, p. 25) suggests, however, that establishing a home, "with all its concrete and metaphorical possibilities provided the foundation for other experiences of 'making it' after being released from prison." O'Brien (2001, p. 64) describes the way women create a web of social relationships as an "enabling environmental niche" that provides both material and psychological support for women transitioning from prison.

Brown (2003, pp. 6–7) captures this point of view:

> Under the guise of rehabilitation, the state attempts to alter the consciousness of women in the hopes that these new selves will leave prison as rational, choice-making and responsible individuals. Penal authorities imagine that their reforms will make a difference in the lives women lead after prison and prevent further troubles with the law. However, I found that women's post-prison experiences look very much like their lives prior to prison in terms of their economic, social, and family troubles. Little attention is paid to the pathways women travel to prison, journeys that are shaped by abuse, poverty and the dynamics of gender inequality.

Parole and Motherhood

In Brown's (2003) view, the fact of motherhood becomes a potent nexus for the control of women. Law and other mechanisms of social control, such as prison and parole, continue to assert control over women and their bodies through their claim of legitimate concerns over the welfare of children. Women on parole are often caught in a net thrown by other social welfare agencies, such as welfare, child protective services, and the like, and are often required to attend multiple programs to address their problems. Referring to these programs as technologies of social control, Brown makes the argument made by most feminist criminologists: In defining criminality and subsequent parole performance in terms of individual choice and responsibility, these programs and services widen the net of social control over women while doing little to improve the actual life chances of the parolee.

For the women in Brown's study of parole, economic dependency and lack of other material options often forced them into living situations not of their choosing. Living with violent men, often in drug-involved or dangerous communities, and with dependent children, limit women's "choices" while on parole. As Brown (2003, p. 150) states:

> Financial instability precludes attaining secure housing and women's economic dependence increases the potential for living in an unstable familial environment. Economic dependency is a common reason that women remain in violent households or households plagued with family troubles and conflict.

O'Brien (2001) sees, too, that developing relationships and making connections on the outside often involves making a decision about continuing prior intimate relationships that may have been sexually exploitative and/or physically dangerous.

Recidivism

National data suggest that, for men, offense history appears to be the most significant predictor of recidivism among male parolees (Langan & Levin, 2002). While substance abuse and lack of employment appear to be the major factors in returning to prison for both women and men, O'Brien (2001) argues that family dynamics have a greater effect on recidivism for women than on men. The roles that families and intimate relationships play in parole performance, as found by both Brown (2003) and O'Brien (2001), are quite different for women and men. Domestic violence, partner drug use, and instability in housing for women and their children combine with the demands of child-related social services to create a more complicated parole period for women offenders.

Overall, the recidivism data seem to suggest that women recidivate (by all measures) at a lower rate than men, but those who do return to criminality and subsequent arrest and imprisonment tend to return more quickly (Langan & Levin, 2002; Owen & Deschenes, 2003). Owen and Deschenes (2003) conducted preliminary analysis of the 1994 BJS release cohort, concentrating on the female subsample. Women had served significantly less time than the men in this release cohort; with two-thirds of the women serving less than twelve months, compared to slightly more than half of the males. Overall, women served a mean time of thirteen months and men served a mean time of twenty months. In terms of recidivism, rates for women were significantly lower than for men across all four standard measures (rearrest, reconviction, return to prison for any reason, and return to prison with a new sentence). About 60 percent of the women in the sample were rearrested, while almost 70 percent of the men were. Forty percent of the women had a new conviction compared to 48 percent of the men. Correspondingly, about 30 percent of the women returned to prison (with only 18 percent the result of a new sentence), compared to 37 percent of the men (with 25 percent the result of a new sentence). For both men and women, those serving time for a property offense were much more likely to have a new arrest than those released in all other offense categories.

Policy Implications

Richie (2001, p. 386) highlights the public policy implications of the reentry process for imprisoned women in suggesting that community needs as well as individual needs should be addressed. She states:

> [Women] need families that are not divided by public policy, streets and homes that are safe from violence and abuse, and health and mental health services that are accessible. The challenges women face must be met with expanded opportunity and a more thoughtful criminal justice policy. This would require a plan for reinvestment in low-income communities in this country that centers around women's needs for safety and self-sufficiency.

Bloom, Owen, and Covington (2003) argue for a new vision for the criminal justice system: one that recognizes the behavioral and social differences between female and male offenders that have specific implications for gender-responsive policy and practice. Developing gender-responsive policies, practices, programs, and services target women's pathways to criminality by providing effective interventions that address the intersecting issues of substance abuse, trauma, mental health, and economic marginality. Gender-appropriate sanctions and interventions would recognize the low risk to public safety created by the typical offenses committed by female offenders. Bloom, Owen, and Covington (2003, p. 76) propose six guiding principles for gender-responsiveness in criminal justice (see Figure 13.1).

Conclusion

Women's pathways to prison must be understood within the context of their lives. This context is informed by the three central issues that shape their lives before imprisonment: multi-

FIGURE 13.1 *Gender-Responsive Principles*

1. Gender	Acknowledge that gender makes a difference.
2. Environment	Create an environment based on safety, respect, and dignity.
3. Relationships	Develop policies, practices, and programs that are relational and promote healthy connections to children, family, significant others, and the community.
4. Services and Supervision	Address the issues of substance abuse, trauma, and mental health through comprehensive, integrated, culturally relevant services and appropriate supervision.
5. Economic and Social Status	Improve women's economic/social conditions by developing their capacity to be self-sufficient.
6. Community	Establish a system of community supervision and reentry with comprehensive, collaborative services.

Source: Bloom, B., Owen, B., & Covington, S. (2003). *Gender-Responsive Strategies: Research, Practice, and Guiding Principles for Women Offenders.* Washington, DC: National Institute of Corrections.

plicity of abuse, disrupted family lives and personal relationships, and drug use. Given this background, spiraling marginality and subsequent criminality are common results (Owen, 1998). Combined with a public policy that criminalizes drug use and other survival criminal behavior, the outcome is ever-increasing rates of imprisonment for women.

The subordinate status of women in society also contributes to the imprisonment binge. Female criminality is based on the need for women, excluded from conventional institutions and subjected to the triple jeopardy of discrimination due to race, class, and gender, to survive conditions not of their own making (Chesney-Lind & Palmore, 2004; Owen, 1998; Pollock, 2002).

The story of women in prison reflects their status in society—a status that reflects embedded racism and sexism, devaluation of women and girls, and open tolerance of violence against women and girls in a male-dominated society. Women's prisons—perhaps even more so than men's prisons—have become places for people who have no standing in the conventional world.

The problems of women have become more criminalized as society ignores the context of women's lives. Instead, prison has become the unilateral response to social and political problems that shape the pathways to prison. Because many of these women are poor, from minority communities, and behave in ways outside middle-class sensibilities, prison has become the uniform response to problems created by inequality and gender discrimination. These issues are best addressed outside the punitive custodial environment. However, the upward spiral in the number of women in prison represents a serious failure of conventional society and public policy (Owen, 1999).

Under current policy, these complex problems are laid at the feet of the prison by a society unwilling or unable to confront the problems of women on the margin. Women confined in U.S. prisons are enmeshed in a criminal justice system that is ill-equipped and confused about handling their problems—the problems that brought them to prison and the problems they confront during their incarceration. The prison, with its emphasis on security and population management and its deemphasis on treatment and programs, is unable to respond to the real needs of women victimized by criminal justice and drug policy. Women in prison represent a very specific failure of conventional society—and public policy—to recognize the damage done to women through the oppression of patriarchy, economic marginalization, and the far reaching effects of such short-sighted and detrimental policies as the war on drugs and overreliance on incarceration as social control (Owen, 1999). The story of the women in prison, however, is not hopeless. Many women have survived circumstances far more damaging than a prison term and most will continue to survive in the face of insurmountable odds (Owen, 1998).

Review Questions

1. What does the author mean by stating that crime and social control are gendered? What evidence does she offer? What evidence counters this assertion?

2. This chapter argues that women have a different pathway to prison than men. Describe the nature of these differences in terms of life experiences and offense patterns.

3. According to Owen, the history of women's prisons has been shaped by gender. List at least three ways that gender and historical gender expectations influenced this development.

Discuss how this may be different in contemporary times.

4. A variety of issues affecting women in prison were described in this chapter. Which of these issues are unique to women and which have some implications for men as well? Which of these issues are an inevitable outcome of incarceration? Which issues could be addressed through changing the operations of prison?

5. All prisoners face significant challenges when released to the community. Why does the author suggest that women have different kinds of prob-

lems at release? What should be done to help women solve these problems when released from prison?

6. Six principles for gender-responsiveness conclude the chapter. Take each principle and discuss at least two ways these principles could be applied to the prison. How would the prison change if these principles were adopted?

7. Describe the typical female inmate. What do these characteristics tell us about female offenders?

Key Terms

Gender
Gender-responsiveness
Imprisonment binge
Triple jeopardy
Multiple marginality

War on drugs
Pathways
Arbitrary rule enforcement
New generation prisons

References

Acoca, L. (1998). Defusing the time bomb: Understanding and meeting the growing health care needs of incarcerated women in America. *Crime & Delinquency* 44 (1), 49–70.

Amnesty International. (1999). *Not part of my sentence: Violations of the human rights watch in custody.* New York: Amnesty International.

Belknap, J. (2001). *The invisible woman: Gender, crime, and justice.* Belmont, CA: Wadsworth.

Bloom, B. (1996). *Triple jeopardy: Race, class and gender as factors in women's imprisonment.* Doctoral dissertation in sociology, University of California.

Bloom, B., & Chesney-Lind, M. (2000). Women in prison: Vengeful equity. In R. Muraskin (Ed.), *It's a crime: Women and justice* (pp. 183–204). Upper Saddle River, NJ: Prentice-Hall.

Bloom, B., & Steinhart, D. (1993). *Why punish the children? A reappraisal of the children of incarcerated parents.* San Francisco CA: National Council on Crime and Delinquency.

Bloom, B., Chesney-Lind, M., & Owen, B. (1994). *Women in California prisons: Hidden victims of the war on drugs.* San Francisco, CA: Center on Juvenile and Criminal Justice.

Bloom, B., Owen, B., & Covington S. (2003). *Gender-responsive strategies: Research, practice, and guiding

principles for women offenders.* Washington DC: National Institute of Corrections.

Brown, M. (2003). *Motherhood on the margin: Rehabilitation and subjectivity among female parolees in Hawaii.* University of Hawaii, Manoa: Department of Sociology, Unpublished dissertation.

Browne, A., Miller, B., & Maguin, E. (1999). Prevalence and severity of lifetime physical and sexual victimization among incarcerated women. *International Journal of Law and Psychiatry* 22 (3–4), 301–322.

Bush-Baskette, S. (1999). The war on drugs: A war against women? In S. Cook & S. Davies (Eds.), *Harsh punishment: International experiences of women's imprisonment* (pp. 211–229). Boston: Northeastern University Press.

Center for Substance Abuse Treatment. (1997). *Practical approaches in the treatment of women who abuse alcohol and other drugs.* Rockville, MD: U.S. Department of Health and Human Services.

Chesney-Lind, M., & Palmore, L. (2004). *The female offender: Girls, women and crime.* Thousand Oaks, CA: Sage.

Eaton, M. (1993). *Women after prison.* Buckingham, UK: Open University Press.

Freedman, E. (1981). *Their sisters' keepers.* Ann Arbor: University of Michigan Press.

Greenfeld, L., & Snell, T. (1999). *Special report: Women offenders.* Washington, DC: U.S. Department of Justice.

Griggs, D. (2004). Unpublished paper submitted to Criminology 130, Department of criminology, California State University, Fresno.

Harlow, C. W. (1999). *Prior abuse reported by inmates and probationers.* Washington, DC: U.S. Department of Justice.

Harrison, P., & Beck, A. (2003). Prisoners in 2002. Washington, DC: U.S. Department of Justice.

Human Rights Watch Women's Rights Project. (1996). *All too familiar: Sexual abuse of women in U.S. state prisons.* New York: The Ford Foundation.

Irwin, J. (2004). *The warehouse prison: Disposal of the new dangerous class.* Los Angeles: Roxbury Press.

Irwin, J., & Owen, B. (forthcoming). Harm and the contemporary prison. In A. Liebling & S. Maruna (Eds.), *The effects of imprisonment.* Devon, UK: Willam Publishing.

Johnson, R. (2002). *Hard time: Understanding and reforming the prison.* Belmont, CA: Wadsworth.

Johnson, R. (1997). Race, gender and the American prisons: Historical observations. In J. Pollock (Ed.), *Prisons: Today and tomorrow* (pp. 26–32). Gaithersburg, MD: Aspen Press.

Kassebaum, P. (1999). *Substance abuse treatment for women offenders: Guide to promising practices.* Rockville, MD: U.S. Department of Health and Human Services.

Kurshan, N. (1992). Women and imprisonment in the United States. In W. Churchill & J. Vander Wall (Eds.), *Cages of steel* (pp. 331–358). Washington, DC: Maisonneuve Press.

Langan, P. A., & Levin, D. J. (2002). *Recidivism of prisoners released in 1994.* Washington, DC: U.S. Department of Justice.

Legal Services for Prisoners with Children. (2004). Retrieved March 3, 2004 from http://prisonerswithchildren.org/issues/health.htm.

Leonard, E. (2002). *Convicted survivors: The imprisonment of battered women who kill.* Albany, NY: State University of New York Press.

Lord, E. (1995). A prison superintendent's perspective on women in prison. *Prison Journal* 75 (2), 257–269.

Mauer, M., Potler, C., & Wolf, R. (1999). *Gender and justice: Women, drugs and sentencing policy.* Washington, DC: The Sentencing Project.

Merlo, A. V. (1995). Female criminality in the 1990s. In A. V. Merlo & J. M. Pollock (Eds.), *Women, law and social control* (pp 119–134). Boston: Allyn and Bacon.

McClellan, D. (1994). Disparity in the discipline of male and female inmates in Texas prisons. *Women and Criminal Justice* 5 (2), 71–97.

Moss, A. (1999). Sexual misconduct among staff and inmates. In P. Carlson & J. Garrett (Eds.), *Prison and jail administration: Practice and theory* (pp. 185–195). New York: Aspen Publishers.

O'Brien, P. (2001). *Making it in the "free world": Women's transition from prison.* Albany: State University Press of New York.

Owen, B. (2004). *Changing lives: A pathways perspective* In progress.

Owen, B., & Deschenes, E. P. (2003). *Gender and recidivism: A gendered review of the 1994 BJS recidivism data.* Paper presented to the American Society of Criminology, November 21. Denver, Colorado.

Owen, B. (2003). Differences with a distinction: Women offenders and criminal justice practice. In B. Bloom (Ed.), *Gendered justice: Addressing female offenders* (pp. 25–44). Durham, NC: Carolina Academic Press.

Owen, B. (1999). Women and imprisonment in the United States: The gendered consequences of the U.S. imprisonment binge. In S. Cook & S. Davies (Eds.), *Harsh punishments: International experiences of women's imprisonment* (pp. 81–98). Boston: Northeastern University Press.

Owen, B. (1998). *In the mix: Struggle and survival in a women's prison.* New York: State University of New York Press.

Owen, B., & Bloom, B. (1995). Profiling women prisoners: Findings from national survey and California sample. *The Prison Journal* 75 (2), 165–185.

Pollock, J. M. (2002). *Women, prison, and crime* (2nd ed.). Pacific Grove, CA: Brooks/Cole: Belknap.

Pollock, J. M. (1998). *Counseling women in prison.* Thousand Oaks, CA: Sage.

Pollock, J. M. (1999). *Criminal women.* Cincinnati, OH: Anderson Publishing.

Pollock, J. M. (1995). Gender, justice, and social control. In A. Merlo & J. Pollock (Eds.), *Women, law and social control* (pp. 3–35). Boston: Allyn and Bacon.

Rafter, N. (1985). *Partial justice: State prisons and their inmates, 1800–1935.* Boston: Northeastern University Press.

Raeder, M. (2003). Legal considerations with regard to women offenders. In B. Bloom, B. Owen, & S. Covington (Eds.), *Gender-responsive strategies: Research, practice, and guiding principles for women offenders* (pp. 107–130). Washington, DC: National Institute of Corrections.

Richie, B. (1996). *Compelled to crime: The gendered entrapment of battered black women.* New York: Routledge

Richie, B. (2001). Challenges incarcerated women face as

they return to their community: Findings from life history interviews. *Crime and Delinquency* 47 (3), 368–389.

Singer, M., Bussey, J., Song, L., & Lunghofer, L. (1995). The psychosocial issues of women serving time in jail. *Social Work* 40 (1), 103–114.

Smith, B.V. (2001). Sexual abuse against women in prison. *Criminal Justice* 16 (1), 30–38.

Steffensmeir, D., & Allan, E. (1998). The nature of female offending: Patterns and explanations. In R. Zupan (Ed.), *Female offenders: Critical perspectives and interventions* (pp. 5–30). Gaithersburg MD: Aspen Publishing.

Teplin, L., Abraham, K., & McClelland, G. (1996). Prevalence of psychiatric disorders among incarcerated women. *Archives of General Psychiatry* 53, 505–512.

Widom, C. (1995). *Victims of childhood sexual abuse— Later criminal consequences.* Research in Brief. Washington, DC: Office of Justice Programs, National Institute of Justice.

Widom, C. (2000). Childhood victimization: Early adversity, later psychopathology. *National Institute of Justice Journal* 242, 2–9.

Women's Prison Association. (2004). *Focus on women and justice: Trends in arrest and sentencing.* Accessed September 4, 2004 at www.wpaonline.org.

Cases Cited

Glover v. Johnson, 478 F.Supp. 1075 (E.D. Mich., 1979)

14

Still "The Best Place to Conquer Girls"*

Girls and the Juvenile Justice System

Meda Chesney-Lind and Katherine Irwin

*This phrase is taken from an inmate file by Rafter (1990, p. 169) in her review of the establishment of New York's Albion Reformatory.

While the stereotype of juvenile delinquency is generally that of a boy delinquent, the juvenile justice system actually has a long but largely unrecognized history of involvement in the policing of girls, particularly in the legal and judicial enforcement of traditional gender roles. Indeed, as the title to this chapter attests, the focus on controlling girls' and women's sexuality was at the center rather than at the periphery of the early history of the juvenile justice system (Rafter, 1990). By the middle of that last century, the chief vehicle for that gendered control was "status offenses" (noncriminal offenses for which only youth could be arrested such as truancy, running away from home, and being "incorrigible") (Chesney-Lind & Shelden, 2004). Because these offenses also involved an essentially judicial system in the moral behavior of youth, they had also become controversial by that time.

Thirty years have now passed since the passage of the landmark Juvenile Justice and Delinquency Prevention Act (JJDPA of 1974). This legislation focused national attention on the treatment of status offenders. In addition, over a decade has passed since the 1992 reauthorization of this same Act; a reauthorization that specifically called for more equitable treatment of girls in the juvenile justice system. For both these reasons, it might well be time to take stock of progress made. Is the juvenile justice system now dispensing justice to girls or is it still haunted by its history of differential and unequal treatment?

A Century of Girls' Justice

In 1974, when the original JJDPA was passed, reformers concerned about judicial abuse of the status offense category by juvenile courts were applying considerable pressure on Congress. Interestingly, although generally concerned about the legal treatment of status offenders, reformers were fairly silent on the status of girls in the system. Based largely on broad constitutional concerns about institutionalization for noncriminal statuses (like mental illness and vagrancy) common during the era, this federal legislation required that states receiving federal delinquency prevention money begin to divert and deinstitutionalize their status offenders. Despite erratic enforcement of this provision and considerable resistance from juvenile court judges, it initially appeared that girls were the clear beneficiaries of the reform. Incarceration of young women in training schools and detention centers across the country fell dramatically in the decades since the JJDPA of 1974, in distinct contrast to patterns found early in the century.

Through the first half of the last century, the juvenile justice system incarcerated increasing numbers of girls. Girls' share of the population in juvenile correctional facilities (both public and private) increased from 19 percent in 1880 to 28 percent in 1923. By 1950, girls had climbed to 34 percent of the total population of youth in custody and in 1960 they were still 27 percent of those in correctional facilities. By 1980, the impact of the JJDPA was clear, and girls had dropped back down to only 19 percent of those in any type of correctional facility (Calahan, 1986).

However, while the impact of deinstitutionalization was gendered in ways that arguably benefited girls, at the time Congress passed the Act, programs for girls in general (and female delinquents in particular) were an extremely low priority. For example, a report completed in 1975 by the Law Enforcement Assistance Administration revealed that only 5 percent of federally funded juvenile delinquency projects were specifically directed at girls, and that only 6 percent of all local monies for juvenile justice were spent on girls (Female Offender Resource Center, 1977, p. 34). This despite the fact that girls were, at the time of the passage of the JJDPA of 1974, a clear majority of those in institutions for status offenses. One study in Delaware done at the time the law was enacted found that first-time female status offenders were more harshly sanctioned (as measured by the decision to institutionalize) than males charged with felonies; for repeat status offenders, the pattern was even starker: Female status offenders were six times more likely than male status offenders to be institutionalized (Datesman & Scarpitti, 1977, p. 70).

Since virtually no programs targeted them and their needs, girls with a history of family dysfunction, physical and sexual abuse, and running away returned to the sometime violent and predatory streets often to be victimized. The public, led by juvenile court judges, pointed to this pattern and clamored for a return to the time-honored means of protecting female status offenders—incarceration (see Chesney-Lind & Shelden, 2004, for a detailed review of this history).

Crucial ground was lost during the Reagan years, including the passage of legislation on "missing and exploited youth" as well as changes to the JJDPA that permitted the incarceration of status offenders in violation of a "valid court order" (Chesney-Lind & Shelden, 2004, p. 177). Years later, it would be revealed that the national hysteria about missing and abducted children was, essentially, a moral panic fueled by extensive media coverage of a few high-profile and highly unusual child abductions. The vast majority of "missing" or "abducted" children, it turned out, were actually children caught in custody battles after contentious divorces or runaway youth (Joe, Laidler, & Chesney-Lind, 1996). However, the laws passed during that period did erode the gains of the deinstitutionalization movement by enhancing the abilities of law enforcement and others to track and hold missing children and publish their pictures so as to "reunite" them with their parents (Joe, Laidler, & Chesney-Lind, 1996).

The tide turned briefly in girls' favor when the 1992 Reauthorization of the JJDPA was passed. This reauthorization was noteworthy precisely because it provided a forum for practitioners, activists, and scholars, all of whom voiced concerns about the deplorable options for and treatment of girls (see Chesney-Lind & Shelden, 2004, for details of these hearings).

A hearing held during the reauthorization of the Act provided an important focus on the issues of gender bias that had long haunted the courts' treatment of and programs for girls, and at that hearing, perhaps for the first time, academics and practitioners who had worked with girls in the juvenile justice system had an opportunity to be heard. As a result of this historic hearing, when the reauthorization was passed, the legislation funded states to begin their own needs assessments for girls in their systems. Specifically, the 1992 Reauthorization of the JJDPA required that each state should:

1. Assess existing programs for delinquent girls and determine the needs for additional programming.
2. Develop a plan for providing gender-specific services to girls.
3. Provide assurance that all youth were treated equitably, regardless of their sex, race, family income, and mental, physical, and emotional abilities.

    Through the "Challenge E" section of this Act, over twenty-five states across the United States applied for and received funding to address these goals. (Belknap, Dunn, & Holsinger, 1997)

The popular "challenge grant" activity created and supported initiatives that had already begun in certain states and rapidly spread to others. While there was optimism that the passage of these new requirements would give birth to a new national focus on girls, the results have been somewhat uneven to date. As an example, the JJDPA required states receiving federal money "to analyze current needs and services for girls and to present a plan for meeting girls' needs" in their State Plans. Yet, a review of plans completed in 2002 by the Children's Defense Fund (CDF) and Girls, Inc. concluded:

> many states had not taken significant steps toward implementing this framework. An overview of current state approaches finds that (1) a significant percentage of states acknowledge the need for gender-specific services; and (2) the majority of current state plans are lacking and inappropriate pertaining to gender issues. (Children's Defense Fund & Girls Inc., 2002, p. 3)

Beyond this, federal efforts to fund grants on girls' issues (both research and practitioner oriented) were initially issued by the Clinton Administration and subsequently cancelled by the Bush Administration on the heels of the September 11th attacks (Ray, 2002). A scaled-back version of the initiative was issued by the Bush Administration in 2003, and while applications were due in September 2003, no one has yet heard about funding.

Research and Girls in the System

A federal focus on girls' issues and programs is clearly long overdue. One of the chief concerns raised at the time of the 1992 legislation was the general lack of information, research, and theories available about the causes and correlates of girls' offending that, in turn, left girls with a set of programs and interventions that were, at best, sorely lacking and, at worst, damaging and counterproductive. Commenting on the state of the field at the time the states were beginning their work, Reitsma-Street and Offord (1991, p. 12) argued that there existed "a collection of policies and services for female offenders . . . propelled, as well as legitimated, by truncated theories and incorrect assumptions." While some programs were based on incomplete theories, others were just plain inappropriate. For example, some services did nothing more than reinforce derogatory and limiting gender stereotypes (like modeling and make-up classes) (Gelsthorpe, 1989; Kempf-Leonard & Sample, 2000; Kersten, 1989; Smart, 1976).

Even more problematic than enacting policies based on faulty information and archaic assumptions, a common practice was to fit girls into programs designed for boys. The philosophy was that if it worked for boys then it might work for girls too. More often than not, these programs, especially the sports activities, were considerably limited compared to what boys received (Kersten, 1989; Mann, 1984). Marian Daniel, the visionary practitioner who started Maryland's female-only probation services unit, put it more bluntly: "For years people have assumed that all you have to do to make a program designed for boys work for girls is to paint the walls pink and take out the urinals" (Chesney-Lind, 2000).

Indeed, emerging research has consistently found that girls confront different risk factors or challenges than boys. Summarizing U.S. and Canadian research, Corrado, Odgers, and Cohen (2000) argued that delinquent girls have high rates of physical and sexual victimization, drug addiction, poor academic achievement, and family conflict and abuse. In addition, studies conducted of runaway youth reveal high rates of sexual and physical abuse among girls, often higher rates than what is found among runaway boys. In a Toronto runaway shelter study, for example, 73 percent of girls and 38 percent of boys reported a history of sexual abuse. Sexual victimization among girls predicted higher rates of drug abuse, petty theft, and prostitution. Interestingly, the same correlation was not found for boys (McCormack, Janus, & Burgess, 1986). A Seattle study of 372 homeless and runaway youth pointed to a similar pattern. In this study, 30 percent of girls and 15 percent of boys reported sexual victimization. In addition, girls were significantly more likely than boys to report being victimized in their homes and on the street after running away (Tyler, Hoyt, Whitbeck, & Cauce, 2001).

The same trends seem to exist for institutionalized girls. In a Florida study of detained girls and boys, Dembo, Williams, and Schmeidler (1993) found that girls were more likely to have abuse histories than boys. In addition, in an expanded study of 2,104 youth in a Florida assessment center, Dembo, Sue, Borden, and Manning (1995) argued that girls' trajectory toward problem behaviors was different than boys'. Where boys' law violations reflected their involvement in a delinquent lifestyle, girls' acting out related "to an abusive and traumatizing home life" (Dembo et al., 1995, p. 21). Similar findings came out of a California Youth Authority (CYA) study in which boys were likely to witness violence and girls were much more likely to be direct victims (Cauffman, Feldman, Waterman, & Steiner, 1998).

Taken together, this research suggests that girls confront a separate pathway into the juvenile justice system, one that is marked by high rates of victimization and family turmoil. Therefore, girls seem to have unique needs that should be addressed with gender-specific programs. Increased attention to girls' experiences and the more precise map of their trajectory into delinquency is one of the positive developments in the last decade and suggests that there is a firm foundation upon which to build a better system for girls. Despite this promising picture, a closer look at girls' status in the juvenile justice system suggests that the work has only just begun. Regardless of the increased information available about girls and the greater attention given to girls' needs, several national juvenile justice trends in the past decade have made meeting the needs of the 1992 Reauthorization Act extremely difficult. In the next sections, we will outline some of these trends and link them to larger social changes and argue how changes in girls' arrest and detention rates complicate the effort to provide girls with equitable treatment.

Girls' Arrest Trends

Since the mid-nineties, girls' and boys' arrest trends have diverged, with boys' arrests peaking in 1993 and girls' arrests continuing to climb. According to FBI reports (Federal Bureau of Investigation [FBI], 2003, p. 239), between 1993 and 2002 girls' arrests increased 6.4 percent, while arrests of boys actually decreased by 16.4 percent (see Figure 14.1). Since 1991, girls' arrest rates have actually increased more dramatically, by 43.5 percent. As a result of these divergent patterns, girls now account for a growing share of those entering the juvenile justice system; in 1991, girls made up 23 percent of all juvenile arrestees; in 2002, they made up 28.8 percent.

What makes this surge most noteworthy is that girls are increasingly being arrested for violent offenses, not traditional status offenses. Between 1991 and 2002, arrests of girls for

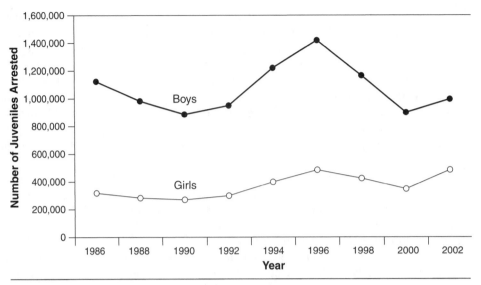

FIGURE 14.1   *Juvenile Arrest Trends by Gender*

Source: Federal Bureau of Investigation. (1995–2002). *Crime in the U.S. 2002*. Washington, DC: U.S. Government Printing Office.

serious violent offenses increased by 42.7 percent and arrests for girls' "other assaults" has increased by 120 percent (FBI, 2003, p. 239; 2001, p. 221). Over the last two decades, increases in girls' arrest rates for a number of violent offenses have outpaced boys' arrest rates. Between 1980 and 2000, for example, girls' arrests for aggravated assault, simple assault, and weapons law violations increased by 121 percent, 257 percent, and 134 percent (respectively). Boys' arrests also increased in these categories, but by much less (28 percent, 109 percent, and 20 percent).

Generally, dramatic percentage increases in girls' arrests should be reviewed with some care, since in the past, some dramatic increases in female participation in "non-traditional offenses" were actually the product of very small base numbers (particularly in the case of murder and forcible rape). However, in the case of girls' participation in the offenses mentioned here (particularly in the case of simple assault), the base numbers involved are relatively substantial, suggesting something significant is occurring. Because girls' and boys' arrest rates have not fluctuated together, Snyder (2001, p. 5) argued that gender-specific factors were most likely at work during the last two decades.

These trends created new challenges and pressures for the juvenile justice system already under criticism for its handling of girls' issues. Historically, girls were most likely to be arrested for status offenses, as noted earlier. In fact, research had long criticized the double standards within the juvenile justice system that seemed to target boys' index offenses through criminal charges and girls' immorality through status offense charges—a pattern that the JJDPA of 1974 seemed to indirectly address (see Chesney-Lind & Shelden, 2004). Three decades later, we have seen significant shifts in girls' arrests with girls more likely to be arrested and enter the juvenile justice system for traditionally "masculine" violations.

One of the first responses to these increases was to offer explanations, the quickest and simplest being that girls were changing. They were becoming increasingly like boys and, thus, were being arrested for violations that were historically viewed as boys' domain. This became an extremely popular explanation and touched off a frenzy of media attention on the topic of girls' violent emancipation (for a review, see Chesney-Lind, 1999). Reports of gun-toting and drug-dealing girl gangsters took center stage in media reports for a short time—that is, until researchers started to investigate these arrest trends more carefully.

Upon closer examination, the surge in girls' violence reported in FBI arrest statistics seemed to be caused by something very different than changes in girls' violent behavior. The first indication that something more complex was occurring came when several self-report data sources failed to corroborate this "surge" in girls' arrests for violence. In fact, self-report studies often found that girls were becoming less violent throughout the 1990s. In the Centers for Disease Control and Prevention's Biennial Youth Risk Behavior Survey, girls self-reported involvement in physical fights decreased. In 1991, 34.2 percent of girls reported being in a fight versus 23.9 percent of girls in 2001. Boys' self-reported violence during the same time also decreased, but more slightly—from 50.2 percent to 43.1 percent (Brener, Simon, Krug, & Lowry, 1999; Centers for Disease Control and Prevention, 1992–2000). A meta-analysis of data collected from 1991 to 1997 revealed that while both male and female violence rates declined, girls' rates declined more dramatically (Brener et al., 1999, p. 444). Girls' decreased rates of self-reported violence were also found in other studies. For example, a matched sample of high-risk youth surveyed in the 1997 National Youth Survey and the 1989 Denver Youth Survey demonstrated significant decreases in girls' involvement in felony and minor assaults (Huizinga, 1997).

It was becoming increasingly clear that although girls were coming into contact with the juvenile justice system at a faster rate than boys for violent offenses, they were, in fact, not behaving more violently. What was changing was the policing of girls' behaviors, particularly the behaviors of girls of color, by official agencies (like police, school officials, and probation officers) in ways that tracked the new focus in the 1990s on youth violence.

To understand how these policing practices emerged, it is important to examine the origins of the movement to get tough on juvenile violence. From 1983 to 1994, the United States experienced a tripling of homicide-victimization rates for black males between the ages of 13 and 17 (Cook & Laub, 1998), an approximately 70 percent increase in youth arrest rates for violent offenses, and a nearly 300 percent growth in youth homicide arrest rates (Snyder & Sickmund, 1999). These statistics led some to call the increased youth violence an "epidemic." Criminologists explained that the epidemic was caused by a combination of the introduction of new crack markets to inner cities, increased distribution of guns among juveniles, and the involvement of gangs in the crack and underground gun markets (all far more relevant to boys' but not girls' violence) (Blumstein, 1995; Blumstein & Cork, 1996; Blumstein & Wallman, 2000). The epidemic and its hypothesized causes ushered in an era of "get tough" anti-youth violence strategies including expelling students for everything from wearing gang attire to bringing weapons to school, installing metal detectors and hiring security guards in schools, conducting random searches of students' lockers, and creating anonymous hotlines for students to report potential violence and threats to authorities.

By 1995, the U.S. violence epidemic waned significantly. Attention to the subject of youth violence, however, did not abate. The collection of sensationalized school shootings, again virtually all male, with the most notorious being the Columbine High School massacre, riveted popular attention. By the late 1990s in the United States, violence prevention legislation and programming also shifted, and in the early 2000s, anti-bullying programs, which promised to improve school climates and increase students' and teachers' feelings of safety (Olweus, Limber, & Mihalic, 2002), became a favorite violence prevention strategy among U.S. school districts. In fact, by March 2004, 34 U.S. states had introduced anti-bullying legislation, most of which required schools districts to adopt anti-bullying policies (Madigan, 2004). These policy initiatives suggest that the strategy to combat the youth violence epidemic of the 1980s and early 1990s translated into an effort to do something about bullying by the early 2000s.

Many school policies maintained the "get tough" flavor of anti-gang and anti-gun practices from the late 1980s and early 1990s. Instead of placing security guards and metal detectors in hallways, schools employed hall monitors equipped with note pads and pens to report incidents of physical altercations or the use of threatening language. As a result, school officials, community members, and police were becoming increasingly sensitive to the violence problem as it played out in the everyday world of schoolyards, hallways, and other adolescent "hangouts."

It is important to note that anti-violence policies and practices, which had their origins in boys' violence, fell particularly heavily upon all girls and adolescents of color. Examining the specific practices initiated in the "get tough on juvenile crime" spirit not only reveals the mechanisms driving the girls' arrest trends from the 1990s to the early 2000s, but it helps identify an overarching process through which the juvenile justice system disproportionately arrests and detains girls of color—often for crimes of "violence."

Exactly how the tough policies of the last decade have impacted patterns of girls' arrests is a bit complex but important to understand. There are actually three related forces likely at work: *relabeling* (sometimes called "bootstrapping") of girls' status offense behavior, *rediscovery of girls' violence,* and *upcriming* of minor forms of youth violence (including girls' physical aggression) (see Chesney-Lind & Belknap, 2003, for a full discussion of these issues).

Relabeling

Relabeling of behaviors that were once categorized as status offenses (non-criminal offenses like "runaway" and "person in need of supervision") into violent offenses cannot be ruled out in explanations of arrest rate shifts, nor can changes in police practices with reference to domestic violence.

The recent focus on mandatory arrest as a policy for domestic violence cases has had a very real, and one would hope, unintended consequence: a dramatic increase in the numbers of girls and women arrested for this form of "assault." A California study, for example, found that the female share of domestic violence arrests increased from 6 percent in 1988 to 16.5 percent in 1998 (Bureau of Criminal Information and Analysis, 1999). African American girls and women had arrest rates roughly three times that of white girls and women in 1998: 149.6 per 100,000 compared to 46.4 (Bureau of Criminal Information and Analysis, 1999).

Such an impression is supported by case file reviews of girls' cases. Acoca's (1999) study of nearly 1,000 girls' files from four California counties found that while a "high percentage" of these girls were charged with "person offenses," a majority of these involved assault. Further, "a close reading of the case files of girls charged with assault revealed that most of these charges were the result of non-serious, mutual combat, situations with parents" (Acoca, 1999, p. 7). Acoca details cases that she regards as typical including: "father lunged at her while she was calling the police about a domestic dispute. She (girl) hit him." Finally, she reports that some cases were quite trivial in nature including a girl arrested "for throwing cookies at her mother" (Acoca, 1999, pp. 7–8). In another study, a girl reported that she was arrested for "assault" for throwing a Barbie doll at her mother (Belknap, Winter, & Cady, 2001). In a number of these instances, the possibility that the child, not the parent, is actually the victim cannot be completely ignored, particularly when girls and defense attorneys keep reporting such a pattern. Marlee Ford, an attorney working with the Bronx Defenders Office, commented, "Some girls have been abused all their lives. . . . Finally, they get to an age where they can hit back. And they get locked up" (Russ, 2004, p. 20).

Rediscovery and "Upcriming"

Girls have always been more violent than their stereotype as weak and passive "good girls" would suggest. A review of the self-reported data cited earlier indicates that girls do get into fights, and they even occasionally carry weapons; as an example, in 2001, about a quarter of girls reported that they were in a physical fight, and about one in twenty carried a weapon (Centers for Disease Control and Prevention, 1992–2002). Until recently, girls' aggression, even their physical aggression, was trivialized rather than criminalized. Law enforcement, parents, social workers, and teachers were once more concerned with controlling girls' sexuality than they were with their violence, but recent research, which we will review below, suggests that may be changing. So, in part, the contemporary focus on girls' violence is actually a "rediscovery" of female violence that has always existed, although at much lower rates than boys' violence.

A related phenomenon, *upcriming,* is likely also involved in the increases in girls' arrests. Upcriming refers to policies (like zero tolerance policies) that increase the severity of criminal penalties associated with particular offenses. It has long been known that arrests of youth for minor or "other" assaults can range from schoolyard scuffles to relatively serious, but not life-threatening, assaults (Steffensmeier & Steffensmeier, 1980). Currie (1998) adds to this the fact that these "simple assaults without injury" are often "attempted," "threatened," or "not completed." A few decades ago, schoolyard fights and other instances of bullying were largely ignored or handled informally by schools and parents. But at a time when official concern about youth violence is almost unparalleled and zero tolerance policies proliferate, school principals are increasingly likely to call police onto their campuses. It should come as no surprise that youthful arrests in this area are up as a consequence—with both race and gender implications. Specifically, while African American children represent only 42 percent of the public school enrollment, they constitute 61 percent of the children charged with a disciplinary code violation. And these violations have serious consequences; according to a U.S. Department of Education's report, 25 percent of all African American students, nationally, were suspended at least once over a four-year period (Harvard Civil Rights Project, 2000, p. vi).

These trends in girls' arrests for violent offenses should not let us lose sight of the fact that large numbers of girls were also being arrested and referred to court for traditional female offenses, like runaway and larceny-theft (the bulk of which for girls was shoplifting). In 2001, girls' runaway arrests exceeded those of boys'—the only offense category where this is true. These two offense categories account for a third (33.2 percent) of female juvenile arrests but far less (16.4 percent) of boys' arrests (FBI, 2003, p. 239). These simultaneous trends—arrests of girls for historically male and historically female offenses—have also further complicated the efforts to craft gender-specific or responsive ways to address girls' needs. Essentially, the juvenile justice system is being pressured to respond to the violent behavior of youth, including girls, while it still also faces all the complexities presented by more traditional girl offenders, who have always been the recipients of what have been described as "throwaway services for throwaway girls" (Wells, 1994). And, as we have already suggested, the two groups often share more in common with each other than conventional wisdom might predict.

Juvenile Justice in the New Millennium

At the same time that the juvenile justice system was becoming increasingly punitive and intolerant of juvenile violence—evidenced in the zero tolerance policies and practices in response to the youth violence epidemic and the spate of school shootings—another, contradictory trend also emerged. The last decade has also signaled a return to an emphasis on protecting girls that justified the court's earliest involvement with female youth during the child-saving era.

Despite the emphasis in the original JJDPA of 1974 to divert status offenders—a group that is dominated by girls—from formal court processing, between 1990 and 1999, the number of delinquency cases coming into juvenile courts involving girls increased by 59 percent (from 250,000 to 398,600) compared to a 19 percent increase for males (from 1,066,900 to 1,274,500) (Stahl, 2003). Looking at specific offense types, the report observed: "The growth in cases involving females outpaced the growth in cases involving males in all offense categories. For both males and females, simple assault cases increased more than any other person offense, "136 percent for females and 80 percent for males" (Stahl, 2003, p. 1).

The increasing referral of girls to formal court processing may, in fact, be an ironic outcome of the 1990s research on girls' needs in the juvenile justice system. For example, by the mid-1990s research agendas had made it clear that girls confronted an entirely different set of circumstances in and out of the system. The overwhelming presence of victimization at home or on the streets gave a clear indication that young female offenders had different histories and service needs than boys.

A particularly poignant example of the balance between punitive and protective policies over girls characterizing this era was the 1995 Washington State "Becca's Bill" implemented in response to the murder of Rebecca Headman, a 13-year-old chronic runaway. After a series of runaway incidents and repeated calls to the police by her parents, Rebecca was murdered while on the streets. Under Becca's Bill, apprehended runways could be detained in a crisis residential center for up to seven days. Between 1994 and 1997, youth detention rates increased by 835 percent in Washington State and, by 1997, girls made up 60 percent of the detained population (Sherman, 2000). According to Sherman (2000), while Becca's Bill was designed to save youths (mostly girls) from the streets in Washington by placing them in detention, there were no long-term community-based programs for runaway girls. In addition, as we will explain later, detention centers were certainly not universally safe havens for girls.

According to Corrado et al. (2000), the reliance on detention rather than treatment in the community was a trend in Canada as well. Looking at delinquency data and sentencing practices leading up to girls' detentions, Corrado et al. (2000, p. 193) found that "the sentencing recommendations made by youth justice personnel are primarily based on the desire to protect female youth from high-risk environments and street-entrenched lifestyles." Furthermore, they argue that reliance on detention came partly because of the:

> . . . inability of community-based programs to protect certain female youth, the difficulties these programs have in getting young female offenders to participate in rehabilitation programs, when they are not incarcerated, and the presence of some, albeit usually inadequate, treatment resources in custodial institutions. (Corrado et al., 2000, p. 193)

The balance between punitive and protective juvenile justice practices affects girls in another way. At the same time that detention and arrest were being used to protect girls from the dangers of the streets, many jurisdictions were cracking down on youths' probation and court order violations. Although designed to get tough on repeat index offenders, sentencing youth to detention for probation and court order violations, in practice, did not distinguish between status and index offenses. Therefore, girls were placed in a precarious position under this practice. Status-offending girls could be swept into detention through policies designed to protect them from the dangers of the streets, and, in the end, could be charged as criminal offenders through contempt of court and probation violations. In fact, as a study by the American Bar Association and National Bar Association [ABA and NBA] (2001) found, this happened frequently in the 1990s. According to this study, girls in the U.S. juvenile justice system between 1991 and 1999 were more likely than boys to not only be detained, but to return to detention after being released. This was, in large part, through contempt of court, probation, and parole violations.

There was an inherent irony in the protective-punitive confluence that underlies the arrest and, as we shall see, detention rates of girls during the 1990s and early 2000s. On one hand, although practitioners are becoming increasingly aware of girls' needs, specifically to address their extensive abuse histories, there are consistent reports of inadequate community-based programs to meet these needs. Therefore, in some jurisdictions, detaining girls has become the only "program" available. On the other hand, we also find a system that has become increasingly intolerant and punitive of certain offenses, such as violent crimes, contempt of court, and probation and parole violations. This sets up a troubling trajectory toward incarceration for girls and one in which they were likely to find themselves either ignored and pushed aside when outside of the system, or set up for failure and certain punishment when they did become involved in the juvenile justice system.

Girls' Detention Trends

One indicator of the increasingly punitive nature of the juvenile justice system in the years after the 1992 Reauthorization Act was the rising detention rates among girls. Between 1989 and 1998, girls' detentions rose by 56 percent compared to a 20 percent expansion seen in boys' detentions (see Figure 14.2), and the "large increase was tied to the growth in the number of delinquency cases involving females charged with person offenses (157 percent)" (Harms, 2002, p. 1)

In addition to a distinctly gendered pattern in these increases, there also seemed to be clear race-based differences. For example, a study conducted by the ABA and NBA (2001) revealed that nearly half of girls in secure detention in the United States were African American. This is particularly interesting given that white girls made up a clear majority (65 percent) of the at-risk population (ABA and NBA, 2001, p. 20).

More worrisome is the fact that, despite the hype about violent girls, it was relatively minor offenses that actually *kept* girls in detention. Nearly half (40.5 percent) of all the girls in detention in the United States in 2001 were being held for either a status offense or a "technical violation" of the conditions of their probation, compared to only 25.3 percent of the boys (Sickmund, Sladky, & Kang, 2004) (see Figure 14.3). Girls being detained for "violent" offenses were far more likely than boys to be held on "other person" offenses like simple assault (as opposed to more serious, Part One violent offenses like aggravated assault, robbery, and murder). Well over half (57.3 percent) of the girls but less than a third of the boys in detention (32.4 percent) were held for these minor forms of violence (Sickmund et al., 2004).

Another troubling gender and race-based pattern in the use of detention was the reliance on private facilities since the early 1980s. The use of private facilities has a particular importance for girls, as they tend to make up a larger proportion of the institutionalized population in private vs. public facilities. Also interesting to note is the fact that 45 percent of the girls in private settings were detained for status offenses in 1997 (Snyder & Sickmund, 1999). This is compared to 11 percent of boys who were detained in private facilities for status offenses.

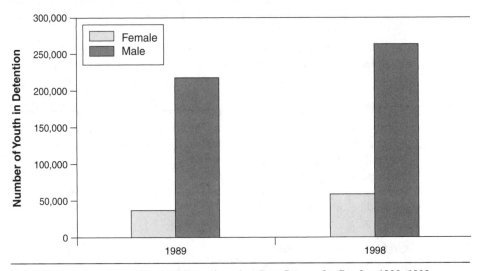

FIGURE 14.2   *Number of Youth in Detention: One Day Census, by Gender, 1989–1998*

Source: Compiled from Harms, P. (2002). *Detention in Delinquency Cases, 1989–1998* (p. 1). Washington, DC: U.S. Department of Justice.

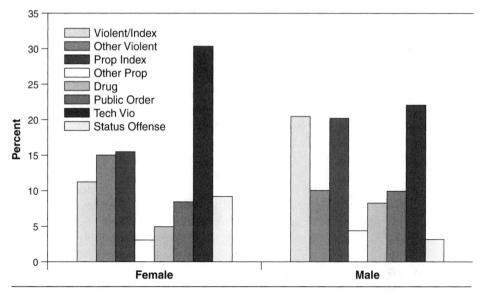

FIGURE 14.3 *Offenses of Detained by Gender by Percentage, 2001*

Source: OJJDP, 2004. *Census of Juveniles in Residential Placement Databook,* Offense Profile of Detained Residents, www.ojjdp.ncjurs.org/ojstatbb/openpage.asp.

The use of private facilities presents some new and unique problems to the creation of equity in the juvenile justice system. Some have argued that the increasing trend to rely on private facilities has, in essence, created a bifurcated, or "two-track," juvenile justice system: one for white girls and another for girls of color. In 1997, whites made up 33 percent of the public detention population and 45 percent of individuals held in private facilities (Snyder & Sickmund, 1999). This disparity might be explained by looking at how girls' cases are handled. In her study of one Los Angeles district from 1992–1993, Miller (1994) discovered that white girls were significantly more likely to be recommended for placement in treatment facilities than Latinas and African American girls. In fact, 75 percent of white girls received treatment recommendations compared to only 34 percent of Latinas and 30 percent of African American girls who received similar recommendations. Looking closely at probation officers' written reports, Miller found a surprising trend where white girls' offenses were more likely to be described as resulting from abandonment and low self-esteem and non-white girls' offenses were attributed to lifestyle choices (Miller, 1994).

This trend has been corroborated in other studies. Robinson's (1990) examination of girls in a social welfare and a juvenile justice sample in Massachusetts revealed that 74 percent of girls in the welfare sample were white and 53 percent of girls in the juvenile justice sample were black. Although white girls seemed to be more likely to come into contact with the welfare rather than the juvenile justice system, Robinson found remarkably similar histories within both populations, especially with regard to their high rates of sexual victimization. One difference was that white girls tended to be charged with status offenses and non-white girls received criminal charges.

Another disturbing trend, present in the earlier data on the offenses for which girls were detained, might be described as the "re-detention" of girls. Essentially, once girls were released on probation in the 1990s, they were more likely than boys to return to detention—usually for a technical violation of the conditions of their probation. A study by the ABA and NBA (2001, p. 20) not only found that girls were more likely than boys to be detained, but that they were more likely "to be sent back to detention after release. Although girls' rates of recidivism are lower than those of boys, the use of contempt proceedings and probation and parole violations make it more likely that, without committing a new crime, girls will return to detention."

Thus, in reviewing the data on detention practices, particularly the role played by minor aggressive offenses and technical violations, which are essentially proxies for status offenses, one can see the way in which the juvenile justice system has essentially married the protectionist logic to the new punitive emphasis in ways that distinctly disadvantage girls, particularly girls of color. And, while those in the system may argue that they are forced to detain girls "for their own protection," a review of the conditions in these facilities as well as the services provided, suggests that they are anything but protective.

Girls' Experiences in Detention

There is considerable evidence to suggest that, like their experiences outside of institutions, girls' confront vastly different environments and obstacles than boys face while being detained. This trend has continued despite the fact that over half of all states have committed themselves to improving conditions for girls in the juvenile justice system, assessing girls' unique needs, and designing better programs for them. One enduring trend is that there continues to be a lack of programs for girls. In 1998, for example, Ohio judges reported that there were few sentencing options for girls. Two-thirds of judges surveyed disagreed with the statement that "there are an adequate number of treatment programs for girls," while less than one-third of judges disagreed with this statement regarding services for boys (Holsinger, Belknap, & Sutherland, 1999). In a San Francisco study, Schaffner, Shorter, Schick, and Frappier (1996, p. 1) concluded that girls were "out of sight, out of mind" and that girls tended to linger in detention centers longer than boys. In fact, 60 percent of girls were detained for more than seven days, while only 6 percent of boys were detained that long.

Another concern noted by researchers examining the girls held in detention in Philadelphia was the "misdiagnosis of mental health issues" (Ambrose, Simpkins, & Levick, 2000, p. 1). As the Female Detention Project found, 81 percent of the girls studied had reported experiencing a trauma of some sort (sexual abuse, physical abuse, witnessing violence, and abandonment). The girls were diagnosed with "Oppositional Defiant Disorder" (ODD) instead of "Posttraumatic Stress Disorder" despite the fact that, according to the researchers, "many of the girls reported symptoms that are characteristics of Posttraumatic Stress Disorder, but not ODD." Significantly, while ODD is "characterized by a persistent pattern of negativistic, hostile, disobedient and defiant—but not violent—behavior," most of these girls were detained for assaults, many school-related. As a consequence of misdiagnosis, the girls were not getting the specific kind of treatment that they needed, many had used alcohol and other drugs, been hospitalized for psychiatric reasons, and about half had attempted suicide (Ambrose et al., 2000, p. 2).

There is also some evidence that girls are more vulnerable than boys to experiencing sexual abuse while being detained. In their study of 200 girls in California juvenile justice halls, Acoca and Dedel (1998, p. 6), found several examples of abuse including "consistent use by staff of foul and demeaning language, inappropriate touching, pushing and hitting, isolation, and deprivation of clean clothing." In addition, girls underwent strip searches while being supervised by male staff.

Lack of female staff seems to place girls in vulnerable positions while being detained. In addition to increasing the chances that female wards will be abused by male staff, the lack of female staff also limits the programs and activities available for girls. Staff shortages in the Miami-Dade County Juvenile Detention Center for girls, for example, resulted in decreased outdoor recreation for girls. Ledermen and Brown (2000) reported that girls sometimes went as long as two weeks without outdoor recreation and were sometimes "locked down" due to shortage of staff. On some days, staff shortages resulted in girls' inability to attend school.

Why do girls languish in detention? The answers are not too hard to find, unfortunately, once one begins to review the literature on probation officers' (and other court officials') attitudes toward female delinquents. Research has consistently revealed that despite their less serious offense profile, girls in the juvenile justice system are regarded as "more difficult" to work with (Baines & Alder, 1996; Belknap et al., 1997). A recent study of probation files in Arizona revealed stark gender and cultural stereotypes that worked against girls. Specifically, the authors found that "common images found in girls' probation files included girls fabricating reports of abuse, acting promiscuously, whining too much and attempting to manipulate the court system." Girls were universally seen as "harder to work with," "had too many issues," and were "too needy" (Gaarder, Zatz, & Rodriquez, 2004, p. 14). Even when girls were abused, they were somehow partially responsible for the abuse in the eyes of probation officers:

> They feel like they're the victim. They try from, "Mom kicked me out" to "Mom's boyfriend molested me" or "My brother was sexually assaulting me." They'll find all kinds of excuses to justify their actions. Because they feel if I say I was victimized at home that justifies me being out on the streets. . . . (Gaarder et al., 2004, p. 16)

Gender and Training Schools—Girls' Victimization Continues

Girls were 13 percent of youth "committed" to residential placements in 2001, up from 11.8 percent in 1997. That period actually saw an 8.8 percent increase in girls' commitments compared to a 1.5 percent decrease in boys' commitments (Sickmund et al., 2004). Girls are also being committed for different and less serious offenses than boys. In 2001, for example, roughly a third of girls (31.8 percent) were committed for either status offenses or technical violations, compared to only 14.2 percent of boys. Over half (54 percent) of the girls committed for a "person" offense were committed for non-index violent crimes (meaning simple assault); only 27.6 percent of boys doing time for violent offenses were committed for these less serious assaults (Sickmund et al., 2004).

Exactly how this works can be seen in a recent study of 444 incarcerated youth in Ohio (Holsinger, Belknap, & Sutherland, 1999). These researchers found that girls were just as likely as boys to be incarcerated for violent offenses and that approximately half of the youths incarcerated reported being charged with violent offenses. On the surface, this suggests that incarcerated Ohio girls were just as violent as boys. Upon closer examination, however, researchers discovered glaring gender differences in the severity of violent offenses, and, as

Belknap et al. (1997) reported, focus group data with incarcerated girls revealed consistent accounts of girls being incarcerated for minor infractions, and in some cases, for defending themselves. As a case in point, one girl revealed during a focus group interview that she was incarcerated for bringing a weapon to school. After being taunted and threatened by a boy at school and receiving no protection from school authorities, she hid a knife in her sock. While school authorities did not intervene in the boy's harassment, they did enforce the zero tolerance for weapons policy against the girl (Belknap et al., 1997).

Conditions in girls' residential facilities, like those found in detention centers, also suggest that while court officials often talk of protecting girls, the environments in training schools, if anything, fail to deliver on that promise. In fact, several recent scandals suggest that like their adult counterparts (women's prisons), juvenile prisons are often unsafe for girls in ways that are uniquely gendered. Take a recent investigation of conditions in the Hawaii Youth Correctional Facility in the summer of 2003 by the American Civil Liberties Union [ACLU]. According to the ACLU report, there were no female guards on duty at night in the girls' ward, one reported case of rape of a girl by a male guard, and several reports of girls exchanging sex for cigarettes. The report also noted that male guards made sexual comments to female wards, talked about their breasts, and discussed raping them. While wards noted that rape comments decreased after the rape incident, White (2003, p. 16) wrote, "wards expressed concern that the night shift is comprised entirely of male guards, and they feel vulnerable after the rape because male guards could enter their cells at any time."

The ACLU report also discovered that wards reported being watched by male guards while they changed clothes and used the toilet. Male guards were also present when girls took showers. And, like their counterparts in detention, girls had not received outdoor recreation for a week due to lack of supervising staff, and girls were told that the situation might last for up to a month (White, 2003). While critics of the ACLU report commented that the wards made up stories and severely exaggerated tales of abuse, in April 2004, the guard implicated in the rape charge pleaded guilty to three counts of sexual assault and one count of "terroristic threatening of a female ward" (Dingeman, 2004). Although comprising a plea bargain, the legal rape case uncovered details indicating that the sexual abuse was more severe and alarming than wards originally reported to the ACLU.

Other scandals have surfaced at girls' institutions (see Chesney-Lind & Shelden, 2004), and all of these incidents suggest that while authorities often use institutionalization as a means of "protecting" girls from the dangers of the streets and in their homes, many of the institutions that house girls perpetuate the gendered victimization that pervades girls' lives outside of these institutions.

Girls and Juvenile Justice: What Does the Future Hold?

The recently reauthorized Juvenile Justice and Delinquency Prevention Act of 2002 supports the continued focus on girls. Specifically, the act requires states, again, to create "a plan for providing needed gender-specific services for the prevention and treatment of juvenile delinquency" and denotes a category of funding for "programs that focus on the needs of young girls at risk of delinquency or status offenses" (Sharp & Simon, 2004). Perhaps this time, as more girls enter the various juvenile justice systems, the states will take more seriously the unique needs of girls.

Recent reports from a number of national organizations such as the American Bar Association, the National Bar Association (ABA and NBA, 2001), and the Child Welfare League (Sharp & Simon, 2004) have, once again, focused critical attention on the unmet needs of girls in the juvenile justice. Beyond the continued claim that girls lack adequate gender-specific programming, there is also the undeniable fact that the girls in the juvenile justice system need considerable advocacy. As this chapter has indicated, girls are currently caught between multiple trends in the juvenile justice system—trends that confront them with new and more severe levels of disadvantage than they experienced in the 1970s and 1980s. In the arena of contemporary justice trends, girls, especially girls of color, are bearing the brunt of "tough on crime" policies specifically in the form of mandatory arrest and zero tolerance initiatives toward youth violence. For example, where boys' arrest rates for violence peaked in 1994 (and have been declining since), girls' violence arrest rates have continued to climb since the early 1980s. In several twists and contortions of policies, laws, and initiatives meant to protect girls from victimization, we find that tough on violence responses have been deployed in ways that actually harm girls.

While the punitive turn in criminal justice has lashed out against girls in new ways, girls in the juvenile justice system continue to face the system's historic impulse to use correctional facilities to "protect" them. However traditional this protective pattern may be, it also confronts girls with a new set of challenges as legal initiatives like Washington State's Becca's Bill exemplifies. Instead of unabashedly sweeping up female status offenders into the system for their protection, as was a common practice critiqued by the 1994 and 2002 JJDPA Acts, legal initiatives like Becca's Bill turn status violators into criminal offenders. It seems that the juvenile court judges' desire to regain the ability to detain youth charged with status offenses has withstood the efforts of critics and reformers (Chesney-Lind & Pasko, 2004).

Ultimately, the juvenile justice system's unfortunate return to its historic (and problematic) pattern of "protecting" girls, coupled with a simultaneous "get tough" trend permeating the entire criminal justice system, has had very negative consequences for girls, particularly girls of color. We find that girls are systematically being reclassified from status offenders "in need of protection and supervision" into criminals deserving strict control and harsh punishment.

What are the prospects for gender-specific programming, assuming that we could get it right? It has also been three decades since the second wave of feminism presumably rekindled a national focus on women's rights, yet girls and women remain a very low priority when it comes to public as well as private funding.

Youth services all too often translate into "boys' services" as can be seen in a 1993 study of the San Francisco Chapter of the National Organization for Women. The study found that only 8.7 percent of the programs funded by the major city organization funding children and youth programs "specifically addressed the needs of girls" (Siegal, 1995). Not surprisingly, then, a 1995 study of youth participation in San Francisco afterschool or summer sports programs found only 26 percent of the participants were girls (Siegal, 1995).

Likewise, problems exist with delinquency programming; in a list of "potentially promising programs" identified by the Office of Juvenile Justice and Delinquency Prevention, there were 24 programs cited specifically for boys and only two for girls. One program for incarcerated teen fathers had no counterpart for incarcerated teen mothers (Girls Incorporated, 1996). And things are apparently no better in the area of private funding. A 2003 study conducted by the Washington Women's Foundation reviewed 12,000 grants given by DC-area foundations in 2002 and 2003, and determined that only 7 percent of a total of $441 million dollars went to programs serving girls or women (E.Viner, personal communication, October 21, 2003). Clearly, the sexism that has long haunted public policy relating to girls programming haunts the world of private funding as well. In short, the prospects are about as dim as they were three decades ago in the area of program funding.

Conclusion

What are some key themes that must be addressed to adequately meet the needs of girls in the juvenile justice system? While space does not permit a full discussion of the rich emerging literature on programming for girls, it is clear that the gendered pathways that bring girls into the system provide a good starting point for crafting gender responsive programming (see Chesney-Lind & Shelden, 2002; OJJDP, 2004).

Clearly, programs must address girls' unique problems with both physical and sexual victimization, a pattern that begins when they are very young and often continues. Dealing with the trauma associated with this victimization should address depression, issues of relational as well as direct aggression, self-medication with drugs, and the inevitable problems that arise with survival strategies that girls develop to deal with abuse (running away; depending on older, inappropriate, and often exploitative males). Girls, particularly girls of color, are also the victims of educational neglect and have severe housing and employment issues, often made more complicated by early motherhood and growing health problems.

Efforts to highlight gender, though, should avoid pathologizing girls and should also build on the considerable resilience that exists in this population. They should also seek to avoid stereotypical and dated notions of femininity that have long haunted juvenile justice programming (especially in girls' facilities) and remember that paying attention to a girl's cultural background is critical. Girls who enter this system are often very clear about their need to be heard, often eager to connect (especially with members of their own ethnic group who understand their problems and can provide culturally responsive ways to begin healing and reconnecting). Girls, according to those who enjoy working with them, are able to articulate their problems and are clear about needing to find spaces to rebuild lives that were often shredded by forces over which they had no control.

Advocacy for more of this sort of programming is critical, since it is clear that the girls in the juvenile justice system cannot wait another generation for things to change. As their numbers increase daily in the detention centers and training schools, and as the scandals in those facilities become more common, it is long past time to pay attention to girls. Imagine how different the juvenile justice system would look if we, as a nation, decided to take girls' sexual and physical victimization seriously and arrested the perpetrators rather than criminalizing girls' survival strategies and jailing them for daring to escape.

Review Questions

1. What role have status offenses played in girls' delinquency? Why do some critics of the juvenile justice system argue that these offenses have criminalized girls' survival strategies?

2. How did the deinstitutionalization of status offenders impact girls? Why did the movement fall short?

3. Are girls getting more violent? Why or why not?

4. What role does gender play in girls' violence?

5. What is meant by gender specific or responsive programming? Why is it necessary for today's juvenile justice system to develop?

6. What are private facilities for girls? What has changed in juvenile justice regarding their utilization?

7. Explain the institutionalization trends for girls. What is unique about them?

Key Terms

Status offenses
Juvenile Justice and Delinquency Prevention Act
Bootstrapping
Upcriming
Zero tolerance
Becca's Bill

Oppositional defiant disorder and posttraumatic stress disorder
Technical violations
Challenge grant activity
Gender responsive programming

References

Acoca, L. (1999). Investing in girls: A 21st century challenge. *Juvenile Justice* 6, 1, 3–13.

Acoca, L., & Dedel, K. (1998). *No place to hide: Understanding and meeting the needs of girls in the California juvenile justice system.* San Francisco: National Council on Crime and Delinquency.

Ambrose, A. M., Simpkins, S., & Levick, M. (2000). *Improving the conditions for girls in the juvenile justice system: The female detention project.* Washington, DC: American Bar Association.

American Bar Association and the National Bar Association. (2001). *Justice by gender: The lack of appropriate prevention, diversion and treatment alternatives for girls in the justice system.* Washington, DC: American Bar Association.

Baines, M., & Alder, C. (1996). Are girls more difficult to work with? Youth workers' perspectives in juvenile justice and related areas. *Crime & Delinquency* 42, 3, 467–485.

Belknap, J., Dunn, M., & Holsinger, K. (1997, February). *Moving toward juvenile justice and youth-serving systems that address the distinct experience of the adolescent female.* Gender Specific Work Group Report to the Governor. Columbus, OH: Office of Criminal Justice Services.

Belknap, J., Winter, E., & Cady, B. (2001). *Assessing the needs of committed delinquent and pre-adjudicated girls in Colorado: A focus group study.* A Report to the Colorado Division of Youth Corrections. Denver, CO: Division of Youth Corrections.

Blumstein, A. (1995). Youth violence, guns, and the illicit-drug industry. *The Journal of Criminal Law & Criminology* 86, 10–34.

Blumstein, A., & Cork, D. (1996, Winter). Linking gun availability to gun violence. *Law and Contemporary Problems* 59, 5–24.

Blumstein, A., & Wallman, J. (2000). *The crime drop in America.* Cambridge: Cambridge University Press.

Brener, N. D., Simon, T. R., Krug, E. G., & Lowry, R. (1999). Recent trends in violence-related behaviors among high school students in the United States. *Journal of the American Medical Association* 282, 5, 330–446.

Bureau of Criminal Information and Analysis. (1999). *Report on arrests for domestic violence in California, 1998.* Sacramento: State of California, Criminal Justice Statistics Center.

Calahan, M. (1986). *Historical corrections statistics in the United States, 1850–1984.* Washington, DC: Bureau of Justice Statistics.

Cauffman, E., Feldman, S. S., Waterman, J., & Steiner, H. (1998). Posttraumatic stress disorder among female juvenile offenders. *Journal of the American Academy of Child and Adolescent Psychiatry* 31, 1209–1216.

Centers for Disease Control and Prevention. (1992–2002). *Youth risk behavior surveillance—United States, 1991–2001.* CDC Surveillance Summaries. U.S. Department of Health and Human Services. Atlanta: Centers for Disease Control.

Chesney-Lind, M. (1999). Media misogyny: Demonizing "violent" girls and women. In J. Ferrel & N. Websdale (Eds.), *Making trouble: Cultural representations of crime, deviance, and control* (pp. 115–141). New York: Aldine.

Chesney-Lind, M. (2000). What to do about girls? In M. McMahon (Ed.), *Assessment to assistance: Programs for women in community corrections* (pp. 139–170). Lanham, MD: American Correctional Association.

Chesney-Lind, M., & Belknap, J. (2003). Trends in delinquent girls' aggression and violent behavior: A review of the evidence. In M. Putallaz & P. Bierman (Eds.), *Aggression, antisocial behavior and violence among girls: A developmental perspective* (in press). New York: Guilford Press.

Chesney-Lind, M., & Pasko, L. (2004) *The female offender: Girls, women and crime* (2nd ed.). Thousand Oaks: Sage.

Chesney-Lind, M., & Shelden, R. (2004). *Girls, delinquency and juvenile justice* (3rd ed.). Belmont, CA: Thompson-Wadsworth.

Children's Defense Fund and Girls Incorporated. (2002, August). *Overview of gender provisions in state juvenile justice plans.* Washington, DC: Children's Defense Fund and Girls Incorporated.

Cook, P. J., & Laub, J. H. (1998). The unprecedented epidemic in youth violence. In M. Tonry & M. H. Moore (Eds.), *Youth violence. Crime and justice: A review of research* (pp. 27–64). Chicago: University of Chicago Press.

Corrado, R., Odgers, C., & Cohen, I. M. (2000). The incarceration of female young offenders: Protection for whom? *Canadian Journal of Criminology* 2, 189–207.

Currie, E. (1998). *Crime and punishment in America.* New York: Metropolitan Books.

Datesman, S., & Scarpitti, F. (1977). Unequal protection for males and females in the juvenile court. In T. N. Ferdinand (Ed.), *Juvenile delinquency: Little brother grows up.* Newbury Park, CA: Sage.

Dembo, R., Sue, S. C., Borden, P., & Manning, D. (1995). *Gender differences in service needs among youths entering a juvenile assessment center: A replication study.* Paper presented at the Annual Meeting of the Society of Social Problems, Washington, DC.

Dembo, R., Williams, L., & Schmeidler, J. (1993). Gender differences in mental health service needs among youths entering a juvenile detention center. *Journal of Prison and Jail Health* 12, 73–101.

Dingeman, R. (2004). Ex-guard guilty in sex assault. *Honolulu Advertiser.* Posted April 30, 2004 on http://the.honoluluadvertiser.com/article/2004/apr/30/in/in14a.html.

Federal Bureau of Investigation. (2001). *Crime in the U.S. 2000.* Washington, DC: U.S. Government Printing Office.

Federal Bureau of Investigation. (2003). *Crime in the U.S. 2002.* Washington, DC: U.S. Government Printing Office.

Female Offender Resource Center. (1977). *Little sisters and the law.* Washington, DC: American Bar Association.

Gaarder, E., Zatz, M. S., & Rodriguez, N. (2004). Criers, liars and manipulators: Probation officers' views of girls. *Justice Quarterly* 21, 547–548.

Gelsethorpe, L. (1989). *Sexism and the female offender.* Aldershot, England: Gower Publishing.

Girls Incorporated. (1996). *Prevention and parity: Girls in juvenile justice.* Indianapolis: Girls Incorporated National Resource Center.

Harms, P. (2002). *Detention in delinquency cases, 1989–1998.* OJJDP Fact Sheet #1. Washington, DC: U.S. Department of Justice.

Harvard Civil Rights Project. (2000, June 15–16). *Opportunities suspended: The devastating consequences of zero tolerance and school discipline.* Report from A National Summit on Zero Tolerance. Washington, DC: U.S. Government Printing Office.

Holsinger, K., Belknap, J., & Sutherland, J. L. (1999). *Assessing the gender specific program and service needs for adolescent females in the juvenile justice system.* A Report to the Office of Criminal Justice Services. Columbus, OH: Office of Criminal Justice Services.

Huizinga, D. (1997). *Over-time changes in delinquency and drug use: The 1970s to the 1990s.* Unpublished report. Washington, DC: Office of Juvenile Justice and Delinquency Prevention.

Joe, K., Laidler, K. A., & Chesney-Lind, M. (1996). Running away from home: Rhetoric and reality in troublesome behavior. *Journal of Contemporary Criminal Justice* 12 (2), May.

Kempf-Leonard, K., & Sample L. L. (2000). Disparity based on sex: Is gender-specific treatment warranted? *Justice Quarterly* 17, 89–128.

Kersten, J. (1989). The institutional control of girls and boys. In M. Cain (Ed.), *Growing up good: Policing the behavior of girls in Europe* (pp. 129–144). London: Sage.

Lederman, C. S., & Brown, E. N. (2000). Entangled in the

shadows: Girls in the juvenile justice system. *Buffalo Law Review* 48, 909–925.

Madigan, E. (2004). Bullying by school kids gets lawmakers' attention. Stateline.org. Retrieved June 19, 2004 from http://www.stateline.org/stateline/.

Mann, C. R. (1984). *Female crime and delinquency*. Birmingham: University of Alabama Press.

McCormack, A., Janus, M. D., & Burgess, A. W. (1986). Runaway youths and sexual victimization: Gender differences in an adolescent runaway population. *Child Abuse and Neglect* 10, 387–395.

Miller, J. (1994). Race, gender and juvenile justice: An examination of disposition decision-making for delinquent girls. In M. D. Schwartz & D. Milovanovic (Eds.), *The intersection of race, gender and class in criminology*. New York: Garland Press.

Olweus, D., Limber, S., & Mihalic, S. (2002). *Blueprints for violence prevention: Bullying prevention program*. Denver, CO: Center for the Study and Prevention of Violence, Institute of Behavioral Science, University of Colorado at Boulder.

Office of Juvenile Justice and Delinquency Prevention. (1998). *Guiding principles for promising female programming: An inventory of best practices*. Nashville, TN: Green Peters and Associates.

Office of Juvenile Justice and Delinquency Prevention. (2004). *Census of juveniles in residential placement databook, offense profile of detained residents*. Retrieved June 5, 2004 from www.ojjdp.ncjurs.org/ojstatbb/openpage.asp.

Rafter, N. H. (1990). *Partial justice: Women, prisons and social control*. New Brunswick, NJ: Transaction Books.

Ray, D. (2002, March 20). Letter to Glenda MacMullin, American Bar Association. Re: National Girl's Institute.

Reitsma-Street, M., & D. R. Offord. (1991). Girl delinquents and their sisters: A challenge for practice. *Canadian Social Work Review* 8, 11–27.

Robinson, R. (1990). *Violations of girlhood: A qualitative study of female delinquents and children in need of services in Massachusetts*. Unpublished doctoral dissertation, Brandeis University.

Russ, H. (2004, February). The war on catfights. *City Limits* 19–22.

Schaffner, L., Shorter, A. D., Shick, S., & Frappier, N. S. (1996). *Out of sight, out of mind: The plight of girls in the San Francisco juvenile justice system*. San Francisco: Center for Juvenile and Criminal Justice.

Sharp, C., & Simon, J. (2004). *Girls and the juvenile justice system: The need for more gender responsive services*. Washington, DC: Child Welfare League.

Sherman, F. (2000). What's in a name? Runaway girls pose challenges for the justice system. *Women, Girls and Criminal Justice* 1 (2), 19–20, 26.

Sickmund, M., Sladky, T. J., & Kang, W. (2004). *Census of juveniles in residential placement databook*. Washington, DC: U.S. Department of Justice. Available from http://www.ojJJDPAp.ncjrs.org/ojstabb/cjrp/.

Siegal, N. (1995, October 4). Where the girls are. *San Francisco Bay Guardian*, pp. 19–20.

Smart, C. (1976). *Women, crime and criminology: A feminist critique*. London: Routledge and Kegan Paul.

Snyder, H. N., & Sickmund, M. (1999). *Juvenile offenders and victims: 1999 national report* (NCJ 178257). Washington, DC: U.S. Department of Justice, Office of Justice Programs, Office of Juvenile Justice and Delinquency Prevention.

Snyder, H. N. (2001). *Law enforcement and juvenile crime. Juvenile offenders and victims national report*. Washington, DC: U.S. Department of Justice, Office of Justice Programs, Office of Juvenile Justice and Delinquency Prevention.

Snyder, H. N. (2002). *Juvenile arrests 2000*. Washington, DC: U.S. Department of Justice, Office of Justice Programs, Office of Juvenile Justice and Delinquency Prevention.

Stahl, A. (2003, September). Delinquency cases in juvenile courts. *OJJDP Fact Sheet #31*. Washington, DC: U.S. Department of Justice.

Steffensmeier, D. J., & Steffensmeier, R. H. (1980). Trends in female delinquency: An examination of arrest, juvenile court, self-report, and field data. *Criminology* 18, 62–85.

Tyler, K. A., Hoyt, D. R., Whitbeck, L. B., & Cauce, A. M. (2001). The impact of childhood sexual abuse or later sexual victimization among runaway youth. *Journal of Research on Adolescence* 11, 151–176.

Viner, E. (2003, October, 21). Personal communication with the author (Chesney-Lind).

White, B. (2003). American Civil Liberties Union report on the Hawaii Youth Correctional Facility June 3–July 23. Available: http://www.acluhawaii.org/pages/news/030826youthcorrection.html.

Wells, R. (1994). America's delinquent daughters have nowhere to turn for help. *Corrections Compendium* 19 (11), 4–6.

15

Intersectionality of Race/Ethnicity, Class, and Justice

Women of Color

Janice Joseph

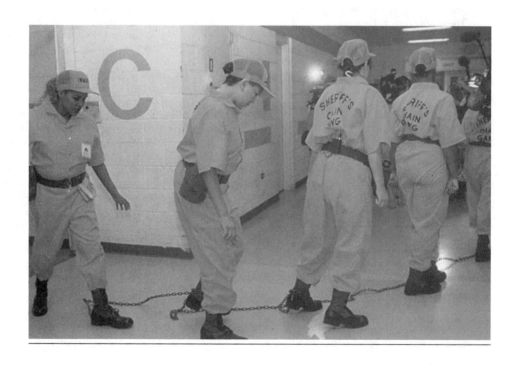

Traditionally, race/ethnicity, class, and gender have been analyzed autonomously as sources of oppression. Each on its own, or in combination, shape or structure the life course of an individual. In other words, they determine a person's access to economic and political power and choices that individuals can make in U.S. society. In general, men have more choices than women; wealthy people have more choices than poor people; and members of the majority group have more avenues available to them than members of minority groups. When these factors are combined, it is evident that wealthy white males have access to the greatest number of choices in the course of their lives, while poor minority women seem to have the fewest (Chigwada-Bailey, 2003).

The interplay of race/ethnicity, class, and gender affect women of color (Asian, African American, Latina/Hispanic, and Native Americans) who are faced with the greatest number of oppressions and are marginalized in U.S. society. Minority men have certain privileges given to them (compared with minority women) in a sexist society. Class-oppressed whites have access to more opportunities and privileges than women of color in a racist society, whether they are men or women. Women of color have to contend with the effects of racism, sexism, and classism simultaneously, and these oppressions are reflected in the system of justice in the United States. Yet there are very few analyses that examine the experiences of women of color and the justice system. Very often their experiences are included within those of men of color or analyzed with those of white women.

This chapter examines how race/ethnicity, class, and gender and their intersections have structured the justice system in United States—a system that has long been racialized, class-based, and gendered. Specifically, it focuses on how women of color experience gendered, racialized, and class-based justice with regard to criminalization and victimization.

Conceptual Framework

The terms *race* and *ethnicity* remain problematic in the way they are conceptualized and used in public discourses. However, the term "race" often refers to a person's biological and physical makeup. Based on this definition, the major racial groups are Caucasian, Negroid, and Mongoloid. Yet, it is difficult, if not impossible, to differentiate races of people based on biological characteristics. In fact, race is a social, cultural, and political construct formulated by the dominant groups in society in order to categorize people based on visible differences (Walker, Spohn, & DeLone, 2000). Consequently, the different categories of races based on skin color is a myth. There is no race of people, for example, who can be considered "white" based on skin color. Likewise, the so-called "black race" does not apply to the group of people presently regarded as "black" because skin color varies among this heterogeneous population. In fact, some people who are referred to as "blacks" (which is used interchangeably with African Americans) exhibit similar biological characteristics of people who are categorized as "whites." These biological differences used to identify groups of people are, therefore, superficial and are not true identifiers of differences between groups of people. However, in U.S. society, racial categories based on biological distinctiveness have become the normative way to identify people, individually and collectively.

The term *ethnicity* comes from the Greek word *ethnos,* which means nation. It is a more inclusive term than race and is used to identify a group of people who share a common cultural heritage. Members of an ethnic group often have a unique history, distinctive behavior patterns, and culture. Within a particular race, there are several ethnic groups because all racial groups contain subgroups with distinct cultural identity. Likewise within one ethnic group because there can be several racial groups. Among "whites," for example, there are Italian Americans, Greek Americans, and Irish Americans; likewise, among "blacks," there are African Americans, African Caribbean people, and Africans. Among Asians, there are Chinese, Japanese, Filipinos, and South Koreans. Ethnic groups also have the tendency to create enclaves within a host country. The only officially recognized ethnic group in this country is Hispanics—people of Spanish descent—and they are concentrated mainly in California, Texas, New York, Florida, and Illinois (U.S. Census Bureau, 2001).

Due to the emergence of new states, the end of the Cold War, and economic and cultural globalization, there have been massive increases in all forms of international population movements from one country to another, creating large numbers of ethnic minorities. In England there are ethnic groups from India, China, the Caribbean region, Africa, and other European countries. In France, there are African minorities; in Italy, large groups of Albanians and Yugoslavs. As more countries become multicultural, the issues of ethnicity and cultural identity continue to be of great importance globally, resulting in the interconnectedness of cultures as well as ethnic conflict all over the world.

The definition and the measure of the term *social class* have been problematic for criminologists. Consequently, there are numerous definitions and measures of class position. However, the common measure is usually based on an economic continuum of power, income, wealth, and prestige. It involves the distribution of social (both material and nonmaterial) resources within the society. Class stratification is central to social stratification in the United States. Social class placement is largely determined by a person's access to, and control of, social resources. The higher one's social class, the more access and control over certain resources (social and political) that person has. On the other hand, the lower the social class, the less control a person has over certain resources.

Within U.S. society, race/ethnicity and class are often intertwined because people of color are likely to be poor (Robinson, 2002). Blacks, Native Americans, and Hispanics (people of color) occupy the lowest socioeconomic status in U.S. society. They earn less than whites, have higher rates of poverty and diseases, and have lower educational attainment. In 2002, for example, 8 percent of whites compared with 10 percent Asians, 22 percent Hispanics, and 24 percent blacks were classified as poor. Likewise, 2002 data show the per capita income for whites was $26,142; for Asians $24,131; for Blacks, $15,441; and for Hispanics $13,487 (DeNavas-Walt, Cleveland, & Webster, 2003).

Justice

There are two major approaches to the understanding of justice. In the United States, when a criminal hurts someone, he or she is viewed as deserving of punishment under a retributive rationale. In this sense, justice is defined as including impartiality, fairness, and equality for everyone. Justice dictates that guilty people should be punished for their actions, and the innocent should go free. There is also no justice if any group is singled out for differential treatment under the law (Robinson, 2002). This conception of justice is represented by the figure of a blindfolded woman with a scale in one hand, indicating that justice is blind. It is the basis of the U.S. ideal of equal treatment for all under the law.

There is, however, another conception of justice from the victim's perspective. Victims tend to see justice as being served when society takes what they view as "appropriate" action to punish the perpetrator based on his or her culpability and the harm the crime caused to the victim. The scales of justice are balanced when the harm inflicted on victims results in punishment for the offender. In essence, justice is more than the system's response to criminals, but includes its response to the needs of victims as well.

Many people believe that the justice system is flawed since it is administered with a great deal of bias. Like other social institutions, the justice system reflects the values of the dominant class and the major racial group, which have the power to make and enforce the laws and policies of society. It is administered based on the values of the political, economic, and social elite.

Race/Ethnicity, Class, and Crime

In the past twenty-five years, researchers have focused on the effects of race and ethnicity on the administration of justice. Official data have consistently indicated that certain racial and ethnic groups (African Americans, Native Americans, and Hispanics) are overrepresented in the criminal justice system. Several studies have examined the overrepresentation of different racial and ethnic groups through multiple points in the criminal justice process, such as arrests, adjudication, and sentencing. The findings have been contradictory and controversial resulting in two different perspectives which explain this overrepresentation of minorities in the criminal justice system. One perspective states that the system is not discriminatory but rather that certain racial and ethnic groups commit more crimes than other groups. Wilbanks (1987) contended that although the practice of the U.S. criminal justice system may have been significantly racist in the past, the system today is, by and large, objective in its processing of criminal defendants (see also D'Alessio & Stolzenberg, 2003). On the other hand, there are those who concluded that the criminal justice system is essentially racist because it discriminates against people of color (see Bushway & Piehl, 2001; Everett & Wojtkiewicz, 2002; Mann, 1996).

Criminologists have argued that there is a correlation between social class and crime. They contend that members of the lower class are more prone to crime than those of the upper classes. Numerous traditional and contemporary mainstream theories have tried to explain the relationship between social class, crime, and criminal justice (see Cohen, 1955; Merton, 1938; Miller, 1958; Shaw & McKay, 1942; Vold, Bernard, & Snipes, 1998). Reiman (1998) argued that there is a class bias at every stage in the justice system. He demonstrated in his book, *The Rich Get Richer and the Poor Get Prison,* that the criminal system punishes the poor severely while ignoring the harmful acts of the wealthy, such as environmental and corporate crimes.

It is quite evident from the race/ethnicity-class nexus that the majority of the criminals in this society are primarily poor people of color. When gender is added to race/ethnicity and class, it is the women of color who are affected most by crime and justice as they are the fastest growing population in the criminal justice system. With three strikes against her, a poor woman of color has to contend with a justice system that is neither color-, class-, nor gender-blind.

Women of Color

The term *women of color* refers to women of African, Asian, Native American, and Hispanic backgrounds. These women share distinct cultural backgrounds and visible physical traits that make them distinct from the major group—white women. Because of their distinctiveness, they are more vulnerable to the racial/ethnic, class, and gender inequities in U.S. society. In addition, while white women, as a category, are often portrayed as models of self-respect, self-control, and modesty—even sexual purity, women of color have faced negative stereotypes.

Black women are often categorized into four stereotypical groups: mammy, Jezebel, matriarch, and Sapphire. The mammy image originated in the South during the time of slavery—she is depicted as a dark overweight woman with large buttocks, large breasts, and a friendly smile showing her white teeth; she is content with her state of being (Mullings, 1997). The Jezebel stereotype portrays black women as lascivious, seductive, alluring, worldly, beguiling, tempting, lewd, promiscuous, and even predatory. The matriarch serves as the head of household. She is seen as a bad mother who is responsible for low educational attainment, crime, and delinquency, but also is known for her independence and strength (Mullings, 1997). The Sapphire is the black woman who uses the "hands-on-hip, finger-pointing style" and verbally puts down the black man, showing his lack of virtues and morality (Jewell, 1992). The most recent stereotype of the black woman, presently dominating U.S. popular culture, is that of the "angry black woman" who is driven, outspoken or opinionated, achievement-oriented, and loud-mouthed. She is represented by Omarosa Manigault-Stallworth of NBC's hit series *The Apprentice* (Jones, 2004).

Latina women are often portrayed as sexy, submissive women of little virtue. They continue to be portrayed in television and films as promiscuous and dishonorable, hot-blooded, and fiery. Implicit in this depiction is the notion that they are immoral, seductive, and unscrupulous. They are also portrayed as lazy, aggressive, ignorant, and poor (Castro, 1998).

Asians are viewed as the "model minority," who are diligent and hardworking. The Asian woman is seen as submissive, deferential, and exotic. She has been portrayed as the "China Doll/Lotus Blossom" in the popular *Madame Butterfly* opera and its silver-screen variations, but she has also has earned the "Dragon Lady" reputation: scheming, subversive, sexually adept, and driven (Xing, 1998). Asian women are also seen as devious and mysterious, and in "the American imagination, Asian women are depicted as ultra-feminine sexual objects for white men" (Feng, 1996, p. 27).

Europeans apply two paradoxical stereotypes to Native American women. Both are based on her relationship with the white man. One image of the Native American woman is the "squaw" who constitutes the inferior, subservient, meek, and lustful woman and who becomes the white man's sexual partner. Native Americans reject the use of the word "squaw" in reference to Native American women because in the Algonquin languages it means *vagina*. The second image is that of the esteemed "princess" who is the guide, protector, helper, comforter, lover, and rescuer of the white man and represents civilization. The "princess" is often portrayed as slightly darker than whites and with distinct white features, while the "squaw" is depicted as darker, fatter, and cruder than the "princess" (Feagin & Feagin, 2002).

Like all women, women of color experience different levels of social control not experienced by white men or their male counterparts. The informal social control restricts a woman of color's choices and opportunities through her life. Because of gender oppression, they are often subordinated to their male relatives within the family, thus creating different notions of masculinity and femininity. In the past, schools controlled women of color by teaching them values and goals of the prevailing white male upper classes. Because they exist in a culture of white dominance, they have had to deal with a formal system of social control that isolates and degrades them and one that attempts to teach submission to authority through power and force. The formal system of control represents the economic elite, thus alienating women of color from the economic and social processes. They are overrepresented in the lowest paying jobs and tokenized in professional and high-paying positions. Consequently, they have been disempowered, marginalized, and underrepresented in positions of power and control. The legal system controls women of color by its almost total failure to respond to issues that concern women the most, such as intimate partner abuse, sexual harassment, and rape (see Rafter, 1981, p. 84).

Theoretical Perspectives

Within criminology, the intersection of race, ethnicity, class, and gender and the effects of these factors on crime and justice have rarely been examined. Mainstream criminology has historically been concerned with the study of white working-class men and boys. It presents a male-centered approach to the understanding of crime and justice and has been developed from male subjects and validated by androcentric studies. Lynch (1996) suggested that traditional criminology does not speak to the many ways in which class, gender, and race/ethnicity affect the life course of individuals, their access to crime, the criminal justice system's response to people, and the chance that a person will be labeled as a criminal. In general, it appears that traditional criminological theory seems to be basically racist and sexist because it unwittingly focuses on the interests and values of white males and boys while ignoring other social groups in the society.

Critical/radical criminologists concentrate on how those with economic and political power have the ability to influence and shape the law. Thus, they contend that the law is based on the values and interests of the upper classes. Lynch (1996, p. 4) reported that radical criminologists have recently come to recognize race and gender (along with class) as forces that affect "how people behave, how others react to and define that behavior, who has the power to define and label behaviors, and how law and law enforcement are organized and focused to control behavior." They now argue that those of the dominant race, class, and gender are most likely to control the legal and the criminal justice processes so that criminal behavior will reflect the definitions of the powerful elite. Despite radical criminologists' attempt to address race/ethnicity and gender in their theory, what seems to be conspicuously missing is a comprehensive examination of the intersection of race/ethnicity, class, and gender and their impact on crime and justice.

Feminist Criminology.   One of the purposes of feminist criminology is to provide an understanding of crime and criminal justice from a woman's perspective. Feminist criminologists criticize "malestream" criminology for ignoring and misrepresenting women in its inquiry. It focuses on gender relations central to understanding (criminal) behavior. Early feminist criminology (see Adler, 1975; Simon, 1975) proposed that as educational and occupational opportunities increase for women so would women's participation in criminal activities. Klein (1973) suggested that the low rates of women's arrests are related to their roles of subservient wife and mother, and Naffine (1996) criticized the male criminologist for his choice of subject to study. Other feminist criminologists have contended that research examining gender differences in participation in crime should place more emphasis on studying women and crime (Daly & Chesney-Lind, 1988; Heidensohn, 1995; Smart, 1976). Because feminist criminologists do not speak with one voice, Jaggar and Rothenberg (1984) and Walby (1990) identified several feminist frameworks—including liberal feminism, traditional Marxism, and radical feminism—that are used to explain the oppression of women.

Traditionally, feminists applied their theories, which were based on the most privileged type of woman, to all women. Typically, they view the conception of "woman" to mean white, middle-class heterosexual woman and "race" to mean blacks, in particular, black men (hooks, 1981). Lewis (1977) noted that because feminist theories focus exclusively upon the effects of sexism, they have been of limited applicability to minority women subjected to the constraints of both racism and sexism. However, over the past thirty years, feminist perspectives have expanded to be more inclusive of all types of women, especially black women.

Danner (1996) attempted to utilize a feminist perspective to examine race/ethnicity, gender, class, and criminalization. She posited that social feminism provides an excellent foundation to explore the implications of the intersection of gender, race/ethnicity, and class. She argued that socialist feminists recognize that gender, class, and race interact in fundamental ways that result in important differences in life experiences for groups and persons. She also suggested that poor ethnic women have few advantages because they may experience domination by men of their own class and ethnic group as well as by elite persons with power. Danner (1996, p. 40) presented the thesis that women's criminality should be viewed as resulting from a matrix of control and domination rather than simply a violation of the law: "Criminalization is foremost a mechanism of social control."

The black feminist movement was formed to address the ways sexism, racism, and classism influence the lives of black women whose needs were ignored by the black men of the black liberation movement and white women in the women's movement. Black feminist thought examines issues such as negative images, disenfranchisement, freedom, multiple oppressions, and justice from black women's perspectives. It offers an insight into the particular situation of black women and criticizes the social and legal systems that are supposed to provide legitimate and equal treatment for everyone in U.S. society (Johnson, 2003). In examining the issues of race/ethnicity, and class, some black feminists argue that the examination of race is more significant than sexism or class because many black women view racism as a more powerful cause of their subordinate position than sexism (see Lewis, 1977). Others such as hooks (1981), Joseph (1981), Dill (1983), Daly and Stevens (1995), and Davis (1981) argued that the experiences of black women should be considered within the context of all forms of inequality—class, race, and gender—as they are an integral part of the lives of these women. A few black feminists argue that black (minority) women occupy a range of multiple positions that have implications for their relationships to social systems and highlighted the importance of examining the racial and class experiences of black women within the private sphere of their families as well as their relationship to the public sphere (see Carby, 1982; Mama, 1989).

The different versions of feminist criminology, however, have yet to comprehensively examine the interrelationship between race/ethnicity, class, and gender within the context of the experiences of women of color. By not examining the interrelationship between these sources of oppression, feminist criminologists are unable to disentangle the complex matrix of oppressions faced by women of color and how these affect their lives.

Race/Ethnicity, Class, and Gender Intersectionality

Proponents of intersectionality have long argued that individuals possess multiple identities (based on race/ethnicity, class, and gender) that simultaneously interact with each other. For example, one cannot understand sexism within this capitalist society without taking into account the dynamics of class relations and racism. Likewise, race/ethnicity must be understood within the context of capitalism because it is embedded within class relations. Class relations are also intertwined with those emerging from patriarchy, primarily sexism and racism. So class struggles are fought on multiple fronts, and so too are racism and sexism fought on various levels (Muszynski, 1989). In other words, it is important to explore the racialization of gender and the gendering of race within the capitalist system. Despite the interdependence of these identifiers, most studies of marginal groups have used a unidimensional approach by analyzing marginalization along one dimension—race/ethnicity, class, or gender.

A race/ethnicity, class, and gender intersectionality framework analyzes ways these three strands of inequality work simultaneously to affect social life. This approach focuses on the disempowerment of marginalized people and attempts to capture the consequences of the interaction between the other two forms of subordination. It addresses the manner in which racial, sexist, class-based, and ethnic oppression create inequalities that determine the positions of individuals in society. It basically examines how the systems of racism, sexism, classism, and ethnic discrimination overlap and interrelate to each other.

The intersection literature resulted from the work of women of color, such as Crenshaw (1989) and Hill-Collins (1993), who have argued that the "intersectionality" of oppression must be taken into consideration when discussing the experiences and life chances of women of color in the United States (Crenshaw, 1989; Crenshaw, 1991; Hill-Collins, 2000). For example, Hill-Collins (2000, p. 18) notes:

> Intersectionality refers to particular forms of intersecting oppressions, for example, intersections of race and gender, or of sexuality and nation. Intersectional paradigms remind us that oppression cannot be reduced to one fundamental type, and that oppressions work together in producing injustice.

These authors state that research needs to examine the "whole person," rather than attempting to break individuals up into their component parts (i.e., race, separate from gender, separate from class). They further indicate that individuals possess one identity that encompasses multiple and intersecting oppressions. What they are saying is that individuals should not be viewed as atomized subsets but as (complete) entities.

Most proponents of intersectionality present the argument that the multiple oppressions of racism, classism, and gender are not additive, but, in fact, mutually exponential. Anderson and Collins (1995), for example, asserted that if a person is a member of the lower class and a minority woman, she will not experience simply the negative additive effects of being female, minority, and lower class. Rather, her experiences will result from how these forces intersect with each other through the social and economic structure. The effect is contextual, not mathematical. Lynch (1996) echoed similar sentiments when he stated that to live as a lower-class minority woman means something different than "adding together" the effects of being a woman, being minority, and being lower class. Understanding such experiences goes beyond statistics (Lynch, 1996). Chigwada-Bailey (2003, p. 19) noted that "it is not simply a question of adding together the effects of these various aspects of disadvantage, rather of considering ways in which, when they intersect and interact, they compound one another—the argument being that the whole is greater than the sum of the parts."

The intersectionality of race, class, and gender is referred to by various terms; for example, triple oppression, interrelation, cumulative effects, interconnections (Belkhir, 1994); interactive, triadic relation, overlapping, interactive systems (Belkhir, 1993); multiple jeopardy, simultaneous oppressions, multiplicative, simultaneous, interconnected systems of a whole (Barnett, Brewer, & Kuumba, 1999). Irrespective of what term is used, the fact remains that justice is administered in this society based on race/ethnicity, class, and gender. According to Barak (2000, para. 37–39):

1. Each of these categories of social difference share similarities and dissimilarities of justice, especially as these relate to power resources and to the allocation and distribution of rewards and punishments in society.
2. The systems of privilege and inequality derived from the social statuses of class, race, and gender, share distinct as well as integrative, or overlapping and accumulating, affects on the type of crime control that various groups of people receive.
3. There are connections and linkages between these systems of difference, inequality, and privilege as each, separately and together, helps reproduce the social divisions of hierarchy and stratification that dynamically affect people's life experiences, inside and outside, the criminal justice system.

Race/Ethnicity, Class, Criminalization, and Justice

Women of color are more likely than white women to be arrested, charged with more serious offenses, prosecuted, convicted, and to serve time in prison (Allard, 2002 ; Chesney-Lind, 1997; Greenfield & Snell, 1999; Miller, 2001). Research continues to show that once women of color are arrested and convicted, they are disproportionately sent to prison while white women are more likely to be placed on probation (Greenfield & Snell, 1999). In addition, black females in the United States had a 5.6 percent chance of going to prison in 2001, which was almost as high as that for white males (5.9 percent) (Bureau of Justice Statistics, 2003).

Although a disproportionate number of women of color in comparison to white women are processed through the criminal justice system, this does not necessarily mean that women of color are more criminal than white women, but instead that they experience justice differently from white women. Because women of color are seen as capable of committing crimes and not seen as victims, they are often blamed wholly for their crimes. Consequently, they do not benefit from decision makers' ability to use mitigating circumstances that can keep individuals out of the system. White women, on the other hand, are not totally blamed for their crimes, benefit from mitigating circumstances, and are often viewed as needing help rather than punishment. This means that for white women, the line between offender and victim is blurred and can be crossed (see Chigwada-Bailey, 2003).

Lynch (1996, p. 20) stated that "who the law reacts to as an offender and victim, who the law protects and discriminates against, both as statute and as a process, depends upon the race, class, and gender of the parties involved." Since crime often reflects racial/ethnic, sexist, and class power, women of color are often criminalized more often than any other group. Richie, Tsenin, and Widom (2000) noted that the most marginalized women in this society are susceptible to involvement in illegal behavior (criminalization) and gender abuse (victimization). However, they often receive very little justice either as a criminal or a victim.

Criminalization

According to Beirne and Messerschmidt (1991, p. 24), "criminalization refers to the process whereby criminal law is selectively applied to social behavior." Danner (1996, p. 31) argued that the criminal justice system "assists in the maintenance of inequality through a process of criminalization whereby the law is selectively applied in a manner detrimental to those groups and persons most disadvantaged in unequal relations." She also acknowledged that not all women experience criminalization to the same extent because of inequality across race, ethnicity, and class based on the distribution of material resources. Danner (1996) reported that not all group members are equally vulnerable to criminalization because it is not the relatively privileged members of the groups who are criminalized, but it is often the poor women who receive the "criminal" label.

The so-called "drug war" illustrates one of the most glaring examples of racial-gender-class biases in the justice system. The redefinition of drug addiction as a legal problem rather than a public health issue has provided a rationale for states to pass anti-drug legislation and to expand the powers of law enforcement officers who often engage in overpolicing communities of color. Many women of color become involved in the drug trade as a way of generating fast, easy money to support their children and maintain the household. Although many of them may be receiving public assistance, the funds are often not enough to take care of a child. If they worked and reported their income, their benefits will be reduced (see Langston, 2003). For many of these women, the prospect of the financial reward from illegal drugs makes facing the risk worth it. Other women find themselves trapped in powerless relationships with men involved in trafficking or are denied access to legal and sustainable means to support their family (Drug Policy Alliance, 2004). A study on female drug couriers found that many of the women were unaware that they were carrying drugs; often the parcel they were carrying was called "a gift for a friend." Abusive boyfriends coerced others with threats of violence and death (Huling, 1995).

Since the 1980s, feminist research about women and illegal drugs has indicated that men are not subjected to the same gendered and patriarchal forms of legal, medical, and social regulation by the state. In addition, illegal drug users are not all treated alike: "Being poor is another strike against a woman, as being a woman of color" (Boyd, 2003, p. 13). The drug war has more or less become both racialized, feminized, and class-based.

One aspect of the war on drug is the "criminalization" of drug use and pregnancy, especially cocaine (see Chapter 4 for a complete discussion of the criminalization of women who use drugs during pregnancy). Although research indicates that white and minority pregnant women use illegal drugs during pregnancy at similar or equal rates, African American women are ten times more likely than white women to be reported to child welfare agencies for prenatal drug use (Chasnoff, Landress, & Barrett, 1990; Neuspiel, 1996; Paltrow, Cohen, & Carey, 2000). According to Kershnar and Paltrow (2001), African American and Latina women account for 80 percent of those prosecuted for delivering drug-exposed babies.

In the Supreme Court case, *Ferguson et al. v. the City of Charleston et al.* (2001), in which the policy of drug testing pregnant women without their consent and prosecuting the mothers for "distributing an illegal substance" to an unborn child through the umbilical cord was challenged, 29 out of the 30 prosecuted under the policy were African American women (Roberts, 1997). As discussed in Chapter 4, the U.S. Supreme Court found that the testing and giving of the information to the police were unconstitutional. The fetus-protection law epitomizes how racism and patriarchy function as reinforcing systems of domination that help to determine "who the criminals are, what constitutes a crime, and which crimes society treats most seriously" (Roberts 1993, p. 1945).

Research continues to show that people of color are stopped and arrested more often than white people on the basis of "profiling" (Harris, 1999; Knowles & Persico, 2001). This practice of stopping, searching, or targeting for investigation an individual on the basis of race, national origin, or ethnicity or class is linked to the drug war. A survey indicated that one in four black women complained that they are profiled by the police (Hutchinson, 2001a). Although there seems to be very little extensive research that specifically examines police stops and arrests of women of color on the streets, one can assume these women, like the men of color, experience (ethnic) profiling by police officers.

There is a common perception that drug couriers are primarily minority women so racial profiling by the U.S. Customs Service occurs at airports nationwide. This type of ethnic-gender profiling is evident in the practices at U.S. airports where people of color are more likely to be searched than white people. Many women of color have been subjected to strip searches, x-rays, body cavity searches, administration of laxatives, monitored bowel movements, and other search procedures (see American Civil Liberties Union, 2002). The U.S. Government Accounting Office (2000) reported that black, Asian, and Hispanic women were nearly three times as likely to be strip-searched at major airports such John Fitzgerald Kennedy International Airport (JFK) in New York, O'Hare International Airport in Chicago, Los Angeles International Airport (LAX), and Miami International Airport, as men of those races. For example, the likelihood of being strip-searched for black men was .0506; and the likelihood was .1421 for black women (.1421/.0506 equals 2.81, or nearly 3 times). The U.S. Government Accounting Office also reported that some passengers who were more likely to be subjected to more intrusive personal searches were not more likely, or even as likely, to be found carrying contraband. This was quite evident in cases of black women who were U.S.

citizens and who were nine times more likely than white women who were U.S. citizens to be x-rayed, frisked, or patted down but were less than half as likely to be found carrying contraband as white women (U.S. Government Accounting Office, 2000).

Women of Color and the Courts

The interplay between race/ethnicity, class, and gender continues in the courts. The treatment of minority poor women during adjudication is different from that of white wealthy women. One study, for example, found that when judges ask white women about the father(s) of their children, they are trying to ascertain whether the father(s) have been economically supportive. However, when they ask black mothers the same question, they are trying to find out if their children have different fathers, or whether the women have a record of promiscuity or prostitution (Hudson, 1988, cited in Chigwada-Bailey, 2003). The courts, therefore, tend to focus on the economic status and well-being of white women while the sexual lifestyle of the black women is seen as significant. These stereotypes and emphases often result in differential treatment in the courts for white and black women (Chigwada-Bailey, 2003).

Farnsworth and Teske (1995) found that white women, in comparison to African American women, were twice as likely to have their charges of assault at arrest changed to non-assault at sentencing. They also reported that whites were more likely to receive reduced charges while African Americans were more likely to receive probation.

Women of Color and Incarceration

Today, more than 2 million people are behind bars and, while women continue to represent a minority of those behind bars, in recent years their numbers have increased at nearly double the rate for men. They are the fastest growing segment of the U.S. imprisonment binge. In the crusade to get tough on crimes, policymakers have gotten tough on women, especially women of color. Due to mandatory sentences, "three strikes and you're out" legislation, and harsh drug laws, more and more women of color, especially black and Latina women, are under the supervision of corrections. In fact, two-thirds of the women in prison in the United States are women of color (New York State Department of Correctional Services, 2002).

Although African Americans comprise only 12.2 percent of the population and 13 percent of drug users, they make up 38 percent of those arrested for drug offenses and 59 percent of those convicted of drug offenses. The rate of imprisonment of black women is more than eight times the rate of imprisonment of white women; the rate of imprisonment of Hispanic women is nearly four times the rate of imprisonment of white women (Amnesty International, 1999). In New York, for example, in 2001, 91 percent of women under custody for a drug offense were women of color: 54 percent were African American and 37 percent were Latina (New York State Department of Correctional Services, 2002). On June 30, 2001, 49 percent of the female prisoners in Florida prison system were black and many were incarcerated for drug violations (Florida Department of Corrections, 2001).

The higher arrest rates for African Americans and Latina women reflect selective enforcement in these communities where drug use and sales are more likely to take place in open-air drug markets. The well-known disparity between crack cocaine and powder cocaine in the Federal Sentencing Guidelines dictates a ratio of 1:100 in punishing the two types of drugs despite the fact that they are chemically identical. Obviously, the harsher punishment is directed to crack, a drug more common among poor blacks (Drug Policy Alliance, 2004).

Race/Ethnicity, Class, Victimization, and Justice

How society responds to the victimization of women is based on that woman's status in society. Thus, certain women are not protected by the criminal justice system from crimes that threaten them. Because of their race/ethnicity, class, and gender statuses, women of color are more vulnerable to all forms of violence and victimization and they often find it difficult to achieve justice for their victimization. Police, prosecutors, and the courts often ignore or lightly punish rape, sexual abuse, and assaults against black women (Hutchinson, 1999). With regard to intragroup violence against women, minority communities, often perceived as prone to violence, are commonly treated differently by the justice system and "this normalization of violence categorizes violence against minority women as normal and that against dominant women as deviant resulting in the differential reckoning of real victims" (Adelman, Erez & Shalhoub-Kevorkian, 2003, p. 114).

Domestic Violence

The problem of domestic violence is serious for all women, but more frequent for women of color and low-income women of color who experience the highest rates of domestic violence (Raj & Silverman, 1999; Rennison & Welchans, 2000; Wyatt, Axelrod, Chin, Carmona, & Loeb, 2000). Poverty puts women at added risk for sustaining physical and psychological injury. Since women and children of color constitute disproportionate numbers of the poor, domestic violence tends to be more prevalent in communities of color because of poverty (Sen, 1999).

Now, with mandatory arrest policies, police often arrest both partners in a dispute, with the claim that both partners were being violent (Ammons, 2002; Sen, 1999). So many women of color simply will not call the police for fear of what will happen to them or their abusive partners in the hands of law enforcement officers. The police have the power to determine who is a legitimate and deserving victim. Based on their perception of minority communities, they sometimes question the credibility of an abused minority woman's complaints. Many abused women of color experience either "gendered racism," "racialized sexism," or "classism" when they contact the justice system (see Adelman et al., 2003). These women are often subjected to racism in white society, sexism in a male-dominated society, classism in this capitalist society, or a combination of all three when they call the police (many of whom are white).

According to Ammons (2002), police trainees are frequently told that physical violence is an acceptable part of life among black poor residents. Consequently, when black women are treated for domestic violence-related injuries in inner-city hospitals, protocols for wife beating are rarely introduced or followed. Ammons also noted that the mental health system deals differently with black and white women who are in abusive relationships.

Native American women experience the highest rate of violence of any group, yet the justice system has done little to protect them from these assaults (see Pope, 2004). In one case, a Native Alaskan woman who had been held hostage and dragged across the lawn by an intimate partner called the police. The responding officer proceeded to tell her to undress so he could examine her bruises. He also falsely claimed that the woman was drunk at the time of the incident despite a hospital report that refuted this. The woman's attacker was never convicted (Bhungalia, 2001).

In the southern states, where large numbers of Mexicans reside, police often view woman battering as a routine event and, therefore, believe that arresting the batterer is a waste of time because they consider violence to be endemic to the Mexican culture (Ferraro, 1989). The injustice increases for battered women of color who have multiple issues, such as substance abuse, a criminal record, homelessness, mental illness, and prostitution. They face barriers to receiving services and benefits and are not taken seriously as victims by the criminal justice system (Gilfus, 2002).

Sexual Abuse

Historically, it was believed that women of color could not be raped because they lacked the basic respectability that enabled them to be credible victims. In addition, it is a common myth that black, Latino, and Chicano cultures are inherently violent and that women of these cultures experience the violence of rape as "natural." When a woman of color cries "rape," it often lacks legitimacy because society has created stereotypes of minority women, especially black women, as promiscuous and loose (Grana, 2002). When a woman of color reports a rape to the police, she is often blamed more than a white woman would be blamed. Sometimes the police take no action or show only a minimal response when a woman of color has been attacked. Black women, for example, are less likely than white women to have a rape case come to trial and lead to conviction (Bart & O'Brien, 1985; Hill-Collins, 2000) because sexual violence committed against women of color is perceived to be insignificant.

Controlling for legal factors, LaFree (1980) analyzed how the race of victim and defendant affected the outcome of rape cases. His "sexual stratification" thesis holds that black women are less likely to be protected by the law when the offender is white and other factors are taken into consideration (e.g., use of a weapon; type of evidence). In addition, if she is raped by a white man, he is also less likely than a man of color to be convicted for the crime.

It is clear that racial, class, and gender positioning put women of color at a high risk for rape. However, because of the injustices in the criminal justice system, women of color are often reluctant to report sexual violence. Because of racist stereotypes, police and the courts sometimes respond with skepticism and cynicism when a woman of color reports a rape, thus minimizing the seriousness of the violence. For many women of color, this second victimization by representatives of the criminal justice system may sometimes be worse than the actual rape. Consequently, many of these women remain silent, especially if the perpetrator is of the same race, thus allowing the sexual violence to continue.

Other Forms of Victimization

Homicide now ranks as the major cause of death of young black women. Hutchinson (2001b) reported that in St. Louis where five women were murdered, police were slow to investigate and even refused the assistance of the Federal Bureau of Investigation. Although the police explained the lack of resources and the fact that the murders did not fit the pattern of serial killing, Hutchinson argued that the police were slow to respond because, with one exception, all the victims were black, poor, and had long personal histories of drug-use and prostitution. The murders of these women did not create public outrage because poor black women have been portrayed by racial and gender stereotypes, and the media often magnify and sensationalize crimes by black men against white women, while ignoring crimes against black women. Likewise in Ciudad Juarez, Mexico, in the past decade, more than 300 women have been murdered. Victims were killed brutally: Many were raped or beaten before being strangled or stabbed to death. A number of the bodies bore signs of torture or mutilation. The motives for the murders of these young women included drug trafficking, the machismo culture, and prostitution. The Mexican authorities have been accused of being inept, corrupt, and even complicit in the killings since very little was done to find the killers of these young women (NPR, 2003).

Consequences of Differential Justice

The disparate justice for women of color has clear moral, political, and economic ramifications for communities of color as well as the individual. Given the high rate of incarceration of women of color, there are many children who are without their mothers. Currently, there are an estimated 14 million African American children who have a parent in prison and, over the course of childhood, these numbers would be considerably higher. Also, this record number of children are now growing up with the stigma of having a parent in prison. Moreover, the separation from their children may make it difficult for women of color to maintain ties with their children, and this separation can also put these children at risk of involvement in the criminal justice system (Mauer, 2003).

The large-scale incarceration of men of color is having drastic effects on the women of color and the family, especially in the black community. When these men are sentenced to prison, many times they leave behind a wife/girlfriend and/or children. The man's absence is even more prominently felt when the woman has to fill the role of financial provider, caretaker, and struggle to rebuild a family structure. This is especially problematic since women are underpaid relative to men in the workforce, and many of these women do not have the necessary skills to obtain a job that would pay a living wage necessary to support them and their children (see Mauer, 2003). Consequently, many of these women are then "compelled" to turn to the informal drug economy as means of survival (see Langston, 2003).

The disproportionate imprisonment of men of color has consequences on family formation and stability as well. Given the dramatic rates of imprisonment for young black men in particular, many communities of color now have a highly uneven ratio of men to women. One study finds that in the 10 percent of neighborhoods in Washington, DC, that are most heavily affected by incarceration, the gender ratio is an estimated 62 men per 100 women (Braman, 2002). In addition, these women have to sometimes also cope with the fact that their sons or brothers are incarcerated as well.

Most ex-felons are denied certain rights once they are released from prison. The disenfranchisement laws deny the right to vote to those who have drug felony convictions. As a result, 1.4 million African American men, or 13 percent of the African American adult male population, and an increasing segment of the black female population are disenfranchised (Drug Policy Alliance, 2003; Mauer, 2003). Other consequences include the denial of public benefits. Tenants who apply for public housing can be denied admission if they have been convicted of a felony drug offense or if they are in a drug treatment program and are currently known to be using illegal drugs. In addition, the Anti-Drug Abuse Act of 1988 contains a "one-strike" law that allows housing officials to evict public housing residents or visitors who have been convicted of a felony. This has disproportionately affected elderly women of color whose relatives have been arrested. Women with criminal records may also lose welfare (TANF), food stamps, and Medicaid (Drug Policy Alliance, 2003). These policies may make it very difficult for women of color to legally obtain food, housing, health care, drug treatment, and income for themselves and their children.

Policy Implications

Women of color are marginalized by virtue of their identities based on class, race/ethnicity, and gender and they have been subjected to social, economic, and political oppressions within the justice system. The solutions to race, class, and gender inequities reside both inside and outside of the criminal justice system (Barak et al., 2001). The following are some suggestions on how to minimize the injustices that women of color faced in this society:

1. The social and economic inequities generated by racism, classism, and sexism should be eliminated. In employment, education, and in other arenas, women of color are sometimes subjected to discrimination because they are not members of the racially or ethnically dominant groups in society. Society can reduce this exclusion by providing more economic and social opportunities for these women.

2. Government needs to develop holistic and multidisciplinary services for people of color. These services also need to be culturally sensitive because services that are not based solely on the experiences of the majority group will be of little benefit to those whose lives are shaped by multiple oppressions.

3. The large-scale "war on drugs" needs to be deescalated and shifted from the law enforcement into the medical arena. In other words, drugs should be treated as a health problem, as is done in many countries in Europe, rather than a criminal justice problem. By shifting the emphasis on the "war on drugs," the number of people of color entangled in the criminal justice system will be reduced drastically and resources can be used for rehabilitation.

4. Employment opportunities in the criminal justice system for people of color need to increase as an approach to reforming the system. At the present time, the criminal justice system is practically white and operates to the benefit of those who control it. A culturally diverse system could help to bring fairness and equality for all who come into contact with it.

5. There needs to be more legal protection for women of color who are victims of violence. Criminal justice personnel need to be educated about the extent to which racist, sexist, and classist attitudes in the justice system result in the revictimization of abused women, and the system needs to be monitored to determine to what extent it meets the needs of female victims in communities of color.

6. The government needs to change its discriminatory laws and policies (minimum mandatory sentences and drug-related polices) based on class, race/ethnicity, and gender. In addition, society needs a more integrative and social form of justice that addresses the realities of class, race, and gender (Barak et al., 2001).

Conclusion

This chapter discussed the race/ethnicity, class, and gender nexus and justice. The chapter investigated the complexities of race/ethnicity, class, and gender as they interact to produce criminals and victims and a system of unequal justice for women of color. The evidence indicates that because the system of justice is based on whiteness, masculinity, and elitism, women of color experience repressive "justice" instead of equal justice. This further reinforces their trilogy of racial/ethnic, class, and gender oppression. In other words, the system of justice has failed to protect the most powerless and vulnerable members of society but instead reinforces the inequities of poverty, racism, and sexism. Campbell (cited by Chandler & Kingery, 2002, p. 91) described this injustice by stating that:

> Today justice is bought and sold, fluctuating by economics for those who may or may not be able to afford appetites. Laws are legislated for or by a financially privileged group. Also "who you know" and "money talks" dictate where and what type of incarceration one endures. A corrupt system such as ours is not about safety or justice, especially not for people of color, women. . . .

The slogans "justice for all" and "equal opportunity" are clearly ideals that are far from reality for poor women of color. The criminal justice system has failed to achieve its goals of doing justice and the blindfolded woman with a scale in one hand symbolizing justice does not represent the experiences of women of color who are poor. For many of them, Justitia— Lady Justice—is race/ethnic, class, and gender conscious and her scales are out of balance. Race/ethnicity, class, and gender do matter in the way justice is administered in this society. Martin Luther King said, "injustice anywhere is a threat to justice everywhere." He no doubt would be saddened to find that the injustice against people of color may be as prevalent today as during his lifetime.

Justice will not be achieved by simply criminalizing more elite white males. Nor will it be achieved by responding less to their victimization. Racially diversifying the criminal justice agencies will not achieve justice either. What is necessary is for society to examine and address the social injustices and oppressions that women of color face in the larger society (poverty, sexism, racism) so that they will not be replicated in the justice system. The future challenge is for the scales of justice to be rebalanced so that there will be justice for all, irrespective of a person's race, ethnicity, class, or gender.

Review Questions

1. Explain the intersectionality perspective of race/ethnicity, class, and gender.

2. What is the black feminist perspective on race/ethnicity, class, and gender?

3. Discuss the relationship between class, race/ethnicity, and crime.

4. How has the "war on drugs" adversely affected women of color?

5. Discuss the ethnic-gender profiling of women of color at U.S. airports. Why has it occurred?

6. Discuss the police response to women of color who have experienced domestic violence.

7. What steps can society take to improve the economic, social, and educational status of poor minority women?

Key Terms

Race
Ethnicity
Justice
Intersectionality

Criminalization
Women of color
Disproportionate representation
Profiling

References

Adelman, M., Erez, E., & Shalhoub-Kevorkian, N. (2003). Policing violence against minority women in multicultural societies: Community and the politics of exclusion. *Police & Society: An Interdisciplinary Journal of Law Enforcement and Criminology* 7, 105–133.

Adler, F. (1975). *Sisters in crime.* New York: McGraw-Hill.

Allard, P. (2002). *Life sentences: Denying welfare benefits to women convicted of drug offenses.* Washington, DC: The Sentencing Project.

American Civil Liberties Union. (2002). *Stop racial profiling at American airports!* http://www.aclu.org/PolicePractices/PolicePractices.cfm?ID=9968&c=118

Ammons. L. L. (2002). *The plight of black battered women.* Arte Sana. http://www.arte-sana.com/articles/plight_black_women_article.htm. Retrieved June 12, 2004.

Amnesty International. (1999). *Not part of my sentence: Violations of the human rights of women in custody.* http://www.amnestyusa.org/rightsforall/women/report/index.html#TopOfPage.

Anderson, M. L., & Collins. P. H. (1995). *Race, class and gender* (2nd ed.). Belmont, CA: Wadsworth.

Barak G. (2000, October). Class, race, and gender in criminology and criminal justice: Ways of seeing difference. Symposium speech delivered at the Second Annual Conference on Race, Gender and Class Project in New Orleans on October 20, 2000. http://www.greggbarak.com/whats_new.html

Barak, G., Flavin, J. M., & Leighton, P. S. (2001). *Class, race, gender, and crime: Social realities of justice in America.* Los Angeles, CA: Roxbury Publishing Company.

Barnett, B. M., Brewer, R., & Kuumba, M. B. (1999). New directions in race, gender and class studies: African American experiences. *Race, Gender & Class* 6 (2), 7–28.

Bart, P., & O'Brien, P. (1985). *Stopping rape: Successful survival strategies.* New York: Pergamon Press

Bart, P. B., & O'Brien, P. H. (1985). Ethnicity and rape avoidance: Jews, white Catholics and Blacks. In P. B. Bart & P. H. O'Brien (Eds.), *Stopping rape: Successful survival strategies* (pp. 70–92). New York: Pergamon Press.

Beirne, P., & Messerschmidt, J. (1991). *Criminology.* San Diego: Harcourt Brace Jovanovich.

Belkhir, J. (1993). Introduction: Integrating race, sex and class in our disciplines. *Race, Sex and Class* 1 (1), 3–11.

Belkhir, J. (1994). The "failure" and revival of Marxism on race, gender and class issues. *Race, Sex and Class* 2 (1), 79–107.

Bhungalia, L. (2001). Native American women and violence. *National NOW Times.* http://www.now.org/nnt/spring-2001/nativeamerican.html. (Spring). Retrieved June 13, 2004.

Boyd, S. C. (2003). *From witches to crack moms: Women, drug law, and policy.* Durham, NC: Carolina Academic Press.

Braman, D. (2000). Families and incarceration. In M. Mauer & M. Chesney-Lind, (Eds.), *Invisible punishment: The collateral consequences of mass imprisonment* (pp. 117–35). New York: The New Press.

Bureau of Justice Statistics. (2003, August 17). *More than 5.6 million U.S. residents have served or are serving time in state or federal prisons.* http://www.ojp.usdoj.gov/bjs/pub/press/piusp01pr.htm. Retrieved June 10, 2004.

Bushway, S. D., & Piehl, A. M. (2001). Judging judicial discretion: Legal factors and racial discrimination in sentencing. *Law & Society Review* 35 (4), 733–764.

Carby, H. (1982). White women listen! Black feminism and the boundaries of sisterhood. In The Centre for Contemporary Cultural Studies (Ed.), *The empire strikes back* (pp. 212–235). London: Hutchinson.

Castro, D. O. (1998). Stereotyping by the media: "Hot blood and easy": Mass media and the making of racist Latino/a stereotypes. In C. R. Mann & M. S. Zata (Eds.), *Images of color: Image of crime* (pp. 134–144). Los Angeles: Roxbury Publishing Company.

Chandler, C., & Kingery, C. (2002). Speaking out against state violence: Activist HIV positive women prisoners redefine social justice. In J. Silliman & A. Bhattacharjee (Eds.), *Policing the national body: Race, gender, and criminalization* (pp. 81–102). Cambridge, MA: South End Press.

Chasnoff, I. J., Landress, H. J., & Barrett, M. E. (1990). The prevalence of illicit-drug or alcohol use during pregnancy and discrepancies in mandatory reporting in Pinellas County, Florida. *New England Journal of Medicine* 322, 1202–1206.

Chesney-Lind, M. (1989). Girls' crime and woman's place: Toward a feminist model of female delinquency. *Crime & Delinquency* 35, 5–29.

Chesney-Lind, M. (1997). *The female offender.* Thousand Oaks, CA: Sage.

Chesney-Lind, M. & Daly, K. 1988. Feminism and criminology. *Justice Quarterly* 5, 499–527.

Chigwada-Bailey, R. (2003). *Black women's experience of criminal justice, race, gender and class: A discourse on disadvantage.* Winchester, UK: Waterside Press.

Cohen, A. K. (1955). *Delinquent boys.* Chicago, IL: University of Chicago Press.

Collins, P. (2000). *Black feminist thought: Knowledge, consciousness and the politics of empowerment* (2nd ed.). New York: Routledge Press.

Collins, P. H. (1993). Toward a new vision: Race, class, and gender as categories of analysis and connection. *Race, Sex, & Class* 1(1), 25–45.

Crenshaw, K. (1989). Demarginalizing the intersection of race and sex: A black feminist critique of anti-discrimination doctrine, feminist theory and antiracist politics. *Chicago Legal Forum* 139–167.

Crenshaw, K. (1991). Mapping the margins: Intersectionality, identity, politics and violence against women of color. *Stanford Law Review* 43, 1241–1299.

D'Alessio, S. J., & Stolzenberg, L. (2003). Race and the probability of arrest. *Social Forces* 81 (4), 1381–1397.

Daly, K., & Chesney-Lind, M. (1988). Feminism and criminology. *Justice Quarterly* 5, 497–538.

Daly, K., & Stevens, D. J. (1995). The "dark figure" of criminology: Towards a black and multicultural feminist agenda for theory and research. In N. H. Farter & F. Heidensohn (Eds.), *International feminist perspectives in criminology: Endangering a discipline* (pp. 189–215). Philadelphia: Open University Press.

Danner, J. E. M. (1996). Gender inequality and criminalization: A socialist feminist perspective on the legal social control of women. In M. D. Schwartz & D. Milovanovic (Eds.), *Race, gender, and class in criminology: The intersection* (pp. 29–45). New York: Garland Publishing.

Davis, A. (1981). *Women, race, and class.* New York: Vintage.

DeNavas-Walt, C., Cleveland, R., & Webster, B. H. (2003). *U.S. Census Bureau, Current Population Reports, P60–221, Income in the United States: 2002.* Washington, DC: U.S. Government Printing Office.

Dill, B. (1983). Race, class, and gender: Prospects for an all-inclusive sisterhood. *Feminist Studies* 9 (1), 131–150.

Drug Policy Alliance. (2003). *Barriers to re-entry for convicted drug offenders.* http://www.lindesmith.org/library/factsheets/barriers/ (April). Retrieved May 26, 2004.

Drug Policy Alliance. (2004). *Race and the drug war.* http://www.lindesmith.org/race/index.cfm. Retrieved May 26, 2004.

Estrand, M., & Blume, J. (2000). *U.S. Customs Service: Better targeting of airline passengers for personal searches could produce better results.* Washington, DC: General Accounting Office.

Everett, R. S., & Wojtkiewicz, R. A. (2002). Difference, disparity, and race/ethnic bias in federal sentencing. *Journal of Quantitative Criminology* 18 (2), 189–211.

Farnsworth, M., & Teske, R. (1995). Gender difference in felony court processing: Three hypotheses of disparity. *Women & Criminal Justice* 6, 23–44.

Feagin, J. R., & Feagin, C. B. (2002). *Racial and ethnic relations* (7th ed.). Upper Saddle River, NJ: Prentice Hall.

Feng, P. (1996). Redefining Asian American masculinity: Steven Okazaki's American sons. *Cineaste* 22 (3) 27–29.

Ferraro K. (1989). Policing domestic violence. *Social Problems* 36 (1), 61–74.

Florida Department of Corrections. (2001, October). *Status Report on Female Offenders.* Tallahassee, FL: Retrieved on June 13, 2004 from http://www.dc.state.fl.us/pub/Females/status102001/index.html.

Gilfus, M. E. (2002). *Women's experiences of abuse as a risk factor for incarceration.* Retrieved on March 11, 2005 from www.vaw.umn.edu/documents/vawnet/arincarceration/arincarceration.pdf.

Grana, S. L. (2002). *Women and (in)justice: The criminal and civil effects of the common law on women's lives.* Boston: Allyn and Bacon.

Greenfield, L. A., & Snell, T. L. (1999). *Women offenders* (NCJ 175688). Washington, DC: U.S. Department of Justice.

Harris, D. A. (1999). The stories, the statistics, and the law: Why "driving while black" matters. *Minnesota Law Review* 84, 265–326.

Heidensohn, F. (1995). *Women and crime* (2nd ed.). New York: New York University Press.

Hill-Collins, P. (2000). *Black feminist thought: Knowledge, consciousness and the politics of empowerment* (2nd ed.). New York: Routledge Press.

hooks, b. (1981). *Ain't I a woman.* Boston: South End Press.

Hudson, B. (1988). *Content analysis of social enquiry reports written in the Borough Haribgey.* Unpublished report, Middlesex Area Probation Service.

Huling, T. (1995). Women drug couriers: Sentencing reform needed for prisoners of war. *Criminal Justice* 9 (4), 15–19, 58–61.

Hutchinson, E. O. (1999, May 26). Los Angeles shooting—Are black women the new menace to society. *Pacific News Service.* Retrieved on June 13, 2004 from http://www.tbwt.com/views/feat/feat1206.asp.

Hutchinson, E. O. (2001a). *Black women say they are race profiling targets too. The Hutchinson report.* Retrieved on June 12, 2004 from http://www.thehutchinsonreport.com/070201feature.html (July 2).

Hutchinson, E. O. (2001b). *Poor black female—Cheap lives.* University of Dayton School of Law. Retrieved on June 12, 2004 from http://academic.udayton.edu/race/05intersection/Gender/gender01.htm (November 26).

Jaggar, A., & Rothenberg, P. S. (1984). *Feminist frameworks.* New York: McGraw-Hill.

Jewell, S. K. (1992). *From Mammy to Miss America and beyond.* New York: Routledge.

Johnson, P. C. (2003). *Voices of African American women in prison: Inner lives.* New York: New York University Press.

Jones, V. E. (2004, April 20). *The angry black woman: Tart-tongued or driven and no-nonsense, she is a stereotype that amuses some and offends others. Boston*

Globe. Retrieved on July 31, 2004 from http://www.boston.com/news/globe/living/articles/2004/04/20/the_angry_black_woman/.

Joseph, G. (1981). The incompatible menage à trois: Marxism, feminism, and racism. In L. Sargent (Ed.), *Women and revolution* (pp. 91–107). Boston: South End Press.

Kershnar, S., & Paltrow, L. (2001, Summer). *Pregnancy, parenting and drug use: Which women? Which harms?* Harm Reduction Coalition. Retrieved on June 13, 2004 from http://www.harmreduction.org/news/summer01/kershnar.htm.

Klein, D. (1973). *The etiology of female crime: A review of the literature.* Albany: State University of New York Press

Klein, D. (1995). Crime through gender's prism: Feminist criminology in the United States. In N. H. Rafter & F. Heidensohn (Eds.), *International feminist perspectives in criminology: Engendering a discipline* (pp. 216–240). Philadelphia: Open University Press.

Knowles, J., & Persico, N. (2001). Racial bias in motor vehicles: Theory and evidence. *Journal of Political Economy* 109, 203–229.

LaFree, G. (1980). The effects of sexual stratification by race on official reaction to rape. *American Sociological Review* 45, 842–854.

Langston, S. (2003). The reality of women of color in the prison system. *Journal of Ethnicity in Criminal Justice* 1 (2), 85–93.

Lewis, D. K. (1977). A response to inequality: Black women, racism, and sexism. *Signs: Journal of Women in Culture and Society* 3 (2), 339–361.

Lynch, M. J. (1996). Class, race, and criminology: Structured choices and the life course. In M. D. Schwartz & D. Milovanovic (Eds.), *Race, gender, and class in criminology: The intersection* (pp. 3–28). New York: Garland Publishing.

Mama, A. (1989). Violence against black women: Gender, race and state response. *Feminist Review* 32, 30–49.

Mann, C. (1996). *When women kill.* Albany: State University of New York Press.

Mauer, M. (2003). *Invisible punishments: Block housing, education, voting.* Retrieved on May 25, 2004 from http://www.sentencingproject.org/pdfs/mauer-focus.pdf.

Merton, R. K. (1938). Social structure and anomie. *American Sociological Review* 3:672–682.

Miller, S. L. (2001). The paradox of women arrested for domestic violence: Criminal justice professionals and service providers respond. *Violence Against Women* 7, 1339–1376.

Miller, W. B. (1958). Lower-class culture as a generating milieu of gang delinquency. *Journal of Social Issues* 14, 5–19.

Minnesota Center Against Violence and Abuse. Retrieved on June 26, 2004, from http://www.vaw.umn.edu/documents/vawnet/arincarceration/arincarceration.html.

Mullings, L. (1997). *On our own terms.* New York: Routledge.

Mumola, C. J. (2000, August). *Incarcerated parents and their children.* Washington, DC: U.S. Department of Justice, Bureau of Justice Statistics.

Muszynski, A. (1989). What is patriarchy? In J. Vorst (Ed.), *Race, class, gender: Bonds and barriers* (pp. 65–83). Winnipeg, Manitoba: Society for Socialist Studies.

Naffine, N. (1996). *Feminism and criminology.* Philadelphia: Temple University Press.

Neuspiel, D. R., (1996). Racism and perinatal addiction. *Ethnicity and Disease* 6, 47–55.

New York State Department of Correctional Services (2002, March). *Women in prison fact sheet.* New York: Correctional association of New York. Retrieved on June 14, 2004, from http://www.corrassoc.org/images/Fact_Sheets_2002.pdf.

NPR. (2003). *Who's killing the women of Juarez? Mexican city haunted by decade of vicious sex crimes.* Retrieved on August 26, 2004, from http://www.npr.org/features/feature.php?wfId=1171962.

Olson, D. E., Lurigio, A. J., & Seng, M. (2000). A comparison of female and male probationers: Characteristics and case outcomes. *Women & Criminal Justice* 11, 65–80.

Paltrow, L. (2001). The war on drugs and the war on abortion: Some initial thoughts on the connections, intersection and the effects. *Southern University Law Review* 28 (3), 201–253.

Paltrow, M. L., Cohen, D. S., & Carey, C. A. (October, 2000). Year 2000 Overview: Governmental responses to pregnant women who use alcohol and other drugs. *Women's Law Project,* 1–78. Philadelphia. Retrieved on May 24, 2004 from http://www.csdp.org/news/news/gov_response_review.pdf.

Pope, A. (2004). B.C. court ignores aboriginal women's plea. *Canadian Dimension* 38(3), 10–11.

Rafter, N. (1981). Marxist feminism. *Crime and Delinquency* 27, 81–87.

Raj, A., & Silverman, J. (2002). Violence against immigrant women. *Violence Against Women* 8, 367–398.

Reiman, J. (1998). *The rich get richer and the poor get prison: Ideology, class, and criminal justice.* Boston: Allyn and Bacon.

Rennison, C., & Welchans, S. (2000). *Intimate partner violence* (NCJ 178247). Washington, DC: Bureau of Justice Statistics. Retrieved June 1, 2004.

Richie B. E., Tsenin K., & Widom C. S. (2000). *Women and girls in the criminal justice system.* Washington, DC: U.S. Department of Justice.

Roberts, D. (1997). *Killing the black body.* New York: Pantheon Books.

Roberts, D. E. (1993). Crime, race, and reproduction. *Tulane Law Review* 67 (6), 1945–1977.

Robinson, M. B. (2002). *Justice blind? Ideal and realities of American criminal justice.* Upper Saddle River, NJ: Prentice Hall.

Sen, R. (1999). Between a rock and a hard place: Domestic violence in communities of color. *ColorLines Magazine* 2 (1). Retrieved on June 14, 2004 from http://www.arc.org/C_Lines/CLArchive/story2_1_07.html.

Shaw, C., & McKay, H. (1942). *Juvenile delinquency and urban areas.* Chicago: University of Chicago Press.

Simon, R. J. (1975). *Women and crime.* Lexington, MA: Lexington Books.

Smart, C. (1976). *Women, crime, and criminology: A feminist critique.* London: Routledge and Kegan Paul.

U.S. Census Bureau. (2001). *Hispanics in United States.* Washington, DC: Author.

U.S. General Accounting Office. (2000, March). U.S. Customs Service better service targeting of airline passengers for personal searches could produce better results. Washington, DC: U.S. Government Printing Office.

Vold, G. B., Bernard., T. J., & Snipes, J. B., (1998) *Theoretical criminology* (4th ed.). New York: Oxford University Press.

Walby, S. (1990). *Theorizing patriarchy.* Cambridge, MA: Basil Blackwell.

Walker, S., Spohn, C., & DeLone, M. (2000). *The color of justice: Race, ethnicity, and crime in America.* Belmont, CA: Wadsworth Publishing Company.

Wilbanks, W. (1987). *The myth of a racist criminal justice system.* Monterey, CA: Brooks/Cole.

Wyatt, G. E., Axelrod, J., Chin, D., Carmona, J. V., & Loeb, T. B. (2000). Examining patterns of vulnerability to domestic violence among African American women. *Violence Against Women* 6, 495–514.

Xing, J. (1998). *Asian America through the lens: History, representations, and identity.* Lanham, MD: Altamira Press.

Cases Cited

Ferguson v. City of Charleston, 532 U.S. 67, 121 S.Ct. 1281, 149 L.Ed.2d 205 (2001)

Whitner v. State, 328 S.C. 1, 492 S.E.2d 777, 1997

Part VI

Conclusion

In this section, we summarize the previous chapters, assess the progress that women have made in criminal justice professions, and examine the implications of our policies toward female victims and offenders. Although women have made significant gains, most notably in the legal profession, they have not enjoyed similar successes in law enforcement. Overall, women have not made the inroads into the criminal justice–related professions envisioned ten years ago.

Women are increasingly being arrested for drug offenses, and many of them are serving sentences in prison for these drug crimes. Rather than focusing on punitive incarceration policies, the criminal justice system could strive to engage in collaborative programs that would make it possible for offenders and their families to receive treatment and remain in the community. In addition, greater attention has to be paid to HIV/AIDS infection, particularly among adolescent and young women. Some of the recent initiatives in states to increase drug treatment options for offenders suggest that there may be changes in this area in the next ten years.

Women who have been victimized by rape and domestic violence are often the same women who are serving time in our prisons and jails. This commonality illustrates the importance of taking a more proactive stance to prevent the victimization of women and girls. At the very least, we need to educate children about treating each other with dignity and respect. Strategies designed to empower girls and young women have to be implemented. These include helping men and women communicate more candidly. Although we have made considerable progress in domestic violence awareness, there are still women whose economic conditions prevent them from leaving these relationships.

Throughout this book, the contributors have attempted to illustrate the economic marginalization of women in our society. Women have traditionally been paid less than men, and they have less political power than men. Women's representation in the labor force is expected to increase slightly in the next six years. The status of women affects their ability to shape public policy. Without a seat in the state legislature, in the Congress, or in the Governor's office, it is unlikely that the conditions women confront are likely to change. We conclude with some recommendations for the future.

16

Assessing Progress and Imagining the Future for Women and Justice

Alida V. Merlo

In the preceding chapters, we examined how the law, social control, and justice have affected women. We focused on female professionals, offenders, and victims, along with female health issues like AIDS and drug use. As Bailey explains in Chapter 2, the imagery of women affects our perceptions of women—and it is powerful. Bailey encourages us to examine those images carefully and challenge the stereotypical portrayals in popular culture that can influence how women are treated in the criminal justice system.

Although some significant strides have been made in dealing with victims of rape and domestic violence, much remains to be done in the areas of women's health, drug use, treatment of women offenders, employment, and sexual harassment awareness and prevention. Additionally, we now understand much more clearly that women's criminality is often preceded by their victimization. By providing women with the requisite support and assistance, we may be able to prevent their involvement in both violent crime and property crime. To facilitate these changes, women will need to identify relevant issues and elect officials who are willing to introduce and support legislation to address them. Women must also organize formal and informal networks to share their knowledge and experiences and to support one another.

Women in Law-Related Professions

In examining the status of women in the United States as professionals, one is struck by the uneven nature of their progress. On the one hand, women are making some modest gains professionally. In the first edition of this book, we celebrated the appointment and confirmation of Judge Ruth Bader Ginsburg to the U.S. Supreme Court; the female Secret Service agents who were assigned to guard President Clinton; the appointment of the first woman Attorney General, Janet Reno; and the appointment of Sheila Widnail as the Secretary of the Air Force (Merlo, 1995a). The increasing number of women entering college and professional schools suggests that more women are making significant contributions to the field and are securing the requisite academic background to pursue their professional goals. However, women continue to be paid significantly less than their male counterparts, and the career mentoring that is so beneficial for men does not seem to be readily available to women (Department for Professional Employees, AFL-CIO, 2004).

In addition, female attorneys, police officers, and correctional officers report that their male colleagues and supervisors are hostile to them and that sexual harassment is still evident. It is surprising that the perception that women are violating sexual stereotypes by pursuing careers in fields traditionally occupied by men continues to be so powerful in the United States. Although women are represented in these professions, it seems as though the gains women made in these fields in the 1970s have had little or no impact.

Women, the Law, and the Judiciary

In the first edition of this book, women comprised more than one-third of the admissions to law schools. Currently, women comprise approximately half of law school enrollments (American Bar Association, 2003). The number of female attorneys has increased almost tenfold since 1971. In 1971, 3 percent of attorneys were women; in 2003, 27 percent of all attorneys were women (American Bar Association, 1995a, 2003). These data demonstrate tremendous progress when compared to 1875 when Miss Lavinia Goodell was denied admission to the Wisconsin bar by the Wisconsin Supreme Court. In his opinion for the court, Chief Justice Edward G. Ryan stated, "There are many employments in life not unfit for female character. The profession of law is surely not one of these. . . . Womanhood is moulded [*sic*] for gentler and better things" (*In re the Motion to Admit Miss Lavinia Goodell to the Bar of this Court,* 39 Wis. 232 [Wis. 1875], quoted in Trial 1992, p. 22).

Despite the increase in the number of women admitted to the bar, women have not made many strides in their attempts to become partners in the prestigious law firms. Bernat persuasively argues in Chapter 7 that despite the initial progress that the elite law firms made in recruiting and hiring female attorneys, the progress has been dissipating and glass ceilings continue to limit women's movement to partnership status. Clearly, this is not the kind of progress that we envisioned ten years ago.

Unfortunately, there is too little mentoring of female associates in large law firms. This may be due, in part, to the fact that those women who have recently been made partners do not have the extra time and energy to assist new female associates. The dearth of women partners in the large firms suggests that those who are offered a partnership are really trailblazers. They may fear that they will be perceived as not "holding their own" if they fail to produce; thus, they may hinder the progress of the next group of female associates being considered for partnerships. Also, some female professionals take the attitude that "If I made it without help, why can't you?"

In 1995, Pollock and Ramirez reported that Gender Status Reports in many states indicated that female attorneys experienced discrimination in hiring and promotion. Stohr and Bostaph present evidence in Chapter 3 that discrimination continues, and also that it extends beyond hiring and promotion. Stohr and Bostoph (Chapter 3) and Bernat (Chapter 7) also found substantial evidence that gender bias exists in the courtroom for both victims and their attorneys. Bernat notes that the consequences of gender bias are significant and serious and include economic disadvantage, inequity, and emotional distress. Clearly, a greater commitment has to be made in the courts to create an environment that is more gender neutral for male and female victims and attorneys.

Another area where women have made some progress in the last twenty years is in the judiciary. In 1995, women comprised 12 percent of the judges on the federal bench (American Bar Association, 1995b). Today, women comprise 20.6 percent of the federal judiciary in large part due to President Clinton's efforts to appoint more women judges (Gendergap.com, 2004).

Women who have made impressive gains in these areas need to share their knowledge and experience with recent law school graduates and undergraduate students. If students and law school graduates understand the realities of working in the profession and how best to prepare for them, they will be better equipped to work successfully in this male-dominated profession and to make it more inclusive. They will also have forged the requisite support network to facilitate reaching their future goals.

Women in Law Enforcement

Although criminal justice professionals' salaries are not commensurate with those of partners in large firms, the picture is strikingly familiar. Women have made some progress in employment in police agencies, but they constitute a very small percentage of the professionals. In 2004, there were 2,100 Secret Service agents in the United States, and women comprised approximately 11 percent of the total (Personal Communication, Secret Service Public Affairs Department, October 22, 2004). Their representation is worse in most state law enforcement agencies. As Scarborough and Garrison illustrated in Chapter 5, in nineteen states women comprise less than 5 percent of state troopers. After thirty-five years, women have not substantially increased their presence in state law enforcement agencies.

On the local level, the number of women police officers is slightly higher. Women have made their greatest strides in large municipal departments. For example, in Los Angeles, 19 percent of Los Angeles police officers are women (Personal Communication, Los Angeles Police Department Recruitment Office, October 28, 2004). Most of the data indicate that nationally women now comprise approximately 10 percent of municipal police organizations and 12 percent of employees in county departments (Maguire & Pastore, 2004, pp. 44–45). Unfortunately, these data belie any claim that women have made significant strides in law enforcement in thirty-five years.

For women, progress in policing refers to the opportunity to be hired and to complete the training academy successfully. Little has changed since the first edition of this book in terms of their ability to be promoted. In some instances, the progress that women have made has been induced by lawsuits, legislation, and federal requirements for funding. Although Heather Fong's recent appointment to Chief in San Francisco is noteworthy, it is not characteristic of other women's experiences in law enforcement in terms of their ability to move up the ranks in police departments in the United States. Women comprise a small number of upper-level positions in law enforcement, and there is little evidence to suggest that that will change anytime soon.

Harassment and Discrimination in the Profession

Currently, women who opt for employment in a law-related field continue to confront a hostile work environment. As Scarborough and Garrison reported in their chapter, in 2003 sexual harassment and hostility at work were concerns voiced by the female participants at the International Association of Women Police. Not only are these attitudes pervasive, but there is evidence that they are fostered in the police academy training. In a participant observation study of police academy training, Prokos and Padavic (2002, p. 454) present evidence that the message of the curriculum suggests that it is permissible to exclude women, to antagonize them, and to make it clear that women are not the equals of male recruits. These attitudes pose a considerable hurdle for female recruits and their more experienced female colleagues.

Although 40 to 80 percent of female workers reported sexual harassment according to a study of twenty-three nations conducted by the Internal Labor Office, Gratch (1995) noted that the incidence of sexual harassment experienced by working women is related to the nature of the occupation examined and the manner in which data were collected. For women who work in traditional female fields like social work, the incidence is less than for women who work in traditional masculine organizations like the military. The costs of sexual harassment extend beyond the physiological, psychological, and economic costs incurred by the victim. Sexual harassment results in the agency's loss of productivity, replacement costs when personnel are sick or resign, and a greater threat to public safety because victims and perpetrators may be distracted and less focused on the danger they are confronting. Additionally, there are the costs that the government must absorb related to the investigation and prosecution of sexual harassment cases (Gratch, 1995).

Although the public and the private sector have made some progress in preventing and addressing discrimination and sexual harassment, there is still plenty of evidence of their existence in the workplace. Consider the recent settlements in corporate America. In 2004, Morgan Stanley paid $54 million to end a lawsuit initiated by dozens of women employees who cited evidence that the firm had refused them promotions and pay increases. In reaching the settlement, Morgan Stanley offered to take additional steps to prevent such practices in the future (Kelly & DeBaise, 2004, pp. A1–A2). Merrill Lynch and Smith Barney also settled sex discrimination suits in the late 1990s. Each of these companies has paid out over $100 million to settle these cases (McGeehan, 2004, p. C7). Clearly, discrimination continues to be a costly and demoralizing influence in the workplace for women.

In the first edition of this book, Hale and Bennett (1995) and Gratch (1995) recommended emphasizing the theme of cooperation among all officers in academy training and throughout the officer's career. Part of that training has to be aimed at debunking myths about police work and stressing that women and men as well as black, Hispanic, and Asian officers are equally capable. It is imperative that every police agency commit to a policy of equal treatment and establish ongoing programs to eliminate bias and harassment. Without a formal and continuous program, women and minorities will continue to be treated differently rather than equally.

Women in Corrections

Despite the fact that women have been involved in various capacities in police work and corrections for a long time, Farkas contends in Chapter 6 that the challenges for women in corrections continue into the new millennium. Traditionally, women have been involved in the helping professions as social workers and counselors who have worked primarily with women and children. Women in corrections initially focused their efforts on juvenile and adult female offenders. In correctional institutions, they were assigned to work as matrons, guards, or counselors in institutions for boys, girls, or adult women. Women began to be employed in nonclerical work or nonmatron in all-male adult correctional institutions after Congress amended Title VII of the 1964 Civil Rights Act in 1972.

Although many law enforcement and corrections agencies have endeavored to reduce discrimination and harassment, much remains to be done. Women still tend to be assigned the less desirable jobs and are treated in a paternalistic and sexualized manner. In the first edition of this book, we noted that women comprised less than 10 percent of police (U.S. Department of Justice, 1993) and approximately 17 percent of correctional officers in the adult systems (Maguire, Pastore, & Flanagan, 1993, p. 98). In both areas, women's presence had been positively perceived both by the public and the inmates. In Chapter 6, Farkas reports that women's employment in correctional officer positions has increased. By 2000, they comprised 28 percent of the officers in jails, 24 percent of those in state facilities, and 14 percent of the officers in the federal system (American Correctional Association, 2003).

As Stohr and Bostoph illustrate in Chapter 3, there are differences in women's representation based upon population. In smaller communities, as few as 5 percent of the local law enforcement officers are women. In 1995, we anticipated that line officers would continue to become more professional. That professionalization, accompanied by the retirement of older more traditional officers and changes in society's attitudes, continues to portend a more receptive environment for women.

Women in correctional institutions like their colleagues in law and law enforcement continue to confront harassment, and, consequently, stress. One problem that women experienced in the 1970s, 1980s, and 1990s that still persists is the lack of female colleagues similarly situated that women can tap for emotional support and assistance when dealing with hostile working conditions and coworkers (Pogrebin & Poole, 1997, 1998). As Farkas's research illustrates, without other officers, networking organizations, or simply the opportunity to share work experiences, women working in corrections will continue to feel isolated and less able to cope with the difficulties that create stress.

How would a more proportional female representation in police departments alter the workplace? Would the incidence of police brutality and corruption decrease? A greater number of female correctional officers might humanize the prison environment and might lead to a reduction in the number of inmate-staff assaults. Once women have a greater presence in these organizations, it will be useful to study their impact.

Assessing Women's Progress in Employment.   More women are employed in law enforcement agencies and organizations today, but they have not made the inroads we envisioned in 1995. Although we applaud the gains in some of the larger departments where women comprise close to 20 percent of the police, we are concerned about how little effect the increasing number of women entering college, studying criminal justice, and indicating a desire to work in the field has had on their likelihood of employment in law enforcement. Their continued underrepresentation in law enforcement agencies is unsettling.

By far, the greatest progress has occurred in the law. The number of women attending law school has increased, and more women are practicing law. However, there, too, the gains, as demonstrated by their representation as partners in major law firms, continue to be modest. Some of the best opportunities for women might be in the federal judiciary where women are now 20.6 percent of all judges (gendergap.com, 2004). Every president has the opportunity to nominate candidates for positions to the federal judiciary, but not all presidents have enthusiastically embraced this challenge. Clearly, the president and the Senate have to be made aware that there should be more opportunities for women in the federal judiciary in the next five years.

In addition, in law enforcement, corrections, and the legal profession, there is a dire need for mentoring and networking. Despite their limited representation and the sometimes overwhelmingly negative environments they have to work in, women must get the message out to potential or new recruits, and to their female colleagues, that they can make a change and that they need to work together. In some instances, this mutual support might involve recruiting women, helping a colleague to address harassment, identifying stressful situations, explaining departmental policies, or simply providing a coworker with empathy and consideration.

Controlling Women's Bodies

The criminal justice system's emphasis on female drug use has resulted in the prosecution and conviction of women who use drugs during their pregnancy. As Bagley and Merlo illustrate in Chapter 4, primarily poor and minority women have been subject to harsh sanctions for their drug use, including the removal and placement of their children. One of the most notorious states is South Carolina, but at least thirty-five states have prosecuted women for substance abuse during pregnancy (Jos, Perlmutter, & Marshall, 2003). These prosecutions tend to focus on poor women who use crack cocaine during pregnancy.

It is misguided and discriminatory to define and target poor minority women who use drugs during pregnancy as criminals. The same is true of HIV-positive women who are pregnant or who engage in sexual intercourse. The concern for the fetus or for another party that these kinds of laws are designed to protect does not translate into prenatal care, drug treatment programs, or counseling and nutritional programs for teenagers and unmarried women. Noticeably absent is any mention of the father's drug use and the impact it may have on the fetus. Although Bagley and Merlo do not advocate the prosecution of fathers who use drugs, they recognize how quickly the fetal abuse path can subject women's everyday activities like working or exercising to scrutiny.

Perhaps most discouraging is the government's continued reliance on the criminal justice system to deal with drug abuse. By comparison, drug treatment slots are significantly cheaper than prison beds. The relationship between drug and alcohol use and criminal behavior should prompt legislators and policymakers to establish drug treatment programs specifically targeted for pregnant women and women with children. Unfortunately, there does not seem to be a commitment to prevent crime and enhance the welfare of mothers and children.

Evidence shows that AIDS in women is increasing faster than among men. The women most affected by the spread of AIDS are predominantly women of color and poor women. Bagley and Merlo recommend that high-quality health care be made available to all AIDS victims. At the same time, there has to be funding for education and prevention programs. These programs must honestly explain the victimization and risk factors and assist teenagers in protecting themselves. Society can reduce the incidence of AIDS victimization among women and children by eliminating restrictions on the purchase of injection equipment or government's distribution of this equipment to addicts and through increased funding for drug prevention and treatment programs, HIV/AIDS can be addressed.

Applying criminal sanctions to poor and minority women who abuse drugs will not result in healthier babies. If anything, there is some concern that these policies continue to discourage women from seeking prenatal care. Similarly, providing women with HIV/AIDS the requisite education, prevention, and treatment programs will go a long way in decreasing the spread of the disease. The school systems have to go beyond an "abstinence only" policy for teaching youth about safe sexual activities and incorporate meaningful information designed to make them aware of the seriousness of the disease, the techniques for preventing the spread of HIV/AIDS, and the treatment options.

Female Victims

Our progress in addressing the issues of female victims of rape has been uneven. The changes that have occurred in society in the areas of rape prevention and awareness are commendable, and the revision of rape laws since the 1970s has resulted in more protection for the victim. However, the vast majority of the public still perceives rape as an act committed by a stranger. As Southerland and Southerland demonstrate in their analysis of victim research in Chapter 8, that perception is inaccurate.

Rape Victimization

Southerland and Southerland illustrate the significance of rape victimization. In the 2002 National Crime Victimization Study, two-thirds of all rapes were acquaintance rapes (U.S. Department of Justice, 2003). Clearly, the prevention of acquaintance rape should be a priority. In the first edition of this book, Southerland (1995) elucidated a strategy involving societal responsibility, individual awareness, and self-protection (Rozee, Bateman, & Gilmore 1991). Of the three areas, societal responsibility continues to merit the greatest attention. The development of educational awareness and prevention programs at colleges and universities in the last fifteen years has helped students to communicate better with one another and to reinforce the view that violence is an unacceptable way for men and women to deal with one another.

Johnson, Palileo, and Gray (1992, p. 41) argued that in order to achieve nonexploitive sexual relations between men and women, a major barrier—ambiguity in sexual communications—must be overcome. This is a formidable task. It necessitates candid discussions about acquaintance rape and illustrates that more aggressive awareness and prevention policies have to be initiated as early as in the junior high school years. Sexual communication awareness involves, in part, listening to the other person and respecting his or her decisions. Such efforts can reduce the incidence of rape victimization and promote a greater sensitivity and understanding between men and women.

Battered Women

In terms of societal awareness, tremendous progress has been made in domestic violence. In the last thirty years—with the assistance of researchers, practitioners, the media, and women's groups—the public has become informed, sensitized, and increasingly intolerant of violence toward women. Concerned citizens prompted legislators in many states to draft legislation that allows victims to secure restraining orders against their abusers and to authorize law enforcement agencies and organizations to establish policies for the arrest and detention of abusers. In addition, Kindschi Gosselin notes in Chapter 9, that there are more shelters and support services for battered women in the United States today. Clearly, significant strides have been made in this area.

Since the first edition of this book, states have touted protection orders as a way to preclude further abuse. In some states, these orders include provisions regarding custody and visitation of minor children. As Kindschi Gosselin reports, their role in preventing abuse is recognized in The Violence Against Women Act of 1994, which makes them enforceable in all states, not just the one where the victim resides. This kind of interstate cooperation was rare ten years ago.

Research has also enhanced our knowledge of domestic violence. Recent evidence suggests that intimate violence is more widespread and more severe in neighborhoods that are characterized by economic disadvantage. Women who live in a household that is economically distressed and also in a neighborhood that is disadvantaged are most at risk (Benson & Fox, 2004, p. ii). Clearly, more has to be done to provide training and job opportunities for women living in poverty.

The victimization of women and girls receives more attention today than in the past. In addition, victimization has attained prominence in our understanding of criminal offending.

However, to initiate a more proactive approach to rape, acquaintance rape, and intimate partner abuse, more emphasis has to be placed on education. These initiatives will require the support of the local, state, and federal governments, but they are important for reducing the cycle of violence in society and for preparing women to assume roles in society that will prevent them from being victims or rape and abuse.

Female Offenders and the System's Response

Several themes dominate the literature and arrest statistics on female offenders over the last twenty years. First, women are not as involved in crimes as men are in U.S. society. Second, women who engage in crime tend to concentrate on property crimes like larceny/theft, drug abuse violations, and fraud. When women do engage in violent crimes like homicide and assault, they do so as a last resort, usually after repeated abuse. Third, according to official data, women's involvement in criminal activity has increased for some crimes, but their involvement is not commensurate with the dramatic increase in the number of women sentenced to incarceration. Fourth, women who are convicted and sentenced to prison often experience an additional hardship, the loss or separation of their children. Fifth, women are sometimes singled out for different or special (not necessarily better) treatment. Sixth, the majority of women who are currently incarcerated in prisons and jails could be more humanely and effectively dealt with in the community.

In order to understand the officially recorded increases in female criminality, Merlo (1995b) examined three explanations: the economic marginalization of women in American society, increased formal social control, and drug use. Recent census data indicate that more and more women are heads of single-parent households; and despite increases in white single-parent households, they are far more prevalent in the black community. There were over 11 million children under the age of 18 living below the poverty level in 2001, and 30 percent of them were black. Black women continue to be the head of the households where these children live (U.S. Census Bureau, 2003). Median weekly earnings for men and women continue to illustrate the disparity. In 2002, women who worked full time had weekly median earnings of $528, and men had weekly median earnings of $676 (U.S. Department of Labor, 2002).

The increase in formal social control played a significant role in officially recorded arrests of women in the first edition of this book, and that trend continues. As police agencies become more bureaucratic, more professional, more skilled at recordkeeping, and more formalized in terms of policies and procedures for handling deviant behavior, a greater number of arrests are likely to occur and to be documented (Feinman, 1986; Steffensmeier & Streifel, 1992). Although the more formalized training, practices, techniques, and computer-assisted technology facilitate police work, these factors alone do not fully explain the increases in female arrests for drug abuse violations and assault in recent years.

Women, Crime, and Drugs

In Chapter 10, Davis, Merlo, and Pollock reexamine drug use as an important factor in explaining female criminality. If the increase in female arrests for property crimes during the last twenty years is related to economic marginalization, increased social control, and drug use, it is possible for the government to intervene and to improve the status quo. The government can make drug treatment programs available to all, not just to those who have private health insurance. The government also must establish drug treatment programs that will accept pregnant women and women who have children. For too long, these women have been excluded or discouraged from entering drug treatment programs. Unfortunately, since this book was first published, we have not made significant progress in providing drug treatment programs for women.

Simultaneously, there must be a commitment to drug education and prevention programs. Programs have to be initiated in elementary school, and they need to declare alcohol and tobacco as dangerous drugs. It is important for drug and alcohol education programs to both realistically portray the harm and the costs incurred and to offer strategies to prevent the abuse from occurring.

In Chapter 11, McShane and Williams further explain the role that drugs has played in female criminality. Women are not the major drug dealers or drug "kingpins" in the United States. However, female drug arrests have increased, convictions of women for drug crimes have increased, and more women are now serving prison sentences for drug crimes. McShane and Williams advocate gender specific treatment programs for women who are using drugs. Once again, the "one size fits all" model of drug treatment programming in prisons, jails, and in the community does not adequately address the unique needs of women. Specifically, women require programs that accept children, that provide some assistance with transportation, and that include aftercare and job opportunities. In addition, greater attention has to be focused on the social problems in our communities. Although illegal drugs have dominated the crime agenda for over twenty years, comparatively little attention has been directed toward improving the economic conditions of women and children.

The poverty of these neighborhoods has to be alleviated, not only by removing physically decaying buildings, but also by providing citizens with decent housing and educational, vocational, and counseling services. Every effort should be made to assist single teenage mothers to finish high school and to pursue advanced training or attend college. These efforts will greatly improve the future of children currently living in poverty.

Women Involved in Violent Crime

Americans appear to be fascinated by certain kinds of criminals—such as women who engage in homicide. As Benekos demonstrates in Chapter 12, women are not socialized to act violently, and in those instances when they do kill, the incidence is far less for female offenders than it is for men. Women tend to kill and to be killed by men with whom they are acquainted and whose racial characteristics are the same.

When a woman kills, the research indicates that she usually is in a marital or intimate relationship and that her motivation is self-defense. The fact that women are at a greater risk of being victims and perpetrators of homicide in family or intimate relationships suggests that society should embark on a course of action to prevent these behaviors. Specifically, Benekos recommends more shelters, community-based victim services, improving the economic position of women, and a coordinated criminal justice system response, including specially trained police and prosecutors, to help to reduce spousal homicide. Such a network of community services and programs would send the clear message that violence is unacceptable for resolving difficulties and that society will assist victims of violence to safety.

Women's involvement in crime and drugs is complex, and frequently it is preceded by their prior violent victimization. In the intervening ten years since the first edition was published, we have learned a great deal. We now know that in order to prevent women from engaging in crime, from larceny and drug possession to homicide, it is important to prevent the victimization of our children. From child maltreatment to sexual victimization, every effort must be made to keep children safe. In addition, there has to be more emphasis on community resources that are designed to provide children with a positive role model and an experience where they can achieve some success. Finally, education, vocational training, counseling, parenting classes, and support services have to be promoted and made available in all communities. These programs do not constitute a "quick fix," but they do have the potential as a more "complete fix" than our previous efforts.

Women in Prison and Jail

The dramatic increase in the number of women in prison and in jail in the United States over the last ten years has been the subject of considerable discussion and debate. In Chapter 13, Owen discusses these trends. Currently, women comprise approximately 7 percent of the prison population in the United States and about 12 percent of the jail population (Harrison & Karberg, 2004, p. 8).

Owen contends that violent offenses account for the increase in male prisons, but for women it is drug offenses that explain the exponential increase. Drug abuse is especially prevalent among female offenders. Although there is evidence that drug use is related to female criminality, drug use alone cannot fully account for the increase in the incarceration of women. In the first edition, Chesney-Lind and Pollock (1995) concluded that the chances of being sentenced to some period of incarceration have significantly increased, in part because of mandatory sentencing statutes and other types of legislative reform, but also because the criminal justice system was getting tougher on those arrested for criminal activity. The get-tough ideology coupled with the media characterization of violent crime and the politics of criminal justice policy continue to adversely affect the criminal justice system's approach to offenders (Merlo & Benekos, 2000).

Prisons for Women: Characteristics and Considerations. With the increase in the number of women incarcerated, states have moved to construct new prisons for female offenders. Many of the states have abandoned the reformatory model of the past and now build larger institutions for women with many of the same characteristics of male prisons. Although the number of prisons for women is much smaller when compared to men, men still have the "luxury" of being assigned to a prison that accommodates their classification risk. For women, there are usually only one or two prisons available in an entire state. Some women serve their sentence in a prison setting that is much higher security than is warranted and with little opportunity for reclassification. Even more problematic is when states with small female inmate populations decide to contract with other states to hold their inmates. For all practical purposes, these kinds of policies preclude family visitation and involvement in the woman's rehabilitation.

Women have had to litigate for most improvements in prison. Nonetheless, women still confront difficulties in programming in prisons. Frequently, the drug treatment programs that are offered are not gender specific and female drug users are an afterthought.

The demographic characteristics of incarcerated women today as well as those of the 1970s, the 1980s, and the 1990s are surprisingly similar. According to Pollock, women in prison tend to be increasingly minority group members, and they continue to be undereducated, underemployed, or unemployed before incarceration and mothers of young children. In addition, contemporary female inmates often are serving time for drug crimes, and they report that they have drug problems (Pollock, 2002, p. 53).

The fact that the majority of women in prison are mothers poses significant problems for offenders and institutional administrators. According to Pollock (2002, p. 107), almost a quarter of a million children have a mother in jail or prison in the United States. There are many hurdles to overcome for the mother and child to maintain a relationship: visitation schedules, distance and travel time, costs, willingness of service providers to facilitate visitation, institutional policies and procedures, and length of incarceration. Research documents how critical it is for women to be able to visit their children and participate in their lives even though they cannot be present physically.

A number of institutions for women have attempted to facilitate maternal involvement with their children, but a great deal remains to be done (see Pollock, 2002). Ten years ago Chesney-Lind and Pollock (1995) recommended more widespread use of alternative sanctions for nonviolent women offenders. Specifically, states and local governments could create more community-based halfway house programs and rely more heavily on probation. These kinds of initiatives are not the goal in contemporary correctional policies, which embody a conservative get-tough ideology (Merlo & Benekos, 2000).

As the chapter authors have illustrated, in the last ten years we have continued incarcerating women for property and drug crimes. These offenders do not pose a serious risk to public safety. There is no empirical evidence that the greater utilization of community-based alternatives for women in previous decades resulted in women's engaging in repeated serious crime. Given the costs of incarceration, both economic and social, and the disruption of families that results, we should embark on a strategy to reduce the prison population and increase probation and community-based services.

In addition, greater attention has to be paid to the conditions in communities that foster women's involvement in drug crimes. Rather than focusing on arresting and prosecuting drug offenders, more resources have to be directed to understanding why women are using drugs and what can be done to assist them. Once again, there is no "quick fix" for this problem. However, there is an opportunity to utilize an enlightened and humane approach.

Juvenile Female Offenders: Differential Processing and Treatment

Although a great deal of our attention has been focused on women and the criminal justice system, Chesney-Lind and Irwin discuss the progress the juvenile justice system has made in its treatment of girls since the enactment of the Juvenile Justice and Delinquency Prevention Act of 1974 and its subsequent amendments in Chapter 14. Typically, our system of justice has determined that male and female juvenile offenders are the same, and that treatment programs can be duplicated rather than specifically tailored for boys or girls. However, research does not support that position.

Despite the media portrayal of girls becoming more violent, Chesney-Lind and Irwin found that rather than a change in girls' offending patterns, the reality is that they are more likely to be referred to the courts by law enforcement officers, school officials, and probation officers. In short, it is our responses to these behaviors rather than an increase in the behaviors themselves, that help to explain these changes in formal processing. Girls are still more likely than boys to be referred to the juvenile justice system for running away and shoplifting.

There is evidence of a possible transition occurring. Chesney-Lind and Irwin cite the recent reauthorization of the Juvenile Justice and Delinquency Prevention Act in 2002 in which Congress directed states to continue to focus on gender-specific treatment and prevention programs for girls. However, they contend that much more needs to be done to eliminate the physical and sexual victimization of girls that ultimately may lead them to delinquent behavior.

Historically, the juvenile justice system's response to girls has been remarkably consistent. It continues to focus on status offenses and to maintain a double standard when it comes to processing girls and boys for these kinds of behaviors in the system. If society is committed to deterring girls' delinquency, more resources have to be directed toward preventing their victimization long before they are juvenile court referrals. Efforts to address violent victimization will go a long way in preventing juvenile court involvement.

The Intersection of Race/Ethnicity, Gender, Class, and Criminal Justice

In Chapter 15, Joseph explains how the intersection of race/ethnicity, class, and gender disproportionately affects women of color in the United States. Women of color are more vulnerable to inequities based on race/ethnic background, class, and gender than the majority population of white women. Whether they are working as professionals, being victimized by rape or abuse, or actively participating in criminal activity, these women experience different treatment.

For women of color, the criminal justice system is not a level playing field. As Bagley and Merlo (Chapter 4) and McShane and Williams (Chapter 11) illustrated, it is poor women of color who have frequently been singled out for prosecution in cases involving the delivery of a controlled substance to a newborn baby. The consequences of this "special treatment" are substantial. Women of color have additional obstacles related to rehabilitation and reintegration in society that white women do not have to address.

In terms of their victimization, poor minority women are less likely to be believed by the criminal justice system when they are the victims of rape or intimate partner violence. Joseph recommends specific training and education programs that will improve their economic standing as well as systemic changes. From the training academy to professional development programs, criminal justice professionals have to be sensitized to attitudes that condone or ignore the victimization of women of color and learn to overcome them. In employment, criminal justice agencies and organizations have to recruit more minority women, and additional efforts have to be directed at providing a work environment that is supportive and inclusive.

During the last ten years, the criminal justice system has continued the trend of disproportionate minority arrests, convictions, and incarceration. Today, there is an opportunity to reduce this overrepresentation. Improving the economic condition of minority children and their mothers, providing better housing, initiating more educational and vocational opportunities, and strengthening families with community support services can potentially improve the current status of minority women. These kinds of strategies could reduce their likelihood of victimization as well as their involvement in criminal activity. In addition, greater emphasis has to be placed on making the professionals in the criminal justice system more representative of the population. These steps will go a long way to make criminal justice agencies more diverse and to ensure fair processing and treatment to victims and offenders.

Strategies for the Incorporation of Women and Women's Perspectives in Law

In this final chapter, we have reviewed and summarized the authors' contributions and identify a strategy to ameliorate the status of women and to empower them to formulate legislation and policies that include and represent more women in contemporary society. Part of the problem can be traced to the differences in pay between men and women. The wage gap that persists between men and women is one manifestation of the deleterious consequences of the images of women in our society. These images are related to the perception that women do not deserve the same pay as men. In 2002, women's income was 77 percent of men's. For Black and Latina women, the situation was even worse; 67 percent and 55 percent respectively (Professional Women: Vital Statistics, 2004). Equal pay affects women in all kinds of occupational categories, from professional and technical women to women working in the service industry. Not only does it affect them throughout their working lives, but it also affects them in retirement when their social security checks are less than their male counterparts (Professional Women: Vital Statistics, 2004).

Women's Progress in Education and Politics

There is plenty of evidence that women are pursuing advanced degrees. In 2004, women are expected to receive 58 percent of all the bachelor's and master's degrees, 46 percent of all the professional degrees, and 44 percent of all the doctoral degrees (Professional Women: Vital Statistics, 2004). Women have attained the advanced degrees, but they have yet to receive equal pay. This is one of the challenges of the new millennium that continues to limit women's progress and to diminish their worth. Greater attention has to be focused on the wage gap and elected officials, beginning with the president, must make it a priority to close the earnings gap.

To address the problems women encounter as professionals, offenders, and victims that we have discussed in the preceding chapters will require a change in public policy. Legislation needs to be enacted. In this arena, the limited progress of women is most striking. In the 108th Congress in 2004, there were 60 women and 383 men in the U.S. House of Representatives and fourteen women in the Senate (Center for American Women and Politics, 2004a). Without equal or at least more proportionate representation, little progress can be made.

In 1995, female representatives comprised 10.3 percent of the House of Representatives; in 2004, they comprised 13.8 percent. In 1995, women held 25.9 percent of statewide elective offices; and in 2004, they held 26 percent. With respect to the state legislatures, women held 20.6 percent of such seats in 1995, and 22.5 percent in 2004 (Center for Women and Politics, 2004a). These data belie the notion that women have made great strides in getting elected to office.

In order to understand why there is a dearth of women involved in politics on the national level, it is instructive to examine the status of women at other levels of government. In 2004, women were governors in nine states, attorneys general in five states, state comptrollers in three states, and public service commissioners in four states (Center for Women and Politics, 2004a). On the local level, the data are pretty similar. Of the 100 largest cities in the United States, a woman is the mayor in fourteen of them. These kinds of elected public offices provide women with the expertise and exposure to enable them to run for national office.

Money, Voting, and the Gender Gap. Another impediment to women being elected to office is funding. In 1985, Ellen Malcolm founded EMILY'S ("Early Money Is Like Yeast") List to give Democratic women who ran for office some money to make it possible for them to appeal to more traditional funding groups (Donovan, 1992, p. 3270). As one might expect, female candidates have to rely on the generosity of female voters to sustain a campaign. Female donors comprise a smaller donor base, and they have less income than men. These two factors place potential female candidates in jeopardy and give any male candidate the advantage (Donovan, 1992, p. 3273). As a result, female candidates are much more dependent upon small contributions than men are (Donovan, 1992, p. 3269).

Women's participation in government is further impeded by the lack of solidarity and uniformity of women voters. Female voters have voted at a higher rate than men in the last five presidential elections. That voter turnout is a reversal of the voting trends that had existed for most of the years since women began to vote in 1920. Women now vote in higher numbers than men (Center for American Women and Politics, 2004a).

Larger numbers of women voted in the 2004 presidential election than in previous elections. In addition, more women register to vote than men. However, for approximately seventy years, women were more likely to follow their husbands' lead in elections (Donovan, 1992, p. 3270). It was not until the presidential election of 1980 that the signs of a "gender gap" in male and female voting patterns emerged. Not only is the women's rate of participation higher, but they have been more likely to vote for Democratic candidates (Cook, 1992, p. 3265).

In the 2004 election, more women than men voted for John Kerry, but the gender gap was smaller than in previous elections (Center for American Women and Politics, 2004b). Typically, the gender gap indicates a ten-percentage-point difference between men and women (Center for American Women and Politics, 2004a). The number of women who are registered and who have voted suggest that there is an opportunity for a woman-centered agenda to emerge in politics.

Consensus Building and Action. Despite the fact that the majority of voters are women, there do not seem to be any controversial gender-specific issues that prompt women to organize. For example, women did not march or demonstrate considerably for the enactment of family leave legislation. And yet, women were the force behind the changes in rape laws that occurred in the last twenty years, and in domestic violence awareness, prevention, and response programs and policies. Who or what determines which issues are priorities on the national agenda while others are relegated only minor importance or are virtually ignored? Part of the explanation has to lie in the fact that women are grossly underrepresented in local governing bodies like county commissions, state legislatures, governorships, and Congress.

Additionally, women who wish to get elected and reelected must rely on funding from men and male-dominated organizations. Despite the success of EMILY'S List, women are only recently starting to write checks for candidates of their choice, and their checks (like their median incomes) when compared to male donors are minuscule. Contributions enable candidates to take their campaigns to television and radio, to advertise in the newspapers, to travel, and to meet with voters.

The appointment of Janet Reno as attorney general, Ruth Bader Ginsburg as an associate justice of the Supreme Court, Jacqueline Elders as surgeon general, and Madeleine Albright as secretary of state in the 1990s may have sent a message that when women are given the opportunity, they can do the job better or at least as effectively as their male colleagues. Once again, networking and career mentoring are critical. Women who are elected to public office in the Senate, Congress, state legislature, city council, and county governing board (as well as women who are working in private and public agencies that establish and implement policy) must cooperate and facilitate the career advancement of other women. It is only through such a concerted, long-term effort that any significant changes can be made.

The progress that women made in the last century is noteworthy, but it demonstrates that women cannot wait their turn in the expectation that society, the government, or other social institutions will care for them. In order to alter the status quo, women will have to pursue a strategy for change actively. That strategy involves women helping women on the local, state, regional, and national scene.

Women will need to identify and develop plans to address the issues that significantly affect large numbers of women. Issues include drug treatment, rape victimization, intimate partner violence, research on women's health, prenatal care, women and children living in poverty, equal employment opportunities, sexual harassment, and education on sex roles. Women also have to continue to endeavor to make the criminal justice system and social policies more responsive to them as female professionals, victims, and offenders. It is a laudable and achievable goal.

Review Questions

1. Explain the changes that have occurred in the field of law. Have women made significant strides? In what areas are they likely to be represented? Why?

2. Discuss the representation of women in law enforcement and corrections. What are some of the barriers they encounter? How can these barriers be addressed?

3. Explain the costs of sexual harassment. How can it be prevented?

4. Discuss the factors that may affect a correctional officer's interactions with inmates. Do you think

that an increase in the number of women in law enforcement and corrections would change these organizations? How?

5. Discuss women and drug use. How is drug use related to female criminality?

6. What can society do to prevent drug abuse? What can be done to help drug abusers?

7. What are some strategies that society can undertake to prevent violence?

8. How do you explain the increase in the number of women incarcerated in state and federal prisons?

9. Discuss the female offender. What specific programs need to be introduced in jails and prisons? What alternative sentencing strategies could be utilized?

10. Discuss acquaintance rape. What can be done to prevent it?

11. Explain society's response to domestic violence. What do you recommend for the future?

12. Explain women's participation in government. What is EMILY'S List? How can women's increased representation affect their future? Why?

Key Terms

"Quick fix"
EMILY'S List
Gender gap
Wage gap
Title VII of the Civil Rights Act of 1964
Lavinia Goodell

Morgan Stanley settlement
Violence and victimization
Violence against Women Act of 1994
Ruth Bader Ginsburg
Juvenile Justice and Delinquency Prevention Act

References

American Bar Association. (1995a). *Unfinished business: Overcoming the Sisyphus factor.* A report from the American Bar Association Commission on Women in the Profession. Chicago: American Bar Association.

American Bar Association. (1995b). *Women in the law: A look at the numbers.* A report from the American Bar Association Commission on Women and the Profession. Chicago: American Bar Association.

American Bar Association. (2003). *National lawyer population survey.* Chicago: ABA Market Research Department.

American Correctional Association. (2003). *Directory of adult and juvenile correctional departments, agencies, probation and parole authorities.* Lanham, MD: American Correctional Association.

Bagley, K., & Merlo, A. V. (1995). Controlling women's bodies. In A. V. Merlo & J. M. Pollock (Eds.), *Women, law, and social control* (pp. 135–154). Boston: Allyn and Bacon.

Benson, M. L., & Fox, G. L. (2004, September). *When violence hits home: How economics and neighborhood play a role.* Research in Brief. National Institute of Justice, Office of Justice Programs. Washington, DC: U.S. Department of Justice.

Center for American Women and Politics. (2004a). *The gender gap and the 2004 women's vote: Setting the record straight.* Retrieved on October 30, 2004 from http:// www.cawp.rutgers.edu/.

Center for American Women and Politics. (2004b). *Gender gap persists in the 2004 election.* Retrieved November 7, 2004 from http://www.cawp.rutgers.edu/.

Chesney-Lind, M., & Pollock, J. M. (1995). Women's prisons: Equality with a vengeance. In A. V. Merlo &

J. M. Pollock (Eds.), *Women, law, and social control* (pp. 155–176). Boston: Allyn and Bacon.

Cook, R. (1992). Democratic clout is growing as the gender gap widens. *Congressional Quarterly Weekly Report* 50, October 17, pp. 3265–3268.

Department for Professional Employees, AFL-CIO. (2004). *DPE: Public policy: Issue fact sheets: Fact sheet 2004: Professional women: Vital statistics.* Retrieved on October 16, 2004 from http://www.dpeaflcio.org/policy/factsheets/fs_2004_Professional_Women.htm.

Donovan, B. (1992). "Women's campaigns fueled mostly by women's checks." *Congressional Quarterly Weekly Report* 50, October 17, pp. 3269–3273.

Feinman, C. (1986). *Women in the criminal justice system.* New York: Praeger Publishers.

Flanagan, T. J., & Maguire, K. (Eds.). (1992). *Sourcebook of criminal justice statistics, 1991.* U.S. Department of Justice, Bureau of Justice Statistics. Washington, DC: U.S. Government Printing Office.

Gender gap in government: The Federal government. (2004). htttp://www.gendergap.com/government.htm.

Gratch, L. (1995). Sexual harassment among police officers: Crisis and change in the normative structure. In A. V. Merlo & J. M. Pollock (Eds.), *Women, law, and social control* (pp. 55–77). Boston: Allyn and Bacon.

Hale, D. C, & Bennett, C. L. (1995). Realities of women in policing: An organizational cultural perspective. In A. V. Merlo & J. M. Pollock (Eds.), *Women, law, and social control* (pp. 41–54). Boston: Allyn and Bacon.

Harrison, P. M., & Karberg, J. C. (2004, May). *Prison and jail inmates at midyear 2003.* Bureau of Justice Statistics Bulletin, pp. 1–12. Washington, DC: U.S. Department of Justice, Office of Justice Programs.

Johnson, G. D., Palileo, G. J., & Gray, N. B. (1992, January). Date rape on a southern campus: Reports from 1991. *Sociology and Social Research* 76, 37–41.

Jos, P. H., Perlmutter, M., & Marshall, M. F. (2003). Substance abuse during pregnancy: Clinical and public health approaches. *Journal of Law, Medicine, and Ethics* 31, 340–347. Retrieved March 23, 2004 from the Lexis-Nexis database.

Kelly K., & DeBaise, C. (2004). Morgan Stanley settles bias suit for $54 million. *The Wall Street Journal,* 13 July, A1, A2.

Maguire, K., Pastore, A. L., & Flanagan, T. (Eds.). (1993). *Sourcebook of criminal justice statistics—1992.* U.S. Department of Justice, Bureau of Justice Statistics. Washington, DC: U.S. Government Printing Office.

Maguire, K., & Pastore, A. L. (Eds.). (2004). *Sourcebook of criminal justice statistics.* [Online]. Retrieved on August 15, 2004 from www.albany.edu/sourcebook/.

McGeehan, P. (2004). Discrimination on Wall Street? Run the numbers and weep. *New York Times,* 14 July, C1, C7.

Merlo, A. V. (1995a). Charting a course for the future. In A. V. Merlo & J. M. Pollock (Eds.), *Women, law, and social control* (pp. 241–264). Boston: Allyn and Bacon.

Merlo, A. V. (1995b). Female criminality in the 1990s. In A. V. Merlo & J. M. Pollock (Eds.), *Women, law, and social control* (pp. 119–135). Boston: Allyn and Bacon.

Merlo, A. V., & Benekos, P. J. (2000). *What's wrong with the criminal justice system: Ideology, politics, and the media.* Cincinnati, OH: Anderson Publishing.

New York Times. (1993). President's safety is now often a woman's work. July 6, A7.

Personal Communication, Los Angeles Police Department Recruiting Office, October 28, 2004.

Personal Communication, Secret Service, Public Affairs Division, October 25, 2004.

Pogrebin, M., & Poole, E. (1997). The sexualized work environment: A look at women jail officers. *The Prison Journal* 77 (1), 41–57.

Pogrebin, M., & Poole, E. (1998). Women deputies in jail work. *Journal of Contemporary Criminal Justice* 14 (2), 117–134.

Pollock, J. M. (1995). Gender, justice, and social control. In A. V. Merlo & J. M. Pollock (Eds.), *Women, law, and social control* (pp. 3–36). Boston: Allyn and Bacon.

Pollock, J. M. (1995). Women in corrections: Custody and the "caring ethic." In A. V. Merlo & J. M. Pollock, (Eds.), *Women, law, and social control* (pp. 97–116). Boston: Allyn and Bacon.

Pollock, J. M., & Ramirez, B. (1995). Women in the legal profession. In A. V. Merlo & J. M. Pollock, (Eds.), *Women, law, and social control* (pp. 79–95). Boston: Allyn and Bacon.

Pollock, J. M. (2002). *Women, prison, and crime* (2nd ed.). Belmont, CA: Wadsworth Thomson Learning.

Professional Women: Vital Statistics. Fact sheet 2004-1. Retrieved on October 16, 2004 from http:www.dpeaflcio.org/policy/factsheets/fs_2004_Professional_Women.htm.

Prokos, A., & Padavic, I. (2002, August). There oughtta be a law against bitches: Masculinity lessons in police academy training. *Gender, Work and Organization* 9 (4), pp. 439–459.

Rozee, P. D., Bateman, P., & Gilmore, T. (1991). The personal perspective of acquaintance rape prevention: A three tier approach. In A. Parrot & L. Bechhofer (Eds.), *Acquaintance rape: The hidden crime* (pp. 337–354). New York: John Wiley and Sons.

Southerland, M. D. (1995). Assaultive sex: The victim's perspective. In A. V. Merlo & J. M. Pollock (Eds.), *Women, law, and social control* (pp. 179–202). Boston: Allyn and Bacon.

Steffensmeier, D., & Streifel, C. (1992, March). Time-series analysis of the female percentage of arrests for property crimes, 1960–1985: A test of alternative explanations. *Justice Quarterly* 9, 77–103.

Trial. (1992, August). Miss Goodell, go home. *Trial* 28, 22.

U.S. Bureau of the Census. (2003). *Statistical abstract of the United States:2003* (123rd ed.). Washington, DC: U.S. Government Printing Office.

U.S. Bureau of the Census. (1992). *Statistical abstract of the United States: 1992* (112th ed.). Washington, DC: U.S. Bureau of the Census.

U.S. Department of Justice. (2003). *Criminal victimization in the United States, 2002 statistical tables.* (NCJ200561.) Retrieved on July 14, 2004 from http://www.ojp.usdoj.gov/bjs/pub/pdf/cvus02.pdf.

U.S. Department of Justice. (1993). *Uniform crime reports for the United States, 1992.* Washington, DC: U.S. Government Printing Office.

U.S. Department of Justice. (2002). *Uniform crime reports for the United States, 2002.* Washington, DC: U.S. Government Printing Office. Retrieved on July 7, 2004 from http://www.fbi.gov/ucr/cius_02/html/web/arrested/04-table42.html.

U.S. Department of Labor, Bureau of Justice Statistics. (2002). *Usual weekly earnings of wage and salary workers: Third quarter 2002.* Retrieved on August 20, 2004 from ftp://ftp.bls.gov/pub/news.release/History/wkyeng.10212002.news.

Index